West's Law School Advisory Board

JESSE H. CHOPER
Professor of Law and Dean Emeritus,
University of California, Berkeley

JOSHUA DRESSLER
Professor of Law, Michael E. Moritz College of Law,
The Ohio State University

YALE KAMISAR
Professor of Law Emeritus, University of San Diego
Professor of Law Emeritus, University of Michigan

MARY KAY KANE
Professor of Law, Chancellor and Dean Emeritus,
University of California,
Hastings College of the Law

LARRY D. KRAMER
President, William and Flora Hewlett Foundation

JONATHAN R. MACEY
Professor of Law, Yale Law School

ARTHUR R. MILLER
University Professor, New York University
Formerly Bruce Bromley Professor of Law, Harvard University

GRANT S. NELSON
Professor of Law, Pepperdine University
Professor of Law Emeritus, University of California, Los Angeles

A. BENJAMIN SPENCER
Professor of Law,
Washington & Lee University School of Law

JAMES J. WHITE
Professor of Law, University of Michigan

FEDERAL INCOME TAXATION

CASES, PROBLEMS, AND MATERIALS

■ ■ ■

By

Theodore P. Seto

Professor of Law and Frederick J. Lower, Jr. Chair
Loyola Law School, Los Angeles

AMERICAN CASEBOOK SERIES®

A Thomson Reuters business

Mat #40904011

Thomson Reuters created this publication to provide you with accurate and authoritative information concerning the subject matter covered. However, this publication was not necessarily prepared by persons licensed to practice law in a particular jurisdiction. Thomson Reuters does not render legal or other professional advice, and this publication is not a substitute for the advice of an attorney. If you require legal or other expert advice, you should seek the services of a competent attorney or other professional.

American Casebook Series is a trademark registered in the U.S. Patent and Trademark Office.

© 2013 Thomson Reuters
    610 Opperman Drive
    St. Paul, MN 55123
    1–800–313–9378

Printed in the United States of America

ISBN: 978–0–314–92706–4

This book is dedicated to my wife Prof. Sande Buhai—who provided essential emotional support, put up with the agony of its writing, and read proofs without complaint—and my daughters Genny, Sami, and Kira—for whom I am trying to make the future a better and more comprehensible place.

PREFACE

For several years, I have been experimenting with new ways to teach basic income taxation. The results have been spectacular. My students emerge with extraordinary technical skills and an enthusiasm for tax and tax policy that lead many to opt for extended tax education. This book is my first attempt to embody the approach I've developed in a set of published, rigorous, problem-based instructional materials.

It presents the U.S. income tax system as a set of answers to six fundamental design questions: (1) What should we tax? (2) How can annually-applied rules be structured so as to measure tax base income correctly over time? (3) How should we account for the time value of money? (4) What adjustments should we make for non-arm's-length relationships? (5) How can we distinguish between the costs of producing income, on the one hand, and consumption, on the other? And (6) how should we accommodate ability-to-pay and other distributive concerns?

My experience to date suggests that a systems design approach to the teaching of tax has significant advantages.

First, it allows the integration of theory with intense practical training. The book envisions that classroom time will be devoted heavily to interactive problem-solving. I generally require students to submit short written answers to the book's "Problems for Discussion" in advance of class. (I do not grade them.) This allows discussion to proceed at a very high level and permits me to embed existing rules in theory while ensuring that my students acquire saleable practical skills.

Second, a systems design approach gives students a more global understanding of what is at stake in public debates about tax. How should we think about the definition of "marriage" for tax purposes? What is the effect of "100 percent bonus depreciation" on effective tax rates? Why are corporate expenditures for executive jets deductible while purchases of oscilloscopes by public school science teachers may not be? Should the costs of assisted reproduction be deductible? What about the costs of religious education? How would abolition of the estate tax affect the income tax system? In my view, well-educated tax students should be able to read tax debates in blogs and newspapers critically. A systems design approach gives them the ability to do so.

Third, it is possible that our tax system will see major changes within the near future. If so, students who have learned tax as just another bunch of rules and cases will find themselves with little to show for their time and money. A systems design approach makes educational obsolescence less likely. Any replacement system will have to address the same fundamental questions that frame our current rules. Most suggested replacements—even the most apparently radical—address many of the same questions in the same ways. Students with a systems design perspective will be better prepared for change.

Consistent with its broader approach, the book is also unusual in the extent to which it discusses transfer and payroll taxation, enforcement issues, and tax expenditures. Thus, for example, it includes several gift and estate tax cases on issues where the transfer and income tax systems collide. It explores the difference between employees and independent contractors. It includes two cases on substantiation, an issue often overlooked in more conventional casebooks. And it includes a significant excerpt from the 2013 Tax Expenditure Budget.

Finally, what the book is not. The book is intentionally *not* a treatise. It is a set of instructional materials. It often omits topics or details that students emerging from a basic tax course are unlikely to remember a year later. In places, it does not explain the relevant rules at all, forcing students to derive their answers directly from the Code and regulations. I am a former big-firm tax and hiring partner; my purpose is to train competent tax lawyers, not to produce yet another reference work. If you find that I have omitted topics you believe essential, I would very much appreciate your views. My intention is to revise and improve these materials interactively over the next several years. Whether or not you adopt them, I hope you will read and enjoy! I have learned a lot writing them.

THEODORE P. SETO

September 2012

Summary of Contents

	Page
Preface	v
Table of Cases	xxiii

PART 1. WHAT SHOULD WE TAX? AN INTRODUCTION TO THE U.S. INCOME TAX SYSTEM

Chapter 1. The Concept of Income — 4

Subch.
- A: Source — 4
- B: Non–Cash Receipts — 13

Chapter 2. Systemic Exclusions — 16

Subch.
- A: The Role of Markets in the Measurement of Income, Non–Market Exchanges, and Imputed Income — 16
  - 1: The Role of Markets in the Measurement of Income — 16
  - 2: Income From Non–Market Exchanges — 19
  - 3: Imputed Income — 23
- B: Psychic or Incidental Income and the Primary Purpose Test — 25
- C: Employee Benefits — 30
  - 1: Code Section 119 — 30
  - 2: Code Section 132 — 36
- D: Gifts, Bequests, and Inheritances — 37
- E: Government–Provided Benefits and the General Welfare Doctrine — 48

Chapter 3. The Federal Income Tax Base — 57

Subch.
- A: Haig–Simons and the Comprehensive Tax Base — 57
- B: Tax Expenditures — 65
- C: Mechanics of the Federal Income Tax — 96
  - 1: Regular Tax — 96
  - 2: Floors and Phase-outs — 97
  - 3: Capital Gains and Losses — 99
  - 4: Alternative Minimum Tax — 101

Chapter 4. Deduction of Interest: An Introduction to Tax Arbitrage — 104
  - 1: Trade or Business Interest — 104
  - 2: Investment Interest — 104
  - 3: Interest on Debt Incurred or Continued to Purchase or Carry Tax–Exempt Obligations — 106

Subch.

    4: Passive Activity Interest 107
    5: Personal Interest and Home Mortgage Interest 109
    6: Interest on Educational Loans 110

PART 2. COMPLETE ACCOUNTING

Chapter 5. Basis 114

Chapter 6. Accounting Methods 117

Subch.
A: Cash Method 118
    1: Methods of Payment 119
    2: Constructive Receipt 123
    3: Cash Equivalence 126
    4: Economic Benefit 129
    5: Successful Deferral 135
    6: Prepaid Expenses 143
B: Accrual Method 145
    1: All–Events Test 145
    2: Economic Performance 147
    3: Prepaid Income 147
C: Section 83 150

Chapter 7. Recoveries 153

Subch.
A: Recoveries With Respect to Items With Basis 153
    1: Recovery of Basis v. Income 153
    2: Installment Sales 156
B: Recoveries With Respect to Items Without Basis 157
    1: Damages on Account of Personal Physical Injury or Sickness 157
    2: Amounts Received Through Accident or Health Insurance 167

Chapter 8. Debt 171

Subch.
A: Basic Rules 171
B: Debt Discharges 173
    1: Debt Discharge Income 173
    2: Purchase Price Adjustments 175
    3: Contested Liability Exception 177
    4: Insolvency Exception 179
    5: The Creditor's Side: Bad Debt? 180
C: Crane and Tufts 185
D: Zarin v. Commissioner 197

Chapter 9. Nonrecognition 213

Subch.
A: Like–Kind Exchanges 213
B: Involuntary Conversions 218
C: Sale of a Principal Residence 222

Summary of Contents

	Page
Chapter 10. Balancing Entries	**224**

Subch.
A: Tax Benefit Rule: Recovery of an Item Previously Deducted 225
B: Tax Detriment Rule: Repayment of Income Previously Included 227

PART 3. TIME VALUE OF MONEY

Chapter 11. Unstated Interest **233**
Subch.
A: Below–Market Loans 233
B: Original Issue Discount (OID) 238

Chapter 12. Capital Expenditures **242**
Subch.
A: Effective Rates of Tax 242
   1: The IRR Function 242
   2: Computing Effective Rates of Tax 244
   3: Effect of Expensing 247
   4: Nondistortive Cost Recovery 249
B: The Capitalization Requirement 252
   1: When Is Capitalization Required? 252
   2: What Amounts Must Be Capitalized? 258
   3: Exceptions 263
C: Cost Recovery 267
   1: Depreciation 267
   2: Amortization 271
   3: Other Cost Recovery Rules 272

PART 4. INTRA–FAMILY AND OTHER NON–ARM'S–LENGTH TRANSFERS

Chapter 13. Entanglement **277**
Subch.
A: Taxation of Entangled Relationships Not Treated as "Marriage" 277
   1: The Challenge of Entanglement 277
   2: Taxation of Support in the Absence of "Marriage" 286
   3: Taxation of Property Divisions in the Absence of "Marriage" 299
B: Taxation of Marriage 303

Chapter 14. Relative Indifference **306**
Subch.
A: Related Party Anti–Abuse Rules 306
   1: Transactions Between Related Parties, in General 307
   2: Purchases of Debt by Related Parties 307
   3: Installment Method Purchases by Related Parties 308
B: Income–Splitting, Joint Filing, and Marriage Bonuses and Penalties .. 310
C: Assignment of Income 315
   1: Income From Services 315
   2: Income From Property 330
D: Basis of Property Acquired by Gift, Inheritance, or Bequest 336
   1: Property Acquired by Gift 336
   2: Property Acquired by Inheritance or Bequest 337

PART 5. BUSINESS OR INVESTMENT VS. PERSONAL EXPENDITURES

Chapter 15.   Costs of Producing Income — 342
Subch.
A: Categories and Their Consequences — 342
    1: In General — 342
    2: Independent Contractor vs. Employee — 346
    3: Trade or Business vs. Other For–Profit Activity — 351
    4: For–Profit vs. Not–For–Profit Activities — 355
B: Specific Requirements — 369
    1: "Ordinary and Necessary" — 369
    2: Not Personal — 380
    3: Not Contrary to Public Policy — 382

Chapter 16.   Specific Types of Expenses — 391
Subch.
A: Entertainment and Business Meals — 391
    1: Complete Disallowance of Unrelated Entertainment — 395
    2: Complete Disallowance of Unsubstantiated Expenses — 397
    3: 50 Percent Disallowance Rule — 397
B: Travel — 402
    1: "Tax Home" and Commuting Expenses — 403
    2: Combined Business and Personal Travel — 407
C: Education — 408
D: Legal Expenses — 414
E: Home Office Expenses — 417

PART 6.   ABILITY TO PAY

Chapter 17.   Family Structure, Income, and Ability to Pay — 421
    1: Personal Exemptions and the Definition of "Dependent" — 421
    2: Head of Household Status — 424
    3: Child Tax Credit — 426
    4: Earned Income Tax Credit — 427

Chapter 18. Nondiscretionary Expenses and Involuntary Personal Losses — 430
Subch.
A: Medical Expense Deduction — 430
    1: "Medical Care" — 430
    2: Gender Reassignment Surgery — 436
    3: Reproductive Services — 447
B: Deduction for State and Local Taxes — 450
C: Personal Casualty Losses — 451

Chapter 19.   Charitable Contributions — 457
Subch.
A: General Rule — 458
B: Eligible Recipient Organizations — 476
    1: Purposes Test — 477
    2: Private Inurement Test — 484

	Page
Subch.	
3: Lobbying and Political Activities Test	488
C: Limitations and Collateral Consequences	515
1: Percentage Limitations	515
2: Limitations on Deduction of Fair Market Value	516
3: Substantiation Requirements	519
Index	531

TABLE OF CONTENTS

	Page
PREFACE	v
TABLE OF CASES	xxiii

PART 1. WHAT SHOULD WE TAX? AN INTRODUCTION TO THE U.S. INCOME TAX SYSTEM

Chapter 1. The Concept of Income 4

Subch.
- A: Source 4
  - *Cesarini v. United States* 4
  - *Notes* 7
  - *Problems for Discussion* 11
  - *Design Considerations* 11
- B: Non–Cash Receipts 13
  - *Rev. Rul. 79–24, 1979–1 C.B. 60* 13
  - *Notes* 13
  - *Problems for Discussion* 14
  - *Design Considerations* 15

Chapter 2. Systemic Exclusions 16

Subch.
- A: The Role of Markets in the Measurement of Income, Non–Market Exchanges, and Imputed Income 16
  - 1: The Role of Markets in the Measurement of Income 16
    - *Turner v. Commissioner* 17
    - *Problems for Discussion* 18
  - 2: Income From Non–Market Exchanges 19
    - *PLR 9608009* 19
    - *Notes* 22
  - 3: Imputed Income 23
    - *Commissioner v. Daehler* 24
    - *Problems for Discussion* 25
    - *Design Considerations* 25
- B: Psychic or Incidental Income and the Primary Purpose Test 25
  - *United States v. Gotcher* 26
- C: Employee Benefits 30
  - 1: Code Section 119 30
    - *Commissioner v. Kowalski* 30
    - *Adams v. United States* 32
    - *Problems for Discussion* 36
  - 2: Code Section 132 36
    - *Problems for Discussion* 37

		Page
Subch.		
D:	Gifts, Bequests, and Inheritances	37
	Commissioner v. Duberstein	37
	Estate of Powell v. United States	43
	Notes	46
	Problems for Discussion	48
E:	Government–Provided Benefits and the General Welfare Doctrine	48
	Graff v. Commissioner	50
	Notes	54
	Problems for Discussion	56

Chapter 3. The Federal Income Tax Base — 57

Subch.

A: Haig–Simons and the Comprehensive Tax Base — 57
    Collins v. Commissioner — 59
    Notes — 64
    Problems for Discussion — 64
    Design Considerations — 64

B: Tax Expenditures — 65
    Analytical Perspectives — 66
    Problems for Discussion — 95

C: Mechanics of the Federal Income Tax — 96
    1: Regular Tax — 96
    2: Floors and Phase-outs — 97
    3: Capital Gains and Losses — 99
        Problems for Discussion — 100
    4: Alternative Minimum Tax — 101

Chapter 4. Deduction of Interest: An Introduction to Tax Arbitrage — 104

    1: Trade or Business Interest — 104
    2: Investment Interest — 104
    3: Interest on Debt Incurred or Continued to Purchase or Carry Tax–Exempt Obligations — 106
    4: Passive Activity Interest — 107
    5: Personal Interest and Home Mortgage Interest — 109
    6: Interest on Educational Loans — 110
        Problems for Discussion — 110

PART 2. COMPLETE ACCOUNTING

Chapter 5. Basis — 114

Philadelphia Park Amusement Co. v. United States — 114
Problems for Discussion — 115

Chapter 6. Accounting Methods — 117

Subch.

A: Cash Method — 118
    1: Methods of Payment — 119
        (a) Checks — 119
            Kahler v. Commissioner — 119
            Problems for Discussion — 120
        (b) Credit Cards — 120
            Rev. Rul. 78–38 — 120
            Problems for Discussion — 121

		Page
Subch.		
	(c) Letters of Credit	121
	Chapman v. United States	121
	Problems for Discussion	123
	2: Constructive Receipt	123
	Miele v. Commissioner	123
	Notes	125
	Problems for Discussion	125
	3: Cash Equivalence	126
	Cowden v. Commissioner	126
	Notes	128
	Problems for Discussion	129
	4: Economic Benefit	129
	Reed v. Commissioner	129
	Notes	134
	Problems for Discussion	135
	5: Successful Deferral	135
	Rev. Rul. 60–31	135
	Minor v. United States	140
	6: Prepaid Expenses	143
	Grynberg v. Commissioner	143
	Problems for Discussion	145
B:	Accrual Method	145
	1: All–Events Test	145
	Flamingo Resort, Inc. v. United States	145
	Notes	147
	2: Economic Performance	147
	Problems for Discussion	147
	3: Prepaid Income	147
	American Automobile Association v. United States	147
	Notes	149
	Problems for Discussion	150
C:	Section 83	150
	Problems for Discussion	151

Chapter 7. Recoveries — 153

Subch.

A:	Recoveries With Respect to Items With Basis	153
	1: Recovery of Basis v. Income	153
	Rev. Rul. 81–277	153
	Problems for Discussion	155
	2: Installment Sales	156
B:	Recoveries With Respect to Items Without Basis	157
	1: Damages on Account of Personal Physical Injury or Sickness	157
	Murphy v. Internal Revenue Service (Murphy II)	157
	Stadnyk v. Commissioner	162
	Notes	166
	Problems for Discussion	167
	2: Amounts Received Through Accident or Health Insurance	167
	Notes	169
	Problems for Discussion	169

	Page
Chapter 8. Debt	171
Subch.	
A: Basic Rules	171
James v. United States	171
Notes	172
Problems for Discussion	173
B: Debt Discharges	173
1: Debt Discharge Income	173
United States v. Kirby Lumber Co.	173
Problems for Discussion	174
2: Purchase Price Adjustments	175
Rev. Rul. 92–99	175
Notes	177
Problems for Discussion	177
3: Contested Liability Exception	177
N. Sobel, Inc. v. Commissioner	177
Problems for Discussion	179
4: Insolvency Exception	179
Notes	179
Problems for Discussion	179
5: The Creditor's Side: Bad Debt?	180
Minneapolis, St. Paul & Sault Ste. Marie R.R. Co. v. United States	180
C: Crane and Tufts	185
Crane v. Commissioner	185
Problems for Discussion	190
Commissioner v. Tufts	191
Notes	197
D: Zarin v. Commissioner	197
Zarin v. Commissioner	197
Zarin v. Commissioner	208
Problems for Discussion	212
Chapter 9. Nonrecognition	213
Subch.	
A: Like–Kind Exchanges	213
Click v. Commissioner	213
Notes	216
Problems for Discussion	217
Design Considerations	218
B: Involuntary Conversions	218
Rev. Rul. 71–41	219
Notes	221
Problems for Discussion	221
C: Sale of a Principal Residence	222
Problems for Discussion	222
Chapter 10. Balancing Entries	224
Subch.	
A: Tax Benefit Rule: Recovery of an Item Previously Deducted	225
Hughes & Luce, L.L.P. v. Commissioner	225
B: Tax Detriment Rule: Repayment of Income Previously Included	227
United States v. Lewis	227
Notes	228

PART 3. TIME VALUE OF MONEY

Chapter 11. Unstated Interest 233
Subch.
A: Below–Market Loans 233
  Dickman v. Commissioner 233
  Problems for Discussion 237
B: Original Issue Discount (OID) 238
  Problems for Discussion 240

Chapter 12. Capital Expenditures 242
Subch.
A: Effective Rates of Tax 242
  1: The IRR Function 242
     Problems for Discussion 244
  2: Computing Effective Rates of Tax 244
     Problems for Discussion 245
  3: Effect of Expensing 247
  4: Nondistortive Cost Recovery 249
B: The Capitalization Requirement 252
  1: When Is Capitalization Required? 252
     INDOPCO, Inc. v. Commissioner 253
     Notes 257
  2: What Amounts Must Be Capitalized? 258
     Commissioner v. Idaho Power Co. 259
  3: Exceptions 263
     (a) Advertising Expenses 263
     (b) Circulation Expenses 263
     (c) Research and Software Development Expenses 264
         Rev. Proc. 2000–50 264
     (d) Bonus Depreciation 265
     (e) Small Business Expensing Election 266
C: Cost Recovery 267
  1: Depreciation 267
     (a) Regular Depreciation 267
     (b) Alternative Depreciation 270
         Problems for Discussion 271
  2: Amortization 271
  3: Other Cost Recovery Rules 272
     (a) Depletion 272
     (b) Start–Up Expenses 272

PART 4. INTRA–FAMILY AND OTHER NON–ARM'S–LENGTH TRANSFERS

Chapter 13. Entanglement 277
Subch.
A: Taxation of Entangled Relationships Not Treated as "Marriage" 277
  1: The Challenge of Entanglement 277
     Pascarelli v. Commissioner 278
     Notes 285
     Problems for Discussion 286
  2: Taxation of Support in the Absence of "Marriage" 286
     United States v. Harris 288
     Green v. Commissioner 291
     Douglas v. Willcuts 294

Subch.

2: Taxation of Support in the Absence of "Marriage"—Continued
   Chief Counsel Advice 201021050 296
   Notes 297
   Problems for Discussion 299

3: Taxation of Property Divisions in the Absence of "Marriage" 299
   Rev. Rul. 74–347 301
   Problems for Discussion 303

B: Taxation of Marriage 303
   Notes 304
   Problems for Discussion 305

Chapter 14. Relative Indifference 306
Subch.

A: Related Party Anti–Abuse Rules 306
   1: Transactions Between Related Parties, in General 307
      Problems for Discussion 307
   2: Purchases of Debt by Related Parties 307
      Problems for Discussion 308
   3: Installment Method Purchases by Related Parties 308
      Problems for Discussion 309

B: Income–Splitting, Joint Filing, and Marriage Bonuses and Penalties 310
   Notes 315

C: Assignment of Income 315
   1: Income From Services 315
      Schuster v. Commissioner 316
      Haeri v. Commissioner 323
      Notes 328
      Problems for Discussion 329
   2: Income From Property 330
      Heim v. Fitzpatrick 330
      Commissioner v. Banks 332
      Notes 335
      Problems for Discussion 336

D: Basis of Property Acquired by Gift, Inheritance, or Bequest 336
   1: Property Acquired by Gift 336
      (a) Basic Rules 336
          Problems for Discussion 337
      (b) Part Gift/Part Sale Transactions 337
          Problems for Discussion 337
   2: Property Acquired by Inheritance or Bequest 337
      (a) Basic Rules 337
          Problems for Discussion 338
      (b) Code Section 1014(e) 338
          Problems for Discussion 339

PART 5. BUSINESS OR INVESTMENT VS. PERSONAL EXPENDITURES

Chapter 15. Costs of Producing Income 342
Subch.

A: Categories and Their Consequences 342

	Page
Subch.	

- 1: In General — 342
  - (a) Expenses of a Trade or Business (Other Than the Trade or Business of Being an Employee) — 342
  - (b) Employee Trade or Business Expenses — 343
  - (c) Expenses of Non–Business Activities Engaged in for Profit — 344
  - (d) Expenses of Activities Not Engaged in for Profit — 345
    - Problems for Discussion — 345
- 2: Independent Contractor vs. Employee — 346
  - Schramm v. Commissioner — 346
  - Notes — 350
- 3: Trade or Business vs. Other For–Profit Activity — 351
  - Snyder v. United States — 352
  - Notes — 354
- 4: For–Profit vs. Not–For–Profit Activities — 355
  - Keating v. Commissioner — 355
  - Problems for Discussion — 359
  - Kurzet v. Commissioner — 359
  - Problems for Discussion — 361
  - Krause v. Commissioner — 362
  - Problems for Discussion — 368

B: Specific Requirements — 369
- 1: "Ordinary and Necessary" — 369
  - Noyce v. Commissioner — 370
  - Wheatland v. Commissioner — 377
  - Notes — 380
- 2: Not Personal — 380
  - Henderson v. Commissioner — 381
- 3: Not Contrary to Public Policy — 382
  - Stephens v. Commissioner — 383

Chapter 16. Specific Types of Expenses — **391**
Subch.

A: Entertainment and Business Meals — 391
- Moss v. Commissioner — 391
- Notes — 394
- Problems for Discussion — 394
- 1: Complete Disallowance of Unrelated Entertainment — 395
  - (a) "Directly Related" — 395
  - (b) "Associated With" — 395
  - (c) Statutory Exceptions — 396
    - Problems for Discussion — 396
- 2: Complete Disallowance of Unsubstantiated Expenses — 397
- 3: 50 Percent Disallowance Rule — 397
  - Boyd Gaming Corporation v. Commissioner — 398
  - Problems for Discussion — 401

B: Travel — 402
- 1: "Tax Home" and Commuting Expenses — 403
  - Rev. Rul. 99–7 — 404
  - Notes — 405
  - Problems for Discussion — 406
- 2: Combined Business and Personal Travel — 407
  - Problems for Discussion — 408

C: Education — 408
- Glenn v. Commissioner — 410
- Notes — 414

		Page
Subch.		
D:	Legal Expenses	414
	Problems for Discussion	416
E:	Home Office Expenses	417
	Problems for Discussion	417

PART 6. ABILITY TO PAY

Chapter 17. Family Structure, Income, and Ability to Pay — 421

1: Personal Exemptions and the Definition of "Dependent" — 421
   Problems for Discussion — 423
2: Head of Household Status — 424
   Heretick v. Commissioner — 424
   Problems for Discussion — 426
3: Child Tax Credit — 426
   Problems for Discussion — 427
4: Earned Income Tax Credit — 427
   Problems for Discussion — 428

Chapter 18. Nondiscretionary Expenses and Involuntary Personal Losses — 430

Subch.

A: Medical Expense Deduction — 430
   1: "Medical Care" — 430
     Havey v. Commissioner — 432
     Notes — 435
     Problems for Discussion — 436
   2: Gender Reassignment Surgery — 436
     O'Donnabhain v. Commissioner — 436
     Problems for Discussion — 447
   3: Reproductive Services — 447
     Magdalin v. Commissioner — 447
     Problems for Discussion — 450
B: Deduction for State and Local Taxes — 450
C: Personal Casualty Losses — 451
   General Counsel Memorandum 35013 (1972), Casualty Losses Under Section 165(c)(3) — 452
   Notes — 456
   Problems for Discussion — 456

Chapter 19. Charitable Contributions — 457

Subch.

A: General Rule — 458
   Rev. Rul. 83–104 — 458
   Hernandez v. Commissioner — 462
   Sklar v. Commissioner — 471
   Problems for Discussion — 476
B: Eligible Recipient Organizations — 476
   1: Purposes Test — 477
     Plumstead Theatre Society, Inc. v. Commissioner — 477
     Problems for Discussion — 484
   2: Private Inurement Test — 484
     Church by Mail, Inc. v. Commissioner — 484
     Problems for Discussion — 488

	Page
Subch.	

- 3: Lobbying and Political Activities Test ... 488
  - (a) Attempting to Influence Legislation ... 488
  - (b) Political Activities ... 490
    - *Branch Ministries v. Rossotti* ... 490
    - *Rev. Rul. 2007–41* ... 495
  - (c) Standing Issues ... 506
    - *In re United States Catholic Conference* ... 506
    - *Problems for Discussion* ... 515
- C: Limitations and Collateral Consequences ... 515
  - 1: Percentage Limitations ... 515
  - 2: Limitations on Deduction of Fair Market Value ... 516
    - *Haverly v. United States* ... 517
  - 3: Substantiation Requirements ... 519
    - *Mohamed v. Commissioner* ... 519
    - *Durden v. Commissioner* ... 526
    - *Problems for Discussion* ... 530

INDEX ... 531

TABLE OF CASES

The principal cases are in bold type. Cases cited or discussed in the text are in roman type. References are to pages. Cases cited in principal cases and within other quoted materials are not included.

Adams v. United States, 218 Ct.Cl. 322, 585 F.2d 1060 (Ct.Cl.1978), **32**
American Auto. Ass'n v. United States, 367 U.S. 687, 81 S.Ct. 1727, 6 L.Ed.2d 1109 (1961), **147**
American Bar Endowment, United States v., 477 U.S. 105, 106 S.Ct. 2426, 91 L.Ed.2d 89 (1986), 458
Armory v. Delamirie, 1 Str. 505 (Kings Bench 1722), 9
Artnell Co. v. Commissioner, 400 F.2d 981 (7th Cir.1968), 150

Bailey (James) v. Commissioner, 88 T.C. No. 72, 88 T.C. 1293 (U.S.Tax Ct.1987), 55
Banks, Commissioner v. 543 U.S. 426, 2005-15 I.R.B. 850, 125 S.Ct. 826, 160 L.Ed.2d 859 (2005), **332,** 414
Best Lock Corp. v. Commissioner, 31 T.C. 1217 (Tax Ct.1959), 263
Big Mama Rag, Inc. v. United States, 631 F.2d 1030, 203 U.S.App.D.C. 448 (D.C.Cir.1980), 489
Bingler v. Johnson, 394 U.S. 741, 89 S.Ct. 1439, 22 L.Ed.2d 695 (1969), 47
Boyd Gaming Corp. v. Commissioner, 177 F.3d 1096 (9th Cir.1999), **398**
Branch Ministries v. Rossotti, 211 F.3d 137, 341 U.S.App.D.C. 166 (D.C.Cir.2000), **490**
Bruun, Helvering v., 309 U.S. 461, 60 S.Ct. 631, 84 L.Ed. 864 (1940), 8

California Federal Life Ins. Co. v. Commissioner, 680 F.2d 85 (9th Cir.1982), 216
Cammarano v. United States, 358 U.S. 498, 79 S.Ct. 524, 3 L.Ed.2d 462 (1959), 382
Carroll v. Commissioner, 418 F.2d 91 (7th Cir. 1969), 408
Cartwright, United States v., 411 U.S. 546, 93 S.Ct. 1713, 36 L.Ed.2d 528 (1973), 17
Cesarini v. United States, 296 F.Supp. 3 (N.D.Ohio 1969), **4**
Chapman v. United States, 527 F.Supp. 1053 (D.Minn.1981), **121**
Cheek v. United States, 498 U.S. 192, 111 S.Ct. 604, 112 L.Ed.2d 617 (1991), 172
Cheh v. Commissioner, T.C. Memo. 1992-658 (U.S.Tax Ct.1992), 352

Chevron, U.S.A., Inc. v. Natural Resources Defense Council, Inc., 467 U.S. 837, 104 S.Ct. 2778, 81 L.Ed.2d 694 (1984), 10
Church By Mail, Inc. v. Commissioner, 765 F.2d 1387 (9th Cir.1985), **484**
Culbertson, Commissioner v., 337 U.S. 733, 69 S.Ct. 1210, 93 L.Ed. 1659 (1949), 316
Click v. Commissioner, 78 T.C. 225 (U.S.Tax Ct.1982), **213**
Clifford, Helvering v., 309 U.S. 331, 60 S.Ct. 554, 84 L.Ed. 788 (1940), 7
Coed Records, Inc. v. Commissioner, 47 T.C. 422 (Tax Ct.1967), 382
Cohan v. Commissioner, 39 F.2d 540 (2nd Cir. 1930), 285
Collins v. Commissioner, T.C. Memo. 1992-478 (U.S.Tax Ct.1992), 16, **59**
Collins v. Commissioner, 412 F.2d 211 (10th Cir.1969), 300
Colvin v. Commissioner, T.C. Memo. 2004-67 (U.S.Tax Ct.2004), 416
Commissioner v. _____ (see opposing party)
Cook v. Commissioner, 80 T.C. 512 (U.S.Tax Ct.1983), 300
Cook v. United States, 904 F.2d 107 (1st Cir. 1990), 300
Correll, United States v., 389 U.S. 299, 88 S.Ct. 445, 19 L.Ed.2d 537 (1967), 402
Coughlin v. Commissioner, 203 F.2d 307 (2nd Cir.1953), 409
Cowden v. Commissioner, 289 F.2d 20 (5th Cir.1961), **126**
Crane v. Commissioner, 331 U.S. 1, 67 S.Ct. 1047, 91 L.Ed. 1301 (1947), **185**

Daehler, Commissioner v., 281 F.2d 823 (5th Cir.1960), **24**
Davis, United States v., 370 U.S. 65, 82 S.Ct. 1190, 8 L.Ed.2d 335 (1962), 300
Deputy v. du Pont, 308 U.S. 488, 60 S.Ct. 363, 84 L.Ed. 416 (1940), 258, 354
Dickman v. Commissioner, 465 U.S. 330, 104 S.Ct. 1086, 79 L.Ed.2d 343 (1984), **233**
Douglas v. Willcuts, 296 U.S. 1, 56 S.Ct. 59, 80 L.Ed. 3 (1935), **294**
Dragovich v. United States Dept. of Treasury, 2012 WL 1909603 (N.D.Cal.2012), 305

Duberstein, Commissioner v. 363 U.S. 278, 80 S.Ct. 1190, 4 L.Ed.2d 1218 (1960), **37**

Durden v. Commissioner, T.C. Memo. 2012-140 (U.S.Tax Ct.2012), **526**

Edwards v. Cuba Railroad Co., 268 U.S. 628, 45 S.Ct. 614, 69 L.Ed. 1124 (1925), 49

E.H. Sheldon & Co. v. Commissioner, 214 F.2d 655 (6th Cir.1954), 263

Eisner v. Macomber, 252 U.S. 189, 40 S.Ct. 189, 64 L.Ed. 521 (1920), 7

Estate of (see name of party)

Farias v. Commissioner, T.C. Memo. 2011-248 (U.S.Tax Ct.2011), 380

Farid–Es–Sultaneh v. Commissioner, 160 F.2d 812 (2nd Cir.1947), 300

Flamingo Resort, Inc. v. United States, 664 F.2d 1387 (9th Cir.1982), **145**

Flowers, Commissioner v., 326 U.S. 465, 66 S.Ct. 250, 90 L.Ed. 203 (1946), 403

France v. Commissioner, T.C. Memo. 1980-215 (U.S.Tax Ct.1980), 431

Fund for the Study of Economic Growth and Tax Reform v. I.R.S., 161 F.3d 755, 333 U.S.App.D.C. 205 (D.C.Cir.1998), 489

Generes, United States v., 405 U.S. 93, 92 S.Ct. 827, 31 L.Ed.2d 62 (1972), 344

Gill v. Office of Personnel Management, 699 F.Supp.2d 374 (D.Mass.2010), 304

Gilmore, United States v., 372 U.S. 39, 83 S.Ct. 623, 9 L.Ed.2d 570 (1963), 415

Glenn v. Commissioner, 62 T.C. 270 (U.S.Tax Ct.1974), **410**

Glenshaw Glass Co., Commissioner v., 348 U.S. 426, 75 S.Ct. 473, 99 L.Ed. 483 (1955), 7

Goedel v. Commissioner, 39 B.T.A. 1 (B.T.A. 1939), 370

Gotcher, United States v., 401 F.2d 118 (5th Cir.1968), **26**

Graff v. Commissioner, 74 T.C. 743 (U.S.Tax Ct.1980), **50**

Graves v. New York ex rel. O'Keefe, 306 U.S. 466, 59 S.Ct. 595, 83 L.Ed. 927 (1939), 167

Green v. Commissioner, T.C. Memo. 1987-503 (U.S.Tax Ct.1987), **291**

Groetzinger, Commissioner v., 480 U.S. 23, 107 S.Ct. 980, 94 L.Ed.2d 25 (1987), 351, 354

Grynberg v. Commissioner, 83 T.C. No. 17, 83 T.C. 255 (U.S.Tax Ct.1984), **143**

Haeri v. Commissioner, T.C. Memo. 1989-20 (U.S.Tax Ct.1989), **323**

Haines v. Commissioner, 71 T.C. 644 (U.S.Tax Ct.1979), 431

Hanover Bank v. Commissioner, 369 U.S. 672, 82 S.Ct. 1080, 8 L.Ed.2d 187 (1962), 22

Harris, United States v., 942 F.2d 1125 (7th Cir.1991), **288**

Haverly v. United States, 513 F.2d 224 (7th Cir.1975), **517**

Havey v. Commissioner, 12 T.C. 409 (Tax Ct.1949), **432**

Heim v. Fitzpatrick, 262 F.2d 887 (2nd Cir.1959), **330**

Heininger, Commissioner v., 320 U.S. 467, 64 S.Ct. 249, 88 L.Ed. 171 (1943), 258

Helvering v. _____ (see opposing party)

Henderson v. Commissioner, T.C. Memo. 1983-372 (U.S.Tax Ct.1983), **381**

Henry v. Commissioner, 36 T.C. 879 (Tax Ct.1961), 369

Heretick v. Commissioner, T.C. Summ.Op. 2003-129 (U.S.Tax Ct.2003), **424**

Hernandez v. Commissioner, 490 U.S. 680, 109 S.Ct. 2136, 104 L.Ed.2d 766 (1989), 47, **462**

Hesse v. Commissioner, 60 T.C. 685 (U.S.Tax Ct.1973), 414

Higgins v. Commissioner, 312 U.S. 212, 61 S.Ct. 475, 85 L.Ed. 783 (1941), 351, 354

Hilton Hotels Corp., United States v., 397 U.S. 580, 90 S.Ct. 1307, 25 L.Ed.2d 585 (1970), 258

Hoover Motor Exp. Co. v. United States, 356 U.S. 38, 78 S.Ct. 511, 2 L.Ed.2d 568 (1958), 382

Howard v. Commissioner, T.C. Memo. 1975–170, p. 414

Hughes & Luce, L.L.P. v. Commissioner, 70 F.3d 16 (5th Cir.1995), **225**

Hunley v. Commissioner, T.C. Memo. 1966-66 (Tax Ct.1966), 16

Husted v. Commissioner, 47 T.C. 664 (Tax Ct.1967), 16

Idaho Power Co., Commissioner v. 418 U.S. 1, 94 S.Ct. 2757, 41 L.Ed.2d 535 (1974), **259**

INDOPCO, Inc. v. Commissioner, 503 U.S. 79, 112 S.Ct. 1039, 117 L.Ed.2d 226 (1992), **253,** 415

In re (see name of party)

International Freighting Corporation v. Commissioner, 135 F.2d 310 (2nd Cir.1943), 14

Interstate Transit Lines v. Commissioner, 319 U.S. 590, 63 S.Ct. 1279, 87 L.Ed. 1607 (1943), 258

Jacobs v. Commissioner, 62 T.C. 813 (U.S.Tax Ct.1974), 431

James v. United States, 366 U.S. 213, 81 S.Ct. 1052, 6 L.Ed.2d 246 (1961), **171,** 229

Kahler v. Commissioner, 18 T.C. 31 (Tax Ct.1952), **119**

Kaiser, United States v., 363 U.S. 299, 80 S.Ct. 1204, 4 L.Ed.2d 1233 (1960), 49

Katz v. Commissioner, T.C. Memo. 1968-16 (Tax Ct.1968), 408

Keating v. Commissioner, 544 F.3d 900 (8th Cir.2008), **355**

Kirby Lumber Co., United States v., 284 U.S. 1, 52 S.Ct. 4, 76 L.Ed. 131 (1931), 7, **173,** 308

Kohen v. Commissioner, T.C. Memo. 1982-625 (U.S.Tax Ct.1982), 414

Kowalski, Commissioner v. 434 U.S. 77, 98 S.Ct. 315, 54 L.Ed.2d 252 (1977), **30**

Krause v. Commissioner, 99 T.C. No. 7, 99 T.C. 132 (U.S.Tax Ct.1992), **362**

Kurzet v. Commissioner, 222 F.3d 830 (10th Cir.2000), **359**

Larsen v. Commissioner, T.C. Memo. 2008-73 (U.S.Tax Ct.2008), 46
Lewis, United States v., 340 U.S. 590, 71 S.Ct. 522, 95 L.Ed. 560 (1951), 9, **227**
Limericks, Inc. v. Commissioner, 165 F.2d 483 (5th Cir.1948), 370
Lincoln Elec. Co., Commissioner v., 176 F.2d 815 (6th Cir.1949), 370
Lincoln Sav. & Loan Ass'n, Commissioner v., 403 U.S. 345, 91 S.Ct. 1893, 29 L.Ed.2d 519 (1971), 258
Lopez v. Commissioner, 2004 WL 2757581 (5th Cir.2004), 352
Lucas v. Earl, 281 U.S. 111, 50 S.Ct. 241, 74 L.Ed. 731 (1929), 311, 316

Magdalin v. Commissioner, T.C. Memo. 2008-293 (U.S.Tax Ct.2008), **447**
Marvin v. Marvin, 134 Cal.Rptr. 815, 557 P.2d 106 (Cal.1976), 298
Massachusetts v. United States Dept. of Health and Human Services, 682 F.3d 1 (1st Cir. 2012), 304
Mayo Foundation for Medical Educ. and Research v. United States, ___ U.S. ___, 131 S.Ct. 704, 178 L.Ed.2d 588 (2011), 9
McKay v. Commissioner, 102 T.C. No. 16, 102 T.C. 465 (U.S.Tax Ct.1994), 415
M.E. Blatt Co. v. United States, 305 U.S. 267, 59 S.Ct. 186, 83 L.Ed. 167 (1938), 8
Merrill v. Fahs, 324 U.S. 308, 65 S.Ct. 655, 89 L.Ed. 963 (1945), 286
Miele v. Commissioner, 72 T.C. 284 (U.S.Tax Ct.1979), **123,** 150
Minneapolis, St. Paul & Sault Ste. Marie R. Co. v. United States, 164 Ct.Cl. 226 (Ct.Cl.1964), **180**
Minor v. United States, 772 F.2d 1472 (9th Cir.1985), **140**
Mississippi Chemical Corp., United States v., 405 U.S. 298, 92 S.Ct. 908, 31 L.Ed.2d 217 (1972), 258
Mohamed v. Commissioner, T.C. Memo. 2012-152 (U.S.Tax Ct.2012), **519**
Moss v. Commissioner, 80 T.C. 1073 (U.S.Tax Ct.1983), **391**
Murphy v. I.R.S. (Murphy II), 493 F.3d 170, 377 U.S.App.D.C. 197 (D.C.Cir.2007), **157**

National Alliance v. United States, 710 F.2d 868, 228 U.S.App.D.C. 357 (D.C.Cir.1983), 489
Newark Morning Ledger Co. v. United States, 507 U.S. 546, 113 S.Ct. 1670, 123 L.Ed.2d 288 (1993), 271
North Am. Oil Consolidated v. Burnet, 286 U.S. 417, 52 S.Ct. 613, 76 L.Ed. 1197 (1932), 9
Northwestern Yeast Co. v. Commissioner, 5 B.T.A. 232 (1926), 263
Noyce v. Commissioner, 97 T.C. No. 46, 97 T.C. 670 (U.S.Tax Ct.1991), **370**
N. Sobel, Inc. v. Commissioner, 40 B.T.A. 1263 (B.T.A.1939), **177**

O'Donnabhain v. Commissioner, 134 T.C. No. 4, 134 T.C. 34 (U.S.Tax Ct.2010), **436**
Old Colony Trust Co. v. Commissioner, 279 U.S. 716, 49 S.Ct. 499, 73 L.Ed. 918 (1929), 14

Palmer v. Commissioner, 302 U.S. 63, 58 S.Ct. 67, 82 L.Ed. 50 (1937), 16
Pascarelli v. Commissioner, 55 T.C. 1082 (U.S.Tax Ct.1971), **278**
Pellar v. Commissioner, 25 T.C. 299 (Tax Ct.1955), 16
Philadelphia Park Amusement Co. v. United States, 130 Ct.Cl. 166, 126 F.Supp. 184 (Ct.Cl.1954), **114**
Plumstead Theatre Society, Inc. v. Commissioner, 74 T.C. 1324 (U.S.Tax Ct.1980), **477**
Poe v. Seaborn, 282 U.S. 101, 51 S.Ct. 58, 75 L.Ed. 239 (1930), 297, 312
Pollock v. Farmers' Loan & Trust Co., 158 U.S. 601, 15 S.Ct. 912, 39 L.Ed. 1108 (1895), 167
Portland Golf Club v. Commissioner, 497 U.S. 154, 110 S.Ct. 2780, 111 L.Ed.2d 126 (1990), 355
Powell, Estate of v. United States, 166 F.Supp.2d 468 (W.D.Va.2001), **43**
Pulliam v. Commissioner, 329 F.2d 97 (10th Cir.1964), 300

Randick v. Commissioner, T.C. Memo. 1976-45 (U.S.Tax Ct.1976), 414
Reed v. Commissioner, 723 F.2d 138 (1st Cir.1983), **129**
Rosenzweig v. Commissioner, 1 T.C. 24 (Tax Ct.1942), 414
Ruehmann v. Commissioner, T.C. Memo. 1971-157 (U.S.Tax Ct.1971), 414
Rutkin v. United States, 343 U.S. 130, 72 S.Ct. 571, 96 L.Ed. 833 (1952), 9

Schlude v. Commissioner, 372 U.S. 128, 83 S.Ct. 601, 9 L.Ed.2d 633 (1963), 149
Schramm v. Commissioner, T.C. Memo. 2011-212 (U.S.Tax Ct.2011), **346**
Schuster v. Commissioner, 800 F.2d 672 (7th Cir.1986), **316**
Shapiro, Estate of v. United States, 634 F.3d 1055 (9th Cir.2011), 286
Sharon v. Commissioner, 591 F.2d 1273 (9th Cir.1978), 409
Sharon v. Commissioner, 66 T.C. 515 (U.S.Tax Ct.1976), 252
Skidmore v. Swift & Co., 323 U.S. 134, 65 S.Ct. 161, 89 L.Ed. 124 (1944), 10
Sklar v. Commissioner, 282 F.3d 610 (9th Cir.2002), **471**
Snyder v. Commissioner, 295 U.S. 134, 55 S.Ct. 737, 79 L.Ed. 1351 (1935), 354
Snyder v. United States, 674 F.2d 1359 (10th Cir.1982), **352**
Soliman, Commissioner v., 506 U.S. 168, 113 S.Ct. 701, 121 L.Ed.2d 634 (1993), 417
Srivastava v. Commissioner, T.C. Memo. Rev. Rul. 60–188, 1960–1 C.B. 28, p. 415
Sunnen, Commissioner v., 333 U.S. 591, 68 S.Ct. 715, 92 L.Ed. 898 (1948), 335

Stadnyk v. Commissioner, 2010 WL 681436 (6th Cir.2010), **162**

Stephens v. Commissioner, 905 F.2d 667 (2nd Cir.1990), **383**

Stolte v. Commissioner, T.C. Memo. 1999-271 (U.S.Tax Ct.1999), 168

Talley v. United States Dept. of Agriculture, 595 F.3d 754 (7th Cir.2010), 336

Tank Truck Rentals, Inc. v. Commissioner, 356 U.S. 30, 78 S.Ct. 507, 2 L.Ed.2d 562 (1958), 370, 382

Tellier, Commissioner v., 383 U.S. 687, 86 S.Ct. 1118, 16 L.Ed.2d 185 (1966), 258, 369, 416

Test v. Commissioner, T.C. Memo. 2000-362 (U.S.Tax Ct.2000), 416

Textile Mills Sec. Corp. v. Commissioner, 314 U.S. 326, 62 S.Ct. 272, 86 L.Ed. 249 (1941), 382

Tso v. Commissioner, T.C. Memo. 1980-399 (U.S.Tax Ct.1980), 431

Tufts, Commissioner v. 461 U.S. 300, 103 S.Ct. 1826, 75 L.Ed.2d 863 (1983), **191**

Turner v. Commissioner, T.C. Memo. 1954-38 (Tax Ct.1954), **17**

United Housing Foundation, Inc. v. Forman, 421 U.S. 837, 95 S.Ct. 2051, 44 L.Ed.2d 621 (1975), 49

United States v. _____ (see opposing party)

United States Catholic Conference (USCC), In re, 885 F.2d 1020 (2nd Cir. 1989), **506**

Walker v. Commissioner, 101 T.C. No. 36, 101 T.C. 537 (U.S.Tax Ct.1993), 405

Wassenaar v. Commissioner, 72 T.C. 1195 (U.S.Tax Ct.1979), 414

Welch v. Helvering, 290 U.S. 111, 54 S.Ct. 8, 78 L.Ed. 212 (1933), 258, 370, 409

Wesenberg v. Commissioner, 69 T.C. 1005 (U.S.Tax Ct.1978), 316

Wilcox, Commissioner v., 327 U.S. 404, 66 S.Ct. 546, 90 L.Ed. 752 (1946), 171

Wheatland v. Commissioner, T.C. Memo. 1964-95 (Tax Ct.1964), **377**

Wild v. Commissioner, 42 T.C. 706 (Tax Ct.1964), 414

Winmill, Helvering v., 305 U.S. 79, 59 S.Ct. 45, 83 L.Ed. 52 (1938), 258

Woodward v. Commissioner, 397 U.S. 572, 90 S.Ct. 1302, 25 L.Ed.2d 577 (1970), 258, 415

Zarin v. Commissioner, 916 F.2d 110 (3rd Cir.1990), **208**

Zarin v. Commissioner, 92 T.C. No. 68, 92 T.C. 1084 (U.S.Tax Ct.1989), **197**

Federal Income Taxation
CASES, PROBLEMS, AND MATERIALS

PART 1

WHAT SHOULD WE TAX? AN INTRODUCTION TO THE U.S. INCOME TAX SYSTEM

■ ■ ■

Every tax system reflects a series of design decisions: what to tax, when to tax it, on whom to impose the tax, and at what rate or rates. This book explores the U.S. income tax system as a series of answers to these and other fundamental design questions. Once we understand how the system answers a particular design question, the system's technical details become easier to understand, remember, and even predict. Indeed, it is not unusual for practitioners to approach a new tax question by asking: "What must the answer be?" and only then exploring the law.

This Part 1 begins with the question: What should we tax?

Since the early part of the 20th century, the U.S. Congress has chosen to tax "income." With almost a century of hindsight, we now understand that this decision is supported by at least three considerations.

First, lower rates for any given revenue target. Mathematically, the revenue raised by a tax equals the average rate times the base. The "base" of a tax is simply "that which is taxed"—in the case of an income tax, "income." Thus, if an economy generates $15 trillion of "income" each year and a tax is imposed on "income" at an average rate of 10 percent, the tax will generate $1.5 trillion per year of revenue. As we narrow the base—for example, by excluding one kind of income or another or by providing more generous deductions or credits—the average rate required to generate the same $1.5 trillion in revenue goes up. The broader a tax's base, the lower the average rate needed to raise any given amount of revenue. Income is one of the broadest tax bases in use today. Using income, broadly defined, as its tax base therefore allows Congress to impose lower rates than might otherwise be required to raise the same amount of revenue using, for example, a tax on consumption or sales.

Second, taxation based on ability to pay. Historically, American voters have preferred that Congress allocate the U.S. tax burden in a manner more or less consistent with ability to pay. Income is an approximate measure of ability to pay; on average, taxpayers with higher income incur less objective sacrifice (however loudly they might complain) than taxpayers with lower income when paying the same dollar amount. Many therefore view an ideal income tax (not necessarily the cluttered system we have in place today) as fairer than possible alternatives. Consider, by contrast, a "head" tax (also known as a "poll" or "capitation" tax) pursuant to which every U.S. resident would pay the same amount of federal taxes per year, regardless of age, income, or ability to pay—the ultimate flat tax. An annual head tax of $3,725 per person, if fully collected, would raise approximately the same total revenue as our individual income tax system currently does, and would clearly be simpler. But because it ignores ability to pay, it would probably be even less popular than our current system. The U.K.'s brief imposition of such a tax in the early 1990s led to nationwide riots and the end of Prime Minister Margaret Thatcher's political career. (Note that imposition of such a tax at the federal level would require amendment of the U.S. Constitution, for reasons discussed in Chapter 6B, Note 1, below.)

Third, minimized economic distortion. Economists believe that taxes should be structured, in general, so as to minimize tax-induced changes in behavior. One way of accomplishing this is to tax whatever it is taxpayers would seek to maximize in the absence of taxation. Assume, for example, that in the absence of taxation publicly reporting corporations attempt to maximize reported book income. If we tax pre-tax book income at a rate of less than 100%, there is no lawful action a corporation can take to reduce taxes that will not also reduce its after-tax book income by an even greater amount. If the corporation is taxed at a rate of 35%, for example, saving $35 in taxes will require it to reduce its pre-tax book income by $100 and its reported after-tax income by $65. If the corporation really does seek to maximize reported book income, therefore, it will never undertake any lawful tax avoidance activity. Taxing whatever it is that taxpayers otherwise seek to maximize minimizes the likelihood of tax-induced behavioral change.

What do individuals seek to maximize? Humans are complex creatures, with multiple and sometimes conflicting motivations. In the economic sphere, however, they commonly seek to maximize income. If so, then all else being equal, using income as our tax base should minimize tax-induced economic distortion. (The closest current contender for minimally-distortive tax base is "consumption," commonly defined as income less savings. We will explore the extent to which our current "income" tax is actually a consumption tax in later chapters.)

In any event, the single most important design decision Congress has made is to tax "income." Chapter 1 explores the concept of income, which is nowhere defined in the Internal Revenue Code. Over time, theoretical income has come to be defined expansively. As you explore this generally accepted definition of income, you may find it useful to keep in mind the reasons income is thought to make sense as a tax base in the first place—breadth, fairness, and nondistortion.

The definition of income outlined in Chapter 1, although widely accepted, turns out to be problematic, picking up many kinds of transactions that most taxpayers simply do not think of as taxable. Chapter 2 explores a series of systemic exclusions that have developed in response, sometimes as a result of action by Congress or the Internal Revenue Service, sometimes less intentionally—for non-market income, imputed income, psychic or incidental income, employee fringe benefits, gifts and bequests, and government-provided benefits. The result, subject to further statutory exclusions, is "gross income"—the beginning point for the tax computation process.

Chapter 3 completes Part 1's overview of the federal income tax system. The generally accepted definition of income introduced in Chapter 1 finds formal expression in the so-called Haig–Simons definition on income: A taxpayer's income for any taxable period equals her change in net worth over that period plus the value of her consumption during that period. Haig–Simons, a variation of which is also sometimes known as the "comprehensive tax base," justifies much of the basic structure of our current income tax system, explored in Chapter 3A.

Nevertheless, Congress has authorized many deviations from Haig–Simons for non-tax reasons. Known as "tax expenditures," these provisions constitute an important and sometimes controversial part of our current system, explored in Chapter 3B. From the formal elegance of Haig–Simons, Chapter 3C then turns to the Rube Goldberg process Congress has decreed for the computation of actual individual tax liability.

Part 1 closes with the interest deductibility rules, for several reasons. First, they are essential to many of the problems in Parts 2 and 3. Second, they illustrate both Haig–Simons and the problem of tax expenditures. Third, they introduce the problem of tax arbitrage and tax abuse more generally. We discover that inconsistent treatment of different parts of a single transaction may allow taxpayers to create non-economic structures that artificially shelter income from tax. The anti-arbitrage rules Congress has enacted in response significantly complicate the answer to the question: "What should we tax?" Our income tax system consists of three types of rules—(1) income-measuring rules consistent with Haig–Simons, (2) tax expenditures, and (3) anti-abuse provisions. In this regard, the interest deductibility rules are nicely representative of the Code as a whole.

CHAPTER 1

THE CONCEPT OF INCOME

■ ■ ■

Principle: All economic value received is, in theory, "income" unless paid for with previously taxed or excluded dollars.

Code: Section 61

Regulations: Section 1.61–1(a)

Subchapter A: Source

Principle: All economic value received, *regardless of its source*, is, in theory, "income" unless paid for with previously taxed or excluded dollars.

Code: Section 61

Regulations: Section 1.61–14(a)

CESARINI v. UNITED STATES
296 F.Supp. 3 (N.D. Ohio 1969)

This is an action by the plaintiffs as taxpayers for the recovery of income tax payments made in the calendar year 1964. Plaintiffs contend that the amount of $836.51 was erroneously overpaid by them in 1964, and that they are entitled to a refund in that amount.

Plaintiffs are husband and wife. In 1957, the plaintiffs purchased a used piano at an auction sale for approximately $15.00, and the piano was used by their daughter for piano lessons. In 1964, while cleaning the piano, plaintiffs discovered the sum of $4,467.00. [They] reported the sum of $4,467.00 on their 1964 joint income tax return as ordinary income. On October 18, 1965, plaintiffs filed an amended return, eliminating the sum of $4,467.00 from the gross income computation, and requesting a refund in the amount of $836.51, the amount allegedly overpaid as a result of the former inclusion of $4,467.00 in the original return for the calendar year of 1964. The Commissioner rejected taxpayers' refund claim in its entirety, and plaintiffs filed the instant action.

Plaintiffs make three alternative contentions in support of their claim. First, that the $4,467.00 found in the piano is not includable in gross income under Section 61. Secondly, even if the retention of the cash constitutes a realization of ordinary income under Section 61, it was due and owing in the year the piano was purchased, 1957, and by 1964, the statute of limitations had elapsed. [Third contention omitted.] The Government asserts that the amount found in the piano is includable in gross income under Section 61(a) [and] that the money is taxable in the year it was actually found, 1964.

The starting point in determining whether an item is to be included in gross income is, of course, Section 61(a), [which] provides in part:

> "Except as otherwise provided in this subtitle, gross income means all income from whatever source derived, including (but not limited to) the following items: . . ."

Subsections (1) through (15) of Section 61(a) then go on to list fifteen items specifically included in the computation of the taxpayer's gross income, and Part II of Subchapter B of the 1954 Code (Sections 71 et seq.) deals with other items expressly included in gross income. While neither of these listings expressly includes the type of income which is at issue in the case at bar, Part III of Subchapter B (Sections 101 et seq.) deals with items specifically excluded from gross income, and found money is not listed in those sections either. This absence of express mention in any of the code sections necessitates a return to the "all income from whatever source" language of Section 61(a), and the express statement there that gross income is "not limited to" the following fifteen examples. Section 1.61–1(a) of the Treasury Regulations reiterates this broad construction of gross income, providing in part:

> "Gross income means all income from whatever source derived, unless excluded by law. Gross income includes income realized in any form, whether in money, property, or services. . . ."

The decisions of the United States Supreme Court have frequently stated that this broad all-inclusive language was used by Congress to exert the full measure of its taxing power under the Sixteenth Amendment to the United States Constitution.

In addition, the Government relies upon an I.R.S. Revenue Ruling which is undeniably on point:

> "The finder of treasure-trove is in receipt of taxable income, for Federal income tax purposes, to the extent of its value in United States Currency, for the taxable year in which it is reduced to undisputed possession." Rev. Rul. 61, 1953–1 Cum. Bull. 17.

In addition to the numerous cases in the Supreme Court which uphold the broad sweeping construction of Section 61(a) found in Treas. Reg. § 1.61–1(a), other courts and commentators writing at a point in time before the ruling came down took the position that windfalls, including found monies, were properly includable in gross income under Section 22(a) of the 1939 Code, the predecessor of Section 61(a) in the 1954 Code. While it is generally true that revenue rulings may be disregarded by the courts if in conflict with the code and the regulations, or with other judicial decisions, plaintiffs in the instant case have been unable to point to any inconsistency between the gross income sections of the code, the interpretation of them by the regulations and the Courts, and the revenue ruling which they herein attack as inapplicable. On the other hand, the United States has shown a consistency in letter and spirit between the ruling and the code, regulations, and court decisions.

Although not cited by either party, the following Treasury Regulation appears in the 1964 Regulations, the year of the return in dispute:

"§ 1.61–14 Miscellaneous items of gross income.

"(a) In general. In addition to the items enumerated in section 61(a), there are many other kinds of gross income .... Treasure trove, to the extent of its value in United States currency, constitutes gross income for the taxable year in which it is reduced to undisputed possession."

This language is the same in all material respects as that found in Rev. Rul. 61, and is undoubtedly an attempt to codify that ruling into the Regulations which apply to the 1954 Code. This Court is of the opinion that Treas. Reg. § 1.61–14(a) is dispositive of the major issue in this case if the $4,467.00 found in the piano was "reduced to undisputed possession" in the year petitioners reported it.

This brings the Court to the second contention of the plaintiffs: that if any tax was due, it was in 1957 when the piano was purchased, and by 1964 the Government was blocked from collecting it by reason of the statute of limitations. This Court finds that the $4,467.00 sum was properly included in gross income for the calendar year of 1964. Problems of when title vests, or when possession is complete in the field of federal taxation, in the absence of definitive federal legislation on the subject, are ordinarily determined by reference to the law of the state in which the taxpayer resides, or where the property around which the dispute centers is located. Since both the taxpayers and the property in question are found within the State of Ohio, Ohio law must govern as to when the found money was "reduced to undisputed possession" within the meaning of Treas. Reg. § 1.61–14 and Rev. Rul. 61.

In Ohio, there is no statute specifically dealing with the rights of owners and finders of treasure trove, and in the absence of such a statute the common-law rule of England applies, so that "title belongs to the finder as against all the world except the true owner." Under Ohio law, the plaintiffs must have actually found the money to have superior title over all but the true owner, and they did not discover the old currency until 1964. Therefore, this Court finds that the $4,467.00 in old currency was not "reduced to undisputed possession" until its actual discovery in 1964, and thus the United States was not barred by the statute of limitations from collecting the $836.51 in tax during that year.

Since it appears to the Court that the income tax on these taxpayers' gross income for the calendar year of 1964 has been properly assessed and paid, this taxpayers' suit for a refund in the amount of $836.51 must be dismissed, and judgment entered for the United States.

NOTES

1. *"Income" in the Supreme Court.*—In *Eisner v. Macomber*, 252 U.S. 189 (1920), the Supreme Court held that stock dividends (dividends paid to corporate shareholders in the form of additional shares of corporate stock) were not "income" within the meaning of the Sixteenth Amendment to the U.S. Constitution and therefore could not be taxed. Income, stated the Court, is "gain derived from labor, from capital, or from both combined." In effect, the Court held that whether receipts were "income" depended on where they came from—on their source. For the next 35 years, lower courts struggled to determine whether particular gains were derived from labor, capital, or both combined—that is, to determine their source. The Court finally resolved the question in *Commissioner v. Glenshaw Glass Co.*, 348 U.S. 426 (1955). At issue was whether a punitive damage award not derived from labor or capital was nevertheless "income." The Court held that it was. Punitive damages were income, the Court held, because they were "accessions to wealth, clearly realized, over which the taxpayers have complete dominion." Glenshaw Glass Co. had income because it was wealthier, regardless of the source of its newfound wealth. The bottom-line conclusion of *Macomber*—that stock dividends are not taxable—remains the general statutory rule, now embodied in Code Section 305(a). But *Macomber*'s use of source to define "income" is no longer the law. Instead, we look at whether taxpayer has received economic value, regardless of the source of that value. And even *Glenshaw Glass* is not generally viewed as constitutionally limiting.

The Court has made two other commonly-cited observations about the nature of "income." First, it has said that in enacting what is now Code Section 61, which provides that "gross income includes all income from whatever source derived, including (but not limited to) the following items," Congress intended "to use the full measure of its taxing power within those definable categories." *Helvering v. Clifford*, 309 U.S. 331, 334 (1940). Second, it has suggested that "income" should be given its "plain popular meaning." *United States v. Kirby Lumber Co.*, 284 U.S. 1, 3 (1931).

2. *The realization requirement.*—One of the most important structural features of our system is that, in general, income must be "realized" before it is subject to tax. Indeed, our international tax rules take the position that other countries' taxes are not "income" taxes unless they contain a realization requirement similar to our own. *See* Treas. Reg. § 1.901–2(b)(2)(i)(A).

Here, it is useful to distinguish three different but related concepts: accrual, realization, and recognition. Accrual is a concept borrowed from accounting; accrued income is simply income that has been earned, even if not collected. Gain from the change in value of property, for example, accrues as the property increases in value, even if the property is not sold. Assume that in January, Alice buys 100 shares of stock for $10,000. Over the course of the year, her stock rises in value to $12,000, although she chooses not to sell it. Is she wealthier? Yes, by $2,000. We say that $2,000 of income has "accrued." In *Glenshaw Glass* terms, she has an "accession to wealth." Do we tax her on that accession to wealth? No, because it has not yet been "realized."

Unfortunately, there is no generally accepted definition of realization for tax purposes. In the context of gains from the change in value of property, income is realized when the property is sold; the sale confirms that the increase in value was real. In effect, our system normally treats increases or decreases in value as hypothetical until taxpayer takes them to market. Realization is harder to define in other contexts. *Compare M. E. Blatt Co. v. United States*, 305 U.S. 267 (1938) (value of improvements built by tenant not realized income to landlord in year of installation) *with Helvering v. Bruun*, 309 U.S. 461 (1940) (landlord realizes income in amount of remaining value of tenant-built improvements when tenant abandons lease) (overruled legislatively by Code Sections 109 and 1019). *See also* Leandra Lederman, *"Stranger Than Fiction": Taxing Virtual Worlds*, 82 N.Y.U. L. REV. 1620, 1652 (2007) ("Does an in-world exchange of virtual items in a game world constitute a realization?"). Finally, recognition. An item of income or loss is "recognized" if and when it is taken into account for federal tax purposes. In general, an item of income or loss is "recognized" the moment it is "realized" under taxpayer's method of accounting, although the Code accords nonrecognition treatment to many types of realized gains and losses. *See, e.g.*, Code Sections 1033 (like-kind exchanges), 351 (incorporations), and 721 (partnership contributions).

There are good reasons for our system's realization requirement. Taxing an increase in value (or allowing a loss for a decrease in value) before an asset is sold is often problematic. Determining the asset's value can be difficult; if so, taxing increases in value currently may be expensive and uncertain, inviting annual appraisals and litigation. In addition, taxing increases in value prior to sale may result in tax liability at a time when taxpayer has no cash with which to pay the tax. Nevertheless, as we will see, the realization requirement has profoundly distortive effects on our system, allowing tax on some gains to be deferred for extended periods and other gains to escape tax altogether.

3. *Relevance of non-tax law.*—Unless otherwise provided, the federal tax consequences of a transaction generally follow the non-tax legal consequences of that same transaction. In the U.S., non-tax legal consequences commonly depend on state law. Outside the U.S., they depend on the laws of the relevant nation or territory. This has at least two important implications for tax analysis. First, all tax analysis must begin with an understanding of the non-tax legal consequences of the transaction in question. Second, the same transaction may have different tax consequences in different states or jurisdictions. This, in turn, poses a significant challenge for those writing tax rules. Such rules have to work as intended in a wide variety of non-tax legal environments.

4. *Annual accounting and the statute of limitations.*—In general, income is reported annually and the tax on that income computed annually. With few exceptions (*see, e.g.*, Chapter 6A, Section 1(a), regarding payment by check, below) liability is computed based on the information available as of midnight on the last day of the taxable period. Subsequently obtained information may require adjusting entries in later years, but the original year's return is not generally required or permitted to reflect after-acquired information. *See, e.g., United States v. Lewis*, 340 U.S. 590 (1951), and Chapter 10, below.

The standard three-year statute of limitations with respect to an income tax return begins to run as of the date the return is due (without extensions) or, if later, the date on which the return or any amended return is actually filed. Code Section 6501. Thus, for example, the three-year statute of limitations for individual taxable year 2012 would expire three years after April 15, 2013, or, if later, three years after the return or any amended return is actually filed. Extended or unlimited limitations periods are provided in a variety of situations, including the filing of false or fraudulent returns or willful attempts to evade tax.

5. *Claim of right doctrine.*—What if a taxpayer receives amounts, claiming that he is entitled to them as a matter of non-tax law, even though he happens to be wrong? Under the common law rule invoked in *Cesarini*, for example, the finder does not get good title against the true owner, but only as against the rest of the world. *See, e.g., Armory v. Delamirie*, 1 Str. 505 (Kings Bench 1722). Nevertheless, under Treas. Reg. § 1.61–14, he is required to report the found item as income in the year in which it is "reduced to undisputed possession." So long as he makes claim to the found item, he cannot defer reporting its value as income until the year in which the true owner's rights are extinguished by operation of the non-tax statute of limitations—which is when, as a matter of non-tax law, he actually acquires title.

This aspect of the treasure trove regulation implements a broader rule known as the "claim of right" doctrine, articulated by the Supreme Court in *North American Oil Consolidated v. Burnet*, 286 U.S. 417 (1932). The Court there stated: "If a taxpayer receives earnings under a claim of right and without restriction as to its disposition, he has received income which he is required to return [that is, report to the IRS], even though it may still be claimed that he is not entitled to retain the money, and even though he may still be adjudged liable to restore its equivalent." The claim of right doctrine, in turn, follows from the even broader principle that a gain "constitutes taxable income when its recipient has such control over it that, as a practical matter, he derives readily realizable economic value from it," regardless of whether he has any legal right to it. *Rutkin v. United States*, 343 U.S. 130, 137 (1952). Thus, the fruits of criminal activity constitute "income" even if they do not legally belong to the criminal.

6. *Official administrative guidance.*—The Department of the Treasury and the Internal Revenue Service (the "IRS" or the "Service") issue three principal types of official guidance interpreting the Internal Revenue Code: regulations, revenue rulings, and revenue procedures. Under *Mayo Foundation for Medical Education and Research v. United States*, 562 U.S. ___, 131 S.Ct. 704 (2011), tax regulations issued in accordance with the Administrative

Procedure Act are entitled to so-called *Chevron* deference. Under *Chevron U.S.A. v. Natural Resources Defense Council*, 467 U.S. 837 (1984), a court first asks whether Congress has "directly addressed the precise question at issue." If it has, the statute governs. If it has not, an administrative regulation construing the statute is to be upheld unless it is "arbitrary or capricious in substance, or manifestly contrary to the statute."

Revenue rulings and procedures, by contrast, are issued by the IRS without the benefit of the public notice and comment procedures required for regulations. Revenue rulings and procedures are therefore probably only entitled to so-called *Skidmore* deference, under which deference is given to an agency interpretation only to the degree the court finds it persuasive. *Skidmore v. Swift & Co.*, 323 U.S. 134 (1944).

The deference status of "temporary" regulations is less clear, since they too are issued without the benefit of public notice and comment. Under Code Section 7805(e)(2), however, temporary regulations issued after November 20, 1988, expire three years after they are issued. In theory, "proposed" regulations are not entitled to deference at all, although they do constitute "authority" for purposes of determining whether a taxpayer is subject to penalties for taking a position without "substantial authority" under Code Section 6662(d)(2)(B)(ii) or Code Section 6664(d)(3)(B). *See* Reg. § 1.6662–4(d)(3)(iii).

7. *How U.S. income tax disputes are litigated.*—Unlike some income tax systems, the U.S. system begins with self-assessment. In general, each taxpayer is expected to determine his or her income tax liability honestly and accurately and report that liability on a return filed with the IRS, typically once a year. If the IRS disagrees with a taxpayer's return, it issues a "statutory notice of deficiency." In general, a taxpayer who wishes to contest the IRS's position has two options: she can (1) not pay the contested amount and file a petition for redetermination in the Tax Court, or (2) pay the contested amount and sue for a refund in her local U.S. District Court or the U.S. Claims Court in Washington, DC. The Commissioner of Internal Revenue is a party to all Tax Court cases; if "Commissioner" appears in a case name, therefore, we can infer that taxpayer chose the Tax Court option (*e.g.*, *Commissioner v. Glenshaw Glass Co.*). The United States is generally the defendant in all suits for refund; the fact that "United States" appears in a case name, therefore, indicates that taxpayer chose to pay and then sue (*e.g.*, *Cesarini v. United States*).

Why might a taxpayer prefer one route over the other? Many factors may enter into a taxpayer's decision. *See, e.g.*, Thomas Greenaway, *Choice of Forum in Federal Civil Tax Litigation*, 62 Tax Law. 311 (2009). The Tax Court has procedural rules that are sometimes quite different from the Federal Rules of Civil Procedure. In addition, Tax Court judges are generally well-versed in tax law and theory. A taxpayer with an intuitively attractive but theoretically or technically questionable case, therefore, may prefer to take his case to U.S. District Court, where judges often have no tax training and may be less persuaded by theoretical or technical arguments. The Cesarinis chose this second route.

PROBLEMS FOR DISCUSSION

1-1. While walking to class, Abby finds a $20 bill on the ground. Assume that common law applies. Absent a statutory exclusion, does she have income?

1-2. Bob's grandmother sends him a check for $25 for his birthday. Absent a statutory exclusion, does he have income? (Note that Code Section 102(a) excludes gifts from "gross income." This question asks you to ignore that section.)

1-3. Carol buys a set of wind chimes for $20. She never takes them out of the package. After concluding that she would rather have the money, she sells them on the internet for $20. Does she have income? Does it matter whether the $20 she used to pay for the wind chimes came from taxable wages or from an excludible gift?

1-4. In *Cesarini*, suppose the true owner had come forward in 1964 (the year of the finding) to claim the $4,467 and the governing non-tax rules had honored the true owner's claim. Same result? Suppose he had come forward instead in January 1965 and the governing non-tax rules had again honored his claim. Same result?

1-5. A number of U.S. states have replaced or supplemented the common law rule invoked in *Cesarini* with "finder's statutes," which typically require a finder to either return the found item to the true owner or deposit it with the police or some other central registry for a specified period. *See, e.g.*, N.Y. Pers. Prop. § 252 (McKinney 2011). If the owner does not come forward and claim the deposited property within the specified period, it becomes the property of the finder. Daniel finds the same $4,467 in his piano in 1964, but in a state with a one-year finder's statute, with which he complies. When should he report the income? What if, notwithstanding the finder's statute, he spends the money immediately?

1-6. Assume that *Cesarini* arises in foreign jurisdiction X, the law of which vests full ownership of the $4,467 in the Cesarinis in 1957. Same result?

DESIGN CONSIDERATIONS

Tax systems often tax income from different sources differently. For example, our income tax system taxes income from capital differently than it does income from labor. Instead of saying that income from a particular source is not "income," however, we say that it is income of a particular "character" and then impose special rules on income of that character. Or we may treat receipts from a particular source as "income" but statutorily exclude them from our tax computation. For example, gifts are, in theory, income ("accessions to wealth, clearly realized, over which the taxpayers have complete dominion"), but are excluded from "gross income" by Code Section 102.

There are at least two problems with defining "income" by reference to source. First, it is sometimes quite hard. Between *Macomber* and *Glenshaw Glass*, the Supreme Court's source-based approach generated a great deal of litigation. Second, it may result in taxing some types of receipts but not others, reducing the breadth of the base, violating ability-to-pay norms, and inducing taxpayers to favor activities that produce nontaxable receipts and disfavor activities receipts from which are taxable. In other words, defining income by reference to source may be inconsistent with the reasons we tax income in the first place.

Nevertheless, so-called "schedular" tax systems make source fundamental. An item is taxable under such a system only if a statutory provision explicitly imposes tax on income from the relevant source. One big advantage of schedular taxation is that it can be made significantly less administratively burdensome. A collection method is typically specified for each type of taxed income—for example, withholding—often without requiring filing or other action by the recipient taxpayer at all. The net effect can be a system without any generally-applicable annual filing requirement—an enormous boon to taxpayers that, coincidentally, makes taxes less politically salient and therefore easier for legislatures to impose.

The United States uses source-based income taxation in two principal contexts. First, it taxes nonresident aliens and foreign corporations on just two types of income: "taxable income which is effectively connected with the conduct of a trade or business within the United States" and "fixed or determinable annual or periodical gains, profits, and income" not so connected that are "received from sources within the United States." The latter are subject to a flat tax of 30 percent on gross income, collected through a withholding requirement imposed on payor; payees are not required to file returns at all. The former is subject to most of the standard return filing rules and rates imposed on income earned by U.S. residents generally. Income of nonresident aliens and foreign corporations from other sources is exempt from U.S. tax altogether.

Second, in addition to the income tax, the United States imposes a second major tax on income from labor: the payroll tax, popularly known as "FICA" or, less accurately, the "Social Security tax." Payroll tax is imposed on income from labor at a rate of 15.3%. Half this amount (7.65%) is paid by the employee; the employer withholds this half from the employee's wages and remits it directly to the government. The other half is paid by the employer. The payroll tax consists of two components, a Social Security component (normally 6.2% on each, the employer and the employee) and a Medicare component (1.45% on each). In 2012, the Social Security component is imposed on the first $110,100 of an individual's labor income; amounts in excess of that cut-off are not subject to the Social Security component. The Medicare component, by contrast, is imposed on all wages without limit. Self-employed individuals are subject to a "self-employment" tax that mimics the payroll tax. Code Section 1401 et seq. Roughly three-quarters of all American taxpayers pay more payroll or self-employment tax than income tax. In fiscal year 2012, the payroll tax is expected to raise about $862 billion; the individual income tax, by comparison, about $1,145 billion.

Subchapter B: Non-Cash Receipts

Principle: All economic value received, *regardless of whether received in cash or in kind*, is, in theory, "income" unless paid for with previously taxed or excluded dollars.

Regulations: Section 1.61–2(d)(1)

REV. RUL. 79–24, 1979–1 C.B. 60

FACTS

Situation 1. In return for personal legal services performed by a lawyer for a housepainter, the housepainter painted the lawyer's personal residence. Both the lawyer and the housepainter are members of a barter club, an organization that annually furnishes its members a directory of members and the services they provide. All the members of the club are professional or trades persons. Members contact other members directly and negotiate the value of the services to be performed.

Situation 2. An individual who owned an apartment building received a work of art created by a professional artist in return for the rent-free use of an apartment for six months by the artist.

LAW

Section 1.61–2(d)(1) of the regulations provides that if services are paid for other than in money, the fair market value of the property or services taken in payment must be included in income. If the services were rendered at a stipulated price, such price will be presumed to be the fair market value of the compensation received in the absence of evidence to the contrary.

HOLDINGS

Situation 1. The fair market value of the services received by the lawyer and the housepainter are includible in their gross incomes under section 61 of the Code.

Situation 2. The fair market value of the work of art and the six months fair rental value of the apartment are includible in the gross incomes of the apartment-owner and the artist under section 61 of the Code.

Notes

1. *Expansion of the concept of income.*—Early Code provisions focused primarily on receipts of cash or property. *See, e.g.*, Code Section 1001(b) (amount realized from the disposition of property equals the sum of any

money received plus the fair market value of any property received). As cases arose in which taxpayers received other types of value, however, courts found ways to construe those provisions to encompass receipt of other types of value, sometimes doing violence to the literal language of the provisions in question. *See, e.g., International Freighting Corp. v. Commissioner*, 135 F.2d 310 (2d Cir. 1943) (amount realized on disposition of appreciated property includes value of employee services to be received in return); *Old Colony Trust Co. v. Commissioner*, 279 U.S. 716 (1929) (amount realized includes relief from liability). Over time, therefore, the *Glenshaw Glass* reference to "accessions to wealth" has come to mean "accessions to economic value."

PROBLEMS FOR DISCUSSION

1–7. Emily receives the use of a company-owned laptop computer having a retail value of $3,000 as a perk from her employer, so long as she remains employed by that employer. Were Emily to rent the same computer from a dealer herself, the list rental rate would be $1,000 per year, although neither Emily nor her employer in fact rents the computer from anyone. In the absence of an applicable statutory exclusion, does she have income? If so, how much income does she have?

1–8. While hiking on publicly owned land, Indiana discovers a silver cup. When he gets home, he takes the cup to an appraiser, who tells him it is worth approximately $15,000. Two weeks later, he sells the cup at auction for $12,000. Does he have income? If so, when and how much? Suppose instead that he discovers a chest of historically important papers, which the appraiser also values at approximately $15,000. Same result?

1–9. Genny and Sami are neighbors. On Tuesday, Genny watches Sami's kids for the afternoon; in exchange, Sami watches Genny's kids on Wednesday. It would cost each of them $40 per afternoon to hire a babysitter. Do they have income?

1–10. Henry drives cross-country. Jenny shares the driving and the cost of gas. Does either of them have income? If so, how much?

1–11. Harry and Sally, who are married and live together, agree to divide up the household tasks. He agrees to do the cooking and cleaning. She agrees to take care of the yard and the car. He takes care of the kids on even numbered days, she on odd numbered days. Do they have income? Does it matter whether they are married? Does it matter whether they live in the same house?

1–12. Because he loves to travel, Mario has chosen a career as a pilot for a commercial airline. His job regularly takes him to London, Paris, Vienna, and Athens; while there, he spends his free time sightseeing and soaking in the local culture. He would visit those cities for pleasure even if he were not a pilot. Does he have income by reason of the fact that he gets to fly there for free?

1–13. Your workplace has a kitchen in which free coffee is provided, paid for by your employer. If you drink the coffee, do you have income?

1–14. You send your kids to public school without charge. The town spends $8,000 per year per pupil to provide free public education, which it funds out of taxes on real property. Do you have income? Does it matter whether you pay property taxes?

Design Considerations

Congress could structure our tax system so as to tax only receipts of cash. One can imagine how taxpayers would likely react. Employees, businesses, lenders, landlords, stockholders, partners, and anyone else who could would ask to be paid in non-cash (and therefore nontaxable) value—use of a house, use of a car, free food, free health insurance, free education and child care for their children, and so forth. Our tax base would be smaller; higher rates would therefore be necessary to raise the same amount of revenue. Taxpayers who were compensated in kind would be treated differently from those compensated in cash—even if they had the same ability to pay taxes. And behavior would likely change; more transactions would be structured as non-cash exchanges. By taxing receipts in kind just as we tax cash, our system avoids these problems.

Nevertheless, the decision to tax all economic value received, even unearned value, creates significant line-drawing problems, which we explore in Chapter 2.

CHAPTER 2

SYSTEMIC EXCLUSIONS

■ ■ ■

In this chapter, we explore some of the tools our system uses (or seems to use) to limit the scope of the principles articulated in Chapter 1. Some are statutory and relatively precise. Some are doctrinal. Yet others are poorly understood—taxpayers simply do not report the items in question, the IRS does not assert a deficiency, there is no case law, Congress provides no guidance, and we are left to wonder where lines should be drawn.

Subchapter A: The Role of Markets in the Measurement of Income, Non–Market Exchanges, and Imputed Income

SECTION 1: THE ROLE OF MARKETS IN THE MEASUREMENT OF INCOME

Our tax system relies heavily on "the objective criterion of the market as the mechanism for determining whether [what taxpayer has received has] economic value." *Collins v. Commissioner*, T.C. Memo. 1992–478 (1992). In general, when a taxpayer purchases an item on the open market and has no other relationship to the seller, the price paid is treated as dispositive of the item's value, a rule sometimes known as the "bargain purchase rule." The fact that a taxpayer has had the good fortune to buy a $200 item for $50 in an arm's-length transaction does not trigger $150 of income—even if, as a matter of fact, he is $150 wealthier. Conversely, the fact that he pays $200 for an item worth only $50 does not trigger loss—even if, as a matter of fact, he has suffered a reduction in net worth. *See, e.g., Palmer v. Commissioner*, 302 U.S. 63 (1937); *Husted v. Commissioner*, 47 T.C. 664, 673 (1967); *Hunley v. Commissioner*, 25 T.C.M. (CCH) 355 (1966); *Pellar v. Commissioner*, 25 T.C. 299, 309 (1955).

In the case of receipts in kind, however, there is often no market reference price available. In such cases, we generally require taxpayer to report the "fair market value" of the item. Although no generally applicable statutory or regulatory definition exists, many more narrowly applicable regulations define "fair market value" in terms similar to the following: "the price at which property or the right to use property would change hands between a willing buyer and a willing seller, neither being under any compulsion to buy, sell or transfer property or the right to use property, and both having reasonable knowledge of relevant facts." Treas. Reg. § 53.4958–4(b)(1)(i). *See also* Treas. Reg. § 1.170–1(c)(1), Treas. Reg. § 1.170A–1(c)(2), Treas. Reg. § 1.412(c)(2)–1(c)(1), Treas. Reg. § 1.415(c)–1(b)(5), Treas. Reg. § 1.430(g)–1(c)(1)(ii), Treas. Reg. § 1.704–4(a)(3), Treas. Reg. § 1.737–1(b)(2), Treas. Reg. § 1.897–1(*o*)(2)(ii); Treas. Reg. § 1.1374–7(a), Treas. Reg. § 1.1445–1(g)(7), Treas. Reg. § 20.2031–1(b), Treas. Reg. § 20.2031–3, Treas. Reg. § 20.2031–6(a), Treas. Reg. § 25.2512–1, and Treas. Reg. § 25.2512–3(a). *See United States v. Cartwright*, 411 U.S. 546, 551 (1973) ("The willing buyer-willing seller test of fair market value is nearly as old as the federal income, estate, and gifts taxes themselves").

Importantly, we ignore taxpayer's *subjective* valuation of the item received. We look instead at *objective* market value. For example, if an employee receives free personal use of a Lincoln Town Car, even though he does not like the car and is embarrassed to be seen driving it, in the absence of a statutory exclusion he is taxed on the car's full market rental value. Any other rule would require that we probe taxpayers' idiosyncratic likes and dislikes. In particular, we assume that employees have negotiated for and want whatever they receive from their employers.

A limited exception may apply to items received in kind other than in a conventional market transaction, if circumstances strongly suggest that taxpayer would not actually have paid market price for the item received.

TURNER v. COMMISSIONER
T.C. Memo. 1954–38

The petitioners, husband and wife, reported salary of $4,536.16 for 1948.

Reginald, whose name had been selected by chance from a telephone book, was called on the telephone on April 18, 1948 and was asked to name a song that was being played on a radio program. He gave the correct name of the song and then was given the opportunity to identify a second song and thus to compete for a grand prize. He correctly identified the second song and in consideration of his efforts was awarded a number of prizes, including two round trip first-class steamship tickets for a cruise between New York City and Buenos Aires. The tickets were not transferable and were good only within one year on a sailing date approved by the agent of the steamship company.

The petitioners reported income on their return of $520, representing income from the award of the two tickets. The Commissioner, in determining the deficiency, increased the income from this source to $2,220, the retail price of such tickets.

Reginald negotiated with the agent of the steamship company, as a result of which he surrendered his rights to the two first-class tickets, and upon payment of $12.50 received four round trip tourist steamship tickets between New York City and Rio de Janeiro. The petitioners and their two sons used those tickets in making a trip from New York City to Rio de Janeiro and return during 1948.

The award of the tickets to Reginald represented income to him in the amount of $1,400.

Persons desiring to buy round trip first-class tickets between New York and Buenos Aires in April 1948, similar to those to which the petitioners were entitled, would have had to pay $2,220 for them. The petitioners, however, were not such persons. The winning of the tickets did not provide them with something which they needed in the ordinary course of their lives and for which they would have made an expenditure in any event, but merely gave them an opportunity to enjoy a luxury otherwise beyond their means. Their value to the petitioners was not equal to their retail cost. They were not transferable and not salable and there were other restrictions on their use. But even had the petitioner been permitted to sell them, his experience with other more salable articles indicates that he would have had to accept substantially less than the cost of similar tickets purchased from the steamship company and would have had selling expenses. Probably the petitioners could have refused the tickets and avoided the tax problem. Nevertheless, in order to obtain such benefits as they could from winning the tickets, they actually took a cruise accompanied by their two sons, thus obtaining free board, some savings in living expenses, and the pleasure of the trip. It seems proper that a substantial amount should be included in their income for 1948 on account of the winning of the tickets. The problem of arriving at a proper fair figure for this purpose is difficult. The evidence to assist is meager, perhaps unavoidably so. The Court, under such circumstances, must arrive at some figure and has done so.

Problems for Discussion

2–1. Constance, a contestant on a television game show, wins a lifetime supply of licorice. The prize is nontransferable; Constance may eat as much licorice as she wants across the course of her life, but cannot sell the right to anybody else. Assume that, based on the amount of licorice the average person like Constance consumes in his or her lifetime and Constance's age, the prize has a fair market value of $1,500. Does Constance have income? If so, how much?

SECTION 2: INCOME FROM NON-MARKET EXCHANGES

In *Turner*, the fact that the transaction was not a conventional market transaction affected the *amount* of income taxpayer was deemed to have received, not *whether* he received income. We know, however, that many informal, non-market exchanges are not reported at all, even by the most diligent taxpayers, and that the IRS evidences no interest in requiring that they be reported. Why is not clear. Nor is the scope of the resulting exclusion. *See generally* Douglas Kahn, *Exclusion from Income of Compensation for Services and Pooling of Labor Occurring in a Noncommercial Setting*, 11 Fla. Tax Rev. 683 (2011).

The Treasury's interpretation of the relevant reporting rules offers the barest hint of guidance. Code Section 6045 requires that entities known as "barter exchanges" submit information returns regarding the exchanges they facilitate to the IRS. The purpose is to assist the IRS in taxing the kinds of barter transactions covered by Rev. Rul. 79–24, *supra* p. 14. Treas. Reg. § 1.6045–1(a)(4) defines "barter exchange" as:

> "any person with members or clients that contract either with each other or with such person to trade or barter property or services either directly or through such person. *The term does not include arrangements that provide solely for the informal exchange of similar services on a noncommercial basis.*" (emphasis added)

In other words, the Treasury seems to have decided not to tax "informal exchange[s] of similar services on a noncommercial basis." What kinds of transactions fall into this category?

PLR 9608009
February 23, 1996

This ruling is in response to the request for a ruling concerning whether X, which sponsors a time dollar program, is a barter exchange under section 6045 of the Internal Revenue Code and section 1.6045–1(a)(4) of the Income Tax Regulations.

X is a nonprofit corporation that sponsors a time dollar program through which it supports and coordinates the exchange of services among residents in the Y neighborhood and surrounding neighborhoods. The purpose of the program is to strengthen the community and to increase access to services and resources for all in the community.

X maintains a file of services that members are willing to provide, matches service providers and service recipients, and maintains accounts of hours of service provided under the program. All services are valued equally under the program: one hour of service equals one good neighbor point. Participants in the program commonly provide services such as housekeeping, babysitting, gardening, and errand running.

The definition of a member of the program is a participant who has completed the application, interview, orientation, and reference check process. X does not charge a fee for participation or membership in the program. Members may earn points, within limits, for work in operating the program. X does not have a staff person that receives monetary compensation.

A person may request services through the program by calling or visiting X's office. After X receives a request for services, it looks for a match based on the service requested, time needed, proximity, and other factors. X then contacts a potential provider for availability. Upon accepting a referral, the service provider is responsible for calling the service recipient and arranging the time and place of service. After the service is provided, either the service provider or the service recipient reports the hours of service to X. X then credits the provider's account and debits the recipient's account for the hours of service.

Although a member may use accumulated points at any time, X encourages members to use their points when needed. The taxpayer does not guarantee that a member will be able to receive services for accumulated points. Members cannot transfer points or sell points except that members may donate points to other members in the member's immediate family or household. In unusual circumstances, X may deny a request for service from a participant with a debit balance of 26 good neighbor points or more. Nonprofit community groups approved to participate in the program may receive good neighbor points for hours of service provided by the group's members and use those points to obtain services. Members who are self-employed cannot use points to obtain services for their businesses.

We conclude that X is not a barter exchange within the meaning of section 6045(c)(3) because X's operations provide a means for the informal exchange of similar services on a noncommercial basis and do not result in the creation of contractual rights and obligations among members (or between members and X) for the exchange of property or services.

One element to be considered in determining whether an organization is a barter exchange is the types of services provided by the organization's members. In the present case, the services provided by X's members are primarily domestic or personal services. Thus, X's operations facilitate the exchange of similar services in accordance with section 1.6045–1(a)(4).

Other elements to be considered in determining whether an organization is a barter exchange are whether services are exchanged on a commercial or noncommercial basis and whether the exchange of services is formal or informal.

X facilitates the exchange of services on a noncommercial basis as evidenced by the following considerations. First, all services receive a point value based solely on the number of hours of service provided without regard to the type of service. Second, a member who has performed services does not thereby have a contractual right to receive any services from X or from X's members. Third, the organization does not place any limits on when services must be received. Thus, there could be a gap of several years between the time when a member provides services and the time when the member first receives services. Fourth, a member cannot assign (except to family or household members) the points that he or she has accumulated for services performed. Fifth, X is a community organization whose membership consists primarily of individuals living in the Y area. Sixth, X does not charge a fee for participation or membership in the program. Seventh, the records maintained by X show significant disparities in members' accounts as to the number of hours of services provided and the number of hours of services received. Some members typically receive many more hours of services than they provide, while other members—who are apparently motivated by a desire to serve the community—typically provide many more hours of services than they receive. Based on X's records as of July, 1995, there were at that time approximately [a] active participants over 25 percent of which have performed services but have not received any services in return.

The informal nature of the exchange of services is also evident. X simply links members in need of services with other members who are potential providers of services. It is up to the members, rather than X, to determine whether any services will be performed, to determine the time and place for performance of the services, and to ensure that the services are satisfactorily performed. Also, X does not have any responsibility for crediting the account of the service provider or debiting the account of the service recipient unless a member first contacts X and indicates the number of hours of service provided. Moreover, either member (the service provider or the service recipient) can contact X to indicate the number of hours of service provided, and this information may be provided to X informally through a phone call or postcard.

This ruling is directed only to the taxpayer who requested it. Section 6110(j)(3) of the Code provides that it may not be used or cited as precedent.

No opinion is expressed about the tax consequences of the program under any other provision of the Code. Specifically, no opinion is expressed concerning whether a member earns income as a result of the member's participation in the program.

The tentative nature of the IRS's guidance in this area is clear. PLR 9608009 is a "private letter ruling," which cannot be used or cited as precedent. And the ruling only addresses whether third-party reporting is required, expressly reserving the underlying question of whether members earn "income" by participating in the program. If exchanges in the program do trigger income, of course, the IRS has just given up its principal tool for enforcing payment of taxes on such income. But the ruling does not address the question of taxability directly.

NOTES

1. *Unofficial administrative guidance.*—Although Code Section 6110(a) requires that the text of any IRS "written determination" be made open to public inspection, Code Section 6110(k)(3) prohibits citation or use of such documents as precedent. "Written determinations" subject to these rules include private letter rulings (commonly abbreviated "PLR"), technical advice memoranda ("TAM"), field service advice ("FSA"), Chief Counsel advice and notices ("CCA"), litigation bulletins ("LB"), service center advice ("SCA"), litigation guideline memoranda ("LGM"), information letters, and non-docketed service advice review ("NSAR").

Although written determinations may not be cited or used as precedent, some courts have nevertheless accepted them as evidence of how the IRS interprets the Code. *See, e.g., Hanover Bank v. Commissioner*, 369 U.S. 672, 686 (1962):

> "Persuasive evidence that we are correct in our interpretation . . . may be found in the respondent's own prior construction of the statute. . . . [A]lthough the petitioners are not entitled to rely upon unpublished private rulings which were not issued specifically to them, such rulings do reveal the interpretation put upon the statute by the agency charged with the responsibility of administering the revenue laws. And, because the Commissioner ruled [in private letter rulings the same way we do here], we have further evidence that our construction . . . is compelled by the language of the statute."

See Judy S. Kwok, *The Perils of Bright Lines: Section 6110(K)(3) and the Ambiguous Precedential Status of Written Determinations*, 24 VA. TAX REV. 863 (2005).

In addition, written determinations can be important in assessing the reasonableness of taxpayer positions for penalty purposes. Reg. § 1.6662–4(d)(3)(iii) states:

> "[T]he following are authority for purposes of determining whether there is substantial authority for the tax treatment of an item: Applicable provisions of the Internal Revenue Code and other statutory provisions; proposed, temporary and final regulations construing such statutes; revenue rulings and revenue procedures; tax treaties and regulations thereunder, and Treasury Department and other official explanations of such treaties; court cases; congressional intent as reflected in committee reports, joint explanatory statements of managers included in conference committee reports, and floor statements made prior to enactment by one of a bill's managers; General Explanations of tax legislation prepared by the Joint Committee on Taxation (the Blue Book); private letter rulings and technical advice memoranda issued after October 31, 1976; actions on decisions and general counsel memoranda issued after March 12, 1981 (as well as general counsel memoranda published in pre–1955 volumes of the Cumulative Bulletin); Internal Revenue Service information or press releases; and notices, announcements and other administrative pronouncements published by the Service in the Internal Revenue Bulletin."

SECTION 3: IMPUTED INCOME

"Imputed income" consists of value taxpayer creates for herself, either through her own labor or through the use of her own property. Imputed income is therefore a subset of non-market income. Laypeople, including non-tax lawyers, often find the notion of taxing imputed income difficult to accept. Yet economists treat imputed income as "income," and the reasons underlying the decision to tax income suggest that imputed income should be taxable as well. Why?

Assume that at the beginning of the year, taxpayer A owns a parcel of land worth $50,000. Over the course of the year, using only her own labor and scrap materials she has found, she builds a house on her land worth $100,000. At the end of the year, the land and building, taken together, are worth $150,000. Her net worth has increased by $100,000.

Compare A's situation with that of taxpayer B. He too builds a house on his land, but sells it to a third party for $150,000, using the proceeds to buy a house identical to A's. Both A and B have created value of $100,000. They end up in identical houses and economically identical situations. B has income of $100,000. Shouldn't A be taxed the same way as B?

Taxpayer A's income is imputed; she has created value for himself and not yet taken that value to market. Taxpayer B, by contrast, has taken the created value to market, realizing a gain of $100,000 on the sale of the house he has built. If we tax B but not A, we narrow the tax base, requiring higher rates to raise any given revenue target; we treat A and B differently, even though they have the same ability to pay taxes; and we create an incentive for taxpayers to build their own houses (or grow their own food, raise their own children, or wash their own dishes), even if it would be more efficient to have someone else do it for them.

One might be tempted to conclude that the question is merely one of timing. After all, if and when Taxpayer A places her house on the market, she too will realize the same $100,000 of gain. Even if this were true, timing is not a minor issue, as we will discover in Part 3. But many imputed income problems involve more than just timing.

Consider, for example, C, a lawyer who writes his own will. Assume that he would have had to pay $5,000 to have the will professionally written. D, by contrast, works overtime to earn an additional $5,000 and pays an estate planning lawyer $5,000 to write an identical will. The two end up in the same place, and yet are taxed differently. D has created $5,000 of value and is taxed on $5,000 of gross income. C is not taxed at all, even though he too has created $5,000 of value. What's more, if we do not tax him when he writes his will, the resulting value will never be taxed. As a matter of theory, this difference is hard to justify.

Why are A and C, who create value for themselves but do not take that value to market, exempt from tax? Again, the answer is not clear. Even the most diligent taxpayer does not report this kind of income, the

IRS never challenges its omission, there is no case law on point, and Congress is silent.

What is clear, however, is that if taxpayer runs value he creates for himself through ordinary market channels, it is includible.

COMMISSIONER v. DAEHLER
281 F.2d 823 (5th Cir. 1960)

[Petitioner was employed as a salesman by Anaconda, a real estate broker. Through Anaconda, he purchased real estate listed with another broker for sale at $60,000. Taking into account the fact that if he procured a buyer for the property for $52,500 he would realize a commission of $1,837.50 on the sale, and by reason thereof he could acquire the property for his own account at a cost of $50,662.50, he made a formal offer of $52,500 for the property, and in due course was repaid $1,837.50, which was the commission he would have earned on the sale to an outside party.]

[On July 29, 1952, Anaconda paid petitioner $1,837.50, which amount represented 70 per cent of the $2,625 it had received from Hortt. On Anaconda's record of the sale of the property, $1,837.50 was shown as petitioner's commission. The Withholding Statement (Form W–2) as prepared and filed by Anaconda on behalf of petitioner and showing commissions paid to him did not include the said $1,837.50. Petitioners did not include the $1,837.50 in the commissions they reported on their income tax return for 1952.]

A majority of the Tax Court, five judges dissenting, held that since Daehler was buying for himself he was not acting as a salesman; the $1,837.50 was not income to the taxpayer but a reduction in the purchase price.

> [This] Court in *Commissioner v. Minzer* denied the validity of these distinctions:
>
>> It does not seem to us that the tax incidence is dependent upon the tag with which the parties label the connection between them. The agent or broker, or by whatever name he be called, is to receive or retain a percentage of the premiums on policies procured by him, called commissions, as compensation for his service to the company in obtaining the particular business for it. The service rendered to the company, for which it was required to compensate him, was no different in kind or degree where the taxpayer submitted his own application than where he submitted the application of another. In each situation there was the same obligation of the company, the obligation to pay a commission for the production of business measured by a percentage of the premiums.

These principles are controlling in the instant case. Daehler's commission was a compensatory payment for services. Daehler performed a service for his employer in regard to real estate purchase identical with the services performed in other transactions. The services were worth 30 per cent of $2,625 to the employer. They were worth 70 per cent of $2,625 to the employee. We see no escape from the conclusion that the amount he received from his employer was compensation for the actions he performed growing out of the employer-employee relationship. Compensation for such services is taxable income of whatever kind and in whatever form it is received, short of a specific exception to the broad statutory definition of gross income.

PROBLEMS FOR DISCUSSION

2–2. Suppose Daehler takes vacation time to identify property that the owner, desperate for cash, is willing to sell at a below-market price—say for $40,000 instead of $52,500. He buys the property for $40,000 without any other party becoming involved. He has purchased a $52,500 property for $40,000, in effect earning $12,500 while on vacation. Same result?

2–3. In the course of his work as a broker after the *Daehler* decision is rendered, Daehler comes upon yet another property for which the owner is willing to accept $52,500, on the understanding that the owner will likely have to pay whoever serves as broker $2,500—netting $50,000 for the owner. Daehler persuades the owner to sell the property to him directly for $50,000 without listing it. Same result?

DESIGN CONSIDERATIONS

One context in which legislators do sometimes consider taxing imputed income is that of owner-occupied housing. Prior to 1963, the UK taxed such imputed income. According to the Census Bureau, the aggregate value of owner-occupied housing in the U.S. in 2000 was $10.6 trillion. Imputing income on such a body of currently untaxed assets would result in a significant addition to the tax base, which in turn would permit a correspondingly significant reduction in tax rates without any revenue loss. The Treasury estimates that in fiscal year 2013 imputing income on owner-occupied housing would raise an additional $51.08 billion in revenues. *See* 2013 Tax Expenditure Budget, Item 62, Chapter 3B, below. A homeowner with a salary of $50,000 is clearly in a better position to pay taxes than a renter earning the same salary; some portion of the renter's salary has to be set aside to pay the rent. Omission of the homeowner's imputed income therefore violates ability-to-pay norms. Finally, interest on a home mortgage can be viewed as a cost of producing the imputed income that results from home ownership; we allow such interest to be deducted but do not require the resulting income to be reported.

Subchapter B: Psychic or Incidental Income and the Primary Purpose Test

The term "psychic income" refers to the pleasure or other personal benefit a taxpayer gets from a transaction not primarily intended to benefit him. So, for example, Taxpayer A may love her job. Indeed, she may choose a job she loves, which pays only $50,000 a year, over one she does not, which pays $120,000. If so, we can reasonably infer that the pleasure she takes in the lower-paying job must be worth at least $70,000 per year to her. Such pleasure is value received and therefore, in theory, "income." Similarly, Taxpayer B may enjoy the business trips he is required to take to Paris and the business meals he is required to eat there. (A tough job, but someone has to do it.)

Unfortunately, the market does not tell us much about whether taxpayers receive personal benefits from things they do for ostensibly non-personal reasons. Taxpayer C, also making $50,000 a year, may hate the same job; the market gives us no reliable way to distinguish Taxpayer A from Taxpayer C. Similarly, our business traveler may hate flying or being away from his family. The fact that he takes the trips in question may simply reflect the demands of his business.

Our tax system therefore does not attempt to measure and tax psychic or "incidental" income. Instead, it looks at the principal purpose of the activity in question. If the principal purpose is business, we ignore the value of incidental personal benefits taxpayer receives. If the principal purpose is personal or compensatory, by contrast, we treat the entire activity as includible. In effect, the primary purpose test converts an intractable measurement problem into an administrable yes-or-no question.

UNITED STATES v. GOTCHER
401 F.2d 118 (5th Cir. 1968)

In 1960, Mr. and Mrs. Gotcher took a twelve-day expense-paid trip to Germany to tour the Volkswagen facilities there. The trip cost $1372.30. His employer, Economy Motors, paid $348.73, and Volkswagen of Germany and Volkswagen of America shared the remaining $1023.53. Upon returning, Mr. Gotcher bought a twenty-five percent interest in Economy Motors, the Sherman, Texas Volkswagen dealership, that had been offered to him before he left. Today he is President of Economy Motors in Sherman and owns fifty percent of the dealership. Mr. and Mrs. Gotcher did not include any part of the $1372.30 in their 1960 income. The Commissioner determined that the taxpayers had realized income to the extent of the $1372.30 for the expense-paid trip and asserted a tax deficiency of $356.79. Taxpayers paid the deficiency and thereafter timely filed suit for a refund. The district court held that the cost of the trip was not income or, in the alternative, was income and deductible as an ordinary and necessary business expense. We affirm the district court's determination that the cost of the trip was not income to Mr. Gotcher ($686.15); however, Mrs. Gotcher's expenses ($686.15) constituted income and were not deductible.

The court below reasoned that the cost of the trip to the Gotchers was not income because an economic or financial benefit does not constitute income under section 61 unless it is conferred as compensation for services rendered. This conception of gross income is too restrictive since it is well-settled that section 61 should be broadly interpreted and that many items, including noncompensatory gains, constitute gross income.

The concept of economic gain to the taxpayer is the key to section 61. This concept contains two distinct requirements: There must be an economic gain, and this gain must primarily benefit the taxpayer personally. In some cases, as in the case of an expense-paid trip, there is no direct economic gain, but there is an indirect economic gain inasmuch as a benefit has been received without a corresponding diminution in wealth. Yet even if expense-paid items, as meals and lodging, are received by the taxpayer, the value of these items will not be gross income, even though the employee receives some incidental benefit, if the meals and lodging are primarily for the convenience of the employer....

The trip was made in 1959 when VW was attempting to expand its local dealerships in the United States. In 1959, when VW began to push for its share of the American market, its officials determined that the best way to remove the apprehension about this foreign product was to take the dealer to Germany and have him see his investment first-hand. It was believed that once the dealer saw the manufacturing facilities and the stability of the "new Germany" he would be convinced that VW was for him. Furthermore, VW considered the expenditure justified because the dealer was being asked to make a substantial investment of his time and money in a comparatively new product. Mr. Horton testified that VW could not have asked that this upgrading be done unless it convinced the dealer that VW was here to stay. Apparently these trips have paid off since VW's sales have skyrocketed and the dealers have made their facilities top-rate operations under the VW requirements for a standard dealership.

The activities in Germany support the conclusion that the trip was oriented to business. The Government makes much of the fact that the travel brochure allocated only two of the twelve days to the touring of VW factories. This argument ignores the uncontradicted evidence that not all of the planned activities were in the brochure. There is ample support for the trial judge's finding that a substantial amount of time was spent touring VW facilities and visiting local dealerships. VW had set up these tours with local dealers so that the travelers could discuss how the facilities were operated in Germany. Mr. Gotcher took full advantage of this opportunity and even used some of his "free time" to visit various local dealerships. Moreover, at almost all of the evening meals VW officials gave talks about the organization and passed out literature and brochures on the VW story.

Some of the days were not related to touring VW facilities, but that fact alone cannot be decisive. The dominant purpose of the trip is the critical inquiry and some pleasurable features will not negate the finding of an overall business purpose. Since we are convinced that the agenda related primarily to business and that Mr. Gotcher's attendance was prompted by business considerations, the so-called sightseeing complained of by the Government is inconsequential. Indeed, the district court found that even this touring of the countryside had an indirect relation to business since the tours were not typical sightseeing excursions but were connected to the desire of VW that the dealers be persuaded that the German economy was stable enough to justify investment in a German product. Considering the record, the circumstances prompting the trip, and the objective achieved, we conclude that the primary purpose of the trip was to induce Mr. Gotcher to take out a VW dealership interest.

The question, therefore, is what tax consequences should follow from an expense-paid trip that primarily benefits the party paying for the trip. In several analogous situations the value of items received by employees has been excluded from gross income when these items were primarily for the benefit of the employer. Section 119 excludes from gross income of an employee the value of meals and lodging furnished to him for the convenience of the employer. Even before these items were excluded by the 1954 Code, the Treasury and the courts recognized that they should be excluded from gross income. Thus it appears that the value of any trip that is paid by the employer or by a businessman primarily for his own benefit should be excluded from gross income of the payee on similar reasoning.

In the recent case of *Allen J. McDonnell*, a sales supervisor and his wife were chosen by lot to accompany a group of contest winners on an expense-paid trip to Hawaii. In holding that the taxpayer had received no income, the Tax Court noted that he was required by his employer to go and that he was serving a legitimate business purpose though he enjoyed the trip. The decision suggests that in analyzing the tax consequences of an expense-paid trip one important factor is whether the traveler had any choice but to go. Here, although taxpayer was not forced to go, there is no doubt that in the reality of the business world he had no real choice. The trial judge reached the same conclusion. He found that the invitation did not specifically order the dealers to go, but that as a practical matter it was an order or directive that if a person was going to be a VW dealer, sound business judgment necessitated his accepting the offer of corporate hospitality. So far as Economy Motors was concerned, Mr. Gotcher knew that if he was going to be a part-owner of the dealership, he had better do all that was required to foster good business relations with VW. Besides having no choice but to go, he had no control over the schedule or the money spent. VW did all the planning. In cases involving noncompensatory economic gains, courts have emphasized that the taxpayer still had complete dominion and control over the money to use it as he wished to satisfy personal desires or needs. Indeed, the Supreme Court has defined income as accessions of wealth over which the taxpayer has complete control. Clearly, the lack of control works in taxpayer's favor here.

McDonnell also suggests that one does not realize taxable income when he is serving a legitimate business purpose of the party paying the expenses. The cases involving corporate officials who have traveled or entertained clients at the company's expense are apposite. Indeed, corporate executives have been furnished yachts, taken safaris as part of an advertising scheme, and investigated business ventures abroad, but have been held accountable for expenses paid only when the court was persuaded that the expenditure was primarily for the officer's personal pleasure.

On the other hand, when it has been shown that the expenses were paid to effectuate a legitimate corporate end and not to benefit the officer personally, the officer has not been taxed though he enjoyed and benefited from the activity. Thus, the rule is that the economic benefit will be taxable to the recipient only when the payment of expenses serves no legitimate corporate purpose. The decisions also indicate that the tax consequences are to be determined by looking to the primary purpose of the expenses and that the first consideration is the intention of the payor. The Government in argument before the district court agreed that whether the expenses were income to taxpayers is mainly a question of the motives of the people giving the trip. Since this is a matter of proof, the resolution of the tax question really depends on whether Gotcher showed that his presence served a legitimate corporate purpose and that no appreciable amount of time was spent for his personal benefit and enjoyment.

Examination of the record convinces us that the personal benefit to Gotcher was clearly subordinate to the concrete benefits to VW. The purpose of the trip was to push VW in America and to get the dealers to invest more money and time in their dealerships. Thus, although Gotcher got some ideas that helped him become a better dealer, there is no evidence that this was the primary purpose of the trip. Put another way, this trip was not given as a pleasurable excursion through Germany or as a means of teaching taxpayer the skills of selling. He had been selling cars since 1949. The personal benefits and pleasure were incidental to the dominant purpose of improving VW's position on the American market and getting people to invest money.

The corporate-executive decisions indicate that some economic gains, though not specifically excluded from section 61, may nevertheless escape taxation. They may be excluded even though the entertainment and travel unquestionably give enjoyment to the taxpayer and produce indirect economic gains. When this indirect economic gain is subordinate to an overall business purpose, the recipient is not taxed. We are convinced that the personal benefit to Mr. Gotcher from the trip was merely incidental to VW's sales campaign.

As for Mrs. Gotcher, the trip was primarily a vacation. She did not make the tours with her husband to see the local dealers or attend discussions about the VW organization. This being so the primary benefit of the expense-paid trip for the wife went to Mr. Gotcher in that he was relieved of her expenses. He should therefore be taxed on the expenses attributable to his wife.

Subchapter C: Employee Benefits

Unlike exclusions for non-market income, imputed income, and psychic income (assuming such exclusions are actually founded in law), the exclusion and inclusion of employee benefits are addressed in detail in the Code and Regulations. The reason is simple: employers are required to report their employees' compensation to the IRS and make appropriate withholding; they need guidance about what to report and how much to withhold. The fact that third parties are enlisted to enforce taxes on employee compensation means that the IRS cannot simply ignore the problem.

Some of the Code's employee-benefit rules are exercises in line-drawing—inherently necessary once a decision has been made to tax "income" in all its forms. Others are intended to encourage particular types of taxpayer behavior; the most important in this latter category are probably Code Section 106, which excludes the value of premiums paid by employers to purchase health and accident insurance for their employees, and provisions that allow employees to save for retirement and employers to contribute to their employees' retirement accounts on a tax-deferred basis.

Here, we will focus on rules that perform line-drawing functions, specifically Code Sections 119 and 132. Other employee-benefit rules that might arguably fall into this category include Code Section 117(d), which allows schools to charge reduced tuition to employees and their families, Code Section 127, which allows employers to pay a limited amount of tuition tax-free for the education of their employees, and Code Section 129, which allows employers to cover certain costs of childcare tax-free to enable their employees to work.

SECTION 1: CODE SECTION 119

Code: Section 119

Regulations: Section 1.119–1

COMMISSIONER v. KOWALSKI
434 U.S. 77 (1977)

This case presents the question whether cash payments to [New Jersey] state police troopers, designated as meal allowances, are included in gross income under § 61(a) and, if so, are otherwise excludable under § 119.

The pertinent facts are not in dispute. Respondent is a state police trooper. During 1970, he received a base salary of $8,739.38, and an additional $1,697.54 designated as an allowance for meals.

The State instituted the cash meal allowance for its state police officers in July 1949. Prior to that time, all troopers were provided with midshift meals in kind at various meal stations located throughout the State. A trooper unable to eat at an official meal station could, however, eat at a restaurant and obtain reimbursement. The meal-station system proved unsatisfactory because it required troopers to leave their assigned areas of patrol unguarded for extended periods of time. As a result, the State closed its meal stations and instituted a cash-allowance system. Under this system, troopers remain on call in their assigned patrol areas during their midshift break. Otherwise, troopers are not restricted in any way with respect to where they may eat in the patrol area and, indeed, may eat at home if it is located within that area. Troopers may also bring their midshift meal to the job and eat it in or near their patrol cars.

The meal allowance is paid biweekly in advance and is included, although separately stated, with the trooper's salary. The meal-allowance money is also separately accounted for in the State's accounting system. Funds are never commingled between the salary and meal-allowance accounts. Because of these characteristics of the meal-allowance system, the Tax Court concluded that the "meal allowance was not intended to represent additional compensation."

Notwithstanding this conclusion, it is not disputed that the meal allowance has many features inconsistent with its characterization as a simple reimbursement for meals that would otherwise have been taken at a meal station. For example, troopers are not required to spend their meal allowances on their midshift meals, nor are they required to account for the manner in which the money is spent. With one limited exception not relevant here, no reduction in the meal allowance is made for periods when a trooper is not on patrol because, for example, he is assigned to a headquarters building or is away from active duty on vacation, leave, or sick leave. In addition, the cash allowance for meals is described on a state police recruitment brochure as an item of salary to be received in addition to an officer's base salary and the amount of the meal allowance is a subject of negotiations between the State and the police troopers' union. Finally, the amount of an officer's cash meal allowance varies with his rank and is included in his gross pay for purposes of calculating pension benefits.

The starting point in the determination of the scope of "gross income" is the cardinal principle that Congress in creating the income tax intended "to use the full measure of its taxing power." In the absence of a specific exemption, therefore, respondent's meal-allowance payments are income within the meaning of § 61 since, like the payments involved in *Glenshaw Glass Co.*, the payments are "undeniabl[y] accessions to wealth, clearly realized, and over which the [respondent has] complete dominion."

Respondent contends, however, that § 119 can be construed to be a specific exemption covering the meal-allowance payments to New Jersey troopers. Alternatively, respondent argues that notwithstanding § 119 a specific exemption may be found in a line of lower-court cases and administrative rulings which recognize that benefits conferred by an employer on an employee "for the convenience of the employer"—at least when such benefits are not "compensatory"—are not income within the meaning of the Internal Revenue Code. In responding to these contentions, we turn first to § 119. Since we hold that § 119 does not cover cash payments of any kind, we then trace the development over several decades of the convenience-of-the-employer doctrine as a determinant of the tax status of meals and lodging, turning finally to the question whether the doctrine as applied to meals and lodging survives the enactment of the Internal Revenue Code of 1954.

Section 119 provides that an employee may exclude from income "the value of any meals ... furnished to him by his employer for the convenience of the employer, but only if ... the meals are furnished on the business premises of the employer...." By its terms, § 119 covers meals furnished by the employer and not cash reimbursements for meals. Accordingly, respondent's meal-allowance payments are not subject to exclusion under § 119.

[The Court reviews the convenience-of-the-employer doctrine in prior administrative rulings and court cases.]

Even if we assume that respondent's meal-allowance payments could have been excluded from income under the 1939 Code pursuant to the doctrine we have just sketched, we must nonetheless inquire whether such an implied exclusion survives the 1954 recodification of the Internal Revenue Code.

In enacting § 119, the Congress was determined to "end the confusion as to the tax status of meals and lodging furnished an employee by his employer." [The Court reviews the history of negotiations between the House and the Senate regarding the text of the section.]

Thus § 119 comprehensively modified the prior law, both expanding and contracting the exclusion for meals and lodging previously provided, and it must therefore be construed as its draftsmen obviously intended it to be—as a replacement for the prior law, designed to "end [its] confusion."

ADAMS v. UNITED STATES
218 Ct.Cl. 322 (1978)

The issue in this tax refund suit is whether the fair rental value of a Japanese residence furnished the plaintiffs by the employer of plaintiff Faneuil Adams, Jr., is excludable from their gross income under Section 119.

In 1970 and 1971, Faneuil Adams [hereinafter "plaintiff"] was president of Mobil Sekiyu Kabushiki Kaisha ("Sekiyu"), a Tokyo-based Japanese corporation which was wholly owned by Mobil Oil Corporation

("Mobil"). During those years, Sekiyu employed about 1,500 persons in Japan with sales between $400–700 million each year. It had several thousand service stations in Japan and was also involved in two joint ventures with Japanese companies which owned and operated four refineries.

In order to attract qualified employees for foreign service and to maintain an equitable relationship between its domestic and American foreign-based employees, thereby preventing any employee from gaining a benefit or suffering a hardship from serving overseas, Mobil maintained a compensation policy for its American employees assigned outside the United States. One of the components of the policy involved the procurement by Mobil of housing for such employees, regardless of their position or duties. Mobil first calculated a "U.S. Housing Element" for each American foreign-based employee, based on a survey of the Bureau of Labor Statistics, which reflected the approximate average housing costs in the United States at various family sizes and income levels. Mobil then subtracted from that employee's salary the amount of his particular U.S. Housing Element. If Mobil provided housing to the employee, the employee would include in his gross income for federal tax purposes the U.S. Housing Element amount. If the employee instead obtained his own housing abroad, Mobil reimbursed him for the full amount, subject to certain predetermined limitations based upon reasonableness, and the employee would then include the full amount reimbursed in his gross income.

Pursuant to the above policy, Mobil provided plaintiff with a residence for the years in question. The three-level house, which was built and owned by Sekiyu, was 3 miles from headquarters and consisted of a large living room, dining room, pantry and kitchen, three bedrooms, a den, two bathrooms, two maid's rooms, two garage areas, and a garden and veranda. By American standards the house was not large, but it was apparently choice. Sekiyu felt that it was important to house its chief executive officer in prestigious surroundings because, particularly in Japan, there is less of a distinction than in the United States between business activities and social activities. The effectiveness of a president of a company in Japan is influenced by the social standing and regard accorded to him by the Japanese business community. If the president of Sekiyu had not resided in a residence equivalent to the type provided the plaintiff, it would appear that he would have been unofficially downgraded and slighted by the business community and his effectiveness for Sekiyu correspondingly impaired. Sekiyu, therefore, provided such a house to plaintiff and required him to reside there as a matter of company policy.

The house was also designed so that it could accommodate the business activities of the plaintiff. The den was built specifically for the conduct of business, and the kitchen and living room were sufficiently large for either business meetings or receptions. Plaintiff worked in the house in the evenings and on weekends and held small meetings there for mixed business and social purposes. He regularly used the telephone for business purposes from his home after regular working hours, both for business emergencies and also for communicating with persons in the United States because of the time difference. In addition, he regularly discharged his business entertainment responsibilities in the residence, generally averaging about 35–40 such occasions in a normal year. In 1970 his entertaining declined considerably because of the absence of his wife from Japan for 10 months, but it resumed again in 1971. Plaintiff was provided with two maids, only one of whom was needed for his family's personal requirements.

Plaintiff included in his gross income for federal tax purposes, as the value of the housing furnished him by his employer, the U.S. Housing Element amounts which had been subtracted from his gross salary. Those amounts, which were designed to approximate the average housing costs of a similarly situated person in the United States during 1970 and 1971, totaled $4,439 for 1970 and $4,824 for 1971. However, because the cost of housing in Tokyo in those years was considerably higher than that in the United States, it is agreed by the parties that the fair rental value of the residence furnished plaintiff by Sekiyu was $20,000 in 1970 and $20,599.09 in 1971. Accordingly, upon audit of plaintiff's 1970 and 1971 income tax returns, the Internal Revenue Service, among other adjustments, increased the amounts reported by plaintiff as the value of the housing furnished by Sekiyu to $20,000 in 1970 and $20,599.09 in 1971. Plaintiff has filed suit to recover the sum of $914.24 plus assessed interest as a result of the Internal Revenue Service's inclusion in his gross income of the amounts in excess of the U.S. Housing Element for the 2 years in suit.

Plaintiff contends that the fair rental value of the residence supplied to him by Sekiyu in 1970 and 1971 is excludable from his gross income because of Section 119 of the 1954 Code. [I]n order to qualify for the exclusion of Section 119, each of three tests must be met:

(1) the employee must be required to accept the lodging as a condition of his employment;

(2) the lodging must be furnished for the convenience of the employer; and

(3) the lodging must be on the business premises of the employer.

The Regulations further provide that the first test is met where the employee is "required to accept the lodging in order to enable him properly to perform the duties of his employment."

It is clear that the first requirement of the statute has been met because the plaintiff was explicitly required to accept the residence provided by Sekiyu as a condition of his employment as president of the company. Sekiyu's goal was twofold: first, it wanted to insure that its president resided in housing of sufficiently dignified surroundings to promote his effectiveness within the Japanese business community. Secondly, Sekiyu wished to provide its president with facilities which were sufficient for the conduct of certain necessary business activities at home. Since at least 1954 Sekiyu had required that its chief executive officer reside in the residence provided to plaintiff, as a condition to appointment as president.

As to the "for the convenience of the employer" test, in *United States Junior Chamber of Commerce v. United States*, the court stated,

> "There does not appear to be any substantial difference between the ... 'convenience of the employer' test and the 'required as a condition of his employment' test."

Since it has already been determined that the condition of employment test has been satisfied, on that basis alone it could be held that the convenience of the employer test has also been met.

That the plaintiff also incurred a benefit from this residence and that it was, in part, a convenience to him, does not disturb the conclusion. As noted in *William I. Olkjer*:

> "No doubt the facilities furnished benefited the employee also. The test which the statute provides, however, is that of convenience to the employer. There is no provision to the effect that the employee is to be deprived of his right to exclude from gross income the value of food and lodging otherwise excludable because he, too, is convenienced."

The third and final test is whether the lodging was on the business premises of the employer. Observe first that "[t]he operative framework of [the clause 'on the business premises'] is at best elusive and admittedly incapable of generating any hard and fast line." This question is largely a factual one requiring a commonsense approach. The statute should not be read literally. As noted by the Tax Court in *Lindeman*:

> "[T]he statutory language ordinarily would not permit any exclusion for lodging furnished a domestic servant, since a servant's lodging is rarely furnished on 'the business premises of his employer'; yet the committee report ... shows a clear intention to allow the exclusion where the servant's lodging is furnished in the employer's home."

The phrase, then, is not to be limited to the business compound or headquarters of the employer. Rather, the emphasis must be upon the place where the employee's duties are to be performed. In *United States Junior Chamber of Commerce v. United States*, the court stated, "We think that the business premises of Section 119 means premises of the employer on which the duties of the employee are to be performed." The phrase has also been construed to mean either (1) living quarters that constitute an integral part of the business property, or (2) premises on which the company carries on some substantial segment of its business activities.

Interpretations of the phrase which are limited to the geographic contiguity of the premises or to questions of the quantum of business activities on the premises are too restrictive. Rather, the statutory language "on the business premises of the employer" infers a functional rather than a spatial unity. In Rev. Rul. 75-540, it was determined that the fair rental value of the official residence furnished a governor by the state is excludable from the governor's gross income under Section 119 of the Code. The Ruling noted that the business premises test was met because the residence provided by the state enabled the governor to carry out efficiently the administrative, ceremonial, and social duties required by his office. The governor's mansion, thus, served an important business function in that it was clearly identified with the business interests of the state. It was, in short, an inseparable adjunct.

We are persuaded that where, as here, (1) the residence was built and owned by the employer, (2) it was designed, in part, to accommodate the business activities of the employer, (3) the employee was required to live in the residence, (4) there were many business activities for the employee to perform after normal working hours in his home because of the extensive nature of the employer's business and the high-ranking status of the employee, (5) the employee did perform business activities in the residence, and (6) the residence served an important business function of the employer, then the residence in question is a part of the business premises of the employer.

The three statutory requisites for exclusion are met. Accordingly, pursuant to Section 119 of the 1954 Code, the fair rental value of the residence is excludable from plaintiff's gross income.

Problems for Discussion

2-4. Helen works as an associate at a large law firm. On the last Friday of every month, all of the firm's lawyers have lunch in a private room at a restaurant across the street from the firm's office. The purpose is to give the firm's attorneys an informal opportunity to chat with each other about their work, although conversations commonly stray onto baseball, housing prices, and other non-work topics. Unless the exigencies of work otherwise demand, all of the firm's lawyers are expected to attend. Occasionally, one or more lawyers will be asked to stand and talk about a recent matter he or she has handled. The cost to the firm of providing these lunches is $50 per lawyer per month. Does Helen have gross income by reason of her attendance and consumption of the meal provided?

SECTION 2: CODE SECTION 132

Code: Section 132

Regulations: Sections 1.132–1, –2, –3, –4, –5, –6, and –7

This Section 2 is intended to allow you to develop your statutory and regulatory reading skills. Read the above-referenced sections of the Code and Treasury Regulations as you work through the following problems.

PROBLEMS FOR DISCUSSION

2–5. Leila works as an international tax attorney for American Airlines. During the taxable year, pursuant to her employment agreement, American provides her with the following items. According to the Code and regulatory provisions cited above, how much income does she recognize as a result?

a. Two standby round-trip tickets on American from Los Angeles to Tokyo for Leila and her husband Ari.

b. Two reserved round-trip tickets on American from Los Angeles to Tokyo for Leila and her husband Ari.

c. Items in American's in-flight catalog totaling $1,000 list price, for which Leila pays $700. On average, 30% of American's list price for such items consists of mark-up.

d. Daily lunches at a cafeteria in American's headquarters building (where Leila works) operated by American on a break-even basis.

e. Two seats per month in American's sky-box at Yankee Stadium for Leila and her husband.

f. $1,000 in reimbursement for 40 dinners eaten at a restaurant near American's headquarters over the course of the year to allow Leila to work late on urgent projects.

g. High-end food and lodging worth $5,000 for a week-end strategic planning retreat for American executive personnel.

2–6. Leila works as an international tax attorney for American Airlines. Once a month, she meets at a restaurant near her office with lawyers from an independent law firm that American retains to handle matters not handled in-house. The purpose of such lunch meetings is to discuss matters being handled by that firm. The firm picks up the tab. Does Leila recognize income equal to the value of the lunches she eats? Does it matter whether the law firm includes the cost of such lunches in its monthly bill to American?

Subchapter D: Gifts, Bequests, and Inheritances

Code: Section 102

Regulations: Section 1.102–1 (proposed)

COMMISSIONER v. DUBERSTEIN

363 U.S. 278 (1960)

No. 376, Commissioner v. Duberstein. The taxpayer, Duberstein, was president of the Duberstein Iron & Metal Company, a corporation with headquarters in Dayton, Ohio. For some years the taxpayer's company had done business with Mohawk Metal Corporation, whose headquarters were in New York City. The president of Mohawk was one Berman. The taxpayer and Berman had generally used the telephone to transact their companies' business with each other, which consisted of buying and selling metals. The taxpayer testified, without elaboration, that he knew

Berman "personally" and had known him for about seven years. From time to time in their telephone conversations, Berman would ask Duberstein whether the latter knew of potential customers for some of Mohawk's products in which Duberstein's company itself was not interested. Duberstein provided the names of potential customers for these items.

One day in 1951 Berman telephoned Duberstein and said that the information Duberstein had given him had proved so helpful that he wanted to give the latter a present. Duberstein stated that Berman owed him nothing. Berman said that he had a Cadillac as a gift for Duberstein, and that the latter should send to New York for it; Berman insisted that Duberstein accept the car, and the latter finally did so, protesting however that he had not intended to be compensated for the information. At the time Duberstein already had a Cadillac and an Oldsmobile, and felt that he did not need another car. Duberstein testified that he did not think Berman would have sent him the Cadillac if he had not furnished him with information about the customers. It appeared that Mohawk later deducted the value of the Cadillac as a business expense on its corporate income tax return.

Duberstein did not include the value of the Cadillac in gross income for 1951, deeming it a gift. The Commissioner asserted a deficiency for the car's value against him, and in proceedings to review the deficiency the Tax Court affirmed the Commissioner's determination. It said that "The record is significantly barren of evidence revealing any intention on the part of the payor to make a gift. ... The only justifiable inference is that the automobile was intended by the payor to be remuneration for services rendered to it by Duberstein." The Court of Appeals for the Sixth Circuit reversed.

No. 546, Stanton v. United States. The taxpayer, Stanton, had been for approximately 10 years in the employ of Trinity Church in New York City. He was comptroller of the Church corporation, and president of a corporation, Trinity Operating Company, the church set up as a fully owned subsidiary to manage its real estate holdings, which were more extensive than simply the church property. His salary by the end of his employment there in 1942 amounted to $22,500 a year. Effective November 30, 1942, he resigned from both positions to go into business for himself. The Operating Company's directors, who seem to have included the rector and vestrymen of the church, passed the following resolution upon his resignation: "Be it resolved that in appreciation of the services rendered by Mr. Stanton ... a gratuity is hereby awarded to him of Twenty Thousand Dollars, payable to him in equal installments of Two Thousand Dollars at the end of each and every month commencing with the month of December, 1942; provided that, with the discontinuance of his services, the Corporation of Trinity Church is released from all rights and claims to pension and retirement benefits not already accrued up to November 30, 1942."

The Operating Company's action was later explained by one of its directors as based on the fact that, "Mr. Stanton was liked by all of the Vestry personally. He had a pleasing personality. He had come in when Trinity's affairs were in a difficult situation. He did a splendid piece of work, we felt. Besides that . . . he was liked by all of the members of the Vestry personally." And by another: "(W)e were all unanimous in wishing to make Mr. Stanton a gift. Mr. Stanton had loyally and faithfully served Trinity in a very difficult time. We thought of him in the highest regard. We understood that he was going in business for himself. We felt that he was entitled to that evidence of good will."

On the other hand, there was a suggestion of some ill-feeling between Stanton and the directors, arising out of the recent termination of the services of one Watkins, the Operating Company's treasurer, whose departure was evidently attended by some acrimony. At a special board meeting on October 28, 1942, Stanton had intervened on Watkins' side and asked reconsideration of the matter. The minutes reflect that "resentment was expressed as to the 'presumptuous' suggestion that the action of the Board, taken after long deliberation, should be changed." The Board adhered to its determination that Watkins be separated from employment, giving him an opportunity to resign rather than be discharged. At another special meeting two days later it was revealed that Watkins had not resigned; the previous resolution terminating his services was then viewed as effective; and the Board voted the payment of six months' salary to Watkins in a resolution similar to that quoted in regard to Stanton, but which did not use the term "gratuity." At the meeting, Stanton announced that in order to avoid any such embarrassment or question at any time as to his willingness to resign if the Board desired, he was tendering his resignation. It was tabled, though not without dissent. The next week, on November 5, at another special meeting, Stanton again tendered his resignation which this time was accepted.

The "gratuity" was duly paid. So was a smaller one to Stanton's (and the Operating Company's) secretary, under a similar resolution, upon her resignation at the same time. The two corporations shared the expense of the payments. There was undisputed testimony that there were in fact no enforceable rights or claims to pension and retirement benefits which had not accrued at the time of the taxpayer's resignation, and that the last proviso of the resolution was inserted simply out of an abundance of caution. The taxpayer received in cash a refund of his contributions to the retirement plans, and there is no suggestion that he was entitled to more. He was required to perform no further services for Trinity after his resignation.

The Commissioner asserted a deficiency against the taxpayer after the latter had failed to include the payments in question in gross income. After payment of the deficiency and administrative rejection of a refund claim, the taxpayer sued the United States for a refund in the District Court for the Eastern District of New York. The trial judge, sitting without a jury, made the simple finding that the payments were a "gift," and judgment was entered for the taxpayer. The Court of Appeals for the Second Circuit reversed.

The exclusion of property acquired by gift from gross income under the federal income tax laws was made in the first income tax statute passed under the authority of the Sixteenth Amendment, and has been a feature of the income tax statutes ever since. The meaning of the term "gift" as applied to particular transfers has always been a matter of contention. Specific and illuminating legislative history on the point does not appear to exist. Analogies and inferences drawn from other revenue provisions, such as the estate and gift taxes, are dubious. The meaning of the statutory term has been shaped largely by the decisional law. With this, we turn to the contentions made by the Government in these cases.

First. The Government suggests that we promulgate a new "test" in this area to serve as a standard to be applied by the lower courts and by the Tax Court in dealing with the numerous cases that arise.[6] We reject this invitation. We are of opinion that the governing principles are necessarily general and have already been spelled out in the opinions of this Court, and that the problem is one which, under the present statutory framework, does not lend itself to any more definitive statement that would produce a talisman for the solution of concrete cases. The cases at bar are fair examples of the settings in which the problem usually arises. They present situations in which payments have been made in a context with business overtones—an employer making a payment to a retiring employee; a businessman giving something of value to another businessman who has been of advantage to him in his business. In this context, we review the law as established by the prior cases here.

The course of decision here makes it plain that the statute does not use the term "gift" in the common-law sense, but in a more colloquial sense. This Court has indicated that a voluntarily executed transfer of his property by one to another, without any consideration or compensation therefor, though a common-law gift, is not necessarily a "gift" within the meaning of the statute. For the Court has shown that the mere absence of a legal or moral obligation to make such a payment does not establish that it is a gift. And, importantly, if the payment proceeds primarily from "the constraining force of any moral or legal duty," or from "the incentive of anticipated benefit" of an economic nature, it is not a gift. And, conversely, "(w)here the payment is in return for services rendered, it is irrelevant that the donor derives no economic benefit from it." A gift in the statutory sense, on the other hand, proceeds from a "detached and disinterested generosity," "out of affection, respect, admiration, charity or like impulses." And in this regard, the most critical consideration, as the Court was agreed in the leading case here, is the transferor's "intention." "What controls is the intention with which payment, however voluntary, has been made."

---

6. The Government's proposed test is stated: "Gifts should be defined as transfers of property made for personal as distinguished from business reasons."

Second. The Government's proposed "test," while apparently simple and precise in its formulation, depends frankly on a set of "principles" or "presumptions" derived from the decided cases, and concededly subject to various exceptions; and it involves various corollaries, which add to its detail. Were we to promulgate this test as a matter of law, and accept with it its various presuppositions and stated consequences, we would be passing far beyond the requirements of the cases before us, and would be painting on a large canvas with indeed a broad brush. The Government derives its test from such propositions as the following: That payments by an employer to an employee, even though voluntary, ought, by and large, to be taxable; that the concept of a gift is inconsistent with a payment's being a deductible business expense; that a gift involves "personal" elements; that a business corporation cannot properly make a gift of its assets. The Government admits that there are exceptions and qualifications to these propositions. We think, to the extent they are correct, that these propositions are not principles of law but rather maxims of experience that the tribunals which have tried the facts of cases in this area have enunciated in explaining their factual determinations. Some of them simply represent truisms: it doubtless is, statistically speaking, the exceptional payment by an employer to an employee that amounts to a gift. Others are overstatements of possible evidentiary inferences relevant to a factual determination on the totality of circumstances in the case: it is doubtless relevant to the overall inference that the transferor treats a payment as a business deduction, or that the transferor is a corporate entity. But these inferences cannot be stated in absolute terms. Neither factor is a shibboleth. The taxing statute does not make nondeductibility by the transferor a condition on the "gift" exclusion; nor does it draw and distinction, in terms, between transfers by corporations and individuals, as to the availability of the "gift" exclusion to the transferee. The conclusion whether a transfer amounts to a "gift" is one that must be reached on consideration of all the factors.

Specifically, the trier of fact must be careful not to allow trial of the issue whether the receipt of a specific payment is a gift to turn into a trial of the tax liability, or of the propriety, as a matter of fiduciary or corporate law, attaching to the conduct of someone else. The major corollary to the Government's suggested "test" is that, as an ordinary matter, a payment by a corporation cannot be a gift, and, more specifically, there can be no such thing as a "gift" made by a corporation which would allow it to take a deduction for an ordinary and necessary business expense. As we have said, we find no basis for such a conclusion in the statute; and if it were applied as a determinative rule of "law," it would force the tribunals trying tax cases involving the donee's liability into elaborate inquiries into the local law of corporations or into the peripheral deductibility of payments as business expenses. The former issue might make the tax tribunals the most frequent investigators of an important and difficult issue of the laws of the several States, and the latter inquiry would summon one difficult and delicate problem of federal tax law as an aid to the solution of another.[9] Or perhaps there would be required a trial of the vexed issue whether there was a "constructive" distribution of corporate property, for income tax purposes, to the corporate agents who had sponsored the transfer. These considerations, also, reinforce us in our conclusion that while the principles urged by the Government may, in non-absolute form as crystallizations of experience, prove persuasive to the trier of facts in a particular case, neither they, nor any more detailed statement than has been made, can be laid down as a matter of law.

Third. Decision of the issue presented in these cases must be based ultimately on the application of the fact-finding tribunal's experience with the mainsprings of human conduct to the totality of the facts of each case. The nontechnical nature of the statutory standard, the close relationship of it to the data of practical human experience, and the multiplicity of relevant factual elements, with their various combinations, creating the necessity of ascribing the proper force to each, confirm us in our conclusion that primary weight in this area must be given to the conclusions of the trier of fact.

This conclusion may not satisfy an academic desire for tidiness, symmetry and precision in this area, any more than a system based on the determinations of various fact-finders ordinarily does. But we see it as implicit in the present statutory treatment of the exclusion for gifts, and in the variety of forums in which federal income tax cases can be tried. If there is fear of undue uncertainty or overmuch litigation, Congress may make more precise its treatment of the matter by singling out certain factors and making them determinative of the matters, as it has done in one field of the "gift" exclusion's former application, that of prizes and awards. Doubtless diversity of result will tend to be lessened somewhat since federal income tax decisions, even those in tribunals of first instance turning on issues of fact, tend to be reported, and since there may be a natural tendency of professional triers of fact to follow one another's determinations, even as to factual matters. But the question here remains basically one of fact, for determination on a case-by-case basis.

One consequence of this is that appellate review of determinations in this field must be quite restricted. Where a jury has tried the matter upon correct instructions, the only inquiry is whether it cannot be said that reasonable men could reach differing conclusions on the issue. Where the trial has been by a judge without a jury, the judge's findings must stand unless "clearly erroneous." "A finding is 'clearly erroneous' when although there is evidence to support it, the reviewing court on the entire evidence is left with the definite and firm conviction that a mistake has been committed." The rule itself applies also to factual inferences from undisputed basic facts, as will on many occasions be presented in this

---

9. Justice Cardozo once described in memorable language the inquiry into whether an expense was an "ordinary and necessary" one of a business: "One struggles in vain for any verbal formula that will supply a ready touchstone. The standard set up by the statute is not a rule of law; it is rather a way of life. Life in all its fullness must sup-ply the answer to the riddle." *Welch v. Helvering*, 290 U.S. 111, 115 (1933). The same comment well fits the issue in the cases at bar.

area. And Congress has in the most explicit terms attached the identical weight to the findings of the Tax Court.

Fourth. A majority of the Court is in accord with the principles just outlined. And, applying them to the *Duberstein* case, we are in agreement, on the evidence we have set forth, that it cannot be said that the conclusion of the Tax Court was "clearly erroneous." It seems to us plain that as trier of the facts it was warranted in concluding that despite the characterization of the transfer of the Cadillac by the parties and the absence of any obligation, even of a moral nature, to make it, it was at bottom a recompense for Duberstein's past services, or an inducement for him to be of further service in the future. We cannot say with the Court of Appeals that such a conclusion was "mere suspicion" on the Tax Court's part. To us it appears based in the sort of informed experience with human affairs that fact-finding tribunals should bring to this task.

As to Stanton, we are in disagreement. To four of us, it is critical here that the District Court as trier of fact made only the simple and unelaborated finding that the transfer in question was a "gift." To be sure, conciseness is to be strived for, and prolixity avoided, in findings; but, to the four of us, there comes a point where findings become so sparse and conclusory as to give no revelation of what the District Court's concept of the determining facts and legal standard may be. Such conclusory, general findings do not constitute compliance with Rule 52's direction to "find the facts specially and state separately ... conclusions of law ... thereon." While the standard of law in this area is not a complex one, we four think the unelaborated finding of ultimate fact here cannot stand as a fulfillment of these requirements. It affords the reviewing court not the semblance of an indication of the legal standard with which the trier of fact has approached his task. For all that appears, the District Court may have viewed the form of the resolution or the simple absence of legal consideration as conclusive. While the judgment of the Court of Appeals cannot stand, the four of us think there must be further proceedings in the District Court looking toward new and adequate findings of fact. In this, we are joined by Mr. Justice Whittaker, who agrees that the findings were inadequate, although he does not concur generally in this opinion.

Accordingly, in No. 376, the judgment of this Court is that the judgment of the Court of Appeals is reversed, and in No. 546, that the judgment of the Court of Appeals is vacated, and the case is remanded to the District Court for further proceedings not inconsistent with this opinion. It is so ordered.

ESTATE OF POWELL v. UNITED STATES
166 F. Supp. 2d 468 (W.D. Va. 2001)

The estate of Beverly W. Powell seeks a refund of federal gift taxes allegedly overpaid by the late Mrs. Powell for the 1994 tax year, in the amount of $136,920 plus interest. In addition, the United States has set forth counterclaims though which it seeks to recover allegedly erroneous income tax refunds issued for the 1992 and 1993 tax years. This dispute centers around payments made between 1989 and 1993 from Mrs. Powell's husband, the late Hampton O. Powell, to Jane Hudson–Young. The primary point of contention between the parties is whether the payments were gifts or compensation for services.

Ms. Hudson–Young was employed by the Lane Company from 1956 through 1989, and she worked as the executive secretary to Mr. Powell, the company's chief executive officer, from 1958 until Mr. Powell's retirement in 1984. While Mr. Powell's secretary, Ms. Hudson–Young assisted Mr. Powell with his personal and financial affairs by handling such matters as his personal correspondence, telephone calls to his stockbrokers to place trades at his direction, and record-keeping with respect to his investments, income, and expenses. After Mr. Powell's retirement, Ms. Hudson–Young assumed other duties within the Lane Company, but she did not cease to provide assistance to the Powells. Following her own retirement from the Lane Company, Ms. Hudson–Young continued to assist Mr. and Mrs. Powell with personal and financial matters until Mr. Powell's death in 1994. However, it is not contended by either party that Ms. Hudson–Young was a statutory employee of Mr. and Mrs. [Powell] between 1989 and 1993.

Much of Mr. Powell's wealth derived from his ownership of Lane Company stock. At the end of nearly every year for many years, Mr. Powell had made gifts of Lane Company stock to Ms. Hudson–Young. [Later], Mr. Powell continued to make year-end payments to Ms. Hudson–Young, but instead made his payments in cash. During the years in question, 1989 through 1993, Mr. Powell made $100,000 payments each December to Ms. Hudson–Young. In addition, in April 1989, Mr. Powell made a payment to Ms. Hudson–Young of Conrail stock worth $98,250; and, in May 1989, Mr. Powell made another $100,000 cash payment to Ms. Hudson–Young. In total, Mr. Powell made payments to Ms. Hudson–Young during the years in question of $798,250. Mr. Powell filed gift tax returns for the payments made to Ms. Hudson–Young during the years in question, and Ms. Hudson–Young did not report the payments as income.

In July 1996, after Mr. Lane became the executor of Mrs. Powell's estate following her death in July 1995, he filed amended gift tax returns [for the years 1989 through 1993 to claim that the gifts made during those years should be recharacterized as compensation for personal services] and sought a refund in the amount of $136,920. In August 1996, Mr. Lane also filed amended individual income tax returns for the years 1992 and 1993 on behalf of the late Mr. and Mrs. Powell in which he claimed that the payments made to Ms. Hudson–Young during those years were compensation and that a significant portion of that compensation was deductible from the Powells' taxable income for those years. In response to Mr. Lane's 1992–1993 amended income tax return filings on behalf of the Powells, the Internal Revenue Service paid refunds of taxes, penalties, and interest to the estate of Mrs. Powell in the total amount of $21,794.46. However, the Service disallowed the gift tax refunds claimed by Mr. Lane on the Powells' behalf, and this suit followed.

Both parties have filed motions for summary judgment.

After reviewing the proof submitted by the parties in connection with their respective motions, the Court concludes that this matter is not ripe for decision at the summary judgment stage in favor of either party because both sides have submitted evidence that, if viewed favorably, could lead a reasonable fact-finder to return a verdict in their favor. The pivotal issue is whether the payments made by Mr. Powell to Ms. Hudson–Young are properly classified as gifts or compensation for services. In the seminal case on this issue, *Commissioner of Internal Revenue v. Duberstein*, the Supreme Court declined the Government's request to establish a bright-line test as to the gift-compensation determination.

The gift-compensation inquiry is one that "does not lend itself to any more definite statement that would produce a talisman for the solution of concrete cases."

The fact-intensive inquiry set forth in *Duberstein* and its progeny does not, however, foreclose the possibility that summary judgment could be granted if the undisputed facts demonstrate that a payment was either a gift or compensation in such a way that a reasonable fact finder could only arrive at one conclusion. However, this is not a case where a reasonable fact-finder could only come to one conclusion. Ultimately, the determination of whether the payments in question were gifts or compensation will rest upon the "application of the fact-finding tribunal's experience with the mainsprings of human conduct to the totality of the facts" presented in this case. Therefore, the most appropriate course of action here is for the Court to deny both parties' motions for summary judgment and for this case to proceed to a trial on the merits.

Nevertheless, the Court will address an argument made by Mr. Lane that, if accepted, would necessitate an award of summary judgment in his favor. Specifically, Mr. Lane argues by analogy to section 102(c) of the Internal Revenue Code—which provides that virtually no amount received by an employee from an employer is excludable from the employee's gross income as a gift—that as a matter of law "a detached and disinterested generosity cannot exist where the recipient of such payments performs substantial, continuous, and ongoing financial and investment management services." Assuming that Mr. Lane has put forth evidence sufficient to show that Ms. Hudson–Young's financial and investment services were substantial, continuous, and ongoing, such proof does not establish that payments to Ms. Hudson–Young were compensation as a matter of law. While it may often be the case that payments made to an individual who performs contemporaneous services for the payer are properly treated as compensation rather than gifts, this fact at best establishes a generalization, not a rule of law. See *Goodwin*, 67 F.3d at 152–53 ("Regular, sizable payments made by persons to whom the taxpayer provides services are customarily regarded as a form of compensation and *may* therefore be treated as taxable income.") (emphasis added); *Olk v. United States*, 536 F.2d 876, 879 (9th Cir. 1976) (stating, in the context of a case involving "tokes" received by a casino employee, that a generalization can be made that "receipts by taxpayers engaged in rendering services contributed by those with whom the taxpayers have some personal or functional contact in the course of the performance of the services are taxable income when in conformity with the practices of the area and easily valued"). Although the fact that a payee may have performed contemporaneous services for the payer might be significant to the gift-compensation determination, it is simply one of "the totality of the facts" that must be considered. For this court to hold otherwise would be to create a "talisman" test of the sort specifically rejected by the Supreme Court in *Duberstein*. Thus, for all of the foregoing reasons, the Court will deny the summary judgment motions of both parties.

NOTES

1. *Code Section 102(c)(1).*—In 1986, Congress modified Code Section 102 by adding subsection (c)(1), which limits the circumstances in which a transfer from an employer to an employee can be treated as a gift. There is little authority as to its effect. In *Larsen v. Commissioner*, T.C. Memo. 2008-73, the Tax Court stated:

> "Generally, amounts transferred by or for an employer to, or for the benefit of, an employee are includable in gross income. Sec. 102(c)(1). The legislative history underlying section 102(c) indicates that a payment from an employer to an employee solely for personal reasons can still be a gift if the payment is completely unrelated to the employment relationship and reflects no expectation of a business benefit."

The Treasury has issued proposed regulations that limit gift treatment to "extraordinary transfers to the natural objects of an employer's bounty." Prop. Treas. Reg. § 1.102–1(f)(2). Although published in 1989, these proposed regulations have not yet been issued in final form.

2. *Transfer Taxes.*—As *Estate of Powell* illustrates, the fact that a transfer is treated as a gift does not necessarily mean it escapes federal taxation altogether. In addition to income tax and payroll taxes, the Code imposes estate and gift taxes, known collectively as "transfer taxes."

An estate tax is imposed on the taxable estate of every U.S. decedent. Just as the income tax begins with "gross income," so the estate tax begins with the "gross estate." From the gross estate are subtracted bequests to decedent's surviving spouse, transfers to public, charitable and religious uses, expenses, debts, taxes, losses, and state death taxes. The result is the "taxable estate."

What happens next is conceptually simple but mechanically convoluted. Conceptually, a portion of the taxable estate called the "applicable exclusion amount" is exempt from tax. Any taxable estate in excess of this applicable exclusion amount is then subject to tax. In 2012, the applicable exclusion amount is $5 million; the tax rate imposed on taxable estates in excess of that amount is 35%. In 2013, the applicable exclusion amount is scheduled to drop to $1,000,000 and the rate structure to revert to a progressive schedule that begins at 41% and rises to a high of 55%.

Mechanically, however, there is no exclusion. Instead, Code Section 2010 grants a "unified credit" that reduces the estate tax by the same amount it would have been reduced if the estate had been allowed a deduction equal to the applicable exclusion amount. The effect on estate tax liability is the same.

The gift tax is fully integrated into this estate tax structure. Every year, an individual donor can give up to a specified amount (the "annual exclusion") to an unlimited number of individual recipients without any gift tax consequences. In 2012, the annual exclusion is $13,000. Thus, in 2012 John and Mary can give each of their three children $26,000 per year ($13,000 each) without gift tax consequences. The excess of any gift over the annual exclusion first reduces the donor's estate tax applicable exclusion amount. Once his or her applicable exclusion amount is exhausted, all further gifts in excess of the annual exclusion become taxable. When the donor dies, the estate pays tax on the taxable estate, reduced by any remaining applicable exclusion amount. The applicable exclusion amount of the surviving spouse, if any, is increased by any unused applicable exclusion amount of the decedent. Responsibility for reporting gifts in excess of the annual exclusion and paying any resulting tax is imposed, in the first instance, on the donor.

Estate of Powell illustrates interactions between the transfer tax and income tax systems in an employment context. The transfers to Ms. Hudson–Young were either gifts or compensation. If they were gifts, then Mr. Powell, the donor, was liable for gift tax. If they were compensation, then Ms. Hudson–Young, the recipient, was liable for income tax and amounts paid to her may have constituted expenses incurred for the production of income, entitling Mr. Powell to an income tax deduction under Code Section 212.

3. *Scholarships.*—Code Section 117 excludes from gross income "any amount received as a qualified scholarship by an individual who is a candidate for a degree at an educational organization described in section 170(b)(1)(A)(ii)." Code Section 117(c)(1), in turn, treats as disqualified, "that portion of any amount received which represents payment for teaching, research, or other services by the student required as a condition for receiving the qualified scholarship...." In *Bingler v. Johnson*, 394 U.S. 741 (1969), the Supreme Court held that the Treasury, by regulation, had construed the statute in a manner consistent with "the ordinary understanding of 'scholarships' and 'fellowships' as relatively disinterested, 'no-strings' educational grants, with no requirement of any substantial quid pro quo from the recipients."

4. *Contributions.*—Code Section 170 allows a deduction for contributions to qualified organizations. In *Hernandez v. Commissioner*, 490 U.S. 680 (1989), the Supreme Court stated:

> The legislative history of the "contribution or gift" limitation, though sparse, reveals that Congress intended to differentiate between unrequit-

ed payments to qualified recipients and payments made to such recipients in return for goods or services. Only the former were deemed deductible. The House and Senate Reports on the 1954 tax bill, for example, both define "gifts" as payments "made with no expectation of a financial return commensurate with the amount of the gift." Using payments to hospitals as an example, both Reports state that the gift characterization should not apply to "a payment by an individual to a hospital in consideration of a binding obligation to provide medical treatment for the individual's employees. It would apply only if there were no expectation of any quid pro quo from the hospital."

On this ground, the Court held that payments made to the Church of Scientology to receive services known as "auditing" and "training" were not "contributions" and therefore not deductible. Code Section 170 is explored in greater detail in Chapter 23, below.

PROBLEMS FOR DISCUSSION

2–7. As a favor to his colleague Prof. Lily Roberts, Prof. Mark Kaplan reviews the draft of an article Roberts has written and gives her extensive comments. To thank him, she gives him an expensive bottle of wine. Does the value of the bottle constitute "gross income" to Kaplan?

2–8. Jerry's adult niece is diagnosed with breast cancer. Unfortunately, she has no health insurance and no immediate family members living. Although he does not particularly care for his niece, Jerry feels morally obligated to pay her medical expenses. Does his niece have "gross income" as a result?

2–9. Mark works as an associate in Deborah's law firm. When he and his fiancée get married, they invite Deborah to the wedding. Deborah is delighted to receive the invitation, attends, and gives Mark and his fiancée an expensive gift. Is the gift excludible under Section 102(c)?

2–10. Quarterback Mike Weisman is recruited to attend his state's university with a full athletic scholarship and an invitation to join the university's varsity football team. Does the scholarship constitute "gross income"?

2–11. After graduating from college, Weisman joins an NFL team. Four years later, believing himself morally obligated to repay the scholarships he had received in college, Weisman makes a payment to his university equal to those scholarships received plus interest. Is the payment a "contribution"?

Subchapter E: Government–Provided Benefits and the General Welfare Doctrine

Code: Sections 85 and 86

In 1938, the IRS ruled that Social Security benefits were not includible in gross income. I.T. 3194, 1938–1 C.B. 114. Since then, it has ruled consistently, in a variety of contexts, that "[p]ayments by a governmental unit to an individual under a legislatively provided social benefit program for the promotion of the general welfare that are not basically for services rendered are not includible in the individual's gross income," I.R.S. Notice 99–3, 1999–1 C.B. at 271 (Temporary Assistance to Needy Families payments excludible), a rule sometimes known as the general welfare doctrine.

A few lower court decisions have acknowledged this exclusion. Justice Frankfurter's concurrence in *United States v. Kaiser*, 363 U.S. 299, 305–326 (1960), reviewed the history of the doctrine but, without either endorsing or rejecting it, found it inapplicable to strike benefits paid by unions to strikers. By statute, Congress has overturned the doctrine with respect to two items, making unemployment and Social Security benefits wholly and partially taxable, respectively. Code Sections 85 and 86. Otherwise, the doctrine continues to function in obscurity, exempting from taxation a wide range of governmental benefits given in cash or in kind.

The legal foundation for the exclusion is unclear. The argument most often given is that Congress simply did not intend to tax this kind of receipt. No language in the legislative history of the Code actually supports this argument. Nevertheless, it does seem unlikely that Congress intended to subject governmental benefits and services to income taxation. As the Supreme Court observed in *United States v. Kirby Lumber Co.*, the term "income" is to be construed in light of its "plain popular meaning." And as the Court observed in a non-tax context: "In a real sense, [a rent subsidy] no more embodies the attributes of income or profits than do welfare benefits, food stamps, or other government subsidies." *United Housing Foundation v. Forman*, 421 U.S. 837, 855 (1975) (addressing issues under the securities laws).

Further comfort can be drawn from the history of Code Section 118, the general welfare doctrine's corporate analog, which excludes governmental and other subsidies from corporate income. Section 118 derives from the now-obsolete *Eisner v. Macomber* definition of income: "gain derived from capital, from labor, or from both combined." In 1925, in *Edwards v. Cuba Railroad Co.*, 268 U.S. 628, 633 (1925), the Court ruled that subsidy payments made by the Cuban government to induce a corporate taxpayer to build and operate a railroad were not "income" within the meaning of *Macomber*. Section 118 then codified *Cuba Railroad* and its progeny. The *Macomber* definition has since been abandoned. Nevertheless, one might argue that Congressional intent in enacting early incarnations of the Code should be understood in light of that definition.

Another possible argument is that benefits received under general welfare programs are excludible as gifts. The Supreme Court itself, in *United States v. Kaiser*, upheld a jury finding that strike assistance paid by a union to participating strikers was excludible as a gift. Concurring, Justice Frankfurter justified three IRS rulings on such a gift rationale: (1) Special Ruling of May 11, 1952, holding that disaster relief in the form of food and clothing from the American Red Cross constituted a gift, not income, (2) Revenue Ruling 131, holding that cash disaster relief from a corporation to its employees was similarly "gratuitous and spontaneous" and therefore not income, and (3) Revenue Ruling 57–102, holding that payments to blind persons under Pennsylvania's public assistance law were excludible. Only the third involved payments by a governmental unit under a legislatively provided social benefit program. All three, however, provide support for excluding general welfare payments as gifts.

Finally, by overruling the doctrine only with respect to unemployment (Code Section 85) and Social Security benefits (Code Section 86), Congress may be deemed to have ratified the IRS's prior administrative position in other regards. Even if that position had no Congressional sanction prior to such ratification, it may have such sanction today.

The scope of the doctrine is itself equally unclear. Although today the doctrine is commonly described as excluding certain "payments by a governmental unit," none of the possible rationales for the exclusion—popular meaning, *Macomber*, gift, or ratification—is limited inherently to "payments" or to governmental action. Taxpayers receive an extraordinary range of governmental services every day—public education, subsidized public transportation, police protection, and disaster relief, to name but a few. These services are probably income under comprehensive tax base theory; nevertheless, they have never been thought to be includible. Some rule must exclude their value from income. The general welfare doctrine seems the most likely candidate.

GRAFF v. COMMISSIONER

74 T.C. 743 (1980), *aff'd per curiam*, 673 F.2d 784, 785 (5th Cir. 1982)

At the time of the trial in this case, the petitioner was the owner of a low and moderate income housing project in Irving, Tex., known as the Park Grove Square Apartments (the project). The petitioner built the project under the provisions of Section 236 of the National Housing Act (Section 236), which provided for certain incentives for the builders and sponsors of low and moderate income housing projects. Such incentives included a provision under which HUD made interest reduction payments on behalf of the sponsor to reduce his cost of borrowing money for the construction of the project.

The major issue in this case is whether the interest reduction payments made by HUD on behalf of the petitioner are includable in his gross income under section 61. It is the petitioner's position that he is entitled to deduct the interest payments made by HUD on the mortgage of the section 236 project and that the [same] interest reduction payments are not includable in his gross income because such payments were in the nature of Government subsidies or general welfare benefits which are exempt from taxation. He also maintains that he received no benefit by reason of such payments since he was not obligated to make them, and since they were made under an obligation running from HUD to the mortgagee. The Commissioner now concedes that the interest payments made on behalf of the petitioner are deductible, but he vigorously contends that the interest reduction payments are includable in the petitioner's gross income.

Section 236 was added to the National Housing Act by section 201 of the Housing and Urban Development Act of 1968. Section 236 provided a variety of incentives to encourage the construction of rental and cooperative housing for low and moderate income families. To qualify for such benefits, a sponsor had to be organized as a profit-making corporation, had to be organized for the sole purpose of providing housing, and had to be restricted to a maximum return of 6 percent on initial equity investment in the project. The incentives included Federal insurance of private long-term (40–year) mortgage loans in an amount not in excess of 90 percent of the FHA-determined certified cost of housing projects.

In addition, Section 236 provided for monthly Federal interest reduction payments made by HUD directly to the private mortgagee on behalf of the sponsor-mortgagor. In practice, the sponsor contracted with private sources and secured a mortgage at the current market rate. HUD then made a contract with the mortgagee under which it made the interest reduction payments each month directly to the mortgagee in an amount equal to the difference between the payment required under the mortgage for principal, interest, and mortgage insurance and the payment that would have been required for principal and interest under a mortgage bearing interest at 1 percent.

In connection with the enactment of Section 236, the Internal Revenue Code was also amended to provide several tax benefits for sponsors of Section 236 projects. For example, section 167 allows the owner of a Section 236 project to take advantage of the 200–percent double declining balance method of depreciation; section 1250(a)(1)(C)(ii) provides Section 236 housing with special treatment regarding depreciation recapture; and section 1039 specifically allows the owner of a Section 236 project to defer paying taxes on the gain from the sale of such project upon certain conditions.

A sponsor of a Section 236 project was required to enter into an agreement with HUD regulating the rents to be charged the tenants. The "basic rental charge" for a tenant was determined as if the project were operated by the sponsor under a mortgage calling for 1–percent interest. The tenant was required to pay either the basic rental charge or 25 percent of his income, whichever was greater. However, in no event could the rental charge exceed the fair market rental determined on the basis of operating the project without any Federal assistance in the form of interest reduction payments. Any rentals collected by the sponsor in excess of the basic charges were returned to HUD for deposit in a revolving fund for the purpose of making other interest reduction payments. The family income of the tenants was reexamined every 2 years, and the rent charged the tenants was adjusted accordingly.

Section 101 of the Housing and Urban Development Act of 1968 added Section 235 to the National Housing Act providing for a home-ownership assistance program for low and moderate income families. Such assistance was provided by HUD paying part of the costs of a mortgage obtained by the homeowner in the private mortgage market. Such payments by HUD equaled the difference between 20 percent of the family's adjusted monthly income and the required monthly payment under the mortgage for principal, interest, taxes, mortgage insurance, and hazard insurance. However, in no case could the payment exceed the difference between the required payment under the mortgage for principal, interest, and mortgage insurance and the payment that would be required for principal and interest if the mortgage bore an interest rate of 1 percent.

Since the enactment of Sections 235 and 236, the Internal Revenue Service has issued several rulings and regulations regarding the tax treatment of the payments made by HUD under such programs. Rev. Rul. 75–271, 1975–2 C.B. 23, stated that payments made under Section 235 on behalf of individual homeowners were in the nature of general welfare and, as such, are not includable in the individuals' gross incomes. In March 1976, section 1.163–1(d), Income Tax Regs., was promulgated, and such regulation stated that no interest deduction is allowable for payments made to assist individuals under Section 235.

In Rev. Rul. 76–75, 1976–1 C.B. 14, the IRS set forth its position with regard to the tax treatment of the payments made by HUD on behalf of sponsors of Section 236 projects. Such ruling concluded that the interest reduction payments under Section 236 were includable in the sponsor's income since such payments made up the difference between the fair rental value of the apartments and the rent actually paid by the low and moderate income tenants. The ruling stated that such payments are treated as if they were received by the sponsor as rent and subsequently paid to the mortgagee as part of the interest due under the mortgage obligation. The ruling also held that the interest payments made under Section 236 were deductible as interest by the sponsor and that his basis in the property is not reduced as a result of any such payments.

To resolve the question of whether the interest reduction payments are includable in the petitioner's gross income, we have scrutinized the legislative history surrounding the enactment of Sections 235 and 236. Under general principles of tax law, such payments are taxable to the petitioner. He was the owner of the project; he secured the mortgage on it; and initially, he was obligated to make the payments under such mortgage. When HUD undertook to, and did make, part of such payments on his behalf, he benefited as the owner of the project, and he benefited since he was relieved of his legal obligation to make such payments. The receipt of such benefits causes such payments to be includable in his gross income.

Careful consideration of the nature, function, and operation of the interest reduction payments lead us to conclude that such payments were intended to be a substitute for rent which the sponsor would otherwise have collected from the tenants. Indeed, the statement of congressional purpose of Section 236 was clearly set forth in the first few words of the statute: "For the purpose of reducing rentals for lower income families, the Secretary is authorized to make . . . interest reduction payments on behalf of the owner." The committee reports also indicate that the general purpose of the interest reduction payments was to reduce the ultimate rent paid by the tenants.

The interest reduction payments made on behalf of the sponsor reduced the total operating costs of a Section 236 project by lowering, in effect, the rate of interest on the sponsor's mortgage to 1 percent, thus enabling the sponsor to charge lower rents to the tenants. To ensure that the tenants benefited from the Section 236 program, the rents charged by the sponsor were controlled and if he actually collected rents in excess of those needed to cover his costs, the excess had to be paid over to HUD for use in other projects. Thus, the tenant was intended to be the ultimate beneficiary of the interest reduction payments, and the benefit received by him is in the nature of welfare not taxable to him. However, it was assumed that the sponsor constructed the project for business purposes and that he expected to make a limited profit from its operation. These considerations furnish no reason to believe that the sponsor was to receive a benefit in the nature of welfare.

The petitioner also contends that Sections 235 and 236 were intended to be companion programs and that since the interest reduction payments made to families under the homeownership program of Section 235 are not taxed as income, the interest reduction payments made on behalf of sponsors of Section 236 projects are likewise not taxable. It is true that the programs were intended to complement each other. However, the purpose of the interest reduction payments under Section 236 was fundamentally different from that under Section 235. The payments made under Section 235 directly benefited low and moderate income families who were not capable of homeownership without assistance payments by the Federal Government. As such, the payments are treated as any other form of Government subsidy or benefit which is exempt from taxation. On the other hand, the ultimate beneficiaries of the Section 236 program were the tenants who were enabled to secure housing at rents below the market rates. The payments under Section 236 were not designed to provide subsidies for sponsors of those projects for such sponsors are not in need of Government assistance.

Lastly, the petitioner's claim that the interest reduction payments are analogous to the nontaxable "incidental benefits" received by an employee in the course of business employment is without merit. In *United States v. Gotcher*, the court held that a trip to Germany which Volkswagen of Germany and a dealer of the automobiles provided an employee of the dealer was not income to him. The court found that the trip was to induce the employee to purchase an interest in the dealership and reasoned that there was no economic gain to the employee which "is the key to section

61", and that the value of the expense-paid items would not be income to the employee even though he received some incidental benefit if the primary purpose of such items was to benefit the employer. In the present case, the interest reduction payments were more than mere incidental benefits to the petitioner; they were very substantial benefits since he was relieved of paying the market-rate interest on the mortgage. His benefit was not insignificant and indirect, as he maintains.

NOTES

1. *Benefits held excludible under the general welfare doctrine.*—Among others, the following have been held to be excludible under the general welfare doctrine: lump sum payments under § 204(a) of the Social Security Act (I.T. 3194, 1938–1 C.B. 114), lump sum death payments under §§ 203 and 204(b) of the Social Security Act (I.T. 3229, 1938–2 C.B. 136), monthly payments from the Federal Old Age and Survivors Insurance Trust Fund under § 202 of the Social Security Act (I.T. 3447, 1941–1 C.B. 191), unemployment compensation (I.T. 3230, 1938–2 C.B. 136), disaster relief payments (Rev. Rul. 131, 1953–2 C.B. 112), unemployment compensation payments to federal employees under Title XV of Social Security Act (Rev. Rul. 55–652, 1955–2 C.B. 21), payments to blind persons under a Pennsylvania public assistance law (Rev. Rul. 57–102, 1957–1 C.B. 26), pensions or annuities under the Social Security Act or the Railroad Retirement Act (T.D. 6272, 1957–2 C.B. 30), benefit payments to individuals undergoing training or retraining under the Area Redevelopment Act or the Manpower Development and Training Act of 1962 (Rev. Rul. 63–136, 1963–2 C.B. 19), payments under Title II–A of the Economic Opportunity Act of 1964 and the Manpower Development and Training Act of 1962 (Rev. Rul. 68–38, 1968–1 C.B. 446), monthly payments under § 202 of Title II of the Social Security Act (Rev. Rul. 70–217, 1970–1 C.B. 13), benefits from the Federal Unemployment Trust Fund (Rev. Rul. 70–280, 1970–1 C.B. 13), stipends paid by city to unemployed probationers (Rev. Rul. 72–340, 1972–2 C.B. 31), unemployment benefits paid under the Emergency Unemployment Compensation Act of 1971 (Rev. Rul. 73–154, 1973–1 C.B. 40), payments by the New York Crime Victims Compensation Board to victims of crime or their surviving spouses and dependents (Rev. Rul. 74-4-74, 1974–4–1 C.B. 18), payments to adoptive parents by Maryland State Department of Social Services for support of adoptive child (Rev. Rul. 74-4-153, 1974–4–1 C.B. 20), replacement housing payments under the Housing and Urban Development Act of 1968 (Rev. Rul. 74-4-205, 1974–4–1 C.B. 20), mortgage assistance payments under the National Housing Act (Rev. Rul. 75–271, 1975–2 C.B. 23), grants under § 408 of the Disaster Relief Act Amendments of 1974 (Rev. Rul. 76–144, 1976–1 C.B. 17), trade readjustment allowances paid to unemployed or adversely affected workers under the Trade Act of 1974 (Rev. Rul. 76–229, 1976–1 C.B. 19), relocation payments under § 105(a)(11) of Title I of the Housing and Community Development Act of 1974 (Rev. Rul. 76–373, 1976–2 C.B. 16), home rehabilitation grants provided under the Housing and Community Development Act of 1974 (Rev.

Rul. 76–395, 1976–2 C.B. 16), nonreimburseable grants under the Indian Financing Act of 1974, designed to stimulate Indian entrepreneurship and employment (Rev. Rul. 77–77, 1977–1 C.B. 11), payments by Ohio on behalf of elderly and disabled persons against the cost of winter energy consumption (Rev. Rul. 78–170, 1978–1 C.B. 24), relocation payments under § 105(a)(11) of Title I of the Housing and Community Development Act of 1974, "funded under the 1997 Emergency Supplemental Appropriations Act for Recovery From Natural Disasters to an individual moving from a flood-damaged residence to another residence" (Rev. Rul. 98–19, 1998–1 C.B. 840), Temporary Assistance to Needy Families payments (I.R.S. Notice 99–3, 1999–1 C.B. 271).

2. *Limitation of the doctrine to individual need.*—Both the Tax Court and the IRS have attempted to limit the general welfare doctrine, at least as applied to payments of cash, to situations involving documented individual need. In *Bailey v. Commissioner*, 88 T.C. 1293, 1293 (1987), a taxpayer received a grant from the city's urban renewal agency to restore the façade on a building he owned. In return, taxpayer granted the agency an easement to enter his property to repair the façade at his expense and agreed not to modify the façade without the agency's approval. The taxpayer sought to exclude the grant under the general welfare doctrine. The Court disagreed, noting:

> In each of respondent's revenue rulings in which the general welfare doctrine has been applied, the grant was received under a program requiring the individual recipient to establish need.... Grants received under social welfare programs that did not require recipients to establish individual need have not qualified under respondent's rulings for tax exempt status under the general welfare doctrine.

Similarly, in Revenue Ruling 80–330, 1980–2 C.B. 29, a taxpayer received a grant under the National Historic Preservation Act of 1966 to restore an historic house. The Service declined to apply the general welfare doctrine:

> The payments in this case are distinguished from welfare program payments.... [P]ayments [here] are not based on an individual recipient's personal financial status, health, educational background, or employment status, nor are they intended to improve the living conditions of low-income homeowners.... Thus, the payments are not made under a social benefit program for the promotion of general welfare.

But if the doctrine also applies to receipt of governmental services in kind, individual need—at least in the conventional charitable sense—cannot be a prerequisite to exclusion. Public education and subsidized public transportation, for example, are available to the rich as well as the poor, yet their value has never been thought to be taxable.

3. *Social Security benefits.*—Code Section 86 partially overturns I.T. 3194, 1938–1 C.B. 114, in which the IRS held that Social Security benefits are excludible from gross income. The Social Security program offers two types of benefits. Most are contributory in form—that is, benefits are based on contributions made by or on behalf of the beneficiary. Arguably, such benefits should therefore be taxed as insurance proceeds, not as welfare. The Supplemental Security Income program for persons over age 65 with limited income and for persons with disabilities, by contrast, is clearly a welfare program.

Under Code Section 86, contributory Social Security benefits may be at least partially taxable. If a taxpayer has no other source of income, such benefits remain nontaxable. As a taxpayer's "modified adjusted gross income" increases, however, first 50 percent and then 85 percent of contributory Social Security benefits are included in gross income. This 85 percent inclusion reflects an attempt to bring the taxation of such benefits into conformity with comprehensive tax base theory. Roughly 15 percent of such benefits, on average, represent contributions previously made to the Social Security system. In theory, therefore, roughly 15 percent of a recipient's benefits constitute a return of capital and should not be taxed. The remaining 85 percent, however, represent benefits not previously paid for and should therefore be includible in gross income. Supplemental Security Income payments, by contrast, are not subject to Section 86 and remain fully excludible under the general welfare doctrine.

Problems for Discussion

2–12. Mark attends Pleasantville Community College. All students at the college, regardless of their means, are required to pay $12 per unit in tuition and fees. The college spends an average of $512 per unit to provide its educational services. The state legislature funds the $500 per unit difference. The legislature's purpose is to make higher education generally available to all state residents, regardless of their means. Mark does not come from a low-income household and could, in fact, afford to pay full tuition at a private college. Does Mark have reportable income by reason of the state subsidy?

CHAPTER 3

THE FEDERAL INCOME TAX BASE

■ ■ ■

Subchapter A: Haig–Simons and the Comprehensive Tax Base

Principle: A taxpayer's income for a taxable period equals her change in net worth over that period plus the value of her consumption during that period.

As we have seen, at the core of the U.S. income tax system is a single elegant premise: all economic value received is, in theory, "income" unless paid for with previously taxed or excluded dollars. Thus, for example, if you receive a car and do not pay for it, you have income. If you receive a car and pay for it by working for a month, you still have income because you have not yet been taxed on your labor. But if you receive a car and pay for it with the already-taxed cash you received for your month's labor, you do not have income, because you are paying for the car with already-taxed dollars.

Economist Henry Simons proposed an expanded version of this principle. "Personal income," he said, "may be defined as the algebraic sum of (1) the market value of rights exercised in consumption and (2) the change in the value of the store of property rights between the beginning and the end of the period in question." HENRY C. SIMONS, PERSONAL INCOME TAXATION 50 (1038). In other words:

Income = change in net worth + consumption.

What has come to be known as Haig–Simons analysis justifies much of the basic structure of the U.S. income tax system. We plug the consequences of the transaction we are analyzing into the foregoing equation. If the result is positive, Haig–Simons requires that taxpayer recognize income. If it is negative, taxpayer should be allowed a deduction. If it is zero, taxpayer should neither recognize income nor be allowed a deduction.

1. *Deductibility of the costs of producing income.*—Assume that taxpayer spends $1,000 on costs of producing future income. As a result, taxpayer's net worth goes down by $1,000. Costs incurred to produce future income are not treated as producing personal "consumption"

benefits. The expenditure therefore results in a Haig–Simons loss of $1,000:

Income = change in net worth   + consumption
       = ($1,000)   + $0
       = ($1,000)

It follows that if we are going to tax "income," our system *must* allow taxpayer a $1,000 deduction. And in general it does. *See, e.g.*, Code Sections 162 (trade or business expenses) and 212 (expenses for the production of income).

2. *Nondeductibility of consumption expenditures.*—Assume instead that taxpayer spends $1,000 on food for her family—pure consumption. Her net worth goes down by $1,000, but she also receives $1,000 worth of consumption. Her Haig–Simons income is therefore zero:

Income = change in net worth   + consumption
       = ($1,000)   + $1,000
       = $0

It follows that if we are going to tax "income," our system *cannot* allow taxpayer a deduction. And in general it does not. *See* Code Section 262(a) ("Except as otherwise expressly provided in this chapter, no deduction shall be allowed for personal, living, or family expenses").

3. *Nondeductibility of capital expenditures.*—Assume that taxpayer spends $1,000 to purchase a business asset that will retain value for longer than one taxable year—for example, a used truck that a plumber plans to use only to drive from job to job. The purchase does not change taxpayer's net worth at all. She starts with $1,000 in cash; immediately after the purchase she has a truck worth approximately $1,000. She also has no consumption benefits, since she will use the truck solely to produce income. Her Haig–Simons income is again zero:

Income = change in net worth   + consumption
       = $0   + $0
       = $0

It follows that system intended to tax "income" should not allow any deduction for capital expenditures (expenditures with useful lives that extend significantly beyond the end of the taxable year), even if they are to be used exclusively for the production of income. And in general our system does not. *See, e.g.*, Code Section 263.

4. *Depreciation.*—Over the useful life of that truck, its value will decline; for simplicity's sake, assume that it declines to zero. Thus, over the useful life of the truck, taxpayer's net worth again declines by $1,000. It follows that a system intended to tax "income" *must* allow a deduction for the use of capital items for income-producing purposes over their useful lives. And in general, it does. We call that deduction "depreciation" in the case of tangible assets, *see, e.g.*, Code Sections 167 and 168,

"amortization" in the case of intangible assets, *see, e.g.*, Code Section 197, and "depletion" in the case of mineral deposits, *see, e.g.*, Code Section 611.

5. *Denial of depreciation for personal assets.*—Finally, assume that taxpayer buys the same truck for personal purposes—say, to go camping for fun. Again, taxpayer's net worth does not change by reason of the purchase. Over the useful life of the truck, however, two things happen: first, the truck declines in value by $1,000; second, taxpayer receives consumption benefits from its use. Our system treats the decline in value as the measure of the consumption benefits taxpayer derives: taxpayer experiences a $1,000 decline in net worth exactly offset by $1,000 of consumption value. Her net income over the useful life of the truck is therefore zero. It follows that our tax system should not allow depreciation of personal assets. And it does not. *See, e.g.*, Code Section 167(a) (allowing depreciation for depreciable property only if used in a trade or business or held for the production of income).

The Haig–Simons formulation has had profound effects on how we think about income taxation. It is commonly used to distinguish between core features of the system, on the one hand, and provisions added to accomplish non-tax objectives, on the other. The part of our economy that would ideally be taxed under the Haig–Simons definition is sometimes known as the "comprehensive tax base." Many deductions and exclusions are justified by Haig–Simons; no further explanation of such income-measuring deductions or exclusions is normally thought to be necessary. Others are not so justified; tax theorists commonly justify or criticize deductions or exclusions that are not Haig–Simons income-measuring by reference to values outside the tax system. For example, medical expenses are conventionally treated as consumption; their deduction or exclusion is not thought to be justified by comprehensive tax base theory. The Code Section 213 deduction for medical expenses is therefore commonly treated as reflecting a Congressional decision to subsidize such expenses, not as part of the structure of the tax system itself. Subchapter 3B, below, explores in further detail how such non-income-measuring provisions are systematically identified and quantified.

Comprehensive tax base theory also sometimes affects the decision of specific cases (not always correctly). Applied in the myriad contexts in which taxpayers make, lose, or recover money or other value, the theory commonly appears to tell us what the rule "must" be, even if no statute or regulation has yet addressed the issue.

COLLINS v. COMMISSIONER
T.C. Memo. 1992-478 (1992)

During 1988 petitioner was employed as a ticket seller at the Off-Track Betting (OTB) parlor in Auburn. OTB operates a statewide network of betting parlors that allow patrons to place legal bets on horseraces run in New York State (as well as certain races run elsewhere) without going to the track. Patrons also may cash in winning tickets at OTB.

Petitioner was a compulsive gambler who, while placing bets for OTB patrons in the course of his employment, could not resist the temptation to gamble without paying for the privilege of doing so. On Sunday, July 17, 1988, petitioner decided, as he had on several prior occasions, that he "would like some money" and began placing bets on his own behalf. He punched the bets into his computer terminal, which entered his bets and printed the tickets. When he had done so on prior occasions, petitioner either ended up ahead or lost a small amount, which he covered without being detected by anyone at OTB.

Petitioner appears to have employed a variant of a technique for betting on horseraces in which he bet on the favorite (the horse with the lowest odds) in each race, increasing the amount of each subsequent bet until he would pick a winner, which would recoup his prior losses and provide a modest surplus. This time, however, petitioner encountered a series of losses that caused his gambling fever to spiral out of control.

He started by placing three $20 bets on one horse in the first race at Finger Lakes Race Track. He bet on this horse to win, place (finish second or better), and show (finish third or better), for total bets of $60. This horse did not finish among the top three. Petitioner then tried to recoup his $60 loss by betting $40 in the second race on one horse to win, place, and show, for total bets of $120. This horse also failed to run in the money.

Petitioner bet a total of $600 on the third race, repeating the pattern of dividing his bets equally among win, place, and show bets on the same horse. At this point, petitioner was trying to recoup the losses he had caused his employer, which he knew he would be responsible for. He also intended to appropriate any net winnings. He lost again.

Petitioner bet a total of $1,500 on the fourth race and lost. He skipped the fifth race, but bet another $1,500 on the sixth race and lost. He bet $7,500 on the seventh race and $15,000 on the eighth. Both times he lost.

With two races left that day, petitioner owed OTB $26,280. He bet $25,500 on the ninth race. His horse came in third, so one of his three $8,500 bets paid off, but it paid only $8,925.

By the 10th race, petitioner was down $42,855. He made three bets totaling $28,500 on one horse in the 10th race. He finally caught the winner, which paid a total of $33,250 on his three bets. But petitioner still was behind $38,105, and the racing day was over. Petitioner's bets had totaled $80,280.

At the end of the racing day, petitioner deposited the winning tickets of $42,175 in his cash drawer and told his supervisor, Debbie D'Angelo, that he had "screwed up". D'Angelo called the police, who took petitioner into custody.

This case requires us to return to first principles to pursue the often elusive answer to the fundamental question, "What is income?"

Did Petitioner Have Income?

The question is whether the $80,280 of bets placed by petitioner resulted in embezzlement or theft income. Petitioner argues that the amount of bets he placed was not income to him because he never had control of money or property in that amount.

The Supreme Court's decision in *James v. United States* firmly established the principle that embezzled funds are income to the embezzler. That decision, however, does not stand for the proposition that all misappropriated funds are gross income of the person who illegally misapplied the funds. The decision necessarily confines taxation of an embezzler to circumstances where the embezzler receives a sufficiently cognizable benefit under the normal principles of income taxation.

The Supreme Court began with the "starting point in all cases dealing with the question of the scope of what is included in 'gross income' that the purpose of Congress was 'to use the full measure of its taxing power'." The Court referred to its oft-quoted language describing the breadth of Congress' intent regarding the statutory definition of gross income: all "accessions to wealth, clearly realized, and over which the taxpayers have complete dominion." The Court refined this definition by noting that such a gain exists when the "recipient has such control over it that, as a practical matter, he derives readily realizable economic value from it."

This formulation does not require possession of money or property, as petitioner argues, but rather the realization of gain. The approach requires that we answer the following questions: (1) Was there any "economic value" that petitioner could have "readily realized" from what he stole (the realizable value test)? (2) If what petitioner stole had readily realizable economic value, did he have sufficient "control" over it to derive that value therefrom (the control test)?

As to the realizable value test, common sense tells us that a betting ticket has economic value that can be readily realized. Almost all horseplayers purchase betting tickets at face value; if they did not consider the opportunity to gamble at least as valuable as the face amount of the ticket, they would not bet.

Common sense and experience also tell us that those gamblers who are compulsive, such as petitioner, may misjudge the value of gambling relative to other activities. For some of these individuals, gambling may have a negative "true" value because it can cause misery and shame. Petitioner argues that his compulsion provides a reason to find he had no income. If some people, such as petitioner, are predisposed toward compulsive, self-destructive behavior, that tendency may provide a good reason to regulate or prohibit gambling; it is not a reason to abandon the objective criterion of the market as the mechanism for determining whether the betting tickets that petitioner created and stole had economic value.

We therefore conclude that the betting tickets petitioner stole had value.

The control test asks whether petitioner had sufficient control over the tickets (or, more precisely, the rights evidenced by the tickets) to enable him to realize at least some of their value. This question we also answer affirmatively. Petitioner's past record of avoiding detection by OTB of his illegal activities convinces us that if he had won one of his earlier bets, he could have covered the amount of his bets with his winnings and taken any excess amount. As explained in more detail in our discussion of the value of the gambling tickets, even when petitioner placed very large bets in later races, he always had the opportunity to realize winnings that would reduce his liability to OTB. As a result, petitioner knew he had an economic stake in the outcome of the races on which he bet. He therefore had the opportunity to derive the same or similar gratifications from gambling as any other bettor.

This case presents the same apparent paradox as *Zarin v. Commissioner*. The more petitioner lost, the more he gambled, and the more he gambled, the more income he is deemed to have, "thus equating the pleasure of gambling with increase in wealth." *Zarin v. Commissioner* at 1101 (Tannenwald, J., dissenting). As with our decision in *Zarin v. Commissioner*, the result is made even more harsh by the restriction of section 165(d), which limits wagering loss deductions to the amount of winnings in the same year. Without that limitation, petitioner would have realized no net income from his peculations.

There is another view of petitioner's activities that resolves the paradox and reconciles the harsh result with the notion of gross income for the purpose of an income tax. The Haig–Simons definition of income states that income during a taxable period is properly defined as the sum of (1) the market value of rights exercised in consumption during the period, and (2) the increase in the value of the store of property rights, or wealth, between the beginning and the end of the period. The 16th Amendment does not enact the Haig–Simons definition of income; nonetheless, the definition provides a useful, comprehensive formula for measuring gross income under the annual accounting concept.

The Haig–Simons definition does precisely what the above-quoted dissent in *Zarin* found so paradoxical: it equates "the pleasure of gambling with increase in wealth," but circuitously. Gambling, which may be pleasurable or exciting, is a kind of consumption. Admittedly, it is an odd sort of consumption, because as the tickets are "used up" when the race is run, they have the potential to generate gains that exceed the amount consumed, but this is no more odd than hobby consumption, which is treated the same under section 183 as gambling is treated under section 165(d). The fair market value of rights exercised in consumption counts as much in the income formula as accessions to wealth, so consumption and accessions to wealth are equated for income tax purposes. To say that consumption (or gambling pleasure) and accessions to wealth are treated the same under the Code does not mean that they are the same conceptually. Obviously, there are distinctions between them. The chief distinction is that accessions to wealth increase net worth and are available for future use, while consumption leaves the consumer with only a memory that may fade. The distinctions make no difference. Both consumption and accessions to wealth are parts of income for tax purposes.

How Much Income Did Petitioner Have?

We find that petitioner had $80,280 in gross income.

Respondent argues that theft income is measured by the fair market value of the thing stolen. Fair market value is defined as "the price at which the property would change hands between a willing buyer and a willing seller, neither being under any compulsion to buy or sell and both having reasonable knowledge of relevant facts".

In an economic sense, petitioner's tickets were identical to any legitimate betting ticket. Therefore, the value of petitioner's tickets must have been the same as what other bettors paid—their face amount.

Did Petitioner Nonetheless Realize no Income?

Petitioner claims that he fully recognized in the year of the theft his obligation to repay his victim, and that therefore he did not realize income from his activities. Respondent concedes only that the $42,175 in winning tickets that petitioner left in his drawer at OTB constitutes restitution for which he is entitled to a deduction. We hold for respondent on this point.

Petitioner took the equivalent of money from OTB and intended to repay the face value of the tickets out of his winnings. However, petitioner could not have been reasonably certain that he would be able to repay the tens of thousands of dollars in tickets he took because he had earnings of less than $12,000 per year. He could not have believed that his appropriation would be approved by OTB. He did not make a prompt assignment of assets, and it appears unlikely that he owned sufficient assets to secure the $38,105 he owed. His debt was reduced to judgment in 1989, the following taxable year.

The linchpin of the "consensual recognition" doctrine, which is closely related to the claim of right doctrine, is that the victim must agree in the same taxable year as the theft to treat the transaction as a loan, rather than as an unauthorized taking. At best, it was petitioner who acquiesced in OTB's right to relief in 1988, perhaps because he believed OTB was entitled under state regulations to recover the loss from him. Neither OTB nor its insurance company "consensually recognized" anything during 1988, and the only evidence of petitioner's ability to repay, his 1988 tax return, shows that it was very unlikely that petitioner would be able to repay.

We hold that petitioner is entitled only to a deduction of $42,175, as permitted by respondent, resulting in taxable income in addition to that reported on his return of $38,105. Petitioner may be allowed a deduction for the amounts he actually repays when he repays them, but not before.

NOTES

1. *Realization and imputed income.*—As has been noted, the Haig–Simons definition justifies major structural components of the U.S. income tax system. In two major regards, however, it differs systematically from current rules. First, Haig–Simons does not require realization. Under Haig–Simons, changes in net worth should be taxed currently, without waiting for the property in question to be sold. After all, Bill Gates has both an increase in net worth and a substantial ability to pay taxes even if he never sells his appreciated Microsoft stock. Second, Haig–Simons requires the taxation of imputed income—value created by the taxpayer for himself. All else being equal, a country in which residents own their own homes is better off than a country with identical cash flows in which residents rent. Rentals will show up in cash flows and boost the country's measured GDP; use of owner-occupied homes ordinarily will not. Imputed income has real economic value.

PROBLEMS FOR DISCUSSION

3–1. Terry practices law. During the taxable year, she receives $100,000 in legal fees. She pays $15,000 in rent for her office and spends $30,000 for office furniture and equipment having a useful life of three years. Assume that this office furniture and equipment declines in value by $10,000 each year and are therefore worth $20,000 at the end of the taxable year in question. The foregoing are her only business expenses for the year. She therefore has $55,000 of cash left after paying her office rent and purchasing her office furniture and equipment. Of this amount, she pays $12,000 to rent her apartment, $18,000 for food, clothing, and other living expenses, and $20,000 to purchase a car having a useful life of five years, which she uses for personal purposes. At the end of the year, therefore, she has $5,000 left, which she deposits in her bank account. How much Haig–Simons income does she have for the year? Under Haig–Simons, what is the appropriate treatment of each item received or expended?

3–2. *Collins* was the first case explicitly to invoke Haig–Simons as an aid to decision. As a result of the series of transactions at issue in the case, what was Collins' change in net worth? What was the value of his consumption? Is the *Collins'* court's analysis consistent with Haig–Simons?

DESIGN CONSIDERATIONS

If we accept the Haig–Simons definition, Congress's seemingly simple decision to tax income has major structural implications. In general, we *must* allow a deduction for the costs of producing income. We *should not* allow deductions for personal expenditures. We *should not* allow an immediate deduction for capital costs, but *must* allow a deduction for their use over time in the production of income. This, in turn, means that our tax system *must* have rules to distinguish between income-producing and personal expenses and between capital and non-capital items. Writing administrable rules to draw these lines, we will discover, is not simple. A significant portion of the Code is devoted to these and other problems inherent in the decision to tax income.

Perhaps as a result, although Congress enacts tax legislation frequently, the Code's basic rules rarely change. Seemingly dramatic proposals to reform the U.S. tax system often turn out, on close examination, to change surprisingly little fundamental law. Many "flat tax" proposals, for example, would amend Code Section 1, which defines the individual rate structure, but little else covered in this book.

Subchapter B: Tax Expenditures

The widespread acceptance of comprehensive tax base theory is evidenced by the continued inclusion in the annual budget of the U.S. Government of a "tax expenditure budget," first instituted by Stanley Surrey when he was Assistant Secretary of the Treasury for Tax Policy in 1968. The theory is that expenditures made for non-tax reasons but delivered through the tax system are expenditures nonetheless, and should be treated accordingly in Congress's budgetary deliberations.

Consider, for example, Code Section 46, Item 15 in the 2013 Tax Expenditure Budget excerpted below, which authorizes a credit for electricity produced from wind energy, biomass, geothermal energy, solar energy, small irrigation power, municipal solid waste, or qualified hydropower and sold to an unrelated party. Its purpose is to subsidize alternative energy production. In fiscal 2013, its cost is estimated to be $1.9 billion. One might easily imagine a direct expenditure program in the same amount for the same purpose. Surrey believed that subsidies run through the tax system should be accounted for as expenditures as well.

The tax expenditure budget has elicited two very different reactions. Tax expenditures clearly complicate the law and allow taxpayers who take advantage of them to pay taxes at lower effective rates. For these and other reasons, many believe that all or most tax expenditures should be repealed. In 2010, for example, the bipartisan National Commission on Fiscal Responsibility and Reform, charged with proposing a plan to reduce the national deficit, reflected this view when it stated:

> "America's tax code is broken and must be reformed. In the quarter century since the last comprehensive tax reform, Washington has riddled the system with countless tax expenditures, which are simply spending by another name. These tax earmarks—amounting to $1.1 trillion a year of spending in the tax code—not only increase the deficit, but cause tax rates to be too high. Instead of promoting economic growth and competitiveness, our current code drives up health care costs and provides special treatment to special interests.

The code presents individuals and businesses with perverse economic incentives instead of a level playing field."

As part of its overall deficit reduction proposal, therefore, the Commission recommended eliminating *all* tax expenditures except the child credit and the earned income tax credit, Items 123 and 162, respectively, below.

Not all, however, are willing to equate tax expenditures with direct spending. In debates over whether to cut the deficit by cutting spending or raising taxes, cutting tax expenditures is normally treated as increasing taxes, not as reducing spending. If tax increases are bad, then eliminating tax expenditures must be bad as well.

In any event, the "tax expenditure budget," published as part of the Budget of the United States Government each year, estimates the direct-expenditure equivalent of the Code's deviations from the comprehensive tax base, as described more fully in the excerpt from the 2013 Budget of the United States Government that follows.

Because this book focuses on the fundamental structure of the system, only a few tax expenditures receive significant coverage here. But tax expenditures are profoundly important: according to the Treasury, the total "spent" through the tax expenditure budget is approximately equal to the amount raised by the entire individual income tax. The excerpt that follows offers a brief introduction to this part of the Code. Elsewhere in this book, this excerpt will be referred to as the "2013 Tax Expenditure Budget."

ANALYTICAL PERSPECTIVES

Budget of the U.S. Government, Fiscal Year 2013
(October 1, 2012–September 30, 2013)

17. Tax Expenditures

The Congressional Budget Act of 1974 requires that a list of "tax expenditures" be included in the budget. Tax expenditures are defined in the law as "revenue losses attributable to provisions of the Federal tax laws which allow a special exclusion, exemption, or deduction from gross income or which provide a special credit, a preferential rate of tax, or a deferral of tax liability." These exceptions may be viewed as alternatives to other policy instruments, such as spending or regulatory programs.

Identification and measurement of tax expenditures depends importantly on the baseline tax system against which the actual tax system is compared. The tax expenditure estimates presented in this chapter are patterned on a comprehensive income tax, which defines income as the sum of consumption and the change in net wealth in a given period of time.

Interpreting Tax Expenditure Estimates

The estimates shown for individual tax expenditures do not necessarily equal the increase in Federal revenues (or the change in the budget balance) that would result from repealing these special provisions, for the following reasons.

First, eliminating a tax expenditure may have incentive effects that alter economic behavior. These incentives can affect the resulting magnitudes of the activity or of other tax provisions or Government programs. For example, if capital gains were taxed at ordinary rates, capital gain realizations would be expected to decline, resulting in lower tax receipts. Such behavioral effects are not reflected in the estimates.

Second, tax expenditures are interdependent even without incentive effects. Repeal of a tax expenditure provision can increase or decrease the tax revenues associated with other provisions. For example, even if behavior does not change, repeal of an itemized deduction could increase the revenue costs from other deductions because some taxpayers would be moved into higher tax brackets. Alternatively, repeal of an itemized deduction could lower the revenue cost from other deductions if taxpayers are led to claim the standard deduction instead of itemizing. Similarly, if two provisions were repealed simultaneously, the increase in tax liability could be greater or less than the sum of the two separate tax expenditures, because each is estimated assuming that the other remains in force.

Present–Value Estimates

The annual value of tax expenditures for tax deferrals is reported on a cash basis. Cash-based estimates reflect the difference between taxes deferred in the current year and incoming revenues that are received due to deferrals of taxes from prior years. Although such estimates are useful as a measure of cash flows into the Government, they do not accurately reflect the true economic cost of these provisions.

Tax Expenditure Baselines

A tax expenditure is an exception to baseline provisions of the tax structure that usually results in a reduction in the amount of tax owed. The 1974 Congressional Budget Act, which mandated the tax expenditure budget, did not specify the baseline provisions of the tax law. As noted previously, deciding whether provisions are exceptions, therefore, is a matter of judgment. As in prior years, most of this year's tax expenditure estimates are presented using two baselines: the normal tax baseline and the reference tax law baseline. Tax expenditures may take the form of credits, deductions, special exceptions and allowances, and reduce tax liability below the level implied by the baseline tax system.

The normal tax baseline is patterned on a practical variant of a comprehensive income tax, which defines income as the sum of consumption and the change in net wealth in a given period of time. The normal tax baseline allows personal exemptions, a standard deduction, and deduction of expenses incurred in earning income. It is not limited to a particular structure of tax rates, or by a specific definition of the taxpaying unit.

The reference tax law baseline is also patterned on a comprehensive income tax, but it is closer to existing law. Reference law tax expenditures are limited to special exceptions from a generally provided tax rule that serve programmatic functions in a way that is analogous to spending programs. Provisions under the reference law baseline are generally tax expenditures under the normal tax baseline, but the reverse is not always true. Both the normal and reference tax baselines allow several major departures from a pure comprehensive income tax. For example, under the normal and reference tax baselines:

• Income is taxable only when it is realized in exchange. Thus, the deferral of tax on unrealized capital gains is not regarded as a tax expenditure. Accrued income would be taxed under a comprehensive income tax.

• There is a separate corporate income tax. Under a comprehensive income tax, corporate income would be taxed only once—at the shareholder level, whether or not distributed in the form of dividends.

• Noncorporate tax rates vary by level of income.

• Individual tax rates, including brackets, standard deduction, and personal exemptions, are allowed to vary with marital status.

• Values of assets and debt are not generally adjusted for inflation. A comprehensive income tax would adjust the cost basis of capital assets and debt for changes in the general price level. Thus, under a comprehensive income tax baseline, the failure to take account of inflation in measuring depreciation, capital gains, and interest income would be regarded as a negative tax expenditure (i.e., a tax penalty), and failure to take account of inflation in measuring interest costs would be regarded as a positive tax expenditure (i.e., a tax subsidy).

Although the reference law and normal tax baselines are generally similar, areas of difference include:

Tax rates. The separate schedules applying to the various taxpaying units are included in the reference law baseline. Thus, corporate tax rates below the maximum statutory rate do not give rise to a tax expenditure. The normal tax baseline is similar, except that, by convention, it specifies the current maximum rate as the baseline for the corporate income tax. The lower tax rates applied to the first $10 million of corporate income are thus regarded as a tax expenditure under the normal tax. By convention, the Alternative Minimum Tax is treated as part of the baseline rate structure under both the reference and normal tax methods.

Income subject to the tax. Income subject to tax is defined as gross income less the costs of earning that income. Under the reference tax rules, gross income does not include gifts defined as receipts of money or property that are not consideration in an exchange nor does gross income include most transfer payments from the Government. The normal tax baseline also excludes gifts between individuals from gross income. Under the normal tax baseline, however, all cash transfer payments from the

Government to private individuals are counted in gross income, and exemptions of such transfers from tax are identified as tax expenditures. The costs of earning income are generally deductible in determining taxable income under both the reference and normal tax baselines.

Capital recovery. Under the reference tax law baseline no tax expenditures arise from accelerated depreciation. Under the normal tax baseline, the depreciation allowance for property is computed using estimates of economic depreciation.

Treatment of foreign income. Both the normal and reference tax baselines allow a tax credit for foreign income taxes paid (up to the amount of U.S. income taxes that would otherwise be due), which prevents double taxation of income earned abroad. Under the normal tax method, however, controlled foreign corporations (CFCs) are not regarded as entities separate from their controlling U.S. shareholders. Thus, the deferral of tax on income received by CFCs is regarded as a tax expenditure under this method. In contrast, except for tax haven activities, the reference law baseline follows current law in treating CFCs as separate taxable entities whose income is not subject to U.S. tax until distributed to U.S. taxpayers. Under this baseline, deferral of tax on CFC income is not a tax expenditure because U.S. taxpayers generally are not taxed on accrued, but unrealized, income.

Descriptions of Income Tax Provisions

Descriptions of the individual and corporate income tax expenditures reported on in this chapter follow. These descriptions relate to current law as of December 31, 2011. [Figures given are the estimated revenue losses in FY 2013 from the normal law baseline.]

National Defense

1. *Benefits and allowances to Armed Forces personnel* ($14.9 billion).—Certain housing and meals, in addition to other benefits provided military personnel, either in cash or in kind, as well as certain amounts of pay related to combat service, are excluded from income subject to tax.

2. *Income earned abroad* ($5.8 billion).—U.S. tax law allows U.S. citizens who live abroad, work in the private sector, and satisfy a foreign residency requirement to exclude up to $80,000, plus adjustments for inflation since 2004, in foreign earned income from U.S. taxes. In addition, if these taxpayers receive a specific allowance for foreign housing from their employers, then they may also exclude such expenses to the extent that they do not exceed 30 percent of the earned income inclusion, with geographical adjustments, over 16 percent of the earned income limit. If taxpayers do not receive a specific allowance for housing expenses, they may deduct housing expenses up to the amount by which foreign earned income exceeds their foreign earned income exclusion.

3. *Exclusion of certain allowances for Federal employees abroad* ($1.12 billion).—U.S. Federal civilian employees and Peace Corps members

who work outside the continental United States are allowed to exclude from U.S. taxable income certain special allowances they receive to compensate them for the relatively high costs associated with living overseas. The allowances supplement wage income and cover expenses such as rent, education, and the cost of travel to and from the United States.

4. *Sales source rule exceptions* ($3.73 billion).—The United States generally taxes the worldwide income of U.S. persons, with taxpayers receiving a credit for foreign taxes paid, limited to the pre-credit U.S. tax on the foreign source income. In contrast, the sales source rules for inventory property allow U.S. exporters to use more foreign tax credits by allowing the exporters to attribute a larger portion of their earnings abroad than would be the case if the allocation of earnings was based on actual economic activity.

5. *Income of U.S.-controlled foreign corporations* ($41.81 billion).—Certain active income of foreign corporations controlled by U.S. shareholders is not subject to U.S. taxation when it is earned. The income becomes taxable only when the controlling U.S. shareholders receive dividends or other distributions from their foreign stockholding. The reference law tax baseline reflects this tax treatment where only realized income is taxed. Under the normal tax method, however, the currently attributable foreign source pre-tax income from such a controlling interest is considered to be subject to U.S. taxation, whether or not distributed. Thus, the normal tax method considers the amount of controlled foreign corporation income not yet distributed to a U.S. shareholder as tax-deferred income.

6. *Exceptions under subpart F for active financing income* ($0).—Financial firms may defer taxes on income earned overseas in an active business.

General Science, Space, and Technology

7. *Expensing R & E expenditures* ($5.07 billion).—Research and experimentation (R & E) projects can be viewed as investments because, if successful, their benefits accrue for several years. It is often difficult, however, to identify whether a specific R & E project is successful and, if successful, what its expected life will be. Because of this ambiguity, the reference law baseline tax system would allow of expensing of R & E expenditures. In contrast, under the normal tax method, the expensing of R & E expenditures is viewed as a tax expenditure. The baseline assumed for the normal tax method is that all R & E expenditures are successful and have an expected life of five years.

8. *R & E credit* ($4.23 billion).—The Code allows an R & E credit of 20 percent of qualified research expenditures in excess of a base amount. The base amount is generally determined by multiplying a "fixed-base percentage" by the average amount of the company's gross receipts for the prior four years. The taxpayer's fixed base percentage generally is the ratio of its research expenses to gross receipts for 1984 through 1988. Taxpayers can elect the alternative simplified credit regime, which is

equal to 14 percent (12 percent prior to 2009) of qualified research expenses that exceed 50 percent of the average qualified research expenses for the three preceding taxable years. Prior to January 1, 2009, taxpayers could also elect an alternative incremental credit regime. Under the alternative incremental credit regime the taxpayer was assigned a three-tiered fixed base percentage that is lower than the fixed-base percentage that would otherwise apply, and the credit rate was reduced. The rates for the alternative incremental credit ranged from 3 percent to 5 percent. The research credit expired on December 31, 2011.

Energy

9. *Exploration and development costs* ($0.79 billion).—Under the baseline tax system, the costs of exploring and developing oil and gas wells would be capitalized and then amortized (or depreciated) over an estimate of the economic life of the well. This insures that the net income from the well is measured appropriately each year. In contrast to this treatment, current law allows intangible drilling costs for successful investments in domestic oil and gas wells (such as wages, the cost of using machinery for grading and drilling, and the cost of unsalvageable materials used in constructing wells) to be deducted immediately, *i.e.*, expensed. Because it allows recovery of costs sooner, expensing is more generous for the taxpayer than would be amortization. Integrated oil companies may deduct only 70 percent of such costs and must amortize the remaining 30 percent over five years. The same rule applies to the exploration and development costs of surface stripping and the construction of shafts and tunnels for other fuel minerals.

10. *Percentage depletion* ($1.26 billion).—The baseline tax system would allow recovery of the costs of developing certain oil and mineral properties using cost depletion. Cost depletion is similar in concept to depreciation, in that the costs of developing or acquiring the asset are capitalized and then gradually reduced over an estimate of the asset's productive life, as is appropriate for measuring net income.

In contrast, the Code generally allows independent fuel and mineral producers and royalty owners to take percentage depletion deductions rather than cost depletion on limited quantities of output. Under percentage depletion, taxpayers deduct a percentage of gross income from mineral production. In certain cases the deduction is limited to a fraction of the asset's net income. Over the life of an investment, percentage depletion deductions can exceed the cost of the investment. Consequently, percentage depletion offers more generous tax treatment than would cost depletion, which would limit deductions to an investment's cost.

11. *Alternative fuel production credit* ($0.01 billion).—The Code provides a credit of $3 per oil-equivalent barrel of production (in 2004 dollars) for coke or coke gas during a four-year period for qualified facilities. With the exception of liquefied hydrogen, these facilities must be placed in service before January 1, 2011.

12. *Oil and gas exception to passive loss limitation* ($0.03 billion).—The baseline tax system accepts current law's general rule limiting taxpayers' ability to deduct losses from passive activities against nonpassive income (*e.g.*, wages, interest, and dividends). Passive losses that are unused may be carried forward and applied against future passive income.

An exception from the passive loss limitation is provided for a working interest in an oil or gas property that the taxpayer holds directly or through an entity that does not limit the liability of the taxpayer with respect to the interest. Thus, taxpayers can deduct losses from such working interests against nonpassive income without regard to whether they materially participate in the activity.

13. *Capital gains treatment of royalties on coal* ($0.08 billion).—For individuals in 2011, tax rates on regular income vary from 10 percent to 35 percent, depending on the taxpayer's income. Current law allows capital gains to be taxed at a preferentially low rate that is no higher than 15 percent. Certain sales of coal under royalty contracts qualify for taxation as capital gains rather than ordinary income, and so benefit from the preferentially low 15 percent maximum tax rate on capital gains. Beginning in 2013, the top preferential tax rate on capital gains will be 20 percent.

14. *Energy facility bonds* ($0.03 billion).—The Code allows interest earned on State and local bonds used to finance construction of certain energy facilities to be exempt from tax. These bonds are generally subject to the State private-activity-bond annual volume cap.

15. *Energy production credit* ($1.9 billion).—The Code provides a credit for certain electricity produced from wind energy, biomass, geothermal energy, solar energy, small irrigation power, municipal solid waste, or qualified hydropower and sold to an unrelated party. In addition to the electricity production credit, an income tax credit is allowed for the production of refined coal and Indian coal at qualified facilities.

16. *Energy investment credit* ($1.51 billion).—The Code provides credits for investments in solar and geothermal energy property, qualified fuel cell power plants, stationary microturbine power plants, geothermal heat pumps, small wind property and combined heat and power property. Owners of renewable power facilities that qualify for the energy production credit may instead elect to take an energy investment credit.

17. *Alcohol fuel credits* ($0.11 billion).—The Tax Code provides an income tax credit for ethanol derived from renewable sources and used as fuel. In lieu of the alcohol mixture credit, the taxpayer may claim a refundable excise tax credit. In addition, small ethanol producers are eligible for a separate income tax credit for ethanol production and a separate income tax credit is available for qualified cellulosic biofuel production. With the exception of the cellulosic biofuel credit, these provisions expired on December 31, 2011.

18. *Bio–Diesel tax credit* ($0).—The Code allows an income tax credit for biodiesel used or sold and for bio-diesel derived from virgin sources. In lieu of the bio-diesel credit, the taxpayer may claim a refundable excise tax credit. In addition, small agri-biodiesel producers are eligible for a separate income tax credit for ethanol production and a separate credit is available for qualified renewable diesel fuel mixtures. This provision expired on December 31, 2011.

19. *Credit for alternative motor vehicles and refueling property* ($0.18 billion).—The Code allows a number of credits for certain types of vehicles and property. These are available for alternative fuel vehicle refueling property, fuel cell vehicles and plug-ins (including plug-in electric vehicles, plug-in electric drive motor vehicles, and plug-in conversion kits). The credits for advanced lean burn technology, and for hybrid and alternative motor vehicles, expired on December 31, 2010, while the credit for non-hydrogen refueling stations expired on December 31, 2011.

20. *Exclusion of utility conservation subsidies* ($0.21 billion).—In certain circumstances, public utilities offer rate subsidies to nonbusiness customers who invest in energy conservation measures. These rate subsidies are equivalent to payments from the utility to its customer, and so represent accretions to wealth, income that would be taxable to the customer under the baseline tax system. The Code exempts these subsidies from the non-business customer's gross income.

21. *Credit to holders of clean renewable energy bonds* ($0.07 billion).—The Code provides for the issuance of Clean Renewable Energy Bonds which entitles the bond holder to a Federal income tax credit in lieu of interest. The limit on the volume issued in 2009–2010 is $2.4 billion. As of March 2010, issuers of the unused authorization of such bonds could opt to receive direct payment with the yield becoming fully taxable.

22. *Deferral of gain from dispositions of transmission property to implement FERC restructuring policy* (revenue pick-up of $0.18 billion).—The Code allows utilities to defer gains from the sale of their transmission assets to a FERC-approved independent transmission company. The sale of property must be made prior to January 1, 2012.

23. *Credit for investment in clean coal facilities* ($0.41 billion).—The Code provides investment tax credits for clean coal facilities producing electricity and for industrial gasification combined cycle projects.

24. *Temporary 50 percent expensing for equipment used in the refining of liquid fuels* ($0.53 billion).—The Code provides for an accelerated recovery of the cost of certain investments in refineries by allowing partial expensing of the cost, thereby giving such investments a tax advantage.

25. *Natural gas distribution pipelines treated as 15–year property* ($0.09 billion).—The Code allows depreciation of natural gas distribution pipelines (placed in service between 2005 and 2011) over a 15 year period. These deductions are accelerated relative to deductions based on economic depreciation.

26. *Amortize all geological and geophysical expenditures over two years* ($0.16 billion).—The Code allows geological and geophysical expenditures incurred in connection with oil and gas exploration in the United States to be amortized over two years for non-integrated oil companies.

27. *Allowance of deduction for certain energy efficient commercial building property* ($0.1 billion).—The Code allows a deduction, per square foot, for certain energy efficient commercial buildings.

28. *Credit for construction of new energy efficient homes* ($0.02 billion).—The Code allows contractors a tax credit of $2,000 for the construction of a qualified new energy-efficient home that has an annual level of heating and cooling energy consumption at least 50 percent below the annual consumption of a comparable dwelling unit. The credit equals $1,000 in the case of a new manufactured home that meets a 30 percent standard. This provision expired on December 31, 2011.

29. *Credit for energy efficiency improvements to existing homes* ($0).—The Code provides an investment tax credit for expenditures made on insulation, exterior windows, and doors that improve the energy efficiency of homes and meet certain standards. The Code also provides a credit for purchases of advanced main air circulating fans, natural gas, propane, or oil furnaces or hot water boilers, and other qualified energy efficient property. This provision expired on December 31, 2011.

30. *Credit for energy efficient appliances* ($0.14 billion).—The Code provides tax credits for the manufacture of efficient dishwashers, clothes washers, and refrigerators. The size of the credit depends on the efficiency of the appliance. This provision expired on December 31, 2011.

31. *Credit for residential energy efficient property* ($1.03 billion).—The Code provides a credit for the purchase of a qualified photovoltaic property and solar water heating property, as well as for fuel cell power plants, geothermal heat pumps and small wind property.

32. *Credit for qualified energy conservation bonds* ($0.03 billion).—The Code provides for the issuance of energy conservation bonds which entitle the bond holder to a Federal income tax credit in lieu of interest. The limit on the volume issued in 2009–2010 is $3.2 billion. As of March 2010, issuers of the unused authorization of such bonds could opt to receive direct payment with the yield becoming fully taxable.

33. *Advanced energy property credit* ($0.38 billion).—The Code provides a 30 percent investment credit for property used in a qualified advanced energy manufacturing project. The Treasury Department may award up to $2.3 billion in tax credits for qualified investments.

34. *Advanced nuclear power facilities production credit* ($0).—The Code allows a tax credit equal to 1.8 cents times the number of kilowatt hours of electricity produced at a qualifying advanced nuclear power facility. A taxpayer may claim no more than $125 million per 1,000 MW of capacity. The Treasury Department may allocate up to 6,000 megawatts of credit-eligible capacity.

Natural Resources and Environment

35. *Exploration and development costs* ($0.07 billion).—Certain capital outlays associated with exploration and development of nonfuel minerals may be expensed rather than depreciated over the life of the asset.

36. *Percentage depletion* ($0.59 billion).—Most nonfuel mineral extractors may use percentage depletion (whereby the deduction is fixed as a percentage of revenue and can exceed total costs) rather than cost depletion, with percentage depletion rates ranging from 22 percent for sulfur to 5 percent for sand and gravel. Over the life of an investment, percentage depletion deductions can exceed the cost of the investment. Consequently, percentage depletion offers more generous tax treatment than would cost depletion, which would limit deductions to an investment's cost.

37. *Sewage, water, solid and hazardous waste facility bonds* ($0.58 billion).—The Code allows interest earned on State and local bonds used to finance construction of sewage, water, or hazardous waste facilities to be exempt from tax. These bonds are generally subject to the State private-activity bond annual volume cap.

38. *Capital gains treatment of certain timber* ($0.08 billion).—Certain timber sales can be treated as a capital gain rather than ordinary income and therefore subject to the lower capital-gains tax rate. For individuals in 2011, tax rates on regular income vary from 10 percent to 35 percent, depending on the taxpayer's income. In contrast, current law allows capital gains to be taxed at a preferentially low rate that is no higher than 15 percent. Beginning in 2013, the top preferential tax rate on capital gains will be 20 percent.

39. *Expensing multi-period timber growing costs* ($0.28 billion).—Most of the production costs of growing timber may be expensed under current law rather than capitalized and deducted when the timber is sold, thereby accelerating cost recovery.

40. *Historic preservation* ($0.57 billion).—Expenditures to preserve and restore certified historic structures qualify for an investment tax credit of 20 percent under current law for certified rehabilitation activities. The taxpayer's recoverable basis must be reduced by the amount of the credit. Qualified GO (Gulf Opportunity) Zone expenditures qualify for a 26 percent credit.

41. *Exclusion of gain or loss on sale or exchange of certain brownfield sites* ($0.03 billion).—In general, a tax-exempt organization must pay taxes on income from activities unrelated to its nonprofit status. The Code, however, provides a special exclusion from unrelated business taxable income of the gain or loss from the sale or exchange of certain qualifying brownfield properties.

42. *Industrial CO2 capture and sequestration tax credit* ($0.06 billion).—The Code allows a credit of $20 per metric ton for qualified carbon dioxide captured at a qualified facility and disposed of in secure geological storage. In addition, the provision allows a credit of $10 per metric ton of

qualified carbon dioxide that is captured at a qualified facility and as a tertiary injectant in a qualified enhanced oil or natural gas recovery project.

43. *Deduction for endangered species recovery expenditures* ($0.02 billion).—Farmers can deduct up to 25 percent of their gross income for expenses incurred as a result of site and habitat improvement activities that will benefit endangered species on their farm land, in accordance with site specific management actions included in species recovery plans approved pursuant to the Endangered Species Act of 1973.

Agriculture

44. *Expensing certain capital outlays* ($0.11 billion).—Farmers may expense certain expenditures for feed and fertilizer as well as for soil and water conservation measures as well as other capital improvements.

45. *Expensing multi-period livestock and crop production costs* ($0.17 billion).—The production of livestock and crops with a production period greater than two years (e.g., establishing orchards or constructing barns) is exempt from the uniform cost capitalization rules, thereby accelerating cost recovery.

46. *Loans forgiven solvent farmers* ($0.02 billion).—The baseline tax system requires debtors to include the amount of loan forgiveness as income or else reduce their recoverable basis in the property related to the loan. If the amount of forgiveness exceeds the basis, the excess forgiveness is taxable. However, for bankrupt debtors, the amount of loan forgiveness reduces carryover losses, unused credits, and then basis, with the remainder of the forgiven debt excluded from taxation.

47. *Capital gains treatment of certain income* ($0.83 billion)—Current law allows capital gains to be taxed at a preferentially low rate that is no higher than 15 percent. Certain agricultural income, such as unharvested crops, qualify for taxation as capital gains rather than ordinary income, and so benefit from the preferentially low 15 percent maximum tax rate on capital gains. Beginning in 2013, the top preferential tax rate on capital gains will be 20 percent.

48. *Income averaging for farmers* ($0.09 billion).—Taxpayers may average their taxable income from farming and fishing over the previous three years.

49. *Deferral of gain on sales of farm refiners* ($0.02 billion).—The Code allows a taxpayer who sells stock in a farm refiner to a farmers' cooperative to defer recognition of the gain if the proceeds are re-invested in a qualified replacement property.

50. *Expensing of reforestation expenditures* ($0.08 billion).—The Code provides for the expensing of the first $10,000 in reforestation expenditures with 7–year amortization of the remaining expenses.

Commerce and Housing

51. *Credit union income exemption* ($1.16 billion).—The earnings of credit unions not distributed to members as interest or dividends are exempt from the income tax.

52. *Deferral of income on life insurance and annuity contracts* ($25.15 billion).—The Code provides favorable tax treatment for investment income earned within qualified life insurance and annuity contracts. In general, investment income earned on qualified life insurance contracts held until death is permanently exempt from income tax. Investment income distributed prior to the death of the insured is generally tax-deferred. Investment income earned on annuities benefits from tax deferral.

53. *Small property and casualty insurance companies* ($0.04 billion).—Stock non-life insurance companies are generally exempt from tax if their gross receipts for the taxable year do not exceed $600,000 and more than 50 percent of such gross receipts consists of premiums. Mutual non-life insurance companies are generally tax-exempt if their annual gross receipts do not exceed $150,000 and more than 35 percent of gross receipts consist of premiums. Also, non-life insurance companies with no more than $1.2 million of annual net premiums may elect to pay tax only on their taxable investment income.

54. *Insurance companies owned by exempt organizations* ($0.21 billion).—Generally the income generated by life and property and casualty insurance companies is subject to tax, albeit by special rules. Insurance operations conducted by such exempt organizations as fraternal societies, voluntary employee benefit associations, and others, however, are exempt from tax.

55. *Small life insurance company deduction* ($0.03 billion).—Small life insurance companies (with gross assets of less than $500 million) can deduct 60 percent of the first $3 million of otherwise taxable income. The deduction phases out for otherwise taxable income between $3 million and $15 million.

56. *Exclusion of interest spread of financial institutions* ($0.6 billion).—Consumers and nonprofit organizations pay for some deposit-linked services, such as check cashing, by accepting a below-market interest rate on their demand deposits. If they received a market rate of interest on those deposits and paid explicit fees for the associated services, they would pay taxes on the full market rate and (unlike businesses) could not deduct the fees. The Government thus foregoes tax on the difference between the risk-free market interest rate and below-market interest rates on demand deposits, which under competitive conditions should equal the value added of deposit services.

57. *Mortgage housing bonds* ($1.46 billion).—The Code allows interest earned on State and local bonds used to finance homes purchased by

first-time, low-to-moderate-income buyers to be exempt. These bonds are generally subject to the State private-activity-bond annual volume cap.

58. *Rental housing bonds* ($1.24 billion).—The Code allows interest earned on State and local government bonds used to finance multifamily rental housing projects to be tax-exempt.

59. *Interest on owner-occupied homes* ($100.91 billion).—The Code allows an exclusion from a taxpayer's taxable income for the value of owner-occupied housing services and also allows the owner-occupant to deduct mortgage interest paid on his or her primary and secondary residences as an itemized non-business deduction. In general, the mortgage interest deduction is limited to interest on debt no greater than the owner's basis in the residence, and is also limited to interest on debt of no more than $1 million. Interest on up to $100,000 of other debt secured by a lien on a principal or second residence is also deductible, irrespective of the purpose of borrowing, provided the total debt does not exceed the fair market value of the residence. As an alternative to the deduction, holders of qualified Mortgage Credit Certificates issued by State or local governmental units or agencies may claim a tax credit equal to a proportion of their interest expense.

60. *Taxes on owner-occupied homes* ($22.32 billion).—The Code allows an exclusion from a taxpayer's taxable income for the value of owner-occupied housing services and also allows the owner-occupant to deduct property taxes paid on his or her primary and secondary residences.

61. *Installment sales* ($1.35 billion).—Dealers in real and personal property (*i.e.*, sellers who regularly hold property for sale or resale) cannot defer taxable income from installment sales until the receipt of the loan repayment. Nondealers (*i.e.*, sellers of real property used in their business) are required to pay interest on deferred taxes attributable to their total installment obligations in excess of $5 million. Only properties with sales prices exceeding $150,000 are includable in the total. The payment of a market rate of interest eliminates the benefit of the tax deferral. The tax exemption for nondealers with total installment obligations of less than $5 million is, therefore, a tax expenditure.

62. *Capital gains exclusion on home sales* ($23.44 billion).—The Code allows homeowners to exclude from gross income up to $250,000 ($500,000 in the case of a married couple filing a joint return) of the capital gains from the sale of a principal residence. To qualify, the taxpayer must have owned and used the property as the taxpayer's principal residence for a total of at least two of the five years preceding the date of sale, In addition, the exclusion may not be used more than once every two years.

63. *Imputed net rental income on owner-occupied housing* ($51.08 billion).—Under the baseline tax system, the taxable income of a taxpayer who is an owner-occupant would include the implicit value of gross rental income on housing services earned on the investment in owner-occupied housing and would allow a deduction for expenses, such as interest,

depreciation, property taxes, and other costs, associated with earning such rental income. In contrast, the Code allows an exclusion from taxable income for the implicit gross rental income on housing services, while in certain circumstances allows a deduction for some costs associated with such income, such as for mortgage interest and property taxes.

64. *Passive loss real estate exemption* ($15.38 billion).—In contrast to the general restrictions on passive losses, the Code exempts owners of rental real estate activities from "passive income" limitations. The exemption is limited to $25,000 in losses and phases out for taxpayers with income between $100,000 and $150,000.

65. *Low-income housing credit* ($7.38 billion).—Taxpayers who invest in certain low-income housing are eligible for a tax credit. The credit rate is set so that the present value of the credit is equal to 70 percent for new construction and 30 percent for (1) housing receiving other Federal benefits (such as tax-exempt bond financing), or (2) substantially rehabilitated existing housing. The credit can exceed these levels in certain statutorily defined and State designated areas where project development costs are higher. The credit is allowed in equal amounts over 10 years and is generally subject to a volume cap.

66. *Accelerated depreciation of residential rental property* ($0.09 billion).—Under an economic income tax, the costs of acquiring a building are capitalized and depreciated over time in accordance with the decline in the property's economic value due to wear and tear or obsolescence. This insures that the net income from the rental property is measured appropriately each year. However, the depreciation provisions of the Tax Code are part of the reference law rules, and thus do not give rise to tax expenditures under reference law. Under normal law, however, depreciation allowances reflect estimates of economic depreciation.

67. *Discharge of mortgage indebtedness* ($0.25 billion).—The Code allows an exclusion from a taxpayer's taxable income for any discharge of indebtedness of up to $2 million ($1 million in the case of a married individual filing a separate return) from a qualified principal residence. The provision applies to debt discharged after January 1, 2007, and before January 1, 2013.

68. *Credit for homebuyer* (revenue pick-up of $1.15 billion).—The Code allows a tax credit for home buyers on purchases before May 1, 2010.

69. *Cancellation of indebtedness* (revenue pick-up of $0.02 billion).—Individuals are not required to report the cancellation of certain indebtedness as current income. If the canceled debt is not reported as current income, however, the basis of the underlying property must be reduced by the amount canceled.

70. *Imputed interest rules* ($0.05 billion).—Holders (issuers) of debt instruments are generally required to report interest earned (paid) in the period it accrues, not when paid. In addition, the amount of interest accrued is determined by the actual price paid, not by the stated principal

and interest stipulated in the instrument. In general, any debt associated with the sale of property worth less than $250,000 is excepted from the general interest accounting rules. This general $250,000 exception is not a tax expenditure under reference law but is under normal law. Exceptions above $250,000 are a tax expenditure under reference law; these exceptions include the following: (1) sales of personal residences worth more than $250,000, and (2) sales of farms and small businesses worth between $250,000 and $1 million.

71. *Treatment of qualified dividends* ($21.9 billion).—In 2011 qualified dividends were taxed at a preferentially low rate that is no higher than 15 percent. Beginning in 2013, dividends will be taxed as ordinary income.

72. *Capital gains (other than agriculture, timber, and coal)* ($62.04 billion).—In 2011 capital gains on assets held for more than one year were taxed at a preferentially low rate that is no higher than 15 percent. Beginning in 2013, the top preferential tax rate on capital gains will be 20 percent.

73. *Capital gains exclusion for small business stock* ($0.28 billion).— The Code provides an exclusion of 50 percent (from a 28 percent tax rate) for capital gains from qualified small business stock held by individuals for more than 5 years; 75 percent for stock issued after February 17, 2009 and before September 28, 2010; and 100 percent for stock issued after September 27, 2010 and before January 1, 2012. A qualified small business is a corporation whose gross assets do not exceed $50 million as of the date of issuance of the stock.

74. *Step-up in basis of capital gains at death* ($23.86 billion).— Under the baseline tax system, unrealized capital gains would be taxed when assets are transferred at death. In contrast, capital gains on assets held at the owner's death are not subject to capital gains tax under current law. The cost basis of the appreciated assets is adjusted to the market value at the owner's date of death.

75. *Carryover basis of capital gains on gifts* ($2.07 billion).—Under the baseline tax system, unrealized capital gains would be taxed when assets are transferred by gift. In contrast, when a gift of appreciated asset is made under current law, the donor's basis in the transferred property (the cost that was incurred when the transferred property was first acquired) carries over to the donee. The carryover of the donor's basis allows a continued deferral of unrealized capital gains.

76. *Ordinary income treatment of losses from sale of small business corporate stock shares* ($0.06 billion).—The Code allows up to $100,000 in losses from the sale of small business corporate stock (capitalization less than $1 million) to be treated as ordinary losses and fully deducted.

77. *Depreciation of non-rental-housing buildings* (revenue pick-up of $7.37 billion).—The depreciation provisions of the Code are part of the reference law rules, and thus do not give rise to tax expenditures under

reference law. Under normal law, however, depreciation allowances reflect estimates of economic depreciation.

78. *Accelerated depreciation of machinery and equipment* ($33.18 billion).—The depreciation provisions of the Code are part of the reference law rules, and thus do not give rise to tax expenditures under reference law. Under normal law, however, depreciation allowances reflect estimates of economic depreciation.

79. *Expensing of certain small investments* ($0.94 billion).—Under the reference law baseline, the costs of acquiring tangible property and computer software would be depreciated using the Code's depreciation provisions. Under the normal tax baseline, depreciation allowances are estimates of economic depreciation. However, the Code allows qualifying investments by small businesses in tangible property and certain computer software to be expensed rather than depreciated over time.

80. *Graduated corporation income tax rate schedule* ($3.3 billion).— Because the corporate rate schedule is part of reference tax law, it is not considered a tax expenditure under the reference method. A flat corporation income tax rate is taken as the baseline under the normal tax method; therefore the lower rate is considered a tax expenditure under this concept.

81. *Small issue industrial development bonds* ($0.34 billion).—The Code allows interest earned on small issue industrial development bonds (IDBs) issued by State and local governments to finance manufacturing facilities to be tax exempt. Depreciable property financed with small issue IDBs must be depreciated, however, using the straight-line method. The annual volume of small issue IDBs is subject to the unified volume cap discussed in the mortgage housing bond section above.

82. *Deduction for U.S. production activities* ($14.5 billion).—The Code allows for a deduction equal to a portion of taxable income attributable to domestic production.

83. *Special rules for certain film and TV production* ($0.08 billion).— Taxpayers may deduct up to $15 million per production ($20 million in certain distressed areas) in non-capital expenditures incurred during the year.

Transportation

84. *Deferral of tax on U.S. shipping companies* ($0.02 billion).—The Code allows certain companies that operate U.S. flag vessels to defer income taxes on that portion of their income used for shipping purposes, primarily construction, modernization and major repairs to ships, and repayment of loans to finance these investments. U.S. shipping companies may choose to be subject to a tonnage tax based on gross shipping weight in lieu of an income tax, in which case profits would not be subject to tax under the regular tax rate schedule.

85. *Exclusion of employee parking expenses* ($3.29 billion).—Dedicated payments and in-kind benefits represent accretions to wealth that do not differ materially from cash wages. In contrast, the Code allows an exclusion from taxable income for employee parking expenses that are paid for by the employer or that are received by the employee in lieu of wages. In 2012, the maximum amount of the parking exclusion will be $240 per month. The tax expenditure estimate does not include any subsidy provided through employer-owned parking facilities.

86. *Exclusion of employee transit pass expenses* ($0.56 billion).—The Code allows an exclusion from a taxpayer's taxable income for passes, tokens, fare cards, and vanpool expenses that are paid for by an employer or that are received by the employee in lieu of wages to defray an employee's commuting costs. The maximum amount of the exclusion in 2012 is set at $125 per month.

87. *Tax credit for certain expenditures for maintaining railroad tracks* ($0.08 billion).—Eligible taxpayers may claim a credit equal to the lesser of 50 percent of maintenance expenditures and the product of $3,500 and the number of miles of track owned or leased.

88. *Exclusion of interest on bonds for financing of highway projects and rail-truck transfer facilities* ($0.29 billion).—The Code provides for $15 billion of tax-exempt bond authority to finance qualified highway or surface freight transfer facilities. The authority to issue these bonds expires on December 31, 2015.

Community and Regional Development

89. *Rehabilitation of structures* ($0.02 billion).—The Code allows a 10–percent investment tax credit for the rehabilitation of buildings that are used for business or productive activities and that were erected before 1936 for other than residential purposes. The taxpayer's recoverable basis must be reduced by the amount of the credit. Qualified GO Zone expenditures qualify for a 13 percent credit.

90. *Airport, dock, and similar facility bonds* ($0.97 billion).—The Code allows interest earned on State and local bonds issued to finance high-speed rail facilities and Government-owned airports, docks, wharves, and sport and convention facilities to be tax-exempt. These bonds are not subject to a volume cap.

91. *Exemption of income of mutuals and cooperatives* ($0.12 billion).—The Code provides for the incomes of mutual and cooperative telephone and electric companies to be exempt from tax if at least 85 percent of their revenues are derived from patron service charges.

92. *Empowerment zones and renewal communities* ($0.46 billion).— Qualifying businesses in designated economically depressed areas can receive tax benefits such as an employer wage credit, increased expensing of investment in equipment, special tax-exempt financing, accelerated depreciation, and certain capital gains incentives. A taxpayer's ability to accrue new tax benefits for Empowerment Zones and the DC Enterprise

Zone expired December 31, 2011. A taxpayer's ability to accrue new tax benefits for Renewal Communities expired December 31, 2009.

93. *New markets tax credit* ($0.93 billion).—Taxpayers who make qualified equity investments in a community development entity (CDE), which then makes qualified investments in low-income communities, are eligible for a tax credit received over 7 years. A CDE must first receive an allocation of tax credit from Treasury before it can sell the tax credit to the investor in exchange for the equity investment. The total equity investment available for the credit across all CDEs is $5 billion in 2011, the last year for which allocations can be made.

94. *Expensing of environmental remediation costs* (revenue pick-up of $0.17 billion).—The Code allows taxpayers who clean up certain hazardous substances at a qualified site to expense the clean-up costs, even though the expenses will generally increase the value of the property significantly or appreciably prolong the life of the property.

95. *Credit to holders of Gulf and Midwest Tax Credit Bonds* ($0.05 billion).—Taxpayers that own Gulf and Midwest Tax Credit bonds receive a non-refundable tax credit rather than interest. The credit is included in gross income.

96. *Recovery Zone Bonds* ($0).—The Code allows local governments to issue up $10 billion in taxable Recovery Zone Economic Development Bonds in 2009 and 2010 and receive a direct payment from Treasury equal to 45 percent of interest expenses. In addition, they would be allowed to allocate up to $15 billion in tax exempt Recovery Zone Facility Bonds. These bonds finance certain kinds of business development in areas of economic distress.

97. *Tribal Economic Development Bonds* ($0.48 billion).—The Code was modified in 2009 to allow Indian tribal governments to issue tax exempt "tribal economic development bonds." There is a national bond limitation of $2 billion.

Education, Training, Employment, and Social Services

98. *Scholarship and fellowship income* ($3.29 billion).—Scholarships and fellowships are excluded from taxable income to the extent they pay for tuition and course-related expenses of the grantee. Similarly, tuition reductions for employees of educational institutions and their families are not included in taxable income. From an economic point of view, scholarships and fellowships are either gifts not conditioned on the performance of services, or they are rebates of educational costs. Thus, under the baseline tax system of the reference law method, this exclusion is not a tax expenditure because this method does not include either gifts or price reductions in a taxpayer's gross income. The exclusion, however, is considered a tax expenditure under the normal tax method, which includes gift-like transfers of Government funds in gross income (many scholarships are derived directly or indirectly from Government funding).

99. *HOPE tax credit* ($0.58 billion).—The non-refundable HOPE tax credit allows a credit for 100 percent of an eligible student's first $1,200 of tuition and fees and 50 percent of the next $1,200 of tuition and fees (dollar amounts are for 2011). The credit only covers tuition and fees paid during the first two years of a student's post-secondary education. In 2011, the credit is phased out ratably for taxpayers with modified AGI between $102,000 and $122,000 if married filing jointly ($51,000 and $61,000 for other taxpayers), indexed.

100. *Lifetime Learning tax credit* ($3.92 billion).—The non-refundable Lifetime Learning tax credit allows a credit for 20 percent of an eligible student's tuition and fees, up to a maximum credit per return of $2,000. In 2011, the credit is phased out ratably for taxpayers with modified AGI between $102,000 and $122,000 if married filing jointly ($51,000 and $61,000 for other taxpayers), indexed. The credit applies to both undergraduate and graduate students.

101. *American Opportunity Tax Credit* ($13.71 billion).—The American Opportunity tax credit allows a partially refundable credit of up to $2,500 per eligible student for qualified tuition and related expenses paid during each of the first four years of the student's postsecondary education. The credit is phased out for taxpayers with modified adjusted gross income between $80,000 and $90,000 ($160,000 and $180,000 for married taxpayers filing a joint return). The credit is available for qualified expenses incurred in tax years beginning on or after January 1, 2009 and on or before December 31, 2012.

102. *Education Individual Retirement Accounts (IRA)* ($0.08 billion).—Contributions to an education IRA are not tax-deductible. However, investment income earned by education IRAs is not taxed when earned, and investment income from an education IRA is tax-exempt when withdrawn to pay for a student's education expenses. The maximum contribution to an education IRA in 2011 is $2,000 per beneficiary. In 2011, the maximum contribution is phased down ratably for taxpayers with modified AGI between $190,000 and $220,000 if married filing jointly ($95,000 and $110,000 for other taxpayers).

103. *Student-loan interest* ($0.9 billion).—Taxpayers may claim an above-the-line deduction of up to $2,500 on interest paid on an education loan. In general, interest may only be deducted for the first five years in which interest payments are required, and the maximum deduction is phased down ratably for taxpayers with modified AGI between $60,000 and $75,000 if married filing jointly ($40,000 to $55,000 for other taxpayers), indexed from 2001. However, for tax years beginning on January 1, 2001 and before December 31, 2011, the first five year requirement is suspended, and the phase down range for the deduction is raised. In 2011, the maximum deduction is phased down ratably for taxpayers with modified AGI between $120,000 and $150,000 if married filing jointly ($60,000 and $75,000 for other taxpayers).

104. *Deduction for higher education expenses* ($0).—The baseline tax system would not allow a deduction for personal expenditures. In contrast, the Tax Code provides a maximum annual deduction of $4,000 in 2011 for qualified higher education expenses for taxpayers with adjusted gross income up to $130,000 on a joint return ($65,000 for other taxpayers). Taxpayers with adjusted gross income up to $160,000 on a joint return ($80,000 for other taxpayers) may deduct up to $2,000. This provision expired on December 31, 2011.

105. *Qualified tuition programs* ($1.89 billion).—Some States have adopted prepaid tuition plans prepaid room and board plans, and college savings plans, which allow persons to pay in advance or save for college expenses for designated beneficiaries. Under current law, investment income, or the return on prepayments, is not taxed when earned, and is tax-exempt when withdrawn to pay for qualified expenses.

106. *Student-loan bonds* ($0.66 billion).—Interest earned on State and local bonds issued to finance student loans is tax-exempt under current law. The volume of all such private activity bonds that each State may issue annually is limited.

107. *Bonds for private nonprofit educational institutions* ($2.9 billion).—Interest earned on State and local Government bonds issued to finance the construction of facilities used by private nonprofit educational institutions is not taxed.

108. *Credit for holders of zone academy bonds* ($0.18 billion).—Financial institutions that own zone academy bonds receive a non-refundable tax credit rather than interest. The credit is included in gross income. Proceeds from zone academy bonds may only be used to renovate, but not construct, qualifying schools and for certain other school purposes. Under current law, the total amount of zone academy bonds that may be issued is limited to $1.4 billion in 2009 and 2010 as of March 2010, issuers of the unused authorization of such bonds could opt to receive direct payment with the yield becoming fully taxable. An additional $0.4 billion of these bonds with a tax credit was authorized to be issued before January 1, 2011.

109. *U.S. savings bonds for education* ($0.02 billion).—Interest earned on U.S. savings bonds issued after December 31, 1989 is tax-exempt if the bonds are transferred to an educational institution to pay for educational expenses. The tax exemption is phased out for taxpayers with AGI between $106,650 and $136,650 if married filing jointly ($71,000 and $86,100 for other taxpayers) in 2011.

110. *Dependent students age 19 or older* ($2.8 billion).—Under the baseline tax system, a personal exemption for the taxpayer is allowed. However, additional exemptions for targeted groups within a given filing status would not be allowed. In contrast, the Code allows taxpayers to claim personal exemptions for dependent children who are over the age of 18 and under the age of 24 and who (1) reside with the taxpayer for over half the year (with exceptions for temporary absences from home, such as

for school attendance), (2) are full-time students, and (3) do not claim a personal exemption on their own tax returns.

111. *Charitable contributions to educational institutions* ($4.61 billion).—The Code provides taxpayers a deduction for contributions to nonprofit educational institutions. Moreover, taxpayers who donate capital assets to educational institutions can deduct the asset's current value without being taxed on any appreciation in value. An individual's total charitable contribution generally may not exceed 50 percent of adjusted gross income; a corporation's total charitable contributions generally may not exceed 10 percent of pre-tax income.

112. *Employer-provided educational assistance* ($0.04 billion).—Employer-provided educational assistance is excluded from an employee's gross income even though the employer's costs for this assistance are a deductible business expense. The maximum exclusion is $5,250 per taxpayer.

113. *Special deduction for teacher expenses* ($0).—The baseline tax system would not allow a deduction for personal expenditures. In contrast, under current law educators in both public and private elementary and secondary schools, who work at least 900 hours during a school year as a teacher, instructor, counselor, principal or aide, may subtract up to $250 of qualified expenses when figuring their adjusted gross income (AGI). This provision expired on December 31, 2011.

114. *Discharge of student loan indebtedness* ($0.02 billion).—The Code allows certain professionals who perform in underserved areas or specific fields, and as a consequence have their student loans discharged, not to recognize such discharge as income.

115. *Qualified school construction bonds* ($0.58 billion).—The Code was modified in 2009 to provide a tax credit in lieu of interest to holders of qualified school construction bonds. The national volume limit is $22.4 billion over 2009 and 2010. As of March 2010, issuers of such bonds could opt to receive direct payment with the yield becoming fully taxable.

116. *Work opportunity tax credit (WOTC)* ($0.62 billion).—The Code provides employers with a tax credit for qualified wages paid to individuals. The credit applies to employees who begin work on or before December 31, 2011 and who are certified as members of various targeted groups. The amount of the credit that can be claimed is 25 percent of qualified wages for employment less than 400 hours and 40 percent for employment of 400 hours or more. Generally, the maximum credit per employee is $2,400 and can only be claimed on the first year of wages an individual earns from an employer. However, the credit for long-term welfare recipients can be claimed on second year wages as well and has a $9,000 maximum. Employees must work at least 120 hours to be eligible for the credit. Employers must reduce their deduction for wages paid by the amount of the credit claimed. The credit was extended to certain recently discharged unemployed veterans through December 31, 2012 with a maximum credit of $9,600 for hiring eligible veterans.

117. *Welfare-to-work tax credit* ($0).—An employer is eligible for a tax credit on the first $20,000 of eligible wages paid to qualified long-term family assistance recipients during the first two years of employment. The welfare-to-work credit expired on December 31, 2006. After this date, long-term welfare recipients became a WOTC target group.

118. *Employer-provided child care exclusion* ($1.58 billion).—Up to $5,000 of employer-provided child care is excluded from an employee's gross income even though the employer's costs for the child care are a deductible business expense.

119. *Employer-provided child care credit* ($0).—Current law provides a credit equal to 25 percent of qualified expenses for employee child care and 10 percent of qualified expenses for child care resource and referral services. Employer deductions for such expenses are reduced by the amount of the credit. The maximum total credit is limited to $150,000 per taxable year.

120. *Assistance for adopted foster children* ($0.56 billion).—Taxpayers who adopt eligible children from the public foster care system can receive monthly payments for the children's significant and varied needs and a reimbursement of up to $2,000 for nonrecurring adoption expenses; special needs adoptions receive the maximum benefit even if that amount not spent. These payments are excluded from gross income.

121. *Adoption credit and exclusion* ($0.38 billion).—Taxpayers can receive a refundable tax credit for qualified adoption expenses under current law. The maximum credit is $13,360 per child for 2011, and is phased-out ratably for taxpayers with modified AGI between $182,520 and $222,520. The credit amounts and the phase-out thresholds are indexed for inflation. Taxpayers may also exclude qualified adoption expenses provided or reimbursed by an employer from income, subject to the same maximum amounts and phase-out as the credit. The same expenses cannot qualify for tax benefits under both programs; however, a taxpayer may use the benefits of the exclusion and the tax credit for different expenses.

122. *Employer-provided meals and lodging* ($10.29 billion).—Employer-provided meals and lodging are excluded from an employee's gross income even though the employer's costs for these items are a deductible business expense.

123. *Child credit* ($18.39 billion).—Taxpayers with children under age 17 can qualify for a $1,000 partially refundable per child credit. Any unclaimed credit due to insufficient tax liability may be refundable—taxpayers may claim a refund for 15 percent of earnings in excess of a $3,000 floor, up to the amount of unused credit. Alternatively, taxpayers with three or more children may claim a refund of the amount of payroll taxes paid in excess of EITC received (up to the amount of unused credit) if this results in a larger refund. The maximum credit declines to $500 in 2013 and later years and refundability is restricted to taxpayers who are eligible for the credit under the alternative calculation. The credit is

phased out for taxpayers at the rate of $50 per $1,000 of modified AGI above $110,000 ($75,000 for single or head of household filers and $55,000 for married taxpayers filing separately).

124. *Child and dependent care expenses* ($1.62 billion).—The Code provides parents who work or attend school and who have child and dependent care expenses a tax credit. In 2011, expenditures up to a maximum $3,000 for one dependent and $6,000 for two or more dependents are eligible for the credit. The credit is equal to 35 percent of qualified expenditures for taxpayers with incomes of $15,000. The credit is reduced to a minimum of 20 percent by one percentage point for each $2,000 of income in excess of $15,000.

125. *Disabled access expenditure credit* ($0.02 billion).—The Code provides small businesses (less than $1 million in gross receipts or fewer than 31 full-time employees) a 50–percent credit for expenditures in excess of $250 to remove access barriers for disabled persons. The credit is limited to $5,000.

126. *Charitable contributions, other than education and health* ($39.77 billion).—The Code provides taxpayers a deduction for contributions to charitable, religious, and certain other nonprofit organizations. Taxpayers who donate capital assets to charitable organizations can deduct the assets' current value without being taxed on any appreciation in value. An individual's total charitable contribution generally may not exceed 50 percent of adjusted gross income; a corporation's total charitable contributions generally may not exceed 10 percent of pre-tax income.

127. *Foster care payments* ($0.4 billion).—Foster parents provide a home and care for children who are wards of the State, under contract with the State. However, compensation received for this service is excluded from the gross incomes of foster parents; the expenses they incur are nondeductible.

128. *Parsonage allowances* ($0.77 billion).—The Code allows an exclusion from a clergyman's taxable income for the value of the clergyman's housing allowance or the rental value of the clergyman's parsonage.

129. *Provide an employee retention credit to employers affected by certain natural disasters* ($0).—The Code provides tax credits against the wages paid to eligible employees in selected areas affected by natural disasters such as hurricanes Katrina, Rita, Wilma, and Ike. This provision expired on December 31, 2009.

130. *Exclusion for benefits provided to volunteer EMS and firefighters* ($0).—The Code allows an exclusion from taxable income of certain rebates or reductions of state and local income and property taxes provided by states or localities if the taxpayer is a member of a volunteer emergency response organization. The Tax Code also allows an exclusion from taxable income of certain payments such as reimbursements for expenses or equipment allowances of up to $360 per year provided by states or localities on account of performance of services as a member of a

volunteer emergency response organization. This provision expired on December 31, 2010.

131. *Making work pay tax credit* ($0).—The Code was modified in 2009 to provide for a tax credit in 2009 and 2010 of the lesser of 6.2 percent of an individual's earned income or $400 ($800 for joint filers). It is phased out at a rate of 2 percent of modified AGI above $75,000 ($150,000 for joint filers).

Health

132. *Employer-paid medical insurance and expenses* ($180.58 billion).—Employer-paid health insurance premiums and other medical expenses (including long-term care) are deducted as a business expense by employers, but they are not included in employee gross income.

133. *Self-employed medical insurance premiums* ($5.97 billion).—Self-employed taxpayers may deduct their family health insurance premiums. Taxpayers without self-employment income are not eligible for this special deduction. The deduction is not available for any month in which the self-employed individual is eligible to participate in an employer-subsidized health plan and the deduction may not exceed the self-employed individual's earned income from self-employment.

134. *Medical and health savings accounts* ($2.07 billion).—Individual contributions to Archer Medical Savings Accounts (Archer MSAs) and Health Savings Accounts (HSAs) are allowed as a deduction in determining adjusted gross income whether or not the individual itemizes deductions. Employer contributions to Archer MSAs and HSAs are excluded from income and employment taxes. Archer MSAs and HSAs require that the individual have coverage by a qualifying high deductible health plan. Earnings from the accounts are excluded from taxable income. Distributions from the accounts used for medical expenses are not taxable. The rules for HSAs are generally more flexible than for Archer MSAs and the deductible contribution amounts are greater (in 2011, $3050 for taxpayers with individual coverage and $6,150 for taxpayers with family coverage). Thus, HSAs have largely replaced MSAs.

135. *Medical care expenses* ($9.91 billion).—Personal expenditures for medical care (including the costs of prescription drugs) exceeding 7.5 percent of the taxpayer's adjusted gross income are deductible. For tax years beginning after 2012, only medical expenditures exceeding 10 percent of the taxpayer's adjusted gross income are deductible. However, for the years 2013, 2014, 2015 and 2016, if either the taxpayer or the taxpayer's spouse turns 65 before the end of the taxable year, the threshold remains at 7.5 percent of adjusted income.

136. *Hospital construction bonds* ($4.28 billion).—Interest earned on State and local government debt issued to finance hospital construction is excluded from income subject to tax.

137. *Refundable Premium Assistance Tax Credit* ($0).—For taxable years ending after 2013, the Code provides a premium assistance credit to

any eligible taxpayer for any qualified health insurance purchased through a Health Insurance Exchange. In general, an eligible taxpayer is a taxpayer with annual household income between 100% and 400% of the federal poverty level for a family of the taxpayer's size and that does not have access to affordable minimum essential health care coverage. The amount of the credit equals the lesser of (i) the actual premiums paid by the taxpayer for such coverage or (ii) the difference between the cost of a statutorily-identified benchmark plan offered on the exchange and a required payment by the taxpayer that increases with income.

138. *Credit for employee health insurance expenses of small business* ($1.75 billion).—The Code provides a tax credit to qualified small employers that make a certain level of non-elective contributions towards the purchase of certain health insurance coverage for its employees. To receive a credit, an employer must have fewer than 25 full-time-equivalent employees whose average annual full-time-equivalent wages from the employer are less than $50,000 (indexed for taxable years after 2013). However, to receive a full credit, an employer must have no more than 10 full-time employees, and the average wage paid to these employees must be no more than $25,000 (indexed for taxable years after 2013). A qualifying employer may claim the credit for any taxable year beginning in 2010, 2011, 2012, and 2013 and for up to two years for insurance purchased through a Health Insurance Exchange thereafter. For taxable beginning in 2010, 2011, 2012, and 2013, the maximum credit is 35 percent of premiums paid by qualified taxable employers and 25 percent of premiums paid by qualified tax-exempt organizations. For taxable years beginning in 2014 and later years, the maximum tax credit will increase to 50 percent of premiums paid by qualified taxable employers and 35 percent of premiums paid by qualified tax-exempt organizations.

139. *Charitable contributions to health institutions* ($4.49 billion).— The Code provides individuals and corporations a deduction for contributions to nonprofit health institutions. Tax expenditures resulting from the deductibility of contributions to other charitable institutions are listed under the education, training, employment, and social services function.

140. *Orphan drugs* ($1.12 billion).—Drug firms can claim a tax credit of 50 percent of the costs for clinical testing required by the Food and Drug Administration for drugs that treat rare physical conditions or rare diseases.

141. *Blue Cross and Blue Shield* ($0.59 billion).—Blue Cross and Blue Shield health insurance providers in existence on August 16, 1986 and certain other nonprofit health insurers are provided exceptions from otherwise applicable insurance company income tax accounting rules that substantially reduce their tax liabilities, provided that their percentage of total premium revenue expended on reimbursement for clinical services provided to enrollees is not less than 85 percent for the taxable year.

142. *Tax credit for health insurance purchased by certain displaced and retired individuals* ($0.01 billion).—The Trade Act of 2002 provides a

refundable tax credit of 65 percent for the purchase of health insurance coverage by individuals eligible for Trade Adjustment Assistance and certain Pension Benefit Guarantee Corporation pension recipients. The American Recovery and Reinvestment Act and a subsequent extension increased the credit to 80 percent in coverage months preceding March 2011. The Trade Adjustment Assistance Extension Act of 2011 extended an enhanced credit of 72.5% through December 2013, but eliminated the credit entirely beginning January 1, 2014.

143. *Distributions for premiums for health and long-term care insurance* ($0.36 billion).—The Code provides for tax-free distributions of up to $3,000 from governmental retirement plans for premiums for health and long term care premiums of public safety officers.

Income Security

144. *Railroad retirement benefits* ($0.29 billion).—Railroad retirement benefits are not generally subject to the income tax unless the recipient's gross income reaches a certain threshold under current law. The threshold is discussed more fully under the Social Security function.

145. *Workers' compensation benefits* ($7.79 billion).—Workers compensation, although income to the recipients, are not subject to the income tax under current law.

146. *Public assistance benefits* ($0.75 billion).—The normal tax method considers cash transfers from the Government as part of the recipients' income, and thus, treats the exclusion for public assistance benefits under current law as tax expenditure.

147. *Special benefits for disabled coal miners* ($0.04 billion).—Disability payments to former coal miners out of the Black Lung Trust Fund, although income to the recipient, are not subject to the income tax.

148. *Military disability pensions* ($0.13 billion).—Most of the military pension income received by current disabled retired veterans is excluded from their income subject to tax.

149. *Employer-provided pension contributions and earnings* ($52.33 billion).—Certain contributions to defined benefit pension plans are excluded from an employee's gross income even though employers can deduct their contributions. In addition, the tax on the investment income earned by defined benefit pension plans is deferred until the money is withdrawn.

150. *401(k) type plans* ($72.74 billion).—Individual taxpayers and employers can make tax-preferred contributions to certain types of employer-provided 401(k) plans (and 401(k)-type plans like 403(b) plans and the Federal Government's Thrift Savings Plan). In 2011, an employee could exclude up to $16,500 (indexed) of wages from AGI under a qualified arrangement with an employer's 401(k) plan. Employees age 50 or over could exclude up to $22,000 in contributions (indexed). The 401(k)-type plan contribution limit including both employee and employer contribu-

tions is $49,000 in 2011 (indexed). The tax on contributions made by both employees and employers and the investment income earned by 401(k)-type plans is deferred until withdrawn.

151. *Individual Retirement Accounts (IRAs)* ($19.65 billion).—Individual taxpayers can take advantage of traditional and Roth IRAs to defer or otherwise reduce the tax on the return to their retirement savings. The IRA contribution limit is $5,000 in 2011 (indexed); taxpayers age 50 or over are allowed to make additional "catch-up" contributions of $1,000. Contributions to a traditional IRA are generally deductible but the deduction is phased out for workers with incomes above certain levels who, or whose spouses, are active participants in an employer-provided retirement plan. Contributions and account earnings are includible in income when withdrawn from traditional IRAs. Individuals who make nondeductible contributions to a traditional IRA can still benefit from deferral of tax on earnings. Roth IRA contributions are not deductible, but earnings and withdrawals are exempt from taxation. Income limits also apply to Roth IRA contributions; however, taxpayers at any income level may roll account balances from traditional IRAs into Roth IRAs, after paying income tax on any deduction and accrued income.

152. *Low and moderate-income savers' credit* ($1.13 billion).—The Code provides an additional incentive for lower-income taxpayers to save through a nonrefundable credit of up to 50 percent on IRA and other retirement contributions of up to $2,000. This credit is in addition to any deduction or exclusion. The credit is completely phased out by $56,500 for joint filers, $42,375 for head of household filers, and $28,250 for other filers in 2011.

153. *Self–Employed plans* ($19.58 billion).—Self-employed individuals can make deductible contributions to their own retirement plans equal to 25 percent of their income, up to a maximum of $49,000 in 2011. Total plan contributions are limited to 25 percent of a firm's total wages. The tax on the investment income earned by self-employed SEP, SIMPLE, and qualified plans is deferred until withdrawn.

154. *Employer-provided life insurance benefits* ($2.12 billion).—Employer-provided life insurance benefits are excluded from an employee's gross income even though the employer's costs for the insurance are a deductible business expense, but only to the extent that the employer's share of the total costs does not exceed the cost of $50,000 of such insurance.

155. *Employer-provided accident and disability benefits* ($0.36 billion).—Employer-provided accident and disability benefits are excluded from an employee's gross income even though the employer's costs for the benefits are a deductible business expense.

156. *Employer-provided supplementary unemployment benefits* ($0.04 billion)—Employers may establish trusts to pay supplemental unemployment benefits to employees separated from employment. Investment income earned by such trusts is exempt from taxation.

157. *Employer Stock Ownership Plan (ESOP) provisions* ($1.7 billion).—ESOPs are a special type of tax-exempt employee benefit plan. Employer-paid contributions (the value of stock issued to the ESOP) are deductible by the employer as part of employee compensation costs. They are not included in the employees' gross income for tax purposes, however, until they are paid out as benefits. In addition, the following special income tax provisions for ESOPs are intended to increase ownership of corporations by their employees: (1) annual employer contributions are subject to less restrictive limitations than other qualified retirement plans; (2) ESOPs may borrow to purchase employer stock, guaranteed by their agreement with the employer that the debt will be serviced by his payment (deductible by him) of a portion of wages (excludable by the employees) to service the loan; (3) employees who sell appreciated company stock to the ESOP may defer any taxes due until they withdraw benefits; and (4) dividends paid to ESOP-held stock are deductible by the employer.

158. *Additional deduction for the blind* ($0.04 billion).—The Code allows taxpayers who are blind to claim an additional $1,450 standard deduction if single, or $1,150 if married in 2011.

159. *Additional deduction for the elderly* ($2.78 billion).—The Code allows taxpayers who are 65 years or older to claim an additional $1,450 standard deduction if single, or $1,150 if married in 2011.

160. *Tax credit for the elderly and disabled* ($0.01 billion).—The Code allows taxpayers who are 65 years of age or older, or who are permanently disabled, to claim a tax credit equal to 15 percent of the sum of their earned and retirement income. The amount to which the 15 percent rate is applied is limited to no more than $5,000 for single individuals or married couples filing a joint return where only one spouse is 65 years of age or older and disabled, and up to $7,500 for joint returns where both spouses are 65 years of age or older and disabled. These limits are reduced by one-half of the taxpayer's adjusted gross income over $7,500 for single individuals and $10,000 for married couples filing a joint return.

161. *Casualty losses* ($0.35 billion).—Under the baseline tax system, neither the purchase of property nor insurance premiums to protect its value are deductible as costs of earning income. Therefore, reimbursement for insured loss of such property is not included as a part of gross income, and uninsured losses are not deductible. In contrast, the Code provides a deduction for uninsured casualty and theft losses of more than $100 each, to the extent that total losses during the year exceed 10 percent of the taxpayer's adjusted gross income.

162. *Earned income tax credit (EITC)* ($3.155 billion).—The Code provides an EITC to low-income workers at a maximum rate of 45 percent of income. For a family with one qualifying child, the credit is 34 percent of the first $9,100 of earned income in 2011. The credit is 40 percent of the first $12,780 of income for a family with two or more qualifying

children. The credit is 45 percent of the first $12,780 of income for a family with three or more qualifying children. Low-income workers with no qualifying children are eligible for a 7.65 percent credit on the first $5,980 of earned income. The credit is phased out at income levels and rates which depend upon how many qualifying children are eligible and marital status. Earned income tax credits in excess of tax liabilities owed through the individual income tax system are refundable to individuals.

Social Security

163. *Social Security benefits for retired workers* ($25.62 billion).—The Code may not tax all of the Social Security benefits that exceed the beneficiary's contributions from previously taxed income. Actuarially, previously taxed contributions generally do not exceed 15 percent of benefits, even for retirees receiving the highest levels of benefits. Up to 85 percent of recipients' Social Security and tier 1 railroad retirement benefits are included in (phased into) the income tax base if the recipient's provisional income exceeds certain base amounts. (Provisional income is equal to other items included in adjusted gross income plus foreign or U.S. possession income, tax-exempt interest, and one half of Social Security and tier 1 railroad retirement benefits.) The untaxed portion of the benefits received by taxpayers who are below the income amounts at which 85 percent of the benefits are taxable is counted as a tax expenditure.

164. *Social Security benefits for the disabled* ($8.23 billion).—Benefit payments from the Social Security Trust Fund for disability are fully or partially excluded from a beneficiary's gross incomes. (See provision number 163, Social Security benefits for retired workers.)

165. *Social Security benefits for dependents and survivors* ($3.89 billion).—Benefit payments from the Social Security Trust Fund for dependents and survivors are fully or partially excluded from a beneficiary's gross income.

Veterans Benefits and Services

166. *Veterans death benefits and disability compensation* ($5.65 billion).—All compensation due to death or disability paid by the Veterans Administration is excluded from taxable income under current law.

167. *Veterans pension payments* ($0.34 billion).—Pension payments made by the Veterans Administration are excluded from gross income.

168. *G.I. Bill benefits* ($1.19 billion).—G.I. Bill benefits paid by the Veterans Administration are excluded from gross income.

169. *Tax-exempt mortgage bonds for veterans* ($0.02 billion).—Interest earned on general obligation bonds issued by State and local governments to finance housing for veterans is excluded from taxable income.

General Government

170. *Public purpose State and local bonds* ($36.21 billion).—Interest earned on State and local government bonds issued to finance public-purpose construction (*e.g.*, schools, roads, sewers), equipment acquisition,

and other public purposes is tax-exempt. Interest on bonds issued by Indian tribal governments for essential governmental purposes is also tax-exempt.

171. *Build America Bonds* ($0).—The Code in 2009 allowed State and local governments to issue taxable bonds and receive a direct payment from Treasury equal to 35 percent of interest expenses. Alternatively, State and local governments may issue taxable bonds and the private lenders receive the 35 percent credit which is included in taxable income.

172. *Deductibility of certain nonbusiness State and local taxes* ($46.26 billion).—The Code allows taxpayers who itemize their deductions to claim a deduction for State and local income taxes (or, at the taxpayer's election, state and local sales taxes) and property taxes, even though these taxes primarily pay for services that, if purchased directly by taxpayers, would not be deductible. The election to deduct sales taxes instead of income taxes expires at the end of 2011.

Interest

173. *U.S. savings bonds* ($1.25 billion).—Taxpayers may defer paying tax on interest earned on U.S. savings bonds until the bonds are redeemed.

PROBLEMS FOR DISCUSSION

3–3. Which of the following constitutes a tax expenditure?

a. Code Section 212 allows a deduction for the costs of producing income other than in the course of a trade or business.

b. Code Section 119 excludes the value of meals or lodging furnished to an employee by his employer if specified conditions are met.

c. Code Section 106 excludes the value of premiums paid by employers to insure the health of their employees.

d. Code Section 263 disallows the deduction of expenditures incurred in a trade or business if they have a useful life of more than of one year.

e. The rental value of owner-occupied housing is not included in the income of the occupying owner.

f. Code Section 163(h)(3) allows a deduction for mortgage interest paid on taxpayer's primary and secondary residences.

g. Code Section 174 allows current deduction of research and development costs, including the costs of writing software.

h. Code Section 1(h) reduces the tax rate imposed on long-term capital gains to a maximum of 15 percent.

i. Code Section 262 disallows the deduction of personal expenses, including law school tuition.

Subchapter C: Mechanics of the Federal Income Tax

Code: Sections 55–59, 61–63, 67–68, and 151

Form 1040, Schedules A, B, C, and D, Form 6251: Google "IRS Forms"

The conceptual structure of federal income tax law is elegant and intellectually coherent. The mechanical process through which liability is actually computed, however, embodies multiple layers of political compromise, inconsistently incorporates Haig–Simons, and in consequence sometimes taxes economic income at effective rates greater than 100%, notwithstanding the Code's nominal top rate of 35%. When voters and politicians complain about the system, the Rube–Goldberg-like nature of its computational process is often one of the principal sources of their displeasure. Indeed, without TurboTax and other return preparation software, our individual income tax system might well collapse.

For the most part, this computational process is not what tax lawyers study. Nevertheless, anomalies in the process can sometimes produce unexpected results. Lawyers need therefore to keep the process in mind when giving advice with regard to their clients' financial affairs.

SECTION 1: REGULAR TAX

The computational process begins with "gross income"—that is, theoretical income less "exclusions." Exclusions are amounts excluded from gross income by tax theory, statute, or administrative action. For example, recoveries of capital (when we get back what we have put into an investment) are excluded because they are not income as a matter of theory; the system must allow the exclusion if it is to measure income correctly. Interest on tax-exempt bonds, by contrast, is income in theory, but is excluded by Code Section 103 for reasons external to the tax system. For readers whose principal contact with the income tax system has been their own Form 1040s, it is important to keep in mind that these exclusions occur *before* the reporting process ever begins. Theoretical income itself never appears in the computation. Exclusions are not actually subtracted. Instead, taxpayers are asked to begin by reporting the result: "gross income."

From gross income, the system allows subtraction of what are sometimes called "Section 62 deductions," "non-itemized deductions," or "above-the-line deductions." Code Section 62 does not actually *allow* deductions; it merely tells us *where* in the computational process to take deductions allowed elsewhere in the Code. Subtracting above-the-line deductions from gross income produces "adjusted gross income" or "AGI," which is reported on the last line of the first page of the Form 1040.

Next, taxpayers are asked to make an election: they may either (1) claim their remaining deductions, sometimes known as "itemized deductions" or "below-the-line deductions," on Schedule A or, alternatively, (2) claim a "standard deduction"—in 2012, $5,950 for a single individual or $11,900 for a married couple filing jointly. Regardless of which taxpayers elect, they are also generally allowed to subtract one "personal exemption"—in 2012, $3,800—for each member of their household.

The result of the foregoing operations is "taxable income," to which the system applies the rates of Code Section 1 to compute taxpayer's regular pre-credit tax. From this, the system subtracts credits to produce taxpayers' regular tax liability. Figure A summarizes the regular tax computation.

Figure A

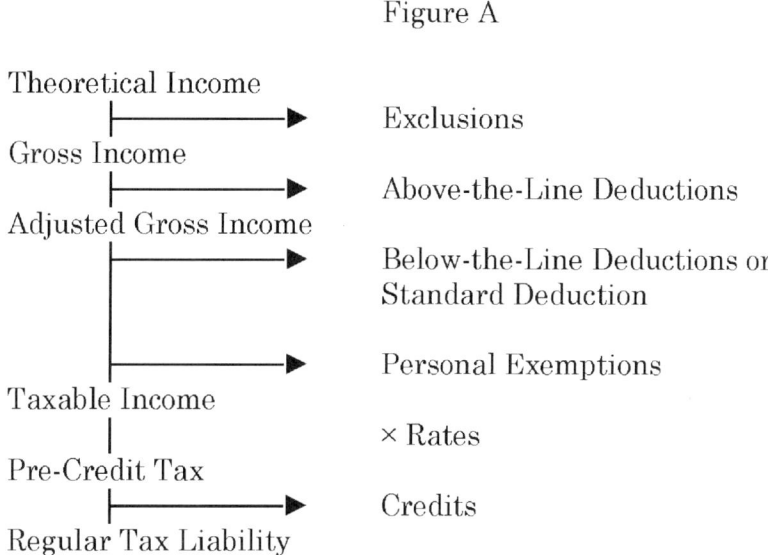

SECTION 2: FLOORS AND PHASE-OUTS

To this point, the regular tax computation might seem relatively straightforward and defensible. Not entirely comfortable with some of its consequences, however, Congress has imposed several complicating limitations—some permanent, some intermittent, depending on the politics of the moment.

Itemized or below-the-line deductions are subject to two limitations. First, under Code Section 67, "miscellaneous itemized deductions" are allowed only to the extent that, in the aggregate, they exceed 2 percent of AGI. All but twelve privileged below-the-line deductions are subject to this limitation. The most common deductions exempt from this "2–percent floor" are those for:

- Interest (Code Section 163),
- Taxes (Code Section 164),
- Casualty or theft losses incurred in a trade or business or in the production of income (Code Section 165(c)(2) & (3)) and gambling losses (Code Section 165(d)),
- Charitable contributions (Code Sections 170 and 642(c)),
- Medical expenses (Code Section 213), and
- Impairment-related work expenses of people with disabilities.

Note one important omission: costs of producing income. In general, trade or business deductions are above-the-line and therefore not subject to the 2–percent floor. Trade or business expenses incurred by "employees," however, are below-the-line and are therefore generally disallowed except to the extent they exceed the 2–percent floor. So are many other income-producing expenses that do not qualify as "trade or business expenses"—for example, many attorneys' fees. One of the perverse results is that economic income from some types of income-producing activity is sometimes taxed at effective rates higher than the Code's nominal rates.

Assume, for example, that taxpayer spends $3,000 of attorneys' fees to recover $10,000 of income. Her economic income is $7,000. (Her attorneys get $3,000; she takes home $7,000.) If the 2–percent floor effectively disallows deduction of her attorneys' fees, she may have to pay a 35 percent tax on her gross recovery ($3,500 = 35 percent times $10,000). If so, the effective tax rate on her economic income is 50 percent (*e.g.*, tax of $3,500 on economic income of $7,000).

Second, Code Section 68 imposes an "overall limitation on itemized deductions" (also sometimes known as "Pease") pursuant to which all but three super-privileged itemized deductions are phased out at higher income levels. The three deductions exempt from the Pease limitation are the deductions for:

- Medical expenses (Code Section 213),
- Investment interest (Code Section 163(d)), and
- Casualty or theft losses incurred in a trade or business or in the production of income (Code Section 165(c)(2) & (3)) and gambling losses (Code Section 165(d)).

One of the justifications given for Pease is that deductions are worth more to taxpayers in higher tax brackets. As a result, a tax expenditure delivered in the form of a tax deduction ends up giving a larger subsidy to high-income taxpayers, which may not be consistent with the purposes of the subsidy itself. Thus, for example, the home mortgage interest deduction (Item 59 in the 2013 Tax Expenditure Budget) delivers a larger subsidy to high-income homeowners than to low-income homeowners. Pease reduces this "upside-down subsidy" effect.

Because Pease affects how the federal tax burden is spread across income classes, however, it is politically contentious. As a result, it is currently suspended, but is scheduled to take effect again in 2013.

A similar political dynamic affects the personal exemption. At higher income levels, the personal exemption deduction is phased out by Code Section 151(d)(3) (sometimes known as "PEP," for "personal exemption phase-out"). The stated justification for PEP is that higher-income taxpayers do not need tax relief if they have more dependents. Like Pease, PEP is currently suspended, but is scheduled to become effective again in 2013.

SECTION 3: CAPITAL GAINS AND LOSSES

Special and more complex rules apply to the taxation of capital gains and losses. An introduction to the mechanics is appropriate here.

For corporations, there are no special capital gain rates. For individuals, capital gains are divided into three categories: a 28–percent group, a 25–percent group, and something called "adjusted net capital gain," which is taxed at a top rate of 15 percent. The 28–percent group includes gain from collectibles—art, rugs, antiques, metals, gems, stamps, coins, and alcoholic beverages—and something called "section 1202 gain"—basically gain from the sale of certain types of small business stock. The 25–percent group consists of something called "unrecaptured section 1250 gain," which is important principally in the context of real estate investments.

The most general category is "adjusted net capital gain." If the tax rate applicable to taxpayer's ordinary income is 25 percent or higher, tax is imposed on adjusted net capital gain at a rate of 15 percent. If the tax rate applicable to taxpayer's ordinary income is less than 25 percent, then in general no tax is imposed on taxpayer's adjusted net capital gain.

Until 2013, adjusted net capital gain consists of (1) net capital gain (excluding gains in the 28–percent and 25–percent categories), plus (2) qualified dividend income. Although dividend income remains ordinary, through the end of 2012 it is taxed at the same rate as net capital gain. In 2013, however, dividends are scheduled to revert to being taxed at ordinary rates.

Net capital gain, in turn, is computed using the Code Section 1222 netting rules. This netting process begins by sorting all gains and losses into long-term and short-term. A long-term capital gain or loss is a gain or loss on a capital asset held for 1 year or more; a short-term capital gain or loss, a gain or loss on a capital asset held for less than 1 year. The purpose of this sorting process is to limit favorable long-term gain treatment (that is, taxation of gains at 15 or zero percent) to assets that have been held for at least a year.

We then add up all long-term capital gains and losses. If the result is a net gain, taxpayer has a "net long-term capital gain." If it is a net loss, taxpayer has a "net long-term capital loss." We do the same with taxpayer's short-term capital gains and losses. Taxpayer's "net capital gain"—the portion of taxpayer's taxable income eligible for special 15 or zero percent rate treatment, ignoring dividends—then equals her net long-term capital gain, if any, reduced by her net short-term capital loss, if any. The effect is to (1) limit favorable rate treatment to gains from assets held for 1 year or more and (2) reduce the amount of taxpayer's income eligible for favorable rate treatment by taxpayer's long-term losses and net short-term losses.

Although long-term capital gains are generally eligible for lower individual rates, deduction of capital losses is limited. Under Code Section 1211, both individual and corporate taxpayers can deduct their capital losses for the year to the extent of their capital gains for the year. Individuals can deduct a further $3,000 of capital losses again ordinary income, if they have any. The portion of any capital loss disallowed under Code Section 1211 is taxpayer's "net capital loss." Note that "net capital gain" and "net capital loss" are not parallel concepts.

Under Code Section 1212(a), corporations are allowed to carry their disallowed capital losses back three years and forward five, subject to the same Code Section 1211 limitations; such carryovers are treated as short-term in the years to which they are carried. Individuals carry all disallowed capital losses forward from year to year, indefinitely. Under Code Section 1212(b), for individuals the excess of the net short-term capital loss over the net long-term capital gain for a year is treated as a short-term capital loss in the next year, and the excess of the net long-term capital loss over the net short-term capital gain for a year is treated as a long-term capital loss in the next year.

PROBLEMS FOR DISCUSSION

3–4. In 2011, Warren incurs the following gains and losses:

Short-term capital gain	$4,000
Short-term capital gain	$3,000
Short-term capital loss	($5,000)
Long-term capital gain	$9,000
Long-term capital loss	($1,000)

What is Warren's net capital gain?

3–5. In 2011, Warren incurs the following gains and losses:

Short-term capital gain	$3,000
Short-term capital loss	($5,000)
Long-term capital gain	$9,000
Long-term capital loss	($1,000)

What is Warren's net capital gain?

3–6. In 2011, XYZ Corp incurs the following:

Short-term capital loss	($21,000)
Long-term capital gain	$5,000

It has no other capital gains or losses but plenty of ordinary income. How much of its loss can XYZ Corp deduct?

3–7. Same facts as in Problem 3–6, but the taxpayer is now Susan, an individual, who also receives $100,000 of ordinary income from her law practice during the year in question. How much of her loss can Susan deduct?

SECTION 4: ALTERNATIVE MINIMUM TAX

Concerned that the foregoing rules permitted some taxpayers to pay too little tax, but politically unwilling to repeal or amend the offending provisions directly, in 1969 Congress enacted a parallel tax system, the alternative minimum tax ("AMT") system. A taxpayer's actual federal income tax liability each year equals the greater of his "regular tax" (as computed above) and something called his "tentative minimum tax." In theory, every taxpayer needs to compute both every year to determine which is greater. For many decades, the AMT was politically obscure, allowing Congress to raise taxes and eliminate deductions with little political push-back. In 2001 and 2003, however, cuts in regular tax rates pushed roughly 30% of all taxpayers into the AMT.

Like the regular tax computation, the AMT computation begins with theoretical income. From theoretical income, it then takes exclusions and deductions computed under rules that are often different from the regular tax rules. For example, deductions subject to the 2–percent floor for regular tax purposes—even income-measuring deductions—are not allowed at all for AMT purposes. State and local income and property taxes are not deductible for AMT purposes. Depreciation is computed under different rules. As a result, basis (which we will study in Chapter 5) and gain or loss are often different for AMT purposes. After taking into account these and other differences, this recomputation produces something known as "alternative minimum taxable income" ("AMTI").

From alternative minimum taxable income, the taxpayer then subtracts something called the "exemption amount," which in 2011 was $74,450 for married couples and surviving spouses and $48,450 for most single taxpayers. The AMT exemption amount is roughly the equivalent of the standard deduction in the regular tax system, except that it phases out at higher income levels—for married couples and surviving spouses whose AMTI exceeds $150,000 and for most single taxpayers whose AMTI exceeds $112,500. This phase-out causes the effective AMT rate to go up, because each dollar of additional income, in addition to being subject to tax, causes a loss of 25 cents of exemption amount in the phase-out range. As a result, within the phase-out range, the top effective AMT rate reaches 35 percent—the same as the top nominal regular tax rate. The effective AMT rate then drops back down to 28 percent for taxpayers at even higher income levels.

Unless Congress acts, the AMT exemption amount is scheduled to fall fairly dramatically in 2012: to $45,000 for married couples and surviving spouses and $33,750 for most single taxpayers. Historically, Congress has enacted an "AMT patch" each year extending the higher AMT exemption amounts year-by-year. In 2012, however, political gridlock has prevented enactment of such a patch. If no such patch is enacted, roughly 25 million additional taxpayers will become subject to AMT, costing taxpayers roughly an additional $100 billion in taxes.

AMTI less the exemption amount is known as the "taxable excess"—the equivalent of "taxable income" in the regular tax system. The AMT then applies a slightly progressive rate structure (beginning at 26 percent and jumping to 28 percent when the taxable excess reaches $175,000) to the taxable excess, yielding "tentative minimum tax." In theory, capital gains are taxed at the same rate for AMT purposes as for regular tax purposes. But capital gains constitute AMTI for exemption amount phase-out purposes. As a result, the top effective AMT rate on capital gains can be as high as 18.75 percent.

In any event, once you have computed your regular tax liability and your tentative minimum tax liability, you compare the two. Conceptually, current law requires that you pay the greater of the two. Mechanically, this is implemented by Code Section 55(a), which provides that if your tentative minimum tax exceeds your regular tax, the difference equals your "alternative minimum tax." It then requires that you pay your regular tax *plus* your alternative minimum tax. Figure B summarizes this computation.

Figure B

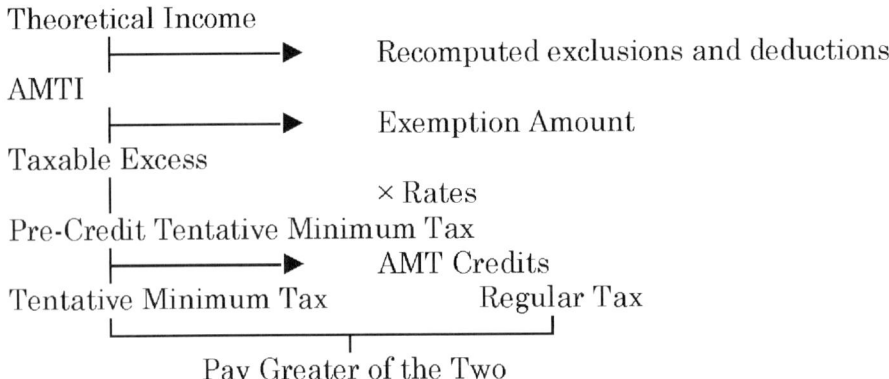

It was once thought that the AMT represented the theoretically pure tax system that Congress would enact if only it could. Politically popular but theoretically unjustified deductions and exclusions would disappear in the AMT computation. The result would be a more or less ideal flat tax on economic income, backing up the flawed but politically more visible regular system. Every taxpayer would therefore have to pay at least some minimum amount of tax on his or her economic income in excess of the exemption amount.

But the current AMT is difficult to justify on this basis. All credits now reduce AMT as well as regular tax; the AMT therefore performs no backup function whatever with respect to credits. On the other hand, of the costs of producing income, only those above the line or exempt from the 2% floor are allowed for AMT purposes. The result is that many costs of producing income are now disallowed for AMT purposes; this in turn means that the AMT taxes many types of income on a gross, rather than net, basis.

A particularly egregious example of this problem was reported by CBS News in 2003. Cindy Spina was the first female on her police force and, regrettably, endured discriminatory treatment from her coworkers. Her tires were slashed, her requests for back-up were ignored, and she faced both formal and informal harassment from superiors and fellow officers. She finally quit and sued under Title VII of the Civil Rights Act of 1964, winning an award of $375,000 compensatory damages, plus attorneys' fees. Then the IRS came to collect its share. All of her attorneys' fees, which had been paid directly to her attorneys, were includible in Spina's gross income for federal income tax purposes, but no deduction was allowed in computing her AMT. As a result, Spina's federal income tax liability on her award was $475,000–$100,000 more than she had actually received, an effective rate of tax of 127% on her actual cash recovery. Congress has since remedied this problem with respect to claims of unlawful discrimination, but the problem remains uncorrected in other contexts. As we will discover in Chapter 7B, the Supreme Court has since confirmed that Spina's tax treatment was proper.

CHAPTER 4

DEDUCTION OF INTEREST: AN INTRODUCTION TO TAX ARBITRAGE

■ ■ ■

The Code's statutory rules reflect the same mix of theoretical elegance and mechanical compromise that characterize the income tax system as a whole. The rules governing deductibility of interest both illustrate this mix and introduce a further source of complexity: the need for anti-abuse rules—in particular, anti-arbitrage rules. In tax, "arbitrage" refers to situations in which different parts of a single deal are taxed in inconsistent ways. In the absence of special (and therefore complicating) rules, inconsistent treatment of different parts of a single transaction may allow taxpayers to create structures that generate artificial tax losses, or otherwise to shelter their income.

SECTION 1: TRADE OR BUSINESS INTEREST

Code: Section 163(a)

Comprehensive tax base theory tells us that interest paid or incurred in the conduct of a trade or business should be deductible. Taxpayer's net worth is reduced by the amount of her interest paid or incurred. She receives no offsetting consumption benefits. Therefore, she incurs a Haig–Simons loss equal to the amount of her trade or business paid or incurred. Consistent with theory, in general Code Section 163(a) allows a deduction for trade or business interest paid or incurred.

SECTION 2: INVESTMENT INTEREST

Principle: Non-corporate taxpayers may deduct investment interest only to the extent of their net investment income.

Code: Section 163(d)

For the same reason, theory tells us that interest paid or incurred in the production of income generally—in particular, investment interest—

should also be deductible. Here, however, the possibility of arbitrage has led Congress to limit deductibility.

Consider the following deal. Taxpayer borrows $1,000,000 to buy an investment asset. Assume he will pay 5% interest ($50,000) per year on the borrowing. Assume also that the asset can reliably be expected to go up in value by the same 5% ($50,000) per year. If things go as expected, the deal will be an economic wash; taxpayer will neither make nor lose money. Each year, taxpayer will gain $50,000 in appreciation and lose the same $50,000 in interest payments. From a Haig–Simons perspective, he should therefore have neither income nor deduction.

We know, however, that because of the realization requirement taxpayer's anticipated gain will not be recognized until he sells the underlying investment asset. If taxpayer is allowed a current deduction for interest paid or incurred on the loan he takes out to buy the asset, he will claim an annual $50,000 deduction. Because he will not have to report the appreciation on the underlying asset until he sells it, he will not have to report the offsetting $50,000 of gain currently. Each year, therefore, he will report a net loss from a deal that in economic reality produces neither income nor loss in any year.

If we allow a current deduction of interest on these facts, we make it relatively simple for taxpayers to structure deals that generate current tax deductions without incurring real economic losses. When taxpayer sells the asset and pays off the debt, of course, he will have to report an equal and offsetting amount of gain. In the meantime, however, he receives the benefit of deferral.

This is tax arbitrage. Haig–Simons requires that taxpayer both report his $50,000 gain each year and claim his $50,000 of interest paid as a deduction each year. If our system were fully consistent with Haig–Simons, it would correctly measure taxpayer's income over time. But it is not. The realization requirement means that taxpayer will not have to report his gain until he sells the asset. The deal just described seeks to take advantage of the fact that the two legs of taxpayer's transaction—the gain leg and the loss leg—are treated inconsistently (or would be in the absence of special rules).

To limit use of deals like this to generate artificial tax deductions, Code Section 163(d) caps the deduction non-corporate taxpayers may take for investment interest to an amount equal to taxpayers' net investment income for the year. Disallowed investment interest deductions then are carried forward from year to year, subject to the same limitations—that is, until taxpayer has net investment income.

How does this solve the problem? Assume, in our hypothetical, that taxpayer borrows the $1,000,000 and buys the investment asset at the beginning of Year 1 and sells the asset and repays the loan at the beginning of Year 4. If he has no other investment income in the intervening period, the resulting interest deductions ($150,000 in all) will be disallowed in Years 1 through 3. At the beginning of Year 4, he will sell the investment asset for $1,150,000, recognizing $150,000 in gain—which constitutes investment income. As a result, the interest deductions disallowed in Years 1 through 3 will be allowed in Year 4, offsetting taxpayer's income from the deal. Under Code Section 163(d), therefore, he will report no net income or loss from the deal in any year, correctly reflecting the underlying economic reality. Problem solved. Sort of.

The astute reader will observe that Code Section 163(d) solves only part of the potential problem. When taxpayer in our hypothetical sells the asset, his gain will likely be long-term capital gain, eligible for favorable rate treatment (*e.g.*, a top rate of 15 percent). The newly freed-up interest deductions will not enter into the Code Section 1222 netting process and will therefore not reduce the "net capital gain" eligible for favorable treatment. Instead, they will be available to shelter ordinary income from other sources—income that would otherwise have been taxed at 35 percent. As a result, he will recognize income taxable at 15 cents on the dollar and an equal amount of loss worth 35 cents on the dollar—a form of arbitrage known as "bracket shift." In addition, the investment interest rules do not apply to entities taxed as corporations, which can structure this kind of deal without having to worry about Code Section 163(d) at all.

SECTION 3: INTEREST ON DEBT INCURRED OR CONTINUED TO PURCHASE OR CARRY TAX-EXEMPT OBLIGATIONS

Principle: In general, expenses of producing tax-exempt income are not deductible.

Code: Sections 103 and 265

Under Code Section 103, interest on state or local bonds is excluded from gross income. Originally, this exclusion was thought to be necessary to avoid infringing on state sovereignty. Today, it is treated as a tax expenditure—a subsidy for state and local borrowing run through the tax system. In the 2013 Tax Expenditure Budget, this subsidy appears in multiple entries, each reflecting a different purpose for which states or localities commonly borrow. See 2013 Tax Expenditure Budget, Items 14, 37, 57, 58, 81, 88, 90, 97, 106, 107, 136, 169, and 170.

The exclusion for tax-exempt interest creates another arbitrage possibility. Assume taxpayer borrows $1,000,000 to buy a tax-exempt bond. He expects to pay 5% interest ($50,000) per year on his loan and to earn 5% ($50,000) per year on his tax-exempt bond. Again, an economic wash: each year, taxpayer will earn $50,000 in tax-exempt interest and pay the same $50,000 in interest on his loan. From a Haig–Simons perspective, he should have neither income nor deduction.

If our rules were to allow a deduction for taxpayer's interest paid, on these facts he would receive a $50,000 deduction each year. Because interest on the underlying bond is exempt from taxation, however, he would never have to report the offsetting $50,000 of interest income.

Again, a simple technique for generating artificial tax deductions without incurring real economic losses.

To limit use of this technique, Code Section 265 provides that, in general, the expenses of producing tax-exempt income are not deductible. Subsection (a)(2), in particular, prohibits the deduction of interest on indebtedness incurred or continued to purchase or carry tax-exempt bonds. In our hypothetical, the loan taxpayer incurs to purchase the tax-exempt bonds is "indebtedness incurred ... to purchase ... tax-exempt bonds." Interest on that loan, therefore, is not deductible. Taxpayer in our hypothetical has no economic income or loss. Under Code Sections 103 and 265 he has no taxable income or loss either.

But there is a problem. Money is "fungible"—by which we mean that taxpayer is unlikely to care (or perhaps even to know) whether he has used borrowed dollars or earned dollars to make a particular purchase. What if, instead of using his business income to pay business expenses, taxpayer borrows to pay those business expenses and uses the business income to purchase tax-exempt bonds? Now, at least in form, the borrowing is incurred to fund business expenses, not to purchase tax-exempt bonds. And yet he still ends up with exempt interest income and an offsetting interest deduction. Or what if taxpayer originally borrows to pay business expenses and now has the wherewithal to repay the loan, but decides to leave the loan outstanding and use the funds he would otherwise have used to repay the loan to buy tax-exempt bonds? Or what if taxpayer could fund his business expenses by selling his tax-exempt bonds, but decides instead to borrow to fund those business expenses so as to avoid having to sell the bonds? In each of these scenarios, taxpayer ends up with exempt interest income and an offsetting, potentially deductible, interest expense.

The somewhat convoluted language of subsection (a)(2)—"interest on indebtedness incurred or continued to purchase or carry [tax-exempt bonds]"—was intended to address at least some of these problems. To "continue" indebtedness is to leave that indebtedness outstanding when one could repay it—so as to be able to purchase or carry tax-exempt bonds. To "carry" tax-exempt bonds is to keep them instead of selling them to fund some other expense. A large body of case law, not easily summarized, has construed this extraordinarily ambiguous language. Suffice it to say that (1) red flags should go up whenever a taxpayer has both tax-exempt interest income and interest deductions, and (2) the closer the connection between the debt and the tax-exempt bonds, the more likely the IRS and the courts will apply the prohibitions of Code Section 265(a)(2).

SECTION 4: PASSIVE ACTIVITY INTEREST

Code: Section 469

Until 1986, the law stood as described in Sections 1 through 3 above. Code Section 163(d) limited the deduction of investment interest to taxpayer's net investment income. Code Section 265 prohibited the deduction of interest on debt incurred or continued to purchase or carry tax-exempt bonds. Otherwise, interest was fully deductible.

Tax lawyers are infinitely ingenious. By 1986, practitioners had developed an array of arbitrage products—more commonly known as "tax shelters"—that relatively modest provisions like Code Section 163(d) and 265 could not shut down. In Chapter 11, when we learn how to construct a classic real estate tax shelter, the serious nature of the challenge such deals posed to tax administration will become clearer.

In response, Congress enacted Code Section 469, which took a different approach to the problem: it moved income or loss from classic tax shelter activities into a series of baskets and provided that, in general, losses in one basket could only be used to offset income from that basket. Disallowed losses within a basket, like disallowed losses under the investment interest rules, could be carried forward until there was income in that basket. When taxpayer ceased to be involved in the relevant activity, any still-disallowed losses were freed up to be applied against taxpayer's other income. The effect was to allow the deduction of true economic losses, but only when taxpayer got out of the tax shelter business that had created those losses in the first place.

Congress defined the term "passive activity" redundantly, to make sure tax counsel could not find a way past the new rules. First, the term includes any trade or business in which taxpayer does not materially participate. Why? Because before 1986, deals had been structured to funnel losses to silent partners—partners in the deal primarily to save taxes. Second, it includes all rental activities. Why? Because the classic tax shelter involved rental real estate. Congress wanted to make sure that all then-extant tax shelters marketed to individuals were caught by the new rules.

The passive activity rules are detailed and complex. Their details, however, are no longer as important to tax practice as they once were—precisely because Code Section 469 proved so effective. Knowing the rules in detail does not normally help a client circumvent them. Exceptions are provided for (1) individuals personally engaged in the rental real estate business more than half of whose personal services are performed pursuant to that business, and (2) individuals with AGIs below $100,000. The classic real estate tax shelter, however, is dead.

In any event, interest paid in connection with a passive activity is now subject to the passive activity rules of Code Section 469. Like other passive losses, such interest may only be deducted to the extent of income in the relevant basket until taxpayer ceases to be engaged in the activity in question.

SECTION 5: PERSONAL INTEREST AND HOME MORTGAGE INTEREST

Prior to 1986, interest on debt incurred for personal purposes—for example, interest on personal credit card debt—was deductible unless disallowed under Code Sections 163(d) or 265. Allowance of this deduction, however, was inconsistent with comprehensive tax base theory, since interest on debt incurred for personal purposes is a cost of consumption. In 1986, therefore, Congress added Code Section 163(h), which provides that, in general, personal interest is not deductible.

The most important exception to this general disallowance rule is for "qualified residence interest"—the home mortgage interest deduction, Item 59 in the 2013 Tax Expenditure Budget, which now costs the federal government about $100 billion a year in foregone revenue.

"Qualified residence interest" consists of interest on "acquisition indebtedness" and interest on "home equity indebtedness," in each case with respect to any "qualified residence" of the taxpayer. A taxpayer can have up to two "qualified residences": his principal residence and any other home used by taxpayer as a residence and chosen by taxpayer to be a "qualified residence" for purposes of these rules.

"Acquisition indebtedness" must meet two requirements: first, it must be incurred in acquiring, constructing, or substantially improving the qualified residence; second, it must be secured by such residence. In general, only the first $1,000,000 of acquisition indebtedness qualifies.

"Home equity indebtedness" consists of any other debt secured by a qualified residence, to the extent it does not exceed taxpayer's equity in the residence, defined as the difference between the fair market value of the residence less the amount of any acquisition indebtedness with respect to such residence. In general, only the first $100,000 of home equity indebtedness qualifies. Under Rev. Rul. 2010–25, indebtedness in excess of $1,000,000 that a taxpayer incurs to acquire, construct, or substantially improve a qualified residence, interest on which may not be deducted because of the $1,000,000 limitation, may qualify instead as home equity indebtedness.

An exception to both of these numerical limitations is provided for mortgage debt incurred on or before October 13, 1987; such debt is automatically treated as acquisition indebtedness and is not subject to the $1,000,000 limitation.

Home mortgage interest, if deductible, is deducted below-the-line, and is therefore only deductible if taxpayer itemizes. It is not subject to the 2–percent floor, but is subject to Pease, the "overall limitation on itemized deductions." Finally, interest on acquisition indebtedness is deductible for AMT purposes; interest on home equity indebtedness is not.

SECTION 6: INTEREST ON EDUCATIONAL LOANS

Under Code Section 221, up to $2,500 of interest on a "qualified educational loan" is deductible. A "qualified educational loan" is a loan incurred to pay qualified higher education expenses of taxpayer, his or her spouse, or one of his or her dependents. The deduction phases out once taxpayer's "modified AGI" exceeds $50,000 ($100,000 in the case of a married couple filing jointly), which limits are adjusted each year for inflation.

Because of the income-based phase-out, this deduction is not of major benefit to many taxpayer, because taxpayers below the phase-out threshold are not likely to be in a high marginal tax bracket. Indeed, the deduction currently costs the government less than a billion dollars a year. Item 103, 2013 Tax Expenditure Budget. Nevertheless, if available, it is taken above-the-line, and therefore is available even to non-itemizers.

PROBLEMS FOR DISCUSSION

4–1. In 2012, Bernie earns $300,000 for his services as an attorney and recognizes $10,000 of capital gain on the sale of stock held for investment. He does not recognize any other gains or losses for the year. The value of his home is $1,000,000. Which items of interest are deductible for regular tax purposes? Are they deductible above the line or below the line? Which items of interest are deductible for alternative minimum tax purposes?

   a. $2,000 of interest paid on a $40,000 debt to National Bank at 5% interest, for funds which he used to expand his law practice,

   b. $25,000 of interest paid on a $500,000 debt to Union Bank at 5% interest, for funds which he deposited in his checking account (he later paid for $400,000 of Google stock with a check drawn on that account),

   c. $5,000 of interest paid on a $100,000 debt to City Bank at 5% interest, for funds which Bernie used to buy California bonds paying 3% interest,

   d. $6,000 of interest paid on personal credit card debt,

   e. $40,000 of interest paid on an $800,000 debt to Metropolitan Bank at 5% interest, secured by a mortgage on the home in which he lives, for funds Bernie used to buy that home,

   f. $1,600 of interest on a $40,000 debt to Canyon Savings and Loan at 4% on a mortgage Bernie took out between 2008 and 2012 to pay for his son's college tuition.

   g. Assume that Bernie's first mortgage from Metropolitan Bank is in the principal amount of $1,500,000 and the value of his home is $2,000,000. Same result?

   h. Assume the facts as given in parts (e) and (f) above. Bernie refinances his second mortgage, increasing the principal amount by $30,000 to pay off his credit card debt. Is the interest on the portion of the second mortgage used to pay off the credit card debt deductible?

i. Assume the facts as given in parts (e) and (f) above. The value of Bernie's home declines to $800,000. Same result?

Part 2

Complete Accounting

■ ■ ■

Principle: Rules for measuring income or loss during particular taxable periods should be construed so as to measure tax base income completely over time.

We now have some idea of what our income tax system is trying to measure. In this Part 2, we explore how Congress, the IRS, and the courts have chosen to measure it. Except where Congress clearly intends mismeasurement, the IRS and the courts generally attempt to construe the Code's accounting rules in a manner consistent with Congress's assumed overall goal: correct measurement of income or loss over time. Sometimes, it will be seen, this requires departure from the Code's literal language.

Part of the problem arises from the fact that our system measures income periodically—generally annually—rather than waiting until transactions are done. Periodic reporting requires rules that can be applied to each period separately, as if it were taxpayer's only taxable period, but that, taken collectively, correctly measure income over multiple periods. Ideally, the Code's accounting rules should require that all items of income and deduction be taken into account once and only once, that no item of deduction or loss be, in effect, deducted twice, and that no item of income be included twice. If the rules operate as they should, the sum of the tax consequences of a series of transactions should exactly equal taxpayer's tax base income or loss from that series of transactions. Except where items are intentionally excluded from the tax base, tax should match economics.

We will discover in Part 3 that complete accounting is not enough; we will also need rules that take into account the time value of money. In this Part, however, we set time-value-of-money problems aside and focus on completeness.

CHAPTER 5

BASIS

■ ■ ■

Principle 1: In general, a taxpayer's basis in an item is increased by investing in the item or recognizing income with respect to it and is reduced by taking cash or property out of the item or recognizing losses or deductions with respect to it.

Principle 2: Costs incurred in acquiring property are included in its basis; costs incurred in selling property reduce taxpayer's "amount realized" on the sale.

Principle 3: Taxpayer's basis in property acquired in a taxable exchange equals the value of the property acquired, not the value of the property given up.

Code: Section 1012

PHILADELPHIA PARK AMUSEMENT CO. v. UNITED STATES
130 Ct.Cl. 166 (1954)

[On August 3, 1934, taxpayer exchanged a bridge, known as "Strawberry Bridge," for a 10–year extension of its franchise from the City of Philadelphia to construct, operate, and maintain a passenger railway in Fairmount Park at its own cost and expense. At issue in the case was the proper amortization and loss on abandonment of the 10–year franchise extension. To determine these, it was necessary to ascertain taxpayer's basis in that extension.]

[T]he cost basis under [Code Section 1012], of the 10–year extension of the franchise was the cost to the taxpayer. The succinct statement in [Code Section 1012] that "the basis of property shall be the cost of such property" although clear in principle, is frequently difficult in application. One view is that the cost basis of property received in a taxable exchange is the fair market value of the property given in the exchange. The other view is that the cost basis of property received in a taxable exchange is the fair market value of the property received in the exchange. As will be seen from the cases and some of the Commissioner's rulings the Commissioner's position has not been altogether consistent on this question. The view that "cost" is the fair market value of the property given is predicated on the theory that the cost to the taxpayer is the economic value relinquished. The view that "cost" is the fair market value of the property received is based upon the theory that the term "cost" is a tax concept and must be considered in the light of the designed interrelationship of [provisions intended correctly to measure taxpayer's gain or loss over time], and the prime role that the basis of property plays in determining tax liability. We believe that when the question is considered in the latter context that the cost basis of the property received in a taxable exchange is the fair market value of the property received in the exchange.

When property is exchanged for property in a taxable exchange the taxpayer is taxed on the difference between the adjusted basis of the property given in exchange and the fair market value of the property received in exchange. For purposes of determining gain or loss the fair market value of the property received is treated as cash and taxed accordingly. To maintain harmony with the fundamental purpose of these sections, it is necessary to consider the fair market value of the property received as the cost basis to the taxpayer. The failure to do so would result in allowing the taxpayer a stepped-up basis, without paying a tax therefor, if the fair market value of the property received is less than the fair market value of the property given, and the taxpayer would be subjected to a double tax if the fair market value of the property received is more than the fair market value of the property given. By holding that the fair market value of the property received in a taxable exchange is the cost basis, the above discrepancy is avoided and the basis of the property received will equal the adjusted basis of the property given plus any gain recognized, or that should have been recognized, or minus any loss recognized, or that should have been recognized.

We, therefore, conclude that the 1934 exchange was a taxable exchange and that the taxpayer is entitled to use as the cost basis of the 10-year extension of its franchise its fair market value on August 3, 1934, for purposes of determining depreciation and loss due to abandonment, as indicated in this opinion.

Accordingly, judgment will be suspended and the question of the value of the extended franchise on August 3, 1934, is remanded to the Commissioner of this court for the taking of evidence and the filing of a report thereon.

PROBLEMS FOR DISCUSSION

5–1. In 2003, while hiking on publicly owned land, Indiana discovers a silver cup. When he gets home, he takes the cup to an appraiser, who tells him it is worth approximately $15,000. Assume that the appraisal is correct. Two years later, in 2005, he sells the cup at auction for $18,000. Does he have income? If so, when and how much? Assume instead that, in 2005, he sells the cup at auction for $14,000. What tax consequences?

5-2. Miyagi purchases an antique car for $5,000 in 2000. In 2010, he sells the car to Daniel for $4,000 cash plus Daniel's beat-up old junker, which is worth $3,000. What is his income or loss? Assume instead that he sells the car to Daniel for $4,000 plus Daniel's promise to keep Miyagi's antique car collection cleaned, waxed, and polished for the next year. Assume Daniel's promise is worth $3,000. Now what is Miyagi's income or loss?

5-3. Melinda incurs $1,000 of out-of-pocket expenses searching for her ideal investment property. She finds an abandoned parking lot in Bakersfield that she expects to go up in value when the convention center planned to be built nearby is finished, and is able to purchase the lot for $30,000. Two years later, she sells the lot for $100,000, but must pay the selling broker $6,000 for his services. What is her gain on the sale?

5-4. Miyagi and Daniel both invest in antique cars. Miyagi gives Daniel his 1954 Austin Healey worth $32,000, in which Miyagi has a basis of $30,000. In exchange, Daniel gives Miyagi his 1936 Ford Roadster worth $40,000, in which Daniel has a basis of $45,000. Daniel does not intend to make a gift to Miyagi by reason of the unequal exchange; he is simply mistaken about the relative value of the two cars. What is Miyagi's gain or loss on the exchange? What is his basis in his newly-acquired Ford Roadster? What is Daniel's gain or loss on the exchange? What is his basis in his newly-acquired Austin Healey?

5-5. After each of the following events, what is Daniel's basis in his partnership interest? You should not need to refer to the cited Code Sections; they are given for informational purposes only.

   a. In 2012, Daniel acquires an interest as a general partner in the Karate–Do partnership in exchange for his contribution of $5,000 in cash to the partnership. Code Sections 721 and 722.

   b. Daniel's allocable share of the taxable income of the partnership for taxable year 2012 is $1,000, which Daniel is required to and does report on his individual income tax return for that year. Code Section 705.

   c. In 2013, Daniel contributes a building with a fair market value of $20,000 and a basis of $15,000 to the partnership. Code Sections 721 and 722.

   d. Daniel's allocable share of the taxable loss of the partnership for taxable year 2013 is $2,000, which Daniel is required to and does report on his individual tax return for that year. Code Section 705.

   e. In 2014, the partnership distributes $10,000 in cash to Daniel. Code Sections 731 and 733.

   f. In 2014, the partnership also distributes a car with a fair market value of $5,000 and a basis of $3,000 to Daniel. Code Sections 731 and 733.

CHAPTER 6

ACCOUNTING METHODS

■ ■ ■

Code: Sections 446 and 448

Code Section 446(a) requires that a taxpayer's income be computed using the method of accounting he uses in keeping his books. Subsection (b) requires that the method used "clearly reflect income." Subsection (c) explicitly permits use of either the cash method or the accrual method. What does all this mean?

Let us begin with the cash and accrual methods.

Assume you have graduated, passed the bar, and are practicing law. In November of Year 1, you complete a matter for which you properly bill the client $100,000. Your client pays you in January of Year 2. When should you report the income? When you earn it in Year 1? Or when you receive it in Year 2?

The answer depends on your method of accounting. If you use the accrual method, you report the income when year earn it, in November of Year 1. If you use the cash method, you report the income when you receive it, in January of Year 2.

In general, the accrual method is more consistent with Haig–Simons. Your net worth goes up once you have done whatever you need to do to earn the $100,000. As a matter of non-tax law, you now own an asset—the right to receive $100,000—commonly known as an "account receivable." If our system taxes accessions to wealth, you should report the $100,000 when it is earned, regardless of when payment is ultimately received. Conversely, an amount you owe should become deductible as soon as you clearly owe it, regardless of when you pay it. Once you have incurred an enforceable obligation, your net worth goes down; as a matter of theory, you should therefore be entitled to take the relevant deduction.

In practice, however, keeping track of when income is earned and obligations are incurred takes extra work, typically by someone specially trained in the accrual method. By contrast, cash receipts and disbursements flowing through a bank account show up automatically on taxpayer's check register or bank statement. If, instead of using the accrual method, we compute taxes by reference to when items are received or paid, we avoid the extra bookkeeping required by that method. Hence, the cash method.

From a design perspective, the cash method poses two related problems. First, it often postpones net income. This postponement is worth money. Consider the hypothetical with which this chapter begins. If the $100,000 is reported in Year 1, the relevant tax is effectively due no later than April 15, Year 2 (when the tax return for Year 1 is due). If, by contrast, the $100,000 is not reportable until Year 2, the relevant tax may not have to be paid until April 15, Year 3. In other words, by deferring the moment the $100,000 is realized from November to January, the cash method defers the relevant tax liability by a full year. Assume that the income is taxed at a rate of 30 percent. If so, the deferred tax will be $30,000. Assume further that the prevailing rate of interest (sometimes known as the "discount rate") is 5 percent. If so, the ability to postpone payment of $30,000 for a year should be worth $1,500 (that is, 5 percent times $30,000). In our hypothetical, therefore, the cash method saves taxpayer $1,500 and costs the Treasury the same amount. $1,500 may not seem like a lot of money. Add enough zeros and it will become interesting. Indeed, deferral constitutes a major part of big-dollar corporate tax practice.

Second, the cash method is relatively easy to manipulate. If we do not want income now, we arrange for amounts owed to us to be paid later, presumably with interest. Thus, in addition to being less consistent with our system's theory of income, the cash method invites taxpayers to alter their behavior solely for purposes of deferring tax.

Income tax system designers are therefore put to a choice between (1) a more expensive accounting method more consistent with the system's underlying theory and less susceptible to manipulation, or (2) a simpler, less expensive accounting method that is both less consistent with theory and easier to game.

Congress, not surprisingly, has adopted a compromise. In general, individuals are permitted to use the cash method. Corporations taxed as separate entities (so-called "C corporations"), partnerships with C corporations as partners, and so-called "tax shelters" are generally required to use the accrual method. Since entities in this latter group almost always employ professional bookkeepers anyhow, the requirement that they use the accrual method for tax purposes is thought to be reasonable.

Subchapter A: Cash Method

Regulations: Section 1.446–1(c)(1)(i)

In general, a taxpayer using the cash receipts and disbursements method of accounting reports income in the year in which such income is actually or constructively received and deducts otherwise deductible expenses in the year in which such expenses are actually paid. An initial question is therefore unavoidable: "What constitutes payment or receipt?"

However we define receipt, we might expect cash method taxpayers to attempt to defer income by not "receiving" it. The IRS and the courts have responded by developing three doctrines that limit taxpayers' ability to play games with the method: the constructive receipt doctrine, the cash equivalence doctrine, and the economic benefit doctrine. As will be seen, the scope and interrelationship of these doctrines is not always clear, nor are the doctrines always successful in preventing income deferral.

SECTION 1: METHODS OF PAYMENT

(a) CHECKS

Principle: Receipt or payment by check is the equivalent of receipt or payment of cash if the check is not issued subject to restrictions and clears in the ordinary course.

KAHLER v. COMMISSIONER
18 T.C. 31 (1952)

[Petitioner was a cash method taxpayer.] Sometime after 5 p.m. on December 31, 1946, petitioner received a check drawn by his employer dated December 31, 1946, in the amount of $4,332.97. This commission check was cashed by petitioner at the drawee bank on January 2, 1947. The total amount of commissions earned by petitioner during 1946 amounted to $5,410.39 from which amount there was subtracted Federal withholding tax plus another small adjustment resulting in the net amount for which the check was made out.

The sole issue is when did the petitioner realize the income represented by the commission check delivered December 31, 1946. Was it in 1946, as determined by respondent, or in 1947, as claimed by petitioner? This, in turn, is based on the question whether the receipt of a check by a cash basis taxpayer after banking hours on the last day of the taxable period constitutes a realization of income.

Under the negotiable instruments law, payment by check is a conditional payment subject to the condition that it will be honored upon presentation; and once such presentation is made and the check is honored, the date of payment relates back to the time of delivery.

In everyday personal and commercial usage, the transfer of funds by check is an accepted procedure. The parties almost without exception think and deal in terms of payment except in the unusual circumstance, not involved here, that the check is dishonored upon presentation, or that it was delivered in the first place subject to some condition or infirmity which intervenes between delivery and presentation.

Under such circumstances, we feel that it is immaterial that delivery of a check is made too late in the taxable year for the check to be cashed in that year. The petitioner realized income upon receipt of the commission check on December 31, 1946.

PROBLEMS FOR DISCUSSION

6–1. At the end of the week, Anna receives a check in the amount of $200 from her employer, reflecting $250 of wages less $50 of state and federal withholding. Because of her low income, she does not have and cannot get a checking account. She therefore takes the check to a check-cashing service, which charges her $20 to cash it. Assume that the $20 fee is standard in the check-cashing business. What is the amount of Anna's income for the week? Does she recognize income when she receives the check or when she cashes it?

(b) CREDIT CARDS

Principle: Payment using borrowed funds is the equivalent of payment of cash.

REV. RUL. 78–38
1978–1 C.B. 67

The Internal Revenue Service has given further consideration to Rev. Rul. 71–216, 1971–1 C.B. 96, which holds that a taxpayer who used a bank credit card to contribute to a qualified charity may not deduct any part of the contribution under section 170(a)(1) of the Internal Revenue Code of 1954 until the year the cardholder makes payment of the amount of the contribution to the bank.

In Rev. Rul. 71–216 the assumption was made that a charitable contribution made by a taxpayer by use of a credit card was tantamount of a charitable contribution made by the issuance and delivery of a debenture bond or a promissory note by the obligor to a charitable organization, as discussed in Rev. Rul. 68–174, 1968–1 C.B. 81, which holds that, under the facts presented, the issuance of a debenture bond or a promissory note represents a mere promise to pay at some future date, and delivery of the bond or note to a charitable organization is not "payment" under section 170 of the Code.

Upon further study, it has been concluded that there are major distinctions between contributions made by the use of credit cards and contributions made by debenture bonds and promissory notes. In Rev. Rul. 68–174, the charitable organization that received the debenture bond or promissory note from the obligor received no more than a mere promise to pay. Conversely, the credit card holder in Rev. Rul. 71–216, by using the credit card to make the contribution, became immediately indebted to a third party (the bank) in such a way that the cardholder could not thereafter prevent the charitable organization from receiving payment.

The credit card draft received by the charitable organization from the credit card holder in Rev. Rul. 71–216 was immediately creditable by the bank to the organization's account as if it were a check.

Since the cardholder's use of the credit card creates the cardholder's own debt to a third party, the use of a bank credit card to make a charitable contribution is equivalent to the use of borrowed funds to make a contribution.

The general rule is that when a deductible payment is made with borrowed money, the deduction is not postponed until the year in which the borrowed money is repaid. Such expenses must be deducted in the year they are paid and not when the loans are repaid.

Accordingly, the taxpayer discussed in Rev. Rul. 71–216, who made a contribution to a qualified charity by a charge to the taxpayer's bank credit card, is entitled to a charitable contribution deduction under section 170(a) of the Code in the year the charge was made and the deduction may not be postponed until the taxpayer pays the indebtedness resulting from such charge.

PROBLEMS FOR DISCUSSION

6–2. In December of Year 1, Sylvia purchases deductible items for her business from Macy's department store, using a Macy's credit card. She does not pay the resulting balance on her credit card until January of Year 2. Assume that the credit card is issued by the same corporation that operates the store. (This is unlikely to be true, but assume it to be true anyway.) Should Sylvia claim the resulting deductions in Year 1 or Year 2? Assume that the credit card is issued by an affiliated corporation, not by the corporation that operates the store. Same result?

(c) LETTERS OF CREDIT

Principle: A letter of credit does not constitute payment until drawn upon.

CHAPMAN v. UNITED STATES
527 F.Supp. 1053 (D. Minn. 1981)

This dispute arises out of a purchase of cattle feed. The plaintiffs, cash basis taxpayers, deducted $30,000 on their joint federal income tax return for the cost of cattle feed. Chapman purchased cattle and feed from the Sun River Cattle Company (the Company). The cost of the feed was $30,000. Chapman paid $15,000 in cash in 1973. The balance of the feed purchase price was due and payable when each cattle lot was sold and was deductible from the proceeds of the sale of each lot prior to disbursing the balance of the proceeds, if any, to Chapman. To insure payment in case the proceeds from the cattle sale failed to cover the cost of the feed, Chapman gave the Company a promissory note for $15,000 and a secured letter of credit from the First National Bank of Minneapolis for the same amount on November 19, 1973.

The Company never drew on the letter of credit, which expired by its own terms on May 15, 1974. However, Chapman deducted $30,000 in 1973 ($15,000 cash plus $15,000 letter of credit) and then increased his income by $15,000 in 1974 when the letter of credit expired unused. The Internal Revenue Service decreased the plaintiffs' 1974 taxable income by $15,000 and disallowed the 1973 deduction of $15,000.

The general rule for cash basis taxpayers is that they must declare income in the taxable year in which it is actually or constructively received and that they may claim deductions for expenses in the taxable year in which they are actually paid. The central issue in this case is what constitutes payment and thus qualifies for a deduction.

A taxpayer is viewed as having paid an expense and is thus entitled to a deduction if the taxpayer uses borrowed funds for the payment. The taxpayer is entitled to the deduction at the time of payment, not at the time the loan is repaid. In addition, if a third party pays an expense on behalf of the taxpayer, the expense is also deductible in the year of payment not in the year the taxpayer repays the third party. However, if the taxpayer gives a promissory note for payment, the taxpayer is entitled to a deduction at the time he or she pays the note not at the time the note is given as payment. The taxpayer who gives a note as payment is denied a deduction even if the note is secured by collateral. A cash basis taxpayer may not deduct an expense while something remains to be done to complete payment.

The plaintiffs argue that they are entitled to the deduction because they paid for the feed with borrowed funds. The defendant argues that the plaintiffs merely gave a promissory note secured by collateral and thus are not entitled to a deduction. The Court finds that the letter of credit is analogous to a promissory note secured by collateral.

The plaintiffs merely promised to pay the expense and secured their payment with the letter of credit. Thus, they are not entitled to a deduction. The parties admit that the bank never paid on the letter of credit. The plaintiffs merely had an obligation to repay the bank if the bank paid the Company.

The critical distinction between the issuance of a letter of credit and the certification of a check is the promissory nature of the bank customer's obligation in the case of a letter of credit. When a bank certifies a check, the drawer's account is debited immediately; thus the drawer has paid at that time. In contrast, when a bank issues a letter of credit, the bank's customer merely pledges collateral but does not pay over the money. Before the customer is obligated to pay, the beneficiary of the credit must present a draft to the issuer of the letter of credit and the issuer must pay the draft. If the issuer does not pay on the letter of credit, the collateral is returned to the customer. [T]he issuer of a letter of credit is not entitled to reimbursement from its customer until the issuer honors a demand for payment.

Thus, a certified check is a cash equivalent but a letter of credit is similar to a consumer credit card waiting to be used. For the reasons stated herein, it is the conclusion of the Court that the letter of credit is not a cash equivalent and that the letter of credit was never drawn against. Therefore, the Court has concluded that the plaintiffs are not entitled to a deduction in 1973.

Problems for Discussion

6–3. Assume that in *Chapman*, the company from which Chapman purchased the feed drew on the letter of credit in 1973. Same result?

SECTION 2: CONSTRUCTIVE RECEIPT

Regulations: Section 1.451–2

MIELE v. COMMISSIONER
72 T.C. 284 (1979)

Fierro and Miele, attorneys, were the sole practitioners in their own law partnership in 1971 and 1972. The law firm maintained its partnership books and filed its Federal partnership income tax returns under the calendar year cash receipts and disbursements method of accounting.

In compliance with Pennsylvania's Code of Professional Responsibility, the law firm preserved the identity of their client's funds and property through segregation and accounting measures. First, the law firm transferred all client advances, including advances for both future client costs and future legal services, to the Fierro and Miele Trustee Account (hereinafter trustee account). Second, the law firm provided an accounting of each client's funds by maintaining a ledger card reflecting all client transactions. When a case was closed, the firm would transfer the earned portion of the prepaid legal fees held in the trustee account to the general partnership account; the unearned portion was refunded to the client.

The law firm would include the prepaid legal fees in income only when the funds were transferred to its general account. For administrative purposes, the firm would transfer funds from the trustee account only about four times a year, and it generally never made any transfers in November or December. Consequently, fees were not always included in income in the year earned and therefore otherwise available to the firm. In fact, $35,623.75 of the $68,199 held in the trustee account at the end of 1972 was earned and available to the firm in 1972 but not transferred to the general account, and not included in income, until 1973.

Petitioners argue the law firm is not taxable on client advances until received, which is when the funds are transferred from the trustee account to the general partnership account. Respondent argues that the client advances are merely prepaid legal fees and are taxable in full when received by the firm regardless of whether they are subsequently transferred to the trustee account. We cannot entirely agree with either party.

The narrow issue presented here is whether the law firm was in receipt of income when the prepaid legal fees were received by it. This in turn depends upon whether the firm received the fees under a claim of right and without restriction as to their disposition.

DR 9–102(A) of the Pennsylvania Code of Professional Responsibility requires the law firm to transfer all client advances received to a special segregated bank account. Moreover, the funds so deposited and segregated may not be commingled with funds belonging to the lawyer or law firm; the firm must maintain records and account to the client for all transactions concerning the funds; and the firm may withdraw only the undisputed amount from the fund when actually due. Violation of the minimum standards set forth in the Disciplinary Rule subjects the firm and its members to disciplinary action. These facts clearly indicate that the prepaid legal fees received by the firm are to be treated as owned by the client until an undisputed amount is due the firm. Under these circumstances, we view the law firm as a mere conduit for passing the client advances to the trustee account. Moreover, the prohibition against commingling these funds with the law firm's and restrictions upon use until an undisputed amount is due clearly indicate the firm did not receive these funds under a claim of right and without substantial restriction as to disposition. Accordingly, we hold that the law firm is not in receipt of income when the payments were actually received. But this is not the end of the matter. Even though the law firm is not taxable on receipt of the payments from the clients, it may be in constructive receipt of amounts held in the trustee account at the end of the year.

The doctrine of constructive receipt requires taxation of income which is subject to the taxpayer's unfettered command and which he is free to enjoy at his own option even though he chooses not to. Income is not constructively received, however, if the taxpayer's control of its receipt is subject to substantial limitations or restrictions. Thus, we must decide whether the funds held in the trustee account are subject to substantial limitations or restrictions which bar the application of constructive receipt doctrine. This, in turn, depends upon when the funds are earned.

DR 9–102(A)(2) provides that client advances belonging solely to the client must be deposited in a segregated bank account, but when the amount becomes due, the law firm may withdraw it. Client advances should be kept separate from the law firm's funds until such time that the firm has an undisputed right to those funds, when the funds are earned. Until the funds are earned, the firm's control of their receipt is subject to a substantial limitation; the firm cannot commingle them with its own funds and use them for its own personal purposes. Consequently, the firm is not free to enjoy the use of the funds until earned.

Fierro testified that $35,623.75 of the 1972 ending balance in the trustee account was earned in 1972 but not included in income until 1973, the year transferred to the law firm's general account. We find the law firm constructively received this amount in 1972. Clearly, all the events defining the firm's right to this amount transpired in 1972 even though, for administrative purposes, it chose not to exercise the right until 1973.

Notes

1. *Exception for deferral by contract.*—As the courts observe in *Cowden v. Commissioner*, Section 3 below, and *Reed v. Commissioner*, Section 4 below, taxpayers are free to enter into contracts pursuant to which receipts (and therefore income) are deferred, even if their purpose in entering into such contracts is explicitly to defer taxation. All that is required is that the relevant contractual provision (1) be entered into before taxpayer becomes unqualifiedly entitled to the amounts in question and (2) be "bona fide." The requirement that the contractual provision be "bona fide" does not necessarily require that consideration be given for the deferral. It does require that the agreement be contractually binding.

Problems for Discussion

6–4. Assume that a cash method law firm performs services in Year 1 and properly bills its client $100,000 for those services.

  a. On December 31, Year 1, the client tenders the firm a check in the amount of $100,000, which the firm accepts. When the firm deposits the check on January 2, Year 2, it clears in the ordinary course. In which year should the firm report the resulting income?

  b. On December 31, Year 1, the client tenders the firm a check in the amount of $100,000, which the law firm declines to accept, seeking to defer the relevant income. The client then tenders the same check on January 2, Year 2, and the firm accepts. The check clears in the ordinary course. In which year should the firm report the resulting income?

  c. On December 31, Year 1, the client tenders the firm a check in the amount of $100,000, but notes that there are not sufficient funds in the account to cover the check and requests that the firm not attempt to deposit it until January 2, Year 2. The law firm accepts the check, but does not attempt to deposit it until January 2, Year 2, at which time the check clears in the ordinary course. In which year should the firm report the resulting income?

  d. On December 31, Year 1, the client tenders the firm a check in the amount of $100,000, but notes that there are not sufficient funds in the account to cover the check and requests that the firm not attempt to deposit it until January 2, Year 2. The law firm declines to accept the check. The client then tenders the same check on January 2, Year 2, and the firm accepts. The check clears in the ordinary course. Same result?

e. Before the law firm is entitled to payment in Year 1, it discusses the timing of payment with its client. Law firm indicates that its goal of income deferral would be furthered by deferring payment until January. Client notes that its cash flow situation would make January payment preferable from its perspective in any event. Law firm and client therefore agree that client will not make payment until January, Year 2. In which year should the firm report the resulting income?

6–5. In Problem 6–4, assume that the client is a cash method taxpayer and the amount paid to the law firm is otherwise deductible. In which of the variations of Problem 6–4 may the client claim the deduction in Year 1? In which must the client wait until Year 2? In each case, why?

SECTION 3: CASH EQUIVALENCE

COWDEN v. COMMISSIONER

289 F.2d 20 (5th Cir. 1961)

In April 1951, Frank Cowden, Sr. and his wife made an oil, gas and mineral lease for themselves and their children to Stanolind Oil and Gas Company. By related supplemental agreements, Stanolind agreed to make "bonus" or "advance royalty" payments in an aggregate amount of $511,192.50. On execution of the instruments $10,223.85 was payable, the sum of $250,484.31 was due "no earlier than" January 5 "nor later than" January 10, 1952, and $250,484.34 was stipulated to be paid "no earlier than" January 5 "nor later than" January 10, 1953. In the deferred payments agreements it was provided that:

> "This contract evidences the obligation of Stanolind Oil and Gas Company to make the deferred payments, and it is understood and agreed that the obligation of Stanolind Oil and Gas Company to make such payments is a firm and absolute personal obligation of said Company, which is not in any manner conditioned upon development or production from the demised premises, nor upon the continued ownership of the leasehold interest in such premises by Stanolind Oil and Gas Company, but that such payments shall be made in all events."

On November 30, 1951, the taxpayer assigned the payments due from Stanolind in 1952 to the First National Bank of Midland, of which Frank Cowden, Sr. was a director. Assignments of the payments due in 1953 were made to the bank on November 20, 1952. For the assignment of the 1952 payments the bank paid the face value of the amounts assigned discounted by $257.43 in the case of Frank Cowden, Sr. and his wife, and

$85.81 in the case of each of their children. For the amounts due in 1953 the discounts were $313.14 for Frank Cowden, Sr. and his wife, and $104.38 for each of their children. The taxpayers reported the amounts received by them from the assignments as long-term capital gains. The Commissioner made a determination that the contractual obligations of Stanolind to make payments in future years represented ordinary income, subject to depletion, to the extent of the fair market value of the obligations at the time they were created. The Commissioner computed the fair market value of the Stanolind obligations, which were not interest bearing, by the deduction of a discount of four per cent, on the deferred payments from the date of the agreements until the respective maturities. Such computation fixed a 1951 equivalent of cash value of $487,647.46 for the bonus payments, paid in 1951 and agreed to be paid thereafter, aggregating $511,192.50. The Commissioner determined that the taxpayers should be taxed in 1951 on $487,647.46, as ordinary income.

As a general rule a tax avoidance motive is not to be considered in determining the tax liability resulting from a transaction. The taxpayers had the right to decline to enter into a mineral lease of their lands except upon the condition that the lessee obligate itself for a bonus payable in part in installments in future years, and the doing so would not, of itself, subject the deferred payments to taxation during the year that the lease was made. Nor would a tax liability necessarily arise although the lease contract was made with a solvent lessee who had been willing and able to pay the entire bonus upon the execution of the lease.

While it is true that the parties may enter into any legal arrangement they see fit even though the particular form in which it was cast was selected with the hope of a reduction in taxes, it is also true that if a consideration for which one of the parties bargains is the equivalent of cash it will be subjected to taxation to the extent of its fair market value. Whether the undertaking of the lessee to make future bonus payments was, when made, the equivalent of cash and, as such, taxable as current income is the issue in this case.

The test in [the Tax Court] seems to be whether the obligation to make the deferred payments is represented by "notes, bonds, or other evidences of indebtedness other than the contract." In this case, the literal [Tax Court] test is met as the obligation of Stanolind to the Cowdens was evidenced by an instrument other than the contract of lease. This instrument is not, however, one of the kind which fall into the classification of notes or bonds. The taxpayers urge that there can be no "equivalent of cash" obligation unless it is a negotiable instrument. Such a test, to be determined by the form of the obligation, is as unrealistic as it is formalistic. The income tax law deals in economic realities, not legal abstractions, and the reach of the income tax law is not to be delimited by technical refinements or mere formalism.

A promissory note, negotiable in form, is not necessarily the equivalent of cash. Such an instrument may have been issued by a maker of doubtful solvency or for other reasons such paper might be denied a ready acceptance in the market place. We think the converse of this principle ought to be applicable. We are convinced that if a promise to pay of a solvent obligor is unconditional and assignable, not subject to set-offs, and is of a kind that is frequently transferred to lenders or investors at a discount not substantially greater than the generally prevailing premium for the use of money, such promise is the equivalent of cash and taxable in like manner as cash would have been taxable had it been received by the taxpayer rather than the obligation. The principle that negotiability is not the test of taxability in an equivalent of cash case such as is before us, is consistent with the rule that men may, if they can, so order their affairs as to minimize taxes, and points up the doctrine that substance and not from should control in the application of income tax laws.

The Tax Court stressed in its findings that the provisions for deferring a part of the bonus were made solely at the request of and for the benefit of the taxpayers, and that the lessee was willing and able to make the bonus payments in cash upon execution of the agreements. It appears to us that the Tax Court, in reaching its decision that the taxpayers had received equivalent of cash bonuses in the year the leases were executed, gave as much and probably more weight to those findings than to the other facts found by it. We are persuaded of this not only by the language of its opinion but because, in its determination of the cash equivalent, it used the amounts which it determined the taxpayers could have received if they had made a different contract, rather than the fair market value cash equivalent of the obligation for which the taxpayers had bargained in the contracts which they had a lawful right to make. We are unable to say whether or not the Tax Court, if it disregarded, as we think it should have done, the facts as it found them as to the willingness of the lessee to pay and the unwillingness of the taxpayers to receive the full bonus on execution of the leases, would have determined that the equivalent bonus obligations were taxable in the year of the agreements as the equivalent of cash. This question is primarily a fact issue. There should be a remand to the Tax Court for a reconsideration of the question submitted in the light of what has been said here.

NOTES

1. *Structure of the cash equivalence doctrine.*—In general, receipt of *any* economic value constitutes income, regardless of its form. If Cowden had received services or property in exchange for his oil and gas interest, he would clearly have recognized income immediately upon that receipt. Why, then, do we need to ask whether what he received is the "equivalent of cash"?

The problem is that as a matter of non-tax law, once we have earned income we are treated as owning an asset representing the right to be paid. If we were to treat receipt of that asset as a "receipt" for cash method accounting purposes, then whenever a cash method taxpayer earns income, he would be required to report the value of that asset immediately, even if he has not yet been paid. This would, in effect, convert all cash method taxpayers into accrual method taxpayers, at least as to income.

It may therefore be useful to think of the cash equivalence doctrine as having two parts. The first is an exception to the general rule that income includes all economic value received. Notwithstanding this rule, in the case of cash method taxpayers income does not include the value of rights to receive income in the future. The second is then an exception to this exception: If a right to receive income in the future is the "equivalent of cash," we require its immediate inclusion nevertheless. When do we require immediate inclusion? In general, when the right to receive future income is effectively convertible immediately into cash. What is unclear from the cases is when this is so. The Tax Court looks for formal indicia of negotiability. The *Cowden* court was unwilling to be so constrained. Compare *Reed v. Commissioner*, below.

2. *Cash equivalent payments.*—Except with respect to payments by check, the cash equivalence doctrine is limited to receipts. Payment by check constitutes payment for cash method purposes so long as the check clears in the ordinary course. Payments in the form of other promises to pay, even if such promises would constitute cash equivalents for receipt purposes, are not payments for purposes of the cash method.

PROBLEMS FOR DISCUSSION

6–6. Why is there no constructive receipt in *Cowden*?

SECTION 4: ECONOMIC BENEFIT

REED v. COMMISSIONER

723 F.2d 138 (1st Cir. 1983)

Reed acquired stock in Reed Electromech Corporation (Electromech) in 1963, when he headed up an investor group which organized Electromech to purchase the assets of another corporation. In 1967, Reed and several of his fellow Electromech shareholders (the selling stockholders) entered into an agreement with Joseph Cvengros, also an Electromech shareholder, granting Cvengros an option to purchase the selling stockholder's stock.

On November 23, 1973, Cvengros exercised his option to purchase the Electromech stock held by the selling shareholders. Shortly thereafter, Reed and his fellow selling shareholders became concerned about the federal income tax implications of a sale in 1973. Reed, in particular, wanted to defer closing until 1974 so that he would have time to make an orderly sale of certain securities ("loss securities"), the capital loss from which he desired to write-off against the capital gain on the Electromech sale. Reed was understandably reluctant to sell the loss securities prior to the December 27 closing, fearing that Cvengros' outside financing might fall through before the closing, thus preventing the Electromech stock sale. On the other hand, Reed believed that after the December 27 closing there would not be enough time remaining in 1973 to properly identify and sell these loss securities in that year. Hence, Reed wanted to postpone closing until January of 1974.

Nevertheless, Cvengros and his financial backer insisted on the December 27, 1973 closing, apparently because the financial backer wanted the stock transaction reflected on his 1973 books. In early December 1973, Reed and Cvengros, desiring to accommodate all involved, orally agreed to modify the purchase-sale agreement to provide that Reed and the other selling shareholders would not be entitled to receive payment for their stocks until January 3, 1974. Both Reed and Cvengros considered the deferred payment provision to be part of the purchase/sale agreement and legally binding. Reed, in fact, indicated that he would not have gone through with the sales transaction if Cvengros had not agreed to the deferred payment provision.

This oral modification was memorialized in a written escrow agreement, executed by Reed and Cvengros immediately prior to the closing on December 27, 1973. Under the terms of the escrow agreement, the stock sales proceeds were to be paid by Cvengros to the escrowee at the December 27, 1973 closing and the escrowee was then to make disbursements of the sales proceeds to a number of selling shareholders, including Reed, on January 3, 1974. Under the agreement, these selling shareholders were not entitled to receive interest, investment income or any other incidental benefits (*e.g.*, bank letter of credit) on the sales proceeds while they were in escrow. The agreement provided for no conditions precedent, other than the passage of time, to the January 3, 1974 payment.

In the Tax Court, the Commissioner argued that Reed recognized a taxable gain from the sale in 1973 rather than in 1974 because: 1) he constructively received the income from the stock sale in 1973; 2) he received an economic benefit (or cash equivalent) in 1973; and 3) the escrow arrangement lacked economic reality, other than as a tax deferral device.

The Tax Court, while recognizing that a cash basis taxpayer such as Reed could postpone income recognition by a bona fide agreement providing for deferred payment, nevertheless held that "when, upon receipt of the [purchased stocks], the buyer deposits the full purchase price in an escrow account to be paid to the seller at a later date and no condition other than the passage of time is placed on the seller's right to receive the escrow funds, courts have held that the seller recognizes income when the buyer deposits funds with the escrowee." The court emphasized that because nothing could have prevented Reed's receipt of the funds once they were deposited with the escrowee, Reed recognized income when Cvengros deposited the funds in escrow in 1973.

A. Constructive Receipt

[U]nder the constructive receipt doctrine, a taxpayer recognizes taxable income when he has an unqualified, vested right to receive immediate payment. However, a taxpayer-seller has the right to enter into an agreement with the buyer that he, the seller, will not be paid until the following year. As long as the deferred payment agreement is binding between the parties and is made prior to the time when the taxpayer-seller has acquired an absolute and unconditional right to receive payment, then the cash basis taxpayer is not required to report the sales proceeds as income until he actually receives them.

Similarly, an existing agreement which has been amended or modified to provide for deferred payment of an amount not yet due serves to postpone income recognition. This is true even though: 1) the purchaser was initially willing to contract for immediate payment; and 2) the taxpayer's primary objective in entering into the deferred payment agreement was to minimize taxes. A deferred payment agreement is considered bona fide and hence given its full legal effect, if the parties intended to be bound by the agreement and were, in fact, legally bound.

While recognizing these principles, the Commissioner claims the escrow modification providing for disbursement of the sales proceeds to Reed in 1974 was not a bona fide arms-length agreement between the Cvengros and Reed and, hence, did not "substantially limit" Reed's access to the sales proceeds deposited in escrow after the December 27, 1973 closing. Instead, the purported escrow modification was nothing more than Reed's self imposed limitation, designed to defer income recognition on proceeds he already had an unqualified, vested right to receive on December 27, 1973. The Commissioner claims the record reveals that Reed could have taken the sales proceeds immediately after the December 27, 1973 closing, had he so requested.

We agree with the Commissioner that a deferred escrow arrangement that is not part of a bona fide agreement between the buyer and the seller-taxpayer, but rather is a "self-imposed limitation" created by the seller-taxpayer, is legally ineffective to shift taxability on escrowed funds from one year to the next. However, in this case the escrow arrangement was the product of an arms-length, bona fide modification to the purchase sale agreement between Reed and Cvengros; it was not Reed's self imposed limitation on the receipt of sales proceeds he had an unqualified, vested right to receive in 1973.

The modification setting up the escrow arrangement was orally agreed upon by the parties in early December, 1973, and, as the Tax Court found, was memorialized in the escrow agreement instruction letter executed prior to closing on December 27, 1973. Thus, the modification became effective prior to the time when Reed had an unqualified right to demand immediate payment under the then existing purchase agreement. As discussed above, an existing purchase-sale agreement can be modified to provide for deferred payment of an amount not already due under the existing agreement, provided the modification is considered by the parties to be legally binding. Both Cvengros and Reed testified that they considered the deferred payment provision to be a legally binding modification, defining their rights and obligations under the purchase-sale agreement. Nothing in the Tax Court's opinion indicates that we should discredit this testimony. In fact, the record reveals that the provision was the product of some arms length negotiations between Cvengros and Reed. Cvengros, at his financial backer's insistance, was initially unwilling to make the deferred payment but agreed to the escrow device after Reed promised to remain on the Electromech Board of Directors following the sale to insure a smooth ownership transaction. And, despite the government's suggestion, on the record here we are unable to say that the deferred payment agreement was any less bona fide or any less a part of the purchase-sale agreement merely because it was not memorialized until just prior to closing.

B. Economic Benefit

The Commissioner next contends that in 1973 Reed received a taxable economic benefit by virtue of Cvengros' deposit of the sales proceeds into the escrow account. The Commissioner argues that upon the December 27, 1973 closing, there were no open transactions remaining and Reed's right to future payment from the escrow account was irrevocable, being conditioned only upon the passage of time; hence, Reed received the "cash equivalent" of the sales proceeds deposited in the escrow account. The Commissioner points out that Reed could have assigned his irrevocable right to receive future payment of the escrow funds.

This argument, which was largely embraced by the Tax Court, is predicated upon a misapplication of various cases the Commissioner says espouse the economic benefit doctrine. These cases held that escrow arrangements were ineffective to defer income tax because of the existence of one of two factors, not present in the instant case: (1) the taxpayer received some present, beneficial interest from the escrow account [*e.g.*, investment or interest income]; (2) the escrow arrangement was the product of the taxpayer's self-imposed limitation on funds the taxpayer had an unqualified, vested right to control.

Specifically, *Kuehner v. Commissioner*, 214 F.2d 437 (1st Cir. 1954), the case upon which the Commissioner principally relies, held that a taxpayer recognized income when the purchase price was deposited with the escrowee because the taxpayer's interest in the escrowed funds constituted a property interest equivalent to cash. The taxpayer's interest in the escrow fund was so viewed because the taxpayer was entitled to investment income earned while the funds were in escrow and hence enjoyed a complete and present economic interest in the funds.

By contrast, in this case Reed was not entitled to receive the income earned from the investment of funds held by the escrowee, but merely obtained an unconditional promise that he would ultimately be paid on January 3, 1974 in accordance with the deferred payment provision.

The Commissioner, however, seizes upon broad language in *Kuehner* as support for the proposition that one who has an unconditional right to future payment from an irrevocable escrow account receives taxable income in the year the escrow account was created. There are three reasons why we do not interpret *Kuehner* as supporting this proposition. First, as the *Kuehner* court apparently recognized, the deposited escrow funds could be characterized as "the equivalent of cash" only if the taxpayer received a present beneficial interest in such funds—*e.g.*, investment income. The *Kuehner* court's discussion of the taxpayer's present, beneficial interest in the escrow funds would have been superfluous if it were holding that the taxpayer's unconditional right to future payment of such funds was the equivalent of cash. Hence, we believe it is reasonable to interpret the *Kuehner* court's discussion of the unconditional nature of a right to future payment as relating to the court's determination of the appropriate value of the economic benefit conferred, the court having determined that the taxpayer had received a present economic benefit.

Second, to apply the Commissioner's interpretation of *Kuehner* to this case would be at odds with the well established principle that a deferred payment arrangement is effective to defer income recognition to a cash basis taxpayer, provided it is part of an arms-length agreement between the purchaser and seller. That the cash basis taxpayer's right to receive future payment of the escrowed proceeds may be characterized as unconditional or irrevocable does not render the contractually binding restriction on the time of payment any less substantial.

Third, to apply the Commissioner's interpretation of *Kuehner* here would require an extension of the economic benefit doctrine that would significantly erode the distinction between cash and accrual methods of accounting. The economic benefit doctrine, a nonstatutory doctrine emerging from and primarily related to the area of the employee deferred compensation, is based on the idea that an individual should be taxed on any economic benefit conferred upon him, to the extent that the benefit has an ascertainable fair market value. However, in applying the economic benefit doctrine to a cash basis taxpayer's contractual right to receive future payment, as we must do here, courts generally go beyond an inquiry into the fair market value of the contract right to ask the separate question of whether the contract right is the equivalent of cash. Without this separate inquiry, the economic benefit doctrine, as applied to a cash basis taxpayer, could be broadly construed to cover all deferred compensation and deferred payment contracts.

In order to meet the cash equivalency requirement for income recognition, a cash basis taxpayer's contractual right to future payment must be reflected in a negotiable note, bond, or other evidence of indebtedness which, like money, commonly and readily changes hands in commerce. And, in addition to being readily transferrable, the evidence of indebtedness received by the taxpayer must be intended as present payment of the amount owed, rather than merely as evidence that payment will be forthcoming in the future.

In this case, it is difficult to conceive Reed's contractual right to future payment, even though unconditional and evidenced by an escrow account, as a right which commonly and readily changes hands in commerce. However, even assuming Reed's right to future payment of the escrowed proceeds was readily transferrable in commerce, the escrow account was not intended by the parties as present payment of the purchase price, but rather was intended to serve as an added assurance that payment would be made in the next year. As such, the escrow account cannot be characterized fairly as the equivalent of cash to Reed in 1973. We would have to ignore the distinction between cash and accrual methods of accounting to adopt a rule requiring immediate recognition of income by a cash basis taxpayer who has a contractual right to future payment from an escrow account, but who has received no present beneficial interest from that account.

The Commissioner alternatively suggests that Reed received a present beneficial interest in the escrow funds in the sense that he could have assigned his right to receive payment under the agreement. This argument proves either too much or too little. It proves too much because any promisee under a contract for deferred payment could conceivably assign his right to receive future payment, provided the contract does not specifically include a non-assignment clause. Hence, to base the economic benefit rule on whether a taxpayer could have assigned his contractual right to future payment would eviscerate the well recognized rule that a taxpayer can defer income recognition pursuant to a bona fide deferred payment agreement. Furthermore, it proves too little in this case because Reed never attempted to make any assignment of his right to receive the escrow funds and thus did nothing to charge himself with any economic benefit to be derived from the funds.

NOTES

1. *Status of the economic benefit doctrine.*—In *Reed*, the IRS correctly summarized the Tax Court's position on the scope of the economic benefit doctrine: a taxpayer has a current "economic benefit," and therefore a current receipt, if he receives a present indefeasible right to the future receipt of cash or other property. The doctrine as commonly applied in the Tax Court has two parts: First, there must be a transfer of identified property in such a fashion that the property is protected from the claims of the transferor's creditors. In other words, it must no longer be subject to the ability or willingness to pay of the payor. Second, the taxpayer's rights must be fully vested. Both conditions were satisfied in *Reed*.

The First Circuit, however, limited the doctrine to situations in which income on the sequestered property accrues to taxpayer's benefit—in property law terms, to situations in which taxpayer receives a present beneficial income interest in the property. It is not clear that all courts accept such a limitation.

PROBLEMS FOR DISCUSSION

6–7. Why did the arrangement in *Reed* not result in constructive receipt of taxable income on December 27, when the sales proceeds were deposited in the escrow account?

6–8. Why did the arrangement in *Reed* not constitute a cash equivalent?

6–9. Assume that any interest earned on the amounts deposited in the escrow account had been payable to the *Reed* taxpayers on January 3, 1974, together with the principal. Same result?

SECTION 5: SUCCESSFUL DEFERRAL

REV. RUL. 60–31

1960–1 C.B. 174

Advice has been requested regarding the taxable year of inclusion in gross income of a taxpayer, using the cash receipts and disbursements method of accounting, of compensation for services received under the circumstances described below.

(1) On January 1, 1958, the taxpayer and corporation X executed an employment contract under which the taxpayer is to be employed by the corporation in an executive capacity for a period of five years. Under the contract, the taxpayer is entitled to a stated annual salary and to additional compensation of 10x dollars for each year. The additional compensation will be credited to a bookkeeping reserve account and will be deferred, accumulated, and paid in annual installments equal to one-fifth of the amount in the reserve as of the close of the year immediately preceding the year of first payment. The payments are to begin only upon (3) termination of the taxpayer's employment by the corporation; (b) the taxpayer's becoming a part-time employee of the corporation; or (c) the taxpayer's becoming partially or totally incapacitated. Under the terms of the agreement, corporation X is under a merely contractual obligation to make the payments when due, and the parties did not intend that the amounts in the reserve be held by the corporation in trust for the taxpayer.

The contract further provides that if the taxpayer should fail or refuse to perform his duties, the corporation will be relieved of any obligation to make further credits to the reserve (but not of the obligation to distribute amounts previously contributed); but, if the taxpayer should become incapacitated from performing his duties, then credits to the reserve will continue for one year from the date of the incapacity, but not beyond the expiration of the five-year term of the contract. There is no specific provision in the contract for forfeiture by the taxpayer of his right to distribution from the reserve; and, in the event he should die prior to his receipt in full of the balance in the account, the remaining balance is distributable to his personal representative at the rate of one-fifth per year for five years, beginning three months after his death.

(2) The taxpayer is an officer and director of corporation A, which has a plan for making future payments of additional compensation for current services to certain officers and key employees designated by its board of directors. This plan provides that a percentage of the annual net earnings (before Federal income taxes) in excess of 4,000x dollars is to be designated for division among the participants in proportion to their respective salaries. This amount is not currently paid to the participants; but, the corporation has set up on its books a separate account for each participant and each year it credits thereto the dollar amount of his participation for the year, reduced by a proportionate part of the corporation's income taxes attributable to the additional compensation. Each account is also credited with the net amount, if any, realized from investing any portion of the amount in the account.

Distributions are to be made from these accounts annually beginning when the employee (1) reaches age 60, (2) is no longer employed by the company, including cessation of employment due to death, or (3) becomes totally disable to perform his duties, whichever occurs first. The annual distribution will equal a stated percentage of the balance in the employee's account at the close of the year immediately preceding the year of first payment, and distributions will continue until the account is exhausted. However, the corporation's liability to make these distributions is contingent upon the employee's (1) refraining from engaging in any business competitive to that of the corporation, (2) making himself available to the corporation for consultation and advice after retirement or termination of his services, unless disabled, and (3) retaining unencumbered any interest or benefit under the plan. In the event of his death, either before or after the beginning of payments, amounts in an employee's account are distributable in installments computed in the same way to his designated beneficiaries or heirs-at-law. Under the terms of the compensation plan, corporation A is under a merely contractual obligation to make the payments when due, and the parties did not intend that the amounts in each account be held by the corporation in trust for the participants.

(3) On October 1, 1957, the taxpayer, an author, and corporation Y, a publisher, executed an agreement under which the taxpayer granted to the publisher the exclusive right to print, publish and sell a book he had written. This agreement provides that the publisher will (1) pay the author specified royalties based on the actual cash received from the sale of the published work, (2) render semiannual statements of the sales, and (3) at the time of rendering each statement make settlement for the amount due. On the same day, another agreement was signed by the same parties, mutually agreeing that, in consideration of, and notwithstanding any contrary provisions contained in the first contract, the publisher shall not pay the taxpayer more than 100x dollars in any one calendar year. Under this supplemental contract, sums in excess of 100x dollars accruing in any one calendar year are to be carried over by the publisher into succeeding ac-counting periods; and the publisher shall not be required

either to pay interest to the taxpayer on any such excess sums or to segregate any such sums in any manner.

(4) In June 1957, the taxpayer, a football player, entered into a two-year standard player's contract with a football club in which he agreed to play football and engage in activities related to football during the two-year term only for the club. In addition to a specified salary for the two-year term, it was mutually agreed that as an inducement for signing the contract the taxpayer would be paid a bonus of 150x dollars. The taxpayer could have demanded and received payment of this bonus at the time of signing the contract, but at his suggestion there was added to the standard contract form a paragraph providing substantially as follows:

> The player shall receive the sum of 150x dollars upon signing of this contract, contingent upon the payment of this 150x dollars to an escrow agent designated by him. The escrow agreement shall be subject to approval by the legal representatives of the player, the Club, and the escrow agent.

Pursuant to this added provision, an escrow agreement was executed on June 25, 1957, in which the club agreed to pay 150x dollars on that date to the Y bank, as escrow and the escrow agent agreed to pay this amount, plus interest, to the taxpayer in installments over a period of five years. The escrow agreement also provides that the account established by the escrow agent is to bear the taxpayer's name; that payments from such account may be made only in accordance with the terms of the agreement; that the agreement is binding upon the parties thereto and their successors or assigns; and that in the event of the taxpayer's death during the escrow period the balance due will become part of his estate.

(5) The taxpayer, a boxer, entered into an agreement with a boxing club to fight a particular opponent at a specified time and place. The place of the fight agreed to was decided upon because of the insistence of the taxpayer that it be held there. The agreement was on the standard form of contract required by the state athletic commission and provided, in part, that for his performance taxpayer was to receive 16x percent of the gross receipts derived from the match. Simultaneously, the same parties executed a separate agreement providing for payment of the taxpayer's share of the receipts from the match as follows: 25 percent thereof not later than two weeks after the bout, and 25 percent thereof during each of the three years following the year of the bout in equal semiannual installments. Such deferments are not customary in prize fighting contracts, and the supplemental agreement was executed at the demand of the taxpayer. Upon the taxpayer's insistence, the agreements also provided than any telecast of the fight must receive his prior consent and that he was to approve or disapprove all proposed sales of radio and motion picture rights.

[T]he individual concerned in each of the situations described above, employs the cash receipts and disbursements method of accounting. Under that method, he is required to include the compensation concerned in gross income only for the taxable year in which it is actually or constructively received. Consequently, the question for resolution is whether in each of the situations described the income in question was constructively received in a taxable year prior to the taxable year of actual receipt.

A mere promise to pay, not represented by notes or secured in any way, is not regarded as a receipt of income within the intendment of the cash receipts and disbursements method.

This should not be construed to mean that under the cash receipts and disbursements method income may be taxed only when realized in cash. For, under that method a taxpayer is required to include in income that which is received in cash or cash equivalent. And, as stated in the above-quoted provisions of the regulations, the "receipt" contemplated by the cash method may be actual or constructive.

It is clear that the doctrine of constructive receipt is to be sparingly used; that amounts due from a corporation but unpaid, are not to be included in the income of an individual reporting his income on a cash receipts basis unless it appears that the money was available to him, that the corporation was able and ready to pay him, that his right to receive was not restricted, and that his failure to receive resulted from exercise of his own choice.

Consequently, it seems clear that in each case involving a deferral of compensation a determination of whether the doctrine of constructive receipt is applicable must be made upon the basis of the specific factual situation involved.

Applying the foregoing criteria to the situations described above, the following conclusions have been reached:

(1) The additional compensation to be received by the taxpayer under the employment contract concerned will be includible in his gross income only in the taxable years in which the taxpayer actually receives installment payments in cash or other property previously credited to his account.

(2) For the reasons in (1) above, it is held that the taxpayer here involved also will be required to include the deferred compensation concerned in his gross income only in the taxable years in which the taxpayer actually receives installment payments in cash or other property previously credited to his account.

In arriving at this conclusion and the conclusion reached in case (1), consideration has been given to section 1.402(b)–1 of the Income Tax Regulations and to Revenue Ruling 57–37, C.B. 1957–1, 18, as modified by Revenue Ruling 57–528, C.B. 1957–2, 263. Section 1.402(b)–1(a)(1) provides in part, with an exception not here relevant, that any contribution made by an employer on behalf of an employee to a trust during a taxable year of the employer which ends within or with a taxable year of the trust for which the trust is not exempt under section 501(a) of the Code, shall be included in income of the employee for his taxable year during which the contribution is made if his interest in the contribution is nonforfeitable at the time the contribution is made. Revenue Ruling 57–37, as modified by Revenue Ruling 57–528, held, inter alia, that certain contributions conveying fully vested and nonforfeitable interests made by an employer into separate independently controlled trusts for the purpose of furnishing unemployment and other benefits to its eligible employees constituted additional compensation to the employees includible, under section 402(b) of the Code and section 1.402(b)–1(a)(1) of the regulations, in their income for the taxable year in which such contributions were made. These Revenue Rulings are distinguishable from cases (1) and (2) in that, under all the facts and circumstances of these cases, no trusts for the benefit of the taxpayers were created and no contributions are to be made thereto. Consequently, section 402(b) of the Code and section 1.402(b)–1(a)(1) of the regulations are inapplicable.

(3) Here the principal agreement provided that the royalties were payable substantially as earned, and this agreement was supplemented by a further concurrent agreement which made the royalties payable over a period of years. This supplemental agreement, however, was made before the royalties were earned; in fact, in was made on the same day as the principal agreement and the two agreements were a part of the same transaction. Thus, for all practical purposes, the arrangement from the beginning is similar to that in (1) above. Therefore, it is also held that the author concerned will be required to include the royalties in his gross income only in the taxable years in which they are actually received in cash or other property.

(4) In arriving at a determination as to the includibility of the 150x dollars concerned in the gross income of the football player, under the circumstances described, in addition to the authorities cited above, consideration also has been given to Revenue Ruling 55–527, C.B. 1955–2, 25, and to the decision in E. T. Sproull v.Commissioner, 16 T.C. 244.

In Revenue Ruling 55–727, the taxpayer, a professional baseball player, entered into a contract in 1953 in which he agreed to render services for a baseball club and to refrain from playing baseball for any other club during the term of the contract. In addition to specified compensation, the contract provided for a bonus to the player or his estate, payable one-half in January 1954 and one-half in January 1955, whether or not he was able to render services. The primary question was whether the bonus was capital gain or ordinary income; and, in holding that the bonus payments constituted ordinary income, it was stated that they were taxable for the year in which received by the player. However, under the facts set forth in Revenue Ruling 55–727 there was no arrangement, as here, for placing the amount of the bonus in escrow. Consequently, the instant situation is distinguishable from that considered in Revenue Ruling 55–727.

In E.T. Sproull v. Commissioner, 16 T.C. 244, affirmed, 194 Fed.(2d) 541, the petitioner's employer in 1945 transferred in trust for the petitioner the amount of $10,500. The trustee was directed to pay out of principal to the petitioner the sum of $5,250 in 1945 and the balance, including income, in 1947. In the event of the petitioner's prior death, the amounts were to be paid to his administrator, executor, or heirs. The petitioner contended that the Commissioner erred in including the sum of $10,500 in his taxable income for 1945. In this connection, the court stated:

> "it is undoubtedly true that the amount which the Commissioner has included in petitioner's income for 1945 was used in that year for his benefit ... in setting up the trust of which petitioner, or, in the event of his death then his estate, was the sole beneficiary ....
>
> "The question then becomes ... was 'any economic or financial benefit conferred on the employee as compensation' in the taxable year. If so, it was taxable to him in that year. This question we must answer in the affirmative. The employer's part of the transaction terminated in 1945. It was then that the amount of the compensation was fixed at $10,500 and irrevocably paid out for petitioner's sole benefit..."

Applying the principles stated in the *Sproull* decision to the facts here, it is concluded that the 150x-dollar bonus is includible in the gross income of the football player concerned in 1957, the year in which the club unconditionally paid such amount to the escrow agent.

(5) In this case, the taxpayer and the boxing club, as well as the opponent whom taxpayer had agreed to meet, are each acting in his or its own right, the proposed match is a joint venture by all of these participants, and the taxpayer is not an employee of the boxing club. The taxpayer's share of the gross receipts from the match belong to him and never belonged to the boxing club. Thus, the taxpayer acquired all of the benefits of his share of the receipts except the right of immediate physical possession; and, although the club retained physical possession, it was by virtue of an arrangement with the taxpayer who, in substance and effect, authorized the boxing club to take possession and hold for him. The receipts, therefore, were income to the taxpayer at the time they were paid to and retained by the boxing club by his agreement and, in substance, at his direction, and are includible in his gross income in the taxable year in which so paid to the club.

MINOR v. UNITED STATES
772 F.2d 1472 (9th Cir. 1985)

Ralph H. Minor is a physician practicing in Snohomish County, Washington. In 1959, he entered into an agreement with the Snohomish County Physicians Corporation (Snohomish Physicians) under which he agreed to render medical services to subscribers of Snohomish Physicians' prepaid medical plan in exchange for fees to be paid by Snohomish Physicians according to its fee schedule.

In 1967, Snohomish Physicians adopted a deferred compensation plan for its participating physicians. Under the voluntary plan, a physician who desired deferred compensation entered into a "Supplemental Agreement" in which the physician and Snohomish Physicians agree that for future services the physician would be paid a designated percentage of the fee he or she would receive under the fee schedule if not participating in the plan. The physician could elect any percentage from 10 per cent to 90 per cent. The balance would go into the deferred compensation fund. Minor's agreement with Snohomish Physicians provided that he would be paid 50 per cent of the scheduled fees through November 30, 1971, and 10 per cent thereafter.

To provide for its obligations under the Supplemental Agreement, Snohomish Physicians established a trust. Snohomish Physicians was the settlor, three physicians, including Minor, were trustees, and Snohomish Physicians was the beneficiary. The trustees, pursuant to instructions from Snohomish Physicians, purchased retirement annuity policies to provide for the payment of benefits under the plan. These benefits would become payable to the physician or to his beneficiaries when he or she retires, dies, becomes disabled, or leaves the Snohomish Physicians service area to practice medicine elsewhere. The physician agrees to continue to provide services to Snohomish Physicians patients until the benefits become payable, to limit his or her practice after retirement, to continue to provide certain emergency and consulting services at Snohomish Physicians' request, and to refrain from providing medical services to competing groups.

On his federal income tax returns for 1970, 1971, and 1973, Minor included in gross income only the 10 per cent of the scheduled fees which he actually received. The remaining 90 per cent, which Minor did not receive, went into the deferred compensation plan trust.

The IRS argues that Minor should have included in his gross income that portion of the fees Snohomish Physicians placed in trust for his future benefit. The IRS relies on the economic benefit doctrine, which is an exception to the well-settled rule that a taxpayer pays income tax only on income which is actually or constructively received by him. In this case, Minor did not actually receive the income the IRS attributes to him nor, the IRS has conceded, did he constructively receive the income. The IRS argues, however, that the economic benefit doctrine applies here because an economic benefit was presently conferred on Minor, although he did not receive and had no right to receive the deferred compensation benefits during the tax year.

The IRS has conceded that Minor did not constructively receive the proceeds of Snohomish Physicians' deferred compensation plan. Although taxation of deferred compensation plans is generally analyzed under the constructive receipt doctrine, the economic benefit doctrine provides an alternate method of determining when a taxpayer receives taxable benefits. Under that doctrine, an employer's promise to pay deferred compensation in the future may itself constitute a taxable economic benefit if the current value of the employer's promise can be given an appraised value. The concept of economic benefit is quite different from that of constructive receipt because the taxpayer must actually receive the property or currently receive evidence of a future right to property.

The economic benefit doctrine is applicable only if the employer's promise is capable of valuation. A current economic benefit is capable of valuation where the employer makes a contribution to an employee's deferred compensation plan which is nonforfeitable, fully vested in the employee and secured against the employer's creditors by a trust arrangement. See Rev.Rul. 60–31, 1960–1 C.B. at 179.

In cases where courts or the IRS have found a current economic benefit to have been conferred, the employer's contribution has always been secured or the employee's interest has been nonforfeitable. If the employee's interest is unsecured or not otherwise protected from the employer's creditors, the employee's interest is not taxable property.

Neither Minor nor any other participants in the deferred compensation plan has any right, title or interest in the trust which holds the annuity contract. The trust, which was established to hold the assets of the deferred compensation plan, was not established pursuant to Minor's Supplemental Agreement, but was created at the initiative of Snohomish Physicians which is both the settlor and beneficiary of the trust. Although Minor incidentally benefits from the trust, he is not a beneficiary. Because Snohomish Physicians has not established any trust in favor of Minor or the other participants, the assets of the trust remain solely those of Snohomish Physicians and subject to the claims of its general creditors.

Minor has pointed out several provisions of the trust agreement which show that the participating physicians had no vested, funded right to the assets of the trust. The IRS in response has cited *Sproull v. Commissioner*, 16 T.C. 244 (1951), aff'd, 194 F.2d 541 (6th Cir.1952), in which a corporation paid over to a trustee compensation for past services rendered by petitioner. The trustee was directed to hold, invest, and pay over this sum to petitioner or his estate in two installments. The Tax Court held the entire trust fund was income to the petitioner in the year it was paid to the trustee. In *Sproull*, the settlor of the trust was the corporation and the beneficiary was the petitioner or his estate. The petitioner exercised substantial control over the money because he could assign or otherwise alienate the trust, had standing to bring an action against the trustee, if needed, and other powers under the trust. In this case Snohomish Physicians is both the settlor and the beneficiary of the trust. Minor's only involvement is as one of the trustees. Because Snohomish Physicians' trust was not established in favor of Minor or the other plan participants, the deferred compensation plan is unfunded. Unfunded plans do not confer a present taxable economic benefit.

SECTION 6: PREPAID EXPENSES

A taxpayer can defer net income in at least two ways: by deferring income recognition or by accelerating the allowance of deductions. Can a cash method taxpayer defer net income by prepaying deductible expenses?

GRYNBERG v. COMMISSIONER
83 T.C. 255 (1984)

During the years 1974 through 1979, petitioners owned several hundred oil and gas leases acquired from the United States government, from various state governments and from private lessors.

Under the lease provisions, petitioners were entitled to search for, extract and sell oil and gas from the properties. Petitioners, however, were also obligated to pay to the lessors a specified annual fee with respect to each lease unless certain conditions enumerated in the various leases were satisfied, such as the commencement of drilling operations or the discovery of specified quantities of oil or gas. This annual fee was referred to as "delay rental." The purpose of delay rental was to compensate the lessor for the delay in the development of drilling or production operations on the properties subject to the leases. Payments of delay rental prevented termination of the leases where drilling or production operations had not commenced. Failure to pay delay rental due on a particular lease would result in automatic termination of the lease.

[F]rom 1971 to the present time, in addition to the delay rental due in the following January, petitioners have prepaid in December of each year delay rental which did not become due until the following February and March. Petitioners deducted the delay rental paid in December with respect to lease anniversary dates occurring in February and March of the following year.

The issue for decision is whether petitioners, who use the cash method of accounting, properly deducted prepayments of delay rental with respect to several oil and gas leases. Petitioners maintain that their tax treatment of prepayments of delay rental has been consistent and therefore that such treatment clearly reflects income.

This case concerns the deductibility of prepaid items solely under the authority of section 162 and section 446(b). Where the deductibility of prepaid items is based on those sections, we believe the test to be applied is clear and relatively straightforward. It is a three-pronged test and is based on well established Federal tax principles which generally are applicable to deductions claimed by cash method taxpayers. Each test is independent and must be satisfied.

The first requirement is that there must have been an actual payment of the item in question. A mere refundable deposit will not support a current deduction. A cash basis taxpayer must actually and irretrievably pay the expense during the taxable year in order to be entitled to a deduction under section 162(a). If the taxpayer retains the unilateral power to require a refund of the money or to redirect its use the transfer is considered a mere deposit and a deduction is not allowed in that year.

The second requirement is that there must have been a substantial business reason for making the prepayment in the year in which it was made. If the prepayment occurred simply to accelerate a tax deduction, no deduction will be allowed in the year of prepayment. This requirement is also based on section 162(a). Unless the prepayment of an item is for a valid business purpose, and not solely for a tax reduction, it "cannot fairly be characterized as an ordinary and necessary business expense" of the year of prepayment.

The third requirement is that prepayment of the item in question must not cause a material distortion in the taxpayer's taxable income in the year of prepayment. Respondent's authority under section 446(b) reaches not only taxpayer's overall method of accounting but also taxpayer's treatment of specific items of income and expense, and there is a heavy burden on the taxpayer to overcome respondent's determination under section 446(b) that taxpayer's method of accounting does not clearly reflect income.

The facts in this case must be analyzed in light of the above three requirements. The prepayments by petitioners of delay rental, at the time of prepayment, effected either an extension or renewal of the leases. No provision of the leases entitled petitioners to a refund of the prepaid delay rental. Accordingly, we find that the prepayments did not constitute mere deposits but irretrievable payments which satisfy the first requirement.

[As to the] issue of whether the prepayments of delay rental involved herein satisfy the second requirement: while there was a legal obligation to pay the delay rental on a periodic basis in order to obtain renewals of the leases, petitioners had no obligation to make delay rental payments in December when the lease renewal dates did not occur and payment of the delay rental was not due until February or March of the following year. Petitioners argue that the prepayments of delay rental were made in order to secure their rights under the leases. This argument is unpersuasive with respect to the prepayments in issue. The general practice of petitioners for all other months was to make the delay rental payments one month in advance. Such practice with respect to the delay rental due in February or March of each year in issue would have secured petitioners' rights under the leases. No reason or business necessity was offered by petitioners herein to explain why it was necessary to prepay sixty to ninety days in advance the delay rental due in February or March of the following year.

[T]he prepayments of delay rental which are in question herein do not satisfy the ordinary and necessary requirements of section 162.

In light of petitioners' failure to satisfy the second requirement, it is not necessary to apply the third requirement to the facts of this case.

Problems for Discussion

6–10. Martin, a cash method taxpayer, entered into a lease of farm land for the period December 1, 1973 to November 30, 1993, for use in his farming business. Yearly rent of $27,000 for the period running from December 1 to November 30 was payable on December 20 of each lease year. On December 20, 1973, Martin paid $27,000 rent for the lease year running from December 1, 1973 to November 30, 1974. Martin deducted this entire amount on his return for the taxable year 1973. Was the deduction appropriate?

Subchapter B: Accrual Method

SECTION 1: ALL-EVENTS TEST

Code: Section 461

Regulations: Section 1.446–1(c)(1)(ii), Section 1.461–4(g)

FLAMINGO RESORT, INC. v. UNITED STATES
664 F.2d 1387 (9th Cir. 1982)

Flamingo is a legal, licensed, gambling casino operating in the State of Nevada. The casino, an accrual basis taxpayer, excluded $676,432.00 of casino receivables in its 1967 tax return. The Commissioner required the accrual of these receivables and authorized an operating reserve fund for bad debts of $130,721. He then assessed a tax deficiency in the amount of $261,942.65, plus interest.

The receivables in dispute arose from uncollected loans extended by Flamingo in the course of its business. In order to facilitate its gambling operations, Flamingo extended credit to some of its customers. That line of credit was proffered only after an extensive credit check of the patron was conducted by the casino. The customer would sign a "marker" signifying his liability for the sum loaned. Approximately sixty percent of the casino's total play resulted from such credit extensions.

Extensive collection efforts were undertaken on behalf of Flamingo to receive payment of those outstanding casino receivables not repaid prior to the patron's departure. Flamingo's estimates of collectability of those receivables ranged as high as ninety-six percent. The extension of credit and high incidence of payment occurred despite the fact that Nevada does not recognize the legal enforceability of gambling debts.

The time of reporting of income of accrual basis taxpayers is governed by the "all events" test. "Under an accrual method of accounting, income is includible in gross income when all the events have occurred which fix the right to receive such income and the amount thereof can be determined with reasonable accuracy." Treas.Reg. s 1.451–1(a).

This case does not involve the question of "reasonable accuracy." Rather the issue is when does the right to receive the income which the "markers" represent become "fixed" for accrual purposes. Commentators and the courts have generally stated that the existence of a definite liability is a prerequisite to the accrual of any obligation. Flamingo, relying on these authorities, contends that because the persons who gave the "markers" for gambling purposes had no legal obligation to repay the casino, the "markers" being void as a matter of law, the "liability" they represent was not "fixed." Rather discharge of the "liability" was contingent on the customer's volition. Therefore, Flamingo should not be required to accrue the "markers."

Flamingo also relies on *H. Liebes & Co. v. Commissioner*, 90 F.2d 932 (9th Cir. 1937). There the issue was when should a debt due an accrual basis taxpayer by the government be accrued. The debt was owed by the government as the result of litigation. This court stated:

> The complete definition would therefore seem to be that income accrues to a taxpayer, when there arises to him a fixed or unconditional right to receive it, if there is a reasonable expectancy that the right will be converted into money or its equivalent.

The court held that the right was fixed immediately upon expiration of the time for appeal by the government from the judgment in favor of the taxpayer. At that point there was a reasonable expectancy that the claim would be converted into money even if the funds to satisfy the judgment had not been appropriated. Although *Liebes* clearly establishes that an obligation must be "fixed" and that there be a "reasonable expectancy" of the obligation being converted into cash or its equivalent, it did not hold that in all situations the existence of a legal liability to pay is a prerequisite to the existence of a "fixed or unconditional right" to receive payment.

Flamingo, as noted earlier, conducted approximately sixty percent of its business through extensions of credit, and its own estimates of collectability on outstanding casino receivables ranged as high as ninety-six percent. The lack of legal liability did not interfere with Flamingo's operation and it is doubtful that legal enforceability of the "markers" would or could increase its recovery rate. Under these circumstances, the obligations of Flamingo's patrons are as "fixed" as it is possible to be and, in fact, no less so than those of other businesses. Flamingo should not be heard to argue that it should be taxed differently from other legitimate businesses. Its inability to enforce its "markers" in court is not a sufficient burden to justify such a differential. The debts which the "markers" represent are, therefore, fixed; there is a reasonable expectancy of collection; and no contention has been made that the amounts cannot be determined with reasonable accuracy.

NOTES

1. *Contested liability exception.*—If an accrual method taxpayer contests its liability to pay an otherwise deductible amount, it may not deduct that amount until the contest is resolved or conceded, unless taxpayer complies with the special procedures of Code Section 461(f).

SECTION 2: ECONOMIC PERFORMANCE

Code: Section 461(h)

Regulations: Section 1.461-4

Until 1984, the all-events test governed accrual of both income and deductions. The addition of Code Section 461(h) in 1984, however, substantially limited accrual and deduction of current commitments to make payments in the future.

PROBLEMS FOR DISCUSSION

6–11. Chrysler, an accrual method automobile manufacturer, offers a warranty with each car that it sells. Assume that it can predict in advance, with high accuracy, the amount that its warranties will cost it in any given year. Chrysler seeks to deduct the expected warranty cost of servicing each car in the year in which the car is sold and the income it recognizes from selling the warranty with respect to that car is reported for federal tax purposes. Would doing so correctly reflect income? May it do so?

6–12. Harolds Club, an accrual method gambling casino in Reno, Nevada, operates progressive slot machines. A progressive slot machine provides a guaranteed jackpot amount that increases as money is gambled through the machine until the jackpot is won or until a maximum predetermined amount is reached. On July 1, Year 1, the guaranteed jackpot amount on one of Harolds Club's machines reaches the maximum predetermined amount of $50,000. On October 1, Year 2, the $50,000 jackpot is paid to Betty. When is the $50,000 deductible?

SECTION 3: PREPAID INCOME

AMERICAN AUTOMOBILE ASSOCIATION v. UNITED STATES
367 U.S. 687 (1961)

The Association is a national automobile club organized as a nonstock membership corporation. It provides a variety of services to the members of affiliated local automobile clubs and those of ten clubs which taxpayer itself directly operates as divisions, but such services are rendered solely upon a member's demand. Its income is derived primarily from dues paid one year in advance by members of the clubs. Memberships may commence or be renewed in any month of the year. For many years, the association has employed an accrual method of accounting and the calendar year as its taxable year. It is admitted that for its purposes the method used is in accord with generally accepted commercial accounting principles. The membership dues, as received, were deposited in the Association's bank accounts without restriction as to their use for any of its corporate purposes. However, for the Association's own accounting purposes, the dues were treated in its books as income received ratably over the 12–month membership period. The portions thereof ratably attributable to membership months occurring beyond the year of receipt, i.e., in a second calendar year, were reflected in the Association's books at the close of the first year as unearned or deferred income. Certain operating expenses were chargeable as prepaid membership cost and deducted ratably over the same periods of time as those over which dues were recognized as income.

The Court of Claims bottomed its opinion on *Automobile Club of Michigan v. Commissioner*, 353 U.S. 180 (1957). The holding of *Michigan* that the system of accounting [reporting dues as income in the months in which such dues entitled the payors to membership benefits] was "purely artificial" was based upon the finding that "substantially all services are performed only upon a member's demand and the taxpayer's performance was not related to fixed dates after the tax year." That is also true here.

It may be true that to the accountant the actual incidence of cost in serving an individual member in exchange for his individual dues is inconsequential, or, from the viewpoint of commercial accounting, unessential to determination and disclosure of the overall financial condition of the Association. That "irregularity," however, is highly relevant to the clarity of an accounting system which defers receipt, as earned income, of dues to a taxable period in which no, some, or all the services paid for by those dues may or may not be rendered. The Code exacts its revenue from the individual member's dues which, no one disputes, constitute income. When their receipt as earned income is recognized ratably over two calendar years, without regard to correspondingly fixed individual expense or performance justification, but consistently with overall experience, their accounting doubtless presents a rather accurate image of the total financial structure, but fails to respect the criteria of annual tax accounting and may be rejected by the Commissioner.

[I]n performing the function of business accounting the method employed by the Association "is in accord with generally accepted commercial accounting principles and practices." It is not to hold that for income tax purposes it so clearly reflects income as to be binding on the Treasury. Likewise, other findings merely reflecting statistical computations of average monthly cost per member on a group or pool basis are without determinate significance to our decision that the federal revenue cannot, without legislative consent and over objection of the Commissioner, be made to depend upon average experience in rendering performance and turning a profit. Indeed, such tabulations themselves demonstrate the inadequacy from an income tax standpoint of the pro rata method of allocating each year's membership dues in equal monthly installments not in fact related to the expenses incurred. Not only did individually incurred expenses actually vary from month to month, but even the average expense varied—recognition of income nonetheless remaining ratably constant. Although the findings below seem to indicate that it would produce substantially the same result as that of the system of ratable monthly recognition actually employed, we consider similarly unsatisfactory, from an income tax standpoint, allocation of monthly dues to gross monthly income to the extent of actual service expenditures for the same month computed on a group or pool basis. In addition, the Association's election in 1954 to change its monthly recognition formula to one which treats one-half of the dues as income in the year of receipt and the other half as income received in the subsequent year, without regard to month of payment, only more clearly indicates the artificiality of its method, at least so far as controlling tax purposes are concerned.

[I]t appears that Congress has long been aware of the problem this case presents. In 1954 it enacted § 452 and § 462, but quickly repealed them. Since that time Congress has authorized the desired accounting only in the instance of prepaid subscription income, which, as was pointed out in *Michigan*, is ratably earned by performance on "publication dates after the tax year." It has refused to enlarge § 455 to include prepaid membership dues. At the very least, this background indicates congressional recognition of the complications inherent in the problem and its seriousness to the general revenue. We must leave to the Congress the fashioning of a rule which, in any event, must have wide ramifications. The Committees of the Congress have standing committees expertly grounded in tax problems, with jurisdiction covering the whole field of taxation and facilities for studying considerations of policy as between the various taxpayers and the necessities of the general revenues. The validity of the long-established policy of the Court in deferring, where possible, to congressional procedures in the tax field is clearly indicated in this case. Finding only that, in light of existing provisions not specifically authorizing it, the exercise of the Commissioner's discretion in rejecting the Association's accounting system was not unsound, we need not anticipate what will be the product of further "study of this entire problem."

NOTES

1. *Partial statutory relief.*—Congress has limited the effect of *American Automobile Association* by Code Sections 455 (prepaid subscription income) and 456 (prepaid membership organization dues). The latter was added shortly after *AAA* was decided, and reversed *AAA* with respect to the American Automobile Association itself.

2. *Deferral of prepaid income notwithstanding* AAA.—*Automobile Club of Michigan, AAA,* and *Schlude v. Commissioner,* 372 U.S. 128 (1963), are sometimes cited for the proposition "that prepaid service income is taxable in

the year received even though the services are to be performed in the future." *Miele v. Commissioner*, 72 T.C. 284 (1979). This is not always so. In *Artnell Co. v. Commissioner*, 400 F.2d 981 (7th Cir. 1968), for example, the court held that "there must be situations where the deferral technique will so clearly reflect income that the Court will find an abuse of discretion if the commissioner rejects it" and remanded for a determination of "whether the White Sox method of accounting did clearly reflect its income," where the time and extent of performance of the future services were certain. *See generally* Luke Roosevelt Hornblower, *The Empire Strikes Out: The IRS & The Ambiguities of Tax Accounting*, 135 TAX NOTES 1045 (2012).

PROBLEMS FOR DISCUSSION

6–13. Assume that in November, Year 1, the AAA receives the annual dues of a member for the 12-month period extending from December, Year 1, to November, Year 2, inclusive. What portion of the dues must be reported in Year 1? Assuming that the AAA can predict its average monthly cost per member with high accuracy, may the AAA deduct the associated expected costs at the same time that it reports the corresponding income?

Subchapter C: Section 83

Code: Section 83

Code Section 83 is one of the most important provisions governing the taxability of employment incentive grants—property, typically company stock, transferred by an employer to an employee to induce him to work harder and stay with the company. Such property is commonly either subject to a substantial risk of forfeiture or not transferrable. Thus, for example, a company might give its employee (or allow the employee to purchase at a discount) company stock subject to the condition that if the employee leaves within a specified period, the stock must be returned.

Subsection (a) sets forth the general rule. At the moment the property becomes transferable or ceases to be subject to a substantial risk of forfeiture, the value of the property at that moment, less any amount the recipient has paid for it, is includible as compensation income. Assume, for example, that a corporation sells 1,000 shares of its stock to its employee for $10 per share. At the time of sale, the stock is worth $15 per share. The sale is subject to a condition: if the employee leaves the employment of the company for any reason before five years have elapsed, the corporation may repurchase the stock for the same $10 per share. Under subsection (a), no income is included in the employee's income at the time of sale. Five years later, when the condition lapses, the employee recognizes compensation income equal to the difference between the value of the stock at the moment of lapse and the amount she had paid for it. Assume the stock is worth $70 per share when the condition lapses. If so, under subsection (a), she recognizes $60 per share of compensation income—a total of $60,000—at the moment of lapse and takes the stock with a basis of $70 per share.

Subsection (b), however, permits a taxpayer in this situation to elect immediate taxation in the year she receives the restricted property. In our hypothetical, if the employee makes the Section 83(b) election, she recognizes $5 per share of compensation income—$5,000 total—at the moment she purchases the shares, taking the stock with a basis of $15 per share. Five years later, when the condition lapses, she does not recognize any further income by reason of the lapse. If she were to sell her shares at that time, she would recognize the remaining $55 per share as long-term capital gain—taxable at a maximum rate of 15%. But she does not recognize any such gain unless and until she sells the shares.

A Section 83(b) election thus fixes the amount of compensation income taxpayer recognizes by reason of the arrangement. Any further appreciation of the transferred property will likely be taxed at capital gains rates. There are two disadvantages, however, to the election. First and most obviously, taxpayer must pay tax earlier. Second, pursuant to subsection (b)(1), if the property is later "forfeited," no deduction is allowed with respect to such forfeiture. Thus, in our hypothetical, if the employee makes the Section 83(b) election, recognizes the $5,000 of compensation income required by that election, later leaves the company within the five year period, and is forced to sell the shares back to the company at $10 per share, she does not get an offsetting $5 per share loss. This loss disallowance rule is inconsistent with Haig–Simons and the correct measurement of taxpayer's income.

Regardless of whether the employee makes the Section 83(b) election, the employer cannot take a deduction for the relevant compensation until the corresponding income is includible to the employee—that is, (1) if a Section 83(b) election is made, at the time of the initial transfer, or (2) if no such election is made, when the restriction lapses or the property becomes transferable. In other words, the employee's election determines the timing of the deduction for her employer.

PROBLEMS FOR DISCUSSION

6–14. As an incentive to its CEO, Megacorp gives her 500,000 shares of its stock in Year 1. At the time of transfer, the stock is worth $10 per share. The transfer is subject to the condition that if the CEO leaves Megacorp's employment for any reason before five years have elapsed, the stock will be forfeited.

   a. Assume the stock is worth $40 per share when the condition lapses. What consequences to the CEO if she does not make the Section 83(b) election? What consequences to the CEO if she does? What if she leaves the company before the five year period has elapsed?

b. Assume the stock is worth $2 per share when the condition lapses. What consequences to the CEO if she does not make the Section 83(b) election? What consequences to the CEO if she does? What if she leaves the company before the five year period has elapsed?

c. What consequences to Megacorp in each of the preceding scenarios?

CHAPTER 7

RECOVERIES

■ ■ ■

Subchapter A: Recoveries With Respect to Items With Basis

SECTION 1: RECOVERY OF BASIS v. INCOME

REV. RUL. 81-277
1981-2 C.B. 14

The payment by a contractor of a sum of money to a buyer in exchange for a release of the buyer's claims against the contractor for failure to fulfill the contract for construction of a plant constitutes a return of capital rather than gross income to the buyer. The cost basis of the plant is adjusted downward to reflect the payment.

ISSUE

Does payment by a contractor of a sum of money to a buyer in exchange for a release of the buyer's claims against the contractor for failure to fulfill a contract result in income to the buyer or a return of capital?

FACTS

In 1969 corporation M agreed to construct a nuclear generating plant for corporation P at a price of 250x dollars. The construction contract specified that M would provide, at no additional cost to P, any additional items that later were determined to be necessary to deliver a complete, safe, licensable, fully operational plant. During the construction period regulatory agencies imposed stricter environmental safeguards on nuclear generating plants than were in effect at the time the contract was signed. Disputes arose between M and P over M's obligation to provide for stricter safeguards and to include them as part of the delivered plant at the original contract price. To the date of the dispute, P has paid M 230x dollars of the contract price of 250x dollars.

The parties eventually settled their dispute by agreeing that the terms of the 1969 contract must be met by both parties. They also agreed that M was responsible to deliver a plant that met the stricter environmental safeguards and that it would cost an additional 40x dollars. P was required to forward 20x dollars to M to complete P's payment obligation under the contract.

In light of these agreements, P paid M 20x dollars, the value of the work performed under the contract but unpaid at the time of the settlement agreement. M and P 40x dollars representing the estimated cost to satisfy the stricter environmental standards rather than completing the plant's construction. Both parties then executed general releases to each other and M ceased its construction activities.

P then contracted with a third party to finish construction of the nuclear generating plant. P eventually had to pay the third party 50x dollars to obtain a plant that satisfied the regulatory agencies' standards.

LAW AND ANALYSIS

Section 61 of the Internal Revenue Code provides that gross income means all income from whatever source derived, including income realized in any form.

Section 1012 of the Code provides that the basis of property is usually its cost. Section 1.1012–1(a) of the Income Tax Regulations provides that cost is the amount paid for property in cash or other property. Section 1016(a) provides that adjustments are made to the basis of property for expenditures, receipts, losses, or other items properly chargeable to the capital account.

Inherent in section 61 of the Code is the concept of economic gain. For a taxpayer to have income under section 61, there must be an economic gain that benefits the taxpayer personally. United States v. Gotcher, 401 F.2d 118 (5th Cir. 1968).

The determination of whether the proceeds received in a lawsuit or received in settlement of a lawsuit constitute income under section 61 of the Code depends on the nature of the claim and the actual basis for recovery. If the recovery represents damages for lost profits, it is taxed as ordinary income. If, however, the recovery is treated as a replacement of capital, the damages received from the lawsuit are treated as a return of capital and are not taxable as income. Payments by the one causing a loss that do no more than restore a taxpayer to the position he or she was in before the loss was incurred are not includible in gross income because there is no economic gain.

In the present situation, the effect of the settlement agreement was that M would compensate P for M's failure to provide a fully operational and licensable plant for 250x dollars as agreed upon under the contract. The payment from M to P of 40x dollars represents the estimated present damages P has incurred because of the breach of contract, determined under the settlement agreement as the estimated additional costs needed to satisfy new regulatory standards that were necessary to deliver a complete, safe, licensable, fully operational plant as required under the contract. P has received no economic gain as a result of the 40x dollars payment and is merely being made whole under the contract. P is being restored to the position that it would have been in if M had fulfilled the terms of the contract.

HOLDING

The 40x dollars payment from M to P represents a return of capital and is not income to P. The basis of the plant in P's hands should be adjusted downward to 210x dollars from its cost basis of 250x dollars (230x dollars plus the 20x dollars payment from P to M) to reflect the 40x dollars payments, and adjusted upward to 260x dollars when P incurs expenses of 50x dollars to finish construction of the plant.

Problems for Discussion

7–1. Dolores, a romance novel author, purchases a home for $200,000. Three months after she moves in, her roof begins to leak badly during a severe thunderstorm. She sues the builder and recovers $50,000. Does she have income? What is her basis in the house? Does it matter what damages she alleges in her complaint?

7–2. Joe the Plumber enters into a contract with a Hollywood magnate to refit the magnate's entire home plumbing system. He expects to make a total of $150,000 in profits on the contract. The contract requires partial payment along the way as specified benchmarks are met. Part way through the work, after Joe has earned $70,000 but been paid only $40,000, a competitor makes false and disparaging remarks to the magnate about Joe, as a result of which the magnate cancels the contract and refuses to pay Joe anything more. Joe sues the competitor for interference with an advantageous business relationship and defamation, among other things, and recovers $110,000 of compensatory damages. How much income does Joe recognize? Does it matter what method of accounting he uses?

7–3. While parked in her law school parking lot, Francine's car is hit and rendered undriveable by another student, who has pulled an all-nighter to get an assignment in on time and is not fit to drive. Before making any repairs, she recovers $10,000 from the other student's insurance company. In each of the following scenarios, how much income does she recognize, and what is her final basis in the car? (For purposes of this problem, assume that all expenditures are capitalized—that is, included in basis—and ignore Code Section 1033.)

   a. She had purchased the car for $15,000. The $10,000 exactly compensates her for the required repairs, which are made by a collision repair shop.

   b. She had purchased the car for $15,000. The $10,000 is to compensate her for the decline in its fair market value by reason of the accident.

Because she had previously worked in a car body shop, she is able to fix the car herself for only $2,000 of out-of-pocket expenses.

c. She had purchased the car for $4,000 and fixed it up herself without incurring any out-of-pocket expenses. Immediately prior to the accident, the car's fair market value was $15,000. The $10,000 exactly compensates her for the required repairs, which are made by a collision repair shop.

d. She had purchased the car for $4,000 and fixed it up herself without incurring any out-of-pocket expenses. Immediately prior to the accident, the car's fair market value was $15,000. The $10,000 is to compensate her for the decline in its fair market value by reason of the accident. Because she had previously worked in a car body shop, she is able to fix the car herself for only $2,000 of out-of-pocket expenses.

SECTION 2: INSTALLMENT SALES

Code: Section 453

When a taxpayer sells property in exchange for an installment note, he may face a tax liability on the resulting gain without receiving any cash with which to pay that tax liability. Code Section 453 therefore allows income from certain installment sales to be taken into account under the installment method.

Under the installment method total gain realized on an installment sale is spread pro rata over the expected payment stream. Assume, for example, that a taxpayer sells land in which he has a basis of $300,000 for a total purchase price of $500,000, realizing $200,000 of gain. Under the purchase agreement, the total purchase price is to be paid in two equal installments—$250,000 in Year 1 and $250,000 in Year 2. Under the installment method, taxpayer spreads his total gain realized pro rata over those two installments. As a result, he recognizes $100,000 of his gain in Year 1 and the remaining $100,000 in Year 2.

The installment method is not available respect to sales of inventory or other "dealer dispositions" (Code Section 453(b)(2)), sales of personal property under revolving credit plans (Code Section 453(k)(1), or sales of publicly traded stock or securities (Code Section 453(k)(2)). Even if it applies, if the obligation is later pledged to secure indebtedness and the sales price is more than $150,000, receipt of the proceeds of such indebtedness may be treated as receipts on the obligation itself, triggering early gain. Code Sections 453A(b)(1) and (d). If in fact the amount of all such obligations exceeds $5,000,000, interest may accrue on tax liabilities deferred. Code Sections 453A(b)(2) and (c).

Subchapter B: Recoveries With Respect to Items Without Basis

SECTION 1: DAMAGES ON ACCOUNT OF PERSONAL PHYSICAL INJURY OR SICKNESS

Code: Section 104(a)(2)

MURPHY v. INTERNAL REVENUE SERVICE (MURPHY II)

493 F.3d 170 (D.C. Cir. 2007)

Marrita Murphy brought this suit to recover income taxes she paid on the compensatory damages for emotional distress and loss of reputation she was awarded in an administrative action she brought against her former employer. Murphy contends that under § 104(a)(2), her award should have been excluded from her gross income because it was compensation received "on account of personal physical injuries or physical sickness." She also maintains that, in any event, her award is not part of her gross income. Finally, she argues that taxing her award subjects her to an unapportioned direct tax in violation of Article I, Section 9 of the Constitution of the United States.

We reject Murphy's argument in all aspects. We hold, first, that Murphy's compensation was not "received ... on account of personal physical injuries" excludable from gross income under § 104(a)(2). Second, we conclude gross income as defined by § 61 includes compensatory damages for non-physical injuries. Third, we hold that a tax upon such damages is within the Congress's power to tax.

In 1994 Murphy filed a complaint with the Department of Labor alleging that her former employer, the New York Air National Guard (NYANG), in violation of various whistle-blower statutes, had "blacklisted" her and provided unfavorable references to potential employers after she had complained to state authorities of environmental hazards on a NYANG airbase. The Secretary of Labor determined the NYANG had unlawfully discriminated and retaliated against Murphy, and remanded her case to an Administrative Law Judge "for findings on compensatory damages."

On remand Murphy submitted evidence that she had suffered both mental and physical injuries as a result of the NYANG's blacklisting her. A psychologist testified that Murphy had sustained both "somatic" and "emotional" injuries, basing his conclusion in part upon medical and dental records showing Murphy had "bruxism," or teeth grinding often associated with stress, which may cause permanent tooth damage. Noting that Murphy also suffered from other "physical manifestations of stress" including "anxiety attacks, shortness of breath, and dizziness," and that Murphy testified she "could not concentrate, stopped talking to friends, and no longer enjoyed 'anything in life,'" the ALJ recommended compensatory damages totaling $70,000, of which $45,000 was for "past and future emotional distress," and $25,000 was for "injury to [Murphy's] vocational reputation" from having been blacklisted. None of the award was for lost wages or diminished earning capacity.

On her tax return for 2000, Murphy included the $70,000 award in her "gross income." As a result, she paid $20,665 in taxes on the award. [She then] filed an amended return in which she sought a refund of the $20,665 based upon § 104(a)(2) of the IRC, which provides that "gross income does not include ... damages ... received ... on account of personal physical injuries or physical sickness." In support of her amended return, Murphy submitted copies of her dental and medical records. [T]he Internal Revenue Service denied her request for a refund. The district court rejected all of Murphy's claims on the merits and granted summary judgment for the Government.

In *Murphy v. IRS*, 460 F.3d 79 (2006) (Murphy I), we concluded Murphy's award was not exempt from taxation pursuant to § 104(a)(2), but also was not "income" within the meaning of the Sixteenth Amendment, and therefore reversed the decision of the district court. The Government petitioned for rehearing en banc, arguing for the first time that, even if Murphy's award is not income, there is no constitutional impediment to taxing it because a tax on the award is not a direct tax and is imposed uniformly. In view of the importance of the issue thus belatedly raised, the panel *sua sponte* vacated its judgment and reheard the case. In the present opinion, we affirm the judgment of the district court based upon the newly argued ground that Murphy's award, even if it is not income within the meaning of the Sixteenth Amendment, is within the reach of the congressional power to tax under Article I, Section 8 of the Constitution.

Section 104(a) provides that "gross income does not include the amount of any damages (other than punitive damages) received ... on account of personal physical injuries or physical sickness."

Murphy points both to her psychologist's testimony that she had experienced "somatic" and "body" injuries "as a result of NYANG's blacklisting [her]," and to the American Heritage Dictionary, which defines "somatic" as "relating to, or affecting the body, especially as distinguished from a body part, the mind, or the environment." Murphy further argues the dental records she submitted to the IRS proved she has suffered permanent damage to her teeth. Murphy contends that "substantial physical problems caused by emotional distress are considered physical injuries or physical sickness."

For its part, the Government argues Murphy's focus upon the word "physical" in § 104(a)(2) is misplaced; more important is the phrase "on account of." In *O'Gilvie v. United States*, the Supreme Court read

§ 104(a)(2) [to be] "applicable only to those personal injury lawsuit damages that were awarded by reason of, or because of, the personal injuries." The Court specifically rejected a "but-for" formulation in favor of a "stronger causal connection." The Government therefore concludes Murphy must demonstrate she was awarded damages "because of" her physical injuries, which the Government claims she has failed to do.

Indeed, as the Government points out, the ALJ expressly recommended, and the Board expressly awarded, compensatory damages "because of" Murphy's nonphysical injuries. In describing the ALJ's proposed award as "reasonable," the Board stated Murphy was to receive "$45,000 for mental pain and anguish" and "$25,000 for injury to professional reputation." Murphy no doubt suffered from certain physical manifestations of emotional distress, but the record clearly indicates the Board awarded her compensation only "for mental pain and anguish" and "for injury to professional reputation." [W]e cannot say the Board, notwithstanding its clear statements to the contrary, actually awarded damages because of Murphy's bruxism and other physical manifestations of stress. At best—and this is doubtful—at best the Board and the ALJ may have considered her physical injuries indicative of the severity of the emotional distress for which the damages were awarded, but her physical injuries themselves were not the reason for the award. The Board thus having left no room for doubt about the grounds for her award, we conclude Murphy's damages were not "awarded by reason of, or because of, ... [physical] personal injuries". Therefore, § 104(a)(2) does not permit Murphy to exclude her award from gross income.

Murphy and the Government agree that for Murphy's award to be taxable, it must be part of her "gross income" as defined by § 61(a) of the IRC, which states in relevant part: "gross income means all income from whatever source derived."

Murphy argues her award is not a gain or an accession to wealth and therefore not part of gross income. Noting the Supreme Court has long recognized "the principle that a restoration of capital [i]s not income; hence it [falls] outside the definition of 'income' upon which the law impose[s] a tax," Murphy contends a damage award for personal injuries—including nonphysical injuries—should be viewed as a return of a particular form of capital—"human capital," as it were. In her view, the Supreme Court in *Glenshaw Glass* acknowledged the relevance of the human capital concept for tax purposes. There, in holding that punitive damages for personal injury were "gross income" under the predecessor to § 61, the Court stated:

> "The long history of ... holding personal injury recoveries nontaxable on the theory that they roughly correspond to a return of capital cannot support exemption of punitive damages following injury to property.... Damages for personal injury are by definition compensatory only. Punitive damages, on the other hand, cannot be considered a restoration of capital for taxation purposes."

By implication, Murphy argues, damages for personal injury are a "restoration of capital."

[T]he Government argues that even if the concept of human capital is built into § 61, Murphy's award is nonetheless taxable because Murphy has no tax basis in her human capital. Under the IRC, a taxpayer's gain upon the disposition of property is the difference between the "amount realized" from the disposition and his basis in the property, 26 U.S.C. § 1001, defined as "the cost of such property," *id.* § 1012, adjusted "for expenditures, receipts, losses, or other items, properly chargeable to [a] capital account," *id.* § 1016(a)(1). The Government asserts, "The Code does not allow individuals to claim a basis in their human capital"; accordingly, Murphy's gain is the full value of the award.

[I]n 1996 the Congress amended § 104(a) to narrow the exclusion to amounts received on account of "personal physical injuries or physical sickness" from "personal injuries or sickness," and explicitly to provide that "emotional distress shall not be treated as a physical injury or physical sickness," thus making clear that an award received on account of emotional distress is not excluded from gross income under § 104(a)(2). As this amendment, which narrows the exclusion, would have no effect whatsoever if such damages were not included within the ambit of § 61, and as we must presume that "[w]hen Congress acts to amend a statute, ... it intends its amendment to have real and substantial effect," the 1996 amendment of § 104(a) strongly suggests § 61 should be read to include an award for damages from nonphysical harms.

For the 1996 amendment of § 104(a) to "make sense," gross income in § 61(a) must, and we therefore hold it does, include an award for nonphysical damages such as Murphy received, regardless whether the award is an accession to wealth.

The taxing power of the Congress is established by Article I, Section 8 of the Constitution: "The Congress shall have power to lay and collect taxes, duties, imposts and excises." There are two limitations on this power. First, as the same section goes on to provide, "all duties, imposts and excises shall be uniform throughout the United States." Second, as provided in Section 9 of that same Article, "No capitation, or other direct, tax shall be laid, unless in proportion to the census or enumeration herein before directed to be taken." We now consider whether the tax laid upon Murphy's award violates either of these two constraints.

Over the years, courts have considered numerous claims that one or another nonapportioned tax is a direct tax and therefore unconstitutional. Although these cases have not definitively marked the boundary between taxes that must be apportioned and taxes that need not be, some characteristics of each may be discerned.

Only three taxes are definitely known to be direct: (1) a capitation, U.S. CONST. art. I, § 9, (2) a tax upon real property, and (3) a tax upon personal property. Such direct taxes are laid upon one's "general ownership of property," as contrasted with excise taxes laid "upon a particular use or enjoyment of property or the shifting from one to another of any power or privilege incidental to the ownership or enjoyment of property."

Murphy and the *amici* supporting her argue the dividing line between direct and indirect taxes is based upon the ultimate incidence of the tax; if the tax cannot be shifted to someone else, as a capitation cannot, then it is a direct tax; but if the burden can be passed along through a higher price, as a sales tax upon a consumable good can be, then the tax is indirect. This, she argues, was the distinction drawn when the Constitution was ratified. As it is clear that Murphy cannot shift her tax burden to anyone else, per Murphy and the *amici*, it must be a direct tax.

The Government, unsurprisingly, backs a different approach; by its lights, only "taxes that are capable of apportionment in the first instance, specifically, capitation taxes and taxes on land," are direct taxes. The Government maintains that this is how the term was generally understood at the time. Moreover, it suggests, this understanding is more in line with the underlying purpose of the tax and the apportionment clauses, which were drafted in the intense light of experience under the Articles of Confederation.

We find it more appropriate to ask whether the tax laid upon Murphy's award is more akin, on the one hand, to a capitation or a tax upon one's ownership of property, or, on the other hand, more like a tax upon a use of property, a privilege, an activity, or a transaction. Even if we assume one's human capital should be treated as personal property, it does not appear that this tax is upon ownership; rather, as the Government points out, Murphy is taxed only after she receives a compensatory award, which makes the tax seem to be laid upon a transaction. Murphy's situation seems akin to an involuntary conversion of assets; she was forced to surrender some part of her mental health and reputation in return for monetary damages. *Cf.* 26 U.S.C. § 1033 (property involuntarily converted into money is taxed to extent of gain recognized).

The Congress may not implement an excise tax that is not "uniform throughout the United States." U.S. CONST. art. I, § 8, cl. 1. A "tax is uniform when it operates with the same force and effect in every place where the subject of it is found." The tax laid upon an award of damages for a nonphysical personal injury operates with "the same force and effect" throughout the United States and therefore satisfies the requirement of uniformity.

For the foregoing reasons, we conclude (1) Murphy's compensatory award was not received on account of personal physical injuries, and therefore is not exempt from taxation pursuant to § 104(a)(2) of the IRC; (2) the award is part of her "gross income," as defined by § 61 of the IRC; and (3) the tax upon the award is an excise and not a direct tax subject to the apportionment requirement of Article I, Section 9 of the Constitution. The tax is uniform throughout the United States and therefore passes constitutional muster.

STADNYK v. COMMISSIONER

105 A.F.T.R.2d 2010–1130, 367 Fed. Appx. 586 (6th Cir. 2010)

On December 11, 1996, Petitioners purchased a used 1990 Geo Storm from Nicholasville Road Auto Sales, Inc. for $3,430.00. Brenda Stadnyk tendered two checks to Nicholasville Auto as partial payment, check number 1080 for $100 and check number 1087 for $1,100, from a checking account with Bank One, Kentucky, N.A. After Petitioners drove approximately seven miles from the dealership, the car broke down. Petitioners spent $479.78 to repair the car. They attempted to call Nicholasville Auto about the Geo Storm, but their calls were ignored, placed on hold for long periods of time, and not returned.

Because of their dissatisfaction with the car, Mrs. Stadnyk contacted Bank One to place a stop payment order on check number 1087 for $1,100. Bank One's record of the stop payment order indicates "dissatisfied purchase" as the reason for the stop payment. However, Bank One incorrectly stamped the check "NSF" for insufficient funds and returned it to Nicholasville Auto. On February 4, 1997, Nicholasville Auto filed a criminal complaint against Mrs. Stadnyk for issuing and passing a worthless check in the amount of $1,100.

At approximately 6:00 p.m. on February 23, 1997, officers of the Fayette County Sheriff's Department arrested Mrs. Stadnyk at her home in the presence of her husband, her daughter, and a family friend, and transported her to the Fayette County Detention Center. She arrived at the detention center at approximately 6:30 p.m., and she was handcuffed, photographed, and confined to a holding area. At approximately 11:00 p.m., Mrs. Stadnyk was transferred to Jessamine County Jail, where she was searched via pat-down and use of an electric wand. Mrs. Stadnyk was required to undress to her undergarments, remove her brassiere in the presence of officers, and put on an orange jumpsuit. She was released on bail at approximately 2:00 a.m. on February 24, 1997. On April 23, 1997, Mrs. Stadnyk was indicted for "theft by deception over $300.00" based on the returned check marked for insufficient funds. These charges were later dropped.

Mrs. Stadnyk testified that she did not suffer any physical injury as a result of her arrest and detention. According to Mrs. Stadnyk, nobody put their hands on her, grabbed her, jerked her around, bruised her, or hurt her. As a result of the incident, Mrs. Stadnyk visited a psychologist every 1.5 to two weeks for approximately eight sessions. The cost of these sessions was covered by Mrs. Stadnyk's insurance and employer. Mrs. Stadnyk did not pay any out-of-pocket medical expenses for physical injury or mental distress as a result of the arrest and detention.

On August 25, 1999, Mrs. Stadnyk filed a Complaint against J.R. Maze, the owner of Nicholasville Auto, Nicholasville Auto, and Bank One. On July 5, 2000, she filed a First Amended Complaint, alleging that Bank

One breached its fiduciary duty of care by improperly and negligently marking her check "NSF" for insufficient funds. Mrs. Stadnyk's First Amended Complaint also included the following claims against J.R. Maze and Nicholasville Auto: malicious prosecution, abuse of process, false imprisonment, defamation, and outrageous conduct. The First Amended Complaint repeated and incorporated by reference these allegations against Bank One.

On March 7, 2002, Bank One agreed to pay Mrs. Stadnyk $49,000 to settle her claims and provide her with a letter of apology. In return, Mrs. Stadnyk agreed to dismiss her complaint against Bank One. The mediation agreement form stated that "Bank One shall pay the total sum of $49,000, by 3/15/02, by official check" and that "[t]he suit shall be dismissed with prejudice with each party to pay their own costs & fees." It contained no language indicating the purpose for which the settlement was paid. On March 14, 2002, Bank One issued a check to Mrs. Stadnyk for $49,000, and on May 3, 2002, Mrs. Stadnyk's complaint against Bank One was dismissed with prejudice.

Petitioners argue that the $49,000 settlement award Mrs. Stadnyk received from Bank One does not classify as income under I.R.C. § 61(a) because Mrs. Stadnyk was made whole—not enriched—by the compensatory damages. Petitioners cite to *Glenshaw* for the proposition that the term "income" for tax purposes is commonly defined as all "accessions to wealth, clearly realized, and over which the taxpayers have complete dominion." According to Petitioners, because Mrs. Stadnyk's award was compensation for something she had lost, not an "accession to wealth," her settlement award does not classify as income under § 61(a).

The fact that the damages award is compensatory does not make it nontaxable. The Supreme Court has found compensatory settlement awards that are not otherwise excluded to be taxable as gross income under I.R.C. § 61(a). While the Supreme Court has never explicitly ruled that compensation received for personal injury is income pursuant to § 61(a), nothing in the Court's analysis of the scope of § 61(a) supports Petitioners' argument that the Court would come to a different conclusion in the context of personal injury awards than in the context of backpay. Settlement awards for back pay, like settlement awards for personal injury, are compensatory in nature because they make the recipient whole.

Furthermore, if damages awards received on account of personal injury were not income, there would be no need for the exclusion laid out in § 104(a)(2), which exempts from income taxation any damages received on account of personal physical injuries or physical sickness.

Accordingly, Mrs. Stadnyk's $49,000 settlement classifies as gross income under § 61(a), and Petitioners can only avoid paying taxes on the damages award if it falls under an exclusion.

The exclusion from § 61(a) at issue in the instant case is contained in § 104(a)(2), which permits taxpayers to exclude from income "the amount of any damages received (whether by suit or agreement and whether as lump sums or as periodic payments) on account of personal physical injuries or physical sickness."

The Supreme Court has held that a taxpayer must meet two independent requirements before a recovery may be excluded under § 104(a)(2). "First, the taxpayer must demonstrate that the underlying cause of action giving rise to the recovery is based upon tort or tort type rights; and second, the taxpayer must show that the damages were received on account of personal injuries or sickness." To satisfy the second prong, the taxpayer must present "concrete evidence demonstrating the precise causal connection" between the taxpayer's asserted personal injuries and the settlement she received.

In 1996, I.R.C. § 104(a)(2) was amended to add the word "physical" to the phrase "personal injuries or sickness." Prior to the amendment, I.R.C. § 104(a)(2) encompassed damages compensating all personal injuries, including non-physical injuries. However, the amendment to I.R.C. § 104(a)(2) expressly limits the type of damages excludable from income to those received "on account of personal physical injuries or physical sickness," and expressly states that emotional distress does not constitute a physical injury or sickness.

Petitioners argue that their settlement award satisfies the two-part test laid out in *Schleier*, and, thus, may be excluded from taxation under § 104(a)(2).

Under the first prong, the question is whether Mrs. Stadnyk's claims against Bank One giving rise to her recovery are based upon tort or tort type rights. Based on the finding that Mrs. Stadnyk alleged tort claims against Bank One in her complaint, we conclude that Mrs. Stadnyk's settlement with Bank One was based on tort or tort type rights.

Having satisfied the first prong, to obtain an exclusion under § 104(a)(2), Mrs. Stadnyk must show that she sustained the damages on account of personal physical injuries or sickness. Under the 1996 Amendment, I.R.C. § 104(a)(2) expressly limits the type of damages excludable from income to personal physical injuries or physical sickness and expressly states that emotional distress does not constitute a physical injury or sickness. Kentucky courts have defined false imprisonment as "any deprivation of the liberty of one person by another or detention for however short a time without such person's consent and against his will, whether done by actual violence, threats or otherwise." The tort of false imprisonment protects personal interest in freedom from physical restraint; the interest is "in a sense a mental one" and the injury is "in large part a mental one."

During her deposition, Mrs. Stadnyk testified that she did not suffer any physical injury as a result of her arrest and detention. According to Mrs. Stadnyk, nobody carrying out her arrest or detention put their hands on her, grabbed her, jerked her around, bruised her, or hurt her. Petitioners' brief concedes that the actions of the police were proper and that Mrs. Stadnyk presumes that she was treated in the same manner as anyone else arrested for passing a bad check. Nothing in the record suggests that Mrs. Stadnyk suffered physical, as opposed to emotional, injuries as a result of Bank One's actions.

The Tax Court correctly noted that "[t]he damages sought by [Mrs. Stadnyk] against Bank One are stated in terms of recovery for nonphysical personal injuries: [e]motional distress, mortification, humiliation, mental anguish, and damage to reputation." These are all emotional injuries, and are thus not excludable under § 104(a)(2).

Despite Mrs. Stadnyk's testimony, Petitioners argue that Mrs. Stadnyk suffered a physical injury because "[p]hysical restraint and detention and the resulting deprivation of [Mrs. Stadnyk's] personal liberty is [itself] a physical injury . . . that Mrs. Stadnyk endured for an eight hour period." Petitioners further argue that Mrs. Stadnyk suffered physical damages in addition to emotional damages because "to be falsely imprisoned, the person must first be physically restrained or held against their will" and "[t]hus the damages received from false imprisonment arise from the person's physical loss of their freedom and the mental suffering and humiliation that accompany this deprivation."

In other words, Petitioners are asking the Court to create a per se rule that every false imprisonment claim necessarily involves a physical injury, even though physical injury is not a required element of false imprisonment under Kentucky law. To be sure, a false imprisonment claim may cause a physical injury, such as an injured wrist as a result of being handcuffed. But the mere fact that false imprisonment involves a physical act—restraining the victim's freedom—does not mean that the victim is necessarily physically injured as a result of that physical act. In the instant case, Mrs. Stadnyk unequivocally testified that she suffered no physical injuries as a result of her physical restraint. Thus, Petitioners have failed to establish that Mrs. Stadnyk suffered from personal physical injuries or physical sickness.

In addition, the Supreme Court has construed the "on account of" phrase to require a direct causal link between the physical injury and the damages recovery in order to qualify for the income exclusion. This direct causal connection must be more than a "but for" link, because a "but for" analysis would "bring virtually all personal injury lawsuit damages within the scope of the provision, since: but for the personal injury, there would be no lawsuit, and but for the lawsuit, there would be no damages." Rather, the "on account of" phrase requires that the damages be awarded by reason of, or because of, a personal physical injury. Petitioners bear the burden of "present[ing] concrete evidence demonstrating the precise causal connection" between the personal physical injuries and the settlement payment.

The settlement agreement does not include any express language of purpose. It only provides that "Bank One shall pay the total sum of $49,000" and that the "suit shall be dismissed with prejudice." Petitioners' only evidence arguably supporting the purpose necessary for exclusion under § 104(a)(2) is Mrs. Stadnyk's testimony that her attorney, the attorney for Bank One, and the mediator all advised her that the settlement proceeds would not be subject to income tax. However, even assuming the attorneys did give her this advice, there is no evidence concerning the basis for the advice. The attorneys may have advised Mrs. Stadnyk based on any number of incorrect beliefs, such as the belief that all personal injury awards are excludable from income, as Petitioner argues here, or the belief that a physical injury was unnecessary. Given that the settlement agreement included no indication that Bank One paid the settlement on account of any physical injury and that all of Mrs. Stadnyk's damages were stated in terms of emotional distress, Petitioners have failed to offer any concrete evidence demonstrating a causal connection between any physical injury and the settlement award.

Thus, Petitioner's settlement award may not be excluded from taxation under § 104(a)(2).

NOTES

1. *Constitutional authority and limitations.*—Article I, Section 8, clause 1 of the United States Constitution grants Congress broad powers to tax and spend. It begins: "The Congress shall have power to lay and collect taxes, duties, imposts and excises, to pay the debts and provide for the common defense and general welfare of the United States . . . "

These broadly stated powers are subject to two explicit limitations, sometimes known as the "uniformity" and "apportionment" clauses. The uniformity clause appears in that same Article I, Section 8, clause 1: "but all duties, imposts and excises shall be uniform throughout the United States; . . ."

The apportionment clause was so important that it appears twice. Article I, Section 2, clause 3 provides: "Representatives and direct taxes shall be apportioned among the several states which may be included within this union, according to their respective numbers, which shall be determined by adding to the whole number of free persons, including those bound to service for a term of years, and excluding Indians not taxed, three fifths of all other Persons." Article I, Section 9, clause 4 then reiterates: "No capitation, or other direct, tax shall be laid, unless in proportion to the census or enumeration herein before directed to be taken."

The purpose of the apportionment clause was to protect slavery. Slave states feared that the new federal government would tax the holding of slaves by imposing either a capitation or head tax, limited to slaves, or a tax on property, also limited to slaves. Both capitation and property taxes were thought to be "direct"—that is, taxes on the things themselves. The apportionment clause required that direct taxes be apportioned among the states in proportion to their populations. The purpose was to make it difficult for an anti-slavery Congress to use direct taxation to inhibit slave-owning.

In *Pollock v. Farmers' Loan & Trust Co.*, 158 U.S. 601 (1895), the Supreme Court held that a tax on income from property was, for constitutional purposes "direct"—that is, equivalent to a tax on the property itself—and therefore invalid unless apportioned among the several states in proportion to their respective populations. Since the federal income tax was not so apportioned, the Court struck down the entire income tax as unconstitutional. The Sixteenth Amendment was proposed and ratified in 1913 to overturn *Pollock*. In a footnote not included in the excerpt reprinted above, the *Murphy* court observes: "Whether that portion of *Pollock* remains good law is unclear," citing *Graves v. New York ex rel. O'Keefe*, 306 U.S. 466, 480 (1939) ("The theory, which once won a qualified approval, that a tax on income is legally or economically a tax on its source, is no longer tenable").

PROBLEMS FOR DISCUSSION

7–4. Jeffrey is arrested while driving in an upper-income neighborhood. It is subsequently determined that the arresting officer did not have probable cause and arrested him primarily because of his skin color. In the course of the arrest, Jeffrey is beaten by the arresting officer, but not so severely as to require medical treatment. Jeffrey sues the officer and the municipality for violation of his civil rights, false arrest, and battery. He recovers $100,000. He does not ask for and the jury does not return a special verdict allocating the $100,000 among the counts in the complaint. How much gross income must Jeffrey report?

7–5. Assume you represent Jeffrey in Problem 6–4. Counsel for the defendants, seeking to avoid adverse publicity for the police department, has approached you with the following settlement offer: Defendants will concede the battery count and pay Jeffrey $80,000 on that count. Jeffrey will concede the civil rights and false arrest counts and receive nothing on those counts. Assume that Jeffrey's marginal tax rate is 35 percent. What should he do?

SECTION 2: AMOUNTS RECEIVED THROUGH ACCIDENT OR HEALTH INSURANCE

Code: Sections 104(a)(3), 105(a), (b), and (c), and 7702B

The interaction between Code Sections 104(b)(3) and 105 can be confusing. The portion of Code Section 104(b)(3) before the final parenthetical sets forth the general rule: gross income does not include amounts received through accident or health insurance for personal injuries or sickness. The phrase "accident or health insurance" is not limited to insurance policies labeled "accident" or "health"; rather, the phrase refers to the risks insured against. Thus, for example, car insurance may qualify as "accident or health insurance" if it insures against the risk of accidental personal injury. Similarly, disability insurance qualifies, since it insures against accident or health risks.

The final parenthetical of Code Section 104(b)(3) sets forth an exception to this general rule for amounts received by an employee (A) attributable to excludible premiums paid by her employer or (B) paid directly by her employer. Recall that under Code Section 106, accident or health insurance premiums paid by taxpayer's employer are excluded from taxpayer's gross income. The final parenthetical, clause (A), tells us that benefits received under an accident or health policy paid for by taxpayer's employer on a tax-excludible basis are *not* excluded from taxpayer's gross income by Code Section 104(b)(3). Clause (B) states similarly that accident or health benefits provided directly by taxpayer's employer (for example, if taxpayer works for a hospital, and her employer provides the medical services itself) are not excluded by Code Section 104(b)(3).

Code Section 105(a) then confirms what the final parenthetical of Code Section 104(b)(3) implies: that amounts received by an employee (A) attributable to excludible premiums paid by her employer or (B) paid directly by her employer *are* includible in gross income—except as otherwise provided in Code Section 105. The two exceptions to this general inclusionary rule appear in Code Section 105, subsections (b) and (c). Subsection (b) excludes amounts paid to cover expenses for the medical care of taxpayer, his spouse, his dependents, and any child of his who has not yet reached age 27. "Medical care" is defined by reference to Code Section 213, explored further in Chapter 22A below. Subsection (c) excludes amounts paid under a type of insurance that was once common but is relatively rare today—employer-provided insurance that pays specified amounts for specified types of permanent injury (*e.g.*, $60,000 for loss of two extremities, or $2,500 per month for loss of hearing). See, e.g., *Stolte v. Commissioner*, T.C. Memo. 1999–271, 78 T.C.M. (CCH) 302 (1999).

The consequences of these provisions can be summarized as follows.

If taxpayer's employer pays for accident or health insurance and the premiums thus paid are excluded from taxpayer's income under Code Section 106, insurance benefits are excluded (1) under Code Section 105(b) if they are for medical care or (2) under Code Section 105(c) if they are for specified types of permanent injury. Otherwise, they are included. Most importantly, benefits from conventional disability insurance policies—which pay a specified amount for the period taxpayer is absent from work—are *included* in gross income if the premiums are paid by taxpayer's employer on a tax-excludible basis.

By contrast, if accident or health insurance premiums are paid out of after-tax dollars, *all* benefits received under such policies are excludible under Code Section 104(b)(3). Conventional disability insurance benefits are *excluded* under that section, notwithstanding the fact that they are replace income that would otherwise be taxable.

The IRS allows employers to offer benefit plans under which employees can elect to have their disability insurance premiums paid with either pre-tax or after-tax dollars. Income-replacement disability benefits paid to employees who choose to have their premiums paid with pre-tax dollars are taxable; the same benefits paid to employees who choose to have their premiums paid with after-tax dollars are not. Rev. Rul. 2004–55, 2004–1 C.B. 1081.

NOTES

1. *Qualified long-term care services.*—Code Section 213 defines "medical care" to include "qualified long-term care services," as that term is defined in Code Section 7702B. The latter section, added in 1996, by the Health Insurance Portability and Accountability Act, is particularly important for people with disabilities. Subsection (c)(1) defines "qualified long-term care services" to include "maintenance or personal care services" required by a "chronically ill individual" and provided pursuant to a plan of care prescribed by a licensed health care practitioner.

2. *Collateral source rule.*—Under the "collateral source" rule, a tortfeasor is liable for damages even if the victim has already been compensated for his injury by insurance. The purpose is to avoid rewarding the tortfeasor for the victim's diligence in insuring himself. *See* RESTATEMENT (SECOND) OF TORTS § 920A(2) (1977) ("Payments made to or benefits conferred on the injured party from other sources are not credited against the tortfeasor's liability, although they cover all or a part of the harm for which the tortfeasor is liable"); Michael I. Krauss & Jeremy Kidd, *Collateral Source and Tort's Soul*, 48 U. LOUISVILLE L. REV. 1 (2009). In a majority of states, this means that a tort victim may be compensated twice for the same injury—once by insurance and a second time by the tortfeasor. His insurance recovery may be excludible under Code Section 104(a)(3) or Code Section 105. His tort recovery may be excludible under Code Section 104(a)(2).

PROBLEMS FOR DISCUSSION

7–6. Carol works for HAL, a computer manufacturer, which provides her with a variety of fringe benefits. One is health insurance, which pays for her medical expenses. A second is long-term disability insurance, which pays 70 percent of her salary if she becomes disabled over an extended period.

    a. In November 2010, Carol's car is hit by a truck while she is driving home from work. She sustains serious injuries and is hospitalized for two months. Her company-provided health insurance policy pays all of her medical costs. Are such payments excluded from gross income? If so, under which Code section?

    b. In January 2011, Carol is released from the hospital to convalesce at home. Her health insurance policy pays for the services of a caretaker 7 days a week, who helps Carol with her physical rehabilitation and medications, cooks for her, keeps house, and helps her with basic personal tasks such as bathing and dressing. Are these payments excluded from gross income?

    c. On February 1, 2011, because she expects to be unable to return to work indefinitely, Carol ceases to be an employee of HAL and begins to collect benefits equal to 70% of her prior HAL salary from her disability insurance policy. Are such payments excluded from gross income? Does it matter whether she paid the premiums on the insurance policy with pre-tax or post-tax dollars?

d. On September 9, 2012, Carol wins a negligence verdict against the truck company for $2,000,000. The jury returns a special verdict, as follows:

Medical expenses	$300,000
Lost income	$1,000,000
Pain and suffering	$200,000
Punitive damages	$500,000
Total	$2,000,000

The $300,000 award for medical expenses reflects future costs that the jury projects will not be covered by Carol's health insurance. The $1,000,000 award for lost income reflects the income she would have earned from HAL for the 5–year period beginning on February 1, 2011, and extending until January 31, 2016—the period during which the jury concludes she is likely to be disabled. (Note that she is already collecting income-replacement benefits equal to 70% of her prior HAL salary from her disability insurance policy for the same period.) Which of these amounts is includible in her gross income?

CHAPTER 8

DEBT

■ ■ ■

Subchapter A: Basic Rules

JAMES v. UNITED STATES
366 U.S. 213 (1961)

[Defendant, convicted in the United States District Court for the Northern District of Illinois, of willfully attempting to evade federal income taxes, appealed. The United States Court of Appeals for the Seventh Circuit affirmed. Certiorari was granted. The Supreme Court had previously held, in *Commissioner v. Wilcox*, 327 U.S. 404 (1946), that embezzled funds were not taxable because the embezzler was required by law to return them.]

The issue before us in this case is whether embezzled funds are to be included in the "gross income" of the embezzler in the year in which the funds are misappropriated.

The facts are not in dispute. The petitioner is a union official who, with another person, embezzled in excess of $738,000 during the years 1951 through 1954 from his employer union and from an insurance company with which the union was doing business. Petitioner failed to report these amounts in his gross income in those years and was convicted for willfully attempting to evade the federal income tax due for each of the years 1951 through 1954.

The starting point in all cases dealing with the question of the scope of what is included in "gross income" begins with the basic premise that the purpose of Congress was "to use the full measure of its taxing power." And the Court has given a liberal construction to the broad phraseology of the "gross income" definition statutes in recognition of the intention of Congress to tax all gains except those specifically exempted. The language of § 22(a) of the 1939 Code, "gains or profits and income derived from any source whatever," and the more simplified language of § 61(a) of the 1954 Code, "all income from whatever source derived," have been held to encompass all "accessions to wealth, clearly realized, and over which the taxpayers have complete dominion." A gain "constitutes taxable income when its recipient has such control over it that, as a practical matter, he derives readily realizable economic value from it." Under these broad principles, we believe that petitioner's contention, that all unlawful gains are taxable except those resulting from embezzlement, should fail.

When a taxpayer acquires earnings, lawfully or unlawfully, without the consensual recognition, express or implied, of an obligation to repay and without restriction as to their disposition, "he has received income which he is required to return, even though it may still be claimed that he is not entitled to retain the money, and even though he may still be adjudged liable to restore its equivalent." In such case, the taxpayer has "actual command over the property taxed—the actual benefit for which the tax is paid," This standard brings wrongful appropriations within the broad sweep of "gross income"; it excludes loans. When a law-abiding taxpayer mistakenly receives income in one year, which receipt is assailed and found to be invalid in a subsequent year, the taxpayer must nonetheless report the amount as "gross income" in the year received. We do not believe that Congress intended to treat a law-breaking taxpayer differently. Just as the honest taxpayer may deduct any amount repaid in the year in which the repayment is made, the Government points out that, "If, when, and to the extent that the victim recovers back the misappropriated funds, there is of course a reduction in the embezzler's income."

We believe that *Wilcox* was wrongly decided and we find nothing in congressional history since then to persuade us that Congress intended to legislate the rule. Thus, we believe that we should now correct the error and the confusion resulting from it, certainly if we do so in a manner that will not prejudice those who might have relied on it. We should not continue to confound confusion, particularly when the result would be to perpetuate the injustice of relieving embezzlers of the duty of paying income taxes on the money they enrich themselves with through theft while honest people pay their taxes on every conceivable type of income.

But, we are dealing here with a felony conviction under statutes which apply to any person who "willfully" fails to account for his tax or who "willfully" attempts to evade his obligation. We believe that the element of willfulness could not be proven in a criminal prosecution for failing to include embezzled funds in gross income in the year of misappropriation so long as the statute contained the gloss placed upon it by *Wilcox* at the time the alleged crime was committed. Therefore, we feel that petitioner's conviction may not stand and that the indictment against him must be dismissed.

NOTES

1. *Criminal tax evasion.*—Under Code Section 7201, any person who "willfully" attempts to evade or defeat any tax imposed by the Code is guilty of a felony. In *Cheek v. United States*, 498 U.S. 192 (1991), the Supreme Court construed this willfulness requirement in the following terms:

"A good-faith misunderstanding of the law or a good-faith belief that one is not violating the law negates willfulness, whether or not the claimed belief or misunderstanding is objectively reasonable. Statutory willfulness, which protects the average citizen from prosecution for innocent mistakes made due to the complexity of the tax laws, is the voluntary, intentional violation of a known legal duty. Thus, if the jury credited Cheek's assertion that he truly believed that the Code did not treat wages as income, the Government would not have carried its burden to prove willfulness, however unreasonable a court might deem such a belief."

PROBLEMS FOR DISCUSSION

8–1. The Elm Street Investment Club loans $1,000,000 to Bernie for 5 years at an annual interest rate of 6%. When Bernie receives the $1,000,000, does he have income? When he repays it, does he have a loss?

8–2. Assume Congress converts our income tax into a pure consumption tax. Does the answer to Problem 8–1 change?

8–3. The Elm Street Investment Club deposits $1,000,000 in Bernie's investment fund. The parties agree that the $1,000,000 will participate in the fund's earnings equally along with other investments in the fund and that any such earnings will be credited to the Club's account. The parties further agree that when the Club requests its money back, the fund will pay the Club all amounts remaining in its account. Unknown to the Club, there actually is no investment fund. Bernie is running a Ponzi scheme that appears from the outside to be legitimate; in fact, however, he intends to repay moneys to his "investors" only to the extent necessary to keep the scheme running. When Bernie receives the $1,000,000, does he have income?

8–4. The Elm Street Investment Club transfers $1,000,000 to Bernie. The Club believes that the $1,000,000 is a loan. Bernie believes that it is payment for services Bernie has performed for the Club. Assume that as a matter of non-tax law, the Club is correct and that Bernie has a legally enforceable obligation to repay the $1,000,000. Does Bernie have income when he receives the $1,000,000? What must happen when he repays the loan?

8–5. In Year 1, the Elm Street Investment Club loans $1,000,000 to Bernie for 5 years at an annual interest rate of 6%. At the end of Year 5, when the loan comes due, Bernie is unable to repay it. Does he have income at that time?

Subchapter B: Debt Discharges

SECTION 1: DEBT DISCHARGE INCOME

UNITED STATES v. KIRBY LUMBER CO.
284 U.S. 1 (1931)

In July, 1923, the plaintiff, the Kirby Lumber Company, issued its own bonds for $12,126,800 for which it received their par value. Later in the same year it purchased in the open market some of the same bonds at less than par, the difference of price being $137,521.30. The question is whether this difference is a taxable gain or income of the plaintiff for the year 1923. By the Revenue Act of (November 23) 1921, c. 136, § 213(a), gross income includes "gains or profits and income derived from any source whatever," and by the Treasury Regulations, "If the corporation purchases and retires any of such bonds at a price less than the issuing price or face value, the excess of the issuing price or face value over the purchase price is gain or income for the taxable year." We see no reason why the Regulations should not be accepted as a correct statement of the law.

In *Bowers v. Kerbaugh–Empire Co.*, 271 U. S. 170 (1926), the defendant in error owned the stock of another company that had borrowed money repayable in marks or their equivalent for an enterprise that failed. At the time of payment the marks had fallen in value, which so far as it went was a gain for the defendant in error, and it was contended by the plaintiff in error that the gain was taxable income. But the transaction as a whole was a loss, and the contention was denied. Here there was no shrinkage of assets and the taxpayer made a clear gain. As a result of its dealings it made available $137,521.30 assets previously offset by the obligation of bonds now extinct. We see nothing to be gained by the discussion of judicial definitions. The defendant in error has realized within the year an accession to income, if we take words in their plain popular meaning, as they should be taken here.

Problems for Discussion

8–6. The Elm Street Investment Club loans Bernie $1,000,000 for 5 years at an annual interest rate of 6%, which amount he uses in his trade or business. In Year 4, it becomes apparent that Bernie is not going to repay the full amount. The parties settle, and Bernie pays the Club $800,000 of principal and receives a full discharge of all of his obligations to the Club. Assume that $15,000 of interest has accrued on the loan but not been paid. How much income does Bernie recognize on the discharge? Does it matter what method of accounting he uses?

8–7. The Elm Street Investment Club loans Bernie $1,000,000 for 5 years. Interest is paid currently. In Year 4, in an arm's-length transaction, Bernie sells the Club a condo in exchange for a reduction in the principal amount of the debt of $200,000–to $800,000. At the time, Bernie has a basis of $140,000 in the condo. How much income does Bernie recognize? What is its character? Assume that, in addition to the foregoing facts, it can be established with certainty that the condo is only worth $150,000. How much income does Bernie recognize? What is its character? Assume instead that it can be established with certainty that the condo is only worth $120,000. How much income does Bernie recognize? What is its character?

8–8. The Elm Street Investment Club loans Bernie $1,000,000 for 5 years. Interest is paid currently. In Year 4, Bernie agrees to supply each member of the Club investment advisory and financial planning services in exchange for a reduction in the principal amount of the debt he owes to the Club of $200,000—reducing the principal amount of the debt to $800,000. How much income does Bernie recognize? What is its character?

8-9. The Elm Street Investment Club loans Bernie $1,000,000 for 5 years. Interest is paid currently. In Year 4, the Club votes to reduce the principal amount of the debt by $200,000—to $800,000. Assume that the transaction is treated as a gift for tax purposes. How much income does Bernie recognize?

SECTION 2: PURCHASE PRICE ADJUSTMENTS

Code: Section 108(e)(5)

REV. RUL. 92-99
1992-2 C.B. 35

If the principal amount of an undersecured nonrecourse debt that arose out of the purchase of property is reduced by the holder of the debt who was not the seller of the property, the debt reduction may not be treated as a purchase price adjustment (in the absence of an infirmity that clearly relates back to the original sale), but results in discharge of indebtedness income under section 61(a)(12) of the Code.

ISSUE

If the principal amount of an undersecured nonrecourse debt that arose out of the purchase of property is reduced by the holder of the debt who was not the seller of the property, does the debt reduction result in discharge of indebtedness income under section 61(a)(12) of the Internal Revenue Code, or is the debt reduction treated as a purchase price adjustment that reduces the basis of the property securing the debt?

FACTS

In 1988, individual A purchased an office building from B for $1,000,000, its fair market value. To pay for the building, A signed a note payable to C, a third-party lender, for $1,000,000. The note bore interest at a fixed market rate payable annually and was secured by the office building. In 1989, when the value of the office building was $800,000 and the outstanding principal on the note was $1,000,000, C agreed to modify the terms of the note by reducing the note's principal amount to $800,000. C's reduction in the note was not based on an infirmity that clearly related back to B's original sale (*e.g.*, B's inducement of a higher purchase price by a misrepresentation of a material fact or by fraud).

LAW AND ANALYSIS

Section 108(e)(5) of the Code permits a debt reduction to be treated as a purchase price adjustment under certain circumstances. Section

108(e)(5) provides that if (A) the debt of a purchaser of property to the seller arising out of the purchase is reduced, (B) the debt reduction does not occur in a title 11 bankruptcy case or when the purchaser is insolvent, and (C) the reduction would be treated as income to the purchaser from the discharge of indebtedness but for paragraph (e)(5), then such reduction will be treated as a purchase price adjustment. This purchase price adjustment treatment will result in a reduction in the basis of the property securing the debt rather than discharge of indebtedness income.

The debt in this case was reduced by an agreement between C (the third-party lender) and A (the purchaser) of the property. Even though the debt arose in connection with the purchase of the property by A from B, it was not a debt of the purchaser (A) "to the seller" (B), as required by section 108(e)(5)(A) of the Code. Thus, the debt reduction by C does not qualify as a purchase price adjustment under section 108(e)(5) of the Code.

In addition, the debt reduction by C is not considered a purchase price adjustment under common law. *See Fifth Avenue–Fourteenth Street Corp. v. Commissioner*, 147 F.2d 453 (2d Cir. 1945), in which the court stated that a purchase price adjustment is limited to a case where the seller-mortgagee agreed to the debt reduction. The Service generally will not follow cases permitting a purchase price adjustment by third-party lenders, such as *Hirsch v. Commissioner*, 115 F.2d 656 (7th Cir. 1940), and *Allen v. Courts*, 127 F.2d 127 (5th Cir. 1942). An agreement to reduce a debt between a purchaser and a third-party lender is not a true adjustment of the purchase price paid for the property because the seller has received the entire purchase price from the purchaser and is not a party to the debt reduction agreement. The debt reduction relates solely to the debt and results in discharge of indebtedness income to the debtor.

Further, the Service will not follow *Commissioner v. Sherman*, 135 F.2d 68 (6th Cir. 1943), involving a third-party lender, to the extent that it relied on *Kerbaugh–Empire* to permit a purchase price adjustment. The Service will, however, treat a debt reduction in third-party lender cases as a purchase price adjustment to the extent that the debt reduction by the third-party lender is based on an infirmity that clearly relates back to the original sale (*e.g.*, the seller's inducement of a higher purchase price by misrepresentation of a material fact or by fraud). No other debt reduction by a third-party lender will be treated as a purchase price adjustment.

The reduction in the note by the third-party lender (C) in this case was not based on an infirmity that clearly relates back to the original sale, so A cannot treat C's debt reduction as a purchase price adjustment. Thus, A realizes $200,000 of discharge of indebtedness income in 1989 under section 61(a)(12) of the Code.

Notes

1. *Scope of the common law purchase price adjustment exception.*— Although it appears that the common law purchase price adjustment exception survived enactment of Code Section 108(e)(5), its scope is unclear. The old common law cases, many decided during or in the aftermath of the Great Depression, frequently characterized discharges as purchase price adjustments on facts that did not appear objectively to support such characterization. Many such cases have not been explicitly overruled. As Rev. Rul. 92–99 illustrates, however, the Service is selective about which such cases it will follow.

Problems for Discussion

8–10. Robert buys a vacant lot for $1,000,000, paying $200,000 in cash and signing a recourse note (not secured by the property) in favor of the seller for the remaining $800,000. Two years later, Robert and the seller agree to reduce the amount of the note to $500,000. At the time, Robert is solvent. What are the tax consequences to Robert?

8–11. Robert buys a vacant lot for $1,000,000, paying $200,000 in cash and signing a recourse note (not secured by the property) in favor of the seller for the remaining $800,000. Two years later, he sells the lot to a third party; in the sale, the third party does not assume Robert's obligations on the note. In Year 4, Robert and the seller agree to reduce the amount of the note to $500,000. At the time, Robert is solvent. What are the tax consequences to Robert?

8–12. In Year 1, Robert purchases deductible legal services for his business for $1,000,000, incurring but not paying a $1,000,000 obligation to the law firm that provides the services. All of the services are provided in Year 1. In Year 2, after disputes about the quality of the services, the parties agree to reduce Robert's obligation to $700,000, which he then pays. What are the tax consequences to Robert? Does it matter what method of accounting he uses? Does it matter whether he contests the liability in Year 1?

SECTION 3: CONTESTED LIABILITY EXCEPTION

N. SOBEL, INC. v. COMMISSIONER

40 B.T.A. 1263 (1939)

For many years [petitioner, an accrual method taxpayer,] had an account with the Bank of United States. In 1929, in a campaign to sell the bank's stock, petitioner was urged to buy 100 stock units, each consisting of a bank share and a share of Bancus Corporation. Petitioner agreed to buy the 100 units for $21,700. On February 25, petitioner issued its 30-day note for $21,700, payable to the bank. The bank accepted the note at a discount and retained the certificate. During the year petitioner suggested a sale of the shares, but was persuaded against it and no sale was made.

The note was renewed from month to month but never was paid, although petitioner was financially able to pay it. The certificate remained with the bank, although during 1930 petitioner's credit position was strong enough to cover the amount of the note. When the note matured on November 26, 1930, petitioner refused to renew, and immediately instituted suit against the bank, demanding rescission of the purchase contract and the loan and a judgment for the interest paid, on the ground that the bank made the loan in violation of law and failed to carry out promises to guarantee the purchaser against loss.

The Superintendent of Banks of the State of New York closed the bank on December 11, 1930, because of insolvency, and on April 21, 1931, brought a countersuit against petitioner for the amount of the note, with interest. Petitioner defended on the ground that the purchase contract and loan were parts of a single transaction which should be rescinded. The proceedings were consolidated for trial and thrice adjourned. They were settled on October 15, 1935, and petitioner agreed to pay $10,850.

The Commissioner disallowed the petitioner's deduction of 1935 of the $10,850 for which it finally in that year settled the litigation over its note. He denied the loss "for the reason that the stock to which it pertained became worthless prior to the taxable year under consideration." He then added to petitioner's gross income the other $10,850 half of the face amount of the note on the ground that this was a gain resulting from the "settlement of an obligation amounting to $21,700 for one-half the face value." The Commissioner argues that the taxpayer bought the shares in 1929, that they became worthless some time before 1935, with the result at that earlier time of a realized and deductible loss of the cost of $21,700; that the note, however, continued as a subsisting liability for its face amount, and its discharge by the payment of one-half its face brought about a gain of the other half, taxable as realized income.

If this were simply a case where a taxpayer bought property, giving its note in payment, and the property became worthless, the rule would apply that a deduction for loss would be available to it only in the year the property became worthless. But the facts are not so certain. There is question whether the taxpayer bought property in 1929 and question as to its liability and the amount thereof, and this question was suspended in litigation until the 1935 compromise agreement with the state superintendent of banks. Until 1935 the loss was not actual and present by any practical test. The litigation was, so far as this record shows, bona fide. There were enough other suits involving similar sales by the bank of its own shares during the 1929 "drive" to indicate that this petitioner was not alone in doubting its ownership of the shares or its liability on the note. Whether it could have avoided either the sale or the note can not be decided in this proceeding, for the claims were compromised and legal rights were never recognized. It can not be said as a postulate that if the litigation had proceeded to judgment it would have established that petitioner invested $21,700 in the shares and owed the full amount of the note. It is not clear that petitioner could rightfully have taken a deduction prior to 1935–not clear enough to carry the correlative denial of the deduction when the final amount was definitely fixed and the loss became actual and present. From every practical standpoint it had no loss until its liability was definitely fixed in 1935 for $10,850. It correctly took the deduction then.

This also establishes that the release of the note was not the occasion for a freeing of assets and that there was no gain under the doctrine of *Kirby Lumber Co. v. United States*.

PROBLEMS FOR DISCUSSION

8–13. What was N. Sobel's economic loss for the period it held the bank stock? What gains or losses was taxpayer ultimately required to report or permitted to take with respect to the transactions in question? Did taxpayer's net tax loss match its net economic loss?

8–14. Under the Service's proposed tax treatment, would taxpayer's net tax loss have matched its net economic loss?

SECTION 4: INSOLVENCY EXCEPTION

Code: Sections 108(a) and 108(b)

NOTES

1. *Abolition of the common law insolvency exception.*—Prior to enactment of Code Section 108(a), courts had recognized a common law insolvency exception to the discharge of indebtedness doctrine. Code Section 108(e)(1) states explicitly that no such common law insolvency exception survived enactment of Code Section 108(a).

PROBLEMS FOR DISCUSSION

8–15. The Elm Street Investment Club deposits $1,000,000 in Bernie's investment fund. The parties agree that the $1,000,000 will participate in the fund's earnings equally along with other investments in the fund and that any such earnings will be credited to the Club's account. The parties further agree that when the Club requests its money back, the fund will pay the Club all amounts remaining in its account. Unknown to the Club, there actually is no investment fund. Bernie is running a Ponzi scheme that appears from the outside to be legitimate, but in fact he intends to repay moneys to his "investors" only to the extent necessary to keep the scheme running. When the scheme collapses, the Club only receives $100,000 of its $1,000,000, because Bernie is insolvent. Does Bernie have gross income in the amount of the $900,000 that he will never pay? What if the Club formally discharges the remainder of the debt in recognition of the fact that he will never pay it?

What if Bernie is not insolvent, but the remainder of the debt is discharged in Bernie's bankruptcy proceeding?

SECTION 5: THE CREDITOR'S SIDE: BAD DEBT?

Code: Section 166

Code Section 166 allows the creditor a deduction for debt that becomes worthless. A "nonbusiness debt" held by a taxpayer other than a corporation generate deductible losses only when wholly worthless; in the year in which it becomes wholly worthless, the resulting loss is treated as a short-term capital loss. The resulting loss therefore enters into the capital gain and loss netting computation for the year and is deductible only to the extent permitted by Code Section 1211. All other bad debts—*e.g.*, nonbusiness debts held by corporations or business bad debts—are deductible when wholly or partially worthless.

These rules place creditor taxpayers in a bind: if they report conservatively, not claiming their bad debts until worthlessness is clear, the IRS may (and commonly does) assert that they should have claimed their deductions earlier—in years that are, unfortunately, closed. This problem is obviated to some extent by Code Section 6651(d)(1), which extends the statute of limitations from three years to seven years with regard to claimed deductions for bad debts or worthless securities. Determining whether and to what extent a debt is "worthless," however, is often difficult.

MINNEAPOLIS, ST. PAUL & SAULT STE. MARIE R.R. CO. v. UNITED STATES
164 Ct.Cl. 226 (1964)

This case can be properly categorized as a study of the toils and tribulations of the railroad industry throughout its undercapitalized expansionary period to its present fight for survival. The presently contested issues involve certain items which the taxpayer claims to have become worthless in 1952 or alternatively in 1954, thus entitling it to a deduction from gross income under section 23 of the Internal Revenue Code of 1939 [predecessor to Code Section 166]. The items in question are taxpayer's secured and unsecured claims against Wisconsin Central Railway.

[Between 1909 and 1924, taxpayer ("Soo") acquired a total of 103,583 shares of Wisconsin Central common stock, having an original cost basis of $4,629,541.13.] From April 15, 1909 forward, Soo operated its own properties, together with those of Wisconsin Central, as a single integrated system with income and expenditures being pooled. At the end of each calendar month, a balance was struck and net income distributed. When Wisconsin Central's gross income was insufficient to cover its necessary monthly expenditures, funds of Soo were temporarily advanced, such advances normally being repaid from the earnings and funds of Wisconsin Central during the immediately succeeding months. [The court then recites an extended history of advances and repayments between the two companies between 1909 and 1954.]

On May 12, 1952, all of the parties in interest, except Wisconsin Central itself and a committee of its preferred stockholders, executed a "Stipulation and Agreement" which fixed an upper limit upon the extent of any possible recovery by Soo upon its claims against Wisconsin Central. [A final plan of reorganization of Wisconsin Central was consummated on March 1, 1954, setting forth the amount Soo would actually receive with respect to debts owed to it by Wisconsin Central.]

Within the time provided by law, Soo filed formal refund claims for the years 1950, 1951, 1952, 1954 and 1955. Soo's refund claims consisted of [among other things] a deduction in 1952, and alternatively in 1954, on account of its advances made to Wisconsin Central prior to December 3, 1932, having first become wholly worthless in 1952 or 1954 and a deduction in 1952, and alternatively in 1954, on account of its secured claims against Wisconsin Central represented by bond interest coupons having first become wholly or partially worthless in 1952 or 1954.

In *Boehm v. Commissioner*, 326 U.S. 287, 292 (1945), the Court reasoned that the language of the statute (after the 1942 amendments) and the regulations promulgated under it require that the loss to be deductible "must have been sustained in fact during the taxable year." We interpret this as meaning that the taxpayer now not only has the burden of proving that the debt had some intrinsic value at the beginning of the year it allegedly became worthless and that it became worthless in the taxable year in question, but also that the taxpayer must show that throughout the entire life of the debt, the evidence reasonably available to him pointed out that it was possessed of some value and had not become wholly worthless.

It is obvious that there is no precise test for determining worthlessness within the taxable year and neither the statutory enactment, its regulations, nor the decisions attempt such an all-inclusive definition. From the numerous decisions, we are taught that a determination of whether or not a debt becomes worthless in a particular year must be confined to the fact of the particular case. Furthermore, it is often impossible to select a single factor or "identifiable event" which clearly establishes the time at which a debt becomes worthless and thus deductible. More often it is a series of events which in the aggregate present a picture establishing that the debt in question has become worthless. Such a decision of necessity requires a practical approach, not a legal test. It must be flexible in nature, varying according to the circumstances of each particular case, so that whatever inferences a court might draw from a particular fact in another case are not binding on the examining court, although the same fact may be present. The Tax Court has aptly said that "worthlessness is not determined by an inflexible formula or slide rule calculation, but upon the exercise of sound business judgment." In making such a determination the taxpayer must follow a rule of reason, avoiding alike the Scyllian role of the "incorrigible optimist" and the Charybdian character of the "stygian pessimist." To be deductible, a debt need not be proven worthless beyond all peradventure, since a bare hope that something might be recovered in the future constitutes no sound reason for postponing the time for taking a deduction. The taxpayer is not required to postpone his entitlement to a deduction in the expectancy of uncertain future events nor is he called to wait until some turn of the wheel of fortune may bring the debtor into affluence.

It appears that the taxpayer must strike a middle course between optimism and pessimism and determine debts to be worthless in the exercise of sound business judgment based upon as complete information as is reasonably obtainable. Once it appears from all the surrounding circumstances that a debt has become worthless, we cannot look to subsequent events to determine if a debt in fact became worthless. The possibility of collection is tested by the facts known at that time and not by hindsight. However, subsequent events may be used to evaluate the soundness of our determination that a debt became worthless in a certain year. Thus our inquiry must be focused on each year in which the debts were in existence without the benefit of subsequent events to help us arrive at our determination.

With this in mind, we now turn to the specific items alleged by the taxpayer to have become worthless in 1952, thus entitling it to a deduction from gross income under section 23 of the Internal Revenue Code of 1939. We shall consider each of the disputed items separately.

As we have stated above, the taxpayer, in determining the point at which a debt became worthless, must exercise sound business judgment based upon as complete information as is reasonably obtainable. Once it appears from all the surrounding circumstances that a debt has become in fact worthless, the taxpayer cannot postpone his entitlement to the deduction. We believe that in the instant situation Soo could not have established from the surrounding circumstances that its secured claim had in fact become worthless. Nor do we believe that Soo's secured claim did in fact become worthless prior to 1952. The secured claim had some value at the beginning of the year (1952) it allegedly became worthless. It is also clear that the execution of the settlement agreement in 1952 effectively rendered the debt wholly worthless. The area of conflict with respect to this item is centered around the question of whether the debt had become wholly worthless prior to 1952 and thus deductible at that time.

[The court reviews the valuations of Wisconsin Central's assets prior to 1952.]

The facts available to the taxpayer in the instant situation at best pointed both ways. We believe that under these circumstances Soo could not, in the exercise of sound business judgment, have determined that the debt had become wholly worthless prior to 1952. The secured claim had a substantial value at the beginning of 1952, and in this respect we note that Soo ultimately received $362,000 worth of new common stock of Wisconsin Central on a secured claim of $1,142,260. The execution of the settlement agreement and subsequent approval by the District Court effectively rendered wholly worthless the debt, except for the specified recovery allowable under the agreement. Moreover, the taxpayer could not have determined that the debt in question had become in fact totally worthless prior to 1952. We say this because Soo's priority participation as a secured creditor was not determined until 1952. Not until 1945 were the claims of the other secured creditors of Wisconsin Central filed. These claims were not finally resolved until 1950. Consequently, throughout the existence of its secured claim, Soo could have reasonably looked to Wisconsin Central's assets for at least partial satisfaction of its secured claim. This is not a situation where the taxpayer is postponing his entitlement to a deduction in the expectancy that some turn of the wheel of fortune may bring the debtor into affluence. Throughout this period, taxpayer could have reasonably looked to the debtor's assets for satisfaction. The fact that at one point the assets appeared to be less than the claimed secured debts is not controlling, since neither the total amount nor the priority of participation of the other secured creditors was finally determined until 1950. A determination that the debt had become totally worthless prior to 1952, in view of the conflicting evidence available, runs contrary to the fact that there was ultimately a substantial recovery on the debt in question. Consequently, we hold that Soo is entitled to take a deduction from gross income in 1952 as provided by section 23(k) of the Internal Revenue Code of 1939, for the loss it suffered on account of its secured claim against Wisconsin Central becoming totally worthless, except for the specified amount recovered under the settlement agreement.

In considering when debts are deductible, the first problem is to determine whether the taxpayer is owed a debt since it is obvious that a taxpayer cannot take a deduction for a worthless debt unless there is a valid debt arising out of an actual debtor-creditor relationship. The defendant strongly urges that the debtor-creditor relationship which might have existed between Wisconsin Central and Soo on account of the monthly running balances, ceased to exist when the lease was terminated. The defendant supports this assertion by making references to the lease agreement between the parties which required Soo to turn over the leased properties at the termination of the lease free from floating indebtedness. There is no dispute that the lease was terminated when the Wisconsin Central went into receivership in 1932. Thus, the defendant contends, whatever sums might have been owing Soo from Wisconsin Central, incurred on account of their joint operation of the leased properties, were wiped out by the provision of the lease. The taxpayer counters by calling our attention to a resolution of the Board of Directors of Wisconsin Central stating in effect that Wisconsin Central acknowledged that the sums paid by Soo from revenues belonging to it in discharge of current liabilities of Wisconsin Central were to be treated as temporary loans and to be repaid from whatever sources. In the alternative the taxpayer contends that if the sum advanced are not treated as debts and thus deductible under section 23(k) of the 1939 Code, Soo is entitled to a loss deduction under section 23(f) of the 1939 Code.

We need not decide this issue since we are of the opinion that even if there was a valid debtor-creditor relationship and the debt survived the termination of the lease, the debt became totally worthless prior to 1952. It is apparent that Soo assumed the Scyllian role of the "incorrigible optimist" with respect to such advances. Here it was the burden of the taxpayer to establish the fact that there was a deductible loss in 1952. It was incumbent upon it to establish not only that the debt had some value in 1952, but also that it had not become worthless prior to that time. Furthermore, the taxpayer had to show that it had become wholly or partially worthless in 1952. The taxpayer contends that this unsecured claim was possessed of substantial value at the beginning of 1952, pointing out the fact that there was a recovery of over $300,000 on a $7 million claim. The taxpayer then argues that the execution in 1952 of the settlement agreement, and its subsequent approval by the District Court, effectively rendered wholly worthless the debt in question, except for the specified recovery allowable under the agreement. However, we are unable to say that the taxpayer has offered any evidence to support its burden of proof that the debt in question always had some value throughout its existence. The taxpayer asserts that from 1932 to 1948, there were substantial recoveries on the open running account, *i.e.*, some $635,000, thus arguing for the continued value of the debt. We are aware that where there are substantial recoveries on an outstanding debt, we are able to draw the inference that the debt in question has not become totally worthless during that period, due to the debtor's ability to repay part of the debt. However, we are unable to draw such an inference in the case at bar. The stipulated facts show that of this sum, $500,000 was due to a determination in 1939 by the receivership court that Wisconsin Central was entitled to return of this amount for materials and supplies advanced to Soo in 1917. The reduction of the alleged outstanding debt was accomplished by a mere bookkeeping entry. Under these circumstances, the resulting reduction of the outstanding debt does not indicate the debtor's ability to repay the debt. We reach the same result with reductions resulting from the delayed receipt of sums earned by Wisconsin Central prior to 1932.

Soo had to look for the satisfaction of its unsecured claim to Wisconsin Central's assets which would be left over after the secured creditors' claims had been satisfied, since it is clear that Wisconsin Central could not meet its obligations from its own revenues. Thus, at that time, it was incumbent upon Soo to make a determination based upon as complete information as was reasonably available, as to the possibility of recovery on the outstanding debt. The evidence shows that throughout Wisconsin Central's receivership and part of its trusteeship, the total value of the assets was not sufficient to satisfy the claims of all the secured creditors.

The general creditors were never allocated any securities under the first ICC reorganization plan. The Commission expressly stated that the recapitalization was due to the improved financial position of Wisconsin Central. The mere fact that there were assets at a later date, due to the debtor's improved financial condition, does not change the result, since the possibility of collection is tested by the facts known at that time and not by hindsight. Soo was not required to postpone its entitlement to a deduction in the expectancy that some turn of the wheel of fortune might bring the Wisconsin Central into affluence, an unlikely event at that time in view of its long history of losses. Thus, the fact of worthlessness could have been reasonably established from all the available information, and it is clear that this event occurred prior to 1952. It follows that the claimed deduction is not available in the years asserted.

The court concludes as a matter of law that plaintiff is entitled to recover, and judgment will be entered to that effect on its claim for refund on account of its secured claim against Wisconsin Central which became worthless in 1952. Soo's claims for refund on account of its unsecured claim, which allegedly became worthless in 1952, are dismissed.

Subchapter C: Crane and Tufts

Code: Section 1014(a)(1) and 1016(a)(2)

Regulations: Section 1.1001–2(a)

CRANE v. COMMISSIONER
331 U.S. 1 (1947)

The question here is how a taxpayer who acquires depreciable property subject to an unassumed mortgage, holds it for a period, and finally sells it still so encumbered, must compute her taxable gain.

Petitioner was the sole beneficiary and the executrix of the will of her husband, who died January 11, 1932. He then owned an apartment building and lot subject to a mortgage, which secured a principal debt of $255,000.00 and interest in default of $7,042.50. As of that date, the property was appraised for federal estate tax purposes at a value exactly equal to the total amount of this encumbrance. Shortly after her husband's death, petitioner entered into an agreement with the mortgagee whereby she was to continue to operate the property—collecting the rents, paying for necessary repairs, labor, and other operating expenses, and reserving $200.00 monthly for taxes—and was to remit the net rentals to the mortgagee. This plan was followed for nearly seven years, during which period petitioner reported the gross rentals as income, and claimed and was allowed deductions for taxes and operating expenses paid on the property, for interest paid on the mortgage, and for the physical exhaustion of the building. Meanwhile, the arrearage of interest increased to $15,857.71. On November 29, 1938, with the mortgagee threatening foreclosure, petitioner sold to a third party for $3,000.00 cash, subject to the mortgage, and paid $500.00 expenses of sale.

Petitioner reported a taxable gain of $1,250.00. Her theory was that the "property" which she had acquired in 1932 and sold in 1938 was only the equity, or the excess in the value of the apartment building and lot over the amount of the mortgage. This equity was of zero value when she acquired it. No depreciation could be taken on a zero value.[2] Neither she nor her vendee ever assumed the mortgage, so, when she sold the equity, the amount she realized on the sale was the net cash received, or $2,500.00. This sum less the zero basis constituted her gain, of which she reported half as taxable on the assumption that the entire property was a "capital asset."

The Commissioner, however, determined that petitioner realized a net taxable gain of $23,767.03. His theory was that the "property" acquired and sold was not the equity, as petitioner claimed, but rather the physical property itself, or the owner's rights to possess, use, and dispose of it, undiminished by the mortgage. The original basis thereof was $262,042.50, its appraised value in 1932. Of this value $55,000.00 was allocable to land and $207,042.50 to building. During the period that petitioner held the property, there was an allowable depreciation of $28,045.10 on the building, so that the adjusted basis of the building at the time of sale was $178,997.40. The amount realized on the sale was said to include not only the $2,500.00 net cash receipts, but also the principal amount of the mortgage subject to which the property was sold, both totaling $257,500.00. The selling price was allocable in the proportion, $54,471.15 to the land and $203,028.85 to the building. The Commissioner agreed that the land was a "capital asset," but thought that the building was not. Thus, he determined that petitioner sustained a capital loss of $528.85 on the land, of which 50% or $264.42 was taken into account, and an ordinary gain of $24.031.45 on the building, or a net taxable gain as indicated.

[T]he dispute in this case is as to the construction to be given the term "property." If "property," as used in [§ 1014], means the same thing as "equity," it would necessarily follow that the basis of petitioner's property was zero, as she contends. If, on the contrary, it means the land and building themselves, or the owner's legal rights in them, undiminished by the mortgage, the basis was $262,042.50.

We think that the reasons for favoring one of the latter constructions are of overwhelming weight. In the first place, the words of statutes—including revenue acts—should be interpreted where possible in their ordinary, everyday senses. The only relevant definitions of "property" to

---

2. This position is, of course, inconsistent with her practice in claiming such deductions in each of the years the property was held. The deductions so claimed and allowed by the Commissioner were in the total amount of $25,500.00.

be found in the principal standard dictionaries are the two favored by the Commissioner, *i.e.*, either that "property" is the physical thing which is a subject of ownership, or that it is the aggregate of the owner's rights to control and dispose of that thing. "Equity" is not given as a synonym, nor do either of the foregoing definitions suggest that it could be correctly so used. Indeed, "equity" is defined as "the value of a property ... above the total of the liens...." The contradistinction could hardly be more pointed. Strong countervailing considerations would be required to support a contention that Congress, in using the word "property," meant "equity," or that we should impute to it the intent to convey that meaning.

In the second place, the Commission's position has the approval of the administrative construction of § [1014]. With respect to the valuation of property under that section, Reg. 101, Art. 113(a)(5)–1, provided that "the value of property as of the date of the death of the decedent as appraised for the purpose of the federal estate tax ... shall be deemed to be its fair market value...." The land and building here involved were so appraised in 1932, and their appraised value—$262,042.50—was reported by petitioner as part of the gross estate. This was in accordance with the estate tax law and regulations, which had always required that the value of decedent's property, undiminished by liens, be so appraised and returned, and that mortgages be separately deducted in computing the net estate. As the quoted provision of the Regulations has been in effect since 1918, and as the relevant statutory provision has been repeatedly reenacted since then in substantially the same form, the former may itself now be considered to have the force of law.

Moreover, in the many instances in other parts of the Act in which Congress has used the word "property," or expressed the idea of "property" or "equity," we find no instances of a misuse of either word or of a confusion of the ideas. In some parts of the Act other than the gain and loss sections, we find "property" where it is unmistakably used in its ordinary sense. On the other hand, where either Congress or the Treasury intended to convey the meaning of "equity," it did so by the use of appropriate language.

A further reason why the word "property" in § [1014] should not be construed to mean "equity" is the bearing such construction would have on the allowance of deductions for depreciation and on the collateral adjustments of basis.

Section [167] permits deduction from gross income of "a reasonable allowance for the exhaustion, wear and tear of property ...." [The depreciation rules] declare that the "basis upon which depletion exhaustion, wear and tear ... are to be allowed" is the basis "provided in section [1014] for the purpose of determining the gain upon the sale" of the property, which is the § [1014] basis "adjusted ... for exhaustion, wear and tear ... to the extent allowed (but not less than the amount allowable) ...."

Under these provisions, if the mortgagor's equity were the § [1014] basis, it would also be the original basis from which depreciation allowances are deducted. If it is, and if the amount of the annual allowances were to be computed on that value, as would then seem to be required, they will represent only a fraction of the cost of the corresponding physical exhaustion, and any recoupment by the mortgagor of the remainder of that cost can be effected only by the reduction of his taxable gain in the year of sale. If, however, the amount of the annual allowances were to be computed on the value of the property, and then deducted from an equity basis, we would in some instances have to accept deductions from a minus basis or deny deductions altogether. The Commissioner also argues that taking the mortgagor's equity as the § [1014] basis would require the basis to be changed with each payment on the mortgage, and that the attendant problem of repeatedly recomputing basis and annual allowances would be a tremendous accounting burden on both the Commissioner and the taxpayer. Moreover, the mortgagor would acquire control over the timing of his depreciation allowances.

Thus it appears that the applicable provisions of the Act expressly preclude an equity basis, and the use of it is contrary to certain implicit principles of income tax depreciation, and entails very great administrative difficulties. It may be added that the Treasury has never furnished a guide through the maze of problems that arise in connection with depreciating an equity basis, but, on the contrary, has consistently permitted the amount of depreciation allowances to be computed on the full value of the property, and subtracted from it as a basis. Surely, Congress' long-continued acceptance of this situation gives it full legislative endorsement.

We conclude that the proper basis under § [1014] is the value of the property, undiminished by mortgages thereon, and that the correct basis here was $262,042.50. The next step is to ascertain what adjustments are required under § [1016]. As the depreciation rate was stipulated, the only question at this point is whether the Commissioner was warranted in making any depreciation adjustments whatsoever.

Section [1016] provides that "proper adjustment in respect of the property shall in all cases be made ... for exhaustion, wear and tear ... to the extent allowed (but not less than the amount allowable ...." The Tax Court found on adequate evidence that the apartment house was property of a kind subject to physical exhaustion, that it was used in taxpayer's trade or business, and consequently that the taxpayer would have been entitled to a depreciation allowance under § [167], except that, in the opinion of that Court, the basis of the property was zero, and it was thought that depreciation could not be taken on a zero basis. As we have just decided that the correct basis of the property was not zero, but $262,042.50, we avoid this difficulty, and conclude that an adjustment should be made as the Commissioner determined.

Petitioner urges to the contrary that she was not entitled to depreciation deductions, whatever the basis of the property, because the law allows them only to one who actually bears the capital loss, and here the loss was not hers but the mortgagee's. We do not see, however, that she has established her factual premise. There was no finding of the Tax Court to that effect, nor to the effect that the value of the property was ever less than the amount of the lien. Nor was there evidence in the record, or any indication that petitioner could produce evidence, that this was so. The facts that the value of the property was only equal to the lien in 1932 and that during the next six and one-half years the physical condition of the building deteriorated and the amount of the lien increased, are entirely inconclusive, particularly in the light of the buyer's willingness in 1938 to take subject to the increased lien and pay a substantial amount of cash to boot. Whatever may be the rule as to allowing depreciation to a mortgagor on property in his possession which is subject to an unassumed mortgage and clearly worth less than the lien, we are not faced with that problem and see no reason to decide it now.

At last we come to the problem of determining the "amount realized" on the 1938 sale. Section [1001(b)], it will be recalled, defines the "amount realized" from "the sale ... of property" as "the sum of any money received plus the fair market value of the property (other than money) received," and § [1001 (a)] defines the gain on "the sale ... of property" as the excess of the amount realized over the basis. Quite obviously, the word "property," used here with reference to a sale, must mean "property" in the same ordinary sense intended by the use of the word with reference to acquisition and depreciation in § [1014], both for certain of the reasons stated heretofore in discussing its meaning in § [1014], and also because the functional relation of the two sections requires that the word mean the same in one section that it does in the other. If the "property" to be valued on the date of acquisition is the property free of liens, the "property" to be priced on a subsequent sale must be the same thing.

Starting from this point, we could not accept petitioner's contention that the $2,500.00 net cash was all she realized on the sale except on the absurdity that she sold a quarter-of-a-million dollar property for roughly one per cent of its value, and took a 99 per cent loss. Actually, petitioner does not urge this. She argues, conversely, that because only $2,500.00 was realized on the sale, the "property" sold must have been the equity only, and that consequently we are forced to accept her contention as to the meaning of "property" in § [1014]. We adhere, however, to what we have already said on the meaning of "property," and we find that the absurdity is avoided by our conclusion that the amount of the mortgage is properly included in the "amount realized" on the sale.

Petitioner concedes that if she had been personally liable on the mortgage and the purchaser had either paid or assumed it, the amount so paid or assumed would be considered a part of the "amount realized." The cases so deciding have already repudiated the notion that there must be an actual receipt by the seller himself of "money" or "other property," in their narrowest senses. It was thought to be decisive that one section of the Act must be construed so as not to defeat the intention of another or to frustrate the Act as a whole, and that the taxpayer was the "beneficiary" of the payment in "as real and substantial (a sense) as if the money had been paid it and then paid over by it to its creditors."

Both these points apply to this case. The first has been mentioned already. As for the second, we think that a mortgagor, not personally liable on the debt, who sells the property subject to the mortgage and for additional consideration, realizes a benefit in the amount of the mortgage as well as the boot.[37] If a purchaser pays boot, it is immaterial as to our problem whether the mortgagor is also to receive money from the purchaser to discharge the mortgage prior to sale, or whether he is merely to transfer subject to the mortgage—it may make a difference to the purchaser and to the mortgagee, but not to the mortgagor. Or put in another way, we are no more concerned with whether the mortgagor is, strictly speaking, a debtor on the mortgage, than we are with whether the benefit to him is, strictly speaking, a receipt of money or property. We are rather concerned with the reality that an owner of property, mortgaged at a figure less than that at which the property will sell, must and will treat the conditions of the mortgage exactly as if they were his personal obligations. If he transfers subject to the mortgage, the benefit to him is as real and substantial as if the mortgage were discharged, or as if a personal debt in an equal amount had been assumed by another.

Therefore we conclude that the Commissioner was right in determining that petitioner realized $257,500.00 on the sale of this property.

Petitioner contends that the result we have reached taxes her on what is not income within the meaning of the Sixteenth Amendment. If this is because only the direct receipt of cash is thought to be income in the constitutional sense, her contention is wholly without merit. If it is because the entire transaction is thought to have been "by all dictates of common-sense . . . a ruinous disaster," as it was termed in her brief, we disagree with her premise. She was entitled to depreciation deductions for a period of nearly seven years, and she actually took them in almost the allowable amount. The crux of this case, really, is whether the law permits her to exclude allowable deductions from consideration in computing gain. We have already showed that, if it does, the taxpayer can enjoy a double deduction, in effect, on the same loss of assets. The Sixteenth Amendment does not require that result any more than does the Act itself.

Problems for Discussion

8–16. Mrs. Crane purchases an apartment building for $15,000,000, putting nothing down, borrowing $15,000,000 from a bank, and giving the

---

37. Obviously, if the value of the property is less than the amount of the mortgage, a mortgagor who is not personally liable cannot realize a benefit equal to the mortgage. Consequently, a different problem might be encountered where a mortgagor abandoned the property or transferred it subject to the mortgage without receiving boot. That is not this case.

bank a non-recourse mortgage to secure the loan. What is her basis in the building?

8–17. Over the ensuing 15 years, Mrs. Crane properly claims $1,000,000 of depreciation per year—for a total of $15,000,000 of depreciation. What is her basis in the building?

8–18. Over the same 15 years, Mrs. Crane pays no principal on the mortgage, but does pay interest as it accrues. To make things simple, assume that her rental income each year exactly equals her interest obligation. At the end of 15 years, Mrs. Crane transfers the building to a third party in an arm's-length transaction for no consideration. What is her amount realized on the transfer? What is her gain?

8–19. In general, does the holding in *Crane* favor taxpayers or the government? In Problems 8–16 through 8–18, would our hypothetical taxpayer be better off or worse off if *Crane* had gone the other way? Why?

8–20. Assume instead that Mrs. Crane has not paid interest as it accrues. At the end of 15 years, in addition to $15,000,000 of principal, she owes $16,000,000 of interest on the mortgage. She transfers the building to a third party in an arm's-length transaction for no consideration. What is her amount realized on the transfer? What is her gain?

8–21. In each of the following situations, what is Mrs. Crane's basis in the acquired property? Does it matter what method of accounting she uses?

   a. She pays for the property with $1,000,000 of borrowed funds, giving the bank a recourse mortgage on the property.

   b. She pays for the property with $15,000,000 of borrowed money, giving the bank a nonrecourse mortgage on the property.

   c. She pays for the property with $15,000,000 of borrowed money, giving the bank her unsecured personal promissory note.

   d. She gives the seller her $15,000,000 promissory note.

   e. She takes the property subject to a $15,000,000 nonrecourse mortgage.

   f. She takes the property subject to a $15,000,000 recourse mortgage. Does it matter whether she assumes the mortgage?

COMMISSIONER v. TUFTS
461 U.S. 300 (1983)

Over 35 years ago, in *Crane v. Commissioner*, 331 U.S. 1 (1947), this Court ruled that a taxpayer, who sold property encumbered by a nonrecourse mortgage (the amount of the mortgage being less than the property's value), must include the unpaid balance of the mortgage in the computation of the amount the taxpayer realized on the sale. The case now before us presents the question whether the same rule applies when the unpaid amount of the nonrecourse mortgage exceeds the fair market value of the property sold.

On August 1, 1970, respondent Clark Pelt, a builder, and his wholly owned corporation, respondent Clark, Inc., formed a general partnership.

The purpose of the partnership was to construct a 120–unit apartment complex in Duncanville, Tex., a Dallas suburb. Neither Pelt nor Clark, Inc., made any capital contribution to the partnership. Six days later, the partnership entered into a mortgage loan agreement with the Farm & Home Savings Association (F & H). Under the agreement, F & H was committed for a $1,851,500 loan for the complex. In return, the partnership executed a note and a deed of trust in favor of F & H. The partnership obtained the loan on a nonrecourse basis: neither the partnership nor its partners assumed any personal liability for repayment of the loan. Pelt later admitted four friends and relatives, respondents Tufts, Steger, Stephens, and Austin, as general partners. None of them contributed capital upon entering the partnership.

The construction of the complex was completed in August 1971. During 1971, each partner made small capital contributions to the partnership; in 1972, however, only Pelt made a contribution. The total of the partners' capital contributions was $44,212. In each tax year, all partners claimed as income tax deductions their allocable shares of ordinary losses and depreciation. The deductions taken by the partners in 1971 and 1972 totalled $439,972. Due to these contributions and deductions, the partnership's adjusted basis in the property in August 1972 was $1,455,740.

In 1971 and 1972, the partnership's rental income was less than expected, and it was unable to make the payments due on the mortgage. Each partner, on August 28, 1972, sold his partnership interest to an unrelated third party, Fred Bayles. As consideration, Bayles agreed to reimburse each partner's sale expenses up to $250; he also assumed the nonrecourse mortgage.

On the date of transfer, the fair market value of the property did not exceed $1,400,000. Each partner reported the sale on his federal income tax return and indicated that a partnership loss of $55,740 had been sustained. The Commissioner of Internal Revenue, on audit, determined that the sale resulted in a partnership capital gain of approximately $400,000. His theory was that the partnership had realized the full amount of the nonrecourse obligation.

Section 1001 governs the determination of gains and losses on the disposition of property. Under § 1001(a), the gain or loss from a sale or other disposition of property is defined as the difference between "the amount realized" on the disposition and the property's adjusted basis. Subsection (b) of § 1001 defines "amount realized": "The amount realized from the sale or other disposition of property shall be the sum of any money received plus the fair market value of the property (other than money) received." At issue is the application of the latter provision to the disposition of property encumbered by a nonrecourse mortgage of an amount in excess of the property's fair market value.

In *Crane v. Commissioner*, this Court took the first and controlling step toward the resolution of this issue. Beulah B. Crane was the sole beneficiary under the will of her deceased husband. At his death in

January 1932, he owned an apartment building that was then mortgaged for an amount which proved to be equal to its fair market value, as determined for federal estate tax purposes. The widow, of course, was not personally liable on the mortgage. She operated the building for nearly seven years, hoping to turn it into a profitable venture; during that period, she claimed income tax deductions for depreciation, property taxes, interest, and operating expenses, but did not make payments upon the mortgage principal. In computing her basis for the depreciation deductions, she included the full amount of the mortgage debt. In November 1938, with her hopes unfulfilled and the mortgagee threatening foreclosure, Mrs. Crane sold the building. The purchaser took the property subject to the mortgage and paid Crane $3,000; of that amount, $500 went for the expenses of the sale.

Crane reported a gain of $2,500 on the transaction. She reasoned that her basis in the property was zero (despite her earlier depreciation deductions based on including the amount of the mortgage) and that the amount she realized from the sale was simply the cash she received. The Commissioner disputed this claim. He asserted that Crane's basis in the property was the property's fair market value at the time of her husband's death, adjusted for depreciation in the interim, and that the amount realized was the net cash received plus the amount of the outstanding mortgage assumed by the purchaser.

In upholding the Commissioner's interpretation, the Court observed that to regard merely the taxpayer's equity in the property as her basis would lead to depreciation deductions less than the actual physical deterioration of the property, and would require the basis to be recomputed with each payment on the mortgage. The Court rejected Crane's claim that any loss due to depreciation belonged to the mortgagee. The effect of the Court's ruling was that the taxpayer's basis was the value of the property undiminished by the mortgage.

The Court next proceeded to determine the amount realized. In order to avoid the "absurdity" of Crane's realizing only $2,500 on the sale of property worth over a quarter of a million dollars, the Court treated the amount realized as it had treated basis, that is, by including the outstanding value of the mortgage. To do otherwise would have permitted Crane to recognize a tax loss unconnected with any actual economic loss. The Court refused to construe one section of the Revenue Act so as "to frustrate the Act as a whole."

Crane, however, insisted that the nonrecourse nature of the mortgage required different treatment. The Court, for two reasons, disagreed. First, excluding the nonrecourse debt from the amount realized would result in the same absurdity and frustration of the Code. Second, the Court concluded that Crane obtained an economic benefit from the purchaser's assumption of the mortgage identical to the benefit conferred by the cancellation of personal debt. Because the value of the property in that case exceeded the amount of the mortgage, it was in Crane's economic interest to treat the mortgage as a personal obligation; only by so doing could she realize upon sale the appreciation in her equity represented by the $2,500 boot. The purchaser's assumption of the liability thus resulted in a taxable economic benefit to her, just as if she had been given, in addition to the boot, a sum of cash sufficient to satisfy the mortgage.

In a footnote, pertinent to the present case, the Court observed:

"Obviously, if the value of the property is less than the amount of the mortgage, a mortgagor who is not personally liable cannot realize a benefit equal to the mortgage. Consequently, a different problem might be encountered where a mortgagor abandoned the property or transferred it subject to the mortgage without receiving boot. That is not this case."

This case presents that unresolved issue. We are disinclined to overrule *Crane*, and we conclude that the same rule applies when the unpaid amount of the nonrecourse mortgage exceeds the value of the property transferred. *Crane* ultimately does not rest on its limited theory of economic benefit; instead, we read *Crane* to have approved the Commissioner's decision to treat a nonrecourse mortgage in this context as a true loan. This approval underlies *Crane*'s holdings that the amount of the nonrecourse liability is to be included in calculating both the basis and the amount realized on disposition. That the amount of the loan exceeds the fair market value of the property thus becomes irrelevant.

When a taxpayer receives a loan, he incurs an obligation to repay that loan at some future date. Because of this obligation, the loan proceeds do not qualify as income to the taxpayer. When he fulfills the obligation, the repayment of the loan likewise has no effect on his tax liability.

Another consequence to the taxpayer from this obligation occurs when the taxpayer applies the loan proceeds to the purchase price of property used to secure the loan. Because of the obligation to repay, the taxpayer is entitled to include the amount of the loan in computing his basis in the property; the loan, under § 1012, is part of the taxpayer's cost of the property. Although a different approach might have been taken with respect to a nonrecourse mortgage loan, the Commissioner has chosen to accord it the same treatment he gives to a recourse mortgage loan. The Court approved that choice in *Crane*, and the respondents do not challenge it here. The choice and its resultant benefits to the taxpayer are predicated on the assumption that the mortgage will be repaid in full.

When encumbered property is sold or otherwise disposed of and the purchaser assumes the mortgage, the associated extinguishment of the mortgagor's obligation to repay is accounted for in the computation of the amount realized. Because no difference between recourse and nonrecourse obligations is recognized in calculating basis,[5] *Crane* teaches that the

---

5. The Commissioner's choice in *Crane* "laid the foundation stone of most tax shelters," by permitting taxpayers who bear no risk to take deductions on depreciable property. Congress recently has acted to curb this avoidance device by forbidding a taxpayer to take depreciation deductions in excess of amounts he has at risk in the investment. Real estate investments,

Commissioner may ignore the nonrecourse nature of the obligation in determining the amount realized upon disposition of the encumbered property. He thus may include in the amount realized the amount of the nonrecourse mortgage assumed by the purchaser. The rationale for this treatment is that the original inclusion of the amount of the mortgage in basis rested on the assumption that the mortgagor incurred an obligation to repay. Moreover, this treatment balances the fact that the mortgagor originally received the proceeds of the nonrecourse loan tax-free on the same assumption. Unless the outstanding amount of the mortgage is deemed to be realized, the mortgagor effectively will have received untaxed income at the time the loan was extended and will have received an unwarranted increase in the basis of his property. The Commissioner's interpretation of § 1001(b) in this fashion cannot be said to be unreasonable.

The Commissioner in fact has applied this rule even when the fair market value of the property falls below the amount of the nonrecourse obligation. Because the theory on which the rule is based applies equally in this situation, we have no reason, after *Crane*, to question this treatment.[11]

Respondents received a mortgage loan with the concomitant obligation to repay by the year 2012. The only difference between that

---

however, are exempt from this prohibition. Although this Congressional action may foreshadow a day when nonrecourse and recourse debts will be treated differently, neither Congress nor the Commissioner has sought to alter *Crane*'s rule of including nonrecourse liability in both basis and the amount realized.

11. Professor Wayne G. Barnett, as amicus in the present case, argues that the liability and property portions of the transaction should be accounted for separately. Under his view, there was a transfer of the property for $1.4 million, and there was a cancellation of the $1.85 million obligation for a payment of $1.4 million. The former resulted in a capital loss of $50,000, and the latter in the realization of $450,000 of ordinary income. Taxation of the ordinary income might be deferred under § 108 by a reduction of respondents' bases in their partnership interests.

Although this indeed could be a justifiable mode of analysis, it has not been adopted by the Commissioner. Nor is there anything to indicate that the Code requires the Commissioner to adopt it. We note that Professor Barnett's approach does assume that recourse and nonrecourse debt may be treated identically.

The Commissioner also has chosen not to characterize the transaction as cancellation of indebtedness. We are not presented with and do not decide the contours of the cancellation-of-indebtedness doctrine. We note only that our approach does not fall within certain prior interpretations of that doctrine. In one view, the doctrine rests on the same initial premise as our analysis here—an obligation to repay—but the doctrine relies on a freeing-of-assets theory to attribute ordinary income to the debtor upon cancellation. According to that view, when nonrecourse debt is forgiven, the debtor's basis in the securing property is reduced by the amount of debt canceled, and realization of income is deferred until the sale of the property. Because that interpretation attributes income only when assets are freed, however, an insolvent debtor realizes income just to the extent his assets exceed his liabilities after the cancellation. Similarly, if the nonrecourse indebtedness exceeds the value of the securing property, the taxpayer never realizes the full amount of the obligation canceled because the tax law has not recognized negative basis.

Although the economic benefit prong of *Crane* also relies on a freeing-of-assets theory, that theory is irrelevant to our broader approach. In the context of a sale or disposition of property under § 1001, the extinguishment of the obligation to repay is not ordinary income; instead, the amount of the canceled debt is included in the amount realized, and enters into the computation of gain or loss on the disposition of property. According to *Crane*, this treatment is no different when the obligation is nonrecourse: the basis is not reduced as in the cancellation-of-indebtedness context, and the full value of the outstanding liability is included in the amount realized. Thus, the problem of negative basis is avoided.

mortgage and one on which the borrower is personally liable is that the mortgagee's remedy is limited to foreclosing on the securing property. This difference does not alter the nature of the obligation; its only effect is to shift from the borrower to the lender any potential loss caused by devaluation of the property. If the fair market value of the property falls below the amount of the outstanding obligation, the mortgagee's ability to protect its interests is impaired, for the mortgagor is free to abandon the property to the mortgagee and be relieved of his obligation.

This, however, does not erase the fact that the mortgagor received the loan proceeds tax-free and included them in his basis on the understanding that he had an obligation to repay the full amount. When the obligation is canceled, the mortgagor is relieved of his responsibility to repay the sum he originally received and thus realizes value to that extent within the meaning of § 1001(b). From the mortgagor's point of view, when his obligation is assumed by a third party who purchases the encumbered property, it is as if the mortgagor first had been paid with cash borrowed by the third party from the mortgagee on a nonrecourse basis, and then had used the cash to satisfy his obligation to the mortgagee.

Moreover, this approach avoids the absurdity the Court recognized in *Crane*. Because of the remedy accompanying the mortgage in the nonrecourse situation, the depreciation in the fair market value of the property is relevant economically only to the mortgagee, who by lending on a nonrecourse basis remains at risk. To permit the taxpayer to limit his realization to the fair market value of the property would be to recognize a tax loss for which he has suffered no corresponding economic loss. Such a result would be to construe "one section of the Act ... so as ... to defeat the intention of another or to frustrate the Act as a whole."

In the specific circumstances of *Crane*, the economic benefit theory did support the Commissioner's treatment of the nonrecourse mortgage as a personal obligation. The footnote in *Crane* acknowledged the limitations of that theory when applied to a different set of facts. *Crane* also stands for the broader proposition, however, that a nonrecourse loan should be treated as a true loan. We therefore hold that a taxpayer must account for the proceeds of obligations he has received tax-free and included in basis. Nothing in either § 1001(b) or in the Court's prior decisions requires the Commissioner to permit a taxpayer to treat a sale of encumbered property asymmetrically, by including the proceeds of the nonrecourse obligation in basis but not accounting for the proceeds upon transfer of the encumbered property.

When a taxpayer sells or disposes of property encumbered by a nonrecourse obligation, the Commissioner properly requires him to include among the assets realized the outstanding amount of the obligation. The fair market value of the property is irrelevant to this calculation. We

Notes

1. *Application of Tufts to recourse debt.*—In Rev. Rul. 90-16, the IRS held that *Tufts* would apply to recourse debt only to the extent of the fair market value of the collateral. Any excess recourse debt discharged would be treated as triggering discharge of indebtedness income. In effect, the IRS adopted Prof. Barnett's proposal, discussed in *Tufts*, footnote 11, but only for recourse debt.

Subchapter D: Zarin v. Commissioner

Code: Section 165(d)

ZARIN v. COMMISSIONER
92 T.C. 1084 (1989)

David Zarin (petitioner) was a professional engineer involved in the development, construction, and management of multi-family housing and nursing home facilities.

Petitioner occasionally stayed at Resorts International Hotel, Inc. (Resorts), in Atlantic City in connection with his construction activities. In June 1978, petitioner applied to Resorts for a $10,000 line of credit to be used for gambling.

The game most often played by petitioner, craps, creates the potential of losses or gains from wagering on rolls of dice. When he played craps at Resorts, petitioner usually bet the table limit per roll of the dice. Resorts quickly became familiar with petitioner. At petitioner's request, Resorts would raise the limit at the table to the house maximum. When petitioner gambled at Resorts, crowds would be attracted to his table by the large amounts he would wager. Gamblers would wager more than they might otherwise because of the excitement caused by the crowds and the amounts that petitioner was wagering. Petitioner was referred to as a "valued gaming patron" by executives at Resorts.

Many casinos extend complimentary services and privileges ("comps") to retain the patronage of their best customers. Beginning in the late summer of 1978, petitioner was extended the complimentary use of a luxury three-room suite at Resorts. Resorts progressively increased the complimentary services to include free meals, entertainment, and 24–hour access to a limousine. By late 1979, Resorts was extending such comps to petitioner's guests as well. By this practice, Resorts sought to preserve not only petitioner's patronage but also the attractive power his gambling had on others.

Patrons of New Jersey casinos may not gamble with currency, but must use chips provided by the casino. Chips may not be used outside the casino where they were issued for any purpose.

Petitioner received chips in exchange for signing counter checks, commonly known as "markers." The markers were negotiable drafts payable to Resorts drawn on petitioner's bank. The markers made no reference to chips, but stated that cash had been received.

At all times pertinent hereto, petitioner intended to repay any credit amount properly extended to him by Resorts and to pay Resorts in full the amount of any personal check given by him to pay for chips or to reduce his gambling debt. Between June 1978 and December 1979, petitioner incurred gambling debts of approximately $2.5 million. Petitioner paid these debts in full.

By January 1980, petitioner was gambling compulsively at Resorts. Petitioner was gambling 12–16 hours per day, 7 days per week in the casino, and he was betting up to $15,000 on each roll of the dice. Petitioner was not aware of the amount of his gambling debts.

During April 1980, petitioner delivered personal checks and markers in the total amount of $3,435,000 that were returned to Resorts as having been drawn against insufficient funds. On April 29, 1980, Resorts cut off petitioner's credit. Shortly thereafter, petitioner indicated to the Chief Executive Officer of Resorts that he intended to repay the obligations.

On November 18, 1980, Resorts filed a complaint in New Jersey state court seeking collection of $3,435,000 from petitioner based on the unpaid personal checks and markers. On March 4, 1981, petitioner filed an answer, denying the allegations and asserting a variety of affirmative defenses.

On September 28, 1981, petitioner settled the Resorts suit by agreeing to make a series of payments totaling $500,000. Petitioner paid the $500,000 settlement amount to Resorts in accordance with the terms of the agreement. The difference between petitioner's gambling obligations of $3,435,000 and the settlement payments of $500,000 is the amount that respondent alleges to be income from forgiveness of indebtedness.

Income from the Discharge of Indebtedness

Respondent contends that the difference between the $3,435,000 in personal checks and markers that were returned by the banks as drawn against insufficient funds and the $500,000 paid by petitioner in settlement of the Resorts suit constitutes income from the discharge of indebtedness. Petitioner argues the settlement agreement between Resorts and himself did not give rise to such income because, among other reasons, the debt instruments were not enforceable under New Jersey law and, in any event, the settlement should be treated as a purchase price adjustment that does not give rise to income from the discharge of indebtedness.

Petitioner argues that gambling and debts incurred to acquire gambling opportunity have always received special treatment at common law and in the Internal Revenue Code and that agreeing with respondent in this case would result in taxing petitioner on his losses. Petitioner relies on *United States v. Hall*, 307 F.2d 238 (10th Cir. 1962), as establishing a rule that the cancellation of indebtedness doctrine is not applicable to the settlement of a gambling debt.

The parties have primarily focused their arguments on whether the debt instruments memorializing the credit transactions were legally enforceable and whether legal enforceability is of significance in determining the existence of income from discharge of indebtedness. Petitioner argues that his debt was unenforceable and thus there was no debt to be discharged and no resulting freeing up of assets because his assets were never encumbered.

Respondent has not proven facts from which we can conclude that the debts were legally enforceable. We must decide, therefore, whether legal enforceability is a prerequisite to recognition of income in this case.

In *United States v. Hall*, the taxpayer transferred appreciated property in satisfaction of a gambling debt of an undetermined amount incurred in Las Vegas, Nevada. The Commissioner sought to tax as gain the difference between the amount of the discharged debt and the basis of the appreciated property. Although licensed gambling was legal in Nevada, gambling debts were nevertheless unenforceable. The Court of Appeals concluded that, under the circumstances, the amount of the gambling debt had no significance for tax purposes. The Court reasoned that, "The cold fact is that taxpayer suffered a substantial loss from gambling, the amount of which was determined by the transfer."

In *Commissioner v. Tufts*, the Supreme Court examined the economic realities associated with the cancellation of a nonrecourse obligation. Although a nonrecourse mortgage does not personally obligate the borrower or create a right against the borrower's general assets, the Supreme Court recognized the necessity of treating nonrecourse obligations as enforceable loans both when the obligations are made and when they are discharged. Thus, upon sale of mortgaged property, the seller-original borrower must include the amount of the nonrecourse mortgage assumed by the purchaser in calculating the amount realized from sale, even when the fair market value of the property is less than the outstanding amount of the nonrecourse obligation. Indicating a concern with symmetry, the Supreme Court observed in *Tufts*:

> "The rationale for this treatment is that the original inclusion of the amount of the mortgage in basis rested on the assumption that the mortgagor incurred an obligation to repay. Moreover, this treatment balances the fact that the mortgagor originally received the proceeds on the nonrecourse loan tax-free on the same assumption. Unless the outstanding amount of the mortgage is deemed to be realized, the mortgagor effectively will have received untaxed income at the time

the loan was extended and will have received an unwarranted increase in the basis of his property."

In the instant case, symmetry from year to year is not accomplished unless we treat petitioner's receipt of the loan from Resorts (*i.e.*, the markers converted to chips) and the subsequent discharge of his obligation to repay that loan in a consistent manner. Petitioner received credit of $3,435,000 from Resorts. He treated these amounts as a loan, not reporting any income on his 1980 tax return. The parties have stipulated that he intended to repay the amounts received. Although Resorts extended the credit to petitioner with the expectation that he would continue to gamble, theoretically petitioner could have redeemed the chips for cash. Certainly if he had won, rather than lost, at gambling, the amounts borrowed would have been repaid.

Petitioner argues that he did not get anything of value when he received the chips other than the "opportunity to gamble," and that, by reason of his addiction to gambling, he was destined to lose everything that he temporarily received. Thus, he is in effect arguing, based on *Hall*, that the settlement merely reduced the amount of his loss and did not result in income.

We conclude here that the taxpayer did receive value at the time he incurred the debt and that only his promise to repay the value received prevented taxation of the value received at the time of the credit transaction. When, in the subsequent year, a portion of the obligation to repay was forgiven, the general rule that income results from forgiveness of indebtedness, section 61(a)(12), should apply.

Legal enforceability of an obligation to repay is not generally determinative of whether the receipt of money or property is taxable. James v. United States, 366 U.S. 213, 219 (1961). Under the "all events test," only the fact of liability and the amount owed need be fixed as of the end of a taxable year in order to give rise to a deduction by an accrual basis taxpayer; legal liability is not required. Unenforceability of an underlying gambling debt is not a bar to the recognition of income by an accrual method gambling casino. Flamingo Resort, Inc. v. United States, 664 F.2d 1387 (9th Cir. 1982). Enforceability may affect the timing of recognition of income; other factors fix the amount to be recognized.

Here the timing of recognition was set when the debt was compromised. The amount to be recognized as income is the part of the debt that was discharged without payment. The enforceability of petitioner's debts under New Jersey law did not affect either the timing or the amount and thus is not determinative for Federal income tax purposes. We are not persuaded that gambling debts should be accorded any special treatment for the benefit of the gambler—compulsive or not.

Petitioner also relies on the principle that settlement of disputed debts does not give rise to income. *N. Sobel, Inc. v. Commissioner*, 40 B.T.A. 1263 (1939). Prior to the settlement, the amount of petitioner's gambling debt to Resorts was a liquidated amount, unlike the taxpayer's debt in *Hall*. There is no dispute about the amount petitioner received. The parties dispute only its legal enforceability, *i.e.*, whether petitioner could be legally compelled to pay Resorts the fixed amount he had borrowed. A genuine dispute does not exist merely because petitioner required Resorts to sue him before making payment of any amount on the debt. The cases cited by petitioner merely require that there be a liquidated debt, *i.e.*, one in which the amount has been determined. In our view, petitioner's arguments concerning his defenses to Resorts' claim, which apparently led to Resorts' agreement to discount the debt, are overcome by (1) the stipulation of the parties that, at the time the debt was created, petitioner agreed to and intended to repay the full amount, and (2) our conclusion that he received full value for what he agreed to pay, *i.e.*, over $3 million worth of chips and the benefits received by petitioner as a "valued gambling patron" of Resorts.

In several different ways, petitioner argues that any income from discharge of his gambling debt was income from gambling against which he may offset his losses; thus, he argues, he had no net income from gambling.

Section 165(d) provides that "Losses from wagering transactions shall be allowed only to the extent of the gains from such transactions." Neither section 165(d) nor section 1.165-10, Income Tax Regs., defines what items are included as gains from wagering transactions. The regulation, however, provides that wagering losses "shall be allowed as a deduction but only to the extent of the gains *during the taxable years* from such transactions." (Emphasis supplied.) Petitioner incurred gambling losses in 1980, but his gain from the discharge of his gambling debts occurred in 1981. That gain is separate and apart from the losses he incurred from his actual wagering transactions. We have no evidence of his actual wagering gains and losses for either year. If we were to effectively allow petitioner to deduct the value of the lost chips from the value of the discharged debt, we would ignore annual accounting and undermine section 165(d) by in effect allowing gambling losses in excess of gambling winnings.

Petitioner argues that the settlement with Resorts should be treated as a purchase price adjustment that does not give rise to income from the discharge of indebtedness. He cites the parties' stipulation, which included a statement that, "Patrons of New Jersey casinos may not gamble with currency. All gambling must be done with chips provided by the casino. Such chips are property which are not negotiable and may not be used to gamble or for any other purpose outside the casino where they were issued." Respondent argues that petitioner actually received "cash" in return for his debts.

Section 108(e)(5) was enacted "to eliminate disagreements between the Internal Revenue Service and the debtor as to whether, in a particular case to which the provision applies, the debt reductions should be treated as discharge income or a true price adjustment."

For a reduction in the amount of a debt to be treated as a purchase price adjustment under section 108(e)(5), the following conditions must be met: (1) The debt must be that of a purchaser of property to the seller which arose out of the purchase of such property; (2) the taxpayer must be solvent and not in bankruptcy when the debt reduction occurs; and (3) except for section 108(e)(5), the debt reduction would otherwise have resulted in discharge of indebtedness income.

In addition to the literal statutory requirements, the legislative history indicates that section 108(e)(5) was intended to apply only if the following requirements are also met: (a) The price reduction must result from an agreement between the purchaser and the seller and not, for example, from a discharge as a result of the bar of the statute of limitations on enforcement of the obligation; (b) there has been no transfer of the debt by the seller to a third party; and (c) there has been no transfer of the purchased property from the purchaser to a third party. S. Rept. No. 96–1035 (1980), 1980–2 C.B. 620, 628.

It seems to us that the value received by petitioner in exchange for the credit extended by Resorts does not constitute the type of property to which section 108(e)(5) was intended to or reasonably can be applied. Petitioner argued throughout his briefs that he purchased only "the opportunity to gamble" and that the chips had little or no value.

We agree that what he received was something other than normal commercial property. He bargained for and received the opportunity to gamble and incidental services, lodging, entertainment, meals, and transportation. Petitioner's argument that he was purchasing chips ignores the essence of the transaction, as more accurately described in his other arguments here quoted. The "property" argument simply overemphasizes the significance of the chips. As a matter of substance, chips in isolation are not what petitioner purchased.

The "opportunity to gamble" would not in the usual sense of the words be "property" transferred from a seller to a purchaser. The terminology used in section 108(e)(5) is readily understood with respect to tangible property and may apply to some types of intangibles. Abstract concepts of property are not useful, however, in deciding whether what petitioner received is within the contemplation of the section.

Obviously the chips in this case were a medium of exchange within the Resorts casino, and in that sense they were a substitute for cash, just as Federal Reserve Notes, checks, or other convenient means of representing credit balances constitute or substitute for cash. Recognition that foreign currency has, for some purposes, been held to be "property" that qualifies as a capital asset is not in point here. Foreign currency fluctuates in United States dollar value, whereas the chips in question do not.

We conclude that petitioner's settlement with Resorts cannot be construed as a "purchase-money debt reduction" arising from the purchase of property within the meaning of section 108(e)(5).

TANNENWALD, J., dissenting:

I think it highly significant that in all the decided cases involving the cancellation of indebtedness, the taxpayer had, in a prior year when the indebtedness was created, received a nontaxable benefit clearly measurable in monetary terms which would remain untaxed if the subsequent cancellation of the indebtedness were held to be tax free. Such is simply not the case herein. The concept that petitioner received his money's worth from the enjoyment of using the chips (thus equating the pleasure of gambling with increase in wealth) produces the incongruous result that the more a gambler loses, the greater his pleasure and the larger the increase in his wealth. Under the circumstances, I think the issue of enforceability becomes critical. In this connection, the repeated emphasis by the majority on the stipulation that Mr. Zarin intended to repay the full amount at the time the debt was created is beside the point. If the debt was unenforceable under New Jersey law, that intent is irrelevant.

I think it significant that because the debts involved herein were unenforceable *from the moment that they were created*, there was no freeing up of petitioners' assets when they were discharged, see *United States v. Kirby Lumber Co.*, and therefore there was no increase in petitioners' wealth that could constitute income. *Cf. Commissioner v. Glenshaw Glass Co.* This is particularly true in light of the fact that the chips were given to Mr. Zarin with the expectation that he would continue to gamble and, therefore, did not constitute an increase in his wealth when he received them in the same sense that the proceeds of a non-gambling loan would.

I find further support for my conclusion from the application of the principle that if there is a genuine dispute as to liability on the underlying obligation, settlement of that obligation will not give rise to income from discharge of indebtedness. *N. Sobel, Inc. v. Commissioner*, 40 B.T.A. 1263 (1939). Respondent simply has not met his burden of showing that the dispute between Resorts and Mr. Zarin was not a genuine dispute as to Mr. Zarin's liability for the underlying obligations, and I believe that, at least as to that debt that was not entered into as required by New Jersey law and was therefore unenforceable, the dispute was in fact genuine. While there is language in *Sobel* indicating that *United States v. Kirby Lumber Co.*, applies when there is a liquidated amount of indebtedness, I do not read that language as requiring that *Kirby Lumber* must apply unless the amount is unliquidated, where there is a genuine dispute as to the underlying liability.

JACOBS, J., dissenting:

In my opinion, petitioner's obligation to Resorts was void *ab initio*, and therefore, I would first hold that petitioner realized income (herein referred to as chip income) in 1980 (a year at issue) to the extent of the value of the chips received.

It is apparent that petitioner left the chips he obtained through the extension of credit by Resorts on Resorts' gambling tables. For had he won, his markers undoubtedly would have been paid, and this case would not be before us. Accordingly, I would next hold that the amount of petitioner's losses from wagering activities in 1980 equalled or exceeded the amount of chip income.

I recognize that section 165(d) limits losses from wagering transactions to the extent of gains from such transactions. In my opinion, for purposes of section 165(d), the chip income constitutes gain from a wagering transaction, because no such income would have been realized but for the wagering transactions in which petitioner's losses occurred. Thus, I would hold that petitioner is entitled to deduct in 1980 his gambling losses to the extent of the chip income.

While I believe the preceding analysis resolves the tax consequences of petitioner's transaction with Resorts, I feel compelled to address the majority's holding that petitioner had income from discharge of gambling indebtedness in 1981.

In my opinion, for tax purposes, an unenforceable debt is a contradiction in terms, an oxymoron. It is like shooting craps without dice. For interest on indebtedness to be deductible under section 163, it is well recognized that the indebtedness must be enforceable. I am unable to discern why the majority imposes a different rule for the inclusion of discharge of indebtedness income. Accordingly, for 1981, I would hold petitioner did not realize discharge of indebtedness income.

RUWE J., dissenting:

Although I agree with much of the majority's reasoning in this case, I dissent from that portion of the opinion which holds that section 108(e)(5) is inapplicable to the transaction at issue. I find no support in the language of the statute or the accompanying legislative history for the majority's determination that the gambling chips purchased by petitioner do not constitute "property" for purposes of section 108(e)(5). Because I believe that petitioner acquired "property" from the casino on credit and subsequently negotiated a reduction of his debt to the casino, I would apply section 108(e)(5) in this case.

This is a fully stipulated case. Since all of the facts were agreed to by the parties, our factual findings are controlled by the stipulation of facts. The parties stipulated that *"chips are property which are not negotiable."* (Emphasis added.) In their briefs, both parties requested that the Court find this as a fact. Despite this, the majority fails to adopt this stipulated fact which is critical to the resolution of this case.

It is unclear whether the majority is saying that it is not persuaded of the fact that the chips were "property" or whether the majority decides that section 108 uses the term "property" in a restricted manner. Given the majority's failure to include in its findings of fact that chips are property, I must assume, for purposes of this dissent, that the majority decides that the stipulation fails to support a factual finding that chips are "property" and also decides that even if they are property in a generic sense, they are not "property" within the meaning of section 108.

[T]he majority finally settles on the conclusion that the gambling chips purchased by petitioner were "something other than normal commercial property." I take this to be a finding of fact since the term "normal commercial property" does not appear in the relevant statutes, regulations, or legislative history.

The majority's legal conclusion seems to be that gambling chips, being other than "normal commercial property," do not constitute "property" within the meaning of section 108(e)(5). In deciding this legal issue of first impression, the majority fails to define either the term "property" as used in section 108(e)(5) or the term "normal commercial property."

If the term "normal commercial property" has a meaning, there is no reason why gambling chips should not be included. As recently stated by the Supreme Court:

> "it would seem that basic concepts of fairness (if there be much of that in the income tax law) demand that [gambling] be regarded as a trade or business just as any other readily accepted activity, such as being a retail store proprietor or, to come closer categorically, as being a casino operator or as being an active trader on the exchanges. *Commissioner v. Groetzinger*, 480 U.S. 23 (1987)."

Chips are certainly "normal commercial property" in a casino's commercial gambling business. If the term "normal commercial property" is meant to preclude the application of section 108(e)(5) to property that is unique or "one of a kind," there is no support for such a conclusion. In any event, neither the statute nor its legislative history restricts its application to "normal commercial property."

The majority concludes that petitioner "received full value for what he agreed to pay, *i.e.*, over $3 million worth of chips." However, the majority concludes that "chips in isolation are not what petitioner purchased." The majority reasons that the value of the chips is really derived from the fact that they give the holder of the chips the opportunity to gamble. This seems akin to saying that a taxpayer who purchases a 99-year leasehold to a vacant lot in midtown Manhattan has not acquired "property" because the value of the leasehold interest is derived from the lessee's "opportunity" to build a large office building. That the chips derive value from the opportunity they afford is no reason why they are not property. A person who purchases chips receives, among other things, the casino's promise to provide a gambling opportunity. In that sense, the opportunity is no different than any other valuable and assignable contract right which we would surely recognize as property. A license is nothing more than a grant of an opportunity to the licensee to do something which he would otherwise be prohibited from doing. Nevertheless, a license is considered property. Similarly, an option, which can also be characterized as nothing more than a grant of an opportunity, constitutes property.

The majority concludes that property within the meaning of section 108(e)(5) includes tangible property and "may apply to some types of intangibles." It then states that "Abstract concepts of property are not useful" in deciding what is property within the contemplation of section 108(e)(5). The opinion then leaves us to wonder what kinds of intangible property might come within the contemplation of the statute or what concepts, abstract or otherwise, were relied upon in construing the meaning of the statute.

The plain language of a statute is the primary source for any interpretation. When that language is not ambiguous, it is conclusive absent a clearly expressed legislative intent to the contrary. The starting point for interpreting a statutory provision is the language of the actual statute. The plain meaning of the statutory language, as enlightened by the contemporaneous legislative history, often indicates the congressional intent behind enactment of a particular statute. In this particular instance, neither the statute nor the accompanying legislative history qualify or restrict the term "property." No attempt has been made to specify any limits on the scope of the term. Instead, the term is used in a broad, comprehensive manner. When Congress intends to restrict the meaning of the term "property," it certainly knows how to do so. See, for example, section 1031(a).

Section 108(e)(5) and the background giving rise to its enactment support its application to the facts in this case. Prior to enactment of section 108(e)(5), case law distinguished between true discharge of indebtedness situations which required recognition of income and purchase price adjustments. A purchase price adjustment occurred when a purchaser of property agreed to incur a debt to the seller but the debt was subsequently reduced because the value of the property was less than the agreed upon consideration. A mere purchase price adjustment does not result in discharge of indebtedness income. See *N. Sobel, Inc. v. Commissioner*, 40 B.T.A. 1263 (1939).

Section 108(e)(5) was enacted "to eliminate disagreements between the Internal Revenue Service and the debtor as to whether, in a particular case to which the provision applies, the debt reductions should be treated as discharge income or a true price adjustment." Its provisions are not elective. It is obvious from the portions of petitioner's brief that one of petitioner's arguments is that the value of what he received was less than the amount of debt incurred. Respondent argues, and the majority finds, that the chips petitioner received were worth the full value of the debt. Thus, this case presents the very controversy that the above-quoted legislative history says Congress tried to eliminate by enacting section 108(e)(5).

For a reduction in the amount of a debt to be treated as a purchase price adjustment under section 108(e)(5), the following conditions must be met: (1) The debt must be that of a purchaser of property to the seller which arose out of the purchase of such property; (2) the taxpayer must be solvent and not in bankruptcy when the debt reduction occurs; and (3) except for section 108(e)(5), the debt reduction would otherwise have resulted in discharge of indebtedness income.

The first condition of section 108(e)(5) has been met since petitioner was the purchaser of property in the form of gambling chips and the debt arose out of these purchases.

As to the second condition of the statute, the stipulation of facts contains no specific statement regarding whether petitioner was solvent and not in bankruptcy when the debt reduction occurred. Respondent bears the burden of proof on the discharge of indebtedness issue, therefore, the absence of evidence cannot benefit respondent. However, petitioner's opening brief stated that petitioner was solvent at the time the debt was reduced and neither respondent's opening nor reply brief disputes this. In any event, had petitioner been insolvent or in bankruptcy, the discharge of indebtedness would have been excluded from income under section 108(a)(1).

The third specific requirement of the statute, that there was discharge of indebtedness income, but for section 108(e)(5), has been met as found by the majority.

In addition to the literal statutory requirements, the legislative history indicates that section 108(e)(5) was intended to apply only if the following requirements are also met: (a) The price reduction must result from an agreement between the purchaser and the seller and not, for example, from a discharge as a result of the running of the statute of limitations on enforcement of the obligation; (b) there has been no transfer of the debt by the seller to a third party; and (c) there has been no transfer of the purchased property from the purchaser to a third party. S. Rept. No. 1035, supra, 1980–2 C.B. at 628.

These requirements have also been met. The settlement agreement indicates that petitioner and Resorts mutually agreed to reduce the amount of indebtedness in order to amicably resolve their differences and terminate their litigation. In that litigation, Resorts alleged a number of counts and petitioner raised a variety of affirmative defenses. The settlement agreement was the result of direct negotiations between petitioner and Resorts.

The second requirement set forth in the legislative history has been met. Resorts did not transfer petitioner's debt to a third party.

The third requirement has also been met. Petitioner did not transfer the property to a third party. Both parties in their briefs acknowledge that petitioner did transfer the property to Resorts in that the chips were lost to Resorts at the gambling tables. The legislative history, however, indicates that application of section 108(e)(5) is precluded only if the purchaser/taxpayer transfers the property to a "third party." Resorts was not a third party; Resorts was the seller/creditor.

The majority decides an issue of first impression by disregarding the plain language of the statute without any justification in the statute or legislative history. The result produced is ironic for both the Court and petitioner. The Court must decide the difficult factual issues that section 108(e)(5) was intended to eliminate while petitioner incurs a huge tax liability, the magnitude of which is in direct proportion to his losses.

I would dispose of this case by assuming that there was discharge of indebtedness income. I would then apply section 108(e)(5) to treat the discharge as a purchase price adjustment. This would result in no taxable income. I respectfully dissent.

ZARIN v. COMMISSIONER

916 F.2d 110 (3rd Cir. 1990)

David Zarin ("Zarin") appeals from a decision of the Tax Court holding that he recognized $2,935,000 of income from discharge of indebtedness resulting from his gambling activities, and that he should be taxed on the income. After considering the issues raised by this appeal, we will reverse.

[The court summarizes the facts.]

The Commissioner of Internal Revenue ("Commissioner") subsequently determined deficiencies in Zarin's federal income taxes for 1980 and 1981, arguing that Zarin recognized $3,435,000 of income in 1980 from larceny by trick and deception. After Zarin challenged that claim by filing a Tax Court petition, the Commissioner abandoned his 1980 claim, and argued instead that Zarin had recognized $2,935,000 of income in 1981 from the cancellation of indebtedness which resulted from the settlement with Resorts.

Agreeing with the Commissioner, the Tax Court decided, eleven judges to eight, that Zarin had indeed recognized $2,935,000 of income from the discharge of indebtedness, namely the difference between the original $3,435,000 "debt" and the $500,000 settlement. Since he was in the seventy percent tax bracket, Zarin's deficiency for 1981 was calculated to be $2,047,245. With interest to April 5, 1990, Zarin allegedly owes the Internal Revenue Service $5,209,033.96 in additional taxes.

Under the Commissioner's logic, Resorts advanced Zarin $3,435,000 worth of chips, chips being the functional equivalent of cash. At that time, the chips were not treated as income, since Zarin recognized an obligation of repayment. In other words, Resorts made Zarin a tax-free loan. However, a taxpayer does recognize income if a loan owed to another party is cancelled, in whole or in part. The settlement between Zarin and Resorts, claims the Commissioner, fits neatly into the cancellation of indebtedness provisions in the Code. Zarin owed $3,435,000, paid $500,000, with the difference constituting income.

Initially, we find that sections 108 and 61(a)(12) are inapplicable to the Zarin/Resorts transaction. Section 61 does not define indebtedness. On the other hand, section 108(d)(1), which repeats and further elaborates on the rule in section 61(a)(12), defines the term as any indebtedness "(A) for which the taxpayer is liable, or (B) subject to which the taxpayer holds property." I.R.C. § 108(d)(1). In order to bring the taxpayer within the sweep of the discharge of indebtedness rules, then, the IRS must show that one of the two prongs in the section 108(d)(1) test is satisfied. It has not been demonstrated that Zarin satisfies either.

Because the debt Zarin owed to Resorts was unenforceable as a matter of New Jersey state law, it is clearly not a debt "for which the taxpayer is liable." I.R.C. § 108(d)(1)(A). Liability implies a legally enforceable obligation to repay, and under New Jersey law, Zarin would have no such obligation.

Moreover, Zarin did not have a debt subject to which he held property as required by section 108(d)(1)(B). Zarin's indebtedness arose out of his acquisition of gambling chips. The Tax Court held that gambling chips were not property, but rather, "a medium of exchange within the Resorts casino" and a "substitute for cash." Alternatively, the Tax Court viewed the chips as nothing more than "the opportunity to gamble and incidental services..." We agree with the gist of these characterizations, and hold that gambling chips are merely an accounting mechanism to evidence debt.

Gaming chips in New Jersey during 1980 were regarded "solely as evidence of a debt owed to their custodian by the casino licensee and shall be considered at no time the property of anyone other than the casino licensee issuing them." N.J.Admin.Code tit. 19k, § 19:46–1.5(d) (1990). Thus, under New Jersey state law, gambling chips were Resorts' property until transferred to Zarin in exchange for the markers, at which point the chips became "evidence" of indebtedness (and not the property of Zarin).

Even were there no relevant legislative pronouncement on which to rely, simple common sense would lead to the conclusion that chips were not property in Zarin's hands. Zarin could not do with the chips as he pleased, nor did the chips have any independent economic value beyond the casino. The chips themselves were of little use to Zarin, other than as a means of facilitating gambling. They could not have been used outside the casino. They could have been used to purchase services and privileges within the casino, including food, drink, entertainment, and lodging, but Zarin would not have utilized them as such, since he received those services from Resorts on a complimentary basis. In short, the chips had no economic substance.

Although the Tax Court found that theoretically, Zarin could have redeemed the chips he received on credit for cash and walked out of the casino, the reality of the situation was quite different. Realistically, before cashing in his chips, Zarin would have been required to pay his outstanding IOUs. New Jersey state law requires casinos to "request patrons to apply any chips or plaques in their possession in reduction of personal checks or Counter Checks exchanged for purposes of gaming prior to exchanging such chips or plaques for cash or prior to departing from the casino area." Since his debt at all times equalled or exceeded the number of chips he possessed, redemption would have left Zarin with no chips, no cash, and certainly nothing which could have been characterized as property.

Not only were the chips non-property in Zarin's hands, but upon transfer to Zarin, the chips also ceased to be the property of Resorts. Since the chips were in the possession of another party, Resorts could no longer do with the chips as it pleased, and could no longer control the chips' use. Generally, at the time of a transfer, the party in possession of the chips can gamble with them, use them for services, cash them in, or walk out of the casino with them as an Atlantic City souvenir. The chips therefore become nothing more than an accounting mechanism, or evidence of a debt, designed to facilitate gambling in casinos where the use of actual money was forbidden. Thus, the chips which Zarin held were not property within the meaning of I.R.C. § 108(d)(1)(B).

In short, because Zarin was not liable on the debt he allegedly owed Resorts, and because Zarin did not hold "property" subject to that debt, the cancellation of indebtedness provisions of the Code do not apply to the settlement between Resorts and Zarin. As such, Zarin cannot have income from the discharge of his debt.

Instead of analyzing the transaction at issue as cancelled debt, we believe the proper approach is to view it as disputed debt or contested liability. Under the contested liability doctrine, if a taxpayer, in good faith, disputed the amount of a debt, a subsequent settlement of the dispute would be treated as the amount of debt cognizable for tax purposes. The excess of the original debt over the amount determined to have been due is disregarded for both loss and debt accounting purposes. Thus, if a taxpayer took out a loan for $10,000, refused in good faith to pay the full $10,000 back, and then reached an agreement with the lendor that he would pay back only $7000 in full satisfaction of the debt, the transaction would be treated as if the initial loan was $7000. When the taxpayer tenders the $7000 payment, he will have been deemed to have paid the full amount of the initially disputed debt. Accordingly, there is no tax consequence to the taxpayer upon payment.

The seminal "contested liability" case is *N. Sobel, Inc. v. Commissioner*, 40 B.T.A. 1263 (1939). There is little difference between the present case and *Sobel*. Zarin incurred a $3,435,000 debt while gambling at Resorts, but in court, disputed liability on the basis of unenforceability. A settlement of $500,000 was eventually agreed upon. It follows from *Sobel* that the settlement served only to fix the amount of debt. No income was realized or recognized. When Zarin paid the $500,000, any tax consequence dissolved.

The Commissioner argues that Sobel and the contested liability doctrine only apply when there is an unliquidated debt; that is, a debt for which the amount cannot be determined. Since Zarin contested his liability based on the unenforceability of the entire debt, and did not dispute the amount of the debt, the Commissioner would have us adopt the reasoning of the Tax Court, which found that Zarin's debt was liquidated, therefore barring the application of *Sobel* and the contested liability doctrine.

We reject the Tax Court's rationale. When a debt is unenforceable, it follows that the amount of the debt, and not just the liability thereon, is in dispute. Although a debt may be unenforceable, there still could be some value attached to its worth. This is especially so with regards to gambling debts. In most states, gambling debts are unenforceable, and have "but slight potential ..." Nevertheless, they are often collected, at least in part. For example, Resorts is not a charity; it would not have extended illegal credit to Zarin and others if it did not have some hope of collecting debts incurred pursuant to the grant of credit.

Moreover, the debt is frequently incurred to acquire gambling chips, and not money. Although casinos attach a dollar value to each chip, that value, unlike money's, is not beyond dispute, particularly given the illegality of gambling debts in the first place. This proposition is supported by the facts of the present case. Resorts gave Zarin $3.4 million dollars of chips in exchange for markers evidencing Zarin's debt. If indeed the only issue was the enforceabilty of the entire debt, there would have been no settlement. Zarin would have owed all or nothing. Instead, the parties attached a value to the debt considerably lower than its face value. In other words, the parties agreed that given the circumstances surrounding Zarin's gambling spree, the chips he acquired might not have been worth $3.4 million dollars, but were worth something. Such a debt cannot be called liquidated, since its exact amount was not fixed until settlement.

To summarize, the transaction between Zarin and Resorts can best be characterized as a disputed debt, or contested liability. Zarin owed an unenforceable debt of $3,435,000 to Resorts. After Zarin in good faith disputed his obligation to repay the debt, the parties settled for $500,000, which Zarin paid. That $500,000 settlement fixed the amount of loss and the amount of debt cognizable for tax purposes. Since Zarin was deemed to have owed $500,000, and since he paid Resorts $500,000, no adverse tax consequences attached to Zarin as a result.

In conclusion, we hold that Zarin did not have any income from cancellation of indebtedness for two reasons. First, the Code provisions covering discharge of debt are inapplicable since the definitional requirement in I.R.C. section 108(d)(1) was not met. Second, the settlement of Zarin's gambling debts was a contested liability. We reverse the decision of the Tax Court and remand with instructions to enter judgment that Zarin realized no income by reason of his settlement with Resorts.

Problems for Discussion

8–22. Assume that in 1980 Zarin purchased deductible services for use in his trade or business, giving in exchange his note in the amount of $3,435,000. Before the end of 1980, he contested the note. The parties settled in 1981, agreeing that Zarin would pay $500,000 on the note, which he did. Does the settlement give rise to discharge of indebtedness income? Does it matter whether Zarin is a cash or accrual method taxpayer?

8–23. Assume that in 1980 Zarin purchased depreciable equipment for use in his trade or business, giving in exchange his note in the amount of $3,435,000. Before the end of 1980, he contested the note. The parties settled in 1981, agreeing that Zarin would pay $500,000 on the note, which he did. Does the settlement give rise to discharge of indebtedness income? Does it matter whether Zarin is a cash or accrual method taxpayer?

8–24. How much Haig–Simons income did the Tax Court conclude Zarin had? How much did Judge Tannenwald conclude Zarin had?

8–25. Sean plays craps at Resorts International, gambling with his own money, and wins $1,000,000, enjoying himself enormously in the process. For U.S. tax purposes, how much gross income does he have? Devon plays craps as well, gambling with his own money, and loses $1,000,000, having a miserable time in the process. Under the Code, how much of a loss is he allowed? Does the Code tax the consumption value of gambling?

8–26. The 3rd Circuit states: "[I]f a taxpayer took out a loan for $10,000, refused in good faith to pay the full $10,000 back, and then reached an agreement with the lender that he would pay back only $7000 in full satisfaction of the debt, the transaction would be treated as if the initial loan was $7000. When the taxpayer tenders the $7000 payment, he will have been deemed to have paid the full amount of the initially disputed debt. Accordingly, there is no tax consequence to the taxpayer upon payment." This statement is commonly viewed as dead wrong. Why?

CHAPTER 9

NONRECOGNITION

■ ■ ■

In general, if a taxpayer realizes income, she is required to recognize it—that is, she is required to report that income on her return. But the Code contains a number of nonrecognition provisions. A nonrecognition provision is simply a provision that says that in this or that circumstance, even if you realize a gain or loss you are not required—or even permitted—to recognize it. Among the more important are Code Section 351 (nonrecognition on exchange of property for corporate stock) and Code Section 721 (nonrecognition on exchange of property for partnership interest), typically studied in courses on business entity taxation.

Here, we will explore two such provisions: Code Section 1031, which accords nonrecognition treatment to "like-kind" exchanges, and Code Section 1033, which accords nonrecognition treatment to involuntary conversions, in each case if specified conditions are met. We will contrast these with Code Section 121, which excludes all or part of the gain on the sale of a taxpayer's principal residence. Code Section 121 is an exclusion provision, not a nonrecognition provision, and usefully illustrates the difference between the two.

Subchapter A: Like–Kind Exchanges

Code: Section 1031

Regulations: Section 1.1031(a)–1

CLICK v. COMMISSIONER
78 T.C. 225 (1982)

We must determine whether petitioner's exchange of farmland for two residential properties, cash, and a note qualifies for nonrecognition treatment under section 1031. Section 1031(a) provides that no gain or loss shall be recognized if property held for productive use in a trade or business or for investment is exchanged solely for property of a like kind which is also "to be held either for productive use in a trade or business or for investment."

To qualify for treatment under section 1031, three requirements must be satisfied: (1) The transaction must be an exchange; (2) the exchange must involve like-kind properties; and (3) both the properties transferred and the properties received must be held either for productive use in a trade or business or for investment. The parties do not question that the transaction at issue constitutes an exchange. Furthermore, they appear to agree that the farmland and the two residences are like-kind properties because the nature and character of the properties, as distinguished from their grade or quality, are substantially the same. The controversy, therefore, centers on whether the two residences received by petitioner Dollie H. Click in the exchange were held for investment.

A taxpayer's intent to hold property for investment must be determined as of the time of the exchange. We must examine the substance of the transaction, rather than the form in which it is cast, when analyzing a purported section 1031 exchange of property. The petitioner bears the burden of proving that she had the requisite investment intent.

In the instant case, respondent proposes to disallow section 1031 nonrecognition treatment on the theory that petitioner's gifts of the residences were part of a prearranged plan. He alleges that petitioner's intent at the time of the exchange was not to hold the houses for investment, but eventually to gift them to her children. Petitioner counters with the assertion that she had no concrete plan to transfer the acquired property to her children at the time of the exchange. Rather, she stated that she took the property because she wanted "something that would grow in value." As such, she claims that she held the houses as an investment until 7 months after the exchange, at which time she decided to gift them to her children.

In *Wagensen v. Commissioner*, 74 T.C. 653 (1980), we considered a factual setting that appears, at first glance, to be analogous to the case at hand. The taxpayer therein exchanged his ranch for another ranch and cash. Nine months later, he made a gift of the new ranch and some cash to his son and daughter. We held that the taxpayer had no concrete plans at the time of the like-kind exchange to make the later gift. First, the facts showed that he did not initiate discussions with his accountants about a gift until after the exchange. Second, he used the acquired ranch in his ranching business during the period between the exchange and the gift. Accordingly, while we found that the general desire to make a gift prior to the time of the exchange is not inconsistent with an intent to hold the acquired ranch for productive use in business or for investment, we also found that, considering the facts presented, the gift was not part of the exchange transaction.

Respondent argues that the *Wagensen* opinion does not control in the instant case because petitioner intended to gift the residences to her children at the time of the exchange, and petitioner never had the requisite investment intent. Furthermore, respondent says that the ranch property exchanged in *Wagensen* was inherently investment or business property, while the houses received herein were personal.

In the instant case, the facts reveal that petitioner suggested to her son and daughter and their spouses as early as mid–1973 that they look for new homes to use as "swap" property. Mr. and Mrs. Highsmith [petitioner's daughter and son-in-law] located the Gierisch residence. Mr. and Mrs. John Click [petition's son and daughter-in-law] located the Tinney residence, which had been the focus of prior inquiry by Mrs. Click in 1973. Such homes suited the personal lifestyles of the two couples and satisfied their desires for larger homes and more land. Only after Marriott made its offer to purchase did petitioner visit the Tinney residence. We cannot believe that petitioner, who was an experienced investor, had an investment intent with respect to property that she did not personally select and had never seen prior to its selection.

Further, petitioner, now 72 years old, was working on an estate plan with her attorney in 1973 and 1974 at the same time that the idea for the exchange of properties developed and at the time of the transaction with Marriott. As a woman with a potentially substantial estate, petitioner had been advised with respect to estate and gift tax liabilities that might arise. Based on the evidence presented, we believe that petitioner's estate planning activities are highly indicative of an intent at the time of the exchange to gift the residences to her children.

Finally, petitioner's testimony indicates that she normally took care of her investments and obtained property insurance therefor. Here, the facts indicate that Mr. and Mrs. Highsmith took out property insurance and paid property taxes on the Gierisch residence for the period from July 9, 1974, through February 8, 1975. In addition, during the same period, Mr. and Mrs. John Click paid for a homeowner's insurance policy on the Tinney residence. They also made substantial expenditures for improvements on the Tinney residence. John Click testified that he treated the property as his own, although he knew he was not the owner. He lived in the house rent free during the 7–month period and spent money on the improvements purportedly to protect his mother's investment. A review of the expenditures indicates that many were for improvements that were more in the nature of personal custom features than for general maintenance. In addition, the fact that Mr. Click did not obtain his mother's approval before making the expenditures further belies petitioner's claim that her children lived in the houses as "caretakers" during the period between the exchange and the gift.

Accordingly, we cannot find that petitioner had an investment intent in accepting the homes as "swap" property. Rather, it appears that her primary purpose was to provide larger homes in which her children and grandchildren could reside. From all of the evidence, we believe that petitioner acquired the residences with the intent of making gifts of them to her children and not to hold as investments for eventual sale. While petitioner was certainly a generous and caring parent and grandparent, her concern for the welfare of her family does not qualify the exchange for nonrecognition treatment under section 1031.

NOTES

1. *Like-kind property.*—In general, real property interests are always treated as of like kind. Treas. Reg. § 1.1031(a)–1(b) provides that "The fact that any real estate involved is improved or unimproved is not material, for that fact relates only to the grade or quality of the property and not to its kind or class." Treas. Reg. § 1031(a)–1(c) further states: "No gain or loss is recognized if . . . a taxpayer who is not a dealer in real estate exchanges city real estate for a ranch or farm, or exchanges a leasehold of a fee with 30 years or more to run for real estate, or exchanges improved real estate for unimproved real estate." (But note that under Code Section 897(e)(1), exchanges of U.S. real property for foreign real property are not eligible for nonrecognition.) Because all U.S. real property is generally treated as of like kind, the single most important practical context in which Code Section 1031 arises is in real estate work.

At the other extreme, Code Section 1031(a)(2) provides that certain types of property are never of like kind—most importantly, property held primarily for sale, stock, bonds, notes or other securities or evidences of indebtedness, and partnership interests. All other types of property fall into an uncertain purgatory, subject to complex regulations and ambiguous case law. *See, e.g.,* Treas. Reg. § 1.1031(a)–2 (additional rules for exchanges of personal property); *California Federal Life Insurance Company v. Commissioner,* 680 F.2d 85 (9th Cir. 1982) (gold coins and Swiss francs not property of like kind).

2. *Deferred exchanges.*—Taxpayer may transfer the property to be given up and only subsequently designate the property to be received by qualifying with the requirements of Code Section 1031(a)(3)(A): (1) the property to be received in the exchange must be *identified* on or before 45 days after the date on which the relinquished property is transferred; and (2) the new property must be *received* by the earlier of (i) 180 days after the date on which the taxpayer transferred the relinquished property, or (ii) the due date of the taxpayers return from the taxable year in which the transfer of the relinquished property occurs, with extensions.

Very commonly, a taxpayer wishing to undertake such an exchange will engage the services of a Code Section 1031 broker. The broker will accept the property to be relinquished, sell it, and deposit the proceeds in escrow (in such a manner as not to put taxpayer in constructive receipt of such proceeds). Taxpayer will then designate the property he wishes to acquire, and the broker will purchase it and transfer it to taxpayer. This is treated as an exchange between taxpayer and broker of the old property for the new, qualifying for nonrecognition treatment so long as the requirements of Code Section 1031 are otherwise met. *See, e.g.,* Treas. Reg. § 1031(k)(1)(b)(3) Example.

PROBLEMS FOR DISCUSSION

9–1. Martha owns an office building in Queens which she uses in her business. It has a fair market value of $1,000,000 and a basis of $300,000. There is no mortgage. She wants to exchange it for some unimproved land in upstate New York, which she plans to hold for investment. The empty land is also worth $1,000,000. In the absence of Code Section 1031, what are the tax consequences of the exchange and what is her basis in the unimproved land she receives in the exchange? Does Code Section 1031 apply? Under Code Section 1031, what are the tax consequences of the exchange?

9–2. Martha owns an office building in Queens which she uses in her business. It has a fair market value of $1,000,000 and a basis of $300,000. There is no mortgage. She wants to exchange it for a piece of unimproved land worth only $900,000, which she plans to hold for investment. She therefore receives $100,000 in cash in addition to the unimproved land. Assuming that Code Section 1031 applies, what are the tax consequences of the exchange?

9–3. Martha owns an office building in Queens which she uses in her business. It has a fair market value of $1,000,000 and a basis of $300,000. There is no mortgage. She wants to exchange it for a piece of unimproved land worth only $900,000, which she plans to hold for investment. To make up for the difference in values, she receives a fully loaded Ferrari worth $100,000 in addition to the unimproved land. Assuming that Code Section 1031 applies, what are the tax consequences of the exchange?

9–4. Martha owns an office building in Queens which she uses in her business. It has a fair market value of $1,000,000 and a basis of $300,000, and is subject to a nonrecourse mortgage in the amount of $100,000. She wants to exchange it for a piece of unimproved land worth $900,000, which she plans to hold for investment. Assuming that Code Section 1031 applies, what are the tax consequences of the exchange?

9–5. Martha owns an office building in Queens which she uses in her business. It has a fair market value of $1,000,000 and a basis of $300,000, and is subject to a nonrecourse mortgage in the amount of $100,000. She wants to exchange it for a piece of unimproved land worth $970,000, subject to a $70,000 mortgage, which she plans to hold for investment. Assuming that Code Section 1031 applies, what are the tax consequences of the exchange?

9–6. Martha exchanges unimproved land in which she has a basis of $150,000 for Phillip's office building, worth $300,000, plus $100,000 in cash. Assuming that Code Section 1031 applies, what are the tax consequences of the exchange?

9–7. Phillip owns an apartment building worth $900,000, which is subject to a $300,000 nonrecourse mortgage. He has a basis of $500,000 in the building.

    a. If he sells the building for cash, how much gain will he recognize for federal income tax purposes?

b. Dana offers to exchange some unimproved land worth $600,000 for Phillip's apartment building. Dana's basis in the land is $700,000. What tax consequences if Phillip accepts Dana's offer?

c. Felicity offers to exchange farmland worth $900,000, subject to a $400,000 mortgage, for Phillip's apartment building, in which she has a basis of $600,000. To equalize values, Felicity offers to give Phillip $100,000 in cash as well. What tax consequences if Phillip accepts Felicity's offer?

9–8. Dana owns unimproved land, held for investment purposes, in a town that has suffered severe long-term damage from hurricanes. She bought the land for $100,000; it is now worth $20,000. She proposes to exchange her land for like-kind investment property worth $15,000, plus $5,000 of cash. What tax consequences?

Design Considerations

Comprehensive tax base theory requires that accrued gains and losses be reported currently, without regard to whether they are realized. Our system's realization requirement represents a significant deviation from that theory. Nonrecognition rules might seem to represent an even further deviation. This fact, however, does not necessarily mean they are unjustified.

One undesirable consequence of the realization requirement is "lock-in." "Lock-in" is an incentive not to sell or exchange investments, even if doing so would redeploy capital to a more economically productive use. A taxpayer holding an asset with large built-in gains may choose to hold onto it even if other investments are more attractive, solely because the tax cost of making the change is both optional (because of the realization requirement) and high (because all accrued gains will be triggered by any realization event). Nonrecognition rules are sometimes viewed as ameliorating lock-in and thereby making capital markets more efficient. They typically apply to transactions through which a taxpayer, although technically making an exchange, is at least arguably merely changing the form of his investment.

Although the foregoing justification is plausible, it is at best inconsistently implemented. We allow tax-free exchanges of office buildings for farmland while prohibiting tax-free exchanges of stock in IBM for stock in Apple Computer. Why? The answer is not clear.

Subchapter B: Involuntary Conversions

Code: Section 1033

A more compelling case for nonrecognition arises when a taxpayer's property is destroyed, or stolen, or taken by eminent domain. As a result, taxpayer may receive either replacement property or, more likely, compensation equal to the value of the property lost. If taxpayer receives monetary compensation, he may use the resulting funds to replace his lost property. In the absence of a nonrecognition provision, however, he will be forced to realize his built-in gain on the original property. Not only has he been deprived of property; he has been forced to recognize taxable income as well.

Code Section 1033 relieves such a taxpayer from gain recognition, so long as he acquires qualifying replacement property within a specified period of time and meets certain other conditions. This relief only applies to property that is "compulsorily or involuntarily converted"—which a statutory parenthetical tells us means: (1) destruction, (2) theft, or (3) condemnation or threat of condemnation.

If taxpayer is not compensated for the conversion, taxpayer has a loss, not a gain, and Code Section 1033 is unnecessary. If taxpayer is compensated for the conversion, he may receive either (1) "property similar or related in service or use to the property so converted" or (2) something else, either cash or some other value. If taxpayer receives "property similar or related in service or use to the property so converted," Code Section 1033(a)(1) provides that he does not recognize gain on the conversion. Nonrecognition is automatic.

The most common form of compensation, however, is money. If taxpayer receives anything other than "property similar or related in service or use to the property so converted," he is subject to Code Section 1033(a)(2), which states that he may still be eligible for nonrecognition treatment if:

(1) he purchases other "property similar or related in service or use to the property so converted" or stock in the acquisition of control of a corporation that owns such other property,

(2) he makes such purchase within a specified time period, and

(3) he affirmatively elects nonrecognition treatment.

REV. RUL. 71-41
1971-1 C.B. 223

The investment of proceeds from condemnation of land and a warehouse held for rental purposes in constructing, on other land the taxpayer owned, a gas station held for rental purposes is a replacement of property similar or related in service or use under section 1033(a) of the Code.

Advice has been requested whether the investment of condemnation proceeds, under the circumstances set forth below, qualifies for the nonrecognition of gain provisions of section 1033 of the Internal Revenue Code of 1954.

The taxpayer, an individual, owned a warehouse which he rented to third parties. The warehouse and the land upon which it was located were condemned by the State and a gain was realized by the taxpayer on the condemnation. The condemnation proceeds were used by the taxpayer to erect a gas station on other land already owned by the taxpayer. The taxpayer rented the gas station to an oil company.

Section 1033(a) of the Code provides, in part, that if property is, as a result of condemnation, compulsorily or involuntarily converted into money and the taxpayer, during the period specified, purchases other property similar or related in service or use to the property so converted, at the election of the taxpayer the gain shall be recognized only to the extent that the amount realized upon such conversion exceeds the cost of the replacement property.

Section 1033(g) of the Code provides, in part, as follows:

(1) Special rule—For purposes of subsection (a), if real property ... held for productive use in trade or business or for investment is ... compulsorily or involuntarily converted, property of a like kind to be held either for productive use in a trade or business or for investment shall be treated as property similar or related in service or use to the property so converted.

The taxpayer in the instant case did not qualify for the special rule under section 1033(g) of the Code as the replacement property (gas station) and the property converted (land and warehouse) were not properties of a "like kind." The specific question is whether the taxpayer can qualify for treatment under section 1033(a) even though he fails to qualify under section 1033(g) of the Code.

Revenue Ruling 64-237, C.B. 1964-2, 319, in applying section 1033(a) of the Code, states that in considering whether replacement property acquired by an investor for the purpose of leasing is similar in service or use to the converted property, attention will be directed primarily to the similarity in the relationship of the service or uses which the original and replacement properties have to the taxpayer owner. In applying this test a determination will be made whether the properties are of a similar service to the taxpayer, the nature of the business risks connected with the properties, and what such properties demand of the taxpayer in the way of management, services, and relations to his tenants.

With respect to the property converted by the State, the taxpayer in the instant case was an investor for the production of rental income. As to the property acquired as replacement, the taxpayer is also an investor for the production of rental income. The mere fact that the taxpayer did not qualify under section 1033(g) of the Code does not preclude the taxpayer from the nonrecognition of gain provisions of section 1033 of the Code if the taxpayer is able to demonstrate that the replacement property is actually similar or related in service or use to the property converted within the meaning of section 1033(a) of the Code.

Accordingly, under the facts of the instant case, it is held that the gas station is property similar or related in service or use within the meaning of section 1033(a) of the Code. The taxpayer at his election will recognize gain upon the involuntarily converted property only to the extent that the amount realized upon such conversion exceeds the cost of the replacement property, provided, the actual replacement took place within the period of time prescribed by section 1033(a)(3)(B) of the Code.

Notes

1. *"Property similar or related in service or use to the property so converted."*—In general, whether replacement property is similar or related in service or use to the converted property is a fact-specific question. In answering this question, the focus is on the taxpayer's use, not on anyone else's. Thus, for example, if taxpayer uses Property 1 to produce rental income, renting to a lessee who operates a book store, and uses Property 2 for the same purpose, renting to a lessee who operates a gas station, the fact that book stores and gas stations are not "similar or related in service or use" is irrelevant. What matters is that taxpayer uses each property for the production of rental income. By contrast, if taxpayer uses the property himself, the two uses must be similar or related. *See, e.g.*, Rev. Rul. 76–319, 1976–2 C.B. 242 (recreational billiards center not sufficiently similar to recreational bowling center to qualify).

Subsection (g)(1) provides a special rule for business or investment real property that is condemned—as opposed to being destroyed or stolen. In such event, it is enough for the real property to be of like kind; and remember that all U.S. real property is deemed to be of like kind.

2. *Time period for acquisition of replacement property.*—Code Section 1033(a)(2)(B) provides that taxpayer has until 2 years after the end of the first taxable year in which any part of the gain would otherwise be recognized to acquire the required replacement property. What does this mean?

Suppose taxpayer's apartment building burns down because of a contractor's negligence in 2002. Taxpayer sues and recovers the value of the building in 2004. Assume that taxpayer's basis in the building was $1,500,000 but that the value (which taxpayer recovers) is $2,000,000. Without some nonrecognition rule, taxpayer will have gain of $500,000 in 2004. The end of the 2004 taxable year (assuming taxpayer uses the calendar year) is midnight, December 31, 2004. This means taxpayer must purchase qualifying replacement property before midnight, December 31, 2006, to qualify for nonrecognition under Code Section 1033.

Problems for Discussion

9–9. Martha's office building is destroyed by fire. She receives $500,000 in insurance to compensate her for the loss. She previously had a $200,000 basis in the building. Assume that all events described below occur within any required time periods.

  a. In the absence of Code Section 1033, what tax consequences?

  b. Martha exchanges undeveloped land that she already owns for a new office building worth $600,000. What tax consequences?

c. Martha buys an apartment building for $400,000 cash. What tax consequences?

d. Martha buys an office building for $100,000 cash plus a $400,000 promissory note secured by the building. What tax consequences?

e. Martha buys a 50–acre parcel of undeveloped land for $600,000. What tax consequences?

f. Same as (e), but Martha's office building was taken by condemnation, not destroyed by a fire. What tax consequences?

Subchapter C: Sale of a Principal Residence

Code: Section 121

Until 1997, Code Section 1034 operated similarly to Code Sections 1031 and 1033 whenever taxpayer sold a principal residence and purchased a new one. So long as taxpayer bought the new principal residence within a specified period, she only recognized gain to the extent of what was effectively her boot. Basis in the new residence was computed using principles having an effect similar to those of Code Sections 1031 and 1033.

At the time, the Code contained a separate provision, Code Section 121, that allowed a one-time exclusion of up to $125,000 of gain on the sale of a principal residence if taxpayer was 55 or over and had owned the property and used it as her principal residence for three or more of the preceding five years.

In 1997, Congress combined these two rules into current Code Section 121. Current Code Section 121 is a true exclusion provision, not a nonrecognition provision. A taxpayer who has owned and used a residence as her principal residence for 2 of the last 5 years may exclude the first $250,000 of gain from the sale of that residence. The only further limitation is that a taxpayer cannot take advantage of this exclusion more than once every two years.

PROBLEMS FOR DISCUSSION

9–10. Martha sells her principal residence for $500,000. She had purchased the residence 10 years ago for $200,000.

a. How much gross income does Martha recognize?

b. Three months later she purchases a new principal resident for $600,000. What consequences?

c. Before selling her old principal residence, Martha moves out and rents it to an unrelated third party for a year. What consequences?

9–11. Bob and Sally, a married couple, make their living by buying homes, living in them, fixing them up, and selling them. In 2000, they buy House #1 for $400,000, move in, and fix it up, incurring $100,000 of out-of-pocket costs in the process. They sell House #1 in 2002 for $1,000,000, realizing an economic profit of $500,000. In 2002, they do the same with House #2, selling it in 2004 and again realizing an economic profit of $500,000. In effect, they earn $250,000 a year from their business of fixing up and flipping homes. How much gross income must they report from this business?

CHAPTER 10

BALANCING ENTRIES

■ ■ ■

The rules discussed in this Part 2 illustrate a single principle: that our system's rules for measuring income or loss during particular taxable periods should be construed so as to measure tax base income completely over time. Except where the system deliberately deviates from economic income, after taking into account all of income effects of a transaction in all of the years the transaction affects, tax should match economics. All items of tax base income and loss should be measured correctly. No item should be included twice, no item deducted twice.

Implicit in most of the Code, this principle finds its clearest expression in two judicially-created balancing entry rules. The first, known as the tax benefit rule, applies when an event occurs in a later year that is inconsistent with a deduction taken in an earlier year. The rule requires taxpayer to report the deducted item as income in the year of the later inconsistent event—even if the item is of a type that would not normally constitute income. Assume, for example, that taxpayer deducts $100 of state income taxes paid in Year 1. In Year 2, he receives a refund of those taxes from the state. We could, of course, permit or require amendment of the Year 1 returns. Such a solution, however, would complicate enforcement of tax statutes of limitation. Instead, we require taxpayer to make, in effect, a balancing entry in the year of recovery.

The second, commonly known as the rule in *United States v. Lewis*, might also be called a tax detriment rule. It provides that when taxpayer includes an item in income in Year 1 and is required to repay that item in a latter year, taxpayer is entitled to a balancing deduction in the year of repayment.

Note that in each case, the balancing entry does not violate the general rule that errors in Year 1, if not corrected within the period set forth in the relevant statute of limitations, cannot be corrected. The balancing entry is justified not by an original error, but by a later event inconsistent with the earlier entry. The rules requiring the balancing entry simply define the tax effects of the later event; and the entry is made in the year of that event.

Subchapter A: Tax Benefit Rule: Recovery of an Item Previously Deducted

Code: Section 111

HUGHES & LUCE, L.L.P. v. COMMISSIONER
70 F.3d 16 (5th Cir. 1995)

Hughes & Luce, L.L.P. is a Texas general partnership engaged in the practice of law. Although the terms of an engagement differ from client to client, Hughes & Luce customarily bills clients separately for out-of-pocket costs paid to third parties for expenses incurred in connection with the firm's representation of those clients. These costs include expenses for court costs, filing fees, expert witness fees, travel and meals, long-distance telephone charges, delivery services, and the like ("Service Costs").

On its income tax returns for the years 1976 through 1989, Hughes & Luce deducted Service Costs as ordinary and necessary business expenses in the year in which the expense was paid. Reimbursements of these costs were included in its ordinary income in the year received. Often the reimbursements were received in a taxable year subsequent to the year in which the Service Costs had been deducted as business expenses.

On March 30, 1992, the IRS began an audit of Hughes & Luce's timely filed 1989 tax return. During the course of this audit, the IRS challenged Hughes & Luce's treatment of the Service Costs. The IRS contended that the firm's payments for Service Costs should be treated as loans to clients. Accordingly, the Service Costs should be neither deductible when paid nor includible in income when reimbursed. For purposes of this case, Hughes & Luce concedes that the Service Costs are properly treated as loans to clients for taxable year 1989 and following.

For the taxable year 1989, Hughes & Luce had deducted Service Costs in the amount of $2,367,535. Reimbursements totaling $2,398,825 were included in income for this same year. Of the total reimbursements, $490,766 was attributable to Service Costs paid and deducted in years prior to 1989. It is these latter reimbursements that are at issue in this case. As the statute of limitations had expired for the years prior to 1989, the IRS was precluded from making an adjustment to those years to disallow the deduction of these Service Costs.

Hughes & Luce essentially contends that none of the reimbursements received in 1989 are taxable income because the IRS determined them to be loan repayments, and loan repayments are not ordinarily includible in income. The IRS counters that the reimbursements received in 1989 but attributable to costs advanced and deducted as expenses in years prior to 1989 are includible in taxable income for 1989 under the tax benefit rule.

The federal income tax is based on an annual accounting system, which is "a practical necessity if [it] is to produce revenue ascertainable and payable at regular intervals." Strict adherence to an annual accounting period, however, may create transactional inequities. The tax benefit rule was adopted in an equitable effort to mitigate some of the inflexibilities of the annual accounting system by approximating the results that would be produced in a system based on transactional rather than annual accounting.

The tax benefit rule includes an amount in income in the current year to the extent that: (1) the amount was deducted in a year prior to the current year, (2) the deduction resulted in a tax benefit, (3) an event occurs in the current year that is fundamentally inconsistent with the premises on which the deduction was originally based, and (4) a nonrecognition provision of the Internal Revenue Code does not prevent the inclusion of gross income. An event is fundamentally inconsistent with the premises on which the deduction was originally based if that event would have foreclosed the deduction had it occurred in the year of the deduction.

The Tax Court held that application of the tax benefit rule was improper in this case because of the "erroneous deduction exception." That exception provides that the tax benefit rule applies only when the original deduction was proper. Because the disbursement of a loan (*i.e.*, Service Cost) is not a proper deduction, the Tax Court concluded that the tax benefit rule did not require Hughes & Luce to include the amount in issue in its 1989 taxable income.

In its opinion, the Tax Court noted candidly that the erroneous deduction exception has been criticized or rejected by many Courts of Appeals. The Tax Court nevertheless applied this exception in the instant case because we had not squarely addressed this issue. We do so now and join the other circuits in rejecting the erroneous deduction exception.

As other courts have observed, the inclusion of the reimbursements in income does not *reopen* the tax liability for the prior years—albeit the result is much the same—and does not implicate the statute of limitations. The only taxable year affected by application of the tax benefit rule is the year in which the reimbursements are received, which year must be open for the rule to apply at all. That these reimbursements are properly treated as loan repayments does not prevent their taxation when, as here, the loan disbursements were erroneously deducted in a prior year as an expense. The tax benefit rule requires taxation because of a previously created tax benefit, regardless of an item's inherent characteristics (*i.e.*, whether repayment of a loan or recovery of a deductible expense) and regardless of whether the original deduction was proper or improper. We therefore reject the erroneous deduction exception and conclude that the tax benefit rule applies regardless of the propriety of the original deduction.

Hughes & Luce also contends that there is no fundamentally inconsistent event in this case because the very nature of "rebillable expenses" is that reimbursement of such expenses is expected. Thus, Hughes & Luce insists, it is improper to invoke the tax benefit rule. This argument misses the mark. In holding that a fundamentally inconsistent event is a requirement to invoke the tax benefit rule, the Supreme Court in *Hillsboro National Bank v. Commissioner*, 460 U.S. 370 (1983), expanded that rule by refusing to limit it to situations involving an actual recovery. The actual recoveries by Hughes & Luce of the Service Costs at issue plainly are fundamentally inconsistent events in that they would have foreclosed the deduction had they occurred in the same year as the disbursements.

The tax benefit rule is said to have two components: an inclusionary component and an exclusionary component. The inclusionary component, illustrated in *Hughes & Luce, L.L.P. v. Commissioner*, requires inclusion of an item previously deducted upon the occurrence in a later year of events inconsistent with that deduction. The exclusionary component, added by Congress in Code Section 111(a), excludes from gross income any recovery "to the extent such amount did not reduce the amount of the tax" in the year of deduction.

Assume, for example, that taxpayer deducts $100 of state income taxes paid in Year 1. Because he is in an AMT posture in Year 1, however, and because state income taxes are not deductible for AMT purposes, he receives no benefit from his Year 1 deduction. In Year 2, he receives a refund of those taxes from the state. By itself, the inclusionary component of the tax benefit rule would require inclusion of the refund, because the refund is inconsistent with the prior deduction. But because taxpayer did not actually benefit from his Year 1 deduction, the exclusionary component reverses this result.

Subchapter B: Tax Detriment Rule: Repayment of Income Previously Included

Code: Section 1341

UNITED STATES v. LEWIS
340 U.S. 590 (1951)

In his 1944 income tax return, respondent reported about $22,000 which he had received that year as an employee's bonus. As a result of subsequent litigation in a state court, however, it was decided that respondent's bonus had been improperly computed; under compulsion of the state court's judgment he returned approximately $11,000 to his employer. Until payment of the judgment in 1946, respondent had at all times claimed and used the full $22,000 unconditionally as his own, in the good faith though "mistaken" belief that he was entitled to the whole bonus.

On the foregoing facts the Government's position is that respondent's 1944 tax should not be recomputed, but that respondent should have deducted the $11,000 as a loss in his 1946 tax return. The Court of Claims, however, held that the excess bonus received "under a mistake of fact" was not income in 1944 and ordered a refund based on a recalculation of that year's tax.

In the *North American Oil* case we said: "If a taxpayer receives earnings under a claim of right and without restriction as to its disposition, he has received income which he is required to return [that is, report], even though it may still be claimed that he is not entitled to retain the money, and even though he may still be adjudged liable to restore its equivalent." Nothing in this language permits an exception merely because a taxpayer is "mistaken" as to the validity of his claim.

Income taxes must be paid on income received (or accrued) during an annual accounting period. The "claim of right" interpretation of the tax laws has long been used to give finality to that period, and is now deeply rooted in the federal tax system. We see no reason why the Court should depart from this well-settled interpretation merely because it results in an advantage or disadvantage to a taxpayer.

What if taxpayer's deduction in the later year does not produce tax savings commensurate with the increase in tax caused by inclusion in the earlier year? Congress has addressed this problem in Code Section 1341. If the amount of the deduction is greater than $3,000, taxpayer's tax in the later year is the lesser of (1) the later year tax computed with the deduction or (2) the later year tax computed without the deduction, minus the decrease in tax in the earlier year that would have resulted if the earlier inclusion had not been made.

Assume, for example, that taxpayer includes $20,000 of commissions in Year 1 under claim of right; as a result, assume that his Year 1 tax increases by $7,000 (35 percent of $20,000). In Year 2, he is forced to return those commissioner and is entitled to a offsetting *United States v. Lewis* deduction. Assume that in Year 2, he is in a 15 percent marginal tax bracket; his tax benefit from the $20,000 deduction is therefore only $3,000. Code Section 1341 provides, in effect, that his tax in Year 2 will be reduced by the greater of the earlier tax detriment ($7,000) and the later tax benefit ($3,000).

NOTES

1. *Scope of* United States v. Lewis *and Code Section 1341.*—In Chapter 1A, Note 5, we observed that the claim of right doctrine follows from the broader principle that a gain "constitutes taxable income when its recipient has such control over it that, as a practical matter, he derives readily realizable economic value from it," regardless of whether he has any legal right to it. Thus, for example, the fruits of criminal activity constitute "income" even if they do not legally belong to the criminal.

Does *United States v. Lewis* apply if the earlier inclusion is required under this broader principle and taxpayer is subsequently required to repay the amounts involved? Yes. The Court so stated, albeit in dictum, in *James v. United States*, 366 U.S. 213 (1961), Chapter 8A above. In Rev. Rul. 65–254, 1965–2 C.B. 50, the IRS confirmed this result and gave it a statutory home, holding that a deduction is allowable under Code Section 165(c)(2), as a loss in a transaction entered into for profit, for the repayment of embezzled funds in the taxable year in which repayment is made. The IRS held, however, that the benefits of Code Section 1341 were limited to repayments of amounts previously included under claim of right. In Rev. Rul. 82–74, 1982–1 C.B. 110, amounts repaid to an insurance company by arsonist were held, similarly, to trigger a loss deductible under Code Section 165(c)(2) but not eligible for the benefits of Code Section 1341. Note that the deduction of reimbursements under this rule may be subject to limitations on public policy grounds. *See* Chapter 15B, Section 3, below.

PART 3

TIME VALUE OF MONEY

■ ■ ■

The rules explored in Part 2 ensure, for the most part, that a taxpayer's income and losses are accounted for *completely* over time—that is, that none are left out or included twice. If those rules operate as they should, the sum of the tax consequences of a series of transactions will exactly equal taxpayer's tax base income or loss from that series of transactions. Complete accounting is an essential beginning. By itself, however, it is not enough. Our system also needs to take into account the time value of money. If it does not, taxpayers will be able to play timing games. Consider the following examples.

Example 1: Mom loans daughter $1,000,000 for one year interest-free. The loan is not a taxable event; neither is the repayment. So long as daughter repays the $1,000,000, neither she nor mom has any income or loss—or so the rules of Part 2 tell us. But note that if the prevailing interest rate is five percent, mom has effectively transferred $50,000 of value to daughter. It is as if daughter paid mom $50,000 of interest for the year and Mom gave that same $50,000 back to Daughter as a gift. Unless our rules recognize that allowing someone to use money without charging them interest is valuable, we open both the income and gift tax systems to potential abuse.

Example 2: X Corp sells an interest-free, 5–year bond with a face value of $1,000,000 on the open market. If the prevailing rate of interest is five percent, compounded annually, for interest-bearing bonds of comparable risk, an economically rational buyer should be willing to pay $783,525 for the interest-free bond in question. If he does, when he receives the $1,000,000 face amount on the bonds five years later, he will have earned a five percent return, compounded annually, on his $783,525 investment. He must, of course, report the difference, $216,475, as income when the debt matures. Economically, this is the equivalent of interest—the amount paid by X Corp for the use of $783,525 for five years. Indeed, in the business world, this is called "original issue discount" and is a common way for borrowing corporations to pay interest. In the absence of special rules, however, a cash-method buyer might be able to characterize the $216,475 difference between what he paid and what he got back as gain from the sale of a capital asset, taxable at capital gains rates. In any event, in the absence of special rules, a cash-method buyer/holder will not have to report income until the debt is repaid in Year 5, even if an accrual-method borrower can accrue the corresponding deduction currently.

These examples only begin to scratch the surface of the time-value-of-money problem. Time value of money explains why we do not allow businesses a current deduction for the cost of assets with extended useful lives. It dictates, at least in theory, the depreciation schedules taxpayers should use in writing off such costs, and explains why accelerated depreciation creates an artificial tax incentive to buy assets for which such depreciation is available. It is also central to the debate over whether we should tax income or consumption. Part 3 explores these issues.

CHAPTER 11

UNSTATED INTEREST

■ ■ ■

The two concrete examples given in the introduction to this Part 3 both involve unstated interest. Each has been addressed by specially targeted statutory provisions.

Subchapter A: Below–Market Loans

Code: Section 7872

Regulations: Proposed Section 1.7872–1(a)

Recall that in Example 1 above, mom loans daughter $1,000,000 for one year interest-free. If the prevailing interest rate is five percent, compounded annually, mom has effectively transferred $50,000 of value to daughter. The Supreme Court first recognized this economic fact in *Dickman v. Commissioner*.

DICKMAN v. COMMISSIONER
465 U.S. 330 (1984)

Paul and Esther Dickman were husband and wife; Lyle Dickman was their son. Paul, Esther, Lyle, and Lyle's wife and children were the owners of Artesian Farm, Inc. Between 1971 and 1976, Paul and Esther loaned substantial sums to Lyle and Artesian. Over this 5–year interval, the outstanding balances for the loans from Paul to Lyle varied from $144,715 to $342,915; with regard to Paul's loans to Artesian, the outstanding balances ranged from $207,875 to $669,733. During the same period, Esther loaned $226,130 to Lyle and $68,651 to Artesian. With two exceptions, all the loans were evidenced by demand notes bearing no interest.

Paul Dickman died in 1976, leaving a gross estate for federal estate tax purposes of $3,464,011. The Commissioner determined that the loans to Lyle and Artesian resulted in taxable gifts to the extent of the value of the use of the loaned funds.

In asserting that interest-free demand loans give rise to taxable gifts, the Commissioner does not seek to impose the gift tax upon the principal amount of the loan, but only upon the reasonable value of the use of the money lent. The taxable gift that assertedly results from an interest-free demand loan is the value of receiving and using the money without incurring a corresponding obligation to pay interest along with the loan's repayment.

What was transferred here was the use of a substantial amount of cash for an indefinite period of time. An analogous interest in real property, the use under a tenancy at will, has long been recognized as a property right. For example, a parent who grants to a child the rent-free, indefinite use of commercial property having a reasonable rental value of $8,000 a month has clearly transferred a valuable property right. The transfer of $100,000 in cash, interest-free and repayable on demand, is similarly a grant of the use of valuable property. Its uncertain tenure may reduce its value, but it does not undermine its status as property. In either instance, when the property owner transfers to another the right to use the object, an identifiable property interest has clearly changed hands.

The right to the use of $100,000 without charge is a valuable interest in the money lent, as much so as the rent-free use of property consisting of land and buildings. In either case, there is a measurable economic value associated with the use of the property transferred. The value of the use of money is found in what it can produce; the measure of that value is interest—"rent" for the use of the funds. We can assume that an interest-free loan for a fixed period, especially for a prolonged period, may have greater value than such a loan made payable on demand, but it would defy common human experience to say that an intrafamily loan payable on demand is not subject to accommodation; its value may be reduced by virtue of its demand status, but that value is surely not eliminated.

Against this background, the gift tax statutes clearly encompass within their broad sweep the gratuitous transfer of the use of money. Just as a tenancy at will in real property is an estate or interest in land, so also is the right to use money a cognizable interest in personal property. The right to use money is plainly a valuable right, readily measurable by reference to current interest rates; the vast banking industry is positive evidence of this reality. Accordingly, we conclude that the interest-free loan of funds is a "transfer of property by gift" within the contemplation of the federal gift tax statutes.

A substantial no-interest loan from parent to child creates significant tax benefits for the lender quite apart from the economic advantages to the borrower. This is especially so when an individual in a high income tax bracket transfers income-producing property to an individual in a lower income tax bracket, thereby reducing the taxable income of the high-bracket taxpayer at the expense, ultimately, of all other taxpayers and the Government. Subjecting interest-free loans to gift taxation minimizes the potential loss to the federal fisc generated by the use of such loans as an income tax avoidance mechanism for the transferor. Gift taxation of interest-free loans also effectuates Congress' desire to supplement the estate tax provisions. A gratuitous transfer of income-producing property may enable the transferor to avoid the future estate tax liability that would result if the earnings generated by the property—rent, interest, or dividends—became a part of the transferor's estate. Imposing the gift tax upon interest-free loans bolsters the estate tax by preventing the diminution of the transferor's estate in this fashion.

Petitioners attack the breadth of the Commissioner's view that interest-free demand loans give rise to taxable gifts. Carried to its logical extreme, petitioners argue, the Commissioner's rationale would elevate to the status of taxable gifts such commonplace transactions as a loan of the proverbial cup of sugar to a neighbor or a loan of lunch money to a colleague. Petitioners urge that such a result is an untenable intrusion by the Government into cherished zones of privacy, particularly where intra-family transactions are involved.

Our laws require parents to provide their minor offspring with the necessities and conveniences of life; questions under the tax law often arise, however, when parents provide more than the necessities, and in quantities significant enough to attract the attention of the taxing authorities. Generally, the legal obligation of support terminates when the offspring reach majority. Nonetheless, it is not uncommon for parents to provide their adult children with such things as the use of cars or vacation cottages, simply on the basis of the family relationship. We assume that the focus of the Internal Revenue Service is not on such traditional familial matters. When the Government levies a gift tax on routine neighborly or familial gifts, there will be time enough to deal with such a case.

Moreover, the tax law provides liberally for gifts to both family members and others; within the limits of the prescribed statutory exemptions, even substantial gifts may be entirely tax free. First, under § 2503(e) of the Code, amounts paid on behalf of an individual for tuition at a qualified educational institution or for medical care are not considered "transfer[s] of property by gift" for purposes of the gift tax statutes. More significantly, § 2503(b) of the Code provides an annual exclusion from the computation of taxable gifts of $10,000 per year, per donee; this provision allows a taxpayer to give up to $10,000 annually to each of any number of persons, without incurring any gift tax liability. The "split gift" provision of Code § 2513(a), which effectively enables a husband and wife to give each object of their bounty $20,000 per year without liability for gift tax, further enhances the ability to transfer significant amounts of money and property free of gift tax consequences. Finally, should a taxpayer make gifts during one year that exceed the § 2503(b) annual gift tax exclusion, no gift tax liability will result until the unified credit of Code § 2505 has been exhausted. These generous exclusions, exceptions, and credits clearly absorb the sorts of *de minimis* gifts petitioners envision and render illusory the administrative problems that petitioners perceive in their "parade of horribles."

We hold, therefore, that the interest-free demand loans shown by this record resulted in taxable gifts of the reasonable value of the use of the money lent.

Dickman created an immediate administrative problem: how to determine "the reasonable value of the use of the money lent" in particular cases. Real world interest rates depend on many things, including the creditworthiness of the borrower, the terms of the loan, and the value of any underlying collateral. At the time, there was no authoritative interest rate tax return preparers could use to comply with the *Dickman* mandate. Chaos threatened.

Congress responded with Code Section 7872, which supersedes *Dickman* and provides mechanical answers to many of the difficult questions *Dickman* raised—including both the appropriate interest rate and the scope of any *de minimis* exceptions.

In general, Code Section 7872 applies to loans at below-market interest rates that fall within any of six categories: (1) gift loans, (2) compensation-related loans, (3) corporation-shareholder loans, (4) tax avoidance loans, (5) "significant effect" loans, and (6) loans to qualified continuing care facilities. Whether a loan is below-market is determined by comparing stated interest on the loan with the "applicable federal rate" computed by the IRS each month pursuant to Code Section 1274(d). *De minimis* exceptions are provided in subsections (c)(2) and (c)(3) for relatively small gift, compensation-related, and corporation-shareholder loans.

In situations to which it applies, Code Section 7872(a)(1) deems a circular flow of cash to have occurred—from lender to borrower, and then back from borrower to lender as interest.

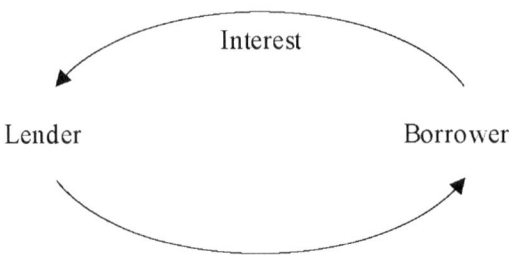

The character of the deemed flow from lender to borrower depends on the relationship between the two. If the lender is mom and the borrower is her daughter, the deemed flow from mom to daughter is probably a gift. If the lender is employer and the borrower is his employee, it is probably compensation. If the lender is a corporation and the borrower is a shareholder, the deemed flow from corporation to shareholder is probably a dividend. If the reverse is true—lender is the shareholder and borrower is the corporation—the deemed flow from shareholder to corporation is probably a contribution to capital. And so on.

The tax consequences of the resulting deemed flows depend on rules outside Code Section 7872. Thus, for example, a deemed receipt of interest by the lender is income under Code Section 61. Whether a deemed payment of interest by the borrower will be deductible is determined under the interest deductibility rules. Gifts are excluded from gross income under Code Section 102, but may be subject to gift tax under Code Section 2501. And so forth.

In the case of demand loans and gift loans, Code Section (a)(2) provides that the resulting flows are deemed to occur annually, on the last day of the calendar year. In the case of all other loans to which Code Section 7872 applies, a more complex computation is specified in subsection (b). In effect, the subsection (b) formula provides that interest will be deemed to be paid annually, and that a lump sum equal to the sum of the present values of all such deemed interest payments will be deemed to have been transferred by lender to borrower on the date the loan is made.

Finally, subsection (d) provides a special rule for gift loans. If this special rule applies, the amount of interest deemed paid by borrower to lender each year is limited to the borrower's "net investment income." In other words, the deemed interest leg is capped. For purposes of this cap, if borrower's net investment income for the year does not exceed $1,000, it is treated as equal to zero. One of the purposes of Code Section 7872 was to prevent high-bracket parents from shifting investment income to their lower-bracket children. In the case of gifts loans, it accomplishes this by deeming parents to have interest income and children to have an interest deduction—in effect, by shifting investment income from borrower to lender at the applicable federal rate. But if the lower-bracket borrower does not have any investment income, there may be no income-shifting abuse. Hence subsection (d).

Because the realization requirement may allow borrowers to earn investment income without having to report any such income for tax purposes, however, this rationale is not entirely persuasive. Perhaps in part for this reason, Congress has limited the special rule of subsection (d) in two important regards. First, it does not apply to any loan the interest arrangements of which have as one of their principal purposes the avoidance of federal tax. Second, it does not apply when loans outstanding between lender and borrower exceed $100,000.

PROBLEMS FOR DISCUSSION

Problem 11–1. Lisa is Amy's adult child. Assume that there are no other loans outstanding between the two and that the applicable federal rate is at all times ten percent, compounded annually. What are the tax consequences of each of the following transactions?

   a. On January 1, Year 1, Amy loans Lisa $5,000 interest-free, repayable on demand. Lisa deposits the $5,000 in a non-interest-bearing checking account and uses the funds to pay for various law school expenses. On January 1, Year 2, Lisa repays the loan in full.

   b. On January 1, Year 1, Amy loans Lisa $5,000 interest-free, repayable on demand. Lisa deposits the $5,000 in an interest-bearing savings account, earning $200 of interest over the course of the year. On January 1, Year 2, Lisa repays the loan in full.

   c. On January 1, Year 1, Amy loans Lisa $20,000 interest-free, repayable on demand. Lisa deposits the $20,000 in a non-interest-bearing checking account and uses the funds to pay for various law school expenses. On January 1, Year 2, Lisa repays the loan in full.

   d. On January 1, Year 1, Amy loans Lisa $30,000 interest-free, repayable on demand. Lisa deposits $10,000 in a non-interest-bearing checking account and uses the funds to pay for various law school expenses. She deposits the remaining $20,000 in an interest-bearing savings account, earning $800 of interest over the course of the year. On January 1, Year 2, Lisa repays the loan in full.

   e. On January 1, Year 1, Amy loans Lisa $150,000 interest-free, repayable on demand. Lisa deposits $40,000 in a non-interest-bearing checking account and uses the funds to pay for various law school expenses. She uses the remaining $110,000 to purchase publicly traded stock, which she sells for $120,000 on December 31, Year 1. On January 1, Year 2, Lisa repays the loan in full.

   f. On January 1, Year 1, Amy loans $100,000 interest-free, repayable on demand, to MichaelCorp, a corporation all of the stock of which is owned by Michael, her daughter Lisa's husband. MichaelCorp invests the $100,000 in junk bonds, earning $15,000 in interest and appreciation on those bonds over the course of the year. On December 31, 2011, MichaelCorp sells the junk bonds, and on January 1, Year 2, repays the loan in full. Neither Michael nor Lisa have any investment income in Year 1.

Subchapter B: Original Issue Discount (OID)

Code: Sections 1272, 1273(a), and 163(e)

Recall that in Example 2 on page 231, X Corp sells an interest-free bond having a face value of $1,000,000, payable at the end of five years. An arm's-length buyer pays X Corp $783,525 for the bond, reflecting the fact that that he could earn five percent, compounded annually, on interest-paying bonds with similar risk. Under Code Section 1273, the difference between the bond's "stated redemption price at maturity," $1,000,000, and its "issue price," $783,525, is called "original issue discount" (OID). The bond in our example has OID of $216,475

($1,000,000 less $783,525). The holder's resulting effective rate of return is called his "yield to maturity." In general, the holder is required to include this yield in income as it accrues, taxable at ordinary rates, and the borrower deducts it as it accrues as well (assuming that it is deductible under the Code's standard interest deductibility rules), in each case regardless of taxpayer's method of accounting.

Computing the statutory "yield to maturity" on bonds with OID can be challenging. In Chapter 12A, you will learn how to compute that yield approximately using the "IRR" function included in most spreadsheet programs; the technical computation required by Code Section 1273, however, can be more difficult. For our purposes, assume that the yield to maturity of the bond in Example 2 is five percent, compounded annually. What then?

Under Code Section 1272, OID accrues at the computed yield to maturity and is added to the bond's issue price, producing an "adjusted issue price" that includes implicit interest accrued but not yet paid. OID then accrues each period on the adjusted issue price as of the end of the preceding period. As adjusted issue price gets larger, the amount of OID that accrues each period gets larger as well. At the end of the 5-year period, the bond's adjusted issue price should exactly equal its "stated redemption price at maturity"—in our example, $1,000,000:

Year	OID (at 5%)	Adjusted Issue Price
0		$783,525
1	$39,176	$822,701
2	$41,136	$863,837
3	$43,192	$907,029
4	$45,352	$952,381
5	$47,619	$1,000,000
Total	$216,475	

Note that this computation spreads the $216,475 of total OID over the 5-year term in a way that correctly reflects buyer's yield to maturity (five percent, compounded annually).

In general, the holder includes each year's OID in income currently, taxable at ordinary rates. In general, the issuer deducts the same amount currently, as if it were interest, subject to the Code's standard rules for the deduction of interest. Thus in Year 1, the holder includes $39,176 of OID as ordinary income, in Year 2, $41,136, and so on, and the issuer deducts the same amount as if it were interest. The amount included in the holder's income is added to his basis in the bond. Code Section 1272(d)(2). When the bond is paid off at the end of five years, therefore, the holder should have a basis of $1,000,000 in the bond and should not recognize any gain or loss on the redemption.

The foregoing rules are subject to exceptions on both sides of the transaction. The requirement that the holder include OID in income as it accrues is subject to five exceptions: for (1) tax-exempt obligations, (2) U.S. savings bonds, (3) short-term debt (debt instruments having fixed terms of not more than one year), (4) obligations issued by natural persons before March 2, 1984, and (5) small ($10,000 or less) loans between natural persons not made in the course of the lender's trade or business. This last exception is not available if one of the principal purposes of the loan is the avoidance of federal tax. In addition, a loan with average annual OID of less than ¼ of 1 percent of the stated redemption price at maturity is treated as having no OID at all.

The rule of Code Section 163(e), which allows the issuer of an OID instrument to deduct OID as it accrues, regardless of his method of accounting, is subject to four exceptions: for (1) short-term obligations (debt instruments having fixed terms of not more than one year), (2) obligations issued by natural persons before March 2, 1984, (3) small ($10,000 or less) loans between natural persons not made in the course of the lender's trade or business, and (4) "applicable high yield discount obligations" issued by a corporation, colloquially known as "junk bonds."

An obligation is an "applicable high yield discount obligation" if it has an initial term of more than five years, a yield to maturity equal to or greater than the applicable federal rate plus five percentage points, and significant OID. A portion of the OID on "applicable high yield discount obligations" is completely nondeductible to issuer; the remainder can only be deducted when paid. The "applicable high yield discount obligation" rules were suspended during the 2008–2010 financial crisis, when almost all corporate bonds with OID would otherwise have become subject to them.

Problems for Discussion

11–2. On which of the following loans does OID income accrue to holder currently? On which is OID deductible currently by issuer?

a. Carol buys interest-free US Treasury bonds having a face value of $1,000,000, payable at the end of five years, for $783,525.

b. Carol buys interest-free US savings bonds having a face value of $1,000,000, payable at the end of five years, for $783,525.

c. Carol buys an interest-free note issued by X Corp having a face value of $1,000,000, payable at the end of five year, for $783,525, reflecting a yield to maturity of five percent, compounded annually.

d. The State of Maryland sells an interest-free bond having a face value of $1,000,000, payable at the end of five years. The buyer pays $783,525 for the bond, reflecting a yield to maturity of five percent, compounded annually.

e. Carol buys an interest-free note from her son Mark for $7,835 for personal reasons. In the note, Mark agrees to pay Carol $10,000 at the end of five years.

f. Carol buys X Corp's interest-free note from X Corp. The note has a face value of $1,000,000, payable at the end of five year, for $567,427, reflecting a yield to maturity of eleven percent, compounded annually. When it is issued, the mid-term AFR is five percent.

CHAPTER 12

CAPITAL EXPENDITURES

■ ■ ■

Unstated interest is not the only context in which time-value-of-money issues arise. Consider a business or investment expenditure that is expected to generate income beyond the end of the taxable year in which the expenditure is made. Should an income tax system allow taxpayer to deduct the entire expenditure immediately? Or should it instead require that taxpayer spread the expense across the expected income stream and deduct only a portion of the expense each year? If the latter, how should the expense be spread and deducted?

In Chapter 3A, we noted that the Haig–Simons definition of income requires that capital expenditures for income-producing purposes not be deducted immediately, since taxpayer's net worth does not decline by the full amount of any such expenditure in the year in which the expenditure is made. We also noted, however, that Haig–Simons requires that we allow such expenditures to be deducted over the "useful life" of the resulting assets. We now explore these requirements in greater detail.

Subchapter A: Effective Rates of Tax

SECTION 1: THE IRR FUNCTION

It is difficult to understand the practical consequences of the tax treatment of capital expenditures without some introduction to a tool familiar to every financial and business planner: internal rate of return. "Internal rate of return" (IRR) is simply a method of computing an investment's or business's effective rate of return, given a projected series of cash flows over time. To use this tool, it is not necessary to understand any difficult mathematics. All that is necessary is to learn how to use the built-in IRR function that comes with every commonly marketed spreadsheet program, including Microsoft Excel and OpenOffice.

Consider the following problem. Taxpayer invests $100 in an asset on December 31, Year 1. He does not experience any income or expense with respect to the asset in Years 2 or 3. On December 31, Year 4, he disposes of the asset and receives $140. What is taxpayer's rate of return on the investment?

To solve this problem using the IRR function, we create a spreadsheet column representing the relevant cash flows:

   −100
      0
      0
    140

Each entry represents the relevant cash flows for one year. In Year 1, taxpayer parts with $100; the relevant cash flow is therefore negative 100. In Years 2 and 3 there are no cash flows. In Year 4, taxpayer receives $140; the relevant cash flow is therefore positive 140.

To compute taxpayer's effective rate of return, we use the IRR function. The function has two arguments. The first is the set of cash flows—the column we just set up. The IRR function reads the column from top to bottom; the top entry is the first cash flow; the bottom entry, the last. The second argument in the function is simply a guess about the rate of return. This guess does not have to be right. The function should return the same answer no matter what guess is entered. Assume that we guess .05. The IRR cell will then contain the following:

   =IRR(column of cash flows,.05)

Push the "enter" button. An instant later we learn that taxpayer's internal rate of return on this investment is 11.87%, compounded annually.

Note how flexible the function is. Assume the same series of cash flows, except that now taxpayer expects to spend an additional $20 on December 31, Year 2, on top of the $100 he invests in Year 1. Our column of cash flows looks like this:

   −100
    −20
      0
    140

What happens to his effective rate of return? The spreadsheet tells us it is now 5.58% per year, compounded annually.

What if, in addition, we project that taxpayer will receive $30 on December 31, Year 3? Now our column of cash flows looks like this:

   −100
    −20
     30
    140

The IRR function tells us that on this series of cash flows, taxpayer's effective rate of return is 14.01% per year, compounded annually.

Any business that can project income and expenses over time can use the IRR function to determine the effective rate of return on its operations and investments. All it needs to do is to list projected cash flows by equally-spaced periods, create an IRR cell, and let the computer do the rest.

PROBLEMS FOR DISCUSSION

12–1. X Corp expects to experience the following net cash expenditures and receipts on a particular investment:

Period 1	–$1,000
Period 2	–$3,000
Period 3	$0
Period 4	$200
Period 5	–$1,000
Period 6	$9,000

What is its effective rate of return on the investment?

12–2. In Problem 12–1, suppose that X Corp's Period 6 receipt ($9,000) is delayed by one year to Period 7 because of difficulties in obtaining required regulatory permits. Otherwise, its net cash expenditures and receipts are the same. What happens to its effective rate of return on the investment?

SECTION 2: COMPUTING EFFECTIVE RATES OF TAX

Now we add in taxes. The rate of return we have computed thus far is pre-tax. We might, therefore, label Column 1 "Pre-tax Cash." Column 2, "Income/Deductions," will list by period all items of taxable income and deduction; Column 3, the tax rate for those items; Column 4, the resulting increases or decreases in tax liability; and Column 5, taxpayer's projected after-tax cash flows.

In the hypothetical we explored in Section 1, assume that (1) the $100 expenditure in Year 1 is not deductible, (2) the $20 expense in Year 2 is deductible against ordinary income, which is taxable at a rate of 35 percent, (3) the $30 receipt in Year 3 is taxable at 35 percent, and (4) the $140 receipt in Year 4 constitutes capital gain taxable at 15 percent to the extent it exceeds taxpayer's basis in the investment (*e.g.*, taxpayer recognizes $40 of capital gain). Our spreadsheet will look something like this:

Year	Pre-tax Cash	Income Deductions	Tax Rate	Tax	After-tax Cash
1	–100	0	35%	0	–100
2	–20	–20	35%	–7	–13
3	30	30	35%	10.5	19.5
4	140	40	15%	6	134

Taxpayer's after-tax cash flow (column 6) will equal his pre-tax cash flow (column 2) minus his taxes (column 5). Note that taxpayer's after-tax cash flow in Year 2 is reduced from $20 out of pocket to $13 out of pocket. This reflects the fact that taxpayer saves $7 in taxes in Year 2 because he is allowed to deduct the $20 expenditure currently. Similarly, his positive after-tax cash flow in Year 3 is reduced from $30 to $19.50 because of the $10.50 he has to pay in taxes on the $30 receipt that year.

The IRR function tells us that on the resulting *after-tax* cash flows, taxpayer's effective rate of return is 11.75 percent per year, compounded annually.

Note what we have just done: we have determined that taxes reduce our investor's effective rate of return from 14.01 percent to 11.75 percent—in other words, by 2.26 percentage points. It is now simple to compute his effective rate of tax. 2.26 percent (his taxes) divided by 14.01 percent (his pre-tax return) equals 16.13 percent. This means that taxpayer's effective rate of tax on the investment is 16.13 percent. Stated more generally:

Effective rate = (pre-tax IRR–after-tax IRR) / (pre-tax IRR)

PROBLEMS FOR DISCUSSION

12–3. Seth purchases an investment for $1,000 at the end of Period 1 and sells it for $2,000 at the end of Period 10, recognizing $1,000 of income on the sale, taxable at a rate of 35 percent.

Period 1	–$1,000
Period 2	$0
Period 3	$0
Period 4	$0
Period 5	$0
Period 6	$0
Period 7	$0
Period 8	$0
Period 9	$0
Period 10	$2,000

a. What is Seth's pre-tax rate of return on this investment?

b. What is his after-tax rate of return on this investment?

c. What is his effective rate of tax?

d. Why is his effective rate of tax lower than his nominal rate of 35 percent?

12–4. On January 1, Year 1, Amos purchased a truck for $200,000 cash. Amos planned to rent the truck out for $60,000 per year for four years and then to sell it for $50,000 on January 1, Year 5. Assume that Amos is allowed to expense the cost of the initial purchase, that he has no other income or expenses from the truck, but plenty of income from other sources to absorb any tax losses, and that all of his income is taxed at 35%. (Ignore Code Section 469 and any other possible limitations on deductibility.)

a. Compute Amos' pre-tax rate of return on the investment.

b. Compute Amos' after-tax rate of return on the investment.

c. Compute Amos' effective rate of tax on the investment.

12–5. On December 31, Year 0, Seth purchased land and an apartment building for $16,000,000 cash. Of the total purchase price, $1,000,000 was properly allocable to the land and $15,000,000 to the building itself. The building contained 60 apartments, each of which was rented for $1,000 per month (for a total of $720,000 per year). There were no other expenses or income.

Assume that for depreciation purposes, the building had a useful life of 15 years and a salvage value of zero and that Seth was permitted to claim a full year's worth of depreciation ($1,000,000) for each of the first 15 years. (Ignore Code Section 469 and any other possible limitations on deductibility.)

Over the 15 years Seth held the land and building, they appreciated at a rate of 3%, compounded annually. As of December 31, Year 15, his basis in the building was zero. On that date, he sold the building and land for $24,927,479, recognizing $23,927,479 in gain. Assume that at all times Seth had plenty of income from other sources that any losses from the building might shelter, that all of his operating income was taxed at a rate of 35%, and that his capital gain from the sale of the land and building was taxable at a rate of 15%.

   a. Compute Seth's pre-tax rate of return on the investment.
   b. Compute Seth's after-tax rate of return on the investment.
   c. Compute Seth's effective rate of tax on the investment.

12–6. On December 31, Year 0, Reuben purchased land and an apartment building for $16,000,000, borrowing $15,000,000 from a bank on a nonrecourse basis and contributing $1,000,000 of his own money. Of the total purchase price, $1,000,000 was properly allocable to the land and $15,000,000 to the building itself.

The mortgage bore interest at an annual rate of 4.8% ($720,000 per year), payable on December 31 of each year. Principal was payable in full on December 31 of Year 15. The building contained 60 apartments, each of which was rented for $1,000 per month (a total of $720,000 per year). There were no other expenses or income. As a result, the building's cash income exactly equaled its cash expenses, and its taxable income exactly equaled its deductible expenses before depreciation.

Assume that for depreciation purposes, the building had a useful life of 15 years and a salvage value of zero and that Reuben was permitted to claim a full year's worth of depreciation ($1,000,000) for each of the first 15 years. (Ignore Code Section 469 and any other possible limitations on deductibility.)

Over the 15 years Reuben held the land and building, they appreciated at a rate of 3%, compounded annually. On December 31, Year 15, he sold the building and land for $24,927,479 and repaid the $15,000,000 principal amount owing on the mortgage, ending up with $9,927,479 in cash. Assume that at all times Reuben had plenty of income from other sources that any losses from the building might shelter, that all of his operating income was taxed at a rate of 35%, and that his capital gain from the sale of the land and building was taxable at a rate of 15%.

   a. Compute Reuben's pre-tax rate of return on the investment.

CH. 12   CAPITAL EXPENDITURES   247

    b. Compute Reuben's after-tax rate of return on the investment.

    c. Compute Reuben's effective tax rate on the investment.

SECTION 3: EFFECT OF EXPENSING

We are now ready to explore how a tax system's treatment of capital expenditures affects effective tax rates. Assume that taxpayer makes an expenditure of $520 in Year 1 and expects to earn $260 in Year 2, $780 in Year 3, and nothing thereafter.

How should we treat taxpayer's $520 expenditure for tax purposes? One possibility would be to allow taxpayer to deduct the expenditure when made—to "expense" it. Assume taxpayer has other income he can shelter with any such deduction and that all income is taxable at 35 percent. If so, taxpayer's pre- and after-tax cash flows will be as follows:

Year	Pre-tax Cash	Taxable Income	Tax Rate	Tax	After-tax Cash
1	−520	−520	35%	−182	−338
2	260	260	35%	91	169
3	780	780	35%	273	507
IRR	50%				50%

His rate of return before taxes is 50%. His rate of return after tax is 50%. Taxes do not reduce his rate of return at all. Although his nominal tax rate is 35 percent, *his effective rate is zero.*

The reason is simple. In Year 1, he receives tax savings of $182 from the government and therefore only has to invest $338 of his own money. If he really wants to invest $520 of his own money, he can "gross up" the investment—that is, invest $520/65%, or $800 pre-tax. The resulting deduction of $800 will give him tax savings of $280; net of these savings, he will end up investing $520 of his own money. His before-and after-tax returns will then look like this:

Year	Pre-tax Cash	Taxable Income	Tax Rate	Tax	After-tax Cash
1	−800	−800	35%	−280	−520
2	400	400	35%	140	260
3	1,200	1,200	35%	420	780
IRR	50%				50%

Now his after-tax cash flows are identical to the pre-tax case flows he would have experienced before grossing up. It is as if the tax system did not exist.

Stated more generally, *if we allow taxpayer to expense his capital investment and he has enough income from other sources to absorb the resulting deduction, his effective rate of tax on income from that investment will be zero.* This result was first observed by MIT economist E. Cary Brown in 1948 and is sometimes known as the Cary Brown equivalence.

There is another way of framing the same result: that expensing has the effect of making the government a partner in taxpayer's investment. At a 35 percent tax rate, the government becomes, in effect, a 35 percent partner. On our original facts, the government kicks in $182 in Year 1 (35 percent of the total investment) and receives back $91 in Year 2 and $273 in Year 3 (35 percent of the total return). The $91 of "taxes" in Year 2 and $273 of "taxes" in Year 3 are really just the government's return on the $182 it puts in up front.

Viewed from this perspective, our taxpayer is not really paying any taxes on his return ($169 in Year 2 and $507 in Year 3; 65 percent of the total return) on his investment ($338; 65 percent of the total investment). Nevertheless, he *appears* to be paying taxes just like everyone else. The government's shares of the partnership's income ($91 in Year 2 and $273 in Year 3) are labeled "taxes" and he pays them to the government.

If we compute his effective tax rate without taking into account the Cary Brown equivalence—as conventional effective tax rate analysis always does—our taxpayer appears to be bearing the same tax burden as everyone else. On our original facts, his total net income over the three year period is $520. His net "taxes" paid on that income total $182 over the same three years. $182 divided by $520 is 35 percent. Our taxpayer therefore appears to be paying taxes at an effective rate of 35 percent, even though the Cary Brown equivalence tells us that his effective rate of tax is in fact zero. A tax system designer ignores time value of money at his peril.

Two further conclusions follow. The first has to do with the relationship between income and consumption. Note that taxpayer in our example is not consuming the $520 in Year 1. He is saving it. By allowing him to deduct this amount up front, we are reducing the amount of his tax base by the amount of his Year 1 savings. Recall that under Haig–Simons:

Income = Change in net worth + Consumption

Therefore:

Consumption = Income–Change in net worth (savings)

Allowing expensing of capital expenditures in Year 1 is equivalent to allowing taxpayer to deduct his savings in Year 1. If we allow capital expenditures to be deducted in full up front, therefore, the effect is to convert, at least partially, what would otherwise be an income tax into a tax on consumption.

You may recall that, at the beginning of Part 1, we noted that after "income," the closest current contender for minimally-distortive tax base was "consumption," commonly defined as income less savings. We also noted that we would eventually explore the extent to which our current "income" tax is actually a consumption tax. We are now at that point. As you explore the current law of expensing and cost recovery in Subchapters B and C below, consider the extent to which, under current law, our system still effectively taxes "income."

Ultimately the difference between an income tax and a consumption tax is simply a timing difference—a time-value-of-money issue. To tax income, we require taxpayers to write off their capital expenditures over time. To tax consumption, we allow taxpayers to write off such expenditures up front. In many respects, our current system more closely resembles the latter—the consumption tax ideal. Under our current system, well-advised owners of capital often do not pay significant effective taxes on their income from capital.

A second further conclusion must by now be obvious: one of the principal functions of the Code's requirement that capital expenditures be capitalized (that is, put into basis) rather than expensed (that is, deducted immediately) is to ensure that income from capital will effectively be subject to tax.

SECTION 4: NONDISTORTIVE COST RECOVERY

Recall that under Haig–Simons, a system intended to tax "income" *must* allow a deduction for the use of capital items for income-producing purposes over their useful lives. Such cost recovery deductions are commonly called "depreciation" in the case of tangible assets, *see, e.g.*, Code Sections 167 and 168, "amortization" in the case of intangible assets, *see, e.g.*, Code Section 197, and "depletion" in the case of mineral deposits, *see, e.g.*, Code Section 611.

Our next question is: If we require all capital expenditures to be capitalized, but allow taxpayer to deduct such expenditures over time, what cost recovery schedule will result in an effective rate of taxation (taking into account the time value of money) equal to his nominal rate? More simply, if taxpayer is subject to a nominal tax rate of 35 percent, what cost recovery schedule will result in an effective rate of 35 percent as well?

The answer is nonintuitive but quite simple: cost recovery is simply a technique for writing off the principal amount of taxpayer's investment. As the investment produces a stream of returns, we need to determine how much of what may appear to be income is really just recovery of his original cost. If we allow a deduction in that amount, we will tax net income correctly each period, and thereby avoid time-value-of-money distortions.

An example may make this easier to understand.

Assume that taxpayer purchases an asset for $100 in Year 0. He expects the asset to generate $25 per year for each of the next five years. At the end of the fifth year, he expects the asset to have a salvage value of

$20 and plans to sell it for that amount. The IRR function tells us that on this series of projected cash flows, taxpayer's effective pre-tax rate of return is 12.54 percent per year, compounded annually.

Our first step is to compute taxpayer's expected cost recovery schedule. To do this, we compute his return each year (Column 3): 12.54 percent times his remaining principal balance at the beginning of that year (Column 5, previous line). Of the $25 he receives each year ($45 in Year 5) (Column 2), part represents return on investment (Column 3); the remainder is just recovery of his original cost (Column 4).

Year	Receipt	=	Return	+	Cost Recovery	Remaining Balance
						100.00
1	25		12.54		12.46	87.54
2	25		10.98		14.02	73.52
3	25		9.22		15.78	54.74
4	25		7.34		17.76	39.98
5	45		5.02		39.98	0.00

The portion representing cost recovery (Column 4) becomes his nondistortive cost recovery schedule, with one adjustment: In Year 5, $20 of the expected cost recovery will come in the form of recovery of basis when he sells the asset for salvage. So of the Year 5 cost recovery of $39.98, $20 represents recovery of basis on the sale of the asset; only the remaining $19.98 should be treated as depreciation, amortization, or depletion.

Note what we have done: Over five years, the asset is expected to decline in value from $100 to $20. We have taken that $80 expected decline and spread it over the five year period as summarized in the following table. Taxpayer's basis in the asset at the end of each cost recovery year is also shown.

Year	Cost Recovery	Ending Basis
1	12.46	87.54
2	14.02	73.52
3	15.78	54.74
4	17.76	39.98
5	19.98	20.00
Total	80.00	

What effect will this cost recovery schedule have on taxpayer's effective rate of tax?

Year	Pre-tax Cash	Cost Recovery	Taxable Income	Tax Rate	Tax	After-tax Cash
	−100		0	35%	0	−100.00
1	25	12.46	12.54	35%	4.39	20.61
2	25	14.02	10.98	35%	3.84	21.16
3	25	15.78	9.22	35%	3.23	21.77
4	25	17.76	7.24	35%	2.53	22.47
5	25 + 20	19.98	5.02	35%	1.76	43.24
IRR	12.54%					8.15%

With this cost recovery schedule, taxpayer's effective tax rate is 35% (12.54 less 8.15, divided by 12.54), exactly equal to his nominal rate.

Stated another way, *a nondistortive cost recovery schedule is one computed in a manner similar to the computation of recovery of principal on a debt instrument with OID.**

How does such a cost recovery schedule relate to taxpayer's Haig-Simons change in net worth? At the end of each year, taxpayer's basis in the asset, using this cost recovery schedule, will exactly equal the present value of his remaining expected cash returns on the investment, discounted at 12.54 percent, the investment's expected yield to maturity. If that yield to maturity is normal in the market, the cost recovery schedule thus computed will exactly reflect the expected decline in fair market value of the asset from one year to the next. In other words, the cost recovery schedule thus computed is consistent with allowing cost recovery deductions equal to each year's expected decline in the fair market value of the asset—sometimes known as Samuelson depreciation. *See* Christopher Hanna, *Tax Theories and Tax Reform*, 59 SMU L. REV. 435 (2006).

Two final observations. First, the asset's nondistortive cost recovery schedule depends on the cash flows the asset is expected to generate. Our example assumes identical cash flows over each of five years. In reality, a particular asset might be expected to generate more revenue earlier in its useful life, or more later. Each set of assumed cash flows will generate a different nondistortive cost recovery schedule. Second, note that even assuming constant cash flows, as our example does, nondistortive cost recovery is backloaded—that is, to produce effective rates of tax equal to nominal rates of tax, the rules must require taxpayer to write off smaller amounts in earlier years and larger amounts in later years.

---

* One important non-intuitive difference should be noted, although it will not affect our understanding of the effect of standard permitted cost recovery methods. In a year with projected receipts smaller than the projected return (that is, yield to maturity times principal balance at the end of the preceding year), nondistortive cost recovery requires *negative* cost recovery in an amount equal to the difference. Recall that what we are trying to do is mimic the taxation of debt instruments with OID. Such instruments always generate taxable income equal to yield to maturity times the deemed principal balance at the end of the preceding year. If our depreciable asset is not projected to produce this much income in a given year, we need to create the difference—hence negative cost recovery. As a practical matter, however, this issue rarely arises; Congress and the IRS might well be excused for ignoring it.

Unless projected income streams are frontloaded, permitted cost recovery schedules that frontload—that is, that allow larger write-offs in early years—are analogous to partial expensing. They result in lower effective rates of tax.

Subchapter B: The Capitalization Requirement

SECTION 1: WHEN IS CAPITALIZATION REQUIRED?

Code: Section 263

Regulation: Sections 1.263(a)–1 and –2

The expensing problem identified in Subchapter A arises whenever a deduction in an earlier period generates tax savings that can be used to help finance income in a later period. When expenses produce income in the same year, allowing taxpayer to deduct such expenses currently does not generally reduce the out-of-pocket investment taxpayer must make to fund them. Stated another way, the expensing problem identified in Subchapter A arises when taxpayer makes an expenditure that produces financial benefits significantly beyond the end of the taxable year in which the expenditure is made. Or in yet another: the problem arises whenever taxpayer makes an expenditure with a "useful life" of more than one year.

Courts address the capitalization/expensing question in a variety of ways. Sometimes they ask whether the expenditure in question is likely to produce future benefits. For assets with limited useful lives, they may ask whether such expected lives are longer than a year. If an expenditure creates a separate and enduring asset, they may view this fact as dispositive. Alternatively, they may ask whether the expenditure is "ordinary" within the meaning of Code Section 162—the implication being that if it is not, it should be capitalized. They may purport to be matching deductions with the income those deductions help generate. Finally, they may ask whether failure to capitalize will have distortive effects on the measurement of taxpayer's income.

In practice, whether particular types of expenditures are capitalized or expensed is sometimes a matter of convention, not principle. A carpenter's hammer, for example, clearly has a useful life of more than one year. The regulations explicitly authorize expensing of this type of item only in the case of farmers. Treas. Reg. § 1.62–12(a) ("The cost of ordinary tools of short life or small cost, such as hand tools, including shovels, rakes, etc., may be deducted."). Yet other types of businesses regularly expense small extended-life items as well, and are upheld when challenged. *See, e.g., Sharon v. Commissioner*, 66 T.C. 515 (1976), *aff'd per curiam*, 591 F.2d 1273 (9th Cir. 1978) (state bar license fee deductible when paid, despite capital nature, by analogy to small tools deduction for farmers). For major items as to which authority or convention does not yet exist, however, law is required.

INDOPCO, INC. v. COMMISSIONER
503 U.S. 79 (1992)

In this case we must decide whether certain professional expenses incurred by a target corporation in the course of a friendly takeover are deductible by that corporation as "ordinary and necessary" business expenses under § 162(a) of the Internal Revenue Code.

Petitioner INDOPCO, Inc., formerly named National Starch and Chemical Corporation and hereinafter referred to as National Starch, manufactures and sells adhesives, starches, and specialty chemical products. In October 1977, representatives of Unilever United States, Inc. expressed interest in acquiring National Starch, which was one of its suppliers, through a friendly transaction. Frank and Anna Greenwall were the corporation's largest shareholders and owned approximately 14.5% of the common. The Greenwalls, getting along in years and concerned about their estate plans, indicated that they would transfer their shares to Unilever only if a transaction tax free for them could be arranged.

Lawyers representing both sides devised a "reverse subsidiary cash merger" that they felt would satisfy the Greenwalls' concerns. Two new entities would be created—National Starch and Chemical Holding Corp. (Holding), a subsidiary of Unilever, and NSC Merger, Inc., a subsidiary of Holding that would have only a transitory existence. In an exchange specifically designed to be tax free under § 351, Holding would exchange one share of its nonvoting preferred stock for each share of National Starch common that it received from National Starch shareholders. Any National Starch common that was not so exchanged would be converted into cash in a merger of NSC Merger, Inc., into National Starch.

In November 1977, National Starch's directors were formally advised of Unilever's interest and the proposed transaction. At that time, Debevoise, Plimpton, Lyons & Gates, National Starch's counsel, told the directors that under Delaware law they had a fiduciary duty to ensure that the proposed transaction would be fair to the shareholders. National Starch thereupon engaged the investment banking firm of Morgan Stanley & Co., Inc., to evaluate its shares, to render a fairness opinion, and generally to assist in the event of the emergence of a hostile tender offer.

Although Unilever originally had suggested a price between $65 and $70 per share, negotiations resulted in a final offer of $73.50 per share, a figure Morgan Stanley found to be fair. Following approval by National Starch's board and the issuance of a favorable private ruling from the Internal Revenue Service that the transaction would be tax free under § 351 for those National Starch shareholders who exchanged their stock for Holding preferred, the transaction was consummated in August 1978.

Morgan Stanley charged National Starch a fee of $2,200,000, along with $7,586 for out-of-pocket expenses and $18,000 for legal fees. The Debevoise firm charged National Starch $490,000, along with $15,069 for out-of-pocket expenses. National Starch also incurred expenses aggregating $150,962 for miscellaneous items—such as accounting, printing, proxy solicitation, and Securities and Exchange Commission fees—in connection with the transaction. No issue is raised as to the propriety or reasonableness of these charges.

On its federal income tax return for its short taxable year ended August 15, 1978, National Starch claimed a deduction for the $2,225,586 paid to Morgan Stanley, but did not deduct the $505,069 paid to Debevoise or the other expenses. Upon audit, the Commissioner of Internal Revenue disallowed the claimed deduction and issued a notice of deficiency. Petitioner sought redetermination in the United States Tax Court, asserting, however, not only the right to deduct the investment banking fees and expenses but, as well, the legal and miscellaneous expenses incurred.

The Tax Court ruled that the expenditures were capital in nature and therefore not deductible under § 162(a) in the 1978 return as "ordinary and necessary expenses." The court based its holding primarily on the long-term benefits that accrued to National Starch from the Unilever acquisition. The United States Court of Appeals for the Third Circuit affirmed, upholding the Tax Court's findings that "both Unilever's enormous resources and the possibility of synergy arising from the transaction served the long-term betterment of National Starch." In so doing, the Court of Appeals rejected National Starch's contention that, because the disputed expenses did not "create or enhance ... a separate and distinct additional asset," see *Commissioner v. Lincoln Savings & Loan Assn.*, 403 U.S. 345, 354 (1971), they could not be capitalized and therefore were deductible under § 162(a).

Section 162(a) of the Internal Revenue Code allows the deduction of "all the ordinary and necessary expenses paid or incurred during the taxable year in carrying on any trade or business." In contrast, § 263 of the Code allows no deduction for a capital expenditure—an "amount paid out for new buildings or for permanent improvements or betterments made to increase the value of any property or estate." The primary effect of characterizing a payment as either a business expense or a capital expenditure concerns the timing of the taxpayer's cost recovery: While business expenses are currently deductible, a capital expenditure usually is amortized and depreciated over the life of the relevant asset, or, where no specific asset or useful life can be ascertained, is deducted upon dissolution of the enterprise. Through provisions such as these, the Code endeavors to match expenses with the revenues of the taxable period to which they are properly attributable, thereby resulting in a more accurate calculation of net income for tax purposes.

The Court also has examined the interrelationship between the Code's business expense and capital expenditure provisions. In so doing, it has had occasion to parse § 162(a) and explore certain of its requirements. For example, in *Lincoln Savings*, we determined that, to qualify for deduction under § 162(a), "an item must (1) be 'paid or incurred during the taxable year,' (2) be for 'carrying on any trade or business,' (3) be an 'expense,' (4) be a 'necessary' expense, and (5) be an 'ordinary' expense." The Court has recognized, however, that the "decisive distinctions" between current expenses and capital expenditures "are those of degree and not of kind," and that because each case "turns on its special facts," the cases sometimes appear difficult to harmonize.

National Starch contends that the decision in *Lincoln Savings* changed these familiar backdrops and announced an exclusive test for identifying capital expenditures, a test in which "creation or enhancement of an asset" is a prerequisite to capitalization, and deductibility under § 162(a) is the rule rather than the exception. We do not agree, for we conclude that National Starch has overread *Lincoln Savings*.

In *Lincoln Savings*, we were asked to decide whether certain premiums, required by federal statute to be paid by a savings and loan association to the Federal Savings and Loan Insurance Corporation (FSLIC), were ordinary and necessary expenses under § 162(a), as Lincoln Savings argued and the Court of Appeals had held, or capital expenditures under § 263, as the Commissioner contended. We found that the "additional" premiums, the purpose of which was to provide FSLIC with a secondary reserve fund in which each insured institution retained a pro rata interest recoverable in certain situations, "serv[e] to create or enhance for Lincoln what is essentially a separate and distinct additional asset." "[A]s an inevitable consequence," we concluded, "the payment is capital in nature and not an expense, let alone an ordinary expense, deductible under § 162(a)."

Lincoln Savings stands for the simple proposition that a taxpayer's expenditure that "serves to create or enhance ... a separate and distinct" asset should be capitalized under § 263. It by no means follows, however, that only expenditures that create or enhance separate and distinct assets are to be capitalized under § 263. We had no occasion in *Lincoln Savings* to consider the tax treatment of expenditures that, unlike the additional premiums at issue there, did not create or enhance a specific asset, and thus the case cannot be read to preclude capitalization in other circumstances. In short, *Lincoln Savings* holds that the creation of a separate and distinct asset well may be a sufficient, but not a necessary, condition to classification as a capital expenditure.

Nor does our statement in *Lincoln Savings* that "the presence of an ensuing benefit that may have some future aspect is not controlling" prohibit reliance on future benefit as a means of distinguishing an ordinary business expense from a capital expenditure. Although the mere presence of an incidental future benefit—"some future aspect"—may not warrant capitalization, a taxpayer's realization of benefits beyond the year in which the expenditure is incurred is undeniably important in determining whether the appropriate tax treatment is immediate deduction or capitalization. *See United States v. Mississippi Chemical Corp.*, 405 U.S. 298, 310 (1972) (expense that "is of value in more than one taxable year" is a nondeductible capital expenditure); *Central Texas Savings & Loan Assn. v. United States*, 731 F.2d 1181, 1183 (CA5 1984) ("While the period of the benefits may not be controlling in all cases, it nonetheless remains a prominent, if not predominant, characteristic of a capital item"). Indeed, the text of the Code's capitalization provision, § 263(a)(1), which refers to "permanent improvements or betterments," itself envisions an inquiry into the duration and extent of the benefits realized by the taxpayer.

In applying the foregoing principles to the specific expenditures at issue in this case, we conclude that National Starch has not demonstrated that the investment banking, legal, and other costs it incurred in connection with Unilever's acquisition of its shares are deductible as ordinary and necessary business expenses under § 162(a).

Although petitioner attempts to dismiss the benefits that accrued to National Starch from the Unilever acquisition as "entirely speculative" or "merely incidental," the Tax Court's and the Court of Appeals' findings that the transaction produced significant benefits to National Starch that extended beyond the tax year in question are amply supported by the record. For example, in commenting on the merger with Unilever, National Starch's 1978 "Progress Report" observed that the company would "benefit greatly from the availability of Unilever's enormous resources, especially in the area of basic technology." Morgan Stanley's report to the National Starch board concerning the fairness to shareholders of a possible business combination with Unilever noted that National Starch management "feels that some synergy may exist with the Unilever organization given a) the nature of the Unilever chemical, paper, plastics and packaging operations ... and b) the strong consumer products orientation of Unilever United States, Inc."

In addition to these anticipated resource-related benefits, National Starch obtained benefits through its transformation from a publicly held, freestanding corporation into a wholly owned subsidiary of Unilever. The Court of Appeals noted that National Starch management viewed the transaction as "swapping approximately 3500 shareholders for one." Following Unilever's acquisition of National Starch's outstanding shares, National Starch was no longer subject to what even it terms the "substantial" shareholder-relations expenses a publicly traded corporation incurs, including reporting and disclosure obligations, proxy battles, and derivative suits. The acquisition also allowed National Starch, in the interests of administrative convenience and simplicity, to eliminate previously authorized but unissued shares of preferred and to reduce the total number of authorized shares of common from 8,000,000 to 1,000.

Courts long have recognized that expenses such as these, "incurred for the purpose of changing the corporate structure for the benefit of future operations are not ordinary and necessary business expenses." Deductions for professional expenses thus have been disallowed in a wide variety of cases concerning changes in corporate structure. Although support for these decisions can be found in the specific terms of § 162(a), which require that deductible expenses be "ordinary and necessary" and incurred "in carrying on any trade or business," courts more frequently have characterized an expenditure as capital in nature because "the purpose for which the expenditure is made has to do with the corporation's operations and betterment, sometimes with a continuing capital asset, for the duration of its existence or for the indefinite future or for a time somewhat longer than the current taxable year." The rationale behind these decisions applies equally to the professional charges at issue in this case.

The expenses that National Starch incurred in Unilever's friendly takeover do not qualify for deduction as "ordinary and necessary" business expenses under § 162(a). The fact that the expenditures do not create or enhance a separate and distinct additional asset is not controlling; the acquisition-related expenses bear the indicia of capital expenditures and are to be treated as such.

Notes

1. *The INDOPCO transaction.*—The "reverse subsidiary cash merger" in *INDOPCO* worked as follows. Step 1: Unilever created a new subsidiary, Holding, which in turn created a new subsidiary, NSC Merger. Step 2: As part of the same transaction in which Unilever contributed assets to Holding in exchange for all of its common stock, participating INDOPCO shareholders contributed their INDOPCO stock to Holding in exchange for shares of preferred stock. Preferred stock typically has a stated yield and a stated redemption value, and may even have a stated term. It often looks very much like debt, but is generally treated as stock for tax purposes. This Step 2 transaction apparently qualified for nonrecognition treatment under Code Section 351, which provides that "No gain or loss shall be recognized if property is transferred to a corporation by one or more persons solely in exchange for stock in such corporation and immediately after the exchange such person or persons are in control . . . of the corporation." As a result, the Greenwalls and other participating INDOPCO shareholders were able to exchange their INDOPCO stock for debt-like preferred shares in Holding without recognizing any built-in gain, taking those preferred shares with carryover basis. Step 3: NSC Merger, Inc. was then merged into Holding, using applicable state statutory merger rules. Under Code Sections 354 and 368, this kind of merger is also accorded nonrecognition treatment. The purpose of this third step was to allow the parties to force out any INDOPCO shareholders who had not voluntarily participated in the Step 2 exchange. Shareholders forced out in a statutory merger have the right to be paid fair market value for their shares, and may have a cause of action for breach of fiduciary duty if they have not been fairly treated. Hence the need for the Debevoise, Plimpton and Morgan Stanley services and fees.

2. *Capitalization in the Supreme Court.*—The Supreme Court has addressed the capitalization requirement repeatedly. Unfortunately, its cases are

sometimes not easily reconciled. In *Welch v. Helvering*, 290 U.S. 111 (1933), the Court held that payments of a former employer's debts to preserve taxpayer's business reputation were capital expenditures—apparently never to be deducted. In *Helvering v. Winmill*, 305 U.S. 79 (1938), it held that brokerage commissions were capital as well. In *Deputy v. Du Pont*, 308 U.S. 488 (1940), it held that expenses incurred by a shareholder to help executives in his company acquire stock were contributions to capital, and therefore nondeductible. It reached the same conclusion in *Interstate Transit Lines v. Commissioner*, 319 U.S. 590 (1943), in the case of a payment by a parent company to cover its subsidiary's operating deficit. By contrast, in *Commissioner v. Heininger*, 320 U.S. 467 (1943), it held that legal expenses incurred in disputing an adverse postal designation were currently deductible as ordinary and necessary expenses, reaching the same result in *Commissioner v. Tellier*, 383 U.S. 687 (1966), with regard to legal expenses incurred in defending against securities fraud charges. In *United States v. Hilton Hotels Corp.*, 397 U.S. 580 (1970), it held that consulting, legal, and other professional fees incurred by the acquiring firm in a minority stock appraisal proceeding were capital expenditures [note that INDOPCO involved similar fees incurred by the *target*, not the acquiring firm]; and in *Woodward v. Commissioner*, 397 U.S. 572 (1970), it reached the same conclusion with regard to legal, accounting, and appraisal expenses incurred in purchasing a minority stock interest. Finally, in *Commissioner v. Lincoln Savings & Loan Assn.*, 403 U.S. 345 (1971), the Court held that required additional premiums paid by a bank to federal insurers were capital expenditures, and in *United States v. Mississippi Chemical Corp.*, 405 U.S. 298 (1972), that cooperatives' required purchases of stock in a bank for cooperatives were not currently deductible. INDOPCO is the Court's most recent capitalization case.

3. *The* INDOPCO *Regulations.*—In response to *INDOPCO*, the Treasury issued new regulations under Code Section 263. Under new Treas. Reg. § 1.263(a)–4, it appears that amounts like those at issue in *INDOPCO* itself would not be required to be capitalized, since they do not create a "separate and distinct intangible asset." In effect, the new regulations seem to accept taxpayer's argument in *INDOPCO* and overturn the rule articulated in that case. *See* Calvin Johnson, *Destroying Tax Base: The Proposed* INDOPCO *Capitalization Regulations*, 99 TAX NOTES 1381 (2003).

SECTION 2: WHAT AMOUNTS MUST BE CAPITALIZED?

Code: Section 263A

Prior to 1987, having determined that capitalization was required, it was then necessary to look to case law, for the most part, to determine which arguably associated costs should be added to basis and which deducted currently. In *Commissioner v. Idaho Power Co.*, below, using principles similar to those explored in Section 1, the Supreme Court held that depreciation claimed on transportation equipment used in the construction of a power plant should be folded into that plant's basis. In 1986, Congress enacted Code Section 263A, which provides detailed capitalization rules for real and tangible personal property produced by taxpayer to be held in inventory or for use in taxpayer's income-producing activity. The pre–263A rules applied in *Idaho Power* continue to govern in other contexts.

COMMISSIONER v. IDAHO POWER CO.
418 U.S. 1 (1974)

This case presents the sole issue whether, for federal income tax purposes, a taxpayer is entitled to a deduction from gross income, under § 167(a) of the Internal Revenue Code of 1954, for depreciation on equipment the taxpayer owns and uses in the construction of its own capital facilities, or whether the capitalization provision of § 263(a)(1) of the Code bars the deduction.

The taxpayer-respondent, Idaho Power Company, is a public utility engaged in the production, transmission, distribution, and sale of electric energy. For many years, the taxpayer has used its own equipment and employees in the construction of improvements and additions to its capital facilities. The major work has consisted of transmission lines, transmission switching stations, distribution lines, distribution stations, and connecting facilities.

During 1962 and 1963, the tax years in question, taxpayer owned and used in its business a wide variety of automotive transportation equipment, including passenger cars, trucks of all descriptions, power-operated equipment, and trailers. Radio communication devices were affixed to the equipment and were used in its daily operations. The transportation equipment was used in part for operation and maintenance and in part for the construction of capital facilities having a useful life of more than one year.

For federal income tax purposes, the taxpayer claimed as a deduction from gross income all the year's depreciation on such equipment, including that portion attributable to its use in constructing capital facilities. The depreciation was computed on a composite life of 10 years and under straight-line and declining-balance methods.

Upon audit, the Commissioner of Internal Revenue disallowed the deduction for the construction-related depreciation. He ruled that that depreciation was a nondeductible capital expenditure to which § 263(a)(1) had application. He added the amount of the depreciation so disallowed to the taxpayer's adjusted basis in its capital facilities, and then allowed a deduction for an appropriate amount of depreciation on the addition, computed over the useful life (30 years or more) of the property constructed. A deduction for depreciation of the transportation equipment to the extent of its use in day-to-day operation and maintenance was also allowed.

The taxpayer asserts that its transportation equipment is used in its "trade or business" and that depreciation thereon is therefore deductible under § 167(a)(1) of the Code. The Commissioner concedes that § 167 may be said to have a literal application to depreciation on equipment used in capital construction, but contends that the provision must be read in light of § 263(a)(1) which specifically disallows any deduction for an amount "paid out for new buildings or for permanent improvements or betterments." He argues that § 263 takes precedence over § 167 by virtue of what he calls the "priority-ordering" terms (and what the taxpayer describes as "housekeeping" provisions) of § 161 of the Code, and that sound principles of accounting and taxation mandate the capitalization of this depreciation.

Since the Commissioner appears to have conceded the literal application of § 167(a) to Idaho Power's equipment depreciation, we need not reach the issue whether the Court of Appeals has given the phrase "used in the trade or business" a proper construction. For purposes of this case, we assume, without deciding, that § 167(a) does have a literal application to the depreciation of the taxpayer's transportation equipment used in the construction of its capital improvements.

Our primary concern is with the necessity to treat construction-related depreciation in a manner that comports with accounting and taxation realities. Over a period of time a capital asset is consumed and, correspondingly over that period, its theoretical value and utility are thereby reduced. Depreciation is an accounting device which recognizes that the physical consumption of a capital asset is a true cost, since the asset is being depleted. As the process of consumption continues, and depreciation is claimed and allowed, the asset's adjusted income tax basis is reduced to reflect the distribution of its cost over the accounting periods affected. The Court stated in *Hertz Corp. v. United States*, 364 U.S. 122, 126 (1960): "(T)he purpose of depreciation accounting is to allocate the expense of using an asset to the various periods which are benefited by that asset." When the asset is used to further the taxpayer's day-to-day business operations, the periods of benefit usually correlate with the production of income. Thus, to the extent that equipment is used in such operations, a current depreciation deduction is an appropriate offset to gross income currently produced. It is clear, however, that different principles are implicated when the consumption of the asset takes place in the construction of other assets that, in the future, will produce income themselves. In this latter situation, the cost represented by depreciation does not correlate with production of current income. Rather, the cost, although certainly presently incurred, is related to the future and is appropriately allocated as part of the cost of acquiring an income-producing capital asset.

The Court of Appeals opined that the purpose of the depreciation allowance under the Code was to provide a means of cost recovery and that this Court's decisions, *e.g.*, *Detroit Edison Co. v. Commissioner*, 319 U.S. 98, 101 (1943), endorse a theory of replacement through "a fund to restore the property." Although tax-free replacement of a depreciating investment is one purpose of depreciation accounting, it alone does not require the result claimed by the taxpayer here. Only last Term, in *United States v. Chicago, B. & Q.R. Co.*, 412 U.S. 401 (1973), we rejected replacement as the strict and sole purpose of depreciation:

> Whatever may be the desirability of creating a depreciation reserve under these circumstances, as a matter of good business and accounting practice, the answer is ... "(d)epreciation reflects the cost of an existing capital asset, not the cost of a potential replacement."

Even were we to look to replacement, it is the replacement of the constructed facilities, not the equipment used to build them, with which we would be concerned. If the taxpayer now were to decide not to construct any more capital facilities with its own equipment and employees, it, in theory, would have no occasion to replace its equipment to the extent that it was consumed in prior construction.

Accepted accounting practice and established tax principles require the capitalization of the cost of acquiring a capital asset. In *Woodward v. Commissioner*, 397 U.S. 572, 575 (1970), the Court observed: "It has long been recognized, as a general matter, that costs incurred in the acquisition ... of a capital asset are to be treated as capital expenditures." This principle has obvious application to the acquisition of a capital asset by purchase, but it has been applied, as well, to the costs incurred in a taxpayer's construction of capital facilities.

There can be little question that other construction-related expense items, such as tools, materials, and wages paid construction workers, are to be treated as part of the cost of acquisition of a capital asset. The taxpayer does not dispute this. Of course, reasonable wages paid in the carrying on of a trade or business qualify as a deduction from gross income. But when wages are paid in connection with the construction or acquisition of a capital asset, they must be capitalized and are then entitled to be amortized over the life of the capital asset so acquired.

Construction-related depreciation is not unlike expenditures for wages for construction workers. The significant fact is that the exhaustion of construction equipment does not represent the final disposition of the taxpayer's investment in that equipment; rather, the investment in the equipment is assimilated into the cost of the capital asset constructed. Construction-related depreciation on the equipment is not an expense to the taxpayer of its day-to-day business. It is, however, appropriately recognized as a part of the taxpayer's cost or investment in the capital asset. The taxpayer's own accounting procedure reflects this treatment, for on its books the construction-related depreciation was capitalized by a credit to the equipment account and a debit to the capital facility account. By the same token, this capitalization prevents the distortion of income that would otherwise occur if depreciation properly allocable to asset acquisition were deducted from gross income currently realized.

An additional pertinent factor is that capitalization of construction-related depreciation by the taxpayer who does its own construction work maintains tax parity with the taxpayer who has its construction work done by an independent contractor. The depreciation on the contractor's equipment incurred during the performance of the job will be an element of cost charged by the contractor for his construction services, and the entire cost; of course, must be capitalized by the taxpayer having the construction work performed. The Court of Appeals' holding would lead to disparate treatment among taxpayers because it would allow the firm with sufficient resources to construct its own facilities and to obtain a current deduction, whereas another firm without such resources would be required to capitalize its entire cost including depreciation charged to it by the contractor.

The presence of § 263(a)(1) in the Code is of significance. Its literal language denies a deduction for "(a)ny amount paid out" for construction or permanent improvement of facilities. The taxpayer contends that depreciation of construction equipment represents merely a decrease in value and is not an amount "paid out," within the meaning of § 263(a)(1). We disagree.

The purpose of § 263 is to reflect the basic principle that a capital expenditure may not be deducted from current income. It serves to prevent a taxpayer from utilizing currently a deduction properly attributable, through amortization, to later tax years when the capital asset becomes income producing. The regulations state that the capital expenditures to which § 263(a) extends include the "cost of acquisition, construction, or erection of buildings." Treas. Reg. § 1.263(a)–2(a). This manifests an administrative understanding that for purposes of § 263(a)(1), "amount paid out" equates with "cost incurred." The Internal Revenue Service for some time has taken the position that construction-related depreciation is to be capitalized. Rev. Rul. 59–380, 1959–2 C.B. 87; Rev. Rul. 55–252, 1955–1 C.B. 319.

There is no question that the cost of the transportation equipment was "paid out" in the same manner as the cost of supplies, materials, and other equipment, and the wages of construction workers. The taxpayer does not question the capitalization of these other items as elements of the cost of acquiring a capital asset. We see no reason to treat construction-related depreciation differently. In acquiring the transportation equipment, taxpayer "paid out" the equipment's purchase price; depreciation is simply the means of allocating the payment over the various accounting periods affected. As the Tax Court stated in *Brooks v. Commissioner*, 50 T.C., at 935, "depreciation—inasmuch as it represents a using up of capital—is as much an 'expenditure' as the using up of labor or other items of direct cost."

Finally, the priority-ordering directive of § 161—or, for that matter, § 261 of the Code—requires that the capitalization provision of § 263(a) take precedence, on the facts here, over § 167(a). Section 161 provides that deductions specified in Part VI of Subchapter B of the Income Tax Subtitle of the Code are "subject to the exceptions provided in part IX." Part VI includes § 167 and Part IX includes § 263. The clear import of

§ 161 is that, with stated exceptions set forth either in § 263 itself or provided for elsewhere (as, for example, in § 404 relating to pension contributions), none of which is applicable here, an expenditure incurred in acquiring capital assets must be capitalized even when the expenditure otherwise might be deemed deductible under Part VI.

We hold that the equipment depreciation allocable to taxpayer's construction of capital facilities is to be capitalized.

SECTION 3: EXCEPTIONS

Several major exceptions exist to the general rule that expenditures producing financial benefits significantly beyond the end of the taxable year must be capitalized, one judicially-created, four statutory.

(a) ADVERTISING EXPENSES

A judicially-created exception for advertising expenses developed when the United States had in place an excess profits tax, under which profits in excess of a specified percentage of "invested capital" were subject to surtax. This structure sometimes gave taxpayers an incentive to argue in favor of capitalization so as to increase "invested capital" and with it the amount of profits exempt from surtax. For excess profits tax purposes, the IRS tended to insist that advertising expenses be deducted currently. In a series of cases beginning with *Northwestern Yeast Co. v. Commissioner*, 5 B.T.A. 232 (1926), and culminating in *E.H. Sheldon & Co. v. Commissioner*, 214 F.2d 655 (6th Cir. 1954), the IRS successfully resisted almost all taxpayer efforts to capitalize advertising. By 1954, the Sixth Circuit could state: "The rule also appears well settled that such an expense cannot be capitalized by the taxpayer in the absence of evidence showing with reasonable certainty the benefits resulting in later years from the expenditure." Since taxpayers were generally unable to show with "reasonable certainty" that any given portion of advertising expenses was properly allocable to future benefits, such expenses effectively became *per se* ordinary, not capital.

The IRS and Tax Court have since retreated from this position with respect to advertising embodied in tangible form—such as product catalogs and billboards. *See, e.g., Best Lock Corp. v. Commissioner*, 31 T.C. 1217 (1959); Rev. Rul. 68–360, 1968–2 C.B. 197. With respect to all other advertising, however, *E.H. Sheldon & Co.* is apparently still followed.

(b) CIRCULATION EXPENSES

Code: Section 173

Code Section 173 permits current deduction of most "expenditures ... to establish, maintain, or increase the circulation of a newspaper, magazine, or other periodical," unless taxpayer elects to capitalize them. Arguably, this is simply an extension and partial codification of the judicially-created rule requiring current deduction of advertising expenses. The 2013 Tax Expenditure Budget does not treat either rule as a tax expenditure.

(c) RESEARCH AND SOFTWARE DEVELOPMENT EXPENSES

Code: Section 174

Regulation: Section 1.174–2

Code Section 174 permits current deduction of "research or experimental expenditures." Congress's evident purpose was to encourage research and development. The 2013 Tax Expenditure Budget treats this as a tax expenditure under the "normal tax baseline" method, but not under the "reference tax law baseline" method. *See* 2013 Tax Expenditure Budget, Item 7. (Note that the revenue loss estimate in the 2013 Tax Expenditure Budget, *supra*, does not take into account the Cary Brown equivalence.)

As a practical matter, one of the most important types of costs treated as currently deductible under Code Section 174 is the cost of writing computer software.

REV. PROC. 2000–50
2000–1 C.B. 601

SECTION 1. PURPOSE

This revenue procedure provides guidelines on the treatment of the costs of computer software.

SECTION 2. DEFINITION

For the purpose of this revenue procedure, "computer software" is any program or routine (that is, any sequence of machine-readable code) that is designed to cause a computer to perform a desired function or set of functions, and the documentation required to describe and maintain that program or routine. It includes all forms and media in which the software is contained, whether written, magnetic, or otherwise. Computer programs of all classes, for example, operating systems, executive systems, monitors, compilers and translators, assembly routines, and utility programs as well as application programs, are included. Computer software also includes any incidental and ancillary rights that are necessary to effect the acquisition of the title to, the ownership of, or the right to use the computer software, and that are used only in connection with that specific computer software. Computer software does not include any data or information base described in § 1.197–2(b)(4) of the Income Tax Regulations (for example, data files, customer lists, or client files) unless the data base or item is in the public domain and is incidental to a computer program. Nor does it include any cost of procedures that are external to the computer's operation.

. . .

SECTION 5. COSTS OF DEVELOPING COMPUTER SOFTWARE

.01 The costs of developing computer software (whether or not the particular software is patented or copyrighted) in many respects so closely resemble the kind of research and experimental expenditures that fall within the purview of § 174 as to warrant similar accounting treatment. Accordingly, the Service will not disturb a taxpayer's treatment of costs paid or incurred in developing software for any particular project, either for the taxpayer's own use or to be held by the taxpayer for sale or lease to others, where:

> (1) All of the costs properly attributable to the development of software by the taxpayer are consistently treated as current expenses and deducted in full in accordance with rules similar to those applicable under § 174(a); or

> (2) All of the costs properly attributable to the development of software by the taxpayer are consistently treated as capital expenditures that are recoverable through deductions for ratable amortization, in accordance with rules similar to those provided by § 174(b) and the regulations thereunder, over a period of 60 months from the date of completion of the development or, in accordance with rules provided in § 167(f)(1) and the regulations thereunder, over 36 months from the date the software is placed in service.

. . .

Recall that the economic effect of permitting the expensing of a capital investment is to tax income from that investment at an effective rate of zero. See Subchapter 12A, Section 3, *supra*. Treating the writing of computer software as the equivalent of scientific research therefore has the effect of exempting software-based industries from federal income taxation. In consequence, *Grand Auto Theft IV* is one of the most heavily tax-subsidized products in the United States today. *See* Calvin Johnson, *Capitalize Costs of Software Development*, 124 TAX NOTES 603 (August 10, 2009).

·

(d) BONUS DEPRECIATION

Code: Section 168(k)

Bonus depreciation was first added as Code Section 168(k) by the Job Creation and Worker Assistance Act in 2002. As originally enacted, the new rule allowed taxpayers to expense 30 percent of the adjusted basis of qualified property. The remaining basis of such property remained subject to the Code's standard depreciation rules, which themselves already permitted accelerated depreciation. Qualified property included new (1) property with a recovery period of 20 years or less, (2) water utility property, (3) non-Code Section 197 computer software, and (4) qualified leasehold improvements. The rule was expanded in May 2003 to allow taxpayers to expense 50 percent of the basis of qualified property.

The original bonus depreciation rules expired, for the most part, at the end of 2004. When the recession hit in 2008, however, the concept was revived, and was eventually expanded to allow taxpayers to expense 100 percent of the basis of qualified property through the end of 2011. Although the President proposed further extension of 100 percent bonus depreciation as part of a larger tax bill, Congressional gridlock prevented its passage. As a result, only 50 percent of the basis of qualified property acquired in 2012 may be expensed under Code Section 168(k), and bonus depreciation is scheduled to disappear altogether in 2013. It would not be surprising, however, if bonus depreciation were to be extended in some form thereafter.

100 percent bonus depreciation has the effect of making expensing the general rule and capitalization the exception—applicable only to items excluded from the definition of "qualified property." This, in turn, has the effect of eliminating effective taxation of income from capital and converting our income tax, in important regards, into a tax on consumption. Unfortunately, expensing only affects the taxation of assets, not the taxation of debt. As a result, bonus depreciation creates significant tax arbitrage opportunities and therefore the possibility of significantly negative—not merely zero—effective tax rates.

(e) SMALL BUSINESS EXPENSING ELECTION

Under Code Section 179, a taxpayer may elect to expense the cost of "section 179 property," which includes tangible property and computer software that constitutes section 1245 property (primarily personal property) and is acquired for use in the active conduct of a trade or business.

The aggregate amount that can be expensed under Code Section 179 is capped; the relevant caps have varied from year to year over the past decade, as follows:

2002	$24,000	
2003	$100,000	
2004	$102,000	($100,000 adjusted for inflation)
2005	$105,000	($100,000 adjusted for inflation)
2006	$108,000	($100,000 adjusted for inflation)
2007	$125,000	
2008	$250,000	
2009	$250,000	
2010	$500,000	

| 2011 | $500,000 |
| 2012 | $138,000 ($125,000 adjusted for inflation) |

In his 2012 budget proposal, the President proposed to extend the 2012 cap of $125,000, adjusted for inflation, indefinitely, but the proposal died as a result of Congressional gridlock. In 2013, the cap is therefore scheduled to revert to $25,000.

The option to expense section 179 property begins to phase out once taxpayer's purchases of such property exceed a threshold amount. The practical effect of this phase-out is to limit the Code Section 179 expensing option to small businesses.

The 2013 Tax Expenditure Budget treats Code Section 179 as a tax expenditure. *See* 2013 Tax Expenditure Budget, Item 79. (Note, again, that the revenue loss estimate in the 2013 Tax Expenditure Budget, *supra*, does not take into account the Cary Brown equivalence.)

Subchapter C: Cost Recovery

Code: Section 167

At least nominally, the general rule is that the Code does not allow taxpayers to deduct capital expenditures up front. Instead, as an asset is used in a trade or business or for investment purposes, Code Section 167 allows taxpayer to write its cost off over its useful life. This write-off is known as depreciation, in the case of tangible property, amortization, in the case of intangible property, or depletion, in the case of mineral deposits.

SECTION 1: DEPRECIATION

Code: Sections 167 and 168

Cost recovery deductions for tangible property, commonly known as "depreciation," are governed by Code Sections 167 and 168. The first allows the deduction. The second specifies the amount of the deduction for tangible property placed in service after its effective date, roughly 1981. The depreciation system now embodied in Code Section 168 is known as the "accelerated cost recovery system," or "ACRS."

(a) REGULAR DEPRECIATION

To understand how depreciation is computed under ACRS, it is useful to have some understanding of how depreciation was computed under prior law. Pre-ACRS, taxpayer estimated the asset's useful life and its salvage value at the end of that useful life. The difference between cost and salvage value was the asset's expected decline in value. Taxpayer then spread the expected decline in value over the asset's useful life using "any reasonable method."

Assume, for example, that taxpayer purchased an asset for $100. He estimated a useful life of four years and a salvage value of $20. The asset's expected decline in value over its useful life was therefore $80. He then spread that expected decline in value over that useful life using any reasonable method. For example, he might spread the expected decline evenly—a method known as "straight-line." If so, he would take a $20 depreciation deduction in each of the four years of the asset's useful life.

Three depreciation methods were *per se* reasonable: straight-line, declining balance switching to straight-line, and sum-of-the-years-digits. Only the first two survived enactment of Code Section 168; we will ignore the third.

Declining balance depreciation began with the "straight-line percentage." This was simply the percentage of total depreciation taken each year under the straight-line method. If, for example, the asset's useful life was three years, 33 percent of total depreciation was taken each year; if its useful life was four years, 25 percent; if ten years, 10 percent; and so on. In applying declining balance depreciation, taxpayers were permitted to use up to 200 percent of the straight-line percentage. This variation was known as the "200 percent declining balance" method, the "double declining balance" method, or "DDB," for short. Taxpayer then claimed depreciation equal to the chosen percentage of his remaining basis each year until the point, if any, at which straight-line depreciation was more favorable. No further depreciation was permitted once basis reached estimated salvage value.

The following example applies the double declining balance method to a $100 asset with a four-year useful life and a $20 salvage value. The straight-line percentage for a four-year asset was 25 percent. Twice that was 50 percent. Each year, therefore, taxpayer could claim depreciation equal to 50 percent of his remaining basis, limited by the estimated salvage value. Thus:

Year	Depreciation	Basis
		100
1	50	50
2	25	25
3	5	20
4	0	20

The most important problem with pre-1981 law was that it was often difficult to estimate an asset's useful life. Taxpayer's expert would swear that taxpayer's new building would only last for 20 years; the IRS's expert would swear that it would likely last for 100; the court would throw its hands up in frustration.

In 1962, the IRS attempted to give taxpayers some security by publishing a list of useful lives it would not challenge. Rev. Proc. 62–21, 1962–2 C.B. 418. In 1971, Congress in effect adopted this system, enacting the Class Lives Asset Depreciation Range ("CLADR" or "ADR") system, which gave taxpayers the option to adopt assumed useful lives (so-called "class lives") and thereby avoid controversy.

Then, in 1981, President Reagan proposed a major tax cut. The resulting legislation included a new approach to depreciation: ACRS. With the stated goal of stimulating investment in depreciable assets, new Code Section 168 specified unrealistically short useful lives and permitted heavily front-loaded methods of depreciation. The result was to lower the effective rate of taxation on income from plant and equipment. ACRS was particularly generous to the real estate, allowing owners to write off the cost of buildings over 15 years. This, in turn, triggered a real estate building boom, with prices escalating at a feverish pace.

In 1986, Congress concluded that it had been too generous and cut back depreciation on real property improvements, specifying a 27.5 year useful life for residential rental property and a 31.5 year useful life for nonresidential real property (*e.g.*, office buildings and shopping malls). These and other 1986 Act changes significantly reduced the Code's artificial incentives for real estate development. The result was a collapse in real estate prices, a collapse of the banking and savings and loan sectors, and a massive taxpayer-funded financial system bailout. Playing with tax write-off rules, history suggests, can produce serious economic dislocations.

In any event, Code Section 168(a) now provides that depreciation shall be determined using "(1) the applicable depreciation method, (2) the applicable recovery period, and (3) the applicable convention."

First, "applicable depreciation method." Three such methods are permitted under ACRS: 200 percent declining balance switching to straight-line, 150 declining balance switching to straight-line, and straight-line. With few exceptions, straight-line is required for real property and 200 percent declining balance switching to straight-line is used for other types of property. Taxpayer may elect to use a *less* favorable method. Thus, for example, a taxpayer entitled to use 200 percent declining balance may elect 150 percent declining balance or straight-line, but few do.

An asset's "applicable recovery period" is simply its statutorily specified useful life. Here, ACRS builds on pre-ACRS law. First, we look up the asset's "class life" in Rev. Proc. 87–56, 1987–2 C.B. 687, successor to the 1962 revenue procedure in which the IRS first gave taxpayers guidance with regard to useful lives. Second, Code Section 168(e)(1) converts the resulting "class life" into a "recovery class." Thus, for example, if an asset has a class life of between 10 and 15 years under the revenue procedure, it is "7–year property." Finally, Code Section 168(c) specifies the "applicable recovery period" for each recovery class. Not surprisingly, "7–year property" has an applicable recovery period of 7 years. Most of the acceleration in ACRS comes from (1) the double declining balance method, and (2) Code Section 168(e)(1), which authorizes the use of unrealistically short useful lives for depreciation purposes.

Finally, the "applicable convention." An asset placed in service on, say, May 24 will be in service for 222 days in its first calendar year. In theory, therefore, a calendar-year taxpayer should be entitled to 222/365 of his first depreciation year's worth of depreciation in taxable Year 1—no more, no less. But allocating depreciation across taxable years in this manner is computationally burdensome. In general, therefore, Code Section 168(d)(1) allows taxpayers to use a "half-year convention." For calendar-year taxpayers, this means that depreciation is computed as if every asset placed in service during a year is placed in service on July 1 of that year. This, in turn, radically simplifies depreciation computations.

Two special applicable convention rules sometimes apply. First, real property is always subject to a "mid-month convention." Second, if taxpayer places more than 40 percent of his newly-acquired depreciable personal property in service during the last quarter of his taxable year, he is required to use a "mid-quarter convention" for all such property.

In practice, Code Section 168 makes depreciation simple and certain. Taxpayer determines the recovery class for each piece of tangible property placed in service during the year and then consults the relevant depreciation percentage tables set forth in Rev. Proc. 87–57, 1987–2 C.B. 687. Here, for example, is the portion of Table 1 from that revenue procedure applicable to 3–year property depreciated using the 200 percent declining balance method and the half-year convention:

Year	Depreciation Percentage
1	33.33
2	44.45
3	14.81
4	7.41

Assume taxpayer purchases 3–year property for $100 and places it in service in Year 1. If Table 1 applies, it tells us that he is entitled to $33.33 of depreciation in Year 1, $44.45 in Year 2, $14.81 in Year 3, and $7.41 in Year 4. The return preparer simply takes taxpayer's initial basis and multiplies it by the percentage specified for the relevant year; the result is taxpayer's allowable depreciation for that year. Over the four-year period, he will write off all of his initial cost of $100.

(b) ALTERNATIVE DEPRECIATION

Code Section 168(g) imposes less favorable depreciation rules on (1) property used predominantly outside the United States, (2) tax-exempt use property, (3) tax-exempt bond financed property, and (4) property that taxpayer elects to depreciate using alternative depreciation. Under alternative depreciation, the recovery period generally equals the asset's class life (40 years for real property) and only straight-line recovery is permitted.

In addition, alternative depreciation is used for AMT purposes. As a result, the bases of depreciable assets are likely to be different for AMT purposes than for regular tax purposes, and gain or loss recognized on the sale of such assets is likely to be different as well.

Ch. 12   Capital Expenditures

PROBLEMS FOR DISCUSSION

12–7. On January 1, Year 1, Amos purchased a truck for $200,000 cash. The truck had a useful life and class life of 4 years and a salvage value of $50,000 at the end of that four year period. Compute Amos's allowable depreciation on the truck under each of the following:

a. Straight-line under Code Section 167.

b. Double declining balance under Code Section 167.

c. Double declining balance switching to straight-line under Code Section 168, using the half-year convention.

d. Expensing under Code Section 179 (assuming a subsection (b)(1) cap of $150,000), remainder depreciated using double declining balance switching to straight-line under Code Section 168, using the half-year convention.

SECTION 2: AMORTIZATION

"Amortization" is the term normally used for cost recovery of intangible assets. Code Section 167 allows the deduction. Code Section 197 requires that property to which it applies be amortized using the straight-line method over 15 years. Intangibles not subject to Code Section 197 are generally amortized using the straight-line method over estimated useful lives.

Again, a little history may be helpful. When one business buys another, the overall purchase price is allocated among the purchased business's separately identifiable assets in accordance with their fair market values. Very often, the overall purchase price paid is greater than the sum of the fair market values of the purchased business's separate assets. Thus, for example, buyer might pay $100 million for a business that has separately identifiable assets worth only $60 million. Only $60 million of the purchase price can properly be assigned to the separately identifiable assets. The remainder is typically assigned to "goodwill"; on the foregoing facts, buyer would be treated as having purchased goodwill for $40 million.

The IRS historically took the position that goodwill had no ascertainable useful life and was therefore not amortizable. Instead, purchaser carried the goodwill on its books until the business was discontinued, at which time the goodwill could be written off. This was not a happy result for taxpayers. In response, taxpayers developed imaginative new intangible assets to which to assign the residual basis in their business purchases—"customer-based intangibles" like customer lists, insurance expirations, subscriber lists, bank deposits, cleaning-service accounts, and drugstore-prescription files, "supplier-based intangibles," "workforce-in-place," and "business books and records"—assets that at least arguably had ascertainable useful lives and could therefore be amortized. In *New-*

ark Morning Ledger Co. v. United States, 507 U.S. 546 (1993), the Supreme Court upheld the assignment of $71,201,395 of basis to an amortizable asset taxpayer had labeled "paid subscribers." The prospect of continued litigation loomed.

Code Section 197 was enacted in response. It specifies a 15–year life for all "amortizable section 197 intangibles." The list of covered assets was intended to encompass all of the innovative intangible asset categories taxpayers had come up with to absorb residual basis in their business purchases. Although the section is not explicitly so structured, separately acquired intangibles are not its primary target. Thus, for example, with some exceptions, self-created intangibles are not covered. Code Section 197(c)(2). Nor are intangibles listed in subsection (e), which attempts to exclude types of intangibles commonly purchased separately—film rights, computer software, mortgage servicing rights, and the like.

SECTION 3: OTHER COST RECOVERY RULES

(a) DEPLETION

Code: Sections 611, 612, and 613

"Depletion" refers to cost recovery of interests in natural resources: minerals, oil and gas, timber, and the like. In general, the resource-holder is entitled to the greater of cost depletion and percentage depletion.

Cost depletion is computed by spreading taxpayer's basis in the depletable property over the number of units of the resource expected to be recovered. As units of the resource are recovered and sold, a proportionate portion of taxpayer's basis is deductible as cost depletion. Treas. Reg. § 1.611–2.

Percentage depletion is only available for resources specified in Code Section 613(b) at the percentages set forth in that section. Taxpayer applies the appropriate percentage to his gross income from the depletable property, regardless of his remaining basis in that property. Each year's percentage depletion is capped, however, at 50 percent of taxpayer's taxable income from the property. Because percentage depletion is not limited to taxpayer's basis, it is common for resource owners to be allowed more cost recovery with respect to qualified resources than their cost. The 2013 Tax Expenditure Budget treats this as a tax expenditure. See 2013 Tax Expenditure Budget, Items 10 and 36.

(b) START–UP EXPENSES

Code: Section 195

Code Section 195 allows taxpayer to elect to amortize the costs of starting up a business over 15 years, beginning in the month in which the trade or business begins. Examples include:

"expenses incurred for the analysis or survey of potential markets, products, labor supply, transportation facilities, etc. Eligible expenses also include startup costs which are incurred subsequent to a decision to establish a particular business and prior to the time when the business begins. For example, startup costs include advertising salaries and wages paid to employees who are being trained and their instructors, travel and other expenses incurred in lining up prospective distributors, suppliers or customers, and salaries or fees paid or incurred for executives, consultants, and for similar professional services."

H.R. Rep. No. 1278, 96th Cong., 2d Sess. 10–11, 1980–2 C.B. 709.

PART 4

INTRA-FAMILY AND OTHER NON-ARM'S-LENGTH TRANSFERS

■ ■ ■

The basic rules of the U.S. tax system assume that individual taxpayers are self-interested—that is, that they care primarily about themselves. A purely self-interested individual maintains separate bank accounts and other financial records and cares a lot whether he or, say, his girlfriend owns a particular piece of property. Significant transfers between such individuals are generally arm's-length value-for-value exchanges. If taxpayers are purely self-interested, we can assume that they will not transfer value to others simply to avoid taxes, since the value of what they give away will almost always exceed any tax saving that may result.

These assumptions fail in a variety of contexts, most notably within families. Spouses commonly care deeply about each other. They commingle assets and liabilities and often do not keep records of their interactions. They may willingly shift income, expenses, assets, or liabilities from one to the other if doing so will reduce their overall tax liabilities.

This creates two related sets of tax system design problems. First, spouses' economic affairs may be so "entangled" as to make application of the system's standard rules unadministrable. Accurately tracing cash flows between entangled partners may be impossible. It may be unclear which spouse owns what or which income is whose. Taxing the innumerable daily deals spouses make ("You pick up the kids; I'll get the groceries") may be unrealistic. Even applying the system's standard rules only to major deals ("You stay home and take care of the kids; I'll support you.") is likely to be problematic.

Second, spouses often do not care where a particular check is deposited, out of whose account a particular bill is paid, who holds title to what, or who is legally the borrower on which debt, at least so long as they remain together. They may be perfectly willing to adjust ownership if doing so will save taxes. We say they are "relatively indifferent" to ownership—that is, they care more about saving taxes than about maintaining the integrity of their separate finances. This relative indifference creates widespread tax avoidance possibilities that our system must and does address.

Entanglement and relative indifference are not limited to spouses. The finances of parents and children raise many of the same issues, although often with special twists. Extended family relationships (grandparents, adult siblings, and the like) can create significant tax avoidance opportunities as well. Nor is relative indifference limited to families. As a matter of non-tax law, to obtain the benefits of limited liability, shareholders must maintain formal separation between their assets and liabilities and those of their corporations. Nevertheless, shareholders may be relatively indifferent as to whether they or their controlled corporations receive income, pay expenses, own property, or owe debt.

CHAPTER 13

ENTANGLEMENT

■ ■ ■

Subchapter A: Taxation of Entangled Relationships Not Treated as "Marriage"

This Subchapter explores how our system taxes individuals in committed, long-term, intimate relationships not treated as "marriage" for federal income tax purposes. Today, these default rules apply only when the Code's special rules for couples treated as "married" do not apply; when they first evolved, however, many applied to married couples as well. As will be seen, the default rules did not work very well then, and do not work very well today. Subchapter B then explores how the Code's special rules for couples treated as "married," enacted largely in response to perceived problems with the default rules, resolve the same issues.

SECTION 1: THE CHALLENGE OF ENTANGLEMENT

As has been noted, individuals in committed, long-term, intimate relationships typically behave differently from the arm's-length actors assumed by the Code's basic rule structure. They do not necessarily keep records of who owns what or owes what. The records they do keep may not accurately reflect their respective beneficial interests. They often commingle assets or use them communally. They engage in countless informal exchanges, some minor, some major. They may even structure basic life choices in reliance on commitments from relationship partners. In short, they become economically "entangled."

Pascarelli v. Commissioner, below, illustrates some of the challenges entangled relationships raise for both taxpayers and courts. As you read the court's discussion of petitioner's lack of records and faulty memory, bear in mind that the trial occurred roughly a decade after the events in question—a not-uncommon gap between taxable year and trial. Notwithstanding the Court's complaints, the *Pascarelli* facts are relatively straightforward. Imagine how much harder its task would have been if DeAngelis and Pascarelli had maintained a joint bank account into which each had made deposits and out of which each had covered daily living expenses. The opinion puzzles over how much Pascarelli spent on DeAngelis's clothing. Imagine its difficulties if they had eaten meals or raised children together.

PASCARELLI v. COMMISSIONER
55 T.C. 1082 (1971)

[In the first of two consolidated cases, the IRS asserted that amounts transferred by DeAngelis to Pascarelli between 1959 and 1963 were compensation income to her; in the second, it asserted that they were gifts subject to transfer tax, for which Pascarelli was secondarily liable as donee.] The primary issue for decision is whether certain funds transferred by Anthony DeAngelis to the petitioner during the years 1959–63 were compensation for services rendered or gifts, or whether the petitioner merely acted as the agent of Mr. DeAngelis in holding such funds to be spent for his purposes and at his direction.

The petitioner met Mr. DeAngelis in 1940 or 1941, at which time she was separated from her first husband. Their close personal relationship began shortly thereafter. In 1941, Mr. DeAngelis lived for a time in the same house with the petitioner and her mother. At that time, the petitioner's mother loaned Mr. DeAngelis between $2,000 and $3,000 that he needed to go into business, and expressed the hope that he "look after" the petitioner in the future. Through all the years of their acquaintance, Mr. DeAngelis made payments to the petitioner in indeterminate amounts; however, such payments were not comparable in amount to the payments made during the years 1959 through 1963. The pre–1959 payments were made to assist the petitioner and her children and were made without restriction as to usage.

In October 1959, the petitioner purchased a house at 63 Berkley Drive, Tenafly, N.J. The full purchase price of the house was $65,000; a downpayment of $40,000 was made. The title to the property was in her name alone; Mr. DeAngelis had no ownership interest in it. From about the time of such purchase through the period here in issue, the house was occupied by the petitioner and Mr. DeAngelis, along with two or three of the petitioner's children. The petitioner's sister, brother-in-law, and young niece also lived there for some period of time during those years. The house had a main floor and a lower floor or basement. The petitioner and her children slept on the main floor, and Mr. DeAngelis occupied the lower floor, which was modified to include a four-room "apartment." In all other respects, Mr. DeAngelis and the petitioner had a relationship akin to that of a husband and wife, with the petitioner in the role of a housewife. She did his washing and cleaning, bought clothing for him, and performed other wifely duties. One important reason for Mr. DeAngelis' sleeping in a separate portion of the house was the presence of the petitioner's teenage children.

The petitioner and Mr. DeAngelis often traveled together, and when they were staying at any place except in the petitioner's home in Tenafly, they stayed as man and wife. In fact, such trips together took place prior to the petitioner's purchase of the house, including a 3–month trip to Spain in 1959. Mr. DeAngelis maintained his principal residence in the petitioner's house in Tenafly until the time he was sent to prison.

Many of the trips on which the petitioner accompanied Mr. DeAngelis during the period with which we are concerned were taken for the purpose of pursuing his business interests. Between the time that they started living together in the petitioner's house in Tenafly and the time of Mr. DeAngelis' business collapse, the house was often used to entertain people who had business relationships with Mr. DeAngelis. The petitioner assisted in such entertainment, both in her home and on the trips away from home.

In 1959, Mr. DeAngelis transferred $41,228.94 directly to the petitioner by means of six checks. In 1960, he transferred $32,500 directly to her by means of 12 checks; he also transferred $2,785 to her through a third party, for a total in 1960 of $35,285. In 1961, he transferred $43,300 directly to her by means of 21 checks. In 1962, he transferred $32,500 directly to her by means of 20 checks; he also transferred $400 to her through a third party, for a total in 1962 of $32,650. In 1963, he transferred $62,800 directly to her by means of 37 checks; he also transferred $1,200 to her through a third party, for a total in 1963 of $64,000. However, in 1963, the petitioner returned $14,000 to Mr. DeAngelis.

In 1959, a brokerage account was opened in the petitioner's name with D. R. Comenzo & Co., a brokerage house. The purpose of the account was to trade in the commodity market. The account was opened with $2,000 which the petitioner contributed. In 1959, Mr. DeAngelis subsequently transferred sums totaling $32,406 into that account. Such transfers were not made as loans to the petitioner. Mr. DeAngelis managed all of the buying and selling activities with respect to such account pursuant to a power of attorney executed by the petitioner; she was not knowledgeable in such matters and did not direct the purchases and sales herself. The petitioner received monthly statements on the status of the account from Comenzo, and she looked at the statements but did not understand their significance. We find that the money in the Comenzo account did in fact belong to the petitioner, and that the sum of $32,406 which Mr. DeAngelis transferred into that account in 1959 constituted a gift to the petitioner in that year.

In 1960, Mr. DeAngelis paid $10,800 directly to John Bellochhio for landscaping work performed on the petitioner's property at 63 Berkley Drive. In the same year, Mr. DeAngelis paid $3,780 directly to Robert Smith for work performed in making improvements to the basement at the same address. The improvements to the basement were done according to Mr. DeAngelis' specifications, as that part of the house served as his living quarters.

The petitioner bought a new Cadillac for herself in 1961, paying approximately $5,526 for it with her check. That Cadillac was traded on another new Cadillac in 1962, with a cash difference of $2,700, which was also paid by the petitioner's check. The cars were used occasionally to pick up Mr. DeAngelis at his place of business in Bayonne, N.J., and drive him home, but the petitioner also used them for her personal errands such as shopping and transporting her children. The petitioner does not know how many miles these cars were driven during the years in issue, and does not know how many miles they were driven for the purpose of picking up Mr. DeAngelis at work. Mr. DeAngelis sometimes used a company car, to which he had access any time he wanted it.

[Between 1959 and 1963, the petitioner transferred substantial amounts to various members of her family.] The petitioner used $8,000 of the funds that Mr. DeAngelis transferred to her to make a loan to Henry Anderson, in order to enable him and his wife to purchase a home. The loan was motivated by the petitioner's personal friendship with the Andersons.

The petitioner sometimes purchased items of clothing for Mr. DeAngelis. Such items included shoes, socks, shirts, ties, and topcoats. We find that the petitioner spent $350 per year during the years 1960, 1961, 1962, and 1963 on articles of clothing for Mr. DeAngelis.

The petitioner entertained and purchased gifts for people with whom Mr. DeAngelis had business dealings. Such entertainment was conducted, and such gifts were purchased, at Mr. DeAngelis' request and with his authorization. The entertainment included parties at the petitioner's home to which a number of Mr. DeAngelis' business associates and their wives were invited; also, the petitioner sometimes took the associates' wives out to dinner, to the theatre, and on shopping trips, in New York City, in Florida, and in other places. Generally, the beneficiaries of the entertainment were not the petitioner's personal friends, and the petitioner paid for most of such entertainment out of the funds transferred to her by Mr. DeAngelis. We find that the petitioner expended a total of $1,500 in 1959 and $5,000 per year in 1960, 1961, 1962, and 1963 for entertainment on Mr. DeAngelis' behalf and at his request. Furthermore, the petitioner bought and paid for certain gifts for people associated with Mr. DeAngelis in business, primarily the wives of such associates. The recipients of these gifts were not the petitioner's personal friends. We find that the petitioner spent a total of $1,000 per year in 1959, 1960, 1961, 1962, and 1963 for such gifts.

The petitioner kept no records of any kind. More specifically, she kept no records of how much money Mr. DeAngelis gave her, of how much she spent on his behalf, of how much she returned to him, of how much he gave her to run the household, of whom she entertained, of how much such entertainment cost, of the extent to which her house was used for Mr. DeAngelis' business purposes, of how many miles she drove her automobiles, of how many miles were put on such automobiles for Mr.

DeAngelis' purposes, or of what gifts she purchased for Mr. DeAngelis' business associates and how much such gifts cost.

The petitioner and Mr. DeAngelis had a very close personal relationship, and the services that she performed with respect to entertainment of his business associates were done in a spirit of cooperation similar to that which might prompt a wife to perform such duties to aid her husband in his business pursuits, and not for the purpose of obtaining compensation. She was not an employee of Mr. DeAngelis at any time during the years in issue. Mr. DeAngelis' dominant reasons for transferring the funds to the petitioner and for transferring the funds to the Comenzo account in her name were love and affection and disinterested generosity, except for the funds which she spent at his direction and on his behalf.

For Federal tax purposes, a gift must proceed from a disinterested and detached generosity, motivated by affection, respect, admiration, charity, or the like, with the most critical factor being the transferor's dominant intention. *Duberstein v. Commissioner*, 363 U.S. 278 (1960). However, when a transfer is made without being motivated by a sense of generosity, but rather with the expectation of an economic benefit flowing to the transfer as a result, then no gift has been made, and the transferee realizes ordinary income to the extent of the excess of the value of what is transferred over the value of the consideration which is returned to the transferor. The mere absence of a legal or moral obligation to make a payment does not establish that such payment is a gift for tax purposes; in fact, such payment is not a gift if made in return for services rendered, or if made because of the incentive of anticipated economic benefit to the payor.

The motivation of Mr. DeAngelis, as transferor, must be determined from an analysis of all the evidence before us pertaining to the relationship between him and the petitioner. The petitioner and Mr. DeAngelis had a close personal relationship dating back nearly 20 years prior to the beginning of the period in issue. The relationship between them may have been influenced by Mr. DeAngelis' gratitude toward the petitioner's mother who assisted him in going into business. Although the petitioner was married to another man for 16 or 17 years in the interim, her relationship with Mr. DeAngelis continued in some form, and he established during that period a pattern of generosity toward her; his payments to her prior to 1959 carried no limitations with respect to the purposes for which they could be used.

During the years in issue, Mr. DeAngelis and the petitioner lived as husband and wife in all respects, except for the facts that they were not legally married and did not occupy the same bedroom at the petitioner's house in Tenafly because of their sensibilities with respect to the feelings of her children, who also lived there. The record indicates that they hope to continue their relationship in the future, and get married someday. Mr. DeAngelis' testimony throughout this case was marked by an attitude of protectiveness toward the petitioner, and a desire not to see her hurt financially by the complex web of circumstances woven by his financial dealings.

These circumstances lead us to find that the petitioner did not perform services for Mr. DeAngelis for the purpose of obtaining compensation, but rather with the same spirit of cooperation that would motivate a wife to strive to help her husband advance in his business. Although it is true, as the respondent contends, that the petitioner's acting as "hostess" to Mr. DeAngelis' business associates and their wives was very valuable to his business, we think it would be artificial and incorrect to conclude that such acts were primarily motivated by a desire to be paid, much as an employee works to receive a salary. Similarly, it would be equally incorrect to conclude that Mr. DeAngelis made payments to the petitioner in order to compensate her for her help in his business. Based on the entire record, we conclude that such payments proceeded from disinterested and detached generosity on the part of Mr. DeAngelis toward the petitioner, and that they were motivated by sentiments of affection, respect, and admiration, all of which were credibly displayed in Mr. DeAngelis' testimony.

The next question is, to what extent were the funds which were undisputedly transferred by Mr. DeAngelis to the petitioner expended by her for Mr. DeAngelis' purposes pursuant to his direction, so that such funds were never really within the control of the petitioner? To the extent that the petitioner has shown that the funds were so expended, they cannot be considered as gifts for tax purposes, as a gift is not complete when the transferor retains dominion over the transferred property, and controls what is to be done with it. To that extent, the petitioner acted merely as a conduit through whom the funds passed, and not as the beneficial owner or recipient of such funds.

It is altogether clear that not all funds transferred to the petitioner by Mr. DeAngelis were to be spent for his purposes. She spent substantial amounts for her own benefit, for the benefit of her family, and for her friends. The two new Cadillacs which she bought for herself in 1961 and 1962 cost about $8,226, and the new Buick that she bought for her daughter in 1961 cost about $3,500. She transferred by check to her relatives a total of $12,570 between 1960 and 1963; also, bank accounts in her name in trust for two of her children showed increments of at least $14,990 during the years in issue.

The petitioner used $8,000 of the funds transferred to her by Mr. DeAngelis to make a loan to the Andersons, a couple whom she described as friends of hers. The record does not indicate whether such loan was ever repaid. The petitioner testified that she did not need or obtain Mr. DeAngelis' authorization to make the loan. Therefore, she has not shown that the proceeds of such loan constituted money spent on Mr. DeAngelis' behalf, despite his testimony that the loan was made with his authorization.

The foregoing items alone account for a total of about $47,286 not expended for Mr. DeAngelis' purposes. Such total does not include any of the clothing that the petitioner purchased for herself and her children, or the myriad other types of personal expenditures which, of necessity, must have followed from her mode of living.

In attempting to determine how much money was spent for Mr. DeAngelis, we are handicapped by the total lack of records of any sort—not even the most informal records exist. Of course, we do not hold the petitioner to the quantum of proof that is required of a taxpayer seeking to deduct travel, entertainment, and gift expenditures from his income as business deductions under section 162 and subject to section 274; the question here is not one of deductions from income, but rather one of determining whether the funds became the property of the petitioner or were merely held by her as an agent. Nevertheless, we cannot base our findings upon mere speculations, and the petitioner must carry her burden of proof by establishing some credible basis for allowing us to decide how much of the money that was transferred to her was not really hers.

When there are no documentary records, and such records are not explicitly required by statute or regulation, this Court can and often does find facts on the basis of oral testimony. In this case, we have the testimony of the petitioner with respect to the money she spent for Mr. DeAngelis' purposes; most of this testimony is very vague and general, except for her statements as to the purposes underlying certain expenditures represented by checks, about which she was specifically questioned by counsel. With respect to virtually every check as to which she testified, the name or business of the payee sheds no light on the question of whether or not the expenditure was made in connection with Mr. DeAngelis' business; thus, such testimony is helpful to the petitioner's case only to the extent that we are willing to take her word for it. Also, we have the testimony of Mr. DeAngelis, which purports to be specific about names and amounts but does not generally fix the year of the alleged expenditure. We use the term "purports to be specific" because most of Mr. DeAngelis' testimony, upon analysis, proves to be nothing more than a collection of estimates, prepared wholly from memory without reference to any sort of data or records; and they contain apparent inconsistencies.

The petitioner's uncertainty as to the facts is demonstrated by her positive testimony to the effect that she spent some of the money that was transferred to hereby Mr. DeAngelis to purchase a fur coat for a Mrs. Salama, the wife of one of Mr. DeAngelis' business associates from Spain. However, on cross-examination, she admitted that she did not really remember whether she paid for the coat with money that she had, or whether she billed the coat to Mr. DeAngelis and had him pay for it. Similarly, she testified that two checks aggregating $526 paid to a photography studio in 1963 "must be" for the photography services ordered by Mr. DeAngelis for a big outside party held for no special occasion; but cross-examination elicited the fact that the petitioner did not really know what the money was paid for and it might have been for pictures taken at an engagement reception held for the petitioner's daughter in a hotel.

Such uncertainty of recollection clearly does not add to the weight to be accorded to her testimony.

Despite our serious doubts as to much of the testimony given by the petitioner and Mr. DeAngelis, we believe that the record establishes nevertheless that the petitioner did expend some money on Mr. DeAngelis' behalf and pursuant to his direction, for the furtherance of his business purposes. The amounts that we have found to be so expended constitute our best estimates based upon the entire record. However, the inexactitude and imprecision revealed by the record have been weighed against the petitioner, as they are of her own making. *Cohan v. Commissioner*, 39 F.2d 540 (C.A. 2, 1930). The *Cohan* rule originated in the context of deductibility of travel and entertainment expenses from income. However, similar estimates have been used in diverse other circumstances in which the taxpayer has not clearly shown the proper figure to be used by the Court. Although the *Cohan* rule is no longer applicable to the deductibility of expenditures for travel and entertainment (sec. 274(d)), it may still be applied in other situations.

Our Findings of Fact set forth our best estimates as to the petitioner's expenditures for Mr. DeAngelis' purposes with respect to clothing (for him), entertainment, and gifts. Beyond such estimates, we feel that we would be indulging in meaningless guesswork.

Next, we deal with the question of whether the amounts that Mr. DeAngelis paid directly to John Bellochhio and Robert Smith, in 1960, for improvements done on the petitioner's real property in Tenafly, were transfers to the petitioner at the time such payments were made, and if so, whether they were transferred as compensation or gifts. The petitioner advances the argument that the payments to John Bellochhio were not equivalent to transfers to her because they involved landscaping work done in order to make the premises more suitable to Mr. DeAngelis' business meetings, and that the payments to Robert Smith were not equivalent to transfers to her because they involved work performed to build an apartment like living space for Mr. DeAngelis use in the basement of the house.

It seems clear to us that Mr. DeAngelis enjoyed the primary use of the basement living quarters during the years that he lived in the house, although it seems that he lived there at the sufferance of the petitioner, there being no indication that his right to occupy those quarters was based upon any legally binding agreement. It is not clear that he derived any more benefit than anyone else living in the house from the landscaping work. However, regardless of such usage, it seems clear that both the improvements to the basement and the landscaping work served to increase the value of the house, which was owned by the petitioner alone. The former, in particular, was an addition of permanent nature. There is no indication in the record that the increase in the value of the real estate as a result of such improvements was less than the cost of such work. Similarly, there is no indication as to the value of Mr. DeAngelis' usage of the basement apartment; but it seems clear that such apartment remained as part of the realty after he took up residence elsewhere. The petitioner has failed to carry her burden of proof on this issue, and therefore, we sustain the respondent's determination that Mr. DeAngelis' payments for improvements to the petitioner's realty were tantamount to payments to her. For the same reasons that we set forth earlier, we hold that such payments were gifts to the petitioner rather than compensation. They constituted a transfer for less than an adequate consideration in money or money's worth. *Commissioner v. Wemyss*, 324 U.S. 303, 306 (1945).

Aside from her contention that the transfers to her and expenditures on her behalf were not gifts, the petitioner has not challenged in any way the respondent's determination with respect to gift tax liability, and therefore we sustain such determination to the extent that we have found the transfers and expenditures to be gifts. It is clear that if the donor's gift tax is not paid when due, then the donee is liable, as transferee, for the amount of such tax liability to the extent of the value of the gifts received. Since Mr. DeAngelis did not pay the gift tax owing for the years in issue, we hold that the petitioner is liable as transferee for the gift tax due from Mr. DeAngelis with respect to the gifts that we have found she received.

NOTES

1. *Cohan Rule.*—In *Cohan v. Commissioner*, 39 F.2d 540 (2d Cir. 1930), George M. Cohan, writer of "You're a Grand Old Flag," "Give My Regards to Broadway," and other famous songs, claimed entertainment and travel expenses that he estimated but could not document. The Board of Tax Appeals disallowed all such expenses. Judge Learned Hand, reversing, reasoned as follows:

> "The Board refused to allow him any part of this, on the ground that it was impossible to tell how much he had in fact spent, in the absence of any items or details. The question is how far this refusal is justified, in view of the finding that he had spent much and that the sums were allowable expenses. Absolute certainty in such matters is usually impossible and is not necessary; the Board should make as close an approximation as it can, bearing heavily if it chooses upon the taxpayer whose inexactitude is of his own making. But to allow nothing at all appears to us inconsistent with saying that something was spent. True, we do not know how many trips Cohan made, nor how large his entertainments were; yet there was obviously some basis for computation, if necessary by drawing upon the Board's personal estimates of the minimum of such expenses. The amount may be trivial and unsatisfactory, but there was basis for some allowance, and it was wrong to refuse any, even though it were the traveling expenses of a single trip."

This has come to be known as "the *Cohan* rule," since overruled in the context of entertainment and travel expenses by enactment of the substantiation requirements of Code Section 274(d).

PROBLEMS FOR DISCUSSION

13–1. The IRS failed to treat any part of the amounts transferred to Pascarelli as rent, even though DeAngelis lived in the basement apartment for all five years at issue. Should it have done so?

13–2. Is application of the *Cohan* rule to the financial affairs of entangled relationships appropriate? The *Pascarelli* Court states: "the inexactitude and imprecision revealed by the record have been weighed against the petitioner, as they are of her own making." Should Pascarelli have kept records "of how much money Mr. DeAngelis gave her, of how much she spent on his behalf, of how much she returned to him, of how much he gave her to run the household, of whom she entertained, of how much such entertainment cost, of the extent to which her house was used for Mr. DeAngelis' business purposes, of how many miles she drove her automobiles, of how many miles were put on such automobiles for Mr. DeAngelis' purposes, or of what gifts she purchased for Mr. DeAngelis' business associates and how much such gifts cost," as the Court seems to suggest?

SECTION 2: TAXATION OF SUPPORT IN THE ABSENCE OF "MARRIAGE"

In the absence of special rules triggered by marriage, the U.S. tax system uses four often mutually inconsistent frames to address entanglement problems raised by inter-partner support. First, as illustrated by *Pascarelli v. Commissioner*, above, and *U.S. v. Harris*, below, voluntary transfers between unmarried partners in long-term intimate relationships, not made on a per-service basis, seem to be treated as gifts, and are therefore excludible for income tax purposes but reportable for gift tax purposes. The same is true of transfers made in anticipation of marriage or pursuant to antenuptial agreements. *See, e.g.*, *Merrill v. Fahs*, 324 U.S. 308 (1945) ("where, pursuant to an antenuptial agreement, taxpayer made transfer in trust for his intended wife in exchange for her release of any right she might acquire as wife or widow in his property, the transfer was not for 'adequate and full consideration in money or money's worth' and was therefore taxable as a 'gift' ").

By contrast, if state law treats such transfers as enforceably compensatory because given for "adequate and full consideration in money or money's worth," they are treated as compensatory for federal tax purposes as well. *Green v. Commissioner*, below, illustrates use of this frame. *Compare Estate of Shapiro v. United States*, 634 F.3d 1055 (9th Cir. 2011) (homemaking services may constitute consideration for claim against estate under Code Section 2053(a)(3)).

Third, state law support obligations are treated like debts. Payment of a debt generally does not result in income to the recipient, a deduction to the payor, or a gift from one to the other. Importantly, *creation* of a support obligation is not itself treated as a transfer. Thus, if A enters into a relationship with B (*e.g.*, parent-child, husband-wife) resulting in a state law obligation that A support B, creation of that obligation is not itself a taxable event—neither a gift nor compensation. When A discharges the obligation by transferring value to B, the transfer is not income to B, not deductible to A, and not reportable as a gift. Conversely, if A's obligation is discharged without payment by A, A has income. *Douglas v. Willcutts*, below, illustrates how, prior to the enactment of Code Section 71, this frame was used to structure the taxation of alimony—not deductible to payor or includible in the income of the recipient. *See* Note, *Federal Tax Aspects Of The Obligation To Support*, 74 HARV. L. REV. 1191 (1961).

As a result, in states that impose statutory support obligations on committed, long-term relationships other than heterosexual marriage, amounts paid by one partner to support the other should be treated as paid in discharge of that obligation, resulting in neither income nor gift. If Pascarelli and DeAngelis had entered into a civil union, for example, state law would likely have imposed support obligations on DeAngelis. His transfers to Pascarelli would then have been made in discharge of those obligations and would not have constituted taxable gifts, regardless of whether they were treated as married for federal tax purposes.

Fourth, Chief Counsel Advice 201021050, below, states that the IRS will respect state community property rules for federal tax purposes if states respect such rules for their own income tax purposes, even when applied to couples not treated as married under federal law. Thus, for example, in California and Washington registered domestic partners and in California married same-sex couples, although not "married" for federal tax purposes, are treated as if each receives 50 percent of the earnings of the working partner; 50 percent of the couple's earnings are then reported on each partner's individual federal income tax return. As a practical matter, this means that partners in committed, long-term relationships subject to state community property rules may not be subject to federal income or gift taxation by reason of the fact that one supports the other. Since B is treated as receiving 50 percent of all amounts that A earns (*e.g.*, B is taxed on that 50 percent and A is not), the fact that A effectively supports B will normally not result in any taxable transfer from A to B.

In sum, how partners in committed, long-term, intimate relationships not treated as married for federal tax purposes will be taxed depends to a significant extent on state law. Partners subject to statutory support obligations will generally be treated as discharging those obligations. Partners subject to community property rules will each be treated as earning 50 percent of the earnings of the couple; expenditures out of each partner's half will not be treated as transfers at all. Unmarried individuals whose partners voluntarily comply with explicit or implicit contractual or other private law obligations will apparently be treated as in receipt of gifts. If they are forced to sue, however, their recoveries will be treated as compensation. And purely voluntary transfers will be treated as gifts.

As a result, the federal tax obligations of partners in committed, long-term, intimate relationships not treated as married vary from state to state. And this, in turn, means that couples in such relationships who move may find that their federal tax treatment changes dramatically as well. Same-sex partners originally married in California (a community property state) who move to Connecticut (a common law property state that recognizes same-sex marriage) and then to Virginia (a state that is constitutionally barred from recognizing formalized same-sex relationships or any incidents thereto) therefore face an extraordinary compliance problem when it comes time to file their state and federal income tax returns.

UNITED STATES v. HARRIS
942 F.2d 1125 (7th Cir. 1991)

David Kritzik, now deceased, was a wealthy widower partial to the company of young women. Two of these women were Leigh Ann Conley and Lynnette Harris, twin sisters. Directly or indirectly, Kritzik gave Conley and Harris each more than half a million dollars over the course of several years. For our purposes, either Kritzik had to pay gift tax on this money or Harris and Conley had to pay income tax. The United States alleges that, beyond reasonable doubt, the obligation was Harris and Conley's. In separate criminal trials, Harris and Conley were convicted of willfully evading their income tax obligations regarding the money, and they now appeal.

Under *Commissioner v. Duberstein*, 363 U.S. 278 (1960), the donor's intent is the "critical consideration" in distinguishing between gifts and income. We reverse Conley's conviction and remand with instructions to dismiss the indictment against her because the government failed to present sufficient evidence of Kritzik's intent regarding the money he gave her. We also reverse Harris' conviction. The district court excluded as hearsay letters in which Kritzik wrote that he loved Harris and enjoyed giving things to her. These letters were central to Harris' defense that she believed in good faith that the money she received was a nontaxable gift, and they were not hearsay for this purpose.

We do not remand Harris' case for retrial, however, because Harris had no fair warning that her conduct might subject her to criminal tax liability. Neither the tax code, the Treasury Regulations, or Supreme Court or appellate cases provide a clear answer to whether Harris owed any taxes or not. The closest authority lies in a series of Tax Court decisions—but these cases favor Harris' position that the money she received was not income to her. Under this state of the law, Harris could not have formed a "willful" intent to violate the statutes at issue. For this reason, we remand with instructions that the indictment against Harris be dismissed. The same conclusion applies to Conley, and provides an alternative basis for reversing her conviction and remanding with instructions to dismiss the indictment.

Current law on the tax treatment of payments to mistresses provided Harris no fair warning that her conduct was criminal. Indeed, current authorities favor Harris' position that the money she received from Kritzik was a gift. We emphasize that we do not necessarily agree with these authorities, and that the government is free to urge departure from them in a noncriminal context. But new points of tax law may not be the basis of criminal convictions. The same reasoning applies to Conley and provides an alternative basis for dismissal of the indictment against her.

The definitive statement of the distinction between gifts and income is in the Supreme Court's *Duberstein* decision, which applies and interprets the definition of income contained in 26 U.S.C. §§ 61. But as the Supreme Court described, the *Duberstein* principles are "necessarily general." It stated, "One struggles in vain for any verbal formula that will supply a ready touchstone. The standard set up ... is not a rule of law; it is rather a way of life. Life in all its fullness must supply the answer to the riddle."

We do not doubt that *Duberstein*'s principles, though general, provide a clear answer to many cases involving the gift versus income distinction and can be the basis for civil as well as criminal prosecutions in such cases. We are equally certain, however, that *Duberstein* provides no ready answer to the taxability of transfers of money to a mistress in the context of a long term relationship. The motivations of the parties in such cases will always be mixed. The relationship would not be long term were it not for some respect or affection. Yet, it may be equally clear that the relationship would not continue were it not for financial support or payments.

Usually, a tax decision by the Supreme Court does not stand by itself. Treasury Regulations add specifics to broad principles, and federal cases apply the broad principles and prevailing regulations to the facts of particular cases. But these usual sources of authority are silent when it comes to the tax treatment of money transferred in the course of long term, personal relationships. No regulations cover the subject, and we have found no appellate or district court cases on the issue.

The most pertinent authority lies in several civil cases from the Tax Court, but these cases favor Harris' position. At its strongest, the government's case against Harris follows the assertions that Harris made, but now repudiates, in a lawsuit she filed against Kritzik's estate. According to her sworn pleadings in that suit, "all sums of money paid by David Kritzik to Lynette Harris ... were made ... in pursuance with the parties' express oral agreement." As Harris' former lawyer testified at her trial, the point of this pleading was to make out a "palimony" claim under the California Supreme Court's decision in *Marvin v. Marvin*, 18 Cal.3d 660, 134 Cal. Rptr. 815, 557 P.2d 106 (1976). Yet, the Tax Court has likened *Marvin*-type claims to amounts paid under antenuptial agreements. Under this analysis, these claims are not taxable income to the recipient:

"In an antenuptial agreement the parties agree, through private contract, on an arrangement for the disposition of their property in the event of death or separation. Occasionally, however, the relinquishment of marital rights is not involved. These contracts are generally enforceable under state contract law. Nonetheless, transfers pursuant to an antenuptial agreement are generally treated as gifts between the parties, because under the gift tax law the exchanged promises are not supported by full and adequate consideration, in money or money's worth."

We do not decide whether *Marvin*-type awards or settlements are or are not taxable to the recipient. The only point is that the Tax Court has suggested they are not. Until contrary authority emerges, no taxpayer could form a willful, criminal intent to violate the tax laws by failing to report *Marvin*-type payments. Reasonable inquiry does not yield a clear answer to the taxability of such payments.

Other cases only reinforce this conclusion. *Reis v. Commissioner*, T.C. Memo 1974–287, is a colorful example. The case concerned the tax liability of Lillian Reis, who had her start as a 16 year old nightclub dancer. At 21, she met Clyde "Bing" Miller when he treated the performers in the nightclub show to a steak and champagne dinner. As the Tax Court described it, Bing passed out $50 bills to each person at the table, on the condition that they leave, until he was alone with Reis. Bing then offered to write a check to Reis for any amount she asked. She asked for $1,200 for a mink stole and for another check in the same amount so her sister could have a coat too.

The next day the checks proved good; Bing returned to the club with more gifts; and "a lasting friendship developed" between Reis and Bing. For the next five years, she saw Bing "every Tuesday night at the [nightclub] and Wednesday afternoons from approximately 1:00 p.m. to 3:00 p.m. ... at various places including ... a girl friend's apartment and hotels where [Bing] was staying." He paid all of her living expenses, plus $200 a week, and provided money for her to invest, decorate her apartment, buy a car, and so on. The total over the five years was more than $100,000. The Tax Court held that this money was a gift, not income, despite Reis' statement that she "earned every penny" of the money. Similarly, in *Libby v. Commissioner*, T.C. Memo 1969–184, the Tax Court accorded gift treatment to thousands of dollars in cash and property that a young mistress received from her older paramour. And in *Starks v. Commissioner*, T.C. Memo 1966–134, the Tax Court did the same for another young woman who received cash and other property from an older, married man as part of "a very personal relationship."

The Tax Court did find that payments were income to the women who received them in *Blevins v. Commissioner*, T.C. Memo 1955–211, and in *Jones v. Commissioner*, T.C. Memo 1977–329. But in *Blevins*, the taxpayer was a woman who practiced prostitution and "used her home to operate a house of prostitution" in which six other women worked. Nothing suggested that the money at issue in that case was anything other than payments in the normal course of her business. Similarly in *Jones*, a woman had frequent hotel meetings with a married man, and on "each occasion" he gave her cash. Here too, the Tax Court found that the relationship was one of prostitution, a point that was supported by the woman's similar relationships with other men.

If these cases make a rule of law, it is that a person is entitled to treat cash and property received from a lover as gifts, as long as the relationship consists of something more than specific payments for specific sessions of sex.

Besides Harris' prior suit, the United States also presented evidence regarding the overall relationship between Harris and Kritzik. Testimony showed that Harris described her relationship with Kritzik as "a job" and "just making a living." She reportedly complained that she "was laying on her back and her sister was getting all the money," described how she disliked when Kritzik fondled her naked, and made other derogatory statements about sex with Kritzik.

This evidence tells us only what Harris thought of the relationship. Again, the Supreme Court in *Duberstein* held that the donor's intent is the "critical consideration" in determining whether a transfer of money is a gift or income. If Kritzik viewed the money he gave Harris as a gift, or if the dearth of contrary evidence leaves doubt on the subject, does it matter how mercenary Harris' motives were? *Duberstein* suggests that Harris' motives may not matter, but the ultimate answer makes no difference here. As long as the answer is at least a close call, and we are confident that it is, the prevailing law is too uncertain to support Harris' criminal conviction.

In short, criminal prosecutions are no place for the government to try out "pioneering interpretations of tax law." The United States has not shown us, and we have not found, a single case finding tax liability for payments that a mistress received from her lover, absent proof of specific payments for specific sex acts. Even when such specific proof is present, the cases have not applied penalties for civil fraud, much less criminal sanctions. The broad principles contained in *Duberstein* do not fill this gap. Before she met Kritzik, Harris starred as a sorceress in an action/adventure film. She would have had to be a real life sorceress to predict her tax obligations under the current state of the law.

GREEN v. COMMISSIONER

T.C. Memo. 1987–503

Petitioner first met the decedent on November 18, 1962, in Boston, Massachusetts. Within a few weeks petitioner had fallen in love with him. The decedent returned her affection and by late December the couple were engaged to be married. Ten months later the decedent begged to be released from the engagement, explaining that he had "a mental problem about marriage." He suggested to petitioner that they forego the legal ceremony, and that she "stay with him without marriage." In return, he promised that he would leave her "everything" when he died. Petitioner reluctantly agreed.

Petitioner characterized her relationship with the decedent as that of "an old-fashioned traditional wife." Although they always maintained separate apartments, she made his life as comfortable as possible; she watched his diet and his health, cared for him when he was ill, kept track of his appointments and concerned herself with his personal needs. She also accompanied the decedent frequently on business related trips and attended meetings and social engagements with him. They were essentially inseparable for the nine years of their relationship and traveled together in the United States and abroad. The couple celebrated the anniversary of their first date every November.

Petitioner, who was employed as a stockbroker, advised the decedent on his business affairs and kept him informed about the value and activity of his investments. Decedent owned and operated a radio station in Boston. Petitioner reported on the stock market activities at his radio station every afternoon. She went to the radio station to wait for him every evening and helped with various tasks.

Although petitioner never saw the decedent's will, he promised her that he had provided for her. After he died, no will could be found. Several months later the decedent's brother, Richard Richmond, discovered a will which left the entire estate, valued at around $7,000,000 to Richard and Dorothy, the decedent's sister.

Petitioner sued the estate for the value of services rendered to the decedent in reliance upon his promise to leave her the entire estate. The jury found for petitioner under the theory of quantum meruit and awarded her $1,350,000. The Supreme Judicial Court of Massachusetts upheld the decision, remanding on the sole issue of the measure of damages. Following that decision, petitioner and the decedent's executor settled the claim for $900,000 payable over two years: $139,311.61 was paid in 1977, and $760,688.39 was paid in 1978.

Petitioner did not include these amounts in income on the returns she filed in 1977 and 1978. The failure to include these sums in income for taxable years 1977 and 1978 is the basis for respondent's determination of a deficiency.

Respondent maintains that the proceeds were neither a gift, bequest nor devise, but were compensation for services rendered by petitioner to the decedent between the years 1962 and 1971. Petitioner claims, on the other hand, that the services she performed were merely "wifely services" and not compensable services within the meaning of section 61. She contends that the payment was a gift or bequest from the decedent and exempt from taxation under section 102. She further maintains that the fact that she had to press her claim through litigation does not alter its essential character as a gratuitous transfer.

We are not required to investigate the relationship between petitioner and the decedent to resolve this question. We have long recognized the rule that "The taxability of the proceeds of a lawsuit, or of a sum received in settlement thereof, depends upon the nature of the claim and the actual basis of recovery." The nature of litigation recovery is determined by reference to the origin and character of the claim which gave rise to the litigation.

The proper inquiry is into the nature of the loss in lieu of which the damages were awarded. If the award of damages was a substitute for income then the damages themselves are income.

In the instant case, petitioner herself characterized the nature of the claim when she sued the estate as a creditor, claiming compensation for past services rendered. She established that the decedent had promised to provide for her through his will. She introduced evidence of the services she had performed. She proved that although she had performed what she promised, the decedent had reneged on his promises. The jury was fully instructed on the elements of recovery under the theory of quantum meruit and held for petitioner under that theory. Because the underlying claim was a suit for earned, but unpaid compensation, that claim dictates the tax treatment for the income received. We therefore conclude that the settlement payment received in lieu of the damages is taxable income to her for the settlement award can go no further than the underlying claim to which it relates.

Petitioner has urged upon us several alternative analytical approaches which allegedly would allow these settlement payments to be excluded from income. After reviewing these arguments, we find that neither has merit.

We first address petitioner's claim that the settlement payments should be excluded from income under section 102. In support of her position, petitioner relies on *Pascarelli v. Commissioner*, 55 T.C. 1082 (1971), a case wherein we held that payments in exchange for "wifely services" are not compensation within the meaning of section 61 even when the provider is not legally a wife. In the *Pascarelli* case, the taxpayer had lived as though she were a wife with the transferor who supported her.

The *Pascarelli* case is factually distinguishable from the instant case because in *Pascarelli* we concluded that the lifetime transfers made to the taxpayer were gifts, specifically transfers that "were motivated by sentiments of affection, respect, and admiration," and that conclusion was supported by the testimony of the transferor. In the case herein, however, we have determined, based on petitioner's lawsuit, that she had a compensatory arrangement with the decedent. Thus, the amounts petitioner received from the estate cannot be characterized as gratuitous transfers.

We are further asked to consider the arrangement between petitioner and the decedent as an antenuptial agreement. In an antenuptial agreement the parties agree, through private contract, on an arrangement for the disposition of their property in the event of death or separation. Frequently, in exchange for the promises of property, one party agrees to relinquish his or her marital rights in other property. Occasionally, however, the relinquishment of marital rights is not involved. These contracts are generally enforceable under state contract law. *See Marvin v. Marvin*, 18 Cal.3d 660, 557 P.2d 106 (1976). Nonetheless, transfers pursuant to an antenuptial agreement are generally treated as gifts between the parties, because under the gift tax law the exchanged promises are not supported by full and adequate consideration, in money or money's worth. *Commissioner v. Wemyss*, 324 U.S. 303 (1945); *Merrill v. Fahs*, 324 U.S. 308 (1945).

Despite initial appeal, we find that this analogy is inapposite. While an exchange of promises was involved in the agreement between petitioner and decedent, there was no contract. In the Massachusetts litigation petitioner was awarded damages under a theory of quantum meruit. The jury was fully instructed on a contract theory of recovery but rejected it. Without a contract there can be no antenuptial agreement. A mere exchange of promises falls short of being an antenuptial agreement. Moreover, it is consistent with petitioner's theory in her litigation with decedent's estate that such exchange of promises be viewed as an arrangement for services to be rendered.

Accordingly, after a careful analysis of all the facts and circumstances we hold that the payments petitioner received in settlement of her claim against the estate of Maxwell E. Richmond constitute taxable income to her in the amounts of $139,311.61 and $760,688.39 during the years 1977 and 1978, respectively. The parties have stipulated that if the payments are deemed to be taxable income, the legal expenses incurred by petitioner are deductible under section 212. Furthermore, the parties agreed that those expenses equalled $52,172.19 in 1977 and $253,562.74 in 1978.

DOUGLAS v. WILLCUTS
296 U.S. 1 (1935)

On September 12, 1923, petitioner, Edward B. Douglas, entered into an agreement with his wife and the Minneapolis Trust Company, by which he transferred securities in trust for his wife's benefit. Out of the income of the trust estate the trustee was to pay Mrs. Douglas annually the sum of $15,000, up to November 6, 1927, and thereafter $21,000. Deficiencies were to be made up in a prescribed manner. Excess income was to be paid to petitioner. On the death of his wife, he was to receive the property free of the trust. Petitioner reserved the right to designate securities for investment, subject, however, to the approval of the trustee acting in that respect on behalf of Mrs. Douglas.

The parties stipulated that the provisions for Mrs. Douglas were "in lieu of, and in full settlement of alimony, and of any and all dower rights or statutory interests in the estate" of her husband, and "in lieu of any and all claims for separate maintenance and allowance for her support."

Three days later, Mrs. Douglas obtained a decree of absolute divorce in a district court of the state of Minnesota. The decree provided: "It is further adjudged and decreed that the defendant provide and create the trust fund as set out in that certain agreement between said parties and the Minneapolis Trust Company as trustee now on file with said trustee, and that the plaintiff have the provision therein made in lieu of all other alimony or interest in the property or estate of the defendant and that neither party have any costs or disbursements herein."

The question in this case relates to the net income of the trust which was distributed to Mrs. Douglas in the years 1927 and 1928. The Commissioner of Internal Revenue determined that these amounts were income to the petitioner. Taxes assessed accordingly were paid by petitioner under protest, claim for refund was disallowed, and this suit was brought to recover the amount paid.

Petitioner contends that the agreement created an irrevocable trust; that under the Revenue Acts petitioner and Mrs. Douglas were separate taxpayers; and that, having accepted the benefits of the trust, she was taxable upon the income she received as beneficiary. The Circuit Court of Appeals decided that the income was taxable to the petitioner, since it went to the discharge of his legal obligation; that is, the income was devoted to payments which petitioner was bound to make under the decree of the Minnesota court.

Amounts paid to a divorced wife under a decree for alimony are not regarded as income of the wife but as paid in discharge of the general obligation to support, which is made specific by the decree. Petitioner's contention that the district court did not award alimony is not supported by the terms of the decree. It described the provision as made "in lieu of all other alimony or interest in the property or estate of the defendant." However designated, it was a provision for annual payments to serve the purpose of alimony, that is, to assure to the wife suitable support. The fact that the provision was to be in lieu of any other interest in the husband's property did not affect the essential quality of these payments. Upon the pre-existing duty of the husband the decree placed a particular and adequate sanction, and imposed upon petitioner the obligation to devote the income in question, through the medium of the trust, to the use of his divorced wife.

We have held that income was received by a taxpayer, when, pursuant to a contract, a debt or other obligation was discharged by another for his benefit. The transaction was regarded as being the same in substance as if the money had been paid to the taxpayer and he had transmitted it to his creditor. The creation of a trust by the taxpayer as the channel for the application of the income to the discharge of his obligation leaves the nature of the transaction unaltered. In the present case, the net income of the trust fund, which was paid to the wife under the decree, stands substantially on the same footing as though he had received the income personally and had been required by the decree to make the payment directly.

CHIEF COUNSEL ADVICE 201021050

On February 24, 2006, the Office of Associate Chief Counsel (Income Tax & Accounting) issued Chief Counsel Advice 200608038 concluding that an individual who is a registered domestic partner in California must report all of his or her income earned from the performance of personal services. In light of a change to California law, effective in 2007, you asked us whether California registered domestic partners should each report half of the community income on their federal returns. You also asked whether individuals who filed returns in accordance with CCA 200608038 must amend those returns.

In 2005, California law significantly expanded the rights and obligations of persons entering into a California domestic partnership for state property law purposes, but not for state income tax purposes. Specifically, the California Domestic Partner Rights and Responsibilities Act of 2003 (the California Act), effective on January 1, 2005, provided that "Registered domestic partners shall have the same rights, protections, and benefits, and shall be subject to the same responsibilities, obligations, and duties under law ... as are granted to and imposed upon spouses." However, the California Act provided that "earned income may not be treated as community property for state income tax purposes."

On September 29, 2006, California enacted Senate Bill 1827. Senate Bill 1827 repealed the language of the California Act providing that earned income was not to be treated as community property for state income tax purposes. Thus, effective January 1, 2007, the earned income of a registered domestic partner must be treated as community property for state income tax purposes (unless the RDPs execute an agreement opting out of community property treatment). As a result of the legislation, California, as of January 1, 2007, treats the earned income of registered domestic partners as community property for both property law purposes and state income tax purposes.

Federal tax law generally respects state property law characterizations and definitions. In *Poe v. Seaborn*, 282 U.S. 101 (1930), the Supreme Court held that for federal income tax purposes a wife owned an undivided one-half interest in the income earned by her husband in Washington, a community property state, and was liable for federal income tax on that one-half interest. Accordingly, the Court concluded that husband and wife must each report one-half of the community income on his or her separate return regardless of which spouse earned the income.

California community property law developed in the context of marriage and originally applied only to the property rights and obligations of spouses. The law operated to give each spouse an equal interest in each community asset, regardless of which spouse is the holder of record.

By 2007, California had extended full community property treatment* to registered domestic partners. Applying the principle that federal law respects state law property characterizations, the federal tax treatment of community property should apply to California registered domestic partners. Consequently, for tax years beginning after December 31, 2006, a California registered domestic partner must report one-half of the community income, whether received in the form of compensation for personal services or income from property, on his or her federal income tax return.

You also asked how to treat a registered domestic partner who reported all of his or her earned income in accordance with CCA 200608038. For tax years beginning before June 1, 2010, registered domestic partners may, but are not required to, amend their returns to report income in accordance with this CCA.

Notes

1. *Community property law.*—A number of western and midwestern states currently use community property rules for married couples. Under a community property system, a couple's property is categorized either as community or separate property. Property acquired during the marriage (other than by gift or inheritance) is generally treated as community property; property is presumed to be community property unless a party can prove it is separate.

Community property is treated as owned 50–50 by the two spouses. Under *Poe v. Seaborn*, 282 U.S. 101 (1930), this means that each spouse will be treated as receiving 50 percent of the couple's income. In addition, on divorce or death each spouse will be treated as having owned 50 percent of the couple's community assets. As a result, on death, only the decedent's 50 percent is included in his or her taxable estate. Currently, California and Washington apply community property rules to same-sex registered domestic partners. California also applies them to same-sex married couples and to opposite-sex registered domestic partners. (In California, opposite-sex couples in which one partner is 62 years of age or older may register as domestic partners, instead of getting married.) By CCA 201012050, the IRS has indicated that it will apply *Poe v. Seaborn* to all couples subject to state law community property regimes, regardless of whether they are "married" for federal tax purposes.

2. *Choice of law: common law property vs. community property.*—Unfortunately, lawyers and clients in common law property states cannot safely ignore community property issues. If a couple is married in New York (a common law property state), is domiciled in New York throughout the

---

* Prior to January 1, 2007, the earned income of a registered domestic partner was treated as community property for state property law purposes but not for state income tax purposes.

marriage, dies or is divorced in New York, and only owns New York property during the marriage, New York law clearly governs who owns what. Similarly, if a couple is married in California (a community property state), is domiciled in California throughout the marriage, dies or is divorced in California, and only owns California property during the marriage, California law governs.

But what if a New York couple owns property in California, or vice versa? What if the couple moves from New York to California? Or from California to New York? Or from California to New York to Texas, which has community property rules somewhat different from California's and does not recognize same-sex relationships? Which state's law determines ownership?

Unfortunately, choice of law rules in this area are murky and inconsistent. It is clear that the court in which any issue is litigated will apply its own state's choice of law rules. Beyond this, the law becomes less clear. Among choice of law rules applied by states in this area are the following: (1) law of the forum governs, (2) law of the domicile of the couple when they married governs, (3) law of the domicile of the couple when the property was acquired governs, (4) law of the state where the property is located governs, (5) law of the state where the couple was domiciled when they divorced governs, and (6) law of the state where decedent was domiciled when he died governs. The two most common are (3) and (4)—domicile when the property was acquired and situs of the property. *See generally* W.S. MCCLANAHAN, COMMUNITY PROPERTY LAW IN THE UNITED STATES, ch. 13 (1982).

In general, a change in domicile does not change the character of property previously acquired by a married couple. Thus, property acquired as community property will generally remain community property when the couple later moves to a common law property state, and vice versa. Some community property states (Arizona, California, and Texas in divorce actions; California, Idaho, and Wisconsin in probate administrations) use "quasi-community property" rules to deal with problems of in-migration—couples moving from common law property states to community property states. How quasi-community property should be treated under *Poe v. Seaborn* is unclear. Because state choice of law rules in this area are inconsistent, it is even possible that a particular piece of property will be both community property and not, depending on which state's laws are deemed controlling for federal tax purposes.

3. *Scope of* Green.—The Tax Court's opinion in *Green* suggests that if the taxpayer had recovered on her contract claim rather than in *quantum meruit*, her recovery might have been treated as a gift, rather than as compensation. This seems odd. A contract to perform services in exchange for financial support would normally generate compensation income. In the leading state court case permitting "palimony" recoveries, *Marvin v. Marvin*, 557 P.2d 106 (1976), the California Supreme Court declined to draw sharp distinctions among possible theories of recovery:

> "The courts should enforce express contracts between nonmarital partners except to the extent that the contract is explicitly founded on the consideration of meretricious sexual services. In the absence of an express contract, the courts should inquire into the conduct of the parties to determine whether that conduct demonstrates an implied contract, agree-

ment of partnership or joint venture, or some other tacit understanding between the parties. The courts may also employ the doctrine of quantum meruit, or equitable remedies such as constructive or resulting trusts, when warranted by the facts of the case."

But if amounts would be compensation for tax purposes if paid pursuant to court order, they should also be compensation for tax purposes if paid voluntarily pursuant to an explicit or implicit contract or because such amounts have been earned. If so, it is hard to reconcile *Green* and *Estate of Shapiro* with *Pascarelli* and *Harris*.

PROBLEMS FOR DISCUSSION

13–3. Leslie and Dana are involved in a committed, long-term intimate relationship that is not treated as "marriage" for federal tax purposes. They have two children. Leslie, a lawyer, earns $200,000 per year and supports the family financially. Dana cares for the children and maintains the household.

a. Dana receives Leslie's financial support in exchange for providing child-care and household services. How will Dana be taxed on this exchange?

b. Assume that Leslie and Dana are registered domestic partners in a state that imposes mandatory community property rules on registered domestic partners. Does your answer change?

13–4. The relationship between Leslie and Dana is dissolved.

a. Assume that they had been married as a matter of state law, but not for federal tax purposes. The state divorce court awards Dana custody of the children, alimony in the amount of $75,000 per year, and child support in the amount of $50,000 per year. How will these payments be treated for federal income tax purposes?

b. Would your answer change if Leslie and Dana are not married as a matter of state law, but the state in which they live recognizes "palimony" and awards Dana custody of the children, alimony in the amount of $75,000 per year, and child support in the amount of $50,000 per year? Does it matter whether the palimony award sounds in contract or quantum meruit?

SECTION 3: TAXATION OF PROPERTY DIVISIONS IN THE ABSENCE OF "MARRIAGE"

Prior to 1984, the federal income tax treatment of a division of property incident to divorce depended on two things: (1) how the couple formally held the property prior to divorce and (2) the rights state law recognized in each spouse to property formally titled in the other.

Where one party to the divorce, typically the wife, accepted specific property in exchange for any marital rights to the husband's property, the transaction was treated as a taxable exchange to the party giving up the property, typically the husband. *United States v. Davis*, 370 U.S. 65 (1962). Thus, in *Davis*, transferor husband was required to recognize gain on property transferred to his ex-wife in settlement of her spousal share claims. A corollary of taxable exchange treatment was that the ex-wife then took the transferred property with fair market value basis. *Farid-Es-Sultaneh v. Commissioner*, 160 F.2d 812 (2d Cir. 1947). A further corollary should have followed as well—that the ex-wife recognized gain on release of her statutory rights, in which she presumably had a basis of zero. But no ex-wives reported such gain and the IRS did not challenge their failure to do so. The *Davis* Court noted: "Under the present administrative practice, the release of marital rights in exchange for property or other consideration is not considered a taxable event as to the wife." The IRS later confirmed this practice in Rev. Rul. 67–221, 1967–2 C.B. 63:

> "Under the terms of a divorce decree and in accordance with a property settlement agreement, which was incorporated in the divorce decree, the husband transferred his interest in an apartment building to his former wife in consideration for and in discharge of her dower rights. The marital rights the former wife relinquished are equal in value to the value of the property she agreed to accept in exchange for those rights. Held, there is no gain or loss to the wife on the transfer and the basis of the property to the wife is its fair market value on the date of the transfer."

In a separate line of cases, however, courts and the IRS held that if a divorce settlement merely divided jointly owned property, the division was nontaxable to both parties, the recipient taking the divided property with carryover basis. After *Davis*, therefore, taxpayers began to assert that state law effectively recognized ownership interests in both parties, even if in form the rights appeared to be merely statutory. *See, e.g., Collins v. Commissioner*, 412 F.2d 211 (10th Cir. 1969), *on remand from* 393 U.S. 215 (1968) (ordering court of appeals to consider effect of state court decision on application of *Davis*); *Pulliam v. Commissioner*, 329 F.2d 97 (10th Cir.), *cert. denied*, 379 U.S. 836 (1964). The effect was to make the property division nontaxable to both parties.

This, in turn, allowed divorcing taxpayers to take conflicting positions, whipsawing the IRS in the process. The ex-husband would contend that the division was not taxable under *Collins* and *Pulliam*; the ex-wife, seeking higher basis, would contend that it was. *Compare Cook v. Commissioner*, 80 T.C. 512 (1983), *aff'd mem.*, 742 F.2d 1431 (2d Cir. 1984) (nontaxable division; no gain to husband), *with Cook v. United States*, 904 F.2d 107 (1st Cir. 1990) (taxable division; wife therefore took property with fair market value basis; wife not bound by prior case because she was not party to it). This possibility of inconsistent positions ultimately led Congress to enact Code Section 1041, discussed in Subchapter B, below.

REV. RUL. 74-347
1974-2 C.B. 26

The award of more than one-half of the jointly-owned property to the wife in a division of property, pursuant to a divorce decree in a noncommunity property State in which the wife's interest in the husband's separately-owned property is not the equivalent of coownership, constitutes a taxable exchange of a portion of the husband's jointly-owned property for the wife's marital rights in his separate property. The husband realizes gain to the extent the fair market value of the jointly-owned property transferred in exchange for the wife's marital rights exceeds the adjusted basis of such property.

A husband and wife were married in 1953 when each had approximately $600 in assets. Neither received an inheritance or gift of any significance during the marriage. Both husband and wife were employed throughout the marriage and their earnings were commingled so that it was impossible to determine whose earnings were used to purchase any given asset.

In 1973, the wife was granted a divorce. The total assets owned by the husband and wife had a net fair market value of $110,000 at the time of the divorce. The jointly-owned property, that is, the property either purchased with the earnings of both the husband and the wife or received by means of a completed gift, consisted of several assets having a combined net fair market value of $70,000. The husband's separately-owned property had a net fair market value of $40,000. The wife owned no property in her own capacity.

The divorce decree awarded the wife jointly-owned property with a net fair market value of $55,000. The husband was awarded the remaining jointly-owned property with a net fair market value of $15,000 and all of his separately-owned property with a net fair market value of $40,000. The adjusted basis of all jointly-owned property received by the wife as $29,500, but $4,000 of such adjusted basis was attributable to personal furniture with a net fair market value of $2,000.

The married couple did not reside in a community property State at the time of the divorce. Under the applicable State law, the wife's interest in her husband's separately-owned property was not the equivalent of coownership since her only rights in her husband's separately-owned property were either inchoate or entitled her to an equitable distribution of property upon divorce.

The specific questions to be considered are (1) whether, under the divorce decree, the unequal division of the jointly-owned property which awarded the wife an excess of such property constitutes a taxable transfer by the husband in satisfaction of the wife's marital rights, and (2) if so, the amount of gain realized by the husband on the transfer.

In *United States v. Davis*, 370 U.S. 65 (1962), the Supreme Court held that there is a taxable event when a husband transfers his property to his wife pursuant to a property settlement incorporated in a divorce decree in exchange for the release of her marital rights. The Court pointed out that the inchoate rights granted a wife in her husband's property by the Delaware law (a common law State) do not even remotely reach the dignity of coownership.

Property may be coowned where (1) title to it is taken jointly under State property law, (2) the State is a community property law State, or (3) State property law is found to be similar to community property law. *See Collins v. Commissioner*, 412 F.2d 211 (10th Cir. 1969), *on remand from* 393 U.S. 215 (1968).

Under the facts stated herein, only the jointly-owned property of the husband and wife is within the scope of the term "coownership."

Accordingly, it is held that since the wife's interest in her husband's separately-owned property was not the equivalent of coownership, the unequal division of jointly-owned property awarded the wife constitutes a taxable exchange of a portion of the husband's jointly-owned property for the wife's marital rights in the husband's separately-owned property.

The net fair market value of the jointly-owned property awarded the wife which was in excess of her one-half half share of such property is determined as follows:

Jointly-owned property received	$55,000
One-half of jointly-owned property	$35,000
Excess received	$20,000

The husband's adjusted basis in the excess jointly-owned property received by the wife is determined by application of the following formula:

> Adjusted basis of excess jointly-owned property received by the wife = Net fair market value of excess jointly-owned property received by the wife/Net fair market value of all jointly-owned property received by the wife x Adjusted basis of all jointly-owned property received by the wife

However, the adjusted basis of all jointly-owned property received by the wife in the above formula does not include the portion of the adjusted basis of any jointly-owned asset which exceeds the net fair market value of such asset for which no loss deduction would otherwise be allowable. For purposes of this formula, therefore, the adjusted basis of all jointly-owned property received by the wife in the instant case is $27,500 ($29,500 less $2,000). Thus, the husband's adjusted basis in the excess jointly-owned property received by the wife is $10,000 ($20,000/$55,000 x $27,500).

Therefore, the husband realized gain the amount of $10,000 (the excess of the amount realized of $20,000 over the adjusted basis of $10,000) as a result of the taxable transfer of the excess jointly-owned property in exchange for the wife's marital rights.

Rev. Rule 74–347 no longer applies to divorces of heterosexual married couples. As will be discussed in Subchapter B below, Code Section 1041 now provides for nonrecognition and carryover basis to all property divisions by reason of divorce in the case of couples treated as "married" for federal tax purposes. The Ruling still applies, however, to divorces of couples not treated as "married" for federal tax purposes.

PROBLEMS FOR DISCUSSION

13–5. The relationship between Leslie and Dana is dissolved.

a. Assume that they had been married as a matter of state law, but not for federal tax purposes. In the divorce, the court orders Leslie to pay Dana $500,000 cash in full discharge of Dana's state-law claims to the couple's marital property. What federal income tax consequences? Does it matter how state law characterizes Dana's interest in property titled in Leslie?

b. Assume that they had been married as a matter of state law, but not for federal tax purposes. Prior to the divorce, Leslie owned Blackacre, an investment property, which has a fair market value of $500,000 and a basis of $200,000. In the divorce, the court awards Blackacre to Dana in full discharge of Dana's state-law statutory spousal share rights. What federal income tax consequences?

c. Assume that Leslie and Dana are registered domestic partners living in a state that imposes mandatory community property rules on registered domestic partners. Do your answers to parts (a) and (b) above change?

Subchapter B: Taxation of Marriage

Code: Sections 71, 1041, 2056, 2513, and 2523

For couples treated as married for federal tax purposes, the Code resolves most of the problems outlined in Subchapter A simply and elegantly.

First, for income tax purposes, the Code ignores informal exchanges between the two spouses, presumably for the reasons discussed in Chapter 2A, Section 2, above. Spouses may enter into formal contracts, and such contracts will generally be given effect for federal tax purposes, *see, e.g.*, Code Section 274(m)(3) (business travel expenses for taxpayer's spouse disallowed unless spouse is an employee of taxpayer), but in the absence of contractual formality, the spouses' daily interactions with each other are simply ignored.

Second, gifts to a spouse are excluded from gift taxation by Code Section 2523. Code Section 2523, in effect, solves the *Pascarelli* problem for couples treated as married for federal tax purposes. Similarly, any property that passes on death from one spouse to another is excluded from estate taxation by Code Section 2056. This reduces the need to determine who owns what at the moment a taxpayer dies, so long as he leaves everything to his spouse. Finally, gifts made by a spouse to a third party are generally treated as having been made half by each spouse, obviating both (1) any need to determine which spouse owns the property at the time of the gift, and (2) any need to first transfer half the property to taxpayer's spouse so as to get the benefit of two annual exclusions under Code Section 2503(b).

Third, Code Section 1041 provides for nonrecognition on a transfer of property from one spouse to another, even if such property is transferred explicitly in exchange for cash or other valuable consideration. The transferee spouse takes the transferred property with carryover basis. In effect, the transfer has no current tax consequences.

Fourth, on divorce, Code Section 71 provides that alimony is deductible to the payor and includible in the income of the payee. To qualify for this treatment, four requirements must be met: (1) the payment must be in cash, (2) the payment must be made pursuant to a divorce or separation instrument, (3) the two ex-spouses cannot be members of the same household at the time the payment is made, and (4) the payments must cease on the death of the payee spouse. Couples can elect out of Code Section 71 treatment (returning to the treatment of alimony under *Douglas v. Willcuts*). In addition, special rules are imposed on heavily front-loaded alimony payments—which the Code partially recharacterizes as property divisions and to that extent become neither deductible nor includible. Code Section 1041 nonrecognition treatment also applies to property transfers between former spouses if such transfers occur within one year after the marriage ends or are related to the cessation of the marriage.

NOTES

1. *"Marriage" for federal tax purposes.*—Section 3 of the Defense of Marriage Act ("DOMA"), 1 U.S.C. § 7, enacted in 1996, provides that:

> In determining the meaning of any Act of Congress, or of any ruling, regulation, or interpretation of the various administrative bureaus and agencies of the United States, the word "marriage" means only a legal union between one man and one woman as husband and wife, and the word "spouse" refers only to a person of the opposite sex who is a husband or a wife.

The IRS has construed this to mean that same-sex couples, even if legally married under the law of the jurisdiction in which they reside, are not "married" for federal tax purposes.

In *Gill v. Office of Personnel Management*, 699 F.Supp.2d 374 (D. Mass. 2010), the court held that Section 3 of DOMA violated the equal protection clause of the Fifth Amendment. The decision of the district court was affirmed sub nom. *Massachusetts v. United States Department of Health and Human Services*, 682 F.3d 1 (1st Cir. 2012), but the mandate of the court was stayed pending appeal.

Gill only addresses whether "marriage," as that term is used in the Code, must be construed to include same-sex "marriage" if authorized by state law. It does not address the status of civil unions or registered domestic partners for federal tax purposes. In *Dragovich v. United States Department of the Treasury*, 2012 WL 1909603 (N.D. Cal. 2012), however, the District Court for the Northern District of California extended the reasoning of *Gill* to registered domestic partnerships. The court held:

> "Because Congress's restriction on state-maintained long-term care plans lacks any rational relationship to a legitimate government interest, but rather appears to be motivated by antigay animus, the exclusion of registered domestic partners of public employees from § 7702B(f)'s list of individuals eligible to enroll in state-maintained long-term care plans violates the Constitution's equal protection guarantee."

Nothing in the court's reasoning limits its conclusion to Code Section 7702B(f). For same-sex couples in registered domestic partnerships or civil unions, *Dragovich*, if upheld on appeal, may mean that such relationships must be treated as the equivalent of "marriage" for other Code purposes as well.

Problems for Discussion

13–6. Leslie and Dana are married for federal tax purposes. They have two children. Leslie, a lawyer, earns $200,000 per year and supports the family financially. Dana cares for the children and maintains the household.

    a. Leslie receives Dana's child-care and household services in exchange for supporting the family. How will Leslie be taxed on this exchange?

    b. Dana receives Leslie's financial support in exchange for providing child-care and household services. How will Dana be taxed on this exchange?

13–7. The relationship between Leslie and Dana is dissolved.

    a. The state divorce court awards Dana custody of the children, alimony in the amount of $75,000 per year, and child support in the amount of $50,000 per year. How will these payments be treated for federal income tax purposes?

    b. In the divorce, the court orders Leslie to pay Dana $500,000 cash in full discharge of Dana's state-law claims to the couple's marital property. What federal income tax consequences?

    c. Prior to the divorce, Leslie owns Blackacre, an investment property, which has a fair market value of $500,000 and a basis of $200,000. In the divorce, the court awards Blackacre to Dana in full discharge of Dana's state-law claims to the couple's marital property. What federal income tax consequences?

    d. Assume that Leslie and Dana live in a community property state. Do your answers to parts (b) and (c) above change?

Chapter 14

Relative Indifference

■ ■ ■

As has been noted, spouses often do not care where a particular check is deposited, out of which account a particular bill is paid, who holds title to what, or who is legally the borrower on a particular debt, at least in the short term. We say they are "relatively indifferent" to ownership—that is, they may care more about saving taxes than about maintaining the integrity of their separate finances. But relative indifference is not limited to spouses. The finances of parents and children raise many of the same issues, as can extended family relationships (grandparents, adult siblings, and the like). Similarly, shareholders may be relatively indifferent as to whether they or their controlled corporations receive income, pay expenses, own property, or owe debt.

As a result, the Code contains hundreds of related-party anti-abuse rules. Subchapter A explores a few representative such rules. Subchapter B then returns to a relative indifference problem particularly important to committed, long-term, intimate relationships: income-splitting, the tax avoidance technique that ultimately led Congress to authorize joint return filing. Subchapter C reviews basic assignment of income principles, and Subchapter D, the effect of entanglement, relative indifference, and other factors on rules governing the basis of property acquired by gift, inheritance, or bequest.

Subchapter A: Related Party Anti–Abuse Rules

The Code includes literally hundreds of statutory related-party anti-abuse rules. This Subchapter explores three representative such rules. Note that the relationships covered by different statutory related-party anti-abuse rules vary from statute to statute. This may reflect the fact that many such rules were enacted in response to specific problems. Congress has never undertaken a comprehensive review of related-party anti-abuse issues.

SECTION 1: TRANSACTIONS BETWEEN RELATED PARTIES, IN GENERAL

Code: Section 267(a)–(d), (g)

PROBLEMS FOR DISCUSSION

14–1. Leslie and Dana are married for federal tax purposes. They have one child, Allan. Leslie also has a sister, Rachel. Leslie owns stock with a fair market value of $200,000, in which he has a basis of $1,000,000. The stock is not publicly traded. He wants to keep the stock in the family, but recognize his $800,000 of built-in loss. What are the federal income tax consequences of each of the following transactions?

   a. Leslie sells the stock to Dana for $200,000 cash.

   b. Leslie sells the stock to Allan for $200,000 cash.

   c. Leslie sells the stock to Allan's wife Sarah for $200,000 cash.

   d. Leslie sells the stock to Rachel for $200,000 cash.

14–2. Same facts as Problem 14–1, except that Leslie and Dana are married for state law purposes but not for federal tax purposes. What are the federal income tax consequences of each of the following transactions?

   a. Leslie sells the stock to Dana for $200,000 cash.

   b. Leslie sells the stock to Allan for $200,000 cash.

14–3. Leslie operates a sole proprietorship, which uses the cash method of accounting. Dana owns all of the stock of Dana Corp, which uses the accrual method of accounting. In Year 1, Dana Corp purchases services from Leslie for $1,000,000 for use in its trade or business. Leslie provides the services in Year 1, but permits Dana Corp to defer payment until some later time. In each of the following scenarios, when will Leslie report the $1,000,000 income and Dana Corp report the corresponding $1,000,000 deduction?

   a. Leslie and Dana are married for federal income tax purposes.

   b. Leslie and Dana are married for state law purposes in a common law state but are not married for federal income tax purposes.

   c. Leslie and Dana are registered domestic partners in a state that imposes mandatory community property rules on registered domestic partners.

SECTION 2: PURCHASES OF DEBT BY RELATED PARTIES

Code: Sections 108(e)(4) and 707(b)(1)

When a debt is discharged for less than the full amount owed, the debtor recognizes debt discharge income. Thus, for example, if a debt of $100,000 is discharged in exchange for a payment of $90,000, the debtor recognizes debt discharge income equal to the $10,000 difference. The same is true if the debtor purchases the debt from the creditor for an amount less than the full amount owed. *See, e.g.*, *United States v. Kirby Lumber Co.*, 284 U.S. 1 (1931). In the foregoing example, if instead of negotiating a discharge the debtor simply purchases the debt from the creditor for $90,000, the debtor recognizes the same $10,000 of debt discharge income.

But what if instead the debtor's *spouse* makes same purchase for $90,000? The debtor may be perfectly happy to have his spouse own his debt. The same may be true if his father purchases the debt, or his wholly-owned corporation. Unless the debt discharge rules treat purchases by related parties as discharges, taxpayers will often be able to circumvent the debt discharge rules.

PROBLEMS FOR DISCUSSION

14–4. Leslie and Dana are married for federal tax purposes. They have one child, Allan. Leslie also has a sister, Rachel. Leslie owes Megabank $100,000. Although he is not insolvent, he has persuaded Megabank that it is unlikely to collect more than $90,000 on the debt. Megabank has therefore agreed to sell the debt to Leslie's nominee for $90,000. What are the federal income tax consequences of each of the following transactions?

    a. Megabank sells Leslie's debt to Dana for $90,000 cash.

    b. Megabank sells Leslie's debt to Allan for $90,000 cash.

    c. Megabank sells Leslie's debt to Allan's wife Sarah for $90,000 cash.

    d. Megabank sells Leslie's debt to Rachel for $90,000 cash.

14–5. Same facts as Problem 14–4, except that Leslie and Dana are married for state law purposes but not for federal tax purposes. What are the federal income tax consequences if Megabank sells Leslie's debt to Dana for $90,000 cash?

14–6. Same facts as Problem 14–4, except that Leslie and Dana are registered domestic partners in a state that imposes mandatory community property rules on registered domestic partners. Leslie owns all of the stock of Leslie Corp. What are the federal income tax consequences if Megabank sells Leslie's debt to Leslie Corp for $90,000 cash?

SECTION 3: INSTALLMENT METHOD PURCHASES BY RELATED PARTIES

Code: Sections 318 and 453(e)

When a taxpayer sells property in exchange for an installment note, he may face a tax liability on the resulting gain without receiving any cash with which to pay that tax liability. As was explored in Chapter 7A, Section 2, Code Section 453 therefore allows income from certain installment sales to be taken into account under the installment method. In general, however, taxpayers only get the benefit of deferral if they also defer receipt of payment. This limits possible abuse.

But what if taxpayer sells an appreciated assets to a related party in exchange for an installment note (with adequate stated interest) providing for payment of the purchase price at the end of 20 years? The related party then turns around and sells that asset to a third party for cash. Unless the Code limits the ability of related parties to do so, taxpayers may be able to obtain extended deferral of gain recognition, while still, in effect, receiving cash on the sale. Code Section 453(e) addresses this problem.

Under Code Section 453(f)(1), a party is related for purposes of Code Section 453(e) if he, she, or it is either (1) a person who bears a relationship described in Code Section 267(b) to the person first disposing of the property, or (2) a person whose stock, if he owned any stock, would be attributed to the person first disposing of the property under Code Section 318(a), other than paragraph (4) thereof.

The cross-reference to Code Section 318(a) asks a hypothetical question, not a real one. In other words, it requires that we perform a thought experiment. Imagine, hypothetically, that the installment basis *buyer* owned some stock. We ask whether that stock would then be deemed owned by the installment basis *seller* under Code Section 318(a)(1), (2), or (3). If so, the two are related for purposes of Code Section 453(e), even if they are not related under Code Section 267(b). (And even if neither of them owns any stock at all.)

Code Section 318(a)(1) ("family attribution") tells us that a person will be deemed to own stock owned by specified family members; Code Section 318(a)(2) ("attribution from" entities) tells us that a person will be deemed to own stock owned by specified partnerships, estates, trusts, and corporations; and Code Section 318(a)(3) ("attribution to" entities) tells us that specified entities will be deemed to own stock owned by specified persons holding interests in such entities. Except as provided in Code Section 318(a)(5)(B) or (C), attribution may apply repeatedly.

Assume, for example, that John and Mary are married and that Mary owns 50 percent of the stock of X Corp. Under family attribution, John will be deemed to own Mary's 50 percent of the stock of X Corp as well. Under "attribution from," John, as deemed 50 percent owner of X Corp, will be deemed to own 50 percent of any stock owned by X Corp. As a result, John and X Corp will be treated as related for installment sales purposes under Code Section 453(f)(1)(A), even though they would not be treated as related under Code Section 267(b).

PROBLEMS FOR DISCUSSION

14–7. Leslie and Dana are married for federal tax purposes. Leslie owns Google stock with a fair market value of $2,000,000, in which he has a basis of

$500,000. He wants to sell the Google stock for cash, but does not want to recognize the $1,500,000 of built-in gain. What are the federal income tax consequences of each of the following transactions?

    a. Leslie sells the Google stock to Dana in exchange for an installment note bearing adequate stated interest, with principal payable at the end of 20 years. Dana then sells the Google stock to a third party for $2,000,000 in cash.

    b. Dana owns all of the stock of Dana Corp. Leslie sells the Google stock to Dana Corp in exchange for an installment note bearing adequate stated interest, with principal payable at the end of 20 years. Dana Corp then sells the Google stock to a third party for $2,000,000 in cash.

    c. In each of parts (a) and (b), is the answer different if Leslie and Dana are married for state law purposes but not for federal tax purposes?

14–8. Same facts as in Problem 14–7, except that Leslie and Dana are registered domestic partners in a state that imposes mandatory community property rules on registered domestic partners. Dana owns all of the stock of Dana Corp. Leslie sells the Google stock to Dana Corp in exchange for an installment note bearing adequate stated interest, with principal payable at the end of 20 years. Dana Corp then sells the Google stock to a third party for $2,000,000 in cash. What federal income tax consequences?

Subchapter B: Income–Splitting, Joint Filing, and Marriage Bonuses and Penalties

Subchapter A suggests that problems of relative indifference can arise whenever parties care more about saving taxes than about maintaining separate finances. A particularly difficult such problem arises in the context of committed, long-term, intimate relationships—a problem known as "income-splitting." It was to address this problem that Congress authorized the filing of joint returns. And it was in the context of joint filing that the problem of marriage bonuses and penalties first became politically salient.

To explore how relative indifference in committed, long-term relationships can create tax avoidance opportunities through income-splitting, it may be useful to construct a simple hypothetical. Assume a two-step rate structure: The first $10,000 of each taxpayer's income is exempt from tax. All income in excess of $10,000 is taxable at a rate of 30%.

	Rate
First $10,000	0%
Income over $10,000	30%

Consider taxpayer H, who earns $40,000 of taxable income per year. If he is single and unattached, his income tax liability will be $9,000 (0% of $10,000 plus 30% of $30,000).

	Rate	Tax
First $10,000	0%	$0
Income over $10,000	30%	$9,000
		$9,000

On the other hand, if he has made a long-term commitment to W, he may be willing to assign half his income to her. He may "income-split." If he does so, and if we give tax effect to that assignment, each of H and W will have taxable income of $20,000 and face a tax liability of $3,000 (0% of $10,000 plus 30% of $10,000).

	Rate	Tax
First $10,000	0%	$0
Income over $10,000	30%	$3,000
		$3,000 x 2

By splitting H's income between the two of them, H and W have cut their total federal income tax liability from $9,000 to $6,000.

The use of income-splitting as a tax-saving technique is limited to situations in which H and W are willing to pool their resources. Suppose H and W have no special relationship. W says to H: "Why don't you assign me half your income ($20,000) to save taxes?" H's response is likely to be: "No way. Doing so will save me taxes, as you suggest, but it will cost me more in foregone income." Purely self-interested taxpayers are not generally willing to transfer half their income to someone else simply to reduce taxes. Income-splitting between individuals is commonly plausible as a tax-saving technique only in committed, long-term relationships.

How can couples income-split? The technique most invulnerable to challenge is for a couple to agree to split income-earning and other common tasks. "Instead of working all-out to earn $40,000, I'll earn $20,000, you earn $20,000, and we'll both take care of the house and the kids." But many other techniques exist.

One is simply to assign half of the earning partner's income to the non-earning partner: "I hereby assign you half of all amounts I earn during our relationship." In *Lucas v. Earl*, 281 U.S. 111 (1930), the Supreme Court held that such bald contractual assignments, without more, would not be given effect for federal tax purposes. Instead, it held, the income would be treated as first having been received by the earning partner, and only then transferred to the non-earning partner pursuant to the assignment. As a result, all of the earning partner's income ends up back in his own return.

There are other ways, however, that one can imagine couples attempting to income-split. A couple might, for example, move the earning spouse's business into a corporation and divide the corporate stock 50–50. Half the earnings of the corporation would then effectively belong to each—even in a common law state. Many interesting such techniques have yet to be tested in court—largely because they were mooted, until recently, by Congress's response to another income-splitting case, *Poe v. Seaborn*, 282 U.S. 101 (1930).

Under Washington's mandatory community property rules, each spouse in *Seaborn* owned half the personal service income earned by the other during the marriage. In addition, the wife was deemed to own half the couple's income-producing property and therefore half the income from that property. The Supreme Court held that her half of the couple's income was properly taxable to her. The Court reasoned:

> '[In *Earl*, w]e held that assuming the validity of the contract under local law, it still remained true that the husband's professional fees, earned in years subsequent to the date of the contract, were his individual income, 'derived from salaries, wages, or compensation for personal service...' The very assignment in that case was bottomed on the fact that the earnings would be the husband's property, else there would have been nothing on which if could operate. That case presents quite a different question from this, because here, by law, the earnings are never the property of the husband, but that of the community.'

In other words, in a community property state, the husband's income does not flow first into the husband's return and then from husband to wife. Half of the income he earns flows directly into the wife's return.

Note what happens to our hypothetical couple under *Seaborn* in a federal tax system based on individual returns. In a common law state, H is subject to a tax of $9,000 on his $40,000 of income. In a community property state, the couple is subject to total tax of only $6,000 on that same $40,000 of income. The effect of *Seaborn* was to place common law states under intense pressure to adopt community property regimes. Several did. Many, however, lobbied Congress to solve the problem at the federal level instead.

Congress's solution, adopted in 1948, was to give married couples the option to file jointly, and to establish separate rates for married couples who accepted that option. For those who decided not to file jointly, Congress established yet another category—married filing separately—with rates that were, for most taxpayers, less favorable.

Once couples filed jointly, as the vast majority did, it no longer mattered whether they income-split. Both income streams were included in the couple's joint return. Couples in community property and common law state were taxed at the same effective rates. Incentives to experiment with more complex ways to income-split were eliminated. The income-splitting problem was solved, or at least so it seemed.

But where to set the joint rates? Congress's solution to the income-splitting problem created a new problem. Remember our hypothetical rate structure for singles: The first $10,000 of taxpayer income is exempt from tax. All income in excess of $10,000 is taxed at a rate of 30%. H earns

$40,000 of taxable income per year. If he is single and unattached, his income tax liability is $9,000 (0% of $10,000 plus 30% of $30,000).

Congress believed it desirable to set H's married-filing-jointly rates so as to make his tax liability "marriage neutral"—that is, to tax him the same way regardless of whether he was married. Unfortunately, the rate schedule required to do so depends on how much his wife earns. If she makes nothing, marriage neutrality requires that we use *exactly the same rate structure for couples filing jointly that we use for singles*: The first $10,000 of the couple's income is exempt from tax. All income in excess of $10,000 is taxed at a rate of 30%. H and W, filing jointly, will still pay $9,000 per year of tax on the same $40,000.

We might call this rate structure the "single-earner endpoint." It lies at one end of a range of plausible joint return rate schedules, hence "endpoint." And it maintains marriage neutrality for couples with a single earner. At the single-earner endpoint, we use the same rate structure for married couples that we do for single taxpayers.

Now consider partners M and N, a two-wage couple. Each makes $20,000. Before they marry, each therefore pays $3,000 of federal income tax—for a total of $6,000 of tax. If we use the same rate structure for couples filing jointly that we use for singles, as we would at the single-earner endpoint, what happens when they marry? Their total income is $40,000. Their total tax liability is now $9,000. Their federal tax liability has just gone up by 50 percent merely because they have married. This result is commonly called a "marriage penalty." If we set our married-filing-jointly rate structure at the single-earner endpoint, couples in which both spouses earn income will end up paying more tax when they get married; our tax system will impose a rate penalty on marriage.

What if we design the joint return rate structure instead to eliminate the marriage penalty on our two-earner couple? We can do this by simply *doubling the boundary points in the schedule*. Our joint return rate schedule will therefore look like this:

	Rate
First $20,000	0%
Income over $20,000	30%

We might call this rate schedule the "two-earner endpoint." Again, it lies at one end of a range of plausible joint return rate schedules, and it maintains marriage neutrality for couples in which the two partners earn equal amounts. It is, in fact, exactly how we would set marriage-neutral rates for couples who income-split—as our hypothetical M and N do.

M and N earn a total of $40,000. If we apply our new rate schedule to their situation, the first $20,000 is exempt, and the last $20,000 is taxable at a rate of 30%. Bingo! $6,000 of tax. The new rate schedule taxes M and N married exactly as they were taxed when they were unmarried. We have achieved marriage neutrality.

But now what happens to our original couple, H and W? Single, H was paying $9,000 of tax. Under married-filing-jointly rates set at the two-earner endpoint, H and W pay only $6,000. In other words, they get a marriage bonus.

If we set the married-filing-jointly rates anywhere between the two endpoints, some couples will get marriage bonuses and some marriage penalties. In fact, it can be proved mathematically that if a rate structure is at all progressive, it is impossible to set joint rates so as to make the system both "marriage neutral" and "couples neutral."

What is "couples neutrality"? Couples neutrality exists when couples with the same income pay the same tax. In our hypothetical, H and W earn $40,000 total; so do M and N. The rate structures we have explored tax the two couples the same amount. They are therefore couples neutral.

We could get rid of both marriage bonuses and marriage penalties by abandoning couples neutrality. The simplest way to do this would be to return to individual filing. A number of academics have urged that we do so. *See, e.g.*, Lawrence Zelenak, *Marriage and the Income Tax*, 67 S. CAL. L. REV. 339 (1994); Edward J. McCaffery, *Taxation and the Family: A Fresh Look at Behavioral Gender Biases in the Code*, 40 UCLA L. REV. 983 (1993); Pamela B. Gann, *Abandoning Marital Status as a Factor in Allocating Income Tax Burdens*, 59 TEX. L. REV. 1 (1980). If we do, then in our hypothetical H pays $9,000 in tax regardless of whether he is married. And M and N each pay $3,000 in tax regardless of whether they are married.

There are at least three problems with this solution. First, the two couples have equal ability to pay. If we return to individual filing, we tax H and W at a significantly higher effective rate than M and N. This is inconsistent with one of the reasons Congress chose to tax income in the first place. Second, it disadvantages traditional couples—couples where the husband works and the wife stays home with the children. Abandoning joint filing is therefore not just a technical fix; it has political ramifications.

Third, H now has a strong incentive to income-split with W. If arrangements exist that will effect income-splitting without too much cost, H and W can cut their total federal tax liability significantly by undertaking such arrangements. Individual filing creates an incentive for taxpayers to change their behaviors solely for tax reasons. We have therefore abandoned our goal of making the tax system nondistortive.

Unfortunately, whether H and W can income-split conveniently is going to depend on their circumstances. If H and W are wage-earners, income-splitting will be harder than if they own their own company and run their own business. If we were to move back to individual returns, therefore, we would likely disadvantage wage-earners while making it possible for interpersonally-committed business owners to cut their tax burdens substantially. Moving back to a system of individual returns therefore has distributional consequences across income classes as well.

Finally, if *Seaborn* remains the law, couples in community property states will income-split automatically, as a matter of law. Couples in common law states will only be able to income-split if they make appropriate economic and legal arrangements. This means that an individual return regime will almost certainly involve geographic tax disparities. Congress might overturn *Seaborn* as to income from labor; but it would be harder to do so as to income from capital. In any event, the problem is not *Seaborn*; the problem is income-splitting.

NOTES

1. *Overturning* Seaborn.—Congress has partially overturned *Seaborn* in two contexts. Code Section 879(a) applies to nonresident alien individuals. In the absence of special rules, half of any community income earned in the United States may escape U.S. taxation merely by reason of the fact that it is attributed to a nonresident alien spouse, who may have no contact whatever with this country. In addition, since U.S. citizens are taxable on their worldwide income, a U.S. citizen married to a resident of a community property country may find herself subject to U.S. tax on half her spouse's earnings solely by reason of foreign community property rules.

To avoid these problems, in the case of nonresident alien individuals Code Section 879(a) disregards community property rules with respect to earned income and trade or business income, but continues to respect those rules with respect to income from property. In effect, the repealer implements the basic assignment of income principles of *Lucas v. Earl* and *Helvering v. Horst*—income from labor is taxed to the person who earns it, income from property to the person who owns the property.

Code Section 66 similarly governs the taxation of community income when a U.S. married couple lives apart and does not in fact pool its earned income. Subsection (a) states that if the couple lives apart at all times during the calendar year and files separate returns, and if no portion of the community earned income is transferred between the separated spouses during the year, such income will be taxed in accordance with the rules of Code Section 879(a). Subsection (b) allows the IRS to deny taxpayer the benefits of community property law if she behaves as if she were solely entitled to community income and fails to notify her spouse of such income on a timely basis. Subsection (c), finally, allows the IRS by regulation to relieve taxpayer of liability for tax on community income if she files separately, does not report that income, and has no reason to know of that income, and taxing her on that income would be inequitable.

Subchapter C: Assignment of Income

SECTION 1: INCOME FROM SERVICES

Principle: Income from services is taxed to the person who has ultimate direction and control over the earning of that income.

Code: Section 482

In *Lucas v. Earl*, 281 U.S. 111 (1930), the Supreme Court declined to give tax effect to a contract pursuant to which each spouse purported to assign half of his or her income to the other during their marriage, stating:

> There is no doubt that the statute could tax salaries to those who earned them and provide that the tax could not be escaped by anticipatory arrangements and contracts however skilfully devised to prevent the salary when paid from vesting even for a second in the man who earned it. That seems to us the import of the statute before us...

In *Commissioner v. Culbertson*, 337 U.S. 733, 739 (1949), Court reaffirmed this holding, calling the holding in *Earl* "the first principle of income taxation: that income must be taxed to him who earns it." In *Wesenberg v. Commissioner*, 69 T.C. 1005 (1978), the Tax Court elaborated further, holding that where more than one person could arguably be said to have earned particular income, it should be taxed to the person having "ultimate direction and control over the earning of the compensation." Under an "agency triangle" approach, this is implemented by looking at contractual formalities. If the third party formally contracts with the taxpayer, income on the contract is taxed to the taxpayer. If the third party formally contracts with taxpayer's assignee, income on the contract is taxed to the assignee.

An alternative approach, illustrated in *Schuster v. Commissioner*, below, is to apply the common law of agency. If taxpayer acts as agent for another, her principal is taxable on the resulting income. If, under the common law of agency, she acts on her own account, she herself is taxable.

Assume, for example, that a law firm associate performs all necessary work on a matter for a client. The client pays the law firm. To whom should the resulting income be taxed? Under the agency triangle approach, we focus on the fact that as a matter of form the client has contracted with the law firm; therefore the law firm is taxable. Under a common law agency approach, we ask whether the associate is acting as an agent under the common law of agency or is acting on his own; if he is acting as an agent, the law firm (as his principal) is taxable on the resulting income; if he is acting on his own, he is. Note that this is true regardless of the fact the law firm gets the money. If we tax the income to the associate, we will then need to account for how the money got to the law firm; but we tax the income to the associate nevertheless.

SCHUSTER v. COMMISSIONER
800 F.2d 672 (7th Cir. 1986)

Schuster, a Roman Catholic nun, is a member of the Order of the Adorers of the Blood of Christ. The Order is a tax-exempt religious organization whose purposes are "to conduct schools and places of learning and to promote education, to advance the cause of religious and social work, to conduct hospitals and institutions for the care and treatment of suffering humanity and to do all and everything necessary or convenient for the accomplishment of any of the purposes or objects and powers above mentioned or incidental thereto."

As a condition of membership in the Order, Schuster was required to make perpetual vows of poverty, chastity, and obedience. In accordance with her vow of poverty, Schuster executed a declaration in which she agreed "never [to] claim or demand, directly or indirectly, any wages, compensation, remuneration, or reward ... for the time or for the services or work that I devote for or with ... [the Order] during the time I may remain there or elsewhere in the name of or upon commission from said [Order]."

Members may withdraw from the Order either with or without official dispensation from the Church.

Members are allowed to secure employment in occupations that relate to the Order's general purposes, subject to approval by a Provincial Superior of the Order. Approval turns upon whether the proposed mission relates to religious and charitable works that promote education, relieve suffering, and otherwise provide assistance to those in need. However, pursuant to a member's vow of obedience, she may not accept employment without approval of the Order. No member can voluntarily terminate her employment without the Order's approval. In addition, each member promises to abide by any direction of the Provincial Superior, even if such direction relates to the performance of the employment itself or requires the member's withdrawal from the employment. The Order has, on occasion, required members to terminate their assigned employment.

Pursuant to their vows, members are not entitled to retain any funds generated by their employment; rather, the Order is entitled to all such funds. After a member transfers such funds to the Order, she maintains no control over the disposition of the funds.

Members generally live in a convent. When, however, a member's employment is not located near a convent, the Order rents a residence for the member. These members living away from the convent submit monthly budget statements of living expenses to the Order, which the Order pays if the expenses are approved. In addition, the Order provides its members with a personal expense allowance.

In October, 1978, Schuster, who has a bachelor's degree in nursing, was awarded an educational grant from the federal government under Section 822(b) of the Public Health Service Act. The award covered the cost of Schuster's tuition, books, fees, living and moving expenses for the Nurse Midwife Program at the University of Mississippi Medical Center. As a condition of receiving the grant, Schuster agreed to reside and practice in a "health man-power shortage area" (as defined in Section 332 of the Public Health Service Act) for a 12–month period upon her completion of the training program. In addition, Schuster agreed to repay in full the amount of the grant if she failed to fulfill the practice commitment.

Upon completion of the Nurse Midwife Program, Schuster obtained permission from the Order to apply and to interview for positions in health manpower shortage areas. One position Schuster applied for was with Su Clinica Familiar ("the Clinic"), a family health service clinic in Raymondville, Texas.

During the year at issue, the National Health Services Corps, a division of the United States Public Health Service, furnished the services of a number of health professionals in its employ to the Clinic. The health professionals provided by the NHSC to the Clinic were employed and compensated by the federal government, and not by the Clinic.

Schuster filed an application for employment with the NHSC in conjunction with her application to the Clinic. She applied for the job in order to fulfill her commitment to practice in a health manpower shortage area. She stated on her application to the NHSC that she would accept a position only if she were assigned to work at the clinic at a salary of at least $16,000.00 per year.

Schuster was interviewed over the telephone by an employee of the NHSC. In late May, 1979, the NHSC paid for Schuster to travel to the Clinic to visit as a prospective NHSC assignee. On June 27, 1979, the Clinic informed the NHSC that it intended to employ Schuster as a staff nurse-midwife beginning on July 23, 1979.

After Schuster was offered employment with the NHSC as a nurse-midwife at the Clinic, she requested and was granted permission from the Order to accept it. Accordingly, on July 1, 1979, Schuster wrote a letter to the NHSC confirming her acceptance of the appointment, effective July 29, 1979.

Also on July 1, 1979, the Acting Provincial Administrator of the Order wrote two letters. One letter was written to the director of the Clinic's nurse-midwifery service, and a second, virtually identical letter, was written to NHSC. These letters stated in part:

> "Sister Francine Schuster has informed us of your recent phone notification of a current job opening in nurse-midwifery at Su Clinica Familiar, Raymondville–Harlingen, Texas. The Community of Adorers of the Blood of Christ would like to contract with you for the services of Sister Francine Schuster, ASC, for the position of nurse-midwife for one year at Su Clinica Familiar. If our offer is acceptable, we request that payment for her services be made to the Adorers of the Blood of Christ."

In response to the letter addressed to the Clinic, the director of the nurse-midwifery service at the Clinic in a July 9, 1979 letter to the Acting Provincial Administrator of the Order, wrote, in pertinent part:

> "Consider this letter as formal acceptance of Sister Francine Schuster on our nurse-midwifery staff. She will be beginning on the pay period

that starts July 23. Sister Francine's checks will be paid to her and she can endorse them and send them to you. I endorse my checks 'paid to the order of the Sisters of St. Mary. Sister Angela Murdaugh.' "

The NHSC did not respond to the July 1, 1979 letter from the Acting Provincial Administrator of the Order.

As an employee of the NHSC, Schuster was a civil service employee subject to the standards of conduct set by the Department of Health, Education and Welfare, and her performance as a midwife was evaluated yearly by means of the Department's employee performance appraisal system. As an NHSC staff member, Schuster qualified for and received continuing professional education at the expense of the federal government. In addition, Schuster was protected against malpractice claims arising from her employment pursuant to Section 224 of the Public Health Service Act.

Schuster's initial annual salary as a nurse-midwife was $15,920, the rate applicable to federal employees at the GS–9 level. During her tenure at the Clinic, Schuster received both a within-grade increase in her salary and an increase pursuant to Executive Order. In addition, Schuster accumulated annual and sick leave at the same rate as did other federal employees with comparable service. The Order did not provide the NHSC or the Clinic with a replacement when Schuster used sick leave.

While employed by the NHSC, Schuster was paid by checks drawn on the United States Treasury and made payable to her individually. Neither the Clinic nor the NHSC imposed any restriction on her use of payroll checks. Schuster endorsed to the Order each check tendered to her, and she mailed each check to a lockbox maintained by the Order in St. Louis.

On her 1980 federal income tax return, Schuster reported that she had received $18,771.20 in wages, but that the compensation was not taxable to her because she had received it as an agent on behalf of the Order. On May 14, 1982, the Commissioner of Internal Revenue issued a notice of deficiency to Schuster reflecting his determination that Schuster's wages were taxable to her individually and not to the Order, because she was not working as an agent of a religious order when she earned her wages.

Schuster argues that her compensation is not includable in her gross income because she received compensation only as an agent acting on behalf of the Order. The Commissioner, on the other hand, argues that Schuster earned the compensation in her individual capacity and that it must be included as a part of her gross income. Because the statute does not address the agency issue, we look elsewhere for guidance in resolving this question.

In *Fogarty v. United States*, 780 F.2d 1005 (Fed. Cir. 1986), the court of appeals thoroughly addressed the issue of whether a member of a religious order, who is subject to a vow of poverty, earns income in an individual, rather than representative, capacity. In that case, the taxpayer, a Roman Catholic priest, accepted employment as an associate professor at the University of Virginia. He received paychecks from the University made payable to him individually. Under canon law of the Catholic Church, Fogarty was not entitled to keep the amounts earned as compensation; instead, the Order received Fogarty's paychecks and provided him with a living expense allowance.

After the IRS determined Fogarty was obligated to report the income as his own, he paid it and sought a refund. His refund claims were denied, and he brought suit in the United States Court of Claims. The court of claims granted summary judgment in favor of the government, from which judgment Fogarty appealed.

The Court of Appeals for the Federal Circuit affirmed the court of claims' decision, stating that the agency determination is a question of law subject to general rules of agency, to be resolved upon consideration of all the underlying facts. The *Fogarty* court cited six relevant factors in making this determination: 1) the degree of control exercised by the Order over the member; 2) ownership rights between the member and the Order; 3) the purposes or mission of the Order; 4) the type of work performed by the member vis-à-vis the purposes or mission; 5) the dealings between the member and the third-party employer, including the circumstances surrounding inquiries and interviews, and the control or supervision exercised by the employer; and 6) the dealings between the employer and the Order.

After applying these factors to the facts, the court concluded in *Fogarty* that the priest had earned the income in his individual capacity, and affirmed the tax court decision. We agree with the *Fogarty* court's conclusion that the agency determination requires a flexible test which allows consideration of all the relevant factors. Thus, we also adopt such a flexible test in this case requiring and directing a consideration of all the underlying facts.

In adopting this flexible test approach, we reject the so-called "agency triangle" theory relied upon by the Commissioner. Under the "agency triangle" theory, a finding that the income generated by an individual's personal services was actually earned on behalf of a separate and distinct principal is premised upon a preliminary finding that a contract or other express agreement existed between the payor of the income and the alleged principal, in which the alleged principal has expressly granted the payor the right to use the individual's services on the principal's behalf. Thus, the Commissioner argues, absent a contract between the Order and the NHSC, Schuster could not have earned compensation from the NHSC on behalf of the Order.

As support for this theory, the Commissioner cites *Johnson v. United States*, 698 F.2d 372 (9th Cir. 1982). In *Johnson*, a professional athlete, who had conveyed the exclusive rights to his personal services to a corporation, contended that the corporation was taxable on amounts paid directly to it by his employer. The court, however, held that the player, and not the corporation, was to be taxed for the earnings. The court stated that, in order for the corporation to be taxed, two requirements must be met: 1) the corporation must have the right to control the player's services and to negotiate the player's compensation, and 2) the third-party employer must recognize the corporation's control over the player. Because the basketball teams employing the player refused to contract with the corporation, the court found that the second requirement had not been met and that the earnings were properly taxable to the player.

In our view, the two-part test applied by the *Johnson* court and the "agency triangle" theory too narrowly restrict the inquiry into an alleged agency relationship. While the dealings between the third-party employer and the alleged principal are an important factor to be considered in assessing the agency determination, there are several other important factors. A flexible test, allowing consideration of all of those factors, better serves our analysis in attempting to determine whether income is to be taxed against the person or entity who actually earned it or against someone else.

Applying the factors cited by the *Fogarty* court to the facts in the present case, we conclude that Schuster, like Fogarty, earned her wages in her individual capacity, rather than as an agent on behalf of her Order. This conclusion is supported, first, by examining the degree of control the Order exercised over Schuster. The Order required Schuster to take a vow of obedience, under which Schuster was obligated to subjugate her will to that of the Order. However, Schuster remained free to withdraw from the Order at any time. The Provincial Superior approved Schuster's acceptance of the job with the Clinic and Schuster's living expenses. The Order also approved Schuster's request to apply and interview for positions in health manpower shortage areas and her request to accept the position with the Clinic. While, pursuant to Schuster's vow of obedience, the Order retained authority to control Schuster's daily routine, the Order did not in fact exercise such day-to-day control.

Second, Schuster's entitlement to the compensation was clearly superior to the Order's. Schuster's paychecks were made payable to her individually. The fact that she endorsed the checks over to the Order before mailing them to the lockbox maintained by the Order in St. Louis demonstrates the superiority of her control over the wages. In addition, Schuster's receipt of personal benefit from employment perquisites, such as annual and sick leave, continuing professional education, and malpractice protection in return for her services provides further support for a conclusion that what Schuster earned, she earned individually.

The third and fourth factors cited by the *Fogarty* court are best considered together: the purpose of the Order and the type of work performed by the member in light of that purpose. The purposes of the Order, generally stated, were to undertake religious and charitable works that promote education and provide health care. Schuster's employment in providing health care services to patients of the Clinic was indisputably consistent with those purposes. Arguably, in these respects, Schuster was acting as an agent for the Order and not on her own behalf.

However, when the purpose of the Order and the work of the member are considered in light of the fifth and sixth factors suggested by the *Fogarty* court, the conclusion seems inescapable that Schuster was not acting merely as an agent of her Order. Factors five and six from *Fogarty* require an analysis of the dealings between the member, the Order, and the employer, and this analysis is very revealing.

Schuster filed an application for employment with the NHSC. Although she was willing to specify a salary level as a condition of her accepting employment with the NHSC, Schuster said nothing on her application about working as an agent on behalf of her Order. Schuster was interviewed over the telephone by a NHSC employee, but again there was no mention of any agency relationship. Schuster also traveled alone to the Clinic as a prospective NHSC assignee at the NHSC's expense. Then, when offered the job at the Clinic, Schuster wrote a letter dated July 1, 1979, to the NHSC confirming her acceptance. Schuster's employment was in no way conditioned upon her status as a member of the Order. Admittedly, the Acting Provincial Administrator of the Order also wrote a letter on July 1, 1979, which appears to make an employment offer to the NHSC for Schuster's services. But, by Schuster's own admission, she had already accepted an offer on the date the Order's offer was made. All the contact between Schuster and the NHSC, especially as related to her acceptance of employment, which occurred without reference to or conditioned upon her alleged agency relationship with the Order, suggests that Schuster was not operating as an agent of the Order.

In addition, once employed, Schuster was under the direct supervision and control of the Clinic and the NHSC. In her daily tasks, Schuster was supervised by other Clinic employees. Schuster's performance was evaluated under the same employee appraisal system used by the Department of Health, Education and Welfare for other civil service employees. The Order was not supervising her work in a day-to-day sense, as evidenced by the fact that the Provincial Superior or another member of the Order's Placement Board made only periodic visits to the mission site. Though a person may, at times, act as an agent on behalf of two principals, the fact that day-to-day control over Schuster was exercised by the Clinic is, at least, consistent with the conclusion that, in performing her duties as an employee of the Clinic, she was acting on her own behalf.

The dealings between the NHSC, the Clinic, and the Order also evidence a conclusion that Schuster earned wages in her individual capacity. The first contact between the Order, the NHSC, and the Clinic was effected via the July 1, 1979 letters from the Acting Provincial Administrator of the Order to the NHSC and the Clinic. In these letters, Schuster's services were offered and a request was made that her wages be paid directly to the Order. The letters also expressly stated that

Schuster's services "are performed ... on behalf of the Order as its agent." The NHSC did not respond to the letter it received. The Director of the Nurse–Midwifery Service at the Clinic sent a reply letter to the Order that, in addition to conveying a formal acceptance of the Order's offer, took exception with the procedure requested by the Order, directing instead that Schuster's checks would be made payable to her, making her free to endorse them over to the Order, if that was Schuster's choice. At most, there was no agreement regarding the manner in which the paychecks would be written. Moreover, when Schuster accepted payment for her services, she accepted it in the form of paychecks made out to her individually. Her failure to insist on direct payment to the Order further disputes her subsequent claim that she had earned her wages as an agent of the Order.

In practice, the assignment of income doctrine commonly interacts with two related arguments. First, where the taxpayer to which income is purportedly assigned is an entity, the IRS will often assert that the entity is a sham and should be disregarded. Second, where commonly controlled businesses interact other than at arm's-length, Code Section 482 allows the IRS to reallocate items of income and deduction "to prevent evasion of taxes or clearly to reflect ... income." The interaction of these three sets of rules is illustrated in the case that follows.

HAERI v. COMMISSIONER
T.C. Memo. 1989–20

During 1981 and 1982, petitioners were alien residents of the United States residing in San Antonio, Texas. Petitioner Fadhlalla Haeri was an officer and a shareholder in Project Development Corporation (PDC), a Panamanian corporation, and was active as a petroleum consultant for oil companies doing business in the Middle East. PDC was a diversified "umbrella" corporation that owned approximately 30 subsidiaries and maintained a large network of connections and personnel throughout the Middle East.

At the time he ceased to be a full-time consultant with PDC, petitioner was a 47 percent owner of the corporation. The remaining 53 percent of PDC's shares were owned by Hamid Jafar and Hosam Raouf. Petitioner handed over his PDC shares to Jafar to be held in trust for the benefit of petitioner and his family. An irrevocable trust, the Fadhlalla Haeri Trust, was formally established for this purpose on February 9, 1981.

On June 13, 1975, PDC incorporated a wholly-owned subsidiary, Haeri and Associates Limited, S.A. (Haeri & Associates), [under the laws of Panama]. By petitioner's own admission, Haeri & Associates:

> "was formed ... as a vehicle, as a convenient vehicle for me if I needed to have any activity or business activity to channel through it

basically. . . . It is basically a company that I control. . . . One of the main reasons actually it was formed, was to enable me to reside in the United Kingdom as a representative. So Haeri & Associates original purpose was to enable me to have a corporation in the United Kingdom, after 1975 to be its sole employee, to satisfy residence requirements in the UK. But as such, it had no business activity of any significance. . . . Haeri & Associates' main function, actually, if one looks at it, for the record, has really been that consultancy agreement with Ashland. That has been the most, if you like, important or prominent function that it has. And since then there has been no activity under it. Prior to that, for also three or four years, I doubt that there has been any activity."

Thus, although he formally was not a majority shareholder, petitioner exercised actual control over Haeri & Associates.

Beginning in 1975, Ashland Oil, Inc. contracted with Abu Dhabi National Oil Co. (ADNOC) to purchase crude oil supplies. During the world-wide crude oil shortage in 1979, however, ADNOC reduced Ashland's contract from 55,000 to 20,000 barrels a day. In an effort to get its oil allotment restored, Ashland, on November 15, 1979, entered into a consulting agreement with Senior Ventures, S.A. and Metronome Enterprises, S.A.

Despite the efforts of Senior Ventures and Metronome, Ashland's ADNOC oil allotments continued to decline, and Ashland became dissatisfied with the performance under these consulting agreements. Early in 1980, officials of Ashland met with petitioner and asked for his assistance in terminating these unsuccessful arrangements and in negotiating an increase in Ashland's oil allotment. Petitioner was also requested to obtain a release from Hisham Alwan, a Middle Eastern oil broker who had asserted claims against Ashland for commissions relating to crude oil purchases by Ashland from ADNOC.

Effective July 20, 1981, Haeri & Associates and Ashland Industries (Bermuda) Limited (AIBL) entered into an agreement [pursuant to which] Haeri & Associates was to perform [the foregoing] services for AIBL. Pursuant to this agreement, petitioner made two or three visits to the Middle East in an attempt to improve Ashland's crude oil allotments from ADNOC. Although PDC was unable to obtain an increase in Ashland's oil allotment, PDC personnel successfully negotiated the termination of the Senior Ventures and Metronome consulting contracts and obtained a release from Alwan.

AIBL made the following payments to Haeri & Associates during 1981 and 1982:

July 22, 1981	$2,391,919.80
September 4, 1981	195,157.20
November 30, 1981	359,853.60
February 1, 1982	123,953.20
Total	$3,070,883.80

The payments from AIBL to Haeri & Associates were deposited to Haeri & Associates' account at Manufacturers Hanover Bank, Brussels, Belgium, and then immediately transferred to PDC's account in the same bank. Petitioners did not report as income any of the payments from AIBL to Haeri & Associates in 1981 and 1982.

In a statutory notice of deficiency, respondent determined that petitioners [Fadhlalla Haeri and his wife] had additional taxable income of $2,946,930 and $123,954 for 1981 and 1982, respectively, for commissions paid by AIBL to Haeri & Associates. [In other words, the IRS taxed the couple, who were beneficiaries of a trust that owned 47 percent of the stock of PDC, which in turn owned 100 percent of Haeri & Associates, on all amounts paid by AIBL to Haeri & Associates in 1981 and 1982.]

Respondent argues that the fees earned from the AIBL consulting contract were produced by petitioner's professional skill and business reputation and are therefore taxable to petitioner as compensation or business income under section 61. In support of his argument, respondent asserts that Haeri & Associates is a sham corporation.

Haeri & Associates was properly organized in accordance with the General Corporation Law of the Republic of Panama, issued stock, elected directors and officers, maintained a bank account, and performed the AIBL consulting contract. Respondent, however, asks us to disregard Haeri & Associates' corporate existence for tax purposes.

Generally, a corporate entity will be respected for tax purposes absent "exceptional situations where it otherwise would present an obstacle to the due protection or enforcement of public or private rights." The test of whether a corporation will be recognized as a taxable entity was stated by the Supreme Court in *Moline Properties, Inc. v. Commissioner*, 319 U.S. 436, 438–439 (1943), as follows:

> "The doctrine of corporate entity fills a useful purpose in business life. Whether the purpose be to gain an advantage under the law of the state of incorporation or to avoid or to comply with the demands of creditors or to serve the creator's personal or undisclosed convenience, so long as that purpose is the equivalent of business activity or is followed by the carrying on of business by the corporation, the corporation remains a separate taxable entity."

PDC was a diversified holding company that pursued various business operations in many different countries through numerous subsidiary corporations. Initially, PDC organized Haeri & Associates to provide consulting services to European and American oil companies. Subsequently, PDC and petitioner used Haeri & Associates to provide these services to AIBL. Although petitioner could have provided these consulting services in his individual capacity, petitioner and PDC apparently made a business decision to use Haeri & Associates to perform the contract.

Petitioner and PDC organized Haeri & Associates for a business purpose, thus satisfying one of the alternative requirements under *Moline*

Properties. Haeri & Associates, through the efforts of PDC's Middle Eastern network, actually carried on some minimal amount of business activity. Moreover, Haeri & Associates' identity was recognized by entities not controlled by petitioner, including Ashland and Manufacturers Hanover Bank. These facts lead us to the conclusion that Haeri & Associates was not a sham corporation and that it is to be recognized for tax purposes.

Petitioner contends that the consulting fees from AIBL were income to Haeri & Associates, while respondent, relying on the assignment of income doctrine of *Lucas v. Earl*, 281 U.S. 111 (1930), argues that the commissions are taxable to petitioner. The assignment of income doctrine is an essential tool for preventing a taxpayer from assigning income to a corporation to avoid tax liability. A conclusion that Haeri & Associates is not a sham does not preclude application of the assignment of income doctrine; a taxpayer can assign income to a corporation with real and substantial business in an attempt to avoid tax liability.

The principle that income is taxed to the person who earned it is basic to our system of income tax law. In the corporate context, particularly in those cases involving closely-held or one-person personal service corporations, however, this actual earner test may be inadequate. *Johnson v. Commissioner*, 78 T.C. 882 (1982), *affd. without published opinion*, 734 F.2d 20 (9th Cir. 1984).

In *Johnson*, a professional athlete who had conveyed the exclusive rights to his personal services to a corporation contended that the corporation was taxable on amounts paid directly to it by his employer. Recognizing that a corporation can earn income only through the personal services of its employees and agents, we set out two requirements that must be met before a corporation, rather than the service-performing individual, will be considered to control the income earned. As applied in this case, first, Haeri & Associates must have had the right to direct or control petitioner's activities in some meaningful manner. Second, there must have been a contract or similar indication of agreement between Haeri & Associates and AIBL recognizing Haeri & Associates' controlling position.

(The Courts of Appeals for the Federal Circuit and for the Seventh Circuit have rejected the two-part *Johnson* test in favor of a more flexible facts and circumstances approach. *See Schuster v. Commissioner*, 800 F.2d 672 (7th Cir. 1986); *Fogarty v. United States*, 780 F.2d 1005 (Fed. Cir. 1986). We need not resolve any conflict between these tests because we would reach the same result applying the facts and circumstances analysis.)

In this case, there was a contract between Haeri & Associates and the entity benefiting from petitioner's services, AIBL. Although the record contains no evidence that petitioner had a formal employment contract with Haeri & Associates, there is evidence that PDC, Haeri & Associates' parent corporation, controlled petitioner's efforts to preserve its ongoing relationship with Ashland. Under PDC's direction, petitioner was successful in terminating the consulting agreement between AIBL and Senior Ventures, a PDC subsidiary, and negotiating a new consulting agreement between AIBL and Haeri & Associates, another PDC subsidiary.

Petitioner has shown that AIBL recognized Haeri & Associates as controlling petitioner's performance of consulting services. AIBL contracted with Haeri & Associates for petitioner's consulting services; the agreement and subsequent affidavits, pursuant to which petitioner agreed to perform consulting services, were executed by petitioner in his capacity as president of Haeri & Associates; AIBL's payments, in the form of wire transfers and checks, were to Haeri & Associates and not to petitioner individually; and all payments from AIBL to Haeri & Associates under the consulting agreement were immediately transferred to PDC, the parent corporation. Accordingly, because Haeri & Associates controlled the earning of the income, petitioner is not directly taxable on the income received from AIBL during the years in issue.

If we conclude that the commission payments from AIBL were income to Haeri & Associates and not to petitioner individually, respondent argues that this income may be properly allocated to petitioner pursuant to section 482. Section 482 allows the Commissioner to reallocate income actually earned by one member of a controlled group to other members of that group if (1) there are two or more trades, businesses, or organizations, (2) the enterprises are owned or controlled by the same interests, and (3) reallocation of income among the enterprises is necessary to clearly reflect income or to prevent the evasion of taxes.

The standard to be applied in examining dealings between controlled taxpayers is that of an uncontrolled taxpayer dealing at arm's length with another uncontrolled taxpayer. The regulations also provide that "Transactions between one controlled taxpayer and another will be subjected to special scrutiny to ascertain whether the common control is being used to reduce, avoid, or escape taxes."

Petitioner's furnishing of consulting services on behalf of Haeri & Associates to AIBL constituted a trade or business separate from PDC for purposes of section 482. Similarly, petitioner and Haeri & Associates were controlled by the same interests. Section 1.482–1(a)(3), Income Tax Regs., provides that the control may be direct or indirect, whether legally enforceable and however exercisable or exercised. Petitioner testified before the SEC in 1983 that Haeri & Associates was "basically a company that I control."

Section 482, however, does not permit allocation of income merely because the common interests have the power to shift income. A reallocation under section 482 must be based on actual shifting of income. We must, therefore, examine all of the facts and circumstances to determine whether there has been a shifting of income between Haeri & Associates and petitioner.

The issue under section 482 is whether Haeri & Associates and petitioner would have entered into their financial relationship had they been unrelated parties dealing at arm's length. Respondent argues that petitioner would not have agreed to work for no compensation if he had bargained at arm's length with an uncontrolled entity. Although a corporation is not required to pay a salary to an officer who performs services on its behalf, particular scrutiny is necessary when the corporation's only business activity is transacted solely through the efforts of the individual as an employee of that corporation.

Petitioner, who had withdrawn from active business dealings, argues that he intervened in the AIBL transaction on behalf of his corporation, PDC, as an investor not as an employee of Haeri & Associates. Further, petitioner contends that his expected financial return for his time and effort was "income, profit or gain in the form of dividends or enhancement in the value of an investment." These very assertions, however, preclude our determining that the arrangement would have been entered into by an unrelated party dealing at arm's length.

The commission income paid to Haeri & Associates may have been compensation in part for items other than petitioner's services. It was petitioners' burden, however, to present evidence sufficient to establish a more correct allocation and to persuade us that respondent's allocation was arbitrary, capricious, and unreasonable. They have not done so.

NOTES

1. *Taxation of nonresident aliens and foreign corporations.*—Nonresident aliens and foreign corporations are only subject to U.S. income tax on (1) income effectively connected with a U.S. trade or business, and (2) U.S. source income other than income from sales. Compensation income is sourced by reference to the place the services are performed. Thus, where services are performed outside the United States by a nonresident alien or foreign corporation, they are not subject to U.S. income taxation unless the services are effectively connected with the conduct of a U.S. trade or business. There is no reason to believe that the services performed by Haeri & Associates were effectively connected with the conduct of a U.S. trade or business by that corporation. Therefore, if the income in question was earned by Haeri & Associates, it was not subject to U.S. income taxation at all.

U.S. residents and citizens, by contrast, are subject to U.S. income taxation on their world-wide income. At the time, Fadhlalla Haeri was a U.S. resident. As a result of the Tax Court's decision, therefore, the income in question became fully subject to U.S. income tax.

2. *Correlative Adjustments.*—When the IRS successfully argues that income paid to A should actually be taxed to B, at least one additional transaction must be deemed to occur: a transaction or transactions through which the cash, deemed to have gone to B, actually ended up in A. Such additional deemed transactions are known as "correlative adjustments."

Consider the following hypothetical. John owns all of the stock of two corporations, X Corp and Y Corp. X Corp performs $1,000,000 worth of services for Y Corp without compensation. Under Code Section 482, the IRS reallocates $1,000,000 of income from Y Corp to X Corp to conform to arm's-length norms. This requires some deemed transaction or transactions by which the cash, which actually stayed in Y Corp, ends up back in Y Corp. Since the two are related through John, the likely correlative adjustment is to deem X Corp to have distributed $1,000,000 to John, who is then deemed to have contributed the same amount to Y Corp.

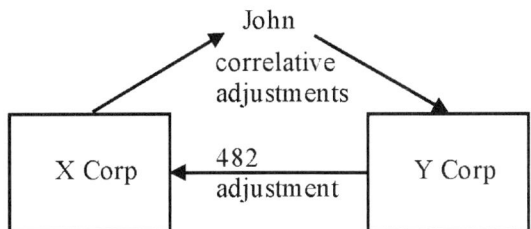

The deemed distribution by X Corp to John will probably be treated as a dividend, taxable to John at a top rate of 15 percent but not deductible to X Corp. The deemed contribution by John to Y Corp will probably be treated as a contribution to capital, excluded from Y Corp's income but increasing John's basis in his Y Corp stock by $1,000,000.

PROBLEMS FOR DISCUSSION

14–9. What might Schuster have done to avoid having her salary taxed to her individually?

14–10. What might Haeri have done to avoid having the amounts paid by AIBL to Haeri & Associates taxed to him personally?

14–11. The compensation at issue in *Haeri* was actually received by PDC, 47% of the stock of which was owned by a trust for the benefit of taxpayer and his family and the remaining 53% of the stock of which was owned by two unrelated individuals. If the compensation was deemed received by Haeri, how did it end up in PDC? What tax consequences flow from the correlative adjustments necessary to get the funds in question from Haeri to PDC?

14–12. In *Minor v. United States*, on page 140 above, the taxpayer entered into an arrangement with Snohomish County Physicians Corporation (of which he was a principal shareholder) pursuant to which 90% of his compensation would be deferred for an extended period. Why was Dr. Minor not personally taxable on the fees collected by the corporation for his services at the time they were collected under sham corporation, assignment of income, or Code Section 482 principles?

SECTION 2: INCOME FROM PROPERTY

Principle: Income from property is taxed to the person who owns the property.

HEIM v. FITZPATRICK
262 F.2d 887 (2nd Cir. 1959)

Plaintiff was the inventor of a new type of rod end and spherical bearing. In September 1942 he applied for a patent thereon. Thereafter on November 17, 1942 he executed a formal written assignment of his invention and of the patents which might be issued for it and for improvements thereof to The Heim Company. The assignment to the Company was made pursuant to an oral agreement, subsequently reduced to a writing dated July 29, 1943, by which it was agreed (1) that the Company need pay no royalties on bearings manufactured by it prior to July 1, 1943; (2) that after that date the Company would pay specified royalties on 12 types of bearings; (3) that on new types of bearings it would pay royalties to be agreed upon prior to their manufacture; (4) that if the royalties for any two consecutive months or for any one year should fall below stated amounts, plaintiff at his option might cancel the agreement and thereupon all rights granted by him under the agreement and under any and all assigned patents should revert to him, his heirs and assigns; and (5) that this agreement is not transferable by the Company.

In August 1943 plaintiff assigned to his wife "an undivided interest of 25 per cent in said agreement with The Heim Company dated July 29, 1943, and in all his inventions and patent rights, past and future, referred to therein and in all rights and benefits of the First Party (plaintiff) thereunder * * *." A similar assignment was given to his son and another to his daughter. Plaintiff paid gift taxes on the assignments. The Company was notified of them and thereafter it made all royalty payments accordingly. As additional types of bearings were put into production from time to time the royalties on them were fixed by agreement between the Company and the plaintiff and his three assignees.

The Commissioner of Internal Revenue decided that all of the royalties paid by the Company to plaintiff's wife and children during the taxable years in suit were taxable to him.

The appellant contends that the assignments to his wife and children transferred to them income-producing property and consequently the royalty payments were taxable to his donees. Judge Anderson, however, was of opinion that: "The income-producing property, *i.e.* the patents, had been assigned by the taxpayer to the corporation. What he had left was a right to a portion of the income which the patents produced. He had the power to dispose of and divert the stream of this income as he saw fit." Consequently he ruled that the principles applied by the Supreme Court in *Helvering v. Horst*, 311 U.S. 112 (1940), and *Helvering v. Eubank*, 311

U.S. 122 (1940), required all the royalty payments to be treated as income of plaintiff.

The question is not free from doubt, but the court believes that the transfers in this case were gifts of income-producing property and that neither *Horst* nor *Eubank* requires the contrary view. In the *Horst* case the taxpayer detached interest coupons from negotiable bonds, which he retained, and made a gift of the coupons, shortly before their due date, to his son who collected them in the same year at maturity. *Lucas v. Earl*, 281 U.S. 111 (1930), which held that an assignment of unearned future income for personal services is taxable to the assignor, was extended to cover the assignment in *Horst*.

In the *Eubank* case the taxpayer assigned a contract which entitled him to receive previously earned insurance renewal commissions. In holding the income taxable to the assignor the court found that the issues were not distinguishable from those in *Horst*. No reference was made to the assignment of the underlying contract.

In the present case more than a bare right to receive future royalties was assigned by plaintiff to his donees. Under the terms of his contract with The Heim Company he retained the power to bargain for the fixing of royalties on new types of bearings, *i.e.* bearings other than the 12 products on which royalties were specified. This power was assigned and the assignees exercised it as to new products. Plaintiff also retained a reversionary interest in his invention and patents by reason of his option to cancel the agreement if certain conditions were not fulfilled. This interest was also assigned. The fact that the option was not exercised in 1945, when it could have been, is irrelevant so far as concerns the existence of the reversionary interest. We think that the rights retained by plaintiff and assigned to his wife and children were sufficiently substantial to justify the view that they were given income-producing property.

In addition to Judge Anderson's ground of decision appellee advances a further argument, namely, that the plaintiff retained sufficient control over the invention and the royalties to make it reasonable to treat him as owner of that income for tax purposes. *Commissioner v. Sunnen*, 333 U.S. 591 (1948). There a patent was licensed under a royalty contract with a corporation in which the taxpayer-inventor held 89% of the stock. An assignment of the royalty contract to the taxpayer's wife was held ineffective to shift the tax, since the taxpayer retained control over the royalty payments to his wife by virtue of his control of the corporation, which could cancel the contract at any time. The argument is that, although plaintiff himself owned only 1% of The Heim Company stock, his wife and daughter together owned 68% and it is reasonable to infer from depositions introduced by the Commissioner that they would follow the plaintiff's advice. Judge Anderson did not find it necessary to pass on this contention. But we are satisfied that the record would not support a finding that plaintiff controlled the corporation whose active heads were the son and son-in-law. No inference can reasonably be drawn that the daughter would be likely to follow her father's advice rather than her husband's or brother's with respect to action by the corporation.

COMMISSIONER v. BANKS
543 U.S. 426 (2005)

The question in these consolidated cases is whether the portion of a money judgment or settlement paid to a plaintiff's attorney under a contingent-fee agreement is income to the plaintiff.

We hold that, as a general rule, when a litigant's recovery constitutes income, the litigant's income includes the portion of the recovery paid to the attorney as a contingent fee.

To clarify why the issue here is of any consequence for tax purposes, two preliminary observations are useful. The first concerns the general issue of deductibility. For the tax years in question the legal expenses in these cases could have been taken as miscellaneous itemized deductions subject to the ordinary requirements, but doing so would have been of no help to respondents because of the operation of the Alternative Minimum Tax (AMT). Alternative minimum taxable income, unlike ordinary gross income, does not allow any miscellaneous itemized deductions.

Second, after these cases arose Congress [added] § 62(a)(19) [now § 62(a)(20)]. The amendment allows a taxpayer, in computing adjusted gross income, to deduct "attorney fees and court costs paid by, or on behalf of, the taxpayer in connection with any action involving a claim of unlawful discrimination." These deductions are permissible even when the AMT applies. Had the Act been in force for the transactions now under review, these cases likely would not have arisen. The Act is not retroactive, however, so while it may cover future taxpayers in respondents' position, it does not pertain here.

The Internal Revenue Code defines "gross income" for federal tax purposes as "all income from whatever source derived." The definition extends broadly to all economic gains not otherwise exempted. A taxpayer cannot exclude an economic gain from gross income by assigning the gain in advance to another party. *Lucas v. Earl*, 281 U.S. 111 (1930); *Commissioner v. Sunnen*, 333 U.S. 591 (1948); *Helvering v. Horst*, 311 U.S. 112 (1940). The rationale for the so-called anticipatory assignment of income doctrine is the principle that gains should be taxed "to those who earned them," a maxim we have called "the first principle of income taxation." The anticipatory assignment doctrine is meant to prevent taxpayers from avoiding taxation through "arrangements and contracts however skillfully devised to prevent [income] when paid from vesting even for a second in the man who earned it." The rule is preventative and motivated by administrative as well as substantive concerns, so we do not inquire whether any particular assignment has a discernible tax avoidance purpose. As *Lucas* explained, "no distinction can be taken according to the motives leading to the arrangement by which the fruits are attributed to a different tree from that on which they grew."

Respondents argue that the anticipatory assignment doctrine is a judge-made antifraud rule with no relevance to contingent-fee contracts of the sort at issue here. The Commissioner maintains that a contingent-fee agreement should be viewed as an anticipatory assignment to the attorney of a portion of the client's income from any litigation recovery. We agree with the Commissioner.

In an ordinary case attribution of income is resolved by asking whether a taxpayer exercises complete dominion over the income in question. In the context of anticipatory assignments, however, the assignor often does not have dominion over the income at the moment of receipt. In that instance the question becomes whether the assignor retains dominion over the income-generating asset, because the taxpayer "who owns or controls the source of the income, also controls the disposition of that which he could have received himself and diverts the payment from himself to others as the means of procuring the satisfaction of his wants." Looking to control over the income-generating asset, then, preserves the principle that income should be taxed to the party who earns the income and enjoys the consequent benefits.

In the case of a litigation recovery the income-generating asset is the cause of action that derives from the plaintiff's legal injury. The plaintiff retains dominion over this asset throughout the litigation. We do not understand respondents to argue otherwise. Rather, respondents advance two counterarguments. First, they say that, in contrast to the bond coupons assigned in *Horst*, the value of a legal claim is speculative at the moment of assignment, and may be worth nothing at all. Second, respondents insist that the claimant's legal injury is not the only source of the ultimate recovery. The attorney, according to respondents, also contributes income-generating assets-effort and expertise-without which the claimant likely could not prevail. On these premises respondents urge us to treat a contingent-fee agreement as establishing, for tax purposes, something like a joint venture or partnership in which the client and attorney combine their respective assets—the client's claim and the attorney's skill—and apportion any resulting profits.

We reject respondents' arguments. Though the value of the plaintiff's claim may be speculative at the moment the fee agreement is signed, the anticipatory assignment doctrine is not limited to instances when the precise dollar value of the assigned income is known in advance. Though *Horst* involved an anticipatory assignment of a predetermined sum to be paid on a specific date, the holding in that case did not depend on ascertaining a liquidated amount at the time of assignment. In each of the cases before us, as in *Horst*, the taxpayer retained control over the income-generating asset, diverted some of the income produced to another party, and realized a benefit by doing so.

We further reject the suggestion to treat the attorney-client relationship as a sort of business partnership or joint venture for tax purposes. The relationship between client and attorney, regardless of the variations in particular compensation agreements or the amount of skill and effort the attorney contributes, is a quintessential principal-agent relationship. The client may rely on the attorney's expertise and special skills to achieve a result the client could not achieve alone. That, however, is true of most principal-agent relationships, and it does not alter the fact that the client retains ultimate dominion and control over the underlying claim. The control is evident when it is noted that, although the attorney can make tactical decisions without consulting the client, the plaintiff still must determine whether to settle or proceed to judgment and make, as well, other critical decisions. Even where the attorney exercises independent judgment without supervision by, or consultation with, the client, the attorney, as an agent, is obligated to act solely on behalf of, and for the exclusive benefit of, the client-principal, rather than for the benefit of the attorney or any other party.

The attorney is an agent who is duty-bound to act only in the interests of the principal, and so it is appropriate to treat the full amount of the recovery as income to the principal. In this respect Judge Posner's observation is apt: "[T]he contingent-fee lawyer [is not] a joint owner of his client's claim in the legal sense any more than the commission salesman is a joint owner of his employer's accounts receivable." In both cases a principal relies on an agent to realize an economic gain, and the gain realized by the agent's efforts is income to the principal. The portion paid to the agent may be deductible, but absent some other provision of law it is not excludable from the principal's gross income.

This rule applies whether or not the attorney-client contract or state law confers any special rights or protections on the attorney, so long as these protections do not alter the fundamental principal-agent character of the relationship. State laws vary with respect to the strength of an attorney's security interest in a contingent fee and the remedies available to an attorney should the client discharge or attempt to defraud the attorney. No state laws of which we are aware, however, even those that purport to give attorneys an "ownership" interest in their fees, convert the attorney from an agent to a partner.

Banks' case involves a further consideration. Banks brought his claims under federal statutes that authorize fee awards to prevailing plaintiffs' attorneys. He contends that application of the anticipatory assignment principle would be inconsistent with the purpose of statutory fee-shifting provisions. In the federal system statutory fees are typically awarded by the court under the lodestar approach, and the plaintiff usually has little control over the amount awarded. Sometimes, as when the plaintiff seeks only injunctive relief, or when the statute caps plaintiffs' recoveries, or when for other reasons damages are substantially less than attorney's fees, court-awarded attorney's fees can exceed a plaintiff's monetary recovery. *See, e.g., Riverside v. Rivera*, 477 U.S. 561 (1986) (compensatory and punitive damages of $33,350; attorney's fee award of $245,456.25). Treating the fee award as income to the plaintiff in such cases, it is argued, can lead to the perverse result that the plaintiff loses money by winning the suit. Furthermore, it is urged that treating statutory fee awards as income to plaintiffs would undermine the effectiveness of fee-shifting statutes in deputizing plaintiffs and their lawyers to act as private attorneys general.

We need not address these claims. After Banks settled his case, the fee paid to his attorney was calculated solely on the basis of the private contingent-fee contract. There was no court-ordered fee award, nor was there any indication in Banks' contract with his attorney, or in the settlement agreement with the defendant, that the contingent fee paid to Banks' attorney was in lieu of statutory fees Banks might otherwise have been entitled to recover. Also, the amendment added by the American Jobs Creation Act [Code Section 62(a)(20)] redresses the concern for many, perhaps most, claims governed by fee-shifting statutes.

NOTES

1. *Application of assignment of income principles outside the related-party context.*—The assignment of income doctrine first came into being and was elaborated in cases involving related parties. In *Commissioner v. Sunnen*, 333 U.S. 591, 605 (1948), for example, the Supreme Court stated:

> "It is in the realm of intra-family assignments and transfers that the *Clifford–Horst* line of cases has peculiar applicability. While specifically relating to short-term family trusts, the *Clifford* case makes clear that where the parties to a transfer are members of the same family group special scrutiny is necessary 'lest what is in reality but one economic unit be multiplied into two or more.' That decision ... recognizes that the fact that the parties are intimately related, causing the income to remain within the family group, may make the transfer give rise to informal and indirect benefits to the transferor so as to make it even more clear that it is just to tax him. ... Moreover, the *Horst* case recognizes that the assignor may realize income if he controls the disposition of that which he could have received himself and diverts payment from himself to the assignee as a means of procuring the satisfaction of his wants, the receipt of income by the assignee merely being the fruition of the assignor's economic gain."

Banks did not involve related parties—attorneys generally being compensated by their clients at arm's-length. *Banks* therefore establishes that the assignment of income doctrine is not restricted to such contexts.

2. *The "kiddie tax."*—Code Section 1(g)(1) in effect taxes a child's "unearned income" at the greater of the child's marginal rate and his parent's marginal rate. This rule eliminates the tax bracket advantages of transferring income-producing property from parent to child in cases to which it applies. The rule covers children under age 18; it also covers children 18 or over who meet the age requirements of Code Section 152(c)(3)(A)—that is, are age 18 or are "students" under age 24—whose earned income does not exceed

half of the amount of the child's support. Code Section 1(g)(7) allows the parent of such a child, in certain limited circumstances, to elect to include the child's unearned income directly on his own return.

PROBLEMS FOR DISCUSSION

14–13. The following facts are adapted from *Talley v. United States Dept. of Agriculture*, 595 F.3d 754 (7th Cir. 2010): The Fair Credit Reporting Act requires that lenders report borrowers' payment history accurately to credit agencies. 15 U.S.C. § 1681s–2. Four times, the Department of Agriculture incorrectly reported that Wayne Talley was behind on a loan that had in fact been paid off. Each time, (1) Talley complained to Trans Union, a credit bureau, which asked the Department whether Talley was indeed delinquent, (2) someone at the Department investigated, concluded that the loan had been repaid, and told Trans Union that Talley had satisfied all of his obligations, and (3) Trans Union corrected Talley's credit history. Each time, the following month the Department again told Trans Union that Talley was tardy in repaying an outstanding loan. Talley sued for damage to his credit rating, recovering $10,000 in compensatory damages and $20,000 in attorney fees under 15 U.S.C. § 1681n(a)(3).

a. Are the $20,000 of attorney fees includible in Talley's income?

b. If they are and if Talley's recoveries in the case are taxable at an effective federal and state combined rate of 40%, how much will Talley take home net of taxes as a result of winning the lawsuit?

Subchapter D: Basis of Property Acquired by Gift, Inheritance, or Bequest

SECTION 1: PROPERTY ACQUIRED BY GIFT

(a) BASIC RULES

Code: Section 1015

If donor and donee were treated as purely self-interested individuals, a gift might well constitute a recognition event. The donor would be deemed to have received value of some sort at least equal to the value of the property transferred; after all, an economically rational actor would only make such a transfer if this were so. The cost to the donee would be zero; his basis would therefore be zero as well.

This is not, however, how the Code treats gifts. Donative transfers in which the donor receives no economic value in return are not treated as realization events. In generally, the donee takes the property with carry-over basis—that is, basis equal to the donor's prior basis in the property.

An exception to pure carry-over basis is provided for property in which donor has a built-in loss. Under Code Section 1015(a), the donee's basis equals the lesser of carry-over basis and the property's fair market value at the time of the gift. This solves a relative indifference problem;

donors might otherwise give properties with built-in losses to related parties who can use those losses.

Finally, Congress has provided a further adjustment to donee's basis equal to the portion of any gift tax paid properly allocable to any built-in gain on the property at the time of the gift.

PROBLEMS FOR DISCUSSION

14–14. Albert owns property with a fair market value of $100,000 and a basis of $30,000. He gifts the property to his son Bob, incurring a gift tax of $10,000 on the transfer. What is Bob's basis in the property?

14–15. Albert owns property with a fair market value of $100,000 and a basis of $170,000. He gifts the property to his son Bob, incurring a gift tax of $10,000 on the transfer. What is Bob's basis in the property?

(b) PART GIFT/PART SALE TRANSACTIONS

Regulations: Section 1.1015–4

PROBLEMS FOR DISCUSSION

14–16. Albert owns property with a fair market value of $100,000 and a basis of $30,000. He sells the property to his son Bob for $50,000, incurring no gift tax on the transfer. What is Bob's basis in the property?

14–17. Albert owns property with a fair market value of $100,000 and a basis of $50,000. He sells the property to his son Bob for $30,000, incurring no gift tax on the transfer. What is Bob's basis in the property?

14–18. Albert owns property with a fair market value of $100,000 and a basis of $170,000. He sells the property to his son Bob for $70,000, incurring no gift tax on the transfer. What is Bob's basis in the property?

SECTION 2: PROPERTY ACQUIRED BY INHERITANCE OR BEQUEST

(a) BASIC RULES

Code: Section 1014(a)

In general, property acquired by inheritance or bequest is received with a basis equal to the property's fair market value on the date of decedent's death. The effect of this extraordinarily generous rule is to wash all built-in gain or loss out of property when its owner dies, without ever taxing that built-in gain or allowing that built-in loss. Assume, for example, that Bill Gates has a negligible basis in his Microsoft stock, which is currently worth in excess of $60 billion. Upon his death, all of his built-in gain will disappear without ever having been taxed. His beneficiaries will take the stock with a basis equal to its fair market value on the date of his death.

This "stepped-up basis" rule is generally justified on administrative grounds: it is often extremely burdensome, if not impossible, for beneficiaries to determine decedent's basis in inherited property.

For this reason, however, the estate tax is sometimes viewed as backing-up the income tax. When Bill Gates dies, although his built-in gain will never be subject to income tax, some portion of his estate may be subject to estate tax. When Congress temporarily repealed the estate tax for decedents dying in 2010, therefore, it substantially limited application of the stepped-up basis rule to property in such estates. *See* Nancy M. Annick, *Plugging the "Gaping Loophole" of the Step–Up in Basis at Death: A Proposal to Apply Carryover Basis to Excess Property*, 8 PITT. TAX REV. 75 (2011). If Congress were to repeal the estate tax again, as some have urged, it would presumably feel some pressure to impose some form of carry-over basis regime on property acquired by bequest or inheritance.

PROBLEMS FOR DISCUSSION

14–19. Albert owns property with a fair market value of $100,000 and a basis of $30,000. He is terminally ill and trying to put his affairs in order. Should he keep the property or sell it?

14–20. Albert owns property with a fair market value of $100,000 and a basis of $170,000. He is terminally ill and trying put his affairs in order. Should he keep the property or sell it?

(b) CODE SECTION 1014(e)

We know that stepped-up basis at death without recognition of gain incorrectly measures income. In most circumstances, this is not a convenient avoidance technique, because taxpayer has to die to take advantage of it.

But there is one situation in which Congress worries about the use of the stepped-up basis rules for tax avoidance purposes. A member of taxpayer's family is about to die. Taxpayer owns property on which he has a large built-in gain. He gives the property to his dying relative. The relative takes the gift with carryover basis; no gain is recognized on the gift. The relative then dies, bequeathing the property back to taxpayer. In the absence of special rules, taxpayer receives the property with stepped-up basis. No one has ever had to pay any tax on the built-in gain.

Code Section 1014(e) deals with this possibility mechanically. If taxpayer gives appreciated property to the decedent and taxpayer (or his spouse) acquires it from decedent upon decedent's death, all within the space of one year, taxpayer (or his spouse) takes the property with carryover, not stepped-up, basis.

PROBLEMS FOR DISCUSSION

14–21. Albert owns property with a fair market value of $100,000 and a basis of $30,000. His father is terminally ill. Albert proposes to gift the property to his father, incurring a gift tax of $10,000 on the transfer. His father will then bequeath the property back to him in his will.

a. What are the federal income tax consequences?

b. What if Albert's father bequeaths the property to Albert's wife instead?

c. What if Albert's father bequeaths the property to Albert's child instead?

PART 5

BUSINESS OR INVESTMENT VS. PERSONAL EXPENDITURES

■ ■ ■

Haig–Simons suggests that the costs of producing income should be deductible, but that personal expenditures should not. In Chapter 4, we explored how this distinction is implemented in the interest deductibility context. This Part 5 explores how it is implemented in the Code more generally.

Chapter 15

Costs of Producing Income

■ ■ ■

Subchapter A: Categories and Their Consequences

SECTION 1: IN GENERAL

Code: Sections 162(a), 212, 183

Regulations: Section 1.183–2

The Code breaks the costs of producing income into three categories: trade or business expenses (Code Section 162), nonbusiness expenses for the production of income (Code Section 212), and expenses of activities not engaged in for profit (Code Section 183). It further divides the first category—trade or business expenses—into two subcategories: trade or business expenses of being an employee, and all other trade or business expenses. This Section 1 summarizes the consequences of these distinctions. The remainder of this Subchapter explores how these distinctions are drawn.

(a) EXPENSES OF A TRADE OR BUSINESS (OTHER THAN THE TRADE OR BUSINESS OF BEING AN EMPLOYEE)

Trade or business expenses other than expenses incurred in the trade or business of being an employee are treated most generously:

• They are deductible above-the-line, reduce adjusted gross income, and are deductible for AMT purposes. Code Section 62(a)(1).

• Interest on trade or business debt (other than the trade or business of being an employee) is deductible. Code Section 163(a) and (h)(2)(A).

• Business bad debts are deductible as ordinary losses whenever such debts become partially or wholly worthless. Code Section 166(a).

• Depreciable assets used in a trade or business are generally eligible for accelerated cost recovery under Code Section 168, bonus depreciation under Code Section 168(k), and small business expensing under Code Section 179.

- If acquisition indebtedness on underwater real property (*e.g.*, where the mortgage exceeds the fair market value) used in a trade or business is discharged to bring the principal balance of the debt down to fair market value, the discharge may be excluded under Code Section 108(a)(1)(D) and (c).

- Individuals engaged in a trade or business may be eligible to deduct costs related to space in their home used for business purposes under Code Section 280A(c).

- If a taxpayer engaged in a trade or business runs a net operating loss ("NOL") in a particular taxable year, taxpayer may carry that NOL back two years and forward 20 and apply it against income in those other years. Code Section 172.

There are a few contexts in which characterization of a taxpayer as engaged in a trade or business may not be advantageous.

- A self-employed individual engaged in a trade or business is subject to a flat 15.3 percent self-employment tax on net earnings from self-employment. Code Sections 1401–1402. *See* Chapter 1A, Design Considerations, above.

- For income tax purposes, she is then entitled to a deduction of half of her self-employment taxes paid. Code Section 164(f).

- Foreign corporations and nonresident alien individuals are taxed on their taxable income effectively connected with a U.S. trade or business, regardless of its source. Code Sections 871(b) and 882(a).

(b) EMPLOYEE TRADE OR BUSINESS EXPENSES

Being an employee is a trade or business for federal tax purposes. Expenses incurred in the course of such a business, however, are less favorably treated:

- In general, such expenses are deductible below-the-line, do not reduce adjusted gross income, and only reduce taxable income to the extent that, together with other itemized deductions, they exceed the standard deduction.*

- With few exceptions, employee business expenses are subject to the 2–percent floor of Code Section 67 and the overall limitation on itemized deductions of Code Section 68.

- If subject to the 2–percent floor, employee business expenses are nondeductible for AMT purposes.

- Interest paid or incurred on debt allocable to the trade or business of being an employee is treated as personal and nondeductible. Code Section 163(h)(2)(A).

---

* Exceptions to this rule are provided for reimbursed expenses, expenses of qualified performing artists, expenses of state officials compensated on a fee basis, and limited expenses incurred by elementary and secondary teachers for books, supplies, computer equipment, and other supplementary classroom materials. Code Section 62(a)(2).

- In theory, an employee's loss on a business bad debt is eligible for ordinary loss treatment like any other business bad debt, but in practice an employee's bad debts are rarely found to be business debts. *See, e.g., United States v. Generes*, 405 U.S. 93 (1972) (dominant motivation of taxpayer was to protect stock holdings, not employment).

(c) EXPENSES OF NON–BUSINESS ACTIVITIES ENGAGED IN FOR PROFIT

Expenses of individuals engaged in activities for profit that do not rise the level of a trade or business—most importantly, investment expenses— are deductible under Code Section 212, not Code Section 162.

- Deductions attributable to property held for the production of rents or royalties and losses from the sale or exchange from property are taken above-the-line (*e.g.*, not itemized). Code Section 62(a)(3) and (4). In general, however, Code Section 212 expenses are deductible below-the-line, do not reduce adjusted gross income, and only reduce taxable income to the extent that, together with other itemized deductions, they exceed the standard deduction.

- Except for investment interest, taxes, and casualty or theft losses, itemized Code Section 212 expenses are subject to the 2–percent floor of Code Section 67.

- If subject to the 2–percent floor, they are nondeductible for AMT purposes.

- Except for investment interest, itemized Code Section 212 expenses are subject to the overall limitation on itemized deductions of Code Section 68.

- There is no general allowance for interest paid or incurred on debt allocable to for-profit activities; interest on debt allocable to property held for investment is deductible, but only subject to the investment interest limitations of Code Section 163(d).

- Investment bad debts are treated as nonbusiness bad debts; a loss on such a debt is treated as a short-term capital loss in the year in which the debt becomes wholly worthless. Code Section 166(d).

- Depreciable assets held for the production of income but not used in a trade or business are generally eligible for accelerated cost recovery under Code Section 168 and bonus depreciation under Code Section 168(k), but not for small business expensing under Code Section 179.

- No deduction is allowed under Code Section 212 for expenses allocable to a convention, seminar, or similar meeting. Code Section 274(h)(7).

- In computing a noncorporate taxpayer's net operating loss for carryover purposes, nonbusiness deductions are allowed only to the extent of nonbusiness income. Code Section 172(d)(4). In effect, therefore, a noncorporate taxpayer's excess Code Section 212 deductions are lost if not used in the year incurred.

(d) EXPENSES OF ACTIVITIES NOT ENGAGED IN FOR PROFIT

In general, the costs of activities not engaged in for profit are personal and nondeductible. Sometimes, however, an activity not engaged in for profit produces gross income nonetheless. We therefore need rules telling us what to do with the costs of the activity in this circumstance. Code Section 183(b) and Treas. Reg. § 1.183–1(b)(1) divide the costs of an activity not engaged in for profit into three categories: (1) costs deductible without regard to whether the activity was engaged in for profit, like home mortgage interest and property taxes, (2) costs, other than costs that result in basis adjustments, that would be allowed if the activity were engaged in for profit, and (3) costs that result in basis adjustments, like depreciation. Category 1 costs are deductible in any event; Category 2 costs are only deductible to the extent income from the activity exceeds Category 1 costs; and Category 3 costs are deductible to the extent income from the activity exceeds costs in Categories 1 and 2.

PROBLEMS FOR DISCUSSION

15–1. Abby and Barb are licensed plumbers. Abby operates a plumbing business as a sole proprietor. Barb performs identical services as an employee of a plumbing company. Each buys and owns her own tools. Each has borrowed to purchase a truck she uses to get from job to job; each pays all of the expenses of operating her truck; their trucks are used solely for business purposes. How are their respective costs of doing business treated for federal income tax purposes?

15–2. Carl and Daniel both buy, hold, and sell real estate for a profit. Some of their properties are rental properties; some are held for appreciation. Some of their properties are purchased subject to mortgages. Each employs one employee to assist in his real estate activities. Carl's activities are such that he is found to be engaged in the trade or business of buying, holding, and selling real estate. Daniel's are not. How are the costs incurred in connection with their real estate activities treated for federal income tax purposes?

15–3. Liz, a movie actress, owns a working horse ranch about two hours drive from Los Angeles. She hires a manager to run the ranch's business operations and retreats to the ranch between movie shoots to get out of the public eye. The ranch loses money every year, as Liz expected it would when she bought it. Nevertheless, its business revenues cover some of its costs, and Liz very much enjoys the hours she spends riding and relaxing there. In its most recent year, the ranch recorded the following income and expenses from operations:

Stud fees and gains from sales	$200,000
Salaries	($120,000)
Property taxes	($20,000)
Depreciation	(140,000)

What portion, if any, of the expenses of the ranch are deductible?

SECTION 2: INDEPENDENT CONTRACTOR vs. EMPLOYEE

Independent contractors are engaged in a trade or business other than the trade or business of providing services as an employee; their expenses are therefore not subject to the less favorable treatment accorded employee business expenses. On the other hand, independent contractors must generally pay their own self-employment taxes. As a result, whether an individual taxpayer is properly characterized as an employee or an independent contractor is often in issue. In general, a taxpayer is an employee for income tax purposes if she is an employee under the common law.

SCHRAMM v. COMMISSIONER
T.C. Memo. 2011–212

Petitioner was an adjunct professor at [Nova Southeastern University] during 2006 and taught online courses in economics. From 1999 to 2007 petitioner taught 4 to 12 online courses per year for NSU. NSU and petitioner entered into a separate employment contract with regard to each course that petitioner taught. During 2006 the period of each contract was 6 weeks. As a condition of his employment, NSU required petitioner to follow various employment policies, including a sexual harassment policy, a drug policy, and a conflict of interest policy. NSU paid petitioner a fixed amount for each course that he taught. In 2006 petitioner received $20,000 from NSU.

NSU provided petitioner with a syllabus for each course he taught that specified the material that was to be covered. Petitioner prepared another more detailed syllabus to set forth specifics regarding the class, such as the assignments and examinations. Petitioner established his own work hours and was able to perform his work from any location via a computer with an Internet connection. However, NSU set the course dates, which established the period within which petitioner's classes were to begin and conclude. NSU also supplied the Web site interface that was used for each course petitioner taught and the services necessary to register and enroll students in the courses. Following the completion of a course, petitioner was required to submit to NSU a report that included an evaluation of his students' learning.

NSU issued petitioner a Form W–2, Wage and Tax Statement, relating to his employment with the university during 2006. NSU withheld

Federal income taxes and employment taxes from the wages it paid to petitioner during the 2006 taxable year.

On or about January 3, 2007, petitioner wrote to NSU requesting clarification of his employment status with the university. On January 8, 2007, NSU's payroll manager, Linda Trosper, sent him a letter advising him that NSU classifies all of its adjunct professors, including petitioner, as employees and not as independent contractors.

On their 2006 Federal income tax return, petitioners reported the amounts petitioner received from NSU as business income on Schedule C, Profit or Loss From Business, rather than on line 7 of the return as wages, salaries, tips, etc. In addition, petitioners claimed business expenses on Schedule C totaling $2,785.63, which were related to petitioner's employment with NSU.

An individual performing services as an employee may deduct expenses incurred in the performance of services as an employee as miscellaneous itemized deductions on Schedule A, Itemized Deductions, to the extent the expenses exceed 2 percent of the taxpayer's adjusted gross income. Itemized deductions may be limited under section 68 and may have alternative minimum tax implications under section 56(b)(1)(A)(i).

An individual who performs services as an independent contractor is entitled to deduct expenses incurred in the performance of services on Schedule C and is not subject to limitations imposed on miscellaneous itemized deductions.

Petitioners argue that petitioner was an independent contractor in 2006 and is thereby entitled to deduct business expenses on Schedule C. Respondent contends that petitioner was a common law employee in 2006 and that his unreimbursed employee expenses are thus properly reportable on Schedule A, subject to the 2–percent-of-adjusted-gross-income limitation.

"Although the income tax treatment of a taxpayer's trade or business expense deductions under section 62(a) depends on whether the taxpayer is '[performing] ... services ... as an employee', subtitle A of the Internal Revenue Code does not define 'employee' ". Under these circumstances, we apply common law rules to determine whether the taxpayer is an employee.

Whether an individual is an employee must be determined on the basis of the specific facts and circumstances involved. Relevant factors include: (1) The degree of control exercised by the principal; (2) which party invests in the work facilities used by the worker; (3) the opportunity of the individual for profit or loss; (4) whether the principal can discharge the individual; (5) whether the work is part of the principal's regular business; (6) the permanency of the relationship; (7) the relationship the parties believed they were creating; and (8) the provision of employee benefits. We consider all of the facts and circumstances of each case, and no single factor is determinative.

The degree of control that the principal exercises over the worker has been referred to as the crucial test in making the determination. The degree of control necessary to find employment status varies with the nature of the services provided by the worker. To retain the requisite degree of control, the principal need not actually direct or control the manner in which the services are performed; it is sufficient if the principal has the right to do so. Where the inherent nature of the job mandates an independent approach, a lesser degree of control exercised by the principal may result in a finding of an employer-employee status.

It is clear that the inherent nature of petitioner's position as an adjunct professor calls for him to follow an independent approach in teaching his classes. However, we believe that NSU either exercised appropriate control over petitioner or had the authority to exercise it in a manner sufficient to render him an employee of the university. For each course petitioner taught, NSU dictated the textbook that he was required to use, the subjects that had to be covered, and the duration of the course. In addition, NSU managed the enrollment of students and supplied the Web site interface used to facilitate instruction in online courses. NSU also required petitioner to follow several of its employment policies, including those dealing with sexual harassment, drug use, and conflicts of interest. It is also of great significance that NSU regarded petitioner as an employee rather than as an independent contractor. Although NSU did not supervise the minute details of petitioner's work, we find that it did exercise the requisite degree of control necessary to establish an employer-employee relationship with him. This factor weighs heavily in favor of a finding that petitioner was a common law employee of NSU.

The fact that a worker provides his or her own tools, or owns a vehicle that is used for work, is indicative of independent contractor status. In addition, maintenance of a home office is consistent with independent contractor status, although alone it does not constitute sufficient basis for a finding of independent contractor status.

NSU bears the cost of maintaining a staff for recruitment, registration, and recordkeeping related to students, and it provides the servers and support required to maintain the online classroom. Petitioner's investment is not substantial, consisting of a computer and office supplies, maintenance of an Internet connection, and the use of a portion of his home as an office. Petitioner's investment in facilities was insubstantial and, thus, insufficient to render him an independent contractor. As a result, we find that this factor is supportive of petitioner's classification as a common law employee.

The opportunity for profit or loss indicates nonemployee status. Petitioner lacked significant opportunity for profit or loss because the amount of pay he received depended only upon the number of classes he taught. The amount petitioner received for teaching a course was not subject to fluctuation and was paid to him in exchange for his working within predetermined starting and ending dates, which were not subject to change. The fact that the wages petitioner received were not subject to change and that the duration of the classes was fixed left him with no more than a negligible risk of loss. When a worker's risk of loss is negligible, this factor weighs in favor of a determination of employee status. The greater risk of profit or loss remained with NSU, whose revenue necessarily fluctuated on the basis of the number of students enrolled relative to the costs involved in running a university.

The employment relationship between NSU and petitioner is governed by a separate contract established for each class section he taught. Copies of the employment contracts were not made a part of the record before the Court. Therefore, we cannot determine with certainty whether the contracts provided the university with the express right to terminate petitioner's employment at any time. However, employers typically have the right to terminate employees at will. Furthermore, because the parties entered into a contract for each specific course, NSU could have ended its long-term relationship with petitioner by electing not to renew the contracts for further courses. In addition, petitioner has failed to provide any evidence to indicate that NSU would be liable for breach of contract if it chose to terminate the relationship before the contract expired. As a result, we find that this factor supports the finding that petitioner was a common law employee.

Where work is part of the principal's regular business, it is indicative of employee status. As an educational institution, NSU's regular business involves the education of students and the evaluation of their work. Petitioner was hired to further NSU's regular business, in that he taught specific courses and then evaluated the students' learning in each course. Petitioner's services were clearly an important part of NSU's primary business. Therefore, we find that this factor supports petitioner's classification as a common law employee.

Permanency of a working relationship is indicative of an employer-employee relationship. In contrast, a transitory work relationship may weigh in favor of independent contractor status.

Petitioner was employed by NSU from 1999 to 2007 and taught 4 to 12 online courses per year during that period. Although NSU and petitioner entered into a separate employment contract with regard to each course that petitioner taught, petitioner maintained a consistent employment relationship with NSU over a period of many years. Petitioner and NSU's decision to continually renew petitioner's contract for more courses indicates that a certain level of stability and continuity existed in their employment relationship. Although the contractual arrangement between the parties did not create an explicit permanent employment relationship, the relationship in practice was continuing in nature. Therefore, we find that this factor weighs in favor of petitioner's being classified as an employee. Furthermore, even if we were to determine that this factor supported petitioner's classification as an independent contractor, it alone would not be sufficient to preclude a finding that he was an employee at NSU on the basis of the other factors examined.

The record indicates that petitioner and NSU considered their relationship to be that of an employer and an employee. NSU withheld Federal income taxes and employment taxes from the wages it paid to petitioner. The withholding of taxes is consistent with a finding that an individual is a common law employee. Furthermore, NSU's payroll manager personally informed petitioner that the university classified him as a common law employee, before petitioners filed their Federal income tax return.

Altogether it is clear that the parties believed that they had established an employer-employee relationship. This factor weighs in favor of petitioner's being treated as a common law employee.

Benefits such as health insurance, life insurance, and retirement plans are typically provided to employees by an employer. Petitioner contends that NSU offers such benefits to other categories of workers, but it neither offered nor provided them to petitioner. However, aside from his testimony at trial, petitioner offered no evidence to substantiate his contention. As a result, while we find that this factor supports petitioner's status as an independent contractor, we decline to place much weight on it in making our ultimate determination, on account of the lack of evidence in the record.

On the basis of a careful consideration of the foregoing factors, in the light of the facts and circumstances particular to this case, we hold that petitioner was a common law employee of NSU for the taxable year 2006.

An individual may deduct unreimbursed employee business expenses as miscellaneous itemized deductions on Schedule A, but only to the extent that the expenses exceed 2 percent of the individual's adjusted gross income. Because we have held that petitioner was a common law employee during the 2006 taxable year, petitioners' claimed business expenses of $2,785.63 must be reported on Schedule A as miscellaneous itemized deductions and, thus, are deductible only to the extent that they exceed 2 percent of petitioners' adjusted gross income.

Notes

1. *Payroll tax safe harbor.*—A safe harbor is available for employers who have in good faith misclassified employees as independent contractors for payroll tax purposes. Under Section 530 of the Revenue Act of 1978, P.L. 95-600, a taxpayer may treat a worker as a non-employee for payroll tax purposes, regardless of the individual's actual status under the common law, if the taxpayer's treatment of the worker for tax purposes has been consistent and a reasonable basis exists for such treatment. A reasonable basis exists if the taxpayer reasonably relies on (1) judicial precedent; (2) a past failure of

the IRS to raise such an employment tax issue on audit; or (3) "long-standing recognized practice of a significant segment of the industry in which such individual was engaged." This safe harbor was extended indefinitely by Section 269(c) of the Tax Equity and Fiscal Responsibility Act of 1982, P.L. No. 97–248. For all other tax purposes, the common law governs.

SECTION 3: TRADE OR BUSINESS vs. OTHER FOR–PROFIT ACTIVITY

In general, expenses incurred in a trade or business are given the most favorable tax treatment; deduction of other expenses incurred to generate income are subject to significant limitations and are sometimes effectively not deductible at all, particularly if taxpayer is in an AMT posture. In *Commissioner v. Groetzinger*, 480 U.S. 23 (1987), the Court stated:

> "[N]ot every income-producing and profit-making endeavor constitutes a trade or business. The income tax law, almost from the beginning, has distinguished between a business or trade, on the one hand, and 'transactions entered into for profit but not connected with ... business or trade,' on the other. We accept the fact that to be engaged in a trade or business, the taxpayer must be involved in the activity with continuity and regularity and that the taxpayer's primary purpose for engaging in the activity must be for income or profit. A sporadic activity, a hobby, or an amusement diversion does not qualify."

Specifically, the Court held, "if one's gambling activity is pursued full time, in good faith, and with regularity, to the production of income for a livelihood, and is not a mere hobby, it is a trade or business"; taxpayer's gambling losses were therefore deductible for AMT purposes. Otherwise, the Court concluded, "in the context of a minimum tax, it is not too extreme to say that the taxpayer is being taxed on his gambling losses, a result distinctly out of line with the Code's focus on income."

Groetzinger has been read to require a two-step inquiry. First, we ask whether the activity was engaged in for profit. Second, we ask whether taxpayer's conduct of the activity rises to the level of a trade or business. If the activity was not engaged in for profit, deductions are governed by Code Section 183. If it was engaged in for profit but was mere "sporadic activity" deductions are governed by Code Section 212. If it was engaged in for profit and taxpayer's conduct constituted a trade or business, deductions are governed by Code Section 162.

Although courts often explore whether taxpayer's activity was full-time or sporadic, the resulting inquiry does not fully explain the case law. In *Higgins v. Commissioner*, 312 U.S. 212 (1941), for example, the Court held that managing one's own investments does not constitute a trade or business for federal income tax purposes, "[n]o matter how large the estate or how continuous or extended the work required may be," even if doing so requires offices and staffs in two cities. *See also* Code Section 864(b)(2) (codifying *Higgins* with regard to foreign taxpayers). On the other, cases in which sporadic non-investment activities are treated as Code Section 212 activities are rare; courts unwilling to find a trade or business in such circumstances often hold instead that taxpayer's activity was not profit-motivated. *See, e.g., Lopez v. Commissioner*, 116 Fed.Appx. 546 (5th Cir. 2004) (Amway distribution activities not engaged in for profit); *Cheh v. Commissioner*, T.C. Memo. 1992–658 (translating materials on nuclear mathematics from Korean into English for the CIA not engaged in for profit).

In practice, Code Section 212 therefore applies primarily to two types of income-generating activity: (1) investments and (2) lawsuits recoveries on which are treated as taxable but not business-related.

One further odd aspect of Code Section 212 merits note: it only authorizes deductions by individuals. Read strictly, therefore, the Code does not authorize corporations to deduct the expenses of profit-motivated activities unless they are incurred in a trade or business. *Higgins*, in particular, suggests that the expenses of managing investments for the corporation's own account should not be deductible. The IRS, however, has never applied *Higgins* against corporate taxpayers.

SNYDER v. UNITED STATES

674 F.2d 1359 (10th Cir. 1982)

Taxpayer, a practicing attorney, testified that he began work on a book of photographs of the Colorado high country in 1972. He expected to publish and sell the finished product. His photographic activities changed markedly as he pursued his book project. Prior to 1972, such activities consisted primarily of taking family snapshots with modest equipment that was inappropriate for a commercial enterprise. In order to produce commercial quality photographs for the book, taxpayer acquired sophisticated large format photographic equipment. He began to devote approximately 30 hours a week to taking pictures. The number of rolls of film taxpayer shot increased from about five or six rolls in 1971 to about 200 rolls in 1972. He also began to keep detailed records of technical data regarding his photographs.

After a year's work, taxpayer had accumulated approximately 3,000 slides and began to send letters to publishers soliciting their interest in his book. He received replies from six or eight publishers who expressed interest, and he traveled to New York to discuss the book with some of them. He testified that the only purpose for his trip to New York was to promote publication of his book. He also traveled to San Francisco, at the expense of Scribners & Sons, to discuss the book with an editor for the Sierra Club. Taxpayer was encouraged by the publishers he met, but none of them offered to buy or publish his book.

The IRS concluded that taxpayers' deductions attributable to the photography book were not allowable under either section 162 or section

212. Accordingly, the IRS found that additional taxes and other amounts of $6,913.41 were due for the years 1972 and 1973. Taxpayer paid that amount, filed a claim for refund, and timely sued to recover the amount paid.

At trial, the district court concluded that taxpayer was not engaged in the "trade or business" of producing a book. The court held that taxpayer's claimed expenses were not appropriate deductions under section 162 or 212 and "at best" the expenses might be capitalized under section 212.

The trial court stated in its oral findings that the taxpayer had "sincere hopes" of selling his photography book to many people, and "does hope to make a profit." Notwithstanding these factual findings of taxpayer's profit motive, the trial court reached the conclusion that the taxpayer was not engaged in the "trade or business" of writing a book, but was trying to produce a literary capital asset.

No citation to any source was provided for these conclusions, and underlying facts other than profit motive were not elaborated upon. This poses a problem for us because the general test for whether a person is engaged in a "trade or business" under section 162 has variously been stated to be "whether the business was undertaken 'in good faith for the purpose of making a profit,'" or whether the taxpayer's primary purpose and intention in engaging in the activity is to make a profit.

The IRS argued below and in this court that an author cannot be in the trade or business of writing if he has not yet produced a book, and it appears from the trial judge's comments during trial that he may have accepted this assertion. If so, the trial judge made his decision based on an erroneous legal conclusion. We find no support for this contention and believe, as a policy matter, that such a position would have an unwarranted and undesirable chilling effect on budding authors who are serious in pursuing a writing career. Section 162 does not require such a result.

The IRS also emphasizes that taxpayer in this case spends 40 hours per week as a lawyer. But he also spent 30 hours a week working on his book in the tax years in question, and we have recognized "the indisputable legal premise that the (taxpayer) . . . might be engaged in carrying on a number of trades or businesses."

The profit motive of the taxpayer is "only significant (under section 162) insofar as it affords a means of distinguishing between an enterprise carried on in good faith as a 'trade or business' and an enterprise merely carried on as a hobby." A taxpayer is clearly not engaged in a trade or business if his predominant purpose is recreation or a hobby. On the other hand, an author may be in a trade or business within the meaning of section 162 if he "participated in that endeavor with a good faith expectation of making a profit."

Even where the taxpayer engages in the activity primarily for profit, such activity does not automatically constitute a "trade or business" under section 162:

"(t)he phrase 'trade or business' (as used in the Tax Code) connotes something more than an act or course of activity engaged in for profit. ... The phrase ... must refer not merely to Acts engaged in for profit, but to extensive activity over a substantial period of time during which the Taxpayer holds himself out as selling goods or services. A taxpayer can show that his activities are a 'business' by demonstrating that he devotes a substantial portion of his time to the activities or that there has been extensive or repeated activity over a substantial period of time."

On remand, if the trial court finds taxpayer was primarily motivated by profit, the court must then determine whether taxpayer devoted sufficient time over a substantial enough period to be in a trade or business under section 162. If the trial court finds that taxpayer was not engaged in a trade or business in the relevant years, it must then determine whether the expenses were deductible under section 212 as ordinary and necessary expenses for the production of income.

NOTES

1. *"Trade or business" in the Supreme Court.*—In *Snyder v. Commissioner*, 295 U.S. 134 (1935), the Court held that an investor had not shown that he "might properly be characterized as a 'trader on an exchange who makes a living in buying and selling securities' "—someone we might today call a day-trader—and therefore entitled to deduct trade or business expenses. In *Deputy v. Du Pont*, 308 U.S. 488 (1940), the Court assumed *arguendo* that taxpayer's activities in conserving and enhancing his estate constituted a trade or business, but disallowed claimed deductions because they were not "ordinary" or "necessary." Justice Frankfurter, concurring, opined that " 'carrying on any trade or business,' involves holding one's self out to others as engaged in the selling of goods or services." In *Higgins v. Commissioner*, 312 U.S. 212 (1941), the Court held that taxpayer's management of his own securities, held for investment, did not constitute a trade or business, even if it required offices and staff. At the time, no equivalent to Code Section 212 existed. The IRS disallowed deduction of the portion of the costs of the offices and staff properly allocable to such management, and the Court upheld the disallowance. Congress immediately overturned the *Higgins* result by enacting the predecessor to Code Section 212. Reviewing this history in *Commissioner v. Groetzinger*, 480 U.S. 23 (1987), the Court stated, "Surely, one who clearly satisfies the Frankfurter adumbration usually is in a trade or business," but concluded that holding one's self out as engaged in the selling of goods or services was not necessary.

2. *Tax-related expenses.*—Code Section 212(3) permits deduction of ordinary and necessary expenses paid or incurred "in connection with the determination, collection, or refund of any tax," whether federal, state, local, or foreign. Treas. Reg. § 1.212–1(*l*) elaborates: "Thus, expenses paid or incurred by a taxpayer for tax counsel or expenses paid or incurred in

connection with the preparation of his tax returns or in connection with any proceedings involved in determining the extent of tax liability or in contesting his tax liability are deductible." In practice, this means that lawyers should always bill their clients separately for matters covered by Code Section 212(3) to facilitate deduction of the resulting fees.

SECTION 4: FOR-PROFIT vs. NOT-FOR-PROFIT ACTIVITIES

Regulations: Section 1.183–2(b)

Code Section 183 is both technically unnecessary and commonly invoked. Even prior to its enactment, the law was clear that in the case of an activity not engaged in for profit, costs of such activity could only be deducted to the extent of income from such activity. In *Portland Golf Club v. Commissioner*, 497 U.S. 154 (1990), for example, the Supreme Court invoked prior law to prevent a nonprofit social club (not subject to Code Section 183) from deducting its losses from nonmember sales against investment income.

Nevertheless, both Code Section 183 and the regulations issued thereunder—in particular Treas. Reg. § 1.183–2(b)—have had a major impact on how courts analyze whether costs purported to have been incurred for the purpose of producing income should be treated. No one case fairly represents the diversity of contexts in which this issue arises. Three are therefore excerpted below. *Keating* explores whether a purported trade or business (horse breeding and boarding) should be treated as a trade or business, *Kuznet* whether a purported investment (a residence on Tahiti) should be treated as an investment, and *Krause* whether net losses from a tax shelter should be treated as having been incurred in a for-profit activity.

KEATING v. COMMISSIONER

544 F.3d 900 (8th Cir. 2008)

In 1996 Nora Keating moved to Williston, North Dakota, where she began work as an emergency room physician and purchased a home on a 10 acre farm. She worked approximately 60 hours per week, preferring two 24 hour shifts and one 12 hour shift because she felt "burned out" from medical school and because it allowed her more full days with her six children. Her average annual salary was $238,134. Her husband at the time, Richard Shearer, worked as a firefighter medic.

Also in 1996, Keating realized a lifelong dream of working with horses when she purchased four Arabians, which she considers the "ballerinas of the horse world." She had always loved horses and had experience owning, caring for, and riding them dating back to high school when she worked in a veterinary clinic, belonged to several riding clubs, and purchased and boarded her first horse at age 15.

When Keating purchased the Arabians in 1996 she spoke with an award winning Arabian horse breeder, two horse trainers, and a veterinarian about training methods, breeding, selection of stallions and mares, and veterinary issues including factors that could result in early termination of pregnancy. She also spoke with people who had been audited for their horse activities; they recommended that she keep good expense records and all receipts. She consulted a certified public accountant regarding tracking receipts and maintaining records.

Although Keating had extensive experience caring for and riding horses, she had no experience in the business of buying, selling, or showing horses, and she presented no evidence at trial that she had consulted anyone regarding the economic or business aspects of breeding, training, or showing horses. Between 1996 and 2002 Keating purchased 13 horses and bred 7, but she sold only 2 horses, each for half of its purchase price.

Keating did not change her work schedule after purchasing the Arabians, but on each day off she spent approximately 7 to 10 hours with the horses. She engaged in their training and feeding, and she also rode them, cleaned their stalls, performed basic veterinary work, and competed in shows. Before a showing she would hire a professional trainer to finish training the horses. Keating and her daughter rode in many shows which gave her great pride, and on four occasions her horses participated in nationally competitive horse shows.

In 2000 Keating built a barn to shelter the horses during the breeding months. In 2001 she began boarding other people's horses, leasing out her own horses, and providing horse clinics, but she did not advertise the boarding and leasing services. She advertised that her horses were for sale by word of mouth, by showing them, and by advertising on three websites; she did not advertise in any written publication.

Between 1996 and 2001, Keating paid both personal and horse activity expenses from the same two or three personal checking accounts. In 2002 she opened a checking account in the name of Nora Ellen Keating Stony Creek Arabians (Stony Creek Arabians) and two new personal checking accounts, but she continued to pay personal and horse activity expenses from all three accounts. For example, she deposited the proceeds from the 2002 sales of the two horses in one of her personal accounts, not the Stony Creek Arabians account. She kept a ledger of total horse activity expenses, retained receipts by month of transaction, and kept records of training, ovulatory cycles, and vaccinations relating to each horse. She did not, however, keep expense records for each individual horse. She had no written business plan and no financial projections relating to her horse activity.

Keating and Shearer filed joint federal income tax returns for 1996 through 2000 and Keating filed individual federal income tax returns for 2001 and 2002, each of which listed "horses" as the principal activity on Form 1040 Schedule F, "Profit or Loss from Farming." The following gross income, expense, and net loss amounts attributable to the horse activity were included on Schedule F:

Year	Gross Income	Expenses	Net Loss
1996	$144	$22,227	$(22,083)
1997	178	22,187	(22,009)
1998	335	48,289	(47,954)
1999	432	44,784	(44,352)
2000	750	50,550	(49,800)
2001	1,200	84,382	(83,182)
2002	1,418	102,550	(101,132)

Keating argues that her horse activity was engaged in for profit. As evidence she cites the facts that she kept good records, spent most of her time outside of work with the horses, and invested her savings, earnings, and retirement funds in the horses with the expectation that they would provide income for her retirement.

An activity is engaged in for profit if the taxpayer has an actual, honest profit objective, even if it is unreasonable or unrealistic. Treasury Regulation § 1.183–2(b) includes a nonexhaustive list of nine factors to consider in determining whether a business is engaged in for profit: (1) the manner in which the taxpayer carries on the activity; (2) the expertise of the taxpayer or her advisors; (3) the time and effort expended by the taxpayer in carrying on the activity; (4) the expectation that assets used in the activity may appreciate in value; (5) the success of the taxpayer in carrying on other similar or dissimilar activities; (6) the taxpayer's history of income or losses in respect to the activity; (7) the amount of occasional profits, if any, which are earned; (8) the financial status of the taxpayer; and (9) any elements of personal pleasure or recreation. No single factor or even a majority of the factors is controlling, and all of the facts and circumstances must be evaluated, giving greater weight to objective facts than to the taxpayer's statement of intent.

The tax court thoroughly analyzed the facts and circumstances of Keating's horse activity as they related to each of the nine factors in Treasury Regulation § 1.183–2(b). It found that five of the factors favored the Commissioner's conclusion that the horse activity was not carried on for profit, four factors were neutral, and none favored Keating's argument that she engaged in the horse activity for profit.

The tax court concluded that the first factor—whether the activity is carried on in a businesslike manner and whether complete and accurate books and records are maintained—favored the Commissioner's finding of liability. It found that she had not carried on the horse breeding activity in a businesslike manner. She commingled her personal and horse funds in her various bank accounts even after opening the Stony Creek Arabians account, made meager efforts at advertising, made relatively small improvements to the grounds and operations, and had no written business plan. It also found that although her books and records were thorough in respect to each horse's vaccinations and ovulatory cycles, her failure to keep track of expenses on a per horse basis and to prepare any financial projections to assess the economics of the activity indicated a lack of profit objective. *See Filios v. Comm'r*, 224 F.3d 16, 23 (1st Cir. 2000) (to indicate profit motive, records generally should assist in cutting expenses, increasing profits, making financial projections, and evaluating overall performance of business). It also found that the books and records were kept by Keating only to "memorialize for tax purposes the existence of the subject transactions."

The tax court found that the second factor—the taxpayer's expertise and preparation with regard to the economic aspects of the business—favored the Commissioner's determination. It said that although Keating consulted with breeders and horse experts regarding breeding and training, she was not an expert and did not seek expert advice regarding the economic aspects of the horse business. *Burger v. Comm'r*, 809 F.2d 355, 359 (7th Cir.1987) (mechanics and economics of activity are separate areas of expertise, and failure to obtain expertise in economics of activity may indicate lack of profit objective). It found that she discussed tracking receipts with a CPA only for tax purposes.

The tax court found that the fourth factor—the expectation that assets used in the activity may appreciate in value—favored the Commissioner's determination because Keating presented no evidence of the value of the horses, making it impossible to determine their current or expected future value. The only two horses Keating sold between 1996 and 2002 were sold for less than half of their purchase price, suggesting that any expectation of appreciation may have been unreasonable.

The tax court concluded that the eighth factor—the financial status of the taxpayer—favored the Commissioner's determination because Keating had a high salary from her work as a physician and had $133,763 in claimed tax savings from the horse activity over seven years. *See* Treas. Reg. § 1.183–2(b)(8) (substantial income from sources other than activity in question may indicate activity not carried on for profit, especially where losses generate substantial tax benefits).

The tax court concluded that the ninth factor—elements of personal pleasure or recreation—favored the Commissioner's determination because the recreational aspects of Keating's horse activity and the fact that her daughter rode recreationally suggest an activity without a profit objective. *See Montagne v. Comm'r*, T.C. Memo. 2004–252 (concession that family enjoyed riding and competing with horses showed lack of profit objective), *aff'd*, 166 Fed.Appx. 265 (8th Cir.2006).

Keating argues that the tax court erred because two of the four factors which it found neutral—factors six and seven regarding the history of income or losses and any occasional profits—favored Keating's position that she engaged in the horse activity for profit. The tax court concluded that these factors were neutral because although Keating had consistent and increasing losses over the seven years at issue, a horse business may have a five to ten year startup phase during which the taxpayer may incur losses before turning a profit. Because Keating's horse activity incurred consistent and increasing losses, however, it was not clear error for the tax court to find these factors neutral rather than in favor of Keating's position.

The tax court did not err in concluding that based on all of the facts and circumstances, including an analysis of the nine factors in Treasury Regulation § 1.183–1(b)(2), a preponderance of the evidence supported the Commissioner's determination that Keating's horse activity was not engaged in for profit.

Problems for Discussion

15–4. What could Keating have done differently that might have changed the result in her case?

KURZET v. COMMISSIONER
222 F.3d 830 (10th Cir. 2000)

[The facts as found by the Tax Court were as follows: In 1984, petitioners Stanley and Anne Kurzet purchased 5.5 acres of oceanfront property on the main island of Tahiti for $1.1 million. On the Tahiti property during the years in issue, petitioners remodeled and renovated a house, installed a solar water heating system, a spa, a culinary water system, and underground utilities, dredged a boat channel, added a satellite TV system, converted the electrical power system to 110 volts, installed a diesel power generator as an alternate source of electricity, and made many other significant improvements.

Petitioner personally designed and worked on many of the projects undertaken at the Tahiti property. Petitioner hired an individual to provide security for the property and to manage and pay repairmen and workmen hired to work on the property.

Generally, twice a year, petitioners traveled from California or Utah to the Tahiti property. Typically, on each trip, petitioners would stay at the Tahiti property for a number of weeks.

Petitioners allege that from 1984 through 1994 their cumulative cash expenditures relating to purchase and improvements undertaken on the Tahiti property totaled $1,760,000.]

Section 212(2) of the Internal Revenue Code provides that an individual may deduct all the ordinary and necessary expenses paid or incurred during the taxable year for the "management, conservation, or maintenance of property held for the production of income." The Kurzets allege that the trial court erred in finding that the Tahiti property was not held for the production of income and that their expenses relating to the Tahiti property were therefore not deductible.

In denying deductions for the Kurzets' Tahiti property, the tax court found that the property "has inherently associated with it extensive recreational and personal aspects" and that the Kurzets did not "satisfy their burden of proof that the Tahiti property was held and managed by them for anything other than personal reasons." The court also noted that the Kurzets did not maintain complete and adequate records with regard to expenditures made on the property and that there was no proof of the unrealized economic gain of $1.94 million dollars on the property claimed by the Kurzets. Specifically, the court determined that "no credible evidence supports either the amount or nature of the claimed expenses petitioners incurred on the Tahiti property, nor the fair market value of the Tahiti property."

In support of their claim that the tax court erred in finding that [their home in Tahiti was not an investment property], the Kurzets point to: (1) the summary of the expenses they incurred on the Tahiti property; (2) the fact that the property was listed for sale in 1989; (3) Kurzet's testimony that he believed that the property increased in value to $3.7 million by 1994; (4) testimony regarding the fact that money was transferred from the United States to Tahiti to improve the property; and (5) testimony from the Kurzets and two of their former employees that the Kurzets spent all of their time in Tahiti working to improve the property and none of it swimming in the ocean or otherwise relaxing.

In light of the factors to be considered under the regulations, we find that the district court did not clearly err in denying the deduction.

The Kurzets' recordkeeping concerning their expenditures relating to the Tahiti property weighs both ways. The treasury regulations indicate that "the fact that the taxpayer carries on the activity in a businesslike manner and maintains complete and accurate books and records may indicate that the activity is engaged in for profit." Thus, conversely, the inadequate record keeping supports the conclusion that an activity was not engaged in for profit. In their opening brief, the Kurzets only point to a conclusory summary of their expenses related to the Tahiti property and testimony of Mrs. Kurzet that she kept track of the money transfers and expenditures related to the Tahiti property on her home computer. This would not satisfy the recordkeeping factor. However, in their reply brief, the Kurzets refer to Joint Exhibit 70BR as evidence of their expenses associated with the Tahiti property. Exhibit 70BR provides a list of every expenditure the Kurzets' made by check and credit card in the years 1987, 1988, and 1989. While these lists describe the general category for every expenditure (e.g., operating supplies, repairs and maintenance, etc.) and are more complete than the other records, we do not find that this evidence necessarily supports the conclusion that the Tahiti property was held for profit. This is because the lists indicate that the Kurzets designated most of their expense entries associated with the Tahiti property as nondeductible personal expenses. By contrast, the Kurzets sought to deduct most expenses associated with their timber farm as business expenses. In addition, adequate recordkeeping is only one of the factors to consider in determining whether the property was being held for profit.

With respect to the second factor, there is no evidence to show that the Kurzets prepared to invest in Tahiti by "extensive study of its accepted business, economic, and scientific practices," or that they sought advice concerning the investment. This is in contrast to their decision to invest in the timber farm.

While the fact that the Kurzets spent considerable time and effort working to improve the property is an indication that they may have purchased the Tahiti property with an eye toward obtaining a profit, this fact does not compel the conclusion that the tax court erred. The Kurzets could easily have sought to make the improvements to the property for the purpose of maximizing their own enjoyment. *See Carkhuff v. Commissioner*, 425 F.2d 1400, 1405 (6th Cir.1970) (finding that improvements that taxpayers had made to a vacation cottage which would have made the cottage suitable for rental also could have been "intended to satisfy the personal tastes and comfort of the taxpayers" and explaining that "[t]he making of repairs and improvements ... does not compel the conclusion that a profit motive was present.").

In addition, although the evidence suggesting that the Kurzets expected the property to appreciate in value carries some weight, we conclude that it does not compel a finding of error on the part of the tax court either. Kurzet testified that he purchased the property because of its "excellent commercial potential" and because he thought it was "an excellent hotel site." There was no evidence, however, to suggest that the Kurzets ever tried to maximize this potential by pursuing development plans with commercial developers or even by renting the property when they were not using it. We also find persuasive the Commissioner's argument that the Kurzets' work to develop the property was, in fact, inconsistent with the intent to develop its commercial potential as a hotel site. In addition, the evidence that the Kurzets put the property on the market in 1989 does not necessarily signify that the property was purchased with the intention of making a profit, particularly in light of the fact that the Kurzets still owned the Tahiti property at the time of the trial in 1995. Finally, while actual appreciation in value may provide some evidence that a property may be held for profit, we conclude that Kurzet's subjective belief as to the value of the property in 1995 is not sufficient to establish a profit motive.

PROBLEMS FOR DISCUSSION

15–5. What could the Kurzets have done differently that might have changed the result in their case?

KRAUSE v. COMMISSIONER

99 T.C. 132 (1992), aff'd sub nom. Hildebrand v. Commissioner, 28 F.3d 1024 (10th Cir.1994), and sub nom. Hill v. Commissioner, 204 F.3d 1214 (9th Cir. 2000)

These consolidated cases are test cases for over 2,000 related cases and for a number of related TEFRA partnerships. Alleged total tax deficiencies at issue in connection with this group of related cases and TEFRA partnerships are in excess of $2 billion.

The particular limited partnerships that are involved in these test cases (namely, Technology–1980 and Barton) were part of two groups of limited partnerships that are referred to in this opinion at various times as the "Manhattan Partnerships", the "Wichita Partnerships", and occasionally as "the partnerships". The partnerships had the stated general objective of, among other things, investing in enhanced oil recovery (EOR) technology for the recovery of oil and natural gas.

Resolution of the issues in these cases is complicated by the extensive record. Trial of these cases lasted 15 weeks. The trial transcript consists of 8,361 pages. Over 1,500 multi-page exhibits were admitted into evidence, and a total of 46 fact witnesses and 28 expert witnesses testified. [Both the statement of facts and the court's analysis of them are severely edited here.]

Throughout the mid to late 1970s and early 1980s, world oil markets were destabilized by war in the Middle East, by the Iranian revolution, by production and export quotas of oil exporting countries, and by other actions of the Organization of Petroleum Exporting Countries. During these years, certain segments of the public, of the oil industry, and of governmental organizations responsible for energy policy reflected a certain hysteria about the worldwide energy crisis and about oil prices.

In the late 1970s, the Carter Administration announced a new national goal for the United States within a decade to achieve energy independence. This goal was to be achieved by increasing the supply of domestic crude oil, by developing new alternate sources of energy, and by conserving existing energy resources. Numerous energy related research and development facilities were established, funded, or subsidized by the Government. Billions of dollars were spent directly by the Federal Government or indirectly through tax incentives to accelerate the development of synthetic fuels, fossil energy research, and EOR technology.

Specifically, regarding the development of EOR technology, in 1979 a tertiary oil incentive program was adopted by the DOE. Under this program, which effectively expired in early 1981, qualified oil producers were allowed to sell oil at market prices, which prices were substantially higher than the controlled prices of crude oil, in order to offset up to the lesser of $20 million or 75 percent of their expenses in qualified EOR projects. Under the Crude Oil Windfall Profit Tax Act of 1980, certain oil recovered through EOR technology qualified for a reduced Federal excise tax, and certain tax credits were made available with respect to the production of oil from tar sands.

In late 1978 or 1979, a number of individuals participated in the formation of tax shelter limited partnerships with the stated general investment objectives of drilling for oil and natural gas and of obtaining the rights to certain EOR technology that might be developed and become valuable if the price of oil continued to rise dramatically in subsequent years.

Petitioners Hildebrand and Wahl invested in one of the Manhattan Partnerships known as Technology–1980. Initially, the individual general partner of Technology–1980 was Richard B. Basile, and the corporate general copartner was Glenda Exploration and Development Corp. (GEDCO), a Texas corporation.

Basile had no experience with oil and gas exploration, production, or investments. Rather, his experience was in selling tax shelters. Basile did not personally investigate the merits of the proposed partnership investments. He did not prepare feasibility studies relating to the partnership, nor did he have such studies prepared.

A number of the individual organizers and promoters of Technology–1980, however, did consult with various experts and did obtain and study various reports that had been prepared relating to, among other things, projections of world oil prices, the extent of oil deposits in Utah and Wyoming tar sands properties, the potential for the recovery of natural gas from the Monroe, Louisiana, natural gas field.

Also, certain economic, financial, accounting, and tax analyses and opinions were obtained by the organizers and promoters of the partnerships. These analyses and these opinions were available to Basile, and much of these analyses and many of these opinions were reflected or summarized in the partnerships' offering memoranda given to prospective investors.

In general, the net losses of Technology–1980 and of Barton are not deductible unless the activities of the partnerships were engaged in with actual and honest profit objectives. Whether activities of partnerships were engaged in with actual and honest profit objectives is analyzed at the partnership level.

The factors set out in the Treasury Regulations under section 183 generally are utilized in determining whether the requisite profit objectives are present under section 162, section 174, and other Internal Revenue Code sections. Those factors, however, are not exclusive, and all of the unique and relevant factors and circumstances of the particular investments at issue are to be considered.

Factors particularly relevant in cases involving new or undeveloped technology, and particularly relevant to our analysis of the profit objective issue in this case are the following: (1) Heavy promotion and marketing on the basis of projected tax benefits and inaccurate information regarding the EOR technology; and (2) the financial structure of the fees and royalties that the partnerships agreed to pay.

Taking into account the factors set out in section 1.183(b)(2), Income Tax Regs., the factors emphasized above, and the extensive testimony of the key participants in these transactions and of the many other witnesses in this case, we conclude that the activities of Technology–1980 and of Barton were not engaged in with actual and honest profit objectives. The stated consideration agreed to by the partnerships for the license of EOR technology and for the lease of tar sands properties bore no relation to the value of that which was acquired, did not conform to industry norms, and precluded any realistic opportunity for profit.

In spite of the fact that a portion of the purported EOR technology licensed by the partnerships in this case might have reached some stage of development by the years in issue (and that additional EOR technology might in subsequent years be developed and become valuable), the estimates used by the partnerships for projected oil recovery from the use and application of the EOR technology licensed by the partnerships are not supported by credible expert testimony in this case and were not reasonable. The use by petitioners' experts of projections of tar sands hydrocarbons or of oil in place, rather than projections of oil reserves, and the failure to take sufficiently into account in their projections the undeveloped, untested status of the EOR technology significantly flaws the projections used by petitioners' experts. Projections based on oil reserves and realistic projected oil recovery therefrom using known and developed EOR technology would have provided a much more realistic basis on which to base the fees in question and a legitimate, acceptable business plan.

The economic projections of Technology–1980 and of Barton, upon which the investments allegedly were based, reflect a series of assumptions and conditions which were acknowledged to be assumptions in the offering memoranda and other material. The validity and reasonableness of those assumptions, however, were never ascertained, nor was any meaningful or credible comment or opinion as to the validity and reasonableness of those assumptions set forth in the offering memoranda or other material.

The economic assumptions made in the partnerships' promotional material apparently did not even take into account or note the abnormal nature and high cost of the license fees and royalties, nor the significant costs of conducting tests and of establishing commercial operations using EOR technology.

With regard to the stated business plan of Technology–1980, petitioners' expert witnesses rely on many of the erroneous assumptions and projections reflected in the partnerships' offering memoranda. Their projections of cash flow are based on assumed production figures from the Monroe, Louisiana, natural gas field as set forth in the offering memorandum. They make erroneous cost estimates in concluding that the royalties

Technology–1980 reasonably would receive just from the natural gas production on the property leased from Glenda Petroleum would be sufficient to pay the entire license and royalty obligations due with regard to the EOR technology and the tar sands properties in Utah and Wyoming, and still produce a reasonable rate of return for the partnerships. Under the agreement between the Manhattan Partnerships and Glenda Petroleum, however, an excessive number of wells was to be drilled by Glenda in the Monroe, Louisiana, natural gas field, and the agreement did not reflect arm's-length terms. The projections of natural gas production from the working interests in the Monroe, Louisiana, natural gas field were excessive.

One of petitioners' expert witnesses theorizes that it would take 10 years to bring the tar sands properties into commercial development using the ElektraFlo technology, at which point in time he speculates that the tar sands property interests of the partnerships would be sold to a major oil company for a sale price of at least $30 million. Another of petitioners' expert witnesses opines that the Barton business plan was a reasonable investment with a high income potential. He, however, bases his report on inappropriate assumptions as to the oil reserves on the property to be leased by Barton, production levels attributable to specific undeveloped EOR technology, and cash flows from joint ventures that did not yet exist.

We found the testimony of respondent's expert witnesses concerning the EOR technology and the structure and reasonableness of the license fees and royalties more credible. The fixed fees to be paid by the partnerships for the EOR technology licenses were not competitive in the oil industry and were contrary to industry norms. All but two of the technologies were undeveloped, untested processes for which no prudent investor would pay any substantial fixed fees, and the TEC and Carmel processes that were developed likely could have been licensed by the partnerships directly from the inventors thereof for running royalties based solely on income realized therefrom.

Petitioners' expert witness regarding the value of the EOR technology license agreement with Elektra did not opine on any specific or general dollar fair market value thereof. The expert witness admitted that the terms of the license agreement were unreasonable but justified in this case on the ground that the unreasonableness of the license agreement somehow could or should be overlooked because of the large amount of money the partnerships were assumed to make from the natural gas drilling program in the Monroe, Louisiana natural gas field. This assumption, among other assumptions, is made in spite of the fact that the original properties assigned to Barton were outside the producing area of the natural gas field and were only exploratory in nature and in spite of the fact that the terms of the drilling agreement with Glenda Petroleum were unfavorable to the partnerships and not at arm's length.

Petitioners did not offer an expert witness regarding the fair market value of the EOR technology licensed from Hemisphere, nor did petitioners offer an expert witness as to the reasonableness of the license agreement with Hemisphere. Rather, petitioners submitted the report of the National Institute of Petroleum Energy Research (NIPER) which merely summarizes NIPER's research with two types of EOR technology and the status generally of EOR technology in the early 1980s, and which provides very general estimates of the amount of oil that might some day be recoverable by someone through the use of EOR technology.

The authors of the NIPER report understood little concerning the terms of the partnerships' license agreements with Elektra and Hemisphere, when the license agreements were entered into, and what technology was included. The NIPER report relies significantly on data from 1980, even though the continuing viability of that data in 1981 and certainly by 1982 was questionable.

Petitioners argue that the business plans of Barton and the other Wichita Partnerships were carefully developed and that the plans were unsuccessful only because of the unexpected decline in world oil and gas prices. More specifically regarding Barton, petitioners argue that the amount of the EOR license fees was based on the number of barrels of oil that were projected to be recovered using EOR technology from the particular properties in which the partnerships obtained working interests. For example, petitioners note that under Barton's EOR license agreement the properties to be acquired were to have not more than 100,000 barrels of oil resources in the ground per partnership unit. Inexplicably, using this maximum number of 100,000 barrels of oil, the promoters of Barton then assumed a 20–percent oil recovery rate using EOR technology, or a total of 20,000 barrels of oil per partnership unit, spread ratably over 10 years or 2,000 barrels of oil a year. The EOR license fee for the right to use the EOR technology acquired by each partnership unit was then set at $2,000 each year or $1 a barrel of projected oil in the ground. Petitioners argue that the 20–percent recovery rate was based on expert opinions, that it was conservative and reasonable, and that $1 a barrel was "a bargain".

We disagree. The estimate of a 20–percent recovery rate using EOR technology that had not been tested in any significant manner on the particular partnership properties was grossly excessive. We believe that by making the license fees due from the partnerships a definite, fixed amount (that was due independently of any successful test of the technology in the properties and independently of any income or oil production from the properties using EOR technology), the license fees were not reasonable, nor realistic. The fixed, definite nature of the license fees flies in the face of the many assumptions and risky, speculative projections on which the stated business plans of the partnerships were based.

If, as petitioners contend, the amount of the license fees related so directly to estimates of recoverable oil in the properties leased by the partnerships and to the utilization or projected utilization of the EOR technology on those properties (and not to the number of partnership units sold), why was accrual of the fees and the amount of the fees not made dependent upon successful pilot tests on the properties of the technology and on actual income realized therefrom or on incremental increased production of oil attributable to the EOR technology (as were the fees Elektra and Hemisphere were to pay for the same technology and as were the license fees to be computed in connection with any sublicenses of the technology by Hemisphere or by the partnerships).

We reiterate that, with respect to the Wichita Partnerships, the properties in which the partnerships were to acquire working interests were not required to have "at least" 100,000 barrels of oil in the ground (which is the basis on which petitioners' argument and computations on this point seem to be made). Rather, the properties were required to have no more than, or not in excess of, 100,000 barrels of oil in the ground. Petitioners' argument and computations do not take into account the possibility that many of the working interests that the Wichita Partnerships might have acquired under this provision could have had much less than 100,000 barrels of estimated oil in the ground and still would have been in compliance with the provisions of the partnership's business plan.

A significant additional flaw in the projections used by the promoters of both the Manhattan and Wichita Partnerships, in the analyses used by petitioners' expert witnesses, and in petitioners' arguments herein, is that world oil prices would continue increasing from 1979 and 1980 prices on a continuing upward spiral for the next 20 years.

With regard to price projections in the 1980 DOE report, we agree with and reiterate what has already been said:

> "The 1980 Department of Energy Report was based on mid–1979 and earlier price figures and was prepared during the world energy crisis of the late 1970's. That crisis was produced mainly by the Iranian Revolution and the related oil embargo. In a sense, the report presented a worst-case scenario as of the period when it was in preparation. The difference between the mid–1979 and the nominal dollar figures shown in the above table demonstrates the rapidly escalating inflation rate during the late 1970's which, by 1981 and 1982, was already being dealt with by the Federal Reserve Board and other Government agencies. The report was neither used by, nor intended to be used by, businessmen as a basis for business decisions."

In support of the value of the EOR technology licenses and the amount of the license fees and royalties, petitioners refer to a transaction in early 1981 by which the Manhattan Partnerships entered into a type of joint venture agreement with Pogo Producing Co., Inc., a publicly traded company, to conduct test drilling operations on the Burnt Hollow tar sands property. Pogo agreed to pay approximately $1.73 million in connection with test wells to be drilled on the Burnt Hollow property in return for a 5–percent undivided interest in the profits from the GEDCO heavy oil joint venture project on the Burnt Hollow property. No representative, however, of Pogo testified at trial, and we know too little about this transaction to give it any credence in considering the value of the EOR technology licenses.

In support of their argument that the partnerships' investments were reasonable, petitioners also rely on certain testimony in this case regarding a number of other apparently large and risky investments in EOR technology by major oil producing companies, some of which apparently involved fixed fees. Such testimony, however, was of a very general nature, was largely given by individuals who were not personally or sufficiently involved with the investments, and does little to bolster the credibility or economic substance of the tax-oriented limited partnership investments at issue in this case.

Petitioners argue that even though no existing, traditional EOR technology had been tested successfully on the Utah and Wyoming tar sands properties, the "portfolio" of EOR technology licensed by Barton and the Wichita Partnerships constituted just the type of unusual, creative combination of EOR technology that might prove valuable on such property. As we have found, however, that portfolio consisted of a package of vague, largely untested ideas, that, if and to the extent ever developed, would likely be available generally in the market place and on much more favorable terms than from the partnerships. We reject petitioners' argument that the portfolio of EOR technology obtained by the partnerships represented anything of any substantial value. The EOR technology license agreements entered into by Technology–1980 with Elektra and by Barton with Hemisphere were essentially valueless.

The multi-million dollar license fees and royalties that Technology–1980 and that Barton (and the other Manhattan and Wichita Partnerships) agreed to pay were excessive. They did not reflect arm's-length obligations, and they are not to be recognized as legitimate obligations of the partnerships. The debt obligations of the partnerships associated therewith did not constitute genuine debt obligations and are to be disregarded.

In summary, presented to us in this case is a chain or multi-layered series of obligations, stacked or multiplied on top of each other via the numerous partnerships to produce debt obligations in staggering dollar amounts, using a largely undeveloped and untested product, in a highly risky, very speculative, and non arm's-length manner in an attempt to generate significant tax deductions for investors. The transactions did not, and do not, constitute legitimate for-profit business transactions.

PROBLEMS FOR DISCUSSION

15–6. What could the organizers in *Krause* have done differently that might have changed the result in that case?

Subchapter B: Specific Requirements

Code Section 162(a) allows as a deduction "all the ordinary and necessary expenses paid or incurred during the taxable year in carrying on any trade or business...." Code Section 212 allows as a deduction "all the ordinary and necessary expenses paid or incurred during the taxable year—(1) for the production or collection of income, [or] (2) for the management, conservation, or maintenance of property held for the production of income...."

As a practical matter, deductions under either section must meet four requirements:

(1) They must be "ordinary and necessary,"

(2) They must not be personal,

(3) They must not be subject to the capitalization requirement, and

(4) Their deduction must not be contrary to public policy.

As will be seen, all four are sometimes or were once treated as aspects of the "ordinary and necessary" requirement itself. As the Supreme Court noted in *Commissioner v. Idaho Power Co.*, above, however, Code Section 263 requires that capital expenses be capitalized regardless of whether they otherwise qualify as "ordinary and necessary." The same logic requires disallowance of personal expenses under Code Section 262, again regardless of whether they otherwise qualify for deduction as ordinary and necessary business or investment expenses. Finally, the requirement that deductions not be contrary to public policy has now, for the most part, been codified. We have explored the capitalization requirement in Chapter 11B. Here we explore the remaining three.

SECTION 1: "ORDINARY AND NECESSARY"

Over time, the phrase "ordinary and necessary" has performed many functions.

(1) *Capital expenses*. It has been used to distinguish current expenses from expenses required to be capitalized. *See, e.g., Commissioner v. Tellier*, 383 U.S. 687, 689–90 (1966) ("The principal function of the term 'ordinary' in § 162(a) is to clarify the distinction, often difficult, between those expenses that are currently deductible and those that are in the nature of capital expenditures, which, if deductible at all, must be amortized over the useful life of the asset.").

(2) *Personal expenses*. It is sometimes used to disallow personal expenses. *See, e.g., Henry v. Commissioner*, 36 T.C. 879 (1961) (costs of yacht flying "1040" flag, purportedly used to attract tax clients, not ordinary and necessary) ("where, as in this case, the expenditures may well have been made to further ends which are primarily personal, ... petitioner must show affirmatively that his expenses were 'necessary' to the conduct of his professions").

(3) *Expenses contrary to public policy.* It has been construed to disallow expenses deduction of which would be contrary to public policy. See, e.g., *Tank Truck Rentals, Inc. v. Commissioner*, 356 U.S. 30 (1958) ("A finding of 'necessity' cannot be made . . . if allowance of the deduction would frustrate sharply defined national or state policies proscribing particular types of conduct, evidenced by some governmental declaration thereof.").

(4) *Expenses unreasonable in amount.* It has been construed to require that deductions be reasonable in amount. See, e.g., *Commissioner v. Lincoln Electric Co.*, 176 F.2d 815, 817 (6th Cir. 1949) ("[T]he element of reasonableness is inherent in the phrase 'ordinary and necessary.' Clearly it was not the intention of Congress to automatically allow as deductions operating expenses incurred or paid by the taxpayer in an unlimited amount."). In practice, however, reasonableness is normally raised where it appears that an alleged business expense may be something else in disguise—*e.g.*, a gift, dividend, or personal expense. See, e.g., *Limericks, Inc. v. Commissioner*, 165 F.2d 483 (5th Cir. 1948) (excessive rents paid to president and principal stockholder of corporate tenant).

(5) *Unusual expenses.* Finally, it is sometimes used to disallow unusual, idiosyncratic, or unique expenditures. See, e.g., *Goedel v. Commissioner*, 39 B.T.A. 1 (1939) ("Where . . . the expenditure is so unusual as never to have been made . . . by other persons in the same business, when confronted with similar conditions, . . . then we do not think the expenditure was ordinary or necessary . . . ."); *Welch v. Helvering*, 290 U.S. 111 (1933) ("Ordinary in this context does not mean that the payments must be habitual or normal in the sense that the same taxpayer will have to make them often. A lawsuit affecting the safety of a business may happen once in a lifetime. The counsel fees may be so heavy that repetition is unlikely. None the less, the expense is an ordinary one because we know from experience that payments for such a purpose, whether the amount is large or small, are the common and accepted means of defense against attack.").

The first question—whether expenses should be capitalized—is explored in Chapter 11B, above. The second—whether expenses should be treated as personal—is explored in Section 2, below. The third—whether expenses should be disallowed as contrary to public policy—is explored in Section 3, below. Here, we focus on the remaining functions of the phrase.

NOYCE v. COMMISSIONER
97 T.C. 670 (1991)

In 1957, petitioner cofounded Fairchild Semiconductor, a pioneer corporation in the semiconductor industry. In 1968, petitioner cofounded Intel Corporation. Upon the formation of Intel, petitioner became the chief executive officer and served in that capacity until 1974 when he became the chairman of the board. In 1979, petitioner became vice chairman of the board and served in that capacity throughout 1983.

Intel was formed as a manufacturer of integrated circuits on silicon chips. Intel generated approximately $1 billion in revenues and employed approximately 7,000 people worldwide in 1983. By June 1989, it generated approximately $3 billion in revenues and employed about 20,000 people worldwide.

Intel has developed and fostered the "Intel Culture." This culture consists of a relatively distinctive operating style, management philosophy, and compensation policy. The Intel culture is summarized by an egalitarian approach to employees where everyone is treated alike in all respects except compensation. The company's open-office concept epitomizes this egalitarian style—there is no executive dining room and there are no private offices or reserved parking spaces for anyone.

Drs. Moore and Grove, who were the chairman of the board and the President, respectively in 1983, set the salaries for all of the Intel officers, including petitioner. During some years, petitioner had asked that his salary as determined by Drs. Moore and Grove be reduced. As a result, petitioner was probably earning less than one-half of the market rate for his position. Petitioner received $105,076 compensation from Intel in 1983.

Petitioner had invested $250,000 in Intel upon its founding. By 1983, petitioner's Intel holdings were worth over $60 million. This represented less than 3 percent of the outstanding Intel stock at that time. Petitioner sold approximately $5 million of Intel stock in 1983.

Over the years, petitioner's role at Intel emerged as that of the company's public representative. During 1983, petitioner fulfilled the function of being Intel's representative to its outside constituencies. Petitioner often "opened doors" to various corporate customers, and for certain major customers of Intel, petitioner's liaison role was crucial.

As vice chairman, petitioner was the governmental affairs liaison and responsible for Intel's public relations. His duties included accepting speaking engagements throughout the United States, performing various governmental and public-service duties, serving as the chairman of the semiconductor Industry Association, serving as a member of various trade associations of the semiconductor industry, and serving as a member of the Presidential Commission on Industrial Competitiveness (the Young Commission). Petitioner was also expected to attend numerous onsite meetings at Intel.

Petitioner also served as a regent of the University of California and as a trustee of Grinnell College during 1983. Petitioner attended Grinnell Board of Trustee meetings as part of his general networking in the educational community and because Grinnell was an Intel stockholder. When petitioner formed Intel in 1968, Grinnell College and two of the Grinnell College trustees each contributed $100,000 to the startup of Intel. The two trustees subsequently contributed their Intel shares to Grinnell College. Service on Grinnell's Board offered petitioner an opportunity to compare his views on trade and competition with other individuals involved in banking, economics, and other areas. Petitioner's service as a University of California Regent allowed him to network with people of significance in commerce, education, science, and government. The Board of Regents is charged with all business aspects of the University of California, including being the final overseer of the energy laboratories in Los Alamos, Livermore, and Berkeley. As part of petitioner's duties as an official of Intel, petitioner was expected to serve on the Grinnell and University of California Boards. Such service was an essential part of networking for the benefit of Intel and provided an opportunity to gain access to people to test and develop ideas on trade and international competition.

In addition to the Board of Regents at the University of California and the Board of Trustees at Grinnell College, petitioner served on the Engineering Advisory Board at Stanford, the Applied Physics Advisory Board at Harvard, and the Electrical Engineering Advisory Board at MIT. Petitioner was also President and chief executive officer of the Semiconductor–Industry Cooperative Consortium, Sematech, whose members include IBM, AT & T, Digital Equipment Corporation, Hewlett–Packard, Texas Instruments, Motorola, National Semiconductor, Intel, Advanced Micro Devices, and Rockwell Corporation.

Petitioner's duties as vice chairman required frequent and extensive travel, some of which was not regularly and easily scheduled. Because of the changing schedules of people with whom petitioner was expected to meet, he was expected to keep a flexible travel schedule.

On April 27, 1983, petitioner purchased a used aircraft, a Cessna Citation M2617U, for $1,260,000 and took delivery in Wichita, Kansas. Since its purchase in 1983, the airplane has not depreciated in economic value. At the time of trial, the bluebook value of the airplane was $1,300,000.

The Cessna Citation M2617U airplane is a twin-turbo jet which has two pilot positions, seats up to six passengers, cruises at 340 knots, and has a range of approximately 1,100 nautical miles. Most turbo jets used in commercial airline travel have a longer range and fly approximately one-third faster. However, the airplane's flying time is comparable to nonstop commercial flights and superior if the commercial flights are not nonstop. The airplane is capable of landing on a 2,800–foot runway, which is within the length of runways at most small town airports. By contrast, commercial airliners need 5,000–6,000–foot runways and, therefore, are limited in the cities they can service.

Petitioner flew the airplane on Intel business. [The court lists flights made in 1983 pursuant to his employment with Intel or in connection with his service as a regent of the University of California and a trustee of Grinnell College.] All these flights, including those to Grinnell College and University of California, were flights within the scope of petitioner's duties for Intel.

Petitioner saved substantial flying time by using the airplane for trips to the Intel site at Hillsboro, the Grinnell College Board of Trustee meetings in Des Moines, and the University of California Board of Regents meeting at Los Alamos. In other cases, commercial flight time was comparable to that of the airplane, but petitioner's freedom from commercial airline schedules allowed him to attend other meetings before or after those trips. Petitioner could accept additional requests for speeches and appearances knowing he would not be dependent upon commercial airline schedules. Because petitioner had access to a private airplane, he was able to squeeze business meetings and appearances into a few hours that otherwise might have taken two days.

[The court compares the costs and flight times of commercially available flights between the destinations flown using his private jet in 1983.] Compared to commercial airlines, for example on the San Jose to Portland trip, the airplane cost approximately four times as much to operate for one person. However, to replicate the schedule and time savings of petitioner's flights via commercial travel would have cost more than the cost of operating the airplane.

The primary issue for decision is whether petitioners may deduct operating expenses and depreciation with respect to use of the airplane for petitioner's travel on behalf of Intel.

A taxpayer is considered to be in the trade or business of being an employee separate and apart from the trade or business of his corporate employer. However, the voluntary payment or guarantee of corporate obligations by corporate officers, employees, or shareholders may not be deducted on the taxpayer's personal return. *Noland v. Commissioner*, 269 F.2d 108, 111 (4th Cir. 1959); *Gantner v. Commissioner*, 91 T.C. 713, 726 (1988), *aff'd*, 905 F.2d 241 (8th Cir. 1990). In *Noland*, the Court stated that:

> "When the corporation, reimbursing its officers and employees for direct expense incurred in furthering its business, does not reimburse an officer for particular expense, that expense prima facie is personal, either because it was voluntarily assumed or because it did not arise directly out of the exigencies of the business of the corporation."

Respondent contends that petitioner voluntarily used his airplane and assumed the airplane expenses and, therefore, is not entitled to the claimed deductions. Petitioners argue that there was no voluntary assumption of corporate obligations because the airplane was used and the expenses were incurred pursuant to written corporate policy. We agree with petitioners.

Respondent's Revenue Ruling 57–502, 1957–2 C.B. 118, acknowledges that a corporate resolution or policy requiring a corporate officer to assume such expenses indicates that they are his expenses as opposed to those of the corporation. In *Gantner*, we disallowed the taxpayer's deduction for expenses and depreciation related to a computer system which he purchased and used in the operation of the Northstar Driving School, Inc.

The taxpayer was an officer and a 50–percent shareholder of Northstar. Even though the taxpayer used the equipment in his employment with the corporation, we found that the deductions were not attributable to the taxpayer's role as an employee noting that "There was no corporate resolution or requirement that petitioner, as an employee, incur those expenses." Similarly, in *Stolk v. Commissioner*, 40 T.C. 345 (1963), *aff'd*, 326 F.2d 760 (2d Cir. 1964), we disallowed a corporate officer's deduction of expenditures for entertainment and gifts, in part, for the taxpayer's failure "to prove that as part of his duties the corporation expected or required him to assume and pay from his own funds any of the disputed expenses, without payment."

In *Lockwood v. Commissioner*, T.C. Memo. 1970–141, the shareholders and officers of Momex agreed that the officers would pay out of their own pocket, without corporate reimbursement, certain travel and entertainment expenses incurred by them on behalf of the corporation. We held that the taxpayer's travel expenses incurred on behalf of the corporation were deductible.

In the instant case, Intel had a written travel reimbursement policy explicitly stating that it expected its officers to incur certain expenses for Intel's benefit, despite the fact that such expenses would not be reimbursed. Reimbursement of such expenses was considered inappropriate in light of the corporate culture and the officers' overall compensation. An example of such expenses is the excess cost of first-class airfare over coach airfare when first-class travel was necessary for business purposes. We find that Intel expected petitioner, as a corporate official, to incur and pay travel expenses in excess of the amount which was reimbursable under its policy. Therefore, we hold that petitioner's use of the airplane and payment of the attendant expenses do not constitute the voluntary assumption of corporate expenses.

Having found that the use and expenses of the airplane were not corporate obligations which were voluntarily assumed, we must decide if the expenses are ordinary and necessary expenses of petitioner's employment. An expense is necessary if it is appropriate and helpful in carrying on the trade or business. An expense is ordinary when the paying thereof is the common and accepted practice in light of the time and place and circumstance.

In Revenue Ruling 70–558, 1970–2 C.B. 35, respondent held that a Federal Government employee who used his privately owned airplane on official business trips was entitled to deduct expenses and depreciation allocable to such use to the extent those amounts exceeded the standard rate travel reimbursements received from the Government. The taxpayer in Revenue Ruling 70–558 was not required by his employer to use his private airplane but was permitted to do so because of the urgency of his trips. For purposes of determining whether petitioner's use of his airplane was ordinary and necessary, we can discern no meaningful distinction between his situation and the facts in Revenue Ruling 70–558.

It is undisputed that petitioner's duties as vice chairman of Intel required frequent and extensive travel, some of which was not regularly or easily scheduled. Furthermore, the parties agree that petitioner's access to the airplane enabled him to reduce significantly his traveling time, thereby allowing him to attend an increased number of meetings and make an increased number of appearances. Consequently, there can be little dispute that use of the airplane was "appropriate and helpful" to the execution of petitioner's duties. Furthermore, respondent's Revenue Ruling 57–502, 1957–2 C.B. 118, states that "a resolution requiring the assumption of such expenses by . . . [a corporate officer] would tend to indicate that they are a necessary expense of his office." Based on all of the foregoing, we find the airplane expenses for the Intel flights were a necessary expense of petitioner's business as a corporate official.

The expenses of using the airplane must also be ordinary in order to be deductible. The principal function of the word "ordinary" in section 162(a) is to clarify the distinction between expenses which are currently deductible and expenses which are capital in nature. The expenses at issue here were not incurred in the acquisition of a capital asset but in the conduct of petitioner's duties as an employee of Intel.

Petitioner traveled by private aircraft only when there was business advantage in doing so. The cost of replicating petitioner's travel schedule and time savings via commercial charter carrier would have exceeded the costs of operating petitioner's airplane. In light of Intel's policies and petitioner's travel requirements, we hold that payment of the excess travel expenses arising from petitioner's use of the airplane was ordinary under the circumstances.

It has been held that for an expense to be considered ordinary and necessary, it must also be reasonable in amount. Respondent argues that the expenses are not ordinary and necessary because petitioners' claimed deduction of $139,369 in connection with the airplane is unreasonable in light of the $105,076 salary petitioner was paid as vice chairman of Intel in 1983. Petitioners argue that in determining reasonableness of the amount of business expenses for purposes of section 162, only out-of-pocket expenses should be considered and that the statutory allowance for depreciation should be excluded from consideration.

Whether depreciation should be included in the amount of expenses in making a reasonableness determination depends on whether it is a "business expense" under section 162. The regulations under section 162 provide in relevant part that "Business expenses deductible from gross income include the ordinary and necessary expenditures directly connected with or pertaining to the taxpayer's trade or business, except items which are used as the basis for a deduction or a credit under provisions of law other than section 162." Sec. 1.162–1(a), Income Tax Regs. Depreciation is not really an "expenditure" but an allowance based on a presumed wasting of a previous capital investment. The authority for deducting an allowance for depreciation in this case is section 168. Therefore, depreciation does not fall under the regulatory rubric of trade or business expense. As such, the section 168 depreciation deduction amount should not be included in the amount of business expense, the reasonableness of which is to be determined.

To hold otherwise would raise serious problems since allowable deductions for depreciation will often not be reflective of economic depreciation. If we were to look simply at the combination of allowable depreciation deductions and other expenditures for a particular year, the combination of these amounts might often seem exorbitant in amount, especially in the early years of operation. Respondent has not argued that we should consider actual economic depreciation. In the instant case, however, the $96,722 depreciation allowance did not reflect actual economic depreciation. The airplane did not decrease in value but increased in value by approximately $340,000 from 1983 to 1989. Therefore, petitioner did not suffer an actual economic loss in addition to his out-of-pocket expenditures of $23,140.

The issue then is whether the $23,140 expended for Intel flights is a reasonable amount of expense under the circumstances. Whether an expenditure is reasonable or not for purposes of section 162 is a question of fact. The parties have stipulated to the fact that replication of petitioner's private airplane flights through a commercial service would have been more costly. Therefore, we hold petitioners are entitled to deduct petitioner's out-of-pocket expenses of operating the airplane with respect to the Intel-related flights to the extent they exceed the reimbursable expenses.

With respect to depreciation, respondent states on brief that he "agrees that if the Court finds that the petitioner flying his own plane is ordinary and necessary that the amount of depreciation is reasonable." Nevertheless, respondent appears to argue that whether depreciation is deductible at all is dependent on whether the asset's use is "ordinary and necessary," and that the combined amount of deductions for depreciation and business expense must be "reasonable" in order to be "ordinary and necessary." Such a position is without support in the law.

Availability of deductions for depreciation on tangible property in this case is dependent solely upon compliance with section 168, which has only two requirements for deduction of depreciation. First, the asset (tangible) must be of a type which is subject to wear and tear, decay, decline, or exhaustion. Second, the property must be used in the taxpayer's trade or business or held for the production of income. The language of the section is unequivocal.

Nowhere in the language of section 168 is there a suggestion that availability of the depreciation deduction is dependent on satisfaction of the requirements of section 162. There simply is no requirement that the use of the depreciable property be "ordinary" or "necessary." The only requirement is that it be used in the taxpayer's trade or business.

Based on the foregoing, we find that petitioners are entitled to deduct depreciation on the airplane to the extent of its use in petitioner's employment.

WHEATLAND v. COMMISSIONER

T.C. Memo. 1964–95

The issue for decision is whether petitioner may deduct in 1959 the cost of three sets of encyclopedias and of certain electronic equipment which he used from time to time in his classroom as a science teacher in elementary school.

In 1959 petitioner was an elementary school teacher in the Sunnyvale School District, Sunnyvale, Calif. He had been a teacher for 11 years. In 1962 petitioner was awarded a lifetime teaching certificate as a general elementary schoolteacher.

As a teacher, petitioner's primary interest was in science education. In 1943 he had been a member of the Navy V–12 program, studying engineering and electronics and his duties in the Navy involved navigation. He attended Long Beach City College where his primary fields of study were mathematics and science. In 1950 he received his A.B. degree from College of the Pacific, and in 1960 he began graduate studies in education at Stanford University. He received his M.A. degree from Stanford in 1962 in education.

Petitioner began teaching in Redwood City, Calif., in 1952, and he was a teacher in the Sunnyvale school district from 1954 to 1962. During this period he also had other jobs in addition to serving as an elementary schoolteacher. These other jobs involved engineering and electronics. From 1952 to 1954 he worked in San Carlos, Calif., as a technician; in 1955 he worked during the summer vacation in Redwood City, Calif., as a test engineer; from 1956 to 1958 he had a position in Palo Alto, Calif., as a maintenance engineer, and from May 1958 to January 1959 he worked as a technician in a computer laboratory.

In January 1959 petitioner obtained a position with Lockheed Aircraft Corporation, Missiles and Space Division, hereinafter called Lockheed, as an associate engineer. In 1962 he was employed by Lockheed as an electronic research engineer. His salary from Lockheed in 1959 was $6,082.62.

Due to his interest in science education, petitioner, in 1959, was a consultant on curriculum for the Sunnyvale school district. In this capacity he advised the superintendent of schools with respect to science curriculum and to the materials to be used in teaching science in the schools. At the elementary school where petitioner taught in 1959 there was a science laboratory library where teaching materials were maintained. Teachers from the elementary school and from nearby junior high schools could use the materials in this library by checking them out for use in the classroom.

In 1959 petitioner purchased parts for the assembly of the following items of electronic equipment for which he paid the following amounts:

High-frequency crossover network	$37.50
Electronic dual sweepscope	370.00
Audio amplifier	85.00
Grid dip oscillator	32.50
Variable oscillator	155.00
Total	680.00

An oscillator is a device similar to a television screen. It has a picture tube and is used for measuring frequency oscillation and for tuning and adjusting electronic components. Had petitioner purchased the oscillators assembled, he would have been required to pay more for them than he did for the component parts. The oscillators and the audio amplifier were assembled in the classroom. Petitioner bought the parts for the other items in laboratory kit form; that is, the parts were in such form that they could be assembled, dissembled, and reassembled many times. In teaching the children in his classes how to assemble the components, petitioner did not solder permanent circuit connections but used clips so that the circuit could be built and rebuilt. Much of the instruction concerning the assembly and reassembly of the components of the foregoing items had no direct connection with general science courses taught elementary school students; the instruction, which included some explanation of computer mathematics, was part of petitioner's program for enrichment of the more advanced students in science.

Petitioner placed the components of the electronic equipment in the science laboratory library at his school, and other teachers from his school and from junior high schools had access to them. On one occasion when he had purchased some equipment at a cost of about $5, he presented the bill to his school for payment, but payment was refused and petitioner had to pay the cost himself.

The high frequency crossover network and the audio amplifier can be used by persons, such as petitioner, who are interested in high fidelity phonograph equipment. Petitioner used some of the items at home particularly during summer vacations.

When petitioner left Sunnyvale school district to do graduate work, he left most of the electronic equipment in the school science library. Some of the equipment was lost or worn out. But petitioner took the audio amplifier with him for use at home and at the date of the trial still had the amplifier and had added speakers to it.

On his return for 1959 petitioner claimed as a deduction from adjusted gross income the above-mentioned cost of the items of electronic equipment. He explained the deduction as "Electronic Test Equipment for

Training & Research." Respondent disallowed the deduction in its entirety.

In 1959 petitioner had four children, ages 1, 2, 7, and 9. In that year he purchased three sets of encyclopedias, published by different publishers, for a total cost of $473, which could be used in the education of children of elementary school age. The school where petitioner was teaching that year had encyclopedias available for the students in the school library, and the children could use them during library periods. But petitioner felt that his students should have available to them a set of encyclopedias in their own classroom for use whenever they needed them, and he requested that his school purchase enough sets so that each classroom could have a set. His request was denied because encyclopedias were available in the library. Consequently, petitioner used the encyclopedias he purchased in his classroom from time to time, and he left one set at the school when he left on sabbatical leave. He used the other two sets at home and at another school where he has taught since 1959. Petitioner would have bought the encyclopedias for his children had he not been a teacher.

Petitioner, on his return for 1959, claimed as a deduction from adjusted gross income the amount of $498, representing "Texts & Encyclopedia." Respondent disallowed the deduction in its entirety.

Petitioner suggested that his expenditures for the books and the electronic equipment which he used at times in his teaching were deductible as expenditures for tools used in his trade or business of teaching. We will assume for purposes of discussion that the cost of tools or other articles used by an employee in his employment could under some circumstances be considered an ordinary and necessary expense in carrying on the taxpayer's trade or business, but we cannot find that the expenditures here involved so qualify.

Section 1.162–1(a), Income Tax Regs., provides that business expenses deductible from gross income include expenditures directly connected with or pertaining to the taxpayer's trade or business, and cases such as *Commissioner v. Heininger*, 320 U.S. 467 (1943), *Robert Lee Henry*, 36 T.C. 879 (1961), and *Alexander P. Reed*, 35 T.C. 199 (1960), stand for the proposition that to qualify as ordinary and necessary business expenses, the expenditures must be directly or proximately related to the taxpayer's trade or business, and they must also be both ordinary and necessary under the circumstances. Here we are doubtful that it can be said that the cost of these books and the equipment was either directly or proximately related to, or a necessary expense of, petitioner's job as a schoolteacher—and we certainly cannot find that it was an ordinary expense of that job.

However laudable petitioner's motives may have been in making available to his pupils reference books in their homeroom and using electronic equipment to illustrate electronics, petitioner himself admitted that the equipment was not directly related to what he was supposed to teach in the sixth grade, and also that neither the books nor the equipment were necessary to carry out his job. Neither did the school authorities think that they were necessary—at least they refused to pay for them. They may have been helpful to the students and appropriate for use in the classroom and in petitioner's teaching, but there is no evidence that they would enhance petitioner's trade or business—that of teaching school.

But it seems to us unquestionable, even if we were to accept the premise that the primary use of these articles was in petitioner's classroom, which we do not, that these were not ordinary expenses of a public schoolteacher. Rather we would think it quite unusual that a public schoolteacher would provide reference books and illustrative equipment for his classroom out of his own funds. Schoolteachers may, at times, do so, but they do not do so ordinarily, even though the result might be to enhance their reputations as dedicated teachers. The money may be well spent, particularly here where it appears that petitioner kept two of the sets of encyclopedias home for use of his children and used a good part of the equipment at home for his own enjoyment, but it was not an ordinary expense of carrying on petitioner's business.

NOTES

1. *Expenses of elementary and secondary teachers.*—Code Section 62(a)(D) provides that for taxable years 2002 through 2011, up to $250 of Code Section 162 expenses incurred by eligible educators "in connection with books, supplies ..., computer equipment ... and other equipment, and supplementary materials used by the eligible educator in the classroom" may be deducted above-the-line. But such expenses must first be deductible under Code Section 162. What kinds of expenses are ordinary and necessary for elementary and secondary school teachers remains unclear. *See, e.g., Farias v. Commissioner*, T.C. Memo. 2011–248 (denying all claimed trade or business expenses of a public school elementary teacher on the authority of *Wheatland*: "To claim a deduction for teaching supplies, it is not enough that the supplies be helpful to the students and appropriate for use in the classroom; they must also be directly related to the taxpayer's job as a teacher and a necessary expense of being a teacher.").

SECTION 2: NOT PERSONAL

Even if specific expenses are "appropriate and helpful in carrying on the trade or business" and "common and accepted practice in light of the time and place and circumstance," *Noyce v. Commissioner*, above, their deduction may still be denied as "personal" under Code Section 262.

HENDERSON v. COMMISSIONER
T.C. Memo. 1983-372, 46 T.C.M. (CCH) 566 (1983)

Respondent determined a deficiency in petitioners' Federal income tax for the taxable year 1977 in the amount of $124. The issue for decision is whether petitioners are entitled to deduct as business expenses amounts paid for a framed print and a live plant for petitioner's office, and for parking fees.

Petitioner was employed in 1977 by the State of South Carolina as an assistant attorney general. As an employee of the State of South Carolina, petitioner was provided an office with furniture and furnishings that consisted of a desk, a desk chair, a work table, a telephone, a dictaphone, a bookcase, a filing cabinet, law books, and two chairs for visitors. Her duties included consulting with public officials and attorneys and others from the private sector, which at times took place in her office.

During 1977, petitioner purchased a framed print for $35 and a live plant for $35 for the purpose of decorating her office. In addition, petitioner paid a total of $180 to rent a parking space located across the street from her office. Petitioner occasionally used her automobile for business purposes when an automobile from the pool of State automobiles was not available.

The only issue is whether petitioner is entitled to a deduction under section 162(a) for amounts paid for a framed print and live plant used to decorate her office, and for amounts paid to rent a parking space. Petitioner contends that the expenses were all ordinary and necessary business expenses deductible under section 162(a). Respondent counters that the expenses were not ordinary and necessary, and that the expenses are nondeductible personal expenses under section 262. We agree with respondent that the expenses constitute nondeductible personal expenses under section 262.

Section 162(a) allows a deduction for all the ordinary and necessary expenses paid or incurred during the taxable year in carrying on any trade or business. However, even assuming an expense meets the requirements of section 162(a), it still may be disallowed if the amount was expended for a personal, living, or family expense. The essential inquiry here is whether a sufficient nexus existed between petitioner's expenses and the "carrying on" of petitioner's trade or business to qualify the expenses for the deduction under section 162(a), or whether they were in essence personal or living expenses and nondeductible by virtue of section 262. Moreover, where both sections 162(a) and 262 may apply, the latter section takes priority over the former.

We find that the amounts paid for the framed print and live plant were expended to improve the appearance of petitioner's office, a personal expense, and only tangentially, if at all, aided her in the performance of her duties as an employee of the State of South Carolina. Her employer had provided her with all the furnishings considered necessary to do her job. No evidence was presented to prove that the presence of the print and plant in her office were either necessary or helpful in performing her required services. "It is not enough that there may be some remote or incidental connection" with the taxpayer's business to support the deduction.

Accordingly, we deny the deduction for these two expenditures.

As to the amounts paid for parking fees, we must likewise deny petitioner the deduction. In *Feistman v. Commissioner*, 63 T.C. 129, 135 (1974), we held that parking fees are nondeductible commuting expenses even where the taxpayer was required by his employer to have his car available for use at work, absent proof that the taxpayer would not have driven his automobile to his place of employment in any event. In the instant case, petitioner has offered no evidence to establish that her employer required her to have her car at her place of employment or that she would not have driven her car to work in any event. In fact, there is no specific evidence that petitioner was required to use her own car on business after she arrived at her office. Accordingly, we deny petitioner a deduction for the parking fees.

SECTION 3: NOT CONTRARY TO PUBLIC POLICY

Code: Sections 162(c), (e), (f), and (g)

Regulations: Sections 1.162–1(a) and 1.212–1(p)

Prior to 1962, the courts held that a deduction under Code Section 162 or 212 was not ordinary and necessary "if allowance of the deduction would frustrate sharply defined national or state policies proscribing particular types of conduct, evidenced by some governmental declaration thereof." *Tank Truck Rentals, Inc. v. Commissioner*, 356 U.S. 30 (1958). On this ground, the courts denied deductions for bribes, kickbacks and other illegal payments, see, e.g., *Coed Records, Inc. v. Commissioner*, 47 T.C. 422 (1967), lobbying expenses, see, e.g., *Cammarano v. United States*, 358 U.S. 498 (1959), and *Textile Mills Securities Corp. v. Commissioner*, 314 U.S. 326 (1941), and fines and penalties, see, e.g., *Hoover Motor Express Co. v. United States*, 356 U.S. 38 (1958).

In 1962, Congress amended Code Section 162 to prohibit deductions for lobbying and political expenses (subsection (e)); in 1969, it added further prohibitions against the deduction, as trade or business expenses, of illegal bribes, kickbacks, and other payments (subsection (c)), fines and penalties (subsection (f)), and antitrust treble damage payments (subsection (g)). The 1969 statutory revisions were clearly intended to supplant the frustration-of-public-policy judicial doctrine as it applied to expenses deductible under Code Section 162. Consistent with this legislative intent,

Treas. Reg. § 1.162–1(a) now provides that: "A deduction for an expense paid or incurred after December 31, 1969, which would otherwise be allowable under section 162 shall not be denied on the grounds that allowance of such deduction would frustrate a sharply defined public policy."

Less clear was the 1969 revisions' effect on the same doctrine as applied to expenses deductible under Code Section 212. Treas. Reg. § 1.212–1(p) provides only that: "The deduction of a payment will be disallowed under section 212 if the payment is of a type for which a deduction would be disallowed under section 162(c), (f), or (g) and the regulations thereunder in the case of a business expense." In addition to leaving open whether additional frustration-of-public-policy grounds may be asserted under Code Section 212, the regulation's failure to cross-reference the Code Section 162(e) prohibition on deduction of lobbying and political expenses leaves open whether lobbying expenses are now deductible under Code Section 212 or are still precluded by the old frustration-of-public-policy doctrine.

Further muddling the picture is Code Section 165, which allows a deduction for "any loss sustained during the taxable year," including losses incurred in a trade or business, subsection (c)(1), and losses incurred in any transaction entered into for profit, subsection (c)(2). Unfortunately, the line between Code Section 162 or Code Section 212 "expenses," on the one hand, and Code Section 165 "losses," on the other, has never been clearly drawn. *See* BORIS BITTKER & LAWRENCE LOKKEN, 1 FEDERAL TAXATION OF INCOME, ESTATES, AND GIFTS ¶ 25.8.5 (3d ed. 1999). Prior to enactment of the 1969 amendments, courts applied the same frustration-of-public-policy limitations to all three. In Rev. Rul. 77–126, 1977–1 C.B. 47, however, the IRS held that the 1969 amendments to Code Section 162 had no effect on the judicially-created frustration-of-public-policy doctrine as applied to Code Section 165. In theory, at least, this leaves open the possibility that whether an otherwise allowable deduction will be disallowed on public policy grounds will depend on whether it is classified as an "expense" under Code Section 162 or 212 (governed by the 1962 and 1969 amendments) or a "loss" under Code Section 165 (governed by the judicially-created frustration-of-public-policy doctrine).

STEPHENS v. COMMISSIONER
905 F.2d 667 (2d Cir. 1990)

In September of 1981, Stephens and other defendants were indicted for participating in a scheme to defraud Raytheon, a Delaware corporation doing business in the United States and in foreign countries. Following a jury trial, Stephens was convicted of four counts of wire fraud, one count of transportation of the proceeds of fraud in interstate commerce, and one count of conspiracy.

Stephens was sentenced on December 3, 1982. Before sentence was pronounced, the Assistant United States Attorney recommended to the court that Stephens be ordered to make restitution to the Raytheon Company. Pointing out that the funds which Stephens had embezzled from the Raytheon Company were frozen in a bank account in Stephens' name in Bermuda, the prosecution suggested that, in addition to whatever custodial and fine requirements the court decided to impose, it sentence Stephens to an additional consecutive period of incarceration and suspend that additional incarceration on condition that restitution to the Raytheon Company be made.

In pronouncing sentence, the sentencing judge agreed that Stephens ought to make restitution to Raytheon. After emphasizing that she "believe[d] a period of imprisonment is absolutely necessary in this case not only for the protection of the public but because we cannot ignore the seriousness of the crimes for which you stand convicted," and "that [Stephens was among] the most culpable," the judge added, "Now, this Court does believe that Raytheon must get its money back. I'm just firmly convinced of that.... I can and shall require restitution from the principals of the [the corporate defendant] because you, in my view, the principals ... defrauded Raytheon.... I'm going to see to it that you give Raytheon its money back."

On each of the counts of wire fraud, Stephens was sentenced to a concurrent 5-year prison term and a $1,000 fine. On the conspiracy count, he was sentenced to a concurrent prison term of 5 years and a $10,000 fine. On the count of interstate transportation of the proceeds of fraud, Stephens was sentenced to a consecutive 5-year prison term and a $5,000 fine; execution of this consecutive prison term, but not the fine, was suspended, and Stephens was placed on 5 years of probation, on the condition that he make restitution to Raytheon in the amount of $1,000,000.

The $1,000,000 represented $530,000 in principal, the amount which was initially embezzled from Raytheon, and $470,000 in interest. Stephens was taxed upon his receipt of the $530,000 in 1976. In 1984, as part of a settlement agreement with Raytheon in connection with two civil actions Raytheon had brought against Stephens, Stephens turned over to Raytheon the $530,000 fund, and executed a $470,000 promissory note, representing the interest. In an Amended 1984 Tax Return, Stephens claimed as a deduction the $530,000 restitution payment. The Commissioner denied this deduction, and Stephens appealed.

In the Tax Court, Stephens contended that the restitution payment was a deductible loss under Section 165. The Commissioner argued that deduction of the payment was barred by Section 162(f). In the alternative, the Commissioner argued that if deductibility was governed by Section 165, rather than by Section 162(f), the deduction of the court-ordered restitution was precluded on public policy grounds.

The Tax Court determined that the allowability of the deduction for the restitution payment was governed by Section 165. In the court's view, such a payment constituted a loss in a "transaction entered into for profit" under Section 165(c)(2), rather than an "ordinary and necessary business expense" described in Section 162(a). Because the deductibility of the payment was not governed by Section 162, the court concluded that Section 162(f), which precludes the deduction of fines and similar penalties as trade or business expenses, was also inapplicable. Nevertheless, the court determined that the public policy considerations embodied in Section 162(f) were relevant in determining whether the payment to Raytheon was deductible under Section 165, reasoning that "it does not follow that the standards, which have been established for the application of section 162(f) to payments which would otherwise be allowable under section 162(a), should not be utilized to determine whether a taxpayer should be denied a deduction for a payment which might otherwise be allowable under section 165(c)(2)."

The Tax Court then considered whether the restitution payment made by Stephens was equivalent to "any fine or similar penalty paid to a government for the violation of any law" within the meaning of Section 162(f). As an initial matter, the court determined that "the fact that the payment in question was made to a private person as restitution rather than to a Government agency in and of itself does not preclude the application of section 162(f)." The court found significant the definition of "fine or similar penalty" in Section 1.162–21(b)(1)(i) of the Treasury Regulations, as including an amount "[p]aid pursuant to conviction or a plea of guilty or nolo contendere for a crime (felony or misdemeanor) in a criminal proceeding." Although the court acknowledged that the payment "had the effect of reimbursing Raytheon for all or part of its loss and, therefore, had a civil aspect," it determined that "[t]he reimbursement-of-loss aspect was merely incidental to the consequences of [taxpayer's] criminal activities." Emphasizing that the payment "was ordered in lieu of an additional prison term and as a condition of probation," the court concluded that the restitution payment was not a deductible loss under Section 165(c)(2).

Stephens appeals from the Tax Court's interpretation of the public policy exception to deductibility under Section 165. Stephens argues that allowing the deduction would not "severely and immediately frustrate" a "sharply defined national or state policy," the test for nondeductibility on public policy grounds under Section 165. Moreover, Stephens asserts, disallowing the deduction results in a tax on his gross income, whereas Congress intended the income tax to be a tax on net income. Finally, Stephens argues that, even assuming Section 162(f) is relevant to deductibility of losses under Section 165, the Tax Court mischaracterized the restitution payment as a fine or similar penalty paid to the government. Because we agree that allowing the deduction would not severely and immediately frustrate a sharply defined national or state policy, we reverse the decision of the Tax Court, and remand for further proceedings.

As Stephens and the Commissioner agree, Stephens' restitution payment is deductible, if at all, pursuant to Section 165(c)(2), which permits an individual to deduct any uncompensated loss sustained during the taxable year, incurred in any transaction entered into for profit, though not connected with a trade or business. 26 U.S.C. § 165(c)(2). Indeed, "[t]he decided cases establish that a restitution payment, such as is involved herein, is not an 'ordinary and necessary' business expense as required by section 162(a) but rather gives rise to a loss in a 'transaction entered into for profit' under section 165(c)(2)." Deductions under Section 165 have been disallowed by the courts, however, where "the allowance of a deduction would 'frustrate sharply defined national or state policies proscribing particular types of conduct'...." *Commissioner v. Tellier*, 383 U.S. 687, 694 (1966) (quoting *Commissioner v. Heininger*, 320 U.S. 467, 473 (1943)). Thus, "the 'test of nondeductibility always is the severity and immediacy of the frustration resulting from allowance of the deduction.'"

For example, in *Tellier*, the Tax Court disallowed a deduction for expenses incurred in the unsuccessful defense of a criminal prosecution. This Court reversed, and the Supreme Court affirmed. Emphasizing that "the 'policies frustrated must be national or state policies evidenced by some governmental declaration of them,'" the Court concluded that "[n]o public policy is offended when a man faced with serious criminal charges employs a lawyer to help in his defense." On the other hand, in *Tank Truck Rentals, Inc. v. Commissioner*, 356 U.S. 30 (1958), the Supreme Court affirmed the disallowance of a deduction of fines paid by a trucking company for violations of state maximum weight laws. In determining the deductibility of the fines, the Court recognized the need to strike a balance between "the congressional intent to tax only net income, and the presumption against congressional intent to encourage violation of declared public policy." Despite the resulting tax on gross income, the Court disallowed the deduction, observing that "[d]eduction of fines and penalties uniformly has been held to frustrate state policy in severe and direct fashion by reducing the 'sting' of the penalty prescribed by the state legislature."

Although *Tellier* and *Tank Truck Rentals* were both decided pursuant to Tax Code provisions relating to business expenses, the test for nondeductibility enunciated in those opinions is applicable to loss deductions under Section 165. Accordingly, the issue before us is whether a deduction for Stephens' restitution payment of embezzled funds to Raytheon so sharply and immediately frustrates a governmentally declared public policy that the deduction should be disallowed.

We note at the outset that "the federal income tax is a tax on net income, not a sanction against wrongdoing.... [T]he statute does not concern itself with the lawfulness of the income that it taxes. Income from a criminal enterprise is taxed at a rate no higher and no lower than income from more conventional sources." *Commissioner v. Tellier*, 383 U.S. at 691. Thus, taxpayers who repay embezzled funds are ordinarily entitled to a deduction in the year in which the funds are repaid. Clearly, no public policy would be frustrated if a restitution payment unrelated to a criminal prosecution were at issue; Stephens would be entitled to a deduction for repaying the embezzled funds to Raytheon.

The Commissioner, however, argues that because Stephens made the restitution payment in lieu of punishment, the deduction should be disallowed. Emphasizing that the sentencing judge suspended the consecutive 5-year sentence on the condition that Stephens make restitution to Raytheon, the Commissioner contends that allowing Stephens a deduction for the restitution payment would take "the sting" out of Stephens' punishment, and therefore would sharply and immediately frustrate public policy. Because Stephens has already paid taxes on the embezzled funds in his 1976 tax return, however, disallowing the deduction for repaying the funds would in effect result in a "double sting." If the deduction were disallowed, Stephens would pay approximately $30,000 in taxes on income he did not retain, in addition to the restitution payment. The sentencing judge made no reference to these tax consequences at the sentencing hearing. Moreover, Stephens received a stern sentence: he was sentenced to five years in prison, and fined a total of $16,000—the $5,000 fine which accompanied the suspended consecutive sentence was not, as we have noted, suspended. We believe that allowing Stephens a deduction for his restitution payment would not severely and immediately frustrate public policy.

However, having reviewed the cases that have sought to elucidate the meaning and scope of the public policy exception under Section 165, and finding them insufficiently decisive, we turn next to Section 162, the Tax Code provision on deductibility of business expenses, as an aid in applying Section 165. Prior to the codification of the public policy exception to deductibility of business expenses, the test for nondeductibility of business expenses and losses was the same: whether the deduction would severely and immediately frustrate a sharply defined national or state policy proscribing particular types of conduct, evidenced by some governmental declaration thereof. In 1969, Congress codified this public policy exception to deductibility of expenses in Section 162 of the Code, limiting the exception to: illegal bribes, kickbacks, and other illegal payments (subsection 162(c)); fines or similar penalties paid to a government for the violation of any law (subsection 162(f)); and a portion of treble damage payments under the antitrust laws (subsection 162(g)). Congress intended these "provision[s] for the denial of the deduction for payments in these situations which are deemed to violate public policy . . . to be all inclusive. Public policy, in other circumstances, generally is not sufficiently clearly defined to justify the disallowance of deductions." S. Rep. No. 552, 91st Cong., 1st Sess., *reprinted in* 1969 U.S. CODE CONG. & ADMIN. NEWS 2027, 2311.

The public policy exception to deductibility under Section 165 was not explicitly affected by the amendments to Section 162. The Internal Revenue Service summarized its view on the impact of the amendments in a Revenue Ruling:

"Congress codified and limited the public policy doctrine in the case of ordinary and necessary business expenses by amending section 162(c) of the Code, adding section 162(f) and (g) in the Tax Reform Act of

1969 ..., and amending section 162(c) in the Revenue Act of 1971.... However, the rules for disallowing a deduction under section 165 of the Code on the grounds of public policy were not limited by Congress but remain the same as they were before 1969. Therefore, disallowance of deductions under section 165 is not limited to amounts of a type for which deduction would be disallowed under section 162(c), (f), and (g) and the regulations thereunder in the case of a business expense."

Rev. Rul. 77–126, 1977–1 C.B. 47, 48. The Tax Court, however, announced a different view: "[t]here is some question whether the public policy doctrine retains any vitality since the enactment of sec. 162(f)." *Medeiros v. Commissioner*, 77 T.C. 1255, 1262 n. 8 (1981). The court observed that "[i]f sec. 162(f) was intended to supplant the public policy doctrine, in all likelihood it would disallow deductions under sec. 165(c)(1) as well as sec. 162(a), as both involved an expenditure incurred in a trade or business."

Though Congress, in amending Section 162, did not explicitly amend Section 165, we believe that the public policy considerations embodied in Section 162(f) are highly relevant in determining whether the payment to Raytheon was deductible under Section 165. Congress can hardly be considered to have intended to create a scheme where a payment would not pass muster under Section 162(f), but would still qualify for deduction under Section 165. It is arguable that the converse is also true, that a payment imposed in the course of a criminal prosecution that does pass muster under Section 162(f) will escape the public policy limitations of Section 165. However, we need not decide in this case whether that is so.

Reference to Section 162(f) supports our conclusion that allowing Stephens a deduction for his restitution payment would not severely and immediately frustrate public policy. Two considerations drawn from Section 162(f) and the cases construing that provision combine to support our conclusion in this case. Whether either consideration alone would suffice is a matter we need not decide.

First, Stephens' restitution payment is primarily a remedial measure to compensate another party, not a "fine or similar penalty," even though Stephens repaid the embezzled funds as a condition of his probation. As the Tax Court summarized in *Waldman v. Commissioner*, 88 T.C. 1384 (1987), *aff'd*, 850 F.2d 611 (9th Cir.1988), "[w]here a payment ultimately serves each of these purposes, *i.e.*, law enforcement (nondeductible) and compensation (deductible), our task is to determine which purpose the payment was designed to serve." Compensatory payments generally "return the parties to the status quo ante." *Colt Industries, Inc. v. United States*, 11 Cl.Ct. 140, 146 (1986) (penalties for violations of the Clean Water Act and Clean Air Act were not compensatory in nature, and therefore not deductible), *aff'd*, 880 F.2d 1311 (Fed.Cir.1989). Under Section 162(f), civil payments, although labelled "penalties," remain deductible if "imposed ... as a remedial measure to compensate another party...."

Our review of the proceedings at Stephens' sentencing convinces us that Stephens' restitution payment was more compensatory than punitive in nature. The sentencing judge, after sentencing Stephens to five years in prison and a fine on each count, reiterated her concern "that Raytheon must get its money back." She then continued,

> "So, this is what I am going to do. On count two, for which you were sentenced to five years and a $5,000 fine, the Court is going to suspend the execution of that sentence, place you on probation and as a condition of your probation, the Court is going to order you to pay restitution in the sum of one million dollars. As to counts one, three, four, five and seven, the Court is going to let those sentences run concurrently."

This excerpt suggests that, after settling on a five-year prison term and a fine as the appropriate sentence, the sentencing judge added the suspended five-year term primarily to "get Raytheon its money back," and not to punish Stephens further. Because the judge suspended the consecutive five-year term on condition "that Raytheon get its money back," the "reimbursement-of-loss aspect," of Stephens' suspended sentence was the primary, not "incidental," purpose of that sentence.

By contrast, in *Waldman*, in which the defendant's entire sentence was suspended on condition that he make restitution, the purpose of the restitution payment was equally compensatory and punitive in nature. Whether or not we would permit use of Section 165 on the facts of *Waldman*, Stephens' situation is distinguishable. Unlike the defendant in *Waldman*, Stephens' sentence consisted of a prison term, fines, and an order to make restitution, supporting the inference that the restitution payment was compensatory in nature, and not in the nature of a fine or penalty. Thus, Stephens' situation resembles that of the petitioners in *Mason and Dixon Lines, Inc. v. United States*, 708 F.2d 1043 (6th Cir.1983), whose fines for trucking violations were punitive and not deductible, but whose liquidated damages payments were compensatory and therefore deductible. While the fines Stephens paid as part of his punishment are obviously not deductible, we find that the restitution payment, which is compensatory in nature, is deductible.

Second, Stephens' payment was made to Raytheon, and not "to a government." The Tax Court found that "the fact that the payment in question was made to a private person as restitution rather than to a Government agency in and of itself does not preclude the application of section 162(f)." In *Waldman*, noting that "[t]he characterization of a payment for purposes of section 162(f) depends on the origin of the liability giving rise to it," the Tax Court disallowed a deduction for restitution payments made as a condition of probation because the "payments ... were ... in satisfaction of ... criminal liability to the State."

To the extent that *Waldman* may be interpreted as suggesting that a restitution payment, ordered in addition to punishment and paid directly to a victim, would not be a deductible loss, we respectfully disagree. In codifying the public policy exception to deductibility of expenses under Section 162, Congress was clear and specific, limiting the exception to bribes, kickbacks and other illegal payments; a portion of treble damage payments; and fines and similar penalties paid to a government. This codification was intended to be "all-inclusive." Whether or not payment to a private party always insulates restitution from the public policy exception of Section 165, it does so on the facts of this case.

We conclude that Stephens' restitution payment was neither a fine or similar penalty, nor paid to the government. Thus, we hold that neither the public policy exception to Section 165, precluding a deduction when it would severely and immediately frustrate public policy to allow it, nor the codification of the public policy exception to deductibility of expenses pursuant to Section 162, bars deduction of Stephens' restitution payment.

Chapter 16

Specific Types of Expenses

∎ ∎ ∎

Subchapter A: Entertainment and Business Meals

Code: Section 274

Regulations: Section 1.274-2

Entertainment and meal expenses have always posed a problem for our income tax system. On the one hand, providing entertainment, meals, and/or beverages is standard business practice in many contexts; failure to do so would sometimes even be viewed as boorish. On the other, recipients clearly receive personal benefits from such expenditures. The problem is raised in its quintessential form when a self-employed taxpayer takes a partner, associate, or client out to lunch. Both clearly receive personal benefits. Yet the lunch may equally clearly be business-related.

MOSS v. COMMISSIONER
80 T.C. 1073 (1983), *aff'd*, 758 F.2d 211 (7th Cir. 1985)

Petitioner, an attorney, was a partner in the law firm Parrillo, Bresler, Weiss & Moss in 1976 and 1977. The firm filed a partnership return for each of the years in question. It took a deduction each year for "meetings and conferences." Petitioner has claimed his share of the firm's expense on his individual return.

Parrillo, Bresler, Weiss & Moss was a firm of six or seven lawyers who specialized in insurance defense work. Their case load was extremely heavy. Most of the lawyers spent the better part of each day participating in or preparing for depositions and trials throughout the greater Chicago area. Judges often held hearings on short notice, thus making it necessary for the firm to assign cases and plan schedules at the last minute.

Robert Parrillo, the senior partner, was responsible for all cases involving the firm's major client. His partners and associates handled the details of these cases, but no final settlements were made without his approval.

The firm had an unwritten policy of meeting every day during the noon recess at the Cafe Angelo, a small, quiet restaurant conveniently located near the courts and the office. Over lunch, the lawyers would decide who would attend various sessions; discuss issues and problems that had come up in the morning; answer questions and advise each other on how to handle certain pending matters; update Mr. Parrillo on settlement negotiations; and, naturally, engage in a certain amount of social banter. Attorneys attended whenever possible for as long as possible; sometimes they ate, at other times they merely joined in the discussions.

The law firm paid for the meals eaten during the noontime meetings. The bill from the Cafe Angelo represents the bulk of the firm's "meeting and conference" expense.

The noon hour was the most convenient and practical time for the firm to have its daily meeting. The courts were almost always in recess at this time, so most attorneys could attend. The more experienced members of the firm were available to advise and educate the fledgling litigators. Parrillo was there to discuss and approve settlements. The Cafe Angelo provided a good location, efficient service, reasonable prices, and a place where judges could locate the attorneys.

In its statutory notice of deficiency, respondent disallowed petitioner's distributive share of the Cafe Angelo expense. The issue for decision is whether petitioner may deduct his share of those expenses in calculating his taxable income.

Petitioner contends that the luncheon meeting expenses are deductible under section 162 as ordinary and necessary business expenses. Respondent, conversely, claims that the lunches are a personal and therefore nondeductible expense. We agree with respondent.

The broad purpose of the Internal Revenue Code is to tax all accessions to wealth, "from whatever source derived." The goal being to tax income, business expenses reduce taxable income. Funds spent on personal consumption, on the other hand, are not deductible. The boundary line dividing personal expenses from business expenses, often obscurely marked, has been a fertile field of battle. In close contests, it is essential to bear in mind that the provisions of section 262 take priority over section 162.

The expense in question is close to that evanescent line dividing personal and business expenses. From the perspective of the partnership, the lunches were a cost incurred in earning their income. The lawyers needed to coordinate assignments and scheduling of their case load, and the noon hour was a logical, convenient time at which to do so. They considered the meeting to be part of their working day, not as an hour of reprieve from business affairs. The individuals did not feel free to make alternate plans, or to eat elsewhere. For this firm, petitioner argues, the meeting was both ordinary and necessary.

The Commissioner focuses not on the circumstances bringing the partnership together each day, but rather on the fact that the individuals were eating lunch while they were together. Rather than to section 162, he looks to section 262, and the regulations which specifically categorize meals as personal expenses. The respondent, in essence, argues that while the meeting may have been ordinary and necessary to the business, the outlay was for meals, a personal item.

The dual nature of the business lunch has long been a difficult problem for legislators and courts alike. The traditional view of the courts has been that if a personal living expense is to qualify under section 162, the taxpayer must demonstrate that it was "different from or in excess of that which would have been made for the taxpayer's personal purposes." *Sutter v. Commissioner*, 21 T.C. 170, 173 (1953).

Following the *Sutter* formula, numerous taxpayers have attempted to deduct the cost of meals eaten under unusual or constraining circumstances. The claims have been denied almost invariably. *See, e.g., Fife v. Commissioner*, 73 T.C. 621 (1980) (attorney may not deduct cost of meals eaten in restaurants due to late client meetings); *Ma–Tran Corp. v. Commissioner*, 70 T.C. 158 (1978) (corporation may not deduct cost of officer's locally consumed meals absent travel or compliance with section 274); *Drill v. Commissioner*, 8 T.C. 902 (1947) (construction worker cannot deduct cost of dinners on nights he worked overtime).

Petitioner relies on *Wells v. Commissioner*, T.C. Memo. 1977–419, 36 T.C.M. (CCH) 1698 (1977), in support of his position. In *Wells*, we denied a deduction claimed by a public defender for the cost of occasional lunch meetings with his staff. The Court noted, however, that in a law firm, "an occasional luncheon meeting with the staff to discuss the operation of the firm would be regarded as an 'ordinary and necessary expense.'" We note, first, that this statement is dictum in a memorandum opinion, and thus not controlling. Second, that case referred to occasional lunches, a far cry from the daily sustenance involved in the case at bar. Even assuming that *Wells* is of any assistance to petitioner, we need not decide where the line between these two cases should be drawn, for we are convinced that outlays for meals consumed 5 days per week, 52 weeks per year would in any event fall on the nondeductible side of it.

In agreeing with the Commissioner on this point, we are well aware that business needs dictated the choice of the noon hour for the daily meeting. In a very real sense, these meetings contributed to the success of the partnership. But other costs contributing to the success of one's employment are treated as personal expenses. Commuting is obviously essential to one's continued employment, yet those expenses are not deductible as business expenses. As this Court stated in *Amend v. Commissioner*, 55 T.C. 320, 325–326 (1970):

> "the common thread which seems to bind the cases together is the notion that some expenses are so inherently personal that they simply cannot qualify for section 162 treatment irrespective of the role played by such expenditures in the overall scheme of the taxpayers'

trade or business. . . . 'A businessman's suit, a saleslady's dress, the accountant's glasses are necessary for their business but the necessity does not overcome the personal nature of these items and make them a deductible business expense.'"

In the instant case, we are convinced that petitioner and his partners and associates discussed business at lunch, that the meeting was a part of their working day, and that this time was the most convenient time at which to meet. We are also convinced that the partnership benefited from the exchange of information and ideas that occurred.

But this does not make his lunch deductible any more than riding to work together each morning to discuss partnership affairs would make his share of the commuting costs deductible. If only the four partners attended the luncheons, petitioner's share of the expenses (assuming they were coequal partners) would have corresponded to his share of the luncheons. This is not an occasion for the general taxpayer to share in the cost of his daily sustenance. Indeed, if petitioner is correct, only the unimaginative would dine at their own expense.

NOTES

1. *Statutory limitations.*—Once taxpayer has established that his claimed entertainment or meal deduction is an "ordinary and necessary" deduction under Code Section 162 or Code Section 212, he must pass additional hurdles imposed by Code Section 274.

Code Section 274 was enacted to curb what Congress perceived to be abusive deduction of entertainment expenses, including meal expenses. It contains three key rules. First, with important exceptions, no such expense is deductible unless it is (1) "directly related to" taxpayer's trade or business or (2) in the case of an expense directly preceding or following a substantial and bona fide business discussion, "associated with" taxpayer's trade or business. Code Section 274(a)(1)(A). Second, no entertainment expense is deductible unless taxpayer substantiates that he is entitled to the deduction by adequate records. Code Section 274(d). Third, with important exceptions, even if an expense is deductible under the foregoing rules, only 50 percent is deductible. Code Section 274(n). In addition, in general Code Section 274(k) disallows the deduction of meal or beverage expenses unless the expense "is not lavish or extravagant under the circumstances" and taxpayer or an employee of taxpayer is present.

PROBLEMS FOR DISCUSSION

16–1. Must the associates in *Moss* report the value of the meals they received as income?

SECTION 1: COMPLETE DISALLOWANCE OF UNRELATED ENTERTAINMENT

Code: Section 274(a)(1)(A)

Code Section 274(a)(1)(A) disallows the deduction of any entertainment expenses, including meal and beverage expenses, even if "ordinary and necessary," unless they (1) are "directly related to" taxpayer's trade or business, or (2) in the case of expenses directly preceding or following a substantial and bona fide business discussion, are "associated with" taxpayer's trade or business.

(a) "DIRECTLY RELATED"

Regulations: Section 1.274–2(c)

An entertainment expense is directly related to taxpayer's trade or business if it is incurred "in a clear business setting directly in furtherance of the taxpayer's trade or business." Treas. Reg. § 1.274–2(c)(4). For example, a lawyer invites her client to lunch to discuss a matter she is handling for him. More generally, an entertainment expense is directly related to taxpayer's trade or business if taxpayer meets a four-part test: (1) he had more than a general expectation of deriving some income or other specific trade or business benefit from the expense, (2) he actively engaged in some bona fide business transaction for that purpose (or was prevented from doing so by reasons beyond his control), (3) the principal character of the event was the active conduct of taxpayer's trade or business (or would have been but for reasons beyond his control), and (4) the expense is allocable to taxpayer and persons with whom he engaged in the active conduct of his trade or business. For example, a lawyer takes the chief financial officer of a corporation she hopes will become a client out to dinner to discuss the structure of his company's employee benefits plans. An expense is not "directly related" to his trade or business if (1) taxpayer was not present, or (2) "the distractions were substantial"—for example, meetings at night clubs, theaters, sporting events or social gatherings like cocktail parties.

(b) "ASSOCIATED WITH"

An entertainment expense that fails the direct relationship test may nevertheless be deductible if it was "associated with the active conduct of trade or business" and "directly preceded or followed a substantial and bona fide business discussion." Treas. Reg. § 1.274–2(d)(1). The expense is "associated with the active conduct of trade or business" if taxpayer "had a clear business purpose in making the expenditure, such as to obtain new business or to encourage the continuation of an existing business relationship." Entertainment directly precedes or follows a business discussion if it occurs on the same day. In addition, under Treas. Reg. § 1.274–2(d)(3)(ii):

"If the entertainment and the business discussion do not occur on the same day, the facts and circumstances of each case are to be considered .... For example, if a group of business associates comes from out of town to the taxpayer's place of business to hold a substantial business discussion, the entertainment of such business guests and their wives on the evening prior to, or on the evening of the day following, the business discussion would generally be regarded as directly preceding or following such discussion."

(c) STATUTORY EXCEPTIONS

The complete disallowance rule of Code Section 274(a)(1)(A) is subject to nine statutory exceptions:

- (1) For food and beverages furnished on taxpayer's business premises primarily for his employees,
- (2) For expenses treated as compensation to an employee,
- (3) For expenses reimbursed by another, subject to conditions,
- (4) For recreational, social, or similar activities primarily for the benefit of employees other than highly compensated employees,
- (5) For expenses directly related to business meetings of employees, stockholders, agents, or directors,
- (6) For expenses necessary to attendance at business league meetings,
- (7) For goods and services made available to the general public,
- (8) For goods and services sold for full consideration, and
- (9) For expenses treated as income to a nonemployee.

PROBLEMS FOR DISCUSSION

16–2. Which of the following expenses are subject to complete disallowance under Code Section 274(a)(1)(A)?

(a) A law firm holds a firm-wide lunch at a nearby restaurant on the last every Friday of every month. At the lunch, substantial firm business is discussed. All lawyers are expected to attend unless otherwise engaged on firm business.

(b) Lawyers at a law firm considering a law student for possible employment take her out to lunch between her morning and afternoon interviews at the firm.

(c) A lawyer and her spouse take a potential client and his spouse out to dinner and the theater. No significant business is discussed.

(d) Louis Tully, a certified public accountant, invites clients to his birthday party. The party is billed and structured as a birthday party. Nevertheless, Louis makes sure to chat briefly about business with all client/guests at some point during the party.

(e) After April 15 has passed, Louis throws a "We're done!" party for his employees, providing food, beverages, and entertainment. His purpose is to enhance morale and give employees a chance to relax after tax filing season.

(f) Each year, a law firm rewards its highest-billing associate by sending her on an all-expenses paid vacation to the European capital of her choice.

SECTION 2: COMPLETE DISALLOWANCE OF UNSUBSTANTIATED EXPENSES

Regulations: Sections 1.274–5 and 1.274–5T

Under Code Section 274(d), no deduction is allowed for entertainment or meal expenses unless taxpayer substantiates by adequate records (A) the amount of such expense, (B) the time and place of the item purchased, (C) its business purpose, and (D) the business relationship to taxpayer of the persons involved. Failure to comply with the substantiation regulations on a timely basis sometimes cannot be remedied after the fact. *See, e.g., Mohamed v. Commissioner*, Chapter 18, below ($18.5 million deduction denied).

SECTION 3: 50 PERCENT DISALLOWANCE RULE

Code: Section 274(n)

Regulation: Section 1.132–6(d)(2)

Code Section 274(n) provides that no deduction for food, beverages, or entertainment shall exceed 50 percent of the amount of the relevant expense. (As originally enacted, and as applied in *Boyd Gaming*, below, the limitation was set at 80 percent.)

In the case of expenses for food or beverages, the 50 percent cap does *not* apply to any entertainment expenses:

- (2) For expenses treated as compensation to an employee,
- (3) For expenses reimbursed by another, subject to conditions,
- (4) For recreational, social, or similar activities primarily for the benefit of employees other than highly compensated employees,
- (7) For goods and services made available to the general public,
- (8) For goods and services sold for full consideration, or
- (9) For expenses treated as income to a nonemployee.

In addition, it does *not* apply to expenses excludible from recipient's gross income as a *de minimis* fringe by reason of Code Section 132(e). Code Section 274(n)(2)(B). In *Boyd Gaming*, below, the Ninth Circuit applied the *de minimis* fringe exception to permit deduction of 100 percent of the costs of employer-provided cafeterias that supplied meals to employees without charge "for the convenience of the employer."

BOYD GAMING CORPORATION v. COMMISSIONER
177 F.3d 1096 (9th Cir. 1999)

This case involves the question whether there really is a "free lunch." In 1986, concerned that the tax laws unfairly allowed high-income taxpayers to structure their business affairs in a manner that generated deductions for personal living expenses, Congress imposed, with certain exceptions, an 80% cap on the amount of deductions for business meals and entertainment. This change, in turn, affected employers who provide "free lunches" to their employees. At issue in this case is whether, under the circumstances here, the employer qualifies for an exception to the 80% cap on deductions associated with "free lunches" furnished to its employees.

Petitioners, California Hotel & Casino, Boyd Gaming Corporation, and their subsidiaries (collectively, "Boyd"), are hotel and casino operators that, for reasons of security and logistics, require their employees to stay on the business premises throughout the work shift. As a consequence of the policy, the employees receive free meals at on-site cafeterias. Boyd contends that it is exempt from the 80% cap on deductions because the meals are provided as a "de minimis fringe" benefit. 26 U.S.C. § 274(n)(2); see 26 U.S.C. § 132(e). Boyd argues that the meals at issue meet the statutory test for "de minimis fringe" benefits because they were furnished to "more than half" the employees for the "convenience of the employer."

During the 1987 and 1988 taxable years, Boyd operated four casino and hotel properties in Las Vegas, Nevada: (i) the Stardust Resort & Casino; (ii) the California Hotel & Casino; (iii) the Fremont Hotel & Casino; and (iv) Sam's Town Hotel & Gambling Hall. These properties are open to the public 24 hours a day, seven days a week. Each property operates an on-site cafeteria facility, separate from the public restaurants, where employees can obtain free meals during their work shifts. In addition, approximately 10% of Boyd's employees (primarily managerial and supervisory personnel) are permitted to eat in the on-site public restaurants at no charge.

During the years at issue, petitioners required their employees to stay on the Properties' premises during their entire shift, except where overridden by union contract or absent permission from a supervisor/manager. An employee who left during his or her shift, without authorization, was subject to disciplinary action, up to and including discharge.

Boyd offers multiple reasons for imposition of the "stay-on-premises" policy, including addressing security and efficiency concerns,[3] maintaining

---
3. Boyd describes the casino environment as one in which vast amounts of cash flow in fast-moving transactions and special security precautions are imposed by state regulations. Many of Boyd's employees handle or have easy access to cash and gambling chips. As a result, each

work force control,[4] handling business emergencies and continuous customer demands, and the impracticality of obtaining meals within a reasonable proximity. In response, the Commissioner argues that the evidence did not support these reasons and, in any event, that there was no business nexus between the "stay-on-premises" requirement and the meals furnished to employees.

This case turns on whether Boyd provided the employee meals for its own "convenience." Before analyzing the issue of "convenience," we first outline the statutes that lead to this test of deductibility.

The "convenience" test, which Boyd must satisfy to be exempt from the 80% cap on food and beverage expenses, stems from the statutory exception to the cap. During the taxable years at issue, 26 U.S.C. § 274(n) limited the amount of a deduction for food or beverages to 80% of the associated expenses. The 80% cap, however, did not apply if the food or beverage expense was "excludable from the gross income of the recipient" under 26 U.S.C. § 132(e). 26 U.S.C. § 274(n)(2). In general, section 132 excludes "de minimis fringe" benefits from an employee's gross income. See 26 U.S.C. § 132(a)(4). Section 132 further defines as a "de minimis fringe" an employer's operation of an eating facility for employees if the facility meets the following criteria:

(A) such facility is located on or near the business premises of the employer, and

(B) revenue derived from such facility normally equals or exceeds the direct operating costs of such facility.

Boyd's facilities were located on the business premises and therefore satisfied subsection (A). For the taxable years at issue, however, Boyd did not charge for the meals and hence could not establish by direct evidence that it met the revenue/operating cost test of subsection (B). Thus, Boyd must rely on a statutory presumption, which treats revenue as equal to operating costs for meals furnished to employees who are entitled to exclude the value of the meals from their gross income pursuant to 26 U.S.C. § 119. 26 U.S.C. § 132(e). Under section 119, an employee may exclude meals furnished on the business premises of the employer for the "convenience of the employer." 26 U.S.C. § 119(a). The applicability of the 80% cap therefore turns on whether Boyd provided the meals at issue for its own convenience.

The term "convenience of the employer" is not defined by statute. IRS regulations, however, consider meals as furnished for the "convenience of the employer" if they are provided for a "substantial noncompensatory business reason." In addition, the regulations define a catch-all

---

property performs special check-out procedures for certain employees before they are permitted to leave the premises. The "stay-on-premises" policy minimizes the number of entries and departures during each work shift, thereby reducing security risks and the costs of security measures.

4. Boyd contends that the "stay-on-premises" requirement allows it to maintain tight control over its workforce, thereby reducing the chances of employees succumbing to the distractions and temptations of the "festive" Las Vegas atmosphere.

provision, which allows an employer to impute a "substantial noncompensatory business reason" for provision of the meals [to employees for whom a specific substantial noncompensatory business reason cannot be shown if a specific substantial noncompensatory business reason is show for a sufficient percentage of employees who receive the benefit].

In 1998, Congress adopted a statutory catch-all provision:

"All meals furnished on the business premises of an employer to such employer's employees shall be treated as furnished for the convenience of the employer if, without regard to this paragraph, more than half of the employees to whom such meals are furnished on such premises are furnished such meals for the convenience of the employer."

26 U.S.C. § 119(b)(4). Section 119(b)(4) was explicitly given retroactive effect. We must examine whether Boyd can satisfy the "convenience of the employer" standard for the requisite number of employees.*

For guidance, we look to the Supreme Court's decision in *Commissioner v. Kowalski*, 434 U.S. 77 (1977). The Court examined the history of section 119 and concluded that the "convenience of the employer" should be measured according to a "business-necessity" theory. Under that theory, the exclusion from gross income applies only when the employee must accept the meals "in order properly to perform his duties."

Kowalski is consistent with our earlier decision, *Caratan v. Commissioner*, 442 F.2d 606 (9th Cir.1971), in which we held that the Tax Court may not substitute a business judgment that is contrary to the unimpeached and uncontradicted evidence presented by the taxpayer. While the taxpayer in *Caratan* offered credible testimony establishing that the farm supervisory personnel at issue needed to be available for duty 24 hours a day and were therefore required to accept lodging on the farm as a condition of employment, the Commissioner put forth no evidence. We specifically rejected the Tax Court's narrow focus on whether the employees could do their jobs without living on the farm, observing that "if the employee must be available for duty at all times, the lodging is, practically speaking, indispensable to the proper discharge" of the employee's duties.

We find *Caratan* analogous to the case now before us. Boyd has adopted a "stay-on-premises" requirement and, as a consequence, furnishes meals to its employees because they cannot leave the casino properties during their shifts. Common sense dictates that once the policy was embraced, the "captive" employees had no choice but to eat on the

---

* In a confusing part of the opinion, omitted in text, the court notes that "between roughly 41% and 48% of Boyd's employees received meals during the 1987 and 1988 taxable years for the 'convenience of the employer.'" The court then finds that Boyd was "a few percentage points short of the 'more than half' threshold." It appears that what the court meant was that between 41% and 48% of *all* of Boyd's employees ate at the cafeterias. This left open the question of what percent of those that did eat at the cafeterias did so for Boyd's convenience. The court ultimately holds that more than half who did eat at the cafeterias did so for Boyd's convenience, thereby meeting the "statutory catch-all" of Code Section 119(b)(4).

premises. As with the lodging in *Caratan*, the furnished meals here were, in effect, "indispensable to the proper discharge" of the employees' duties.

Contrary to the Tax Court's conclusion, no nexus other than the "stay-on-premises" policy was required for the meals to satisfy the *Kowalski* test. Indeed, the Commissioner's argument that the meals must be linked to an employee's specific duties would render the test virtually impossible to satisfy; only restaurant critics and dieticians could meet such a test. The Commissioner's position is also inconsistent with the IRS regulations themselves, which envision that meals furnished to employees who are similarly confined to the business premises during meal times, but for different reasons (*i.e.*, remote location, insufficient eating facilities in the vicinity), are provided for the "convenience of the employer" and satisfy the *Kowalski* test. For these purposes, we can discern no logical distinction between workers isolated by geography and those isolated by employer policy.

We caution that it would not have been enough for Boyd simply to wave a "magic wand" and say it had a policy in order to be entitled to a deduction. Instead, Boyd was required to and did support its closed campus policy with adequate evidence of legitimate business reasons. While reasonable minds might differ regarding whether a "stay-on-premises" policy is necessary for security and logistics, the fact remains that the casinos here operate under this policy. Given the credible and uncontradicted evidence regarding the reasons underlying the "stay-on-premises" policy, we find it inappropriate to second guess these reasons or to substitute a different business judgment for that of Boyd.

As a result of the "stay-on-premises" requirement, "more than half" of Boyd's employees received the free meals for the "convenience of the employer," and thus Boyd is entitled to invoke the catch-all provision of section 119(b)(4). We hold that, for the taxable years at issue, Boyd may deduct 100% of the expenses associated with its employee cafeterias.

PROBLEMS FOR DISCUSSION

16–3. Outline the court's logic in *Boyd Gaming*, beginning with the premise that "more than half the meals were provided for Boyd's convenience" and ending with the conclusion that "Boyd may deduct 100 percent of the expenses associated with its employee cafeterias."

16–4. Is *Boyd Gaming*, which appears to hold that the costs of providing free daily meals to employees "for the convenience of the employer" are 100 percent deductible, consistent with *Moss*, which denies any deduction for the cost of daily business-related meals?

16–5. Which of the following expenses are *not* subject to the 50 percent deduction limitation of Code Section 274(n)?

    (a) Joe's Bar and Grill serves food and beverages to its customers, charging market rates.

(b) A law firm holds a firm-wide lunch at a nearby restaurant on the last every Friday of every month. At the lunch, substantial firm business is discussed. All lawyers are expected to attend unless otherwise engaged on firm business.

(c) A law firm reimburses its associates for the cost of meals incurred when they work late.

(d) Lawyers at a law firm considering a law student for possible employment take her out to lunch between her morning and afternoon interviews at the firm.

(e) A lawyer and her spouse take a potential client and his spouse out to dinner and the theater. Substantial business is discussed.

(f) Each year, a law firm rewards its highest-billing associate by sending her on an all-expenses paid vacation to the European capital of her choice.

(g) After April 15 has passed, Louis Tully, a certified public accountant, throws a "We're done!" party for his employees, providing food, beverages, and entertainment. His purpose is to enhance morale and give employees a chance to relax after tax filing season.

Subchapter B: Travel

Code: Section 162(a)(2)

Regulations: Section 1.911–2(b)

Code Section 162(a)(2) includes among deductible trade or business expenses "traveling expenses (including amounts expended for meals and lodging other than amounts which are lavish or extravagant under the circumstances) while away from home in the pursuit of a trade or business." Expenses deductible under this rule include transportation to and from the destination, meals and lodging while there, and any other business-related expenses of the trip—*e.g.*, transportation from lodging to work site each day. Traveling expenses are subject to the substantiation requirements of Code Section 274(d) and Treas. Reg. §§ 1.274–5 and 1.274–5T, and meals and beverages deducted as traveling expenses are subject to the 50 percent disallowance rule of Code Section 274(h), unless eligible for one of the exceptions to that rule.

Meals may be deducted as traveling expenses, however, only if the trip in question is long enough to require taxpayer to sleep or rest. Originally known as the "overnight rule," this rule was upheld by the Supreme Court in *United States v. Correll*, 389 U.S. 299 (1967). Thus, if taxpayer flies from Boston to Washington in the morning on business, has lunch in Washington, and flies back that evening, he may not deduct the cost of lunch as a travel expense, because his trip is not long enough to require him to sleep or rest. (This will not preclude him from deducting his lunch as a business expense under the rules discussed in Chapter 15A above, if it otherwise qualifies.) If, on the other hand, he flies from Boston to Washington in the morning and returns the next morning, staying overnight, his lunch, dinner, and breakfast are deductible as travel expenses, even if they do not otherwise qualify as business expenses.

SECTION 1: "TAX HOME" AND COMMUTING EXPENSES

Courts have apparently not reached full agreement as to whether a taxpayer's "home" for purposes of Code Section 162(a)(2) is his place of business or his place of residence. As a practical matter, however, any such lingering disagreement has few, if any, discernible consequences. Treas. Reg. § 1.911–2(b), issued under Code Section 911, which allows a U.S. citizen or resident whose "tax home" is in a foreign country to exclude a portion of his foreign earned income from gross income, summarizes the Treasury's view:

> "For purposes of [section 911], the term 'tax home' has the same meaning which it has for purposes of section 162(a)(2) (relating to travel expenses away from home). Thus, under section 911, an individual's tax home is considered to be located at his regular or principal (if more than one regular) place of business, or if the individual has no regular or principal place of business because of the nature of the business, then at his regular place of abode in a real and substantial sense."

In addition, courts have consistently held that a taxpayer who has no regular place of business or no regular place of abode has no "home" to be away from and therefore cannot deduct travel expenses.

In practice, therefore, it may be useful to think of a taxpayer's "tax home" as being subject to a three-part test:

- If taxpayer has a regular or principal place of business, then his tax home is that place of business.

- If he has no regular or principal place of business, then his tax home is his regular place of abode.

- If he has no regular or principal place of business and no regular place of abode, then he has no tax home to be away from and cannot deduct travel expenses.

This, in turn, may explain why standard commuting expenses are disallowed as personal. If taxpayer's place of business is her "home" for Code Section 162(a)(2) purposes, then the standard commuter leaves her "home" to see her family, have dinner, sleep, take a shower, and have breakfast before returning "home"—all personal activities. *Commissioner v. Flowers*, 326 U.S. 465 (1946), the one Supreme Court case to address the problem of commuting expenses, is consistent with this result. In *Flowers*, a lawyer who had his permanent residence in Jackson, Mississippi, but worked in Mobile, Alabama, attempted to deduct his travel costs between Jackson and Mobile and his meals and lodging while in Mobile. The Court denied the deduction: "The added costs in issue ... were incurred solely as the result of taxpayer's desire to maintain a home in Jackson . . . ." In other words, they were personal.

For the most part, the foregoing three-part test is also consistent with exceptions to the general rule of commuting nondeductibility currently recognized by the Tax Court and/or the IRS.

REV. RUL. 99-7
1999-1 C.B. 361

Issue

Under what circumstances are daily transportation expenses incurred by a taxpayer in going between the taxpayer's residence and a work location deductible under § 162(a) of the Internal Revenue Code?

Holding

In general, daily transportation expenses incurred in going between a taxpayer's residence and a work location are nondeductible commuting expenses. However, such expenses are deductible under the circumstances described in paragraph (1), (2), or (3) below.

(1) A taxpayer may deduct daily transportation expenses incurred in going between the taxpayer's residence and a *temporary* work location *outside* the metropolitan area where the taxpayer lives and normally works. However, unless paragraph (2) or (3) below applies, daily transportation expenses incurred in going between the taxpayer's residence and a *temporary* work location *within* that metropolitan area are nondeductible commuting expenses.

(2) If a taxpayer has one or more regular work locations away from the taxpayer's residence, the taxpayer may deduct daily transportation expenses incurred in going between the taxpayer's residence and a *temporary* work location in the same trade or business, regardless of the distance. (The Service will continue not to follow *Walker v. Commissioner*, 101 T.C. 537 (1993).)

(3) If a taxpayer's residence is the taxpayer's principal place of business within the meaning of § 280A(c)(1)(A), the taxpayer may deduct daily transportation expenses incurred in going between the residence and another work location in the same trade or business, regardless of whether the other work location is *regular* or *temporary* and regardless of the distance.

For purposes of paragraphs (1), (2), and (3), the following rules apply in determining whether a work location is *temporary*. If employment at a work location is realistically expected to last (and does in fact last) for 1 year or less, the employment is *temporary* in the absence of facts and circumstances indicating otherwise. If employment at a work location is realistically expected to last for more than 1 year or there is no realistic expectation that the employment will last for 1 year or less, the employment is *not temporary,* regardless of whether it actually exceeds 1 year. If employment at a work location initially is realistically expected to last for 1 year or less, but at some later date the employment is realistically expected to exceed 1 year, that employment will be treated as temporary (in the absence of facts and circumstances indicating otherwise) until the date that the taxpayer's realistic expectation changes, and will be treated as *not temporary* after that date.

The determination that a taxpayer's residence is the taxpayer's principal place of business within the meaning of § 280A(c)(1)(A) is not necessarily determinative of whether the residence is the taxpayer's tax home for other purposes, including the travel-away-from-home deduction under § 162(a)(2).

In *Walker v. Commissioner*, 101 T.C. 537 (1993), with which the IRS states its disagreement in Rev. Rul. 99–7, the Tax Court held that daily transportation expenses incurred in going between the taxpayer's residence and a *temporary* work location *within* that metropolitan area were deductible. The *Walker* result is more consistent with Treas. Reg. § 1.911–2(b) and the three-part test and less discriminatory against blue-collar taxpayers. (White-collar taxpayers are more likely to be able to establish home offices that qualify as places of business; blue-collar taxpayers generally cannot.)

NOTES

1. *Change of tax home.*—The rules summarized in Rev. Rul. 99–7 apply only if the destination work site is "temporary." If taxpayer's work at the new site is "indefinite" rather than "temporary," the new site becomes taxpayer's tax home, and commuting expenses to the site cease to be deductible even if they otherwise meet the requirements of the ruling.

The block language at the end of Code Section 162(a) provides that: "taxpayer shall not be treated as being temporarily away from home during any period of employment if such period exceeds 1 year." Whether employment away from "home" is "indefinite" rather than "temporary" is then governed, in the first instance, by Rev. Rul. 93–86, 1993–2 C.B. 71:

> "[I]f employment away from home in a single location is realistically expected to last (and does in fact last) for 1 year or less, the employment is temporary in the absence of facts and circumstances indicating otherwise. If employment away from home in a single location is realistically expected to last for more than 1 year or there is no realistic expectation that the employment will last for 1 year or less, the employment is indefinite, regardless of whether it actually exceeds 1 year. If employment away from home in a single location initially is realistically expected to last for 1 year or less, but at some later date the employment is realistically expected to exceed 1 year, that employment will be treated as temporary (in the absence of facts and circumstances indicating otherwise) until the date that the taxpayer's realistic expectation changes."

Among the facts and circumstances considered in determining whether taxpayer is "temporarily" away from home, regardless of expectations, is whether he continues to maintain a place of business or residence in the city from which he claims to be "temporarily" away. If he does not, his tax home has probably moved, even if he expects to be at his new work site for less than a year.

Problems for Discussion

16–6. Jeremy, a lawyer, lives in the suburbs of Chicago and works at a law firm downtown. For two weeks, he commutes instead to a client's headquarters in another Chicago suburb and spends his days there reviewing documents for a case he is handling. Are the costs of his commute deductible?

16–7. Adam, a lawyer, uses one room in his house exclusively as his law office. The room constitutes his principal place of business. Adam generally commutes to his client's offices for meetings and to the courts for appearances. Are the costs of these commutes deductible?

16–8. Isabelle, a construction worker who lives in Boston, has no long-term employer. Instead, she takes on temporary jobs, ranging in length from a few weeks to many months.

 (a) Job 1, which is expected to and does last nine months, is in Natick, which is within the Boston metropolitan area. Isabelle commutes roundtrip from her house to the construction site each day. Is the cost of her commute deductible?

 (b) Job 2, which is expected to and does last nine months, is in Springfield, a 90 mile drive from Boston. Isabelle commutes roundtrip from her house in Boston to the construction site each day. Is the cost of her commute deductible?

 (c) Instead of commuting to Job 2 from Boston, Isabelle rents an apartment in Springfield for the nine-month period. On Sunday night, she leaves Boston to drive to Springfield, sleeping in her Springfield apartment Monday through Thursday. On Friday night, she returns to her home in Boston. What expenses can she deduct?

 (d) Assume that Isabelle realistically expects Job 2 to last for nine months. In fact, however, because of environmental regulatory problems, it lasts for 15 months. Does this affect the deductibility of her expenses for travel "while away from home"?

 (e) Isabelle is single. When she takes Job 2, believing that it will last nine months, Isabelle gives up her apartment in Boston and rents an apartment in Springfield. She intends to return to Boston when the job is complete and in fact does so at the end of the nine-month period. Does this affect the deductibility of her expenses for travel "while away from home"?

SECTION 2: COMBINED BUSINESS AND PERSONAL TRAVEL

Regulations: Sections 1.162–2 and 1.274–4

Taxpayers commonly take trips that combine business and pleasure. The regulations break the costs of such trips into two parts: the costs of transportation to and from the destination (*e.g.*, plane fare or intercity mileage) and other costs (*e.g.*, hotel, meals, and the like).

In general, the deductibility of transportation to and from the destination is determined using a "primary purpose" test. Treas. Reg. § 1.162–2(b)(1). If the primary purpose of the trip is business, the costs of such transportation are fully deductible. If the primary purpose is personal, such costs are not deductible at all. In determining the purpose of the trip, the amount of time spent on business activities relative to the amount spent on personal activities is "an important factor." Treas. Reg. § 1.162–2(b)(2).

Nontransportation expenses, by contrast, are allocated expense by expense, regardless of the trip's primary purpose. "[E]xpenses while at the destination which are properly allocable to the taxpayer's trade or business are deductible even though the traveling expenses to and from the destination are not deductible." Treas. Reg. § 1.162–2(b)(1). Consistent with the "tax home" analysis outlined in Section 1, above, commuting expenses within the destination city that are properly allocable to taxpayer's trade or business are deductible—since taxpayer is away from "home" in pursuit of a trade or business.

These general rules are modified, in the case of extended foreign travel with a significant personal component, by Code Section 274(c) and Treas. Reg. § 1.274–4. The modified rules apply if (1) the trip exceeds 7 days, not counting the day of departure, and (2) personal activities make up more than 25 percent of the trip. If they apply, they limit the deductibility of transportation expenses. Transportation expenses subject to these special rules must first pass the standard "primary purpose" test. If they do, they must then be allocated between the business and personal components of the trip; this is generally done by counting the number of days taxpayer spends on business matters. Treas. Reg. § 1.274–4(d)(2). A day is a "business day" if on that day (1) taxpayer was traveling to or returning from his destination, (2) his presence was required at a particular place for a specific and bona fide purpose, (3) during business hours, his principal activity was business activity, or (4) the day was "a Saturday, Sunday, legal holiday, or other reasonably necessary standby day which intervened during that course of the taxpayer's trade or business ... which the taxpayer endeavored to conduct with reasonable dispatch." This is true even if taxpayer engages in more nonbusiness than business activities on such a day.

Although the allocation rules of Treas. Reg. § 1.274–4(d)(2) technically apply only to foreign travel, they are convenient to apply to domestic travel as well. As a result, it is common for taxpayers to use the foreign travel allocation rules to allocate the meal and lodging component of domestic travel expenses. If a day is a "business day" under those allocation rules, they deduct meals and lodging for that day; if it is not, they do not.

PROBLEMS FOR DISCUSSION

16–9. On Thursday, Marla flies from New York to Paris to negotiate a new supply contract for her company. She meets with representatives of the supply company on Friday, then spends the weekend visiting friends. On Monday, meetings are cancelled because the CEO of the supply company is called away on business; she therefore spends the day sightseeing. On Tuesday, the contract is signed and on Wednesday, she flies back to New York. For which days can she deduct the cost of meals and lodging as travel expenses?

Subchapter C: Education

Regulations: Section 1.162–5

As a matter of theory, costs of education can be divided into three categories. First, education for personal purposes—for example, to become a more fully rounded person—is personal; its costs should therefore be nondeductible. Second, education to enter an income-producing profession—for example, to become a lawyer—is capital; its costs should therefore be capitalized and amortized over taxpayer's professional life, or at least become deductible when taxpayer retires. Third, education to maintain or improve skills in an existing trade or business should be deductible if that education has a short useful life or capitalized and amortized if it has a longer useful life.

In this context, however, law only partially follows theory.

First, costs of education for personal purposes are nondeductible. *See, e.g., Carroll v. Commissioner*, 418 F.2d 91 (7th Cir. 1969) (policeman studying philosophy); *Katz v. Commissioner*, 27 TCM (CCH) 87 (1968) (CPA's cost of learning how to fly an airplane). Code Section 274(m)(2) now categorically disallows deduction of expenses for travel as a form of education, presumably on the theory that educational travel is inherently personal.

Second, the costs of education that qualify taxpayer to enter into a new trade or business are nondeductible and nonamortizable. Treas. Reg. § 1.162–5(b) treats as personal or "an inseparable aggregate of personal and capital expenditures" the costs of (1) education required "to meet the minimum educational requirements for qualification in his employment or other trade or business" or (2) education "which is part of a program of study being pursued by him which will lead to qualifying him in a new trade or business." Thus, for example, the costs of a J.D. degree and bar review course cannot be deducted when incurred, amortized over taxpayer's professional life, or deducted when taxpayer ceases to engage in the practice of law. *Sharon v. Commissioner*, 591 F.2d 1273 (9th Cir. 1978), *cert. denied*, 442 U.S. 941 (1979). This result is arguably supported by the Supreme Court's early capitalization decision in *Welch v. Helvering*, 290 U.S. 111 (1933) (payments of a former employer's debts to preserve taxpayer's business reputation personal and capital, apparently never to be deducted), but is inconsistent with modern comprehensive tax base theory. As a result, it is sometimes said that our income tax system disfavors investments in "human capital."

Third, the costs of maintaining or improving skills required in taxpayer's employment or trade or business are currently deductible, Treas. Reg. § 1.162–5(c)(1), as are the costs of education undertaken to meet the express requirements of taxpayer's employer or of applicable law or regulations as a condition of retention taxpayer's established employment relationship, Treas. Reg. § 1.162–5(c)(2). Early on, current deductibility of such costs was justified by "the rather evanescent character of that for which the petitioner spent his money." *Coughlin v. Commissioner*, 203 F.2d 307, 310 (2d Cir. 1953) (allowing deduction as trade or business expense of lawyer's cost of attending NYU's annual Institute on Federal Taxation). Under current regulations, however, such costs are deductible regardless of their useful lives. Thus, for example, a taxpayer already engaged in the trade or business of being a lawyer may deduct the costs of a tax LL.M. degree—which the regulations treat as "maintaining or improving" his skills as a lawyer—even if the degree increases taxpayer's income-producing potential over an extended period.

Importantly, the second principle trumps the third. If education undertaken to maintain or improve skills required in taxpayer's existing trade or business also qualify him for a new trade or business, its costs are not deductible regardless. This reflect the fact that the current regulations, issued in 1967, were intended to avoid reference to taxpayer's intentions and to turn entirely on objectively ascertainable facts. Thus, if a law degree qualifies an accountant to become a lawyer, we treat the costs of that degree as nondeductible even if taxpayer has no intention of ever practicing law and has only studied law to improve his skills as an accountant; objectively, he has the option to become a lawyer.

As the Tax Court holds in *Glenn*, below, the regulations therefore require a comparison between the types of tasks and activities which the taxpayer was engaged in and qualified to perform before the acquisition of the degree, and those which he is qualified to perform afterwards (even if he never does so). If the two types of tasks and activities are significantly different, the educational expense deduction is disallowed.

GLENN v. COMMISSIONER
62 T.C. 270 (1974)

Petitioner received a bachelor's degree in accountancy from Austin Peay State University in 1956. On March 8 of that year, the State Board of Accountancy of Tennessee approved his application to practice as a public accountant, a practice petitioner has continued through the time of the trial in the instant case. From 1959 through 1963, petitioner was employed in Nashville as a staff accountant by John S. Glenn Associates, a firm which merged with the national accounting firm of Peat, Marwick, Mitchell & Co., in 1963. Petitioner continued his employment with Peat, Marwick until 1970.

From approximately the time of the merger, petitioner held the position of senior accountant with Peat, Marwick. As senior accountant, petitioner trained recent college graduates entering the firm, was in charge of audits, and supervised and reviewed the work of other staff accountants before its submission to a manager at the firm. Petitioner was also involved in the setting up of budget and bookkeeping systems for clients of the firm. On numerous dates between 1960 and 1970, petitioner sat for the Tennessee certified public accountant examination. Passing such exam would have enabled petitioner to hold himself out as a certified public accountant, a title considered a prerequisite to promotion to the positions of manager or partner in Peat, Marwick's Nashville office.

Two months prior to the November 1970 C.P.A. exam, petitioner attended a review course for the exam offered by Peat, Marwick for its employees. Petitioner also enrolled in the semiannual certified public accountant review course offered by the University of Alabama. This course, which lasted the entire month of October, covered the general areas of accounting theory and practice, auditing, and commercial law. Petitioner was familiar with all these areas both from prior studies, and from his work in such areas with John S. Glenn Associates and Peat, Marwick. The Alabama course emphasized the organization and analysis of numerous accounting and commercial concepts, with time also devoted to instruction concerning exam-taking techniques. While the course at Peat, Marwick was given in the evening after work, petitioner attended the Alabama course at the University of Alabama campus on a full-time basis for the entire month of October. The daily schedule for the course on weekdays called for a study period between 8 a.m. and 12 noon, lectures and discussions between 1 p.m. and 5 p.m., and discussions and supervised problem work from 7 p.m. to 10 p.m. in the evenings. Lectures, discussions, and supervised problem work sessions were also held on Saturdays between 8 a.m. and 4 p.m.

After completing the review course, petitioner sat for the C.P.A. exam in Memphis on November 4, 5, and 6 of 1970. He was not successful on the exam. Later that year, on December 1, petitioner withdrew from Peat, Marwick, and established his own public accounting firm.

On his 1970 individual return, petitioner [deducted the cost of the Alabama review course and associated travel, meals, and lodging, as trade or business expenses. Respondent disallowed this deduction.]

[The court rejects respondent's argument that the Alabama review course was not "education."]

It is respondent's alternative argument that while the Alabama course may be characterized as having maintained or improved skills required in petitioner's employment, that the course also constituted education, "which will lead to qualifying him in a new trade or business," namely certified public accounting. As respondent correctly points out, if educational expenses are incurred in connection with qualifying for a new trade or business, the fact that they also serve to maintain and improve skills required in a current trade or business does not save such expenses from characterization as either nondeductible personal expenses, or as a nondeductible aggregate of personal and capital expenditures.

The issue as we see it is one of definition; of determining what are the relevant trades or businesses involved in the instant case. It is respondent's contention that the practice of a public accountant constitutes a different trade or business from that of a C.P.A. Petitioner argues that public accountants and C.P.A.'s in Tennessee are members of a single trade or business, namely public accounting, and that his attempt to become a C.P.A. represents an attempt to move within, as opposed to out of, his current trade or business.

We have not found a substantial case law suggesting criteria for determining when the acquisition of new titles or abilities constitutes the entry into a new trade or business for purposes of section 1.162–5(c)(1), Income Tax Regs. What has been suggested, and we uphold such suggestion as the only commonsense approach to a classification, is that a comparison be made between the types of tasks and activities which the taxpayer was qualified to perform before the acquisition of a particular title or degree, and those which he is qualified to perform afterwards. Where we have found such activities and abilities to be significantly different, we have disallowed an educational expense deduction, based on our finding that there had been qualification for a new trade or business.

In the instant case, we find that the differences in potential scope of practice between a public accountant and a C.P.A. in Tennessee are significant, and that petitioner's expenses were incurred in attempting to qualify for a new trade or business. Hence, we hold that the expenses described above are nondeductible.

Under Tennessee law, public accountants and C.P.A.'s are separately licensed by the State after compliance with certain educational and examination requirements. Both types of accountants are considered under State law as practicing public accounting in Tennessee, a practice defined as follows in the State accountancy statute:

" 'Practice' defined. The practice of public accountancy is hereby defined as holding oneself out to the public as skilled in the knowledge, science and practice of accounting; as qualified and ready to render professional services therein as a public accountant or certified public accountant for compensation, and performing such work of an accountant for more than one employer on a fee basis, or otherwise, in any of the following services: auditing; devising and installing systems; recording and presentation of financial information or data; compiling tax returns, preparing financial statements, schedules, reports, and exhibits for publication, credit purposes, use in courts of law and equity, and for other purposes. ..."

The tasks listed in section 62–127, Tenn. Code Ann., are those to which the practice of a public accountant in Tennessee is limited. A C.P.A., however, in addition to being authorized to perform all the above-mentioned operations allowed to be performed by public accountants, is also qualified to perform certain other tasks not permitted the public accountant. He may "(5) advise taxpayers as to their rights and liabilities under federal or state taxing statutes as entail or are based upon accounting procedures; (6) represent taxpayers before governmental departments of the state and of the United States in matters pertaining to taxes." Sec. 62–139, Tenn. Code Ann. Furthermore, and probably most significantly of all, he may hold himself out to the public and sign his name accompanied by the designation that he is a licensed C.P.A.

Although we think the question is extremely close and not entirely free from doubt, we find these differences between the potential practice of a public accountant and that of a C.P.A. to be compelling and significant. The ability to undertake a tax practice appears especially significant. It is common knowledge that clients often look to their accountants for advice on the tax consequences of handling receipts and expenses in a certain way, of electing a particular method of depreciation, and so on. Unlike the public accountant, the C.P.A. is not only able to advise as to such matters, but may also actively represent his client if recourse to a governmental board or agency is deemed appropriate, or is required. Furthermore, unlike the public accountant, the C.P.A. is able to hold himself out to the public as qualified and able to advise and represent clients as to tax matters, thus opening up to him the potential of attracting a substantial practice in tax, an area whose importance in the modern business world is undeniable. In effect, in tax matters, the ability of a C.P.A. is not so unlike that of an attorney, a comparison which clearly cannot be made in the case of a public accountant.

In addition, C.P.A. status is considered in Tennessee, according to the uncontradicted and sworn statement of the secretary of the Tennessee State Board of Accountancy, as representing a higher level of professional competence than the status of public accountant. Thus, it may be expected, as is clearly commonly thought in the business world, that an opinion and certification from a C.P.A. is considered more valuable and authoritative than such from a public accountant. And, at least in petitioner's old firm, Peat, Marwick, advancement to the positions of partner and manager—positions offering wider responsibility and substantial increases in compensation to an accountant—is contingent on the attainment of C.P.A. status.

Petitioner does not dispute that these differences in potential practice between a C.P.A. and public accountant are significant, but raises instead three other arguments. He first points out that, had he passed the exam and become a C.P.A., he would still have been performing the same types of tasks for Peat, Marwick, as he had as a public accountant. While such assertion may be correct, the touchstone of section 1.162–5(c)(1), Income Tax Regs., is only whether or not the education taken will lead to qualification in a new trade or business. Here, as we have found above, the education was directed to so qualify petitioner, and the fact that had he passed the exam, he may not have performed any of the tasks previously not allowed him as a public accountant is simply irrelevant in determining deductibility.

Petitioner next urges that it should be deemed significant that he already had a license to practice public accounting in Tennessee. The possession of a license, he points out, distinguishes his situation from that of an unlicensed accountant attempting to become licensed. For such an accountant could not hold himself out to the public, according to petitioner, as one skilled in the practice of accounting. Petitioner's possession of a license to practice public accounting, however, does not affect our conclusion in the instant case. For, while it is true that petitioner's license set him apart from other unlicensed accountants in Tennessee who could not hold themselves out as skilled and knowledgeable in public accounting, the mere fact that one may be licensed to practice as a public accountant in no way precludes us from finding that there were in fact three types of accounting trades or businesses in Tennessee: unlicensed accounting, public accounting, and certified public accounting. In view of the significant differences in scope of practice between public accountants and C.P.A.'s, we refuse to hold that these two separately licensed groups should be considered to be within one trade or business in Tennessee for purposes of respondent's regulation.

Finally, petitioner cites as requiring a decision in his favor the following example in respondent's regulation:

> "C, while engaged in the private practice of psychiatry, undertakes a program of study and training at an accredited psychoanalytic institute which will lead to qualifying him to practice psychoanalysis. C's expenditures for such study and training are deductible because the study and training maintains or improves skills required by him in his trade or business and does not qualify him for a new trade or business."

As is implicit in our discussion above, however, the issue of whether or not the acquisition of new skills and abilities constitutes a new trade or business involves, essentially, a factual finding as to the significance of such new capabilities. We have found as a fact that there is a significant difference between the potential practice of a public accountant and that of a C.P.A. in Tennessee. That respondent has reached a different conclusion as to psychiatrists and psychoanalysts is simply not controlling on the distinct facts of the instant case.

NOTES

1. *Costs of an LL.M. in Taxation.*—Under the *Glenn* test, the practice of tax law is not treated as a different trade or business from the practice of law in general; the same license generally allows one to practice either. When a taxpayer seeks to deduct the cost of a tax LL.M. degree, therefore, the principal question is usually whether he was actively engaged in the practice of law before he incurred that cost.

A student who takes his tax LL.M. coursework the year immediately after he receives his J.D. typically cannot meet this requirement. He graduates in May or June, takes a bar examination during the summer, begins his LL.M. coursework in the fall, is admitted to the bar later in the fall, completes his LL.M. coursework in the spring, and only then enters the active practice of law. Any legal work he performs during law school or the summer thereafter typically cannot qualify as legal practice because the student is not yet licensed. Students in this posture therefore almost always lose. *See, e.g., Wassenaar v. Commissioner*, 72 T.C. 1195 (1979), *Kohen v. Commissioner*, T.C. Memo. 1982–625, *Randick v. Commissioner*, T.C. Memo. 1976–45. Compare *Ruehmann v. Commissioner*, T.C. Memo. 1971–157 (J.D. student took and passed Georgia bar examination after *second* year of law school and worked *as licensed attorney* during Christmas break of third year and summer between graduation and beginning of LL.M. coursework; held: costs of LL.M. deductible as expenses of current trade or business).

Subchapter D: Legal Expenses

For the most part, the rules governing the deduction of legal expenses are consistent with theory.

First, legal costs of generating current taxable income are deductible under Code Section 162 or Code Section 212, whichever applies. *See, e.g., Commissioner v. Banks*, 543 U.S. 426 (2005), above. Thus, the portion of an ex-spouse's legal fees incurred in winning an award of alimony (taxable to recipient under Code Section 71) is deductible under Code Section 212. *See, e.g., Wild v. Commissioner*, 42 T.C. 706 (1964); *Hesse v. Commissioner*, 60 T.C. 685 (1973) (acq.), *aff'd*, 511 F.2d 1393 (3d Cir. 1975); *Howard v. Commissioner*, T.C. Memo. 1975–170 (allocation required between legal fees incurred in connection with alimony award and those incurred in connection with property division or child support, neither of which is taxable). *See also Rosenzweig v. Commissioner*, 1 T.C. 24 (1942) (legal fees for amounts recovered on suit for infringement of copyright); *Srivastava v.*

Commissioner, T.C. Memo. Rev. Rul. 60–188, 1960–1 C.B. 28 (legal fees incurred in recovering taxable amounts for wrongful termination from employment deductible under Code Section 212).

Second, legal costs of generating tax-exempt income or other current non-taxable items are not deductible under either section. Code Section 265(a)(1). See Chapter 4, Section 3, above. *See, e.g., McKay v. Commissioner*, 102 T.C. 465 (1994), *vacated and remanded on other grounds*, 84 F.3d 433 (5th Cir. 1996) (legal fees for amounts excludible under Code Section 104(a)(2) not deductible).

Third, legal costs subject to the capitalization requirement must be capitalized; if included in the basis of an amortizable asset they can then be amortized over that asset's useful life. *See, e.g., Woodward v. Commissioner*, 397 U.S. 572 (1970); *INDOPCO, Inc. v. Commissioner*, 503 U.S. 79 (1992), above; Treas. Reg. § 1.263(a)–2(d)(2)(i) ("amounts paid to defend or perfect title to real or personal property ... must be capitalized").

Legal fees incurred for tax advice and dispute resolution may, in theory, be either personal or incurred for the production of income. In practice, however, it is often impossible to draw clear lines between the two. Perhaps for this reason, Code Section 212(3) permits the deduction of expenses "in connection with the determination, collection, or refund of any tax." Treas. Reg. § 1.212–1(*l*) elaborates:

> "Expenses paid or incurred by an individual in connection with the determination, collection, or refund of any tax, whether the tax authority be Federal, State, or municipal, and whether the tax be income, estate, gift, property, or any other tax, are deductible. Thus, expenses paid or incurred by a taxpayer for tax counsel or expenses paid or incurred in connection with the preparation of his tax returns or in connection with the proceedings involved in determining the extent of his tax liability or in contesting his tax liability are deductible."

The difficult questions in this area tend not to arise in transactional contexts or where taxpayer is plaintiff; they tend rather to arise when taxpayer is defendant. In civil actions, defendant is almost always resisting efforts by plaintiff to take some of defendant's assets, which are commonly income-producing. Almost all legal fees spent to defend civil actions are therefore, at least arguably, "for the ... conservation ... of property held for the production of income...." Code Section 212(2). In criminal actions, defendant worries about going to jail—an inherently personal indignity—but may also worry about loss of business licenses and reputation and possible loss of business income.

It was in such a context that the Supreme Court, in *United States v. Gilmore*, 372 U.S. 39 (1963), articulated what has come to be known as the "origin of claim" doctrine: "[T]he characterization, as 'business' or 'personal,' of the litigation costs of resisting a claim depends on whether or not the claim *arises in connection with* the taxpayer's profit-seeking activities. It does not depend on the *consequences* that might result to a taxpayer's income-producing property from a failure to defeat the claim." Because the claim Gilmore was resisting arose out divorce, an inherently personal matter, the Court held, the costs of resisting that claim to protect his assets was personal as well. By contrast, in *Commissioner v. Tellier*, 383 U.S. 687 (1966), a stockbroker unsuccessfully resisted criminal charges of securities and mail fraud arising out of his business activities. The Court allowed the deduction.

The origin of claim doctrine is used not only to determine whether legal expenses are deductible at all, but also to determine whether they are deductible as employee trade or business expenses or Code Section 212 expenses. *See, e.g., Test v. Commissioner*, T.C. Memo. 2000–362, *aff'd*, 49 Fed.Appx. 96 (9th Cir. 2002) (employee business expenses).

Gilmore did not involve litigation expenses incurred in *asserting* a claim. Nevertheless, courts have applied the origin of claim doctrine to deny deduction of legal costs incurred in the prosecution of unsuccessful suits to recover taxable income, where taxpayer's claims arise in a personal context and are not primarily profit-motivated. *See, e.g., Colvin v. Commissioner*, T.C. Memo. 2004–67 ("It is the determination of the Court that the expense here arose in connection with the management, conservation, or maintenance of property held for use by petitioner as a personal residence. Assuming without deciding that an ultimate consequence of petitioner's litigation might have been the recovery of taxable income, or the determination, collection, or refund of a tax, the claim for which the expense arose was not in connection with those activities. Petitioner was upset by what he perceived to be the failure of the association to properly manage, conserve, or maintain the condominium property where he resided.").

PROBLEMS FOR DISCUSSION

16–10. How should each of the following legal expenses be treated for federal tax purposes (*e.g.*, deducted under Code Section 162 as a non-employee business expense, deducted under Code Section 162 as an employee business expense, deducted under Code Section 212, deducted under Code Section 183, capitalized under Code Section 263, neither deducted nor capitalized)? Why might taxpayer care?

(a) Jeremy, a lawyer with a large private law firm, incurs legal expenses defending himself against a criminal indictment asserting that he beat his spouse. If convicted, he will lose both his license to practice law and his job. Does it matter whether he is a partner or an associate?

(b) Jeremy, a lawyer with a large private law firm, incurs legal expenses defending himself against a criminal indictment asserting that he embezzled client funds entrusted to him. If convicted, he will lose both his license to practice law and his job. Does it matter whether he is a partner or an associate?

(c) Kathy incurs legal expenses in a Tax Court case in which she asserts that she is entitled to file joint income tax returns with the same-sex spouse to whom she is married as a matter of state law.

(d) Lori incurs legal expenses when she brings suit to quiet title to a large parcel of forested land over which a hiking club asserts it has a right of way easement.

(e) Mike incurs legal expenses in a child support case in which he denies that he was the father of the child in question.

(f) Nicholas is involved in a major traffic accident and is badly injured. He sues and successfully recovers $1.3 million in compensatory damages from the tortfeasor.

(g) Oliver, the tortfeasor in part (f) above, incurs legal fees in his unsuccessful defense.

Subchapter E: Home Office Expenses

Code: Section 280A

Code Section 280A(c)(1) limits the deduction of expenses incurred by reason of the use of part of taxpayer's home as an office. No trade or business deduction is allowed with respect to such use unless a portion of the dwelling is exclusively used on a regular basis (1) as the principal place of business for taxpayer's trade or business, (2) as a place of business used by patients, clients, or customers in meeting or dealing with the taxpayer in the normal course of his trade or business, or (3) in the case of an unattached separate structure, in connection with the taxpayer's trade or business. Effectively overruling *Commissioner v. Soliman*, 506 U.S. 168 (1993), the block language at the end of the subsection states: "the term 'principal place of business' includes a place of business which is used by the taxpayer for the administrative or management activities of any trade or business of the taxpayer if there is no other fixed location of such trade or business where the taxpayer conducts substantial administrative or management activities of such trade or business." In the case of an employee, no trade or business deduction is allowed at all unless such use is for the convenience of his employer.

PROBLEMS FOR DISCUSSION

16–11. Petra, an associate at a major law firm, has set aside a room in her home for use as a home office, so that she can conveniently bill additional time without having to go in to work. There is a bed in the room, on which Petra puts up house guests when her guest room is otherwise occupied. Can she deduct depreciation and other costs with respect to this room?

16–12. Roberta, a self-employed anesthesiologist, has practice privileges at several hospitals in the city within which she lives, but no office at any of them. She performs all of her medical work at the various hospitals, but conducts all the administrative work with respect to her practice in one room in her house set aside exclusively for this purpose. Can she deduct depreciation and other costs with respect to this room?

16–13. Sam, a partner with a large downtown law firm, uses one room in his home to meet clients for whom traveling downtown would be inconvenient. He does not use the room for any other purpose. His principal office is on the top floor of the firm's office building downtown. Can he deduct depreciation and other costs with respect to this room?

PART 6

ABILITY TO PAY

■ ■ ■

Comprehensive tax base theory has enormous explanatory power, but almost no capacity to deal with factors that might affect taxpayers' abilities to pay taxes other than differences in income. Under comprehensive tax base theory, for example, a quadriplegic taxpayer who earns $50,000 but must spend $20,000 for a full-time assistant to help her go to the bathroom, wash, dress, and eat is treated as having equal ability to pay taxes as a "normal" taxpayer who earns the same amount but can choose to spend the same $20,000 on sky-diving, bar-hopping, or long-term investments instead. Comprehensive tax base theory suggests that, as a matter of tax policy, the two should contribute equally to the costs of government.

Congress, by contrast, believes that "[o]ne of the basic tenets of tax policy is that an accurate measurement of ability to pay taxes is essential to tax fairness." *See, e.g.*, STAFF, JOINT COMM. ON TAX'N, 108TH CONG., DESCRIPTION OF REVENUE PROVISIONS CONTAINED IN THE PRESIDENT'S FISCAL YEAR 2005 BUDGET PROPOSAL 8 (Comm. Print 2004). In fact, our system contains a number of features most easily explained—indeed, sometimes explicitly justified by Congress—by reference to ability to pay. The deduction for medical expenses, for example, might be viewed as reflecting Congress's judgment that our hypothetical quadriplegic taxpayer has less ability to pay taxes than her "normal" counterpart. Tax theorists, by contrast, often deny that ability to pay offers meaningful guidance. They therefore commonly reframe such features as tax expenditures included for non-tax reasons. *See, e.g.*, 2013 Tax Expenditure Budget, Item 135 (medical expenses). As a consequence, rules reflecting ability to pay are sometimes less than completely coherent, reflecting tension between academic theory and common-place intuition.

Chapter 16 explores how family structure affects ability to pay and, presumably in consequence, tax liability. In general, larger households pay less tax, all else being equal, than smaller households. The rules themselves, however, are largely uncoordinated and sometimes difficult to justify.

Chapter 17 explores the treatment of other sometimes nondiscretionary demands on taxpayers' resources: medical expenses, state and local taxes, and personal casualty losses. In each case, an argument can be made that taxpayers who face such demands have less ability to pay federal income taxes than taxpayers who do not—again, all else being equal. In each case, however, the Treasury treats the relevant provisions as tax expenditures—provisions included in the Code for reasons having nothing to do with tax policy.

Chapter 18, finally, explores the deduction for charitable contributions. A taxpayer who donates part of her income to charity has less left over for personal consumption purposes or to pay taxes. She may view herself as morally obligated to make such donations—in some sense, involuntary. Taxpayers making such contributions have less ability to pay than taxpayers who do not. In any event, her donations may end up being spent on functions the government might otherwise have been required to perform.

CHAPTER 17

FAMILY STRUCTURE, INCOME, AND ABILITY TO PAY

■ ■ ■

All else being equal, Congress appears to believe that a family with more mouths to feed has less ability to pay taxes, and should therefore pay less in taxes. This intuition is reflected in at least four provisions: (1) under Code Section 151, taxpayers are allowed to claim personal exemptions for themselves and their "dependents," (2) under Code Sections 1(b) and 2(b), a more generous rate structure is allowed for "heads of households," (3) under Code Section 24, a credit is allowed to taxpayers with qualifying children, and (4) under Code Section 32, an earned income tax credit is allowed to low-income working taxpayers, with most of the benefits going to taxpayers with qualifying children. As will be seen, these provisions, although intuitively plausible in concept, are not well-coordinated.

SECTION 1: PERSONAL EXEMPTIONS AND THE DEFINITION OF "DEPENDENT"

Code: Sections 151 and 152

Regulations: Section 1.152-1

In general, Code Section 151 allows a taxpayer to deduct one personal exemption for herself, one for her spouse, and one for each of her dependents. The allowable "exemption amount" is adjusted annually for inflation; in 2012 it is $3,800 per person. Rev. Proc. Rev. 2011-52, 2011-45 I.R.B. Thus in 2012 a family of four is typically entitled to personal exemption deductions totaling $15,200. Combined with the standard deduction (in 2012, $11,900 for a married couple filing jointly), this means that in 2012 the first $27,100 of our hypothetical family-of-four's income is exempt from federal income taxation (although subject to federal payroll taxation). The larger the family, the greater its personal exemption deductions—reflecting Congress's judgment that, all else being equal, larger families have less ability to pay taxes.

At higher income levels, the personal exemption deduction is phased out by Code Section 151(d)(3) ("PEP," for "personal exemption phase-out"). The stated justification for PEP is that higher-income taxpayers do not need tax relief by reason of their additional dependents. PEP is currently suspended, but is scheduled to become effective again in 2013.

The personal exemption rules for the mythic standard American family (mom and dad filing jointly and their non-disabled children) are relatively simple: Children are their parents' "dependents" if they share their parents' principal place of abode for more than half of the parents' taxable year and do not provide more than half of their own support for the calendar year in which their parents' taxable year begins. "Support," for this purpose, includes food, shelter, clothing, medical and dental care, education, and the like, including amounts that would otherwise be excludible from gross income, Treas. Reg. § 1.152–1(a)(2)(ii), but not including scholarships received by "students." Code Section 152(f)(5). In addition, qualifying children must meet an age requirement: as of the close of the calendar year they must be (1) 18 or younger, or (2) if they are "students," 23 or younger. In general, the term "student" means full-time student at an educational organization described in Code Section 170(b)(1)(A)(ii) during each of 5 calendar months during the year.

Many American families—probably a majority—do not fit this stereotype. The Code therefore provides more complex rules to deal with the real world. Under the rules more fully stated, dependents can be viewed as falling into three categories: (1) "qualifying children," (2) "qualifying relatives," and (3) Section 152(d)(2)(H) dependents.

An individual is a "qualifying child" with respect to taxpayer if she (1) is taxpayer's child, brother, sister, stepbrother, or stepsister, or a descendant of any such relative, (2) has the same principal place of abode as taxpayer for more than half of taxpayer's taxable year, (3) is younger than taxpayer and (as of the close of the calendar year) is no more than 18 years old, or, if a "student," no more than 23 years old, (4) does not provide more than half of her own support for the calendar year in which taxpayer's taxable year begins, and (5) does not file a joint return with a spouse. Code Section 152(c). A taxpayer's "children" include legally adopted children, children lawfully placed with taxpayer for adoption, and eligible foster children. Code Section 152(f)(1). If a "qualifying child" is permanently and totally disabled, she need not meet any age requirement. Code Section 152(c)(3)(B). An individual is "permanently and totally disabled" if "he is unable to engage in any substantial gainful activity by reason of any medically determinable physical or mental impairment which can be expected to result in death or which has lasted or can be expected to last for a continuous period of not less than 12 months." Code Section 22(e)(3).

Note that "qualifying children" can include a taxpayer's brothers and sisters, grandchildren, nephews and nieces, and grandnephews and grandnieces who meet applicable age requirements, not just children, and that "qualifying children" can have gross income in excess of the exemption amount so long as they do not provide more than half of their own support.

An individual is a "qualifying relative," by contrast, if she (1) is taxpayer's child or other descendant, brother, sister, stepbrother, or stepsister, parent or other ancestor, stepparent, niece or nephew, or child-in-law, parent-in-law, or sibling-in-law, (2) has gross income of less than the exemption amount ($3,800 in 2012), (3) receives over half of her support from taxpayer, and (4) is not a "qualifying child" of taxpayer. There is no requirement that "qualifying relatives" live with taxpayer or be of any particular age. In addition, many more relationships qualify. But "qualifying relatives," unlike "qualifying children," must have gross income of less than the exemption amount. Code Section 152(d).

Finally, a Section 152(d)(2)(H) dependent is any individual, other than taxpayer's spouse, who (1) has gross income of less than the exemption amount ($3,800 in 2012), (2) receives over half of her support from taxpayer, and (3) has the same principal place of abode as taxpayer and is a member of taxpayer's household. Section 152(d)(2)(H) dependents are technically "qualifying relatives," although they are treated differently from other qualifying relatives in important regards. Anyone other than taxpayer's spouse can qualify, but unlike qualifying relatives generally, Section 152(d)(2)(H) dependents must share taxpayer's abode and be part of taxpayer's household.

PROBLEMS FOR DISCUSSION

17–1. John, whose wife died five years ago, has two children: (1) Amanda is an unmarried 24–year–old who lives and attends law school full-time in another state. When she graduates, she plans to get a full-time job in that state. For the taxable year in question, she has $2,000 of gross income and a full tuition scholarship from her school (tuition is $40,000). John has given her $15,000 towards living expenses for the year. She has borrowed an additional $10,000 to cover her remaining expenses. (2) Bob is an unmarried 20–year–old who lives with John and studies computer programming full-time at a local community college. For the taxable year in question, he has $12,000 of gross income from a part-time job. His father covers the rest of his expenses. John's household also includes Raymond, John's unmarried older brother, who is permanently and totally disabled. Raymond receives Social Security disability payments of $10,800 per year, the remainder of his support (less than half) is provided by John. How many personal exemptions may John claim? Would your answer change if Amanda or Bob attends school part-time?

17–2. Leslie and Dana consider themselves married and were legally married in Massachusetts, but have since moved to a state that does not recognize same-sex marriage. They have two children, Amanda and Bob, both in elementary school. The children are the biological children of Dana, with contributed gametes from an anonymous donor. Their current state of residence does not recognize second-parent adoptions. Dana stays home and takes care of their children. Leslie, a lawyer, supports the family. How many personal exemptions may Leslie claim?

SECTION 2: HEAD OF HOUSEHOLD STATUS

Code: Section 2(b)

A taxpayer is a "head of household," eligible for the more favorable tax rates of Code Section 1(b), if she (1) is neither married nor a surviving spouse, and (2) furnishes more than half the cost of maintaining a household if either (a) the household is her home and the principal place of abode of a qualifying child (subject to limited restrictions) or a qualifying relative if taxpayer is eligible to claim a personal exemption deduction for such qualifying relative, or (b) the household constitutes the principal place of abode of taxpayer's father or mother if taxpayer is eligible to claim a personal exemption deduction for such father or mother. A taxpayer cannot qualify for head of household status solely by reason of having a Section 152(d)(2)(H) dependent.

HERETICK v. COMMISSIONER

T.C. Summ. Op. 2003–129

The sole issue for decision is whether petitioner is entitled to head-of-household filing status under section 2(b). The parties agree that petitioner's status as head-of-household depends upon whether petitioner's home was "the principal place of abode" for Maggie Elizabeth Heretick, petitioner's adult unmarried daughter.

Petitioner and his wife divorced in 1981. They had one child, Maggie Elizabeth Heretick (Maggie), who was born in 1977. Maggie was 22 years old during 1999. Upon graduation from high school in 1995, Maggie enrolled as a full-time student at the University of Richmond. She graduated with a bachelor of science degree in physical science in May 1999. She then entered Medical College of Virginia and thereafter graduated with a degree in sports medicine.

During her college career, including the year at issue, Maggie lived in Richmond, Virginia, in university dormitories. During summer breaks, she alternated living with petitioner and her mother. After Maggie received her degree, but before entering the Medical College of Virginia, she worked on a research project for one of the professors at the Medical College of Virginia. About that time, Maggie rented an apartment in Richmond. Although Maggie occasionally visited both parents from time to time, she never moved to either petitioner's home or his former wife's home. Petitioner maintained a room for her at his home, where Maggie kept clothes and personal belongings. Petitioner acknowledged, however, he was sure that Maggie had similar arrangements with his former wife (Maggie's mother). There is no evidence that Maggie lived with her father, or even her mother, on a permanent basis, or that she intended to do so during 1999.

Section 2(b) provides generally that an individual shall be considered as a head-of-household if such individual is not married at the close of the taxable year and maintains as his home a household which constitutes, for more than one-half of such taxable year, the "principal place of abode" of a son, stepson, or daughter of the taxpayer (as well as other individuals not pertinent here). Petitioner was not married during 1999.

Section 1.2–2(c)(1), Income Tax Regs., provides, in pertinent part:

> The taxpayer and such other person will be considered as occupying the household ... notwithstanding temporary absences from the household due to special circumstances. A nonpermanent failure to occupy the common abode by reason of illness, education, business, vacation, military service, or a custody agreement ... shall be considered temporary absence due to special circumstances. Such absence will not prevent the taxpayer from being considered as maintaining a household if (i) it is reasonable to assume that the taxpayer or such other person will return to the household, and (ii) the taxpayer continues to maintain such household or a substantially equivalent household in anticipation of such return.

Section 12(c) of the Internal Revenue Code of 1939 and section 1(b) of the 1954 Internal Revenue Code, the predecessors of section 2(b) of the 1986 Code, contained substantially the same language. In enacting section 12(c), Congress intended that section:

> to apply where the taxpayer and such other members of the household live together in such household ... (except for temporary absences due to special circumstances). The fact that a child may be at college during the college term does not prevent the home of the taxpayer from also constituting the principal place of abode of the child. However, such home will not be considered as the principal place of abode where the child establishes a separate habitation and only returns for periodic visits. ... [H. Rept. 586, 82d Cong., 1st Sess. (1951), 1951–2 C.B. 434]

In this case, for Maggie's absence to be "temporary" and for petitioner's household to be considered the principal place of abode for his daughter, petitioner must meet the following three requirements: (1) The special circumstances or necessity of the absence must be a type intended by the statute; (2) it must be reasonable for petitioner to assume his daughter would return to the household; and (3) petitioner must have maintained the household in anticipation of such return.

The record does not support a conclusion that Maggie's absence from petitioner's home was temporary during 1999. Maggie completed her undergraduate degree during 1999 at Richmond, Virginia, where she lived and worked part-time for 4 years. She chose to stay in Richmond not only to continue working part-time but also to obtain an advanced degree. More importantly, there is no evidence that petitioner's daughter planned or intended to return to live with petitioner upon completion of her college career, nor did petitioner express any real expectation that his daughter would do so.

Therefore, the Court is unable to conclude that it was reasonable to assume that petitioner's daughter would return to his household or that petitioner maintained the household in anticipation of such return. Accordingly, petitioner does not qualify as "head-of-household" under the facts and circumstances of this case.

PROBLEMS FOR DISCUSSION

17–3. John, whose wife died five years ago, has two children: (1) Amanda is an unmarried 24–year–old who lives and attends law school full-time in another state. When she graduates, she plans to get a full-time job in that state. For the taxable year in question, she has $2,000 of gross income and a full tuition scholarship from her school (tuition is $40,000). John has given her $15,000 towards living expenses for the year. She has borrowed an additional $10,000 to cover her remaining expenses. (2) Bob is an unmarried 20–year–old who lives with John and studies computer programming full-time at a local community college. For the taxable year in question, he has $12,000 of gross income from a part-time job. His father covers the rest of his expenses. John's household also includes Raymond, John's unmarried older brother, who is permanently and totally disabled. Raymond receives Social Security disability payments of $10,800 per year, the remainder of his support (less than half) is provided by John. May John claim head of household status? Would your answer change if Amanda or Bob attends school part-time?

17–4. Leslie and Dana were legally married in Massachusetts, but are not married for federal purposes and have since moved to a state that does not recognize same-sex marriage. They have two children, Amanda and Bob, both in elementary school. The children are the biological children of Dana, with contributed gametes from an anonymous donor. Their current state of residence does not recognize second-parent adoptions. Dana stays home and takes care of their children. Leslie, a lawyer, supports the family. May Leslie claim head of household status?

SECTION 3: CHILD TAX CREDIT

Code: Section 24

In general, Code Section 24 allows a tax credit in the amount of $1,000 for each qualifying child under the age of 17. The credit begins to phase out once taxpayer's income exceeds $110,000 (married filing jointly) or $75,000 (unmarried). A portion of the credit may be refundable—that is, payable to taxpayer even if taxpayer is not liable for any federal income tax.

PROBLEMS FOR DISCUSSION

17–5. John, whose wife died five years ago, has two children: (1) Amanda is an unmarried 24–year–old who lives and attends law school full-time in another state. When she graduates, she plans to get a full-time job in that state. For the taxable year in question, she has $2,000 of gross income and a full tuition scholarship from her school (tuition is $40,000). John has given her $15,000 towards living expenses for the year. She has borrowed an additional $10,000 to cover her remaining expenses. (2) Bob is an unmarried 20–year–old who lives with John and studies computer programming full-time at a local community college. For the taxable year in question, he has $12,000 of gross income from a part-time job. His father covers the rest of his expenses. John's household also includes Raymond, John's unmarried older brother, who is permanently and totally disabled. Raymond receives Social Security disability payments of $10,800 per year, the remainder of his support (less than half) is provided by John. Assuming that his income does not exceed the limitations of Code Section 24(b), for how many child tax credits is John eligible?

17–6. Leslie and Dana were legally married in Massachusetts, but are not married for federal purposes and have since moved to a state that does not recognize same-sex marriage. They have two children, Amanda and Bob, both in elementary school. The children are the biological children of Dana, with contributed gametes from an anonymous donor. Their current state of residence does not recognize second-parent adoptions. Dana stays home and takes care of their children. Leslie, a lawyer, supports the family. Assuming that Leslie's income does not exceed the limitations of Code Section 24(b), for how many child tax credits is Leslie eligible?

SECTION 4: EARNED INCOME TAX CREDIT

Code: Section 32

Section 32, which allows low-income working taxpayers an "earned income tax credit" (EITC), now constitutes the federal government's largest anti-poverty program. The credit is refundable—that is, taxpayer receives cash from the federal government if the credit exceeds her income tax liability for the year.

To be eligible for the EITC, a taxpayer must either (1) have a qualifying child, or (2) be at least 25 but not more than 65 years old, live in the United States, and not be anyone else's dependent. A taxpayer who is someone else's qualifying child is himself ineligible. If taxpayer is married, she can claim the EITC only if she files a joint return.

The amount of the credit to which taxpayer is entitled equals taxpayer's "credit percentage" times so much of taxpayer's "earned income," as does not exceed her "earned income amount." Her "earned income" is basically her includible compensation income (reduced, if applicable, by the deduction for one-half of self-employment taxes allowed pursuant to Code Section 164(f)). Her credit percentage and earned income amount depend on how many "qualifying children" she has. In general, a child is a "qualifying child" for EITC purposes if she is a "qualifying child" for personal exemption purpose, but for EITC purposes the child is not disqualified merely by reason of the fact that she provides for more than half of her own support. In 2012, the credit percentages and earned income amounts are:

Qualifying children	Credit percentage	Earned income amount
None	7.65%	up to $6,210
One	34.00%	up to $9,230
Two	40.00%	up to $13,090
Three or more	45.00%	up to $13,090

Thus, for example, in 2012, a single mother with one child and $10,000 of earned income is entitled to an EITC of $3,138.20 (34% times so much of $10,000 as does not exceed $9,230). If she has two children, her EITC is $4,000 (40% times so much of $10,000 as does not exceed $13,090).

The credit begins to phase out once the greater of the taxpayer's earned income or adjusted gross income exceeds a "threshold phase-out amount." Taxpayer ceases to be eligible for the credit once the greater of her earned income or adjusted gross income exceeds a "completed phase-out amount." Both figures are adjusted for inflation. For 2012, they are as follows:

Qualifying children	Threshold phaseout amount	Completed phaseout amount
None	$7,770	$13,980
One	$17,090	$36,920
Two	$17,090	$41,952
Three or more	$17,090	$45,060

Thus our hypothetical single mother with one child can earn up to $17,090 without losing any of her EITC. Once she begins to earn more than that amount, her EITC phases out, disappearing entirely when her earnings exceed $36,920.

The current special rules for taxpayers with three or more qualifying children are scheduled to terminate in 2013.

For a recent summary of the impact of the EITC on poverty and hours worked, *see* Bruce D. Meyer, *The Effects of the Earned Income Tax Credit and Recent Reforms*, in 24 TAX POLICY AND THE ECONOMY 153 (NBER 2010), *available at* http://www.nber.org/books/brow09-1.

PROBLEMS FOR DISCUSSION

17–7. John, whose wife died five years ago, has two children: (1) Amanda is an unmarried 24–year–old who lives and attends law school full-time in another state. When she graduates, she plans to get a full-time job in that state. For the taxable year in question, she has $2,000 of gross income and a full tuition scholarship from her school (tuition is $40,000). John has given her $15,000 towards living expenses for the year. She has borrowed an additional $10,000 to cover her remaining expenses. (2) Bob is an unmarried 20–year–old who lives with John and studies computer programming full-time at a local community college. For the taxable year in question, he has $12,000 of gross income from a part-time job. His father covers the rest of his expenses. John's household also includes Raymond, John's unmarried older brother, who is permanently and totally disabled. Raymond receives Social Security disability payments of $10,800 per year, the remainder of his support (less than half) is provided by John. How many qualifying children does John have for EITC purposes?

17–8. Leslie and Dana were legally married in Massachusetts, but are not married for federal purposes and have since moved to a state that does not recognize same-sex marriage. They have two children, Amanda and Bob, both in elementary school. The children are the biological children of Dana, with contributed gametes from an anonymous donor. Their current state of residence does not recognize second-parent adoptions. Dana stays home and takes care of their children. Leslie, a lawyer, supports the family. How many qualifying children does John have for EITC purposes? If Dana also has income, is Dana's income taken into account in determining Leslie's earned income or adjusted gross income for EITC purposes?

CHAPTER 18

NONDISCRETIONARY EXPENSES AND INVOLUNTARY PERSONAL LOSSES

■ ■ ■

Tax theorists categorize expenses and losses as "personal"—in effect, as Haig–Simons "consumption"—regardless of whether such expenses or losses are discretionary or voluntary and regardless of whether they give taxpayers pleasure. Nevertheless, taxpayers who incur nondiscretionary expenses or involuntary losses may have less ability to pay taxes than taxpayers who do not, all else being equal. Congress has authorized several deductions that can be justified on this basis. Among the most important are the medical expense deduction, the deduction for state and local taxes, and the deduction for personal casualty losses. By allowing such deductions, Congress has, to some extent, converted our tax on income into a tax on discretionary income.

Subchapter A: Medical Expense Deduction

Code: Section 213

SECTION 1: "MEDICAL CARE"

The traditional justification for the deductibility of medical expenses is that such expenses are, to some extent, involuntary and reduce taxpayer's ability to pay taxes. William D. Andrews, *Personal Deductions in an Ideal Income Tax*, 86 HARV. L. REV. 309, 314 (1972). Code Section 213(a) allows a deduction for the unreimbursed costs of medical care for taxpayer, his spouse, and dependents, but only to the extent such costs exceed 7.5 percent of taxpayer's adjusted gross income. This 7.5 percent threshold is scheduled to increase to 10 percent in 2013.

Code Section 213(d)(1)(A), in turn, sets forth the section's core definition: "medical care" means "amounts paid for the diagnosis, cure, mitigation, or prevention of disease, or for the purpose of affecting any structure or function of the body." As the Tax Court elaborated in a widely-quoted passage in *Havey*, below: "there must be a direct or proximate relation between the expenses and the diagnosis, cure, mitigation, treatment, or prevention of disease or the expense must have been incurred for the purpose of affecting some structure or function of the body." Among the factors to be considered:

- The motive or purpose of the taxpayer

- Whether the expense was incurred at the direction or suggestion of a physician

- Whether the treatment bore directly on the condition in question

- Whether the treatment bore such a direct or proximate therapeutic relation to the condition as to justify a reasonable belief it would be efficacious

- Whether the treatment so proximate in the time to the onset or recurrence of the disease or condition as to make one the true occasion of the other.

Note what is *not* required. It is not required that the expense be medical in the conventional sense. Thus, for example, if taxpayer is advised by a physician to install an elevator in his home so that his wife, who has a heart condition, will not have to climb stairs, and if installation of the elevator does not increase the value of the home, the entire cost of installing the elevator qualifies as a medical expense. Treas. Reg. § 1.213–1(e)(1)(iii). Similarly, the entire cost (including meals, lodging, and the cost of ordinary education) of attending a special school is a medical expense if the resources of the school for alleviating a mental or physical handicap are a principal reason for the individual's presence there. Treas. Reg. § 1.213–1(e)(1)(v)(a).

The term is also *not* limited to mainstream Western medicine. Thus, for example, in *Tso v. Commissioner*, T.C. Memo. 1980–399, the IRS conceded that the use of animal skins, incense, and singing by a Navajo medicine man qualified for the medical expense deduction. Treatment by a Christian Science practitioner may also qualify. Rev. Rul. 55–261, 1955–1 C.B. 307.

Nevertheless, expenditures that are merely beneficial to the general health of the individual, such as exercise equipment, membership in a gym, a much-needed vacation, a program to quit smoking, or a divorce are not deductible as "medical care." *See, e.g.*, Treas. Reg. § 1.213–1(e)(ii) (vacation); *Haines v. Commissioner*, 71 T.C. 644 (1979) (swimming pool); *France v. Commissioner*, 40 T.C. Memo. 1980–215, *aff'd per curiam*, 690 F.2d 68 (6th Cir. 1982) (dance lessons); *Jacobs v. Commissioner*, 62 T.C. 813 (1974) (psychiatrist-recommended divorce).

Two contexts in which the scope of the deduction is currently in significant controversy are treatments for gender identity disorder, explored in Section 2 below and costs of assisted reproduction, explored in Section 3 below.

HAVEY v. COMMISSIONER
12 T.C. 409 (1949)

Petitioner's wife, who is 56 years of age, became ill during the night of October 1, 1943. In the early morning of October 2, 1943, she was taken in an ambulance to Mercy Hospital in Pittsburgh, where she remained until December 3, 1943. Her condition was diagnosed as coronary occlusion. On the tenth day after her admission to the hospital she developed an infarction in the right lower lobe of the lung. She was kept in an oxygen tent for about two weeks. She was critically ill, but her condition improved. She remained in bed for about seven weeks. During the last week of her stay in the hospital she was permitted to walk about. She was taken home by petitioner in a car. A nurse was in attendance and remained with her for about four or five weeks.

After leaving the hospital the activities of petitioner's wife were completely restricted. Her condition improved, but she continued to have pains in her chest and attacks of breathlessness from time to time during the year following. These were due to inadequate coronary circulation following the coronary occlusion. The infarction of the lung had healed.

The cardiologist who attended petitioner's wife advised petitioner to take his wife to the seashore during the humid months of July and August because she lived in an apartment in Pittsburgh and he felt she would be benefited by living at the seashore. He also advised petitioner to take her to Arizona during the winters.

During 1945 petitioner and his wife traveled to and remained at Spring Lake, New Jersey, from June 25 to July 23, inclusive. The petitioner paid the hotel at which they resided the amount of $741.51 which was incurred: $641 for the room and board; $28 for cocktails and the like for petitioner; $12.50 for extra meals; $14 for meal service; $37.50 for garage; and $8.51 for the telephone, newsstand, valet, and postage. The petitioner and his wife also traveled to and remained at Atlantic City, New Jersey, from October 8 to October 18, 1945, inclusive, and paid the hotel where they resided $232.07. He paid the hotel $154 for the room; $39.70 for restaurant; $17.82 for beverages; $12.21 for auto; and $8.34 for telephone, telegrams, and city sales tax. They also traveled to and remained at Remuda Ranch, Wickenburg, Arizona, from November 20 to December 31, inclusive. Petitioner paid $327.58 for transportation to Arizona for himself and wife and $749.56 for expenses incurred at the Ranch, including $659 for room and board; $13.78 for tax; $63 for horses hired; $4.50 for rodeo ticket; and $9.28 for other expenses. The petitioner was not compensated for such expenses by insurance or otherwise.

The trips were beneficial to petitioner's wife. The state of her health was such that petitioner did not feel she should travel alone.

The petitioner and his wife first traveled to Arizona for pleasure in about 1937. At that time they stayed there from two to four weeks. They were there again in 1939, 1940, and 1942. They did not go in 1941 because of wartime restrictions on travel. They had stayed at the Remuda Ranch before 1945. They were also there in 1947. Prior to 1945 they had also been to Atlantic City, but not regularly.

In his 1945 income tax return the petitioner claimed a deduction for medical and dental expenses of $3,179.18, of which respondent disallowed $2,175.83.

Like most statutes, [Code Section 213] is stated in broad and comprehensive terms. The Commissioner's regulations are more detailed and specific. Whether a given deduction falls within the favor of the section is largely a matter of definition and the ascertainment of Congressional intent.

The section was first inserted by the Senate Finance Committee in the Revenue Bill of 1942. In its Report No. 1631 (C.B. 1942-2, pp. 576-577) the committee stated, in part, as follows:

> "The term 'medical care' is broadly defined to include amounts paid for the diagnosis, cure, mitigation, treatment, or prevention of disease, or for the purpose of affecting any structure or function of the body. It is not intended, however, that a deduction should be allowed for any expense that is not incurred primarily for the prevention or alleviation of a physical or mental defect or illness."

In approaching this question it is necessary to have in mind the basic concept of [Code Section 262] that personal, living, and family expenses are not deductible. Thus, many expenses, such as the cost of vacations, though undoubtedly highly and directly beneficial to the general health, or athletic club expenses by means of which an individual keeps physically fit, are not deductible because they fall within the category of personal or living expenses. To be deductible as medical expense, there must be a direct or proximate relation between the expenses and the diagnosis, cure, mitigation, treatment, or prevention of disease or the expense must have been incurred for the purpose of affecting some structure or function of the body.

In determining allowability, many factors must be considered. Consideration should be accorded the motive or purpose of the taxpayer, but such factor is not alone determinative. To accord it conclusive weight would make nugatory the prohibition against allowing personal, living, or family expenses. Thus also it is important to inquire as to the origin of the expense. Was it incurred at the direction or suggestion of a physician; did the treatment bear directly on the physical condition in question; did the treatment bear such a direct or proximate therapeutic relation to the bodily condition as to justify a reasonable belief the same would be efficacious; was the treatment so proximate in the time to the onset or recurrence of the disease or condition as to make one the true occasion of the other, thus eliminating expense incurred for general, as contrasted with some specific, physical improvement?

In the present case deduction is asked of expenses of travel to and maintenance at two resort hotels in New Jersey and a resort ranch in Arizona. Although the physician advised the trips, the record does not specifically link the treatment of coronary occlusion with a change of climate. The generally accepted treatment is restricted activity, rest, and the proper use of certain drugs. During her absence from Pittsburgh, while staying at the New Jersey hotels and at the Arizona ranch, petitioner's wife was not under the care of a physician. In fact, the record is barren of evidence that in 1945 she required the care of a physician in any substantial amount while at home in Pittsburgh. The coronary occlusion occurred in 1943. She has been restricted in activity since that time, but has suffered no further attacks. The infarction of the lung had entirely healed.

We do not question the fact that the trips may have been beneficial to petitioner's wife. There can be no question that carefully chosen changes of climate are beneficial to most persons, or that vacations at appropriate resorts are desirable and conducive to better health. The record fails to show, however, that the benefit derived by the wife was in any respect different from that enjoyed by any vacationer at the same resorts at the same time. Nor is it shown that the change in climate served to cure or alleviate her existing heart condition. Certainly it will not be contended that Congress intended that the Government, by tax deduction, was to assist in financing trips that should be characterized as vacation trips.

We consider it significant, though not conclusive, that in their travels petitioner and his wife did not visit sanitariums or similar establishments equipped to render therapeutic aid. At no time during these trips were medical services sought by the wife. The record shows that, albeit petitioner testified he did not take pleasure trips, he nonetheless had been to Atlantic City on various occasions and had visited Arizona for periods from two to four weeks in 1937, 1939, 1940, and 1941, all of which trips were admittedly taken for vacation purposes. In many aspects the trips to Arizona in 1945 appears to have been a resumption of petitioner's former vacation program.

It is also significant that a period of more than 20 months elapsed between the onset of the disease in question and the first of the 3 trips taken by petitioner and his wife. Although it was testified that the first trip to New Jersey was to obtain relief from the humid months of July and August, they returned from Spring Lake, New Jersey, late in July and spent the remainder of that month and the whole month of August in Pittsburgh. No convincing explanation was advanced to account for the trip to Atlantic City, where they remained for 10 days. It was but a month thereafter, on November 20, 1945, that we find petitioner and his wife at the Remuda Ranch in Arizona, where they remained until December 31. Why this latter period was selected, rather than the more severe winter period which could reasonably have been anticipated in Pittsburgh after January 1, does not appear.

It seems clear to us that the deduction in question may be claimed only where there is a health or body condition coming within the statutory concept and where the expense was incurred primarily for the prevention or alleviation of such condition. An incidental benefit is not enough.

On the entire record, we are not convinced that the travel in connection with which petitioner sustained the expense he seeks to deduct was incurred primarily for the cure, prevention, or alleviation of a disease or physical condition within the meaning of [Code Section 213].

The reliance which petitioner places on an unpublished ruling of the Commissioner in which he allowed travel expenses from New York to Miami, Florida, in a case where the patient was a sufferer from hay fever is clearly misplaced. The facts of that case, the nature of the disease, and the proven effect of the climate thereon readily distinguish that case from the present.

Notes

1. *Transportation.*—Code Section 213(d)(1)(B) allows the deduction of amounts paid "for transportation primarily for and essential to medical care." Code Section 213(d)(2) allows amounts paid for lodging away from home primarily for and essential to medical care themselves to be treated as amounts paid for medical care if (A) that medical care is provided by a physician in a license hospital (or in a medical care facility which is related to, or the equivalent of, a licensed hospital), and (B) there is no significant element of personal pleasure, recreation, or vacation in the travel away from home. Any such deduction for lodging is limited to $50 per night per individual.

2. *Qualified long-term care services.*—Code Section 213(d)(1)(C) extends the definition of "medical care" to include "qualified long-term care services," defined in Code Section 7702B(c) to include, among a list of more obviously medical expenses, "maintenance or personal care services" which (A) are required by a chronically ill individual and (B) are provided pursuant to a plan of care prescribed by a licensed health care practitioner. A "chronically ill individual" is one who has been certified by a licensed health care practitioner as being unable to perform on his own at least 2 activities of daily living (eating, toileting, transferring, bathing, dressing, or continence) for a period of at least 90 days due to a loss of functional capacity or as requiring supervision due to severe cognitive impairment. "Maintenance or personal care services" means care "the primary purpose of which is the provision of needed assistance with any of the disabilities as a result of which the individual is a chronically ill individual."

3. *Medical insurance premiums.*—Code Section 213(d)(1)(D) allows the deduction as medical expense the cost of premiums for insurance covering medical care.

4. *Cosmetic surgery.*—Code Section 213(d)(9) excludes from the definition of medical care "cosmetic surgery or other similar procedures, unless the surgery or procedure is necessary to ameliorate a deformity arising from, or directly related to, a congenital abnormality, a personal injury resulting from an accident or trauma, or disfiguring disease." In effect, the subsection excludes elective cosmetic procedures.

PROBLEMS FOR DISCUSSION

18–1. Which of the following expenses qualifies for deduction as an expense for medical care? On the recommendation of a physician:

(a) Taxpayer, suffering from male pattern baldness, undergoes hair transplant surgery.

(b) Taxpayer, suffering from myopia, buys glasses.

(c) Taxpayer, who is blind, acquires and bears the costs of a seeing-eye dog.

(d) Taxpayer, whose hair has gone grey from age, dyes it back to its "normal" color.

(e) Taxpayer, who is confirmed to be severely allergic to pesticides, purchases more expensive organic foods.

(f) Taxpayer, who has a young child, removed lead-based paint from his residence to protect his child from lead poisoning.

SECTION 2: GENDER REASSIGNMENT SURGERY

In *O'Donnabhain v. Commissioner*, excerpted below, the IRS disallowed costs of treating gender identity disorder (GID) on three grounds: (1) that GID was not a "disease" for purposes of Code Section 213, (2) that there was no scientific proof of the efficacy of the procedures used, and (3) that those procedures were disallowed cosmetic surgery or similar procedures because they were not medically necessary.

O'DONNABHAIN v. COMMISSIONER
134 T.C. 34 (2010)

The issue for decision is whether petitioner may deduct as a medical care expense under section 213 amounts paid for hormone therapy, sex reassignment surgery, and breast augmentation surgery that petitioner contends were incurred in connection with a condition known as gender identity disorder.

Rhiannon G. O'Donnabhain was born a genetic male. However, she was uncomfortable in the male gender role from childhood and first wore women's clothing secretly around age 10. Her discomfort regarding her gender intensified in adolescence, and she continued to dress in women's clothing secretly.

As an adult, petitioner earned a degree in civil engineering, served on active duty with the U.S. Coast Guard, found employment at an engineering firm, married, and fathered three children. However, her discomfort with her gender persisted. She felt that she was a female trapped in a male body, and she continued to secretly wear women's clothing. Petitioner's marriage ended after more than 20 years. After separating from her spouse in 1992, petitioner's feelings that she wanted to be female intensified and grew more persistent.

By mid–1996 petitioner's discomfort with her male gender role and desire to be female intensified to the point that she sought out a psychotherapist to address them. In early 1997, after approximately 20 weekly individual therapy sessions, Ms. Ellaborn's diagnosis was that petitioner was a transsexual suffering from severe gender identity disorder (GID), a condition listed in the Diagnostic and Statistical Manual of Mental Disorders (4th ed.2000 text revision) (DSM–IVTR), published by the American Psychiatric Association.

The World Professional Association for Transgender Health (WPATH), formerly known as the Harry Benjamin International Gender Dysphoria Association, Inc., is an association of medical, surgical, and mental health professionals specializing in the understanding and treatment of GID. WPATH publishes "Standards of Care" for the treatment of GID (hereinafter Benjamin standards of care or Benjamin standards). The Benjamin standards of care were originally approved in 1979 and have undergone six revisions through February 2001.

Summarized, the Benjamin standards of care prescribe a "triadic" treatment sequence for individuals diagnosed with GID consisting of (1) hormonal sex reassignment; *i.e.*, the administration of cross-gender hormones to effect changes in physical appearance to more closely resemble the opposite sex; (2) the "real-life" experience (wherein the individual undertakes a trial period of living full time in society as a member of the opposite sex); and (3) sex reassignment surgery, consisting of genital sex reassignment and/or nongenital sex reassignment.

After diagnosing severe GID in petitioner in early 1997, Ms. Ellaborn administered a course of treatment that followed the Benjamin standards of care.

In February 1997 Ms. Ellaborn referred petitioner to an endocrinologist for feminizing hormone therapy, and petitioner commenced taking hormones in September 1997. She remained on feminizing hormones continuously through the taxable year in issue (2001). After beginning hormone therapy petitioner told Ms. Ellaborn that she felt calmer and better emotionally and that she felt positive about her physical changes. Ms. Ellaborn viewed petitioner's positive reactions to hormone therapy as validation of the GID diagnosis.

In consultation with Ms. Ellaborn, petitioner decided to undertake the Benjamin standards' "real-life" experience; *i.e.*, to present in public as female on a full-time basis in March 2000. Petitioner legally changed her name from Robert Donovan to Rhiannon G. O'Donnabhain and arranged to have the gender designation on her driver's license changed, on the basis of her GID diagnosis. She underwent surgery to feminize her facial features, and with the cooperation of her employer commenced presenting as a female at work around April of that year. Petitioner informed Ms. Ellaborn that her transition at work went smoothly and that the "real-life" experience had been "incredibly easy." Ms. Ellaborn viewed petitioner's positive response to her "real-life" experience as further validation of the GID diagnosis.

Petitioner's anxiety as a result of having male genitalia persisted, however, and Ms. Ellaborn concluded that her prognosis without genital surgical sex reassignment (sex reassignment surgery) was poor, in that petitioner's anxiety over the lack of congruence between her perceived gender and her anatomical sex would continue in the absence of surgery and would impair her ability to function normally in society. In November 2000 Ms. Ellaborn wrote a referral letter to Dr. Toby Meltzer, a board-certified plastic and reconstructive surgeon, with over 10 years' experience specializing in sex reassignment surgery, to secure a place for petitioner on his waiting list.

After three additional therapy sessions with petitioner in mid-2001, Ms. Ellaborn concluded that petitioner had satisfied or exceeded all of the Benjamin standards' criteria for sex reassignment surgery, including time spent satisfactorily on feminizing hormones and in the "real-life" experience. In July 2001 Ms. Ellaborn wrote a second letter to Dr. Meltzer certifying petitioner's GID diagnosis and satisfaction of the Benjamin standards' criteria for sex reassignment surgery, and formally recommending petitioner for the surgery. Another licensed psychotherapist with a doctoral degree in clinical psychology, Dr. Alex Coleman (Dr. Coleman), examined petitioner and provided a second recommendation for her sex reassignment surgery.

In mid-October 2001 petitioner underwent sex reassignment surgery. Dr. Meltzer also performed breast augmentation surgery designed to make petitioner's breasts, which had experienced some development as a result of feminizing hormones, more closely resemble the breasts of a genetic female.

In May 2002 Dr. Meltzer performed follow-up surgery on petitioner to refine the appearance of her genitals and remove scar tissue. In February 2005 Dr. Meltzer performed further surgery on petitioner's face, designed to feminize her facial features.

During 2001 petitioner incurred and paid expenses totaling $21,741 in connection with her hormone therapy, sex reassignment surgery, and breast augmentation surgery. These payments were not compensated for by insurance or otherwise.

On her Federal income tax return for 2001, petitioner claimed an itemized deduction for the foregoing expenditures as medical expenses, which respondent subsequently disallowed in a notice of deficiency.

Since the inception of the medical expense deduction, the definition of deductible "medical care" has had two prongs. The first prong covers amounts paid for the "diagnosis, cure, mitigation, treatment, or prevention of disease" and the second prong covers amounts paid "for the purpose of affecting any structure or function of the body".

The regulations treat "disease" as used in the statute as synonymous with "a physical or mental defect or illness." In addition, to qualify as "medical care" under the regulations, an expense must be incurred "primarily" for alleviation of a physical or mental defect, and the defect must be specific. "[A]n expenditure which is merely beneficial to the general health of an individual, such as an expenditure for a vacation, is not an expenditure for medical care."

The second prong of the statutory definition of "medical care", concerning amounts paid "for the purpose of affecting any structure or function of the body," was eventually adjudged too liberal by Congress. The Internal Revenue Service, relying on the second prong, had determined in two revenue rulings that deductions were allowed for amounts expended for cosmetic procedures (such as facelifts, hair transplants, and hair removal through electrolysis) because the procedures were found to affect a structure or function of the body within the meaning of section 213(d)(1)(A).

In 1990 Congress responded to these rulings by amending section 213 to include new subsection (d)(9) which, generally speaking, excludes cosmetic surgery from the definition of deductible medical care. A review of the legislative history of section 213(d)(9) shows that Congress deemed the amendment necessary to clarify that deductions for medical care do not include amounts paid for "an elective, purely cosmetic treatment".

There appear to be no cases of precedential value interpreting the cosmetic surgery exclusion of section 213(d)(9).

Respondent contends that petitioner's hormone therapy, sex reassignment surgery, and breast augmentation surgery are nondeductible "cosmetic surgery or other similar procedures" under section 213(d)(9) because they were directed at improving petitioner's appearance and did not treat an illness or disease, meaningfully promote the proper function of the body, or ameliorate a deformity. Although respondent concedes that GID is a mental disorder, respondent contends, relying on the expert testimony of Dr. Dietz, that GID is not a disease for purposes of section 213 because it does not arise from an organic pathology within the human body that reflects "abnormal structure or function of the body at the gross, microscopic, molecular, biochemical, or neurochemical levels." Respondent further contends that the procedures at issue did not treat disease because there is no scientific proof of their efficacy in treating GID and that the procedures were cosmetic surgery because they were not medically necessary.

Petitioner maintains that she is entitled to deduct the cost of the procedures at issue on the grounds that GID is a well-recognized mental disorder in the psychiatric field that "falls squarely within the meaning of 'disease' because it causes serious, clinically significant distress and impairment of functioning." Since widely accepted standards of care prescribe hormone treatment, sex reassignment surgery, and, in appropriate circumstances, breast augmentation surgery for genetic males suffering from GID, expenditures for the foregoing constitute deductible "medical care" because a direct or proximate relationship exists between the expenditures and the "diagnosis, cure, mitigation, treatment, or prevention of disease", petitioner argues. Moreover, petitioner contends, because the procedures at issue treated a "disease" as used in section 213, they are not "cosmetic surgery" as defined in that section.

The availability of the medical expense deduction for the costs of hormonal and surgical sex reassignment for a transsexual individual presents an issue of first impression.

Determining whether sex reassignment procedures are deductible "medical care" or nondeductible "cosmetic surgery" starts with the meaning of "treatment" and "disease" as used in section 213. Both the statutory definition of "medical care" and the statute's exclusion of "cosmetic surgery" from that definition depend in part upon whether an expenditure or procedure is for "treatment" of "disease". Under section 213(d)(1)(A), if an expenditure is "for the ... treatment ... of disease", it is deductible "medical care"; under section 213(d)(9)(B), if a procedure "[treats] ... disease", it is not "cosmetic surgery" that is excluded from the definition of "medical care."

Respondent maintains that petitioner's expenditures did not treat "disease" because GID is not a "disease" within the meaning of section 213. Central to his argument is respondent's contention that "disease" as used in section 213 has the meaning postulated by respondent's expert, Dr. Dietz; namely, "a condition ... [arising] as a result of a pathological process ... [occurring] within the individual and [reflecting] abnormal structure or function of the body at the gross, microscopic, molecular, biochemical, or neuro-chemical levels."

As a legal argument for the proper interpretation of "disease", respondent's position is meritless. Respondent cites no authority, other than Dr. Dietz' expert testimony, in support of his interpretation, and we have found none. To the contrary, respondent's interpretation is flatly contradicted by nearly a half century of case-law. Numerous cases have treated mental disorders as "diseases" for purposes of section 213 without regard to any demonstrated organic or physiological origin or cause. These cases found mental conditions to be "diseases" where there was evidence that mental health professionals regarded the condition as creating a significant impairment to normal functioning and warranting treatment.

The absence of any consideration of etiology in the caselaw is consistent with the legislative history and the regulations. Both treat "disease" as synonymous with "a physical or mental defect", which suggests a more colloquial sense of the term "disease" was intended than the narrower (and more rigorous) interpretation for which respondent contends.

In addition, in the context of mental disorders, it is virtually inconceivable that Congress could have intended to confine the coverage of section 213 to conditions with demonstrated organic origins when it enacted the provision in 1942, because physiological origins for mental disorders were not widely recognized at the time. As Dr. Dietz confirmed in his testimony, the physiological origins of various well-recognized mental disorders—for example, panic disorder and obsessive-compulsive disorder—were discovered only about a decade ago. Moreover, Dr. Dietz confirmed that bulimia would not constitute a "disease" under his definition, because bulimia has no demonstrated organic origin, nor would posttraumatic stress disorder. Dr. Dietz was unable to say whether anorexia would meet the definition because he was uncertain regarding the current state of scientific knowledge of its origins. Petitioner's expert, Dr. Brown, testified without challenge that most mental disorders listed in the DSM–IV–TR do not have demonstrated organic causes. Thus, under the definition of "disease" respondent advances, many well-recognized mental disorders, perhaps most, would be excluded from coverage under section 213—a result clearly at odds with the intent of Congress (and the regulations) to provide deductions for the expenses of alleviating "mental defects" generally.

In sum, we reject respondent's interpretation of "disease" because it is incompatible with the stated intent of the regulations and legislative history to cover "mental defects" generally and is contradicted by a consistent line of cases finding "disease" in the case of mental disorders without regard to any demonstrated etiology.

Respondent, while conceding that GID is a mental disorder, argues that GID is "not a significant psychiatric disorder" but instead is a "social construction"—a "social phenomenon" that has been "medicalized."

We conclude that GID is a "disease" within the meaning of section 213. We start with the two case-law factors influencing a finding of "disease" in the context of mental conditions: (1) A determination by a mental health professional that the condition created a significant impairment to normal functioning, warranting treatment, or (2) a listing of the condition in a medical reference text. Both factors involve deference by a court to the judgment of medical professionals.

As noted in our findings, GID is listed as a mental disorder in the DSM–IV–TR, which all three experts agree is the primary diagnostic tool of American psychiatry. GID or transsexualism is also listed in numerous medical reference texts, with descriptions of their characteristics that are similar to those in the DSM–IV–TR.

Even if one accepts respondent's expert Dr. Schmidt's assertion that the validity of the GID diagnosis is subject to some debate in the psychiatric profession, the widespread recognition of the condition in medical literature persuades the Court that acceptance of the GID diagnosis is the prevailing view. Dr. Schmidt's own professed misgivings about the diagnosis are not persuasive, given that he continues to employ the diagnosis in practice, believes that psychiatrists must be familiar with it, and recently gave a GID diagnosis as an expert in another court proceeding. On balance, the evidence amply demonstrates that GID is a widely recognized and accepted diagnosis in the field of psychiatry.

Second, GID is a serious, psychologically debilitating condition. Respondent's characterization of the condition on brief as a "social construction" and "not a significant psychiatric disorder" is undermined by both of his own expert witnesses and the medical literature in evidence. All three expert witnesses agreed that, absent treatment, GID in genetic males is sometimes associated with autocastration, autopenectomy, and suicide. Respondent's expert Dr. Schmidt asserts that remaining ambiguous about gender identity "will tear you apart psychologically." Petitioner's expert Dr. Brown likewise testified that GID produces significant distress and maladaption.

Third, respondent's position that GID is not a significant psychiatric disorder is at odds with the position of every U.S. Court of Appeals that has ruled on the question of whether GID poses a serious medical need for purposes of the Eighth Amendment, which has been interpreted to require that prisoners receive adequate medical care. Seven of the U.S. Courts of Appeals that have considered the question have concluded that severe GID or transsexualism constitutes a "serious medical need" for purposes of the Eighth Amendment. No U.S. Court of Appeals has held otherwise.

In view of (1) GID's widely recognized status in diagnostic and psychiatric reference texts as a legitimate diagnosis, (2) the seriousness of the condition as described in learned treatises in evidence and as acknowledged by all three experts in this case; (3) the severity of petitioner's impairment as found by the mental health professionals who examined her; (4) the consensus in the U.S. Courts of Appeal that GID constitutes a serious medical need for purposes of the Eighth Amendment, we conclude and hold that GID is a "disease" for purposes of section 213.

Respondent also contends that petitioner was not correctly diagnosed with GID, citing his expert Dr. Schmidt's contentions that certain co-morbid conditions such as depression or transvestic fetishism had not been adequately ruled out as explanations of petitioner's condition.

Absent evidence of a patent lack of qualifications, this Court has generally deferred, in section 213 disputes, to the judgment of the medical professionals who treated the patient. All three witnesses who supported petitioner's GID diagnosis interviewed petitioner. Since Dr. Schmidt did not, his analysis is entitled to considerably less weight, and we conclude that there is no persuasive basis to doubt the diagnosis.

Our conclusions that GID is a "disease" for purposes of section 213, and that petitioner suffered from it, leave the question of whether petitioner's hormone therapy, sex reassignment surgery, and breast augmentation surgery "[treated]" GID within the meaning of section 213(d)(1)(A) and (9)(B).

Respondent argues that petitioner's sex reassignment surgery did not "treat" disease within the meaning of section 213(d)(9)(B) because there is insufficient scientific evidence of the surgery's efficacy in treating GID. Petitioner's and respondent's experts disagree regarding the sufficiency of the scientific proof of the surgery's efficacy. Respondent's expert Dr. Schmidt contends that efficacy (beyond patient satisfaction) has not been demonstrated, whereas petitioner's expert Dr. Brown believes there is ample proof of positive therapeutic outcomes.

Even assuming some debate remains in the medical profession regarding acceptance of the Benjamin standards or the scientific proof of the therapeutic efficacy of sex reassignment surgery, a complete consensus on the advisability or efficacy of a procedure is not necessary for a deduction under section 213. *See, e.g., Dickie v. Commissioner*, T.C. Memo. 1999–138 (naturopathic cancer treatments deductible); *Crain v. Commissioner*, T.C. Memo. 1986–138 (holistic cancer treatments deductible but for failure of substantiation); *Tso v. Commissioner*, T.C. Memo. 1980–399 (Navajo "sings" deductible); Rev. Rul. 72–593, 1972–2 C.B. 180 (acupuncture deductible); Rev. Rul. 55–261, 1955–1 C.B. 307 (services of Christian Science practitioners deductible). It is sufficient if the circumstances "justify a reasonable belief the . . . [treatment] would be efficacious." That standard has been fully satisfied here. The evidence is clear that a substantial segment of the psychiatric profession has been persuaded of the advisability and efficacy of hormone therapy and sex reassignment surgery as treatment for GID, as have many courts.

Finally, the Court does not doubt that, as respondent's expert Dr. Schmidt points out in his report, some medical professionals shun transsexual patients and consider cross-gender hormone therapy and sex reassignment surgery unethical because they disrupt what is considered to be a "normally functioning hormonal status or destroy healthy, normal tissue." However, the Internal Revenue Service has not heretofore sought to deny the deduction for a medical procedure because it was considered unethical by some. *See, e.g.*, Rev. Rul. 73–201, 1973–1 C.B. 140 (cost of abortion legal under State law is deductible medical care under section 213); Rev. Rul. 55–261, *supra* (services of Christian Science practitioners deductible). Absent a showing of illegality, any such ground for denying a medical expense deduction finds no support in section 213.

In sum, the evidence establishes that cross-gender hormone therapy and sex reassignment surgery are well-recognized and accepted treatments for severe GID. The evidence demonstrates that hormone therapy and sex reassignment surgery to alter appearance (and, to some degree, function) are undertaken by GID sufferers in an effort to alleviate the distress and suffering occasioned by GID, and that the procedures have positive results in this regard in the opinion of many in the psychiatric profession, including petitioner's and respondent's experts. Thus, a "reasonable belief" in the procedures' efficacy is justified. Alleviation of suffering falls within the regulatory and case-law definitions of treatment, and to "relieve" is to "treat" according to standard dictionary definitions. We therefore conclude and hold that petitioner's hormone therapy and sex reassignment surgery "[treated] ... disease" within the meaning of section 213(d)(9)(B) and accordingly are not "cosmetic surgery" as defined in that section.

We consider separately the qualification of petitioner's breast augmentation surgery as deductible medical care, because respondent makes the additional argument that this surgery was not necessary to the treatment of GID in petitioner's case because petitioner already had normal breasts before her surgery. Because petitioner had normal breasts before her surgery, respondent argues, her breast augmentation surgery was "directed at improving ... [her] appearance and [did] not meaningfully promote the proper function of the body or prevent or treat illness or disease," placing the surgery squarely within the section 213(d)(9)(B) definition of "cosmetic surgery."

We find that petitioner has failed to show that her breast augmentation surgery "[treated]" GID. The Benjamin standards provide that breast augmentation surgery for a male-to-female patient "may be performed if the physician prescribing hormones and the surgeon have documented that breast enlargement after undergoing hormone treatment for 18 months is not sufficient for comfort in the social gender role." The record contains no documentation from the endocrinologist prescribing petitioner's hormones at the time of her surgery. To the extent Ms. Ellaborn's or Dr. Coleman's recommendation letters to Dr. Meltzer might be considered substitute documentation for that of the hormone-prescribing physician, Ms. Ellaborn's two letters are silent concerning the condition of petitioner's presurgical breasts, while Dr. Coleman's letter states that petitioner "appears to have significant breast development secondary to hormone therapy". The surgeon here, Dr. Meltzer, recorded in his presurgical notes that petitioner had "approximately B cup breasts with a very nice shape." Thus, all of the contemporaneous documentation of the condition of petitioner's breasts before the surgery suggests that they were within a normal range of appearance, and there is no documentation concerning petitioner's comfort level with her breasts "in the social gender role."

We find that petitioner's breast augmentation surgery did not fall within the treatment protocols of the Benjamin standards and therefore did not "treat" GID within the meaning of section 213(d)(9)(B). Instead, the surgery merely improved her appearance.

The breast augmentation surgery is therefore "cosmetic surgery" under the section 213(d)(9)(B) definition unless it "meaningfully [promoted] the proper function of the body." The parties have stipulated that petitioner's breast augmentation "did not promote the proper function of her breasts." Although petitioner expressly declined to stipulate that the breast augmentation "did not meaningfully promote the proper functioning of her body within the meaning of I.R.C. § 213", we conclude that the stipulation to which she did agree precludes a finding on this record, given the failure to adhere to the Benjamin standards, that the breast augmentation surgery "meaningfully [promoted] the proper function of the body" within the meaning of section 213(d)(9)(B). Consequently, the breast augmentation surgery is "cosmetic surgery" that is excluded from deductible "medical care."

Finally, respondent argues that petitioner's sex reassignment surgery was not "medically necessary", which respondent contends is a requirement intended by Congress to apply to procedures directed at improving appearance, as evidenced by certain references to "medically necessary" procedures in the legislative history of the enactment of the cosmetic surgery exclusion of section 213(d)(9). Respondent in effect argues that the legislative history's contrast of nondeductible cosmetic surgery with "medically necessary" procedures evidences an intent by Congress to impose a requirement in section 213(d)(9) of medical necessity for the deduction of procedures affecting appearance. We find it unnecessary to resolve respondent's claim that section 213(d)(9) should be interpreted to require a showing of "medical necessity" notwithstanding the absence of that phrase in the statute. That is so because respondent's contention would not bar the deductions at issue, inasmuch as we are persuaded, as discussed below, that petitioner has shown that her sex reassignment surgery was medically necessary.

Respondent's basis for the claim that petitioner's sex reassignment surgery was not medically necessary is the expert report and testimony of his expert, Dr. Schmidt. Dr. Schmidt acknowledges in his report that the definition of medical necessity "varies according to the defining party". Dr. Schmidt never expressly defines the term, but he concludes that sex reassignment surgery is not medically necessary because (1) no "community" standard of care requires it (so that a practitioner's failure to provide the surgery would not constitute malpractice) and (2) in his view a therapist should remain neutral regarding the decision to have the surgery—which makes the surgery, Dr. Schmidt reasons, elective. Taken together, these two factors indicate that the surgery is not medically necessary, in Dr. Schmidt's view. Respondent has not shown that Dr. Schmidt's concept of medical necessity is widely accepted, and it strikes the Court as idiosyncratic and unduly restrictive. Moreover, Dr. Schmidt also expressed the view that sex reassignment surgery has "recognized medical and psychiatric benefits" and is "certainly medically helpful".

Dr. Schmidt conceded in his report that a significant segment of those physicians who are knowledgeable concerning GID believes that sex reassignment surgery is medically necessary, ranging from those who believe such surgery is generally medically necessary in treating GID to those who think it is medically necessary in selected cases. As noted, petitioner's expert Dr. Brown believes that sex reassignment surgery is often the only effective treatment for severe GID, and a number of courts have concurred. Dr. Brown therefore believes the surgery is medically necessary for severe GID. Several courts have also concluded in a variety of contexts that sex reassignment surgery for severe GID or transsexualism is medically necessary.

The mental health professional who treated petitioner concluded that petitioner's GID was severe, that sex reassignment surgery was medically necessary, and that petitioner's prognosis without it was poor. Given Dr. Brown's expert testimony, the judgment of the professional treating petitioner, the agreement of all three experts that untreated GID can result in self-mutilation and suicide, and, as conceded by Dr. Schmidt, the views of a significant segment of knowledgeable professionals that sex reassignment surgery is medically necessary for severe GID, the Court is persuaded that petitioner's sex reassignment surgery was medically necessary.

The evidence amply supports the conclusions that petitioner suffered from severe GID, that GID is a well-recognized and serious mental disorder, and that hormone therapy and sex reassignment surgery are considered appropriate and effective treatments for GID by psychiatrists and other mental health professionals who are knowledgeable concerning the condition. Given our holdings that GID is a "disease" and that petitioner's hormone therapy and sex reassignment surgery "[treated]" it, petitioner has shown the "existence ... of a disease" and a payment for goods or services "directly or proximately related" to its treatment. *See Jacobs v. Commissioner*, 62 T.C. at 818. She likewise satisfies the "but for" test of *Jacobs*, which requires a showing that the procedures were an essential element of the treatment and that they would not have otherwise been undertaken for nonmedical reasons. Petitioner's hormone therapy and sex reassignment surgery were essential elements of a widely accepted treatment protocol for severe GID. The expert testimony also establishes that given (1) the risks, pain, and extensive rehabilitation associated with sex reassignment surgery, (2) the stigma encountered by persons who change their gender role and appearance in society, and (3) the expert-backed but commonsense point that the desire of a genetic male to have his genitals removed requires an explanation beyond mere dissatisfaction with appearance (such as GID or psychosis), petitioner would not have undergone hormone therapy and sex reassignment surgery except in an effort to alleviate the distress and suffering attendant to GID. Respondent's contention that petitioner undertook the surgery and hormone treatments to improve appearance is at best a superficial characterization of the circumstances that is thoroughly rebutted by the medical evidence.

Petitioner has shown that her hormone therapy and sex reassignment surgery treated disease within the meaning of section 213 and were therefore not cosmetic surgery. Thus petitioner's expenditures for these procedures were for "medical care" as defined in section 213(d)(1)(A), for which a deduction is allowed under section 213(a).

PROBLEMS FOR DISCUSSION

18–2. Were the expenses incurred in *O'Donnabhain* "involuntary" in the sense that led Congress to allow a deduction for medical care in Code Section 213(a), or "voluntary" in the sense that led Congress to disallow expenses for cosmetic surgery in Code Section 213(d)(9)?

SECTION 3: REPRODUCTIVE SERVICES

Magdalin, excerpted below, was the first published opinion to address the deductibility of the costs of assisted reproduction. See Katherine Pratt, *Deducting the Costs of Fertility Treatment: Implications of* Magdalin v. Commissioner *for Opposite-Sex Couples, Gay and Lesbian Same-Sex Couples, and Single Women and Men*, 2009 WIS. L. REV. 1283. William Magdalin, a gay man not legally married, attempted to deduct the costs of producing his two children through egg donation and surrogacy. The IRS denied the deduction on the ground that (1) Magdalin did not suffer from medical infertility, and (2) the medical procedures involved did not affect the structure or function of Magdalin's body, although they "affected the structures or functions of the bodies of the unrelated surrogate mothers."

MAGDALIN v. COMMISSIONER
T.C. Memo. 2008–293

Petitioner is a medical doctor licensed to practice medicine in Massachusetts. At all relevant times, his sperm count and motility were found to be within normal limits. He has twin sons from a marriage to his former spouse, Deborah Magdalin. The twins were born through natural processes and without the use of in vitro fertilization (IVF).

In July 2004 petitioner entered into an Anonymous Egg Donor Agreement under which an anonymous donor was to donate eggs to be fertilized with petitioner's sperm and transferred to a gestational carrier using the IVF process. That same month, petitioner also entered into a Gestational Carrier Agreement in which a woman (the first carrier) agreed to become impregnated through the IVF embryo transfer process with the embryo created from the anonymous donor's egg and petitioner's sperm and to bear a child for petitioner. The first carrier gave birth to a child on September 17, 2005.

On November 18, 2005, petitioner entered into a similar Gestational Carrier Agreement with another woman (the second carrier). The second carrier gave birth to a child on August 12, 2006. The donor was not the spouse or dependent of petitioner. Nor was either of the carriers. Both IVF procedures occurred at the Reproduction Science Center (IVF clinic) in Lexington, Massachusetts.

Petitioner paid the following expenses in 2004 relating to the aforementioned agreements: (1) $3,500 for petitioner's legal fees relating to the first donation cycle under the Anonymous Egg Donor Agreement; (2) $500 for the donor's legal fees relating to the Anonymous Egg Donor Agreement; (3) $10,750 for the donor's fees and expenses; (4) $8,000 for the first carrier's fees and expenses; (5) $25,400 to the IVF clinic; and (6) $2,815 for prescription drugs for the first carrier.

In 2005 petitioner paid the following relevant expenses: (1) $750 for petitioner's legal fees relating to the second donation cycle under the Anonymous Egg Donor Agreement; (2) $17,000 for the first carrier's fees and expenses; (3) $14,270 for petitioner's legal fees relating to the Gestational Carrier Agreement with the second carrier; (4) $1,000 for the second carrier's legal fees relating to the Gestational Carrier Agreement; (5) $2,615.10 to the IVF clinic; (6) $300 to Lawrence General Hospital for costs relating to the first carrier's stay during delivery of the first child; (7) $1,181.25 for the first carrier's legal fees relating to legal proceedings concerning a dispute over the issuance of the first child's birth certificate; and (8) $838 for prescription drugs for both carriers. There is no evidence that petitioner was compensated for any of those expenses by insurance or otherwise.

Petitioner filed his 2004 and 2005 Federal income tax returns on time. On Schedules A, Itemized Deductions, included with those returns he deducted medical expenses of $34,050 for 2004 and $28,230 for 2005. On March 22, 2007, respondent issued petitioner a notice of deficiency for his 2004 and 2005 tax years. Therein, respondent disallowed petitioner's claimed medical expense deductions in their entirety. On April 3, 2007, petitioner, who then resided in Massachusetts, filed a timely petition with this Court.

Section 213(a) allows for the deduction of paid expenses "not compensated for by insurance or otherwise, for medical care of the taxpayer, his spouse, or a dependent * * * to the extent that such expenses exceed 7.5 percent of adjusted gross income." The deductibility of the expenses at issue hinges on whether they were paid for petitioner's medical care. If so, they are deductible medical expenses under section 213. If not, they are nondeductible personal expenses under section 262.

The term "medical care" includes amounts paid "for the diagnosis, cure, mitigation, treatment, or prevention of disease, or for the purpose of affecting any structure or function of the body". Sec. 213(d)(1)(A). The regulations provide that "Deductions for expenditures for medical care allowable under section 213 will be confined strictly to expenses incurred primarily for the prevention or alleviation of a physical or mental defect or illness." Sec. 1.213–1(e)(1)(ii), Income Tax Regs.

We have interpreted the statute as requiring a causal relationship in the form of a "but for" test between a medical condition and the expenditures incurred in treating that condition. The "but for" test requires petitioner to prove (1) "that the expenditures were an essential element of the treatment" and (2) "that they would not have otherwise been incurred for nonmedical reasons."

It is also noteworthy that section 213(d)(1)(A), which is not a model of clarity, is phrased disjunctively—it allows for the deduction of any expenses paid "for the diagnosis, cure, mitigation, treatment, or prevention of disease, or for the purpose of affecting any structure or function of the body". Sec. 213(d)(1)(A) (emphasis added); see *Dickie v. Commissioner*, T.C. Memo. 1999–138 ("The deductibility of medical care payments under section 213 is not strictly limited to traditional medical procedures, but it includes payments made for the purpose of affecting any structure or function of the body."). Although the phrase "for the purpose of affecting any structure or function of the body" was historically interpreted by the Internal Revenue Service and the Court to allow taxpayers to deduct the costs of a wide array of cosmetic procedures, Congress felt this was too liberal a tax deduction because it resulted from a personal expense and not a medical one. As a consequence, in 1990 Congress restricted taxpayers' ability to do so.

Petitioner argues that it was his civil right to reproduce, that he should have the freedom to choose the method of reproduction, and that it is sex discrimination to allow women but not men to choose how they will reproduce. While he correctly acknowledges that Internal Revenue Service private letter rulings are "not legal precedent", he refers to Priv. Ltr. Rul. 2003–18–017 (Jan. 9, 2003) to show that "the expenses for egg donor, medical and legal costs are deductible medical expenses".

"Although respondent believes that amounts paid for procedures to mitigate infertility may qualify as deductible medical care", respondent argues that "Petitioner had no physical or mental defect or illness which prohibited him from procreating naturally", as he in fact has, and that "the procedures were not medically indicated." Respondent's position is that the expenses at issue are nondeductible under section 262 because "Petitioner's choice to undertake these procedures was an entirely personal/nonmedical decision."

The expenses at issue were not paid for medical care under the first portion of section 213(d)(1)(A) because the requisite causal relationship is absent. None of the expenses at issue was "incurred primarily for the prevention or alleviation of a physical or mental defect or illness." Sec. 1.213–1(e)(1)(ii), Income Tax Regs. In other words, petitioner had no medical condition or defect, such as, for example, infertility, that required treatment or mitigation through IVF procedures. We therefore need not answer lurking questions as to whether (and, if so, to what extent) expenditures for IVF procedures and associated costs (*e.g.*, a taxpayer's legal fees and fees paid to, or on behalf of, a surrogate or gestational carrier) would be deductible in the presence of an underlying medical condition. We leave such questions for another day. Further, petitioner cannot deduct those expenses under the second portion of the statute because they did not affect a structure or function of his body.

Although petitioner at times attempts to frame the deductibility of the relevant expenses as an issue of constitutional dimensions, under the facts and circumstances of his case, it does not rise to that level. Petitioner's gender, marital status, and sexual orientation do not bear on whether he can deduct the expenses at issue. He cannot deduct those expenses because he has no medical condition or defect to which those expenses relate and because they did not affect a structure or function of his body. Expenses incurred in the absence of the requisite underlying medical condition or defect and that do not affect a structure or function of the taxpayer's body are nondeductible personal expenses within the meaning of section 262.

PROBLEMS FOR DISCUSSION

18–3. If Magdalin had been married to a woman who was physically incapable of bearing children, would the result have been different? Would the reason for her physical incapacity (*e.g.*, removal of her uterus because of cancer v. natural aging) have mattered? Would it have mattered if he was legally married to her?

18–4. If Magdalin had been legally married to another man, would the result have been different?

Subchapter B: Deduction for State and Local Taxes

Code: Section 164

Code Section 164(a) allows a deduction for state and local real property taxes, personal property taxes, and income taxes, among others. One might view such taxes as paid for consumption benefits—road, education, police services, and the like—provided by state or local governments. But the amount of state and local taxes one pays generally varies with income or wealth, not with consumption of state services. The one thing we can say for sure is that a taxpayer forced to pay state or local taxes has less money left over to pay federal income taxes than an otherwise identically situated taxpayer who is not.

Code Section 164(b)(5) allows taxpayers to elect to deduct state and local sales taxes instead of income taxes. The election accommodates residents of states without income taxes. Electing taxpayers can compute the amount of their sales tax deduction either by saving receipts or by referring to tables published by the IRS based on the average consumption by taxpayers of sales-tax-eligible items.

Finally, Code Section 164(f) allows individual taxpayer who pay self-employment taxes to deduct half of those taxes paid. The subsection's purpose is to replicate the treatment of payroll taxes paid or collected by employers. Half of such taxes are paid by (and deductible by) employers; the other half are paid by their employees, although collected and remitted by employers.

Subchapter C: Personal Casualty Losses

Joe's camper, which he uses solely for personal purposes, is picked up by a tornado and thrown half-way across town. Before the tornado, it was worth $10,000. Afterwards, it is worth nothing. How much Haig–Simons income does he have? Clearly, his net worth has declined by $10,000. If the camper had declined in value through ordinary use, we would treat that decline in value as the amount his Haig–Simons consumption. But is having one's property destroyed by a tornado Haig–Simons "consumption"? What about losing it to theft? Arguably not. If not, then under Haig–Simons, Sam should be entitled to a $10,000 deduction, reflecting his $10,000 loss.

The line Code Section 165(c)(3) draws between "fire, storm, shipwreck, or other casualty, or from theft" and ordinary consumption is thus at least arguable consistent with tax base theory. Nevertheless, the Treasury treats the deduction for personal casualty losses as a tax expenditure. 2013 Tax Expenditure Budget, Item 161. And the deduction is structured as a recognition that taxpayer may have a reduced ability to pay taxes, not as the inevitable consequence of tax base theory.

Code Section 165(h)(1) prohibits taking into account the first $100 of any personal casualty loss. Code Section 165(h)(2) then allows any remaining net personal casualty losses (that is, personal casualty losses in excess of personal casualty gains) only to the extent they exceed 10 percent of AGI. "Personal casualty gain" means gain from any involuntary conversion of property by reason of a Code Section 165(c)(3) event—for example, by reason of insurance or tort recovery.

Assume, for example, that Joe, in our opening hypothetical, has AGI of $50,000 for the year. Under (h)(1), we knock off the first $100 of his $10,000 loss; his cognizable loss is therefore $9,900. We disallow the loss to the extent it does not exceed 10 percent of AGI—here, $5,000 (10 percent of $50,000). His deductible loss is therefore $4,900. With an AGI of $50,000, Joe is probably in a 25 percent marginal tax bracket. If so, the deduction saves him $1,225 in taxes. In effect, of his $10,000 loss, the federal government absorbs $1,225.

Because of the mechanical structure of the income tax computation, even the foregoing probably overstates the value of the deduction to the ordinary Joe. Personal casualty losses are subject to the 2 percent floor of Code Section 68. Thus, unless he has other miscellaneous itemized deductions, another $1,000 of the loss will be lopped off by the 2 percent floor. If Joe is single and the loss occurs in 2012, his standard deduction is $5,950. This means that unless he has other significant itemized deductions, the deduction does him no good at all. And this is so notwithstanding the fact that an uninsured $10,000 loss probably hits someone with only $50,000 per year of income fairly hard.

GENERAL COUNSEL MEMORANDUM 35013 (1972), CASUALTY LOSSES UNDER SECTION 165(c)(3)

This is in response to your memorandum dated September 3, 1971, in which you referred a proposed revenue ruling to us for concurrence or comment. The proposed ruling was previously considered by this Office in G.C.M. 34538, Casualty Losses Under Section 165(c)(3) (Jun. 30, 1971). As the result of a conference held on August 25, 1971, you have incorporated certain revisions into the proposed ruling and ask that we now reconsider the matter formally.

Issue

Whether the words "external physical force" should be used in the statement "to be a casualty, the accidental loss must result from some external physical force evidencing an identifiable event of a sudden, unexpected or unusual nature, as must any other casualty loss" in a proposed ruling concerning the effect of *John P. White*, 48 T.C. 430 (1967) (Acq. C.B. 1969–1, 21) on Service casualty loss position?

Conclusion

We conclude that the reference to some "external physical force" should be deleted from the purposed ruling. We recommend that the word "damaging" be inserted to modify "event". The ruling would thus hold that the Service casualty loss position is altered only to the extent that the accidental loss of property can now qualify as a casualty provided the loss results from some identifiable and damaging event of a sudden, unexpected, and unusual nature as must any other casualty loss.

Facts

This Office first considered this case in G.C.M. 33735, Casualty Losses Under Section 165(c)(3), I–2854 (Jan. 25, 1968). At issue there was the effect of *John P. White*, *supra*, on the Service casualty loss position. We concluded that a loss arising where property is lost, *i.e.*, unable to be found, as a result of a qualifying event, is deductible as a casualty loss within the meaning of section 165(c)(3). That G.C.M. also sketched the meaning of the terms "sudden, unexpected, or unusual" as developed in court decisions as follows: to be "sudden" the event must be of a swift, forceful, and precipitous nature and not gradual or progressive; to be "unexpected" the event must be ordinarily unanticipated and one which occurs without the intent of the taxpayer who suffers the loss; and to be "unusual" the event must be extraordinary and nonrecurring, and one that does not commonly occur in the ordinary course of day-to-day living.

In G.C.M. 34538, Casualty Losses Under Section 165(c)(3), I–2854 (Jun. 30, 1971), we were asked to consider a proposed revenue ruling based on G.C.M. 33735. In G.C.M. 34538 we concluded that the word "forceful" should be deleted from the description of the word "sudden". We also revised the definition of the word "unusual" to reflect views expressed in *David Axelrod*, 56 T.C. No. 23 (1971). The present proposed ruling adopts those revisions.

In addition, in G.C.M. 34538, we also recommended that the word "damaging" be inserted to modify the word "event" in the proposed statement of Service position on what constitutes a casualty. A casualty loss would thus be allowed only where there was an identifiable and damaging event, sudden in nature, which results in the loss of property and the event is unexpected and unusual in the context in which it occurs. At the conference held on August 25, 1971, attended by representatives of the Tax Legislative Counsel, your office, and the Interpretative Division, it was recommended that the word "damaging" be deleted from the statement of Service casualty loss position. Representatives of your office suggested that the statement be revised to substitute a reference to some "external physical force" in place of "damaging". The proposed ruling adopts that suggestion as follows:

> "In other words, the Service position is altered only to the extent that the accidental loss of property can now qualify as a casualty provided the loss is caused by some unexpected external force. Therefore, to be a casualty, the accidental loss must result from some external physical force evidencing an identifiable event of a sudden, unexpected, and unusual nature, as must any other casualty loss. . . ."

Analysis

In the G.C.M. 34538 discussion concerning whether the word "forceful" should be included in the description of "sudden", we cited several instances in which casualty loss deductions have been permitted without a showing that the event was "forceful". To illustrate, the Service has taken the position that a casualty loss deduction is allowed for cattle killed as a result of having eaten certain cottonseed feed pellets made in machines lubricated by oil containing chlorinated naphthalene, a poisonous substance. Rev. Rul. 54–395, 1954–2 C.B. 143. Another example is the allowance of a casualty loss deduction where a taxpayer inadvertently threw $* * * into the trash which resulted in the money being burned. See * * *, I–10 (Mar. 10, 1961). In addition, in Rev. Rul. 69–88, 1969–1 C.B. 58 the Service allowed a casualty loss where a taxpayer's personal automobile parked on a frozen lake sank when the ice unexpectedly gave way. Furthermore, we have suggested that casualty loss treatment should not be precluded where property such as household furnishings, the function of which is substantially decorative, is spotted or stained rather than smashed or torn. * * *, I–3502 (Nov. 28, 1968).

Those examples also illustrate interpretative problems that could arise if the term "external physical force" is used in the Service definition of a casualty loss. Before discussing those potential problems, however, the term "external physical force" should be defined. Webster's Seventh New

Collegiate Dictionary (1969) defines "force" as "1 a: strength or energy exerted or brought to bear: cause of motion or change: active power ...". The term "physical" is defined as "1: of, relating to, or according with material things or natural laws as opposed to things mental, moral, spiritual or imagery. 2 a: of, or relating to natural science. b(1): of, or relating to physics: (2): characterized or produced by the forces and operations of physics ...". The term "external" is defined as "1 a: capable of being perceived outwardly ... b(1): having merely the outward appearance of something ... 2 a: of, relating to, or connected with the outside or an outer part. b: applied or applicable to the outside ...". "External physical force" can therefore be broadly interpreted to mean a strength or energy relating to natural laws that can be perceived outwardly. It can also be narrowly interpreted to mean a strength or energy of or relating to physics that is connected with an outside part.

How the term "external physical force" is interpreted can have a significant effect on whether an event qualifies under section 165(c)(3). If narrowly interpreted, in Rev. Rul. 54–395 in which cattle were poisoned, death could be attributed to an "internal chemical reaction" rather than an "external physical force". The burning of the money in * * * could also be termed a "chemical reaction" rather than a "physical force".

Use of the concept "force" can also create problems in labeling the "force" associated with a loss and the degree of "force" necessary to cause a loss. What "force" evidenced the sinking of the car in Rev. Rul. 69–88? Is the spotting or staining of household furnishings caused by a sufficient "force" to constitute a casualty?

While we realize that it may be impossible to formulate a general rule that is applicable in all cases, we believe that the interpretative problems associated with the "external physical force" description are too significant to recommend its inclusion in a formulation of the Service casualty loss position. For that reason we recommend that the term "external physical force" be deleted from the proposed revenue ruling.

We recommend that the word "damaging" be inserted to modify the word "event" in the proposed statement of Service position. A casualty loss would thus be allowed only where there is an identifiable and damaging event, sudden in nature, which results in the loss of the property and the event is unexpected and unusual in the context in which it occurs.

The inclusion of the "damaging" requirement is consistent with previous Service position and case law. Rev. Rul. 66–303, 1966–2 C.B. 55, for example, contains the following statement describing a casualty:

> " 'Casualty' within the meaning of section 165(c)(3) of the Code must include an identifiable event, sudden in nature, fixing a point at which loss to the owner of the damaged property can be measured, and must also be unexpected or unusual in the context in which it occurs."

Also see the discussion in G.C.M. 34538, *supra*, 3–4. Moreover, we have been unable to find any court decisions or revenue rulings that allow a casualty loss deduction where the property for which the loss was claimed had not been damaged.

At the conference held on August 25, 1971, representatives of your office presented a hypothetical fact pattern that they believe illustrates a case in which a casualty loss deduction should be allowed although no damage occurred. Under that fact pattern, an oil tank sitting in an isolated area is struck by lightning. The lightning does not damage the tank but the force of the lightning trips the open-shut valve on the tank. The valve is not damaged but the oil runs out onto the ground and is rendered useless. We believe that the lightning in that case qualifies as a damaging event. Although the oil tank and the valve were not harmed, the oil was damaged as a result of the bolt of lightning. If the lightning was not a damaging event, no loss would have been suffered.

We believe that the use of the term "damaging" in the formulation of the Service casualty loss position is preferable to the reference to an "external physical force". The term "damaging" has two advantages: (1) it makes precise definitional interpretations in each case unnecessary; and (2) an inquiry into the type or degree of "force" causing a loss is not required. Under the "damaging" concept, it is sufficient that property is damaged by an identifiable event, sudden in nature and unexpected and unusual in the context in which it occurs. The "damaging" requirement, moreover, provides proof that a loss has been suffered, an important factor in the administration of section 165(c)(3).

GCM 35013 was part of an internal reevaluation of the IRS's position following the Tax Court's decision in *White v. Commissioner* upholding a personal casualty loss deduction on the following facts:

> "the taxpayer-husband accidentally slammed the car door on his wife's hand after helping her alight from the car. Her diamond engagement ring absorbed the full impact of the blow, which broke two flanges of the setting holding the diamond in place. His wife quickly withdrew her injured hand, shaking it vigorously, and the diamond dropped or flew out of the broken setting. The uninsured diamond was never found, and the taxpayer claimed a casualty loss deduction for its value in the year it was lost."

This reevaluative process resulted in the publication of Rev. Rul. 72–592, 1972–2 C.B. 101, holding that in response to *White v. Commissioner*,

> "the Service position is altered only to the extent that the accidental loss of property can now qualify as a casualty. Such losses must, of course, qualify under the same rules as must any other casualty; namely, the loss must result from some event that is (1) identifiable,

(2) damaging to property, and (3) sudden, unexpected, and unusual in nature."

NOTES

1. *Wagering losses.*—Code Section 165(d) limits the deduction of wagering losses to the amount of taxpayer's wagering gains in the same year. As a result, if taxpayer earns a salary of $100,000 for the year but loses half of it gambling, he still has to pay taxes on his $100,000 salary.

2. *Theft losses.*—Under Code Section 165(e), theft losses are treated as sustained in the year of discovery. Thus, if taxpayer does not discover a theft loss until several years after the theft occurs, he can still deduct the loss.

3. *Worthless securities.*—Code Section 165(g)(1) provides that if a security held as a capital asset becomes worthless, the resulting loss is treated as a capital loss—and therefore subject to the capital loss limitation rules of Code Section 1212—not a Code Section 165 loss.

4. *Personal casualty gains.*—As has been noted, a "personal casualty gain" means gain from an involuntary conversion of property by reason of a Code Section 165(c)(3) event. Only personal casualty losses net of personal casualty gains are deductible, subject, of course, to the limitations of Code Section 165(h). But what if personal casualty gains for the year exceed personal casualty losses? Code Section 165(h)(2)(B) provides that in such event, all such gains and losses will be treated as capital gains and losses, subject to the Code Section 1211 netting rules and Code Section 1212 capital loss limitation rules.

PROBLEMS FOR DISCUSSION

18–5. Which of the following losses is eligible for deduction as a personal casualty loss (ignoring the limitations of Code Section 165(h))? Assume that none of the losses is covered by insurance.

(a) Taxpayer's pet cat throws a tantrum, in the process breaking an expensive vase owned by taxpayer.

(b) A military jet flying overhead emits a sonic boom, shattering the plate glass window in taxpayer's living room.

(c) Taxpayer is repeated cited by his local fire department for failure to clear flammable brush from around his house. He refuses to clear the brush on "liberty" grounds. As a result, when a brush fire sweeps through his neighborhood, his house burns to the ground.

(d) An intense drought kills all of the plants in taxpayer's backyard vegetable garden.

(e) Taxpayer's child is kidnapped for ransom. He recovers his child by paying the kidnappers the amount they demand.

(f) Taxpayer purchases publicly traded stock in Enron based on fraudulent reports of the company's profitability. When the fraudulent nature of the reports becomes public, the stock becomes worthless.

CHAPTER 19

CHARITABLE CONTRIBUTIONS

■ ■ ■

Code: Section 170

Code Section 170(a)(1) allows the deduction of "any charitable contribution"—a deceptively simple introduction to an astonishingly complex and inconsistent set of rules. Added to the U.S. income tax in 1917 in response to concerns that wealthy donors would stop contributing to universities and other institutions of higher learning, the charitable contribution deduction is one of the oldest in the Code. *See* Ellen P. Aprill, *Churches, Politics, and the Charitable Contribution Deduction*, 42 B.C. L. Rev. 843 (2001).

The original rationale for the deduction—to encourage donations for specified types of activities—remains plausible but problematic. One can relatively easily justify incentives for charitable, scientific, or educational giving. Each is arguably a legitimate goal of government. For the most part, the donor group and the group receiving the resulting services do not overlap much; donations therefore generally cannot pay for personal consumption by donors. As a result, it is plausible simply to assume disinterested altruistic motivation; it is also reasonable to worry that in the absence of tax incentives, such donations might decline.

From the outset, however, a deduction was also permitted for contributions to organizations operated for purely religious purposes—primarily churches. Many churches do undertake significant charitable work. But a large portion of the funds spent by any church is spent to provide religious services to churchgoers—the donors themselves. As a matter of tax theory, consumption of religious services is no different from any other kind of consumption. We do not generally allow consumers of educational services to deduct amounts they pay for such services; tax theory offers no reason to treat consumers of religious services differently. In the United States, moreover, it is not clear that encouraging the provision of religious services is a legitimate objective of government. In addition, it is harder to infer a purely altruistic motive for the standard periodic contribution or payment to a church, synagogue, mosque, or temple. Such contributions or payments are expected—sometimes even required—as a condition of receiving the services in question. And empirically, most such contributions or payments would be made even in the absence of tax incentives; the tax benefits provided by Code Section 170 have little measurable incentive effect in the religious context. The net effect of the deduction for contributions or payments for religious services appears to be simply that, all else being equal, itemizing taxpayers who are religiously observant pay lower taxes than those who are not.

None of this necessarily means that a deduction for contributions to churches, synagogues, mosques, or temples is inappropriate. What it does mean is that the charitable contribution deduction lacks a single clear theoretical foundation. This almost certainly contributes to its incoherence and internal inconsistency. As will be seen, the charitable contribution deduction is one of very few areas in which the federal agency charged with administering the law appears to disregard governing Supreme Court precedent. For students and teachers (if for no one else), this poses an interesting question: What is the law?

Subchapter A: General Rule

Principle: A contribution is a voluntary transfer of money or property that is made with no expectation of procuring a financial benefit commensurate with the amount of the transfer.

Code: Sections 170(c) and (f)(8) and 6115

Code Section 170(c) defines a "charitable contribution" as a contribution or gift to any of a list of eligible recipients, the most important of which are commonly called "501(c)(3)'s"—organizations "organized and operated exclusively for religious, charitable, scientific, literary, or educational purposes, or to foster national or international amateur sports competition ..., or for the prevention of cruelty to children or animals." The key question, at least outside the religious context, has always been whether the donor receives some quid pro quo. If he does, then (1) only the portion of his "contribution" in excess of the value of what he receives in exchange can be treated as a charitable contribution and, even then, (2) only if the "excess payment" was made with the intention of making a gift. *United States v. American Bar Endowment*, 477 U.S. 105 (1986).

REV. RUL. 83–104

1983–2 C.B. 46

Issue

Is the taxpayer entitled to a deduction for a charitable contribution under section 170 of the Internal Revenue Code in each of the situations described below?

Facts

In each of the situations described below, the donee organization operates a private school and is an organization described in section 170(c) of the Code. In each situation a taxpayer who is a parent of a child who attends the school makes a payment to the organization. In each situation, the cost of educating a child in the school is not less than the payments made by the parent to the organization.

Situation 1. Organization S, which operates a private school, requests the taxpayer to contribute $400x for each child enrolled in the school. Parents who do not make the $400x contribution are required to pay $400x tuition for each child enrolled in the school. Parents who neither make the contribution nor pay tuition cannot enroll their children in the school. The taxpayer paid $400x to S.

Situation 2. Organization T, which operates a private school, solicits contributions from parents of applicants for admission to the school during the period of the school's solicitation for enrollment of students or while the applications are pending. The solicitation materials are part of the application materials or are presented in a form indicating that parents of applicants have been singled out as a class for solicitation. With the exception of a few parents, every parent who is financially able makes a contribution or pledges to make a contribution to T. No tuition is charged. The taxpayer paid $400x to T, which amount was suggested by T.

Situation 3. Organization U, which operates a private school, admits or readmits a significantly larger percentage of applicants whose parents have made contributions to U than applicants whose parents have not made contributions. The taxpayer paid $400x to U.

Situation 4. Organization V, a society for religious instruction, has as its sole function the operation of a private school providing secular and religious education to the children of its members. No tuition is charged for attending the school, which is funded through V's general account. Contributions to the account are solicited from all society members, as well as from local churches and nonmembers. Persons other than parents of children attending the school do not contribute a significant portion of the school's support. Funds normally come to V from parents on a regular, established schedule. At times, parents are personally solicited by the school treasurer to contribute funds according to their financial ability. No student is refused admittance to the school because of the failure of his or her parents to contribute to the school. The taxpayer paid $40x to V.

Situation 5. Organization W, operates a private school that charges a tuition of $300x per student. In addition, it solicits contributions from parents of students during periods other than the period of the school's solicitation for student enrollments or the period when applications to the school are pending. Solicitation materials indicate that parents of students have been singled out as a class for solicitation and the solicitation materials include a report of W's cost per student to operate the school. Suggested amounts of contributions based on an individual's ability to pay are provided. No unusual pressure to contribute is placed upon individuals with children in the school, and many parents do not contribute. In addition, W receives contributions from many former students, parents of former students, and other individuals. The taxpayer paid $100x to W in addition to the tuition payment.

Situation 6. Church X operates a school providing secular and religious education that is attended both by children of parents who are members of X and by children of nonmembers. X receives contributions from all of its members. These contributions are placed in X's general operating fund and are expended when needed to support all church activities. A substantial portion of the other activities is unrelated to the school. Most members of X do not have children in the school, and a major portion of X's expenses are attributable to its nonschool functions. The methods of soliciting contributions to X from church members with children in the school are the same as the methods of soliciting contributions from members without children in the school. X has full control over the use of the contributions that it receives. Members who have children enrolled in the school are not required to pay tuition for their children, but tuition is charged for the children of nonmembers. Taxpayer, a member of X and whose child attends X's school, contributed $200x to X during the year for X's general purposes.

Law and Analysis

Section 170(a) of the Code provides, subject to certain limitations, for the allowance of a deduction for charitable contributions or gifts to or for the use of organizations described in section 170(c), payment of which is made during the taxable year.

A contribution for purposes of section 170 of the Code is a voluntary transfer of money or property that is made with no expectation of procuring a financial benefit commensurate with the amount of the transfer. (See section 1.170A–1(c)(5) of the Income Tax Regulations and H.R. Rep. No. 1337, 83rd Cong., 2d Sess. A44 (1954).) Tuition expenditures by a taxpayer to an educational institution are therefore not deductible as charitable contributions to the institution because they are required payments for which the taxpayer receives benefits presumably equal in value to the amount paid. (See *Channing v. United States*, 4 F.Supp. 33 (D. Mass), *aff'd per curiam*, 67 F.2d 986 (1st Cir. 1933), *cert. denied*, 291 U.S. 686 (1934).) Similarly, payments made by a taxpayer on behalf of children attending parochial or other church-sponsored schools are not allowable deductions as contributions either to the school or to the religious organization operating the school if the payments are earmarked for such children. (See Rev. Rul. 54–580, 1954–2 C.B. 97.) However, the fact that the payments are not earmarked does not necessarily mean that the payments are deductible. On the other hand, a charitable deduction for a payment to an organization that operates a school will not be denied solely because the payment was, to any substantial extent, offset by the fair market value of the services rendered to the taxpayer in the nature of tuition.

Whether a transfer of money by a parent to an organization that operates a school is a voluntary transfer that is made with no expectation of obtaining a commensurate benefit depends upon whether a reasonable person, taking all the facts and circumstances of the case into account, would conclude that enrollment in the school was in no manner contingent upon making the payment, that the payment was not made pursuant to a plan (whether express or implied) to convert nondeductible tuition into charitable contributions, and that receipt of the benefit was not otherwise dependent upon the making of the payment.

In determining this issue, the presence of one or more of the following factors creates a presumption that the payment is not a charitable contribution: the existence of a contract under which a taxpayer agrees to make a "contribution" and which contains provisions ensuring the admission of the taxpayer's child; a plan allowing taxpayers either to pay tuition or to make "contributions" in exchange for schooling; the earmarking of a contribution for the direct benefit of a particular individual; or the otherwise-unexplained denial of admission or readmission to a school of children of taxpayers who are financially able, but who do not contribute.

In other cases, although no single factor may be determinative, a combination of several factors may indicate that a payment is not a charitable contribution. In these cases, both economic and noneconomic pressures placed upon parents must be taken into account. The factors that the Service ordinarily will take into consideration, but will not limit itself to, are the following: (1) the absence of a significant tuition charge; (2) substantial or unusual pressure to contribute applied to parents of children attending a school; (3) contribution appeals made as part of the admissions or enrollment process; (4) the absence of significant potential sources of revenue for operating the school other than contributions by parents of children attending the school; (5) and other factors suggesting that a contribution policy has been created as a means of avoiding the characterization of payments as tuition.

However, if a combination of such factors is not present, payments by a parent will normally constitute deductible contributions, even if the actual cost of educating the child exceeds the amount of any tuition charged for the child's education.

Holdings

Situation 1. The taxpayer is not entitled to a charitable contribution deduction for the payment to Organization S. Because the taxpayer must either make the contribution or pay the tuition charge in order for his or her child to attend S's school, admission is contingent upon making a payment of $400x. The taxpayer's payment is not voluntary and no deduction is allowed.

Situation 2. The taxpayer is not entitled to a charitable contribution deduction for the payment to Organization T. Because of the time and manner of the solicitation of contributions by T, and the fact that no tuition is charged, it is not reasonable to expect that a parent can obtain the admission of his or her child to T's school without making the suggested payments. Under these circumstances, the payments made by the taxpayer are in the nature of tuition, not voluntary contributions.

Situation 3. The taxpayer is not entitled to a charitable contribution deduction for contributions to Organization U. The Service will ordinarily conclude that the parents of applicants are aware of the preference given to applicants whose parents have made contributions. The Service will therefore ordinarily conclude that the parent could not reasonably expect to obtain the admission of his or her child to the school without making the transfer, regardless of the manner or timing of the solicitation by U. The Service will not so conclude, however, if the preference given to children of contributors is principally due to some other reason.

Situation 4. Under these circumstances, the Service will generally conclude that the payment to Organization V is nondeductible. Unless contributions from sources other than parents are of such magnitude that V's school is not economically dependent upon parents' contributions, parents would ordinarily not be certain that V's school could provide educational benefits without their payments. This conclusion is further evidenced by the fact that parents contribute on a regular, established schedule. In addition, the pressure placed on parents throughout the personal solicitation of contributions by V's school treasurer further indicates that their payments were not voluntary.

Situation 5. Under these circumstances, the Service will generally conclude that the taxpayer is entitled to claim a charitable contribution deduction of $100x to Organization W. Because a charitable organization normally solicits contributions from those known to have the greatest interest in the organization, the fact that parents are singled out for a solicitation will not in itself create an inference that future admissions or any other benefits depend on a contribution from the parent.

Situation 6. The Service will ordinarily conclude that the taxpayer is allowed a charitable contribution deduction of $200x to Organization X. Because the facts indicate that X's school is supported by the church, that most contributors to the church are not parents of children enrolled in the school, and that contributions from parent members are solicited in the same manner as contributions from other members, the taxpayer's contributions will be considered charitable contributions, and not payments of tuition, unless there is a showing that the contributions by members with children in X's school are significantly larger than those of other members. The absence of a tuition charge is not determinative in view of these facts.

HERNANDEZ v. COMMISSIONER
490 U.S. 680 (1989)

Section 170 of the Internal Revenue Code of 1954 permits a taxpayer to deduct from gross income the amount of a "charitable contribution."

The Code defines that term as a "contribution or gift" to certain eligible donees, including entities organized and operated exclusively for religious purposes. We granted certiorari to determine whether taxpayers may deduct as charitable contributions payments made to branch churches of the Church of Scientology in order to receive services known as "auditing" and "training." We hold that such payments are not deductible.

Scientology was founded in the 1950's by L. Ron Hubbard. It is propagated today by a "mother church" in California and by numerous branch churches around the world. The mother Church instructs laity, trains and ordains ministers, and creates new congregations. Branch churches, known as "franchises" or "missions," provide Scientology services at the local level, under the supervision of the mother Church. *Church of Scientology of California v. Commissioner*, 823 F.2d 1310, 1313 (CA9 1987), *cert. denied*, 486 U.S. 1015 (1988).

Scientologists believe that an immortal spiritual being exists in every person. A person becomes aware of this spiritual dimension through a process known as "auditing." Auditing involves a one-to-one encounter between a participant (known as a "preclear") and a Church official (known as an "auditor"). An electronic device, the E-meter, helps the auditor identify the preclear's areas of spiritual difficulty by measuring skin responses during a question and answer session. Although auditing sessions are conducted one on one, the content of each session is not individually tailored. The preclear gains spiritual awareness by progressing through sequential levels of auditing, provided in short blocks of time known as "intensives."

The Church also offers members doctrinal courses known as "training." Participants in these sessions study the tenets of Scientology and seek to attain the qualifications necessary to serve as auditors. Training courses, like auditing sessions, are provided in sequential levels. Scientologists are taught that spiritual gains result from participation in such courses.

The Church charges a "fixed donation," also known as a "price" or a "fixed contribution," for participants to gain access to auditing and training sessions. These charges are set forth in schedules, and prices vary with a session's length and level of sophistication. In 1972, for example, the general rates for auditing ranged from $625 for a 12-½-hour auditing intensive, the shortest available, to $4,250 for a 100-hour intensive, the longest available. Specialized types of auditing required higher fixed donations: a 12-½-hour "Integrity Processing" auditing intensive cost $750; a 12-½-hour "Expanded Dianetics" auditing intensive cost $950. This system of mandatory fixed charges is based on a central tenet of Scientology known as the "doctrine of exchange," according to which any time a person receives something he must pay something back. In so doing, a Scientologist maintains "inflow" and "outflow" and avoids spiritual decline.

The proceeds generated from auditing and training sessions are the Church's primary source of income. The Church promotes these sessions not only through newspaper, magazine, and radio advertisements, but also through free lectures, free personality tests, and leaflets. The Church also encourages, and indeed rewards with a 5% discount, advance payment for these sessions. The Church often refunds unused portions of prepaid auditing or training fees, less an administrative charge.

Petitioners in these consolidated cases each made payments to a branch church for auditing or training sessions. They sought to deduct these payments on their federal income tax returns as charitable contributions under § 170. Respondent disallowed these deductions, finding that the payments were not charitable contributions within the meaning of § 170.

Before trial, the Commissioner stipulated that the branch churches of Scientology are religious organizations entitled to receive tax-deductible charitable contributions under the relevant sections of the Code. This stipulation isolated as the sole statutory issue whether payments for auditing or training sessions constitute "contribution[s] or gift[s]" under § 170.*

The legislative history of the "contribution or gift" limitation, though sparse, reveals that Congress intended to differentiate between unrequited payments to qualified recipients and payments made to such recipients in return for goods or services. Only the former were deemed deductible. The House and Senate Reports on the 1954 tax bill, for example, both define "gifts" as payments "made with no expectation of a financial return commensurate with the amount of the gift." Using payments to hospitals as an example, both Reports state that the gift characterization should not apply to "a payment by an individual to a hospital in consideration of a binding obligation to provide medical treatment for the individual's employees. It would apply only if there were no expectation of any quid pro quo from the hospital."

In ascertaining whether a given payment was made with "the expectation of any quid pro quo," the IRS has customarily examined the external features of the transaction in question. This practice has the advantage of obviating the need for the IRS to conduct imprecise inquiries into the motivations of individual taxpayers. The lower courts have generally embraced this structural analysis. We likewise focused on exter-

---

*The stipulation allowed the Tax Court to avoid having to decide whether the particular branches to which payments were made in these cases qualified under § 170(c)(2) and § 501(c)(3) of the Code as tax-exempt organizations entitled to receive charitable contributions. In a separate case decided during the pendency of this litigation, the Tax Court held that the mother Church in California did not qualify as a tax-exempt organization under § 501(c)(3) for the years 1970 through 1972 because it had diverted profits to its founder and others, had conspired to impede collection of its taxes, and had conducted almost all activities for a commercial purpose. *Church of Scientology of California v. Commissioner*, 83 T.C. 381 (1984). The Court of Appeals for the Ninth Circuit affirmed, basing its decision solely on the ground that the Church had diverted profits for the use of private individuals. It did not address the other bases of the Tax Court's decision. *Church of Scientology of California v. Commissioner*, 823 F.2d 1310 (1987), *cert. denied*, 486 U.S. 1015 (1988).

nal features in *United States v. American Bar Endowment*, 477 U.S. 105 (1986), to resolve the taxpayers' claims that they were entitled to partial deductions for premiums paid to a charitable organization for insurance coverage; the taxpayers contended that they had paid unusually high premiums in an effort to make a contribution along with their purchase of insurance. We upheld the Commissioner's disallowance of the partial deductions because the taxpayers had failed to demonstrate, at a minimum, the existence of comparable insurance policies with prices lower than those of the policy they had each purchased. In so doing, we stressed that "[t]he sine qua non of a charitable contribution is a transfer of money or property without adequate consideration."

In light of this understanding of § 170, it is readily apparent that petitioners' payments to the Church do not qualify as "contribution[s] or gift[s]." As the Tax Court found, these payments were part of a quintessential quid pro quo exchange: in return for their money, petitioners received an identifiable benefit, namely, auditing and training sessions. The Church established fixed price schedules for auditing and training sessions in each branch church; it calibrated particular prices to auditing or training sessions of particular lengths and levels of sophistication; it returned a refund if auditing and training services went unperformed; it distributed "account cards" on which persons who had paid money to the Church could monitor what prepaid services they had not yet claimed; and it categorically barred provision of auditing or training sessions for free. Each of these practices reveals the inherently reciprocal nature of the exchange.

Petitioners do not argue that such a structural analysis is inappropriate under § 170, or that the external features of the auditing and training transactions do not strongly suggest a quid pro quo exchange. Petitioners argue instead that they are entitled to deductions because a quid pro quo analysis is inappropriate under § 170 when the benefit a taxpayer receives is purely religious in nature. Along the same lines, petitioners claim that payments made for the right to participate in a religious service should be automatically deductible under § 170.

We cannot accept this statutory argument for several reasons. First, it finds no support in the language of § 170. Whether or not Congress could, consistent with the Establishment Clause, provide for the automatic deductibility of a payment made to a church that either generates religious benefits or guarantees access to a religious service, that is a choice Congress has thus far declined to make. Instead, Congress has specified that a payment to an organization operated exclusively for religious (or other eleemosynary) purposes is deductible only if such a payment is a "contribution or gift." The Code makes no special preference for payments made in the expectation of gaining religious benefits or access to a religious service. The House and Senate Reports on § 170, and the other legislative history of that provision, offer no indication that Congress' failure to enact such a preference was an oversight.

Second, petitioners' deductibility proposal would expand the charitable contribution deduction far beyond what Congress has provided. Numerous forms of payments to eligible donees plausibly could be categorized as providing a religious benefit or as securing access to a religious service. For example, some taxpayers might regard their tuition payments to parochial schools as generating a religious benefit or as securing access to a religious service; such payments, however, have long been held not to be charitable contributions under § 170. Taxpayers might make similar claims about payments for church-sponsored counseling sessions or for medical care at church-affiliated hospitals that otherwise might not be deductible. Given that, under the First Amendment, the IRS can reject otherwise valid claims of religious benefit only on the ground that a taxpayers' alleged beliefs are not sincerely held, but not on the ground that such beliefs are inherently irreligious, see *United States v. Ballard*, 322 U.S. 78 (1944), the resulting tax deductions would likely expand the charitable contribution provision far beyond its present size. We are loath to effect this result in the absence of supportive congressional intent.

Finally, the deduction petitioners seek might raise problems of entanglement between church and state. If framed as a deduction for those payments generating benefits of a religious nature for the payor, petitioners' proposal would inexorably force the IRS and reviewing courts to differentiate "religious" benefits from "secular" ones. If framed as a deduction for those payments made in connection with a religious service, petitioners' proposal would force the IRS and the judiciary into differentiating "religious" services from "secular" ones. We need pass no judgment now on the constitutionality of such hypothetical inquiries, but we do note that "pervasive monitoring" for "the subtle or overt presence of religious matter" is a central danger against which we have held the Establishment Clause guards.

Accordingly, we conclude that petitioners' payments to the Church for auditing and training sessions are not "contribution[s] or gift[s]" within the meaning of that statutory expression.

[The Court also rejects "petitioners' constitutional claims based on the Establishment Clause and the Free Exercise Clause of the First Amendment."]

We turn, finally, to petitioners' assertion that disallowing their claimed deduction is at odds with the IRS' longstanding practice of permitting taxpayers to deduct payments made to other religious institutions in connection with certain religious practices. They now make two closely related claims. First, the IRS has accorded payments for auditing and training disparately harsh treatment compared to payments to other churches and synagogues for their religious services: Recognition of a comparable deduction for auditing and training payments is necessary to cure this administrative inconsistency. Second, Congress, in modifying § 170 over the years, has impliedly acquiesced in the deductibility of payments to these other faiths; because payments for auditing and training are indistinguishable from these other payments, they fall within the principle acquiesced in by Congress that payments for religious services are deductible under § 170.

Although the Commission demurred at oral argument as to whether the IRS, in fact, permits taxpayers to deduct payments made to purchase services from other churches and synagogues, the Commissioner's periodic revenue rulings have stated the IRS' position rather clearly. A 1971 ruling, still in effect, states: "Pew rents, building fund assessments, and periodic dues paid to a church ... are all methods of making contributions to the church, and such payments are deductible as charitable contributions within the limitations set out in section 170 of the Code." Rev. Rul. 70–47, 1970–1 C.B. 49. We also assume for purposes of argument that the IRS also allows taxpayers to deduct "specified payments for attendance at High Holy Day services, for tithes, for torah readings and for memorial plaques."

The development of the present litigation, however, makes it impossible for us to resolve petitioners' claim that they have received unjustifiably harsh treatment compared to adherents of other religions. The relevant inquiry in determining whether a payment is a "contribution or gift" under § 170 is, as we have noted, not whether the payment secures religious benefits or access to religious services, but whether the transaction in which the payment is involved is structured as a quid pro quo exchange. To make such a determination in this case, the Tax Court heard testimony and received documentary proof as to the terms and structure of the auditing and training transactions; from this evidence it made factual findings upon which it based its conclusion of nondeductibility, a conclusion we have held consonant with § 170 and with the First Amendment.

Perhaps because the theory of administrative inconsistency emerged only on appeal, petitioners did not endeavor at trial to adduce from the IRS or other sources any specific evidence about other religious faiths' transactions. The IRS' revenue rulings, which merely state the agency's conclusions as to deductibility and which have apparently never been reviewed by the Tax Court or any other judicial body, also provide no specific facts about the nature of these other faiths' transactions. In the absence of such facts, we simply have no way (other than the wholly illegitimate one of relying on our personal experiences and observations) to appraise accurately whether the IRS' revenue rulings have correctly applied a quid pro quo analysis with respect to any or all of the religious practices in question. We do not know, for example, whether payments for other faiths' services are truly obligatory or whether any or all of these services are generally provided whether or not the encouraged "mandatory" payment is made.

The IRS' application of the "contribution or gift" standard may be right or wrong with respect to these other faiths, or it may be right with respect to some religious practices and wrong with respect to others. It may also be that some of these payments are appropriately classified as partially deductible "dual payments." With respect to those religions where the structure of transactions involving religious services is established not centrally but by individual congregations, the proper point of reference for a quid pro quo analysis might be the individual congregation, not the religion as a whole. Only upon a proper factual record could we make these determinations. Absent such a record, we must reject petitioners' administrative consistency argument.

Petitioners' congressional acquiescence claim fails for similar reasons. Even if one assumes that Congress has acquiesced in the IRS' ruling with respect to "[p]ew rents, building fund assessments, and periodic dues," the fact is that the IRS' 1971 ruling articulates no broad principle of deductibility, but instead merely identifies as deductible three discrete types of payments. Having before us no information about the nature or structure of these three payments, we have no way of discerning any possible unifying principle, let alone whether such a principle would embrace payments for auditing and training sessions.

JUSTICE O'CONNOR, with whom JUSTICE SCALIA joins, dissenting.

The Court today acquiesces in the decision of the Internal Revenue Service to manufacture a singular exception to its 70-year practice of allowing fixed payments indistinguishable from those made by petitioners to be deducted as charitable contributions. Because the IRS cannot constitutionally be allowed to select which religions will receive the benefit of its past rulings, I respectfully dissent.

The IRS' position here is not based upon the contention that a portion of the knowledge received from auditing or training is of secular, commercial, nonreligious value. Thus, the denial of a deduction in these cases bears no resemblance to the denial of a deduction for religious-school tuition up to the market value of the secularly useful education received. Here the IRS denies deductibility solely on the basis that the exchange is a quid pro quo, even though the quid is exclusively of spiritual or religious worth. Respondent cites no instances in which this has been done before, and there are good reasons why.

When a taxpayer claims as a charitable deduction part of a fixed amount given to a charitable organization in exchange for benefits that have a commercial value, the allowable portion of that claim is computed by subtracting from the total amount paid the value of the physical benefit received. If at a charity sale one purchases for $1,000 a painting whose market value is demonstrably no more than $50, there has been a contribution of $950. The same would be true if one purchases a $1,000 seat at a charitable dinner where the food is worth $50. An identical calculation can be made where the quid received is not a painting or a meal, but an intangible such as entertainment, so long as that intangible has some market value established in a noncontributory context. Hence, one who purchases a ticket to a concert, at the going rate for concerts by the particular performers, makes a charitable contribution of zero even if it is announced in advance that all proceeds from the ticket sales will go to charity. The performers may have made a charitable contribution, but the audience has paid the going rate for a show.

It becomes impossible, however, to compute the "contribution" portion of a payment to a charity where what is received in return is not merely an intangible, but an intangible (or, for that matter a tangible) that is not bought and sold except in donative contexts so that the only "market" price against which it can be evaluated is a market price that always includes donations. Suppose, for example, that the charitable organization that traditionally solicits donations on Veterans Day, in exchange for which it gives the donor an imitation poppy bearing its name, were to establish a flat rule that no one gets a poppy without a donation of at least $10. One would have to say that the "market" rate for such poppies was $10, but it would assuredly not be true that everyone who "bought" a poppy for $10 made no contribution. Similarly, if one buys a $100 seat at a prayer breakfast receiving as the quid pro quo food for both body and soul—it would make no sense to say that no charitable contribution whatever has occurred simply because the "going rate" for all prayer breakfasts (with equivalent bodily food) is $100. The latter may well be true, but that "going rate" includes a contribution.

Confronted with this difficulty, and with the constitutional necessity of not making irrational distinctions among taxpayers, and with the even higher standard of equality of treatment among religions that the First Amendment imposes, the Government has only two practicable options with regard to distinctively religious quids pro quo: to disregard them all, or to tax them all. Over the years it has chosen the former course.

An Assistant Commissioner of the IRS recently explained in a "question and answer guidance package" to tax-exempt organizations that "[i]n contrast to tuition payments, religious observances generally are not regarded as yielding private benefits to the donor, who is viewed as receiving only incidental benefits when attending the observances. The primary beneficiaries are viewed as being the general public and members of the faith. Thus, payments for saying masses, pew rents, tithes, and other payments involving fixed donations for similar religious services, are fully deductible contributions." Although this guidance package may not be as authoritative as IRS rulings, in the absence of any contrary indications it does reflect the continuing adherence of the IRS to its practice of allowing deductions for fixed payments for religious services.

There can be no doubt that at least some of the fixed payments which the IRS has treated as charitable deductions, or which the Court assumes the IRS would allow taxpayers to deduct, are as "inherently reciprocal" as the payments for auditing at issue here. In exchange for their payment of pew rents, Christians receive particular seats during worship services. Similarly, in some synagogues attendance at the worship services for Jewish High Holy Days is often predicated upon the purchase of a general admission ticket or a reserved seat ticket. Religious honors such as publicly reading from Scripture are purchased or auctioned periodically in some synagogues of Jews from Morocco and Syria. Mormons must tithe their income as a necessary but not sufficient condition to obtaining a "temple recommend," *i.e.*, the right to be admitted into the temple. A Mass stipend—a fixed payment given to a Catholic priest, in consideration of which he is obliged to apply the fruits of the Mass for the intention of the donor—has similar overtones of exchange. According to some Catholic theologians, the nature of the pact between a priest and a donor who pays a Mass stipend is "a bilateral contract known as do ut facias. One person agrees to give while the other party agrees to do something in return." A finer example of a quid pro quo exchange would be hard to formulate.

There is no discernible reason why there is a more rigid connection between payment and services in the religious practices of Scientology than in the religious practices of the faiths described above. Neither has respondent explained why the benefit received by a Christian who obtains the pew of his or her choice by paying a rental fee, a Jew who gains entrance to High Holy Day services by purchasing a ticket, a Mormon who makes the fixed payment necessary for a temple recommend, or a Catholic who pays a Mass stipend, is incidental to the real benefit conferred on the "general public and members of the faith," while the benefit received by a Scientologist from auditing is a personal accommodation.

In my view, the IRS has misapplied its longstanding practice of allowing charitable contributions under § 170 in a way that violates the Establishment Clause. It has unconstitutionally refused to allow payments for the religious service of auditing to be deducted as charitable contributions in the same way it has allowed fixed payments to other religions to be deducted. I would reverse the decisions below.

In August 1993, Congress added Code Sections 170(f)(8) and 6115, which require substantiation of charitable contributions in excess of $250. Code Section 6115 requires charitable donees that receive "quid pro quo contributions" in excess of $250 to estimate the value of the goods and services donor is receiving and inform donor that the deductible amount of his contribution is limited to the excess of what he has given over the value of those goods and services. Subsection (b) provides:

> "For purposes of this section, the term 'quid pro quo contribution' means a payment made partly as a contribution and partly in consideration for goods or services provided to the payor by the donee organization. A quid pro quo contribution does not include any payment made to an organization, organized exclusively for religious purposes, for which the taxpayer receives solely an intangible religious benefit that generally is not sold in a commercial transaction outside the donative context."

In October 1993, the IRS and the Church of Scientology announced that they had entered into a "Closing Agreement" resolving all outstanding matters between them. Closing Agreement Between IRS and Church of Scientology, 97 Tax Notes Today 251-24 (Dec. 31, 1997). At least through the end of 1999, the IRS agreed:

> "not to contest the deductibility of Church of Scientology fixed donations in connection with qualified religious services. The phrase 'qualified religious services' means those appearing on the 'Scientology Classification, Gradation and Awareness Chart.' [That chart appears to have included the auditing and training services at issue in *Hernandez*.] If the taxpayer produces an accurate receipt or other documentation from the donee Church of Scientology substantiating (1) the amount of the taxpayer's fixed donation and (2) the qualified religious services with respect to which the donation was made, then ... the full amount of the fixed donation for these services shall be treated as a charitable contribution under Code section 170 and shall not be challenged on that basis."

In other words, the IRS agreed not to enforce the Supreme Court's decision in *Hernandez* against members of the Church of Scientology. Consistent with the Closing Agreement, on November 1, 1993, the IRS obsoleted Rev. Rul. 78-189, 1978-1 C.B. 68, in which it had originally declared payments for such payments nondeductible. *See* Rev. Rul. 93-73, 1993-2 C.B. 75.

The Closing Agreement raised at least two questions: First, if payments for religious services and training (including training to become qualified to serve as an auditor) in the Church of Scientology were deductible, what payments made by taxpayers of other faiths might now be deductible? Second, if the existence of a quid pro quo exchange no longer disqualified a payment as a "charitable contribution" in a religious context, were quid pro quo exchanges still disqualifying in nonreligious contexts?

SKLAR v. COMMISSIONER
282 F.3d 610 (9th Cir. 2002)

The taxpayer-petitioners in this action, Michael and Marla Sklar, challenge the Internal Revenue Service's disallowance of their deductions, as charitable contributions, of part of the tuition payments made to their children's religious schools. Specifically, the Sklars sought to deduct 55% of the tuition, on the basis that this represented the proportion of the school day allocated to religious education. The Sklars contend that these costs are deductible under section 170 of the Internal Revenue Code, as payments for which they have received "solely intangible religious benefits." They also argue that they should receive this deduction because the IRS permits similar deductions to the Church of Scientology, and it is a violation of administrative consistency and of the Establishment Clause to deny them, as Orthodox Jews, the same deduction.

The Sklars assert that the deduction they claimed is allowable under section 170 of the Internal Revenue Code which permits taxpayers to deduct, as a charitable contribution, a "contribution or gift" to certain tax-exempt organizations. Not only has the Supreme Court held that, generally, a payment for which one receives consideration does not constitute a "contribution or gift" for purposes of § 170, *see United States v. American Bar Endowment*, 477 U.S. 105 (1986) (stressing that "[t]he sine qua non of a charitable contribution is a transfer of money or property without adequate consideration"), but it has explicitly rejected the contention made here by the Sklars: that there is an exception in the Code for payments for which one receives only religious benefits in return. *Hernandez v. Commissioner*, 490 U.S. 680 (1989). The taxpayers in *Hernandez*, members of the Church of Scientology, sought to deduct, as charitable contributions under § 170(c), payments made by them to the Church of Scientology in exchange for the religious exercises of "auditing" and "training." The Court affirmed the Tax Court's reading of the statute disallowing the deductions on the following three grounds: (1) Congress had shown no preference in the Internal Revenue Code for payments made in exchange for religious benefits as opposed to other benefits; (2) to permit the deductions the taxpayers demanded would begin a slippery slope of expansion of the charitable contribution deduction beyond what Congress intended; and (3) to permit these deductions could entangle the IRS and the government in the affairs and beliefs of various religious faiths and organizations in violation of the constitutional principle of the separation of church and state. Specifically, the Supreme Court stated that to permit these deductions might force the IRS to engage in a searching inquiry of whether a particular benefit received was "religious" or "secular" in order to determine its deductibility, a process which, the Court said, might violate the Establishment Clause.

Despite the clear statutory holding of *Hernandez*, the Sklars contend that recent changes to the Internal Revenue Code have clarified Congressional intent with respect to the deductibility of these payments. We seriously doubt the validity of this argument. The amendments to the Code appear not to have changed the substantive definition of a deductible charitable contribution, but only to have enacted additional documentation requirements for claimed deductions. Section 170(f) of the Code adds a new requirement that taxpayers claiming a charitable contribution deduction obtain from the donee an estimate of the value of any goods and services received in return for the donation, and exempts from that new estimate requirement contributions for which solely intangible religious benefits are received. Similarly, § 6115 requires that tax-exempt organizations inform taxpayer-donors that they will receive a tax deduction only for the amount of their donation above the value of any goods or services received in return for the donation and requires donee organizations to give donors an estimate of this value, exempting from this estimate requirement contributions for which solely intangible religious benefits are received.

Given the clear holding of *Hernandez* and the absence of any direct evidence of Congressional intent to overrule the Supreme Court on this issue, we would be extremely reluctant to read an additional and significant substantive deduction into the statute based on what are clearly procedural provisions regarding the documentation of tax return information, particularly where the deduction would be of doubtful constitutional validity. We need not, however, decide this issue definitively in this case.[3]

Additionally, the Sklars claim that the IRS engages in a "policy" of permitting members of the Church of Scientology to deduct as charitable contributions, payments made for "auditing," "training," and other qualified religious services, and that the agency's refusal to grant similar religious deductions to members of other faiths violates the Establishment Clause and is administratively inconsistent. They assert that the "policy" is contained in a "closing agreement" that the IRS signed with the Church of Scientology in 1993, shortly after the *Hernandez* decision and the 1993 changes to § 170 of the Internal Revenue Code. Because the IRS erroneously asserted that it is prohibited from disclosing all or any part of the closing agreement, we assume, for purposes of resolving this case, the truthfulness of the Sklars' allegations regarding the terms of that agreement. However, rather than concluding that the IRS's pro-Scientology policy would require it to adopt similar provisions for all other religions, we would likely conclude, were we to reach the issue, that the policy must be invalidated on the ground that it violates either the Internal Revenue Code or the Establishment Clause.

We are required, for purposes of our analysis, to assume the contents of the IRS's policy towards the Church of Scientology, because of the IRS's refusal to reveal to the Sklars, to this court, or even to the Department of Justice, the contents of its closing agreement, although that agreement has apparently been reprinted in the *Wall Street Journal*. [The court rejects the IRS's argument that it prohibited from disclosing the Closing Agreement by Code Section 6103.]

The Sklars contend that because "the IRS has admitted that it permits members of the Church of Scientology to deduct their payments for religious instruction.... in order to avoid violating the First Amendment, [the] IRS must permit adherents of other faiths to deduct their payments for religious instruction." To the extent that the Sklars claim that the Establishment Clause requires that we extend the Scientology deduction to all religious organizations, they are in error for three reasons: First, we would be reluctant ever to presume that Congress or any agency of the government would intend that a general religious preference be adopted, by extension or otherwise, as such preferences raise the highly

---

3. Our concurring colleague may well be correct that *Hernandez* is still controlling of this case and that § 170 has not been amended to permit deductions of contributions for which the consideration consists of "intangible religious benefits." As we have stated in the text, we are strongly inclined to that view ourselves. However, we need not issue a definitive holding on the effect of the statutory amendments here, because we can reject the Sklars' claim on the ground that they have failed to satisfy the requirements for the partial deductibility of dual payments set out in *United States v. American Bar Endowment*, 477 U.S. 105 (1986).

sensitive issue of state sponsorship of religion. In the absence of a clear expression of such intent, we would be unlikely to consider extending a policy favoring one religion where the effect of our action would be to create a policy favoring all. Second, the Supreme Court has previously stated that a policy such as the Sklars wish us to create would be of questionable constitutional validity under *Lemon*, because the administration of the policy could require excessive government entanglement with religion. Third, the policy the Sklars seek would appear to violate section § 170. To the extent that the Sklars are also making an administrative inconsistency claim, we reject that claim on two grounds. First, in order to make an administrative inconsistency claim, a party must show that it is similarly situated to the group being treated differently by the agency. We seriously doubt that the Sklars are similarly situated to the persons who benefit from the Scientology closing agreement because the religious education of the Sklars' children does not appear to be similar to the "auditing", "training" or other "qualified religious services" conducted by the Church of Scientology. Second, even if they were so situated, because the treatment they seek is of questionable statutory and constitutional validity under § 170 of the IRC, we would not hold that the unlawful policy set forth in the closing agreement must be extended to all religious organizations. In the end, however, we need not decide the Establishment Clause claim or the administrative inconsistency claim as the Sklars have failed to show that their tuition payments constitute a partially deductible "dual payment" under the Tax Code.

A "dual payment" (or "quid pro quo payment") under the Tax Code is a payment made in part in consideration for goods and services, and in part as a charitable contribution. I.R.C. § 6115. For example, the purchase, for seventy-five dollars, of an item worth five dollars at a charity auction would constitute a dual payment: five dollars in consideration for goods, and seventy dollars as a charitable contribution. The IRS permits a deduction under § 170 for the portion of a dual payment that consists of a charitable contribution, but not for the portion for which the taxpayer receives a benefit in return. Although the Sklars concede that they received a benefit for their tuition payments, in that their children received a secular education, they claim that part of the payment—the part attributable to their children's religious education—should be regarded as a charitable contribution because they received only an "intangible religious benefit" in return. Leaving aside both the issue, discussed in section I, of whether the tax code does indeed treat payments for which a taxpayer receives an "intangible religious benefit" as a charitable contribution, as well as any constitutional considerations, we are left with the Sklars' contention that their tuition payment was a dual one: in part in consideration for secular education, and in part as a charitable contribution. The Sklars assert that because 45% of their children's school day was spent on secular education, and 55% on religious education, they should receive a deduction for 55% of their tuition payments.

On the record before this court, the Sklars failed to satisfy the requirements for deducting part of a "dual payment" under the Tax Code. The Supreme Court discussed the deductibility of such payments in *United States v. American Bar Endowment*, 477 U.S. 105 (1986), and held that the taxpayer must establish that the dual payment exceeds the market value of the goods received in return. The facts of that case were as follows: The American Bar Endowment ("ABE"), a tax-exempt corporation organized for charitable purposes and associated with the American Bar Association ("ABA"), raised money for its charitable work by providing group insurance policies to its members, all of whom were also members of the ABA. ABE negotiated premium rates with insurers, collected premiums from its members and passed those premiums on to the insurers. Because the group policies purchased by ABE were "experience rated," the group members were entitled to receive, each year, a refund of the portion of their premiums paid above the actual cost to the insurer of providing insurance to the group. Although normally these refunds, called "dividends," would be distributed to individual policyholders, ABE required its members to agree to turn the dividends over to ABE for use in its charitable work. ABE members sought to deduct the dividends as charitable contributions to ABE, claiming that the premiums paid constituted partially deductible "dual payments." The Supreme Court held that the ABE members could not deduct the dividends as charitable contributions because they had not shown that the premiums they paid to ABE exceeded the market value of the insurance they purchased, or that the "excess payment," if any, was made with the intention of making a gift. Because the ABE insurance was no more costly to its members than other policies that were available to them, the taxpayers could not prove that they "purposely contributed money or property in excess of the value of any benefit [they] received in return."

Similarly, the Sklars have not shown that any dual tuition payments they may have made exceeded the market value of the secular education their children received. They urge that the market value of the secular portion of their children's education is the cost of a public school education. That cost, of course, is nothing. The Sklars are in error. The market value is the cost of a comparable secular education offered by private schools. The Sklars do not present any evidence even suggesting that their total payments exceeded that cost. There is no evidence in the record of the tuition private schools charge for a comparable secular education, and thus no evidence showing that the Sklars made an "excess payment" that might qualify for a tax deduction. This appears to be not simply an inadvertent evidentiary omission, but rather a reflection of the practical realities of the high costs of private education. The Sklars also failed to show that they intended to make a gift by contributing any such "excess payment." Therefore, under the clear holding of American Bar Endowment, the Sklars cannot prevail on this appeal.[15]

---

15. Moreover, as the IRS argues in its brief, the Sklars' deduction was properly denied on the alternative ground that they failed to meet the contemporaneous substantiation requirement of

We hold that because the Sklars have not shown that their "dual payment" tuition payments are partially deductible under the Tax Code, and, specifically, that the total payments they made for both the secular and religious private school education their children received exceeded the market value of other secular private school education available to those children, the IRS did not err in disallowing their deductions.

PROBLEMS FOR DISCUSSION

19–1. What kinds of taxpayers may now either challenge the Closing Agreement or demand that its principles be extended to their situations?

19–2. A small unaffiliated church collects just enough in contributions from those who attend worship services to pay its minister and maintain its sanctuary. It has no other sources of income. Under Rev. Rul. 83–104, Situation 4, are contributions to the church deductible?

19–3. Justice O'Connor asserts in her dissent in *Hernandez* that it is impossible to value the intangible religious benefits observant taxpayers receive in the practice of their faiths, and therefore impossible to apply the "dual payment" analysis required by *American Bar Endowment* to religious "contributions." In other contexts, when a taxpayer receives items in kind and there is no reliable market transaction between taxpayer and the supplier of the items to use to determine their value, how does our tax system determine the value of those items?

Subchapter B: Eligible Recipient Organizations

Code: Sections 170(c) and 501(c)

Code Section 170(c) defines "charitable contribution" as a contribution or gift to or for the use of any of five types of eligible recipients. The most general type—the so-called "501(c)(3)"—in fact accounts for almost all charitable contributions. To understand this category, it is easier to begin with Code Section 501, which deals with taxation of the recipient charitable organization itself, rather than with Code Section 170(c), which invokes subsection 501(c)(3) by descriptive cross-reference to deal with taxation of the organization's donors.

Code Section 501 exempts a wide variety of organizations from federal income taxation. The two most important are 501(c)(3)'s and 501(c)(4)'s. To qualify as a 501(c)(3), an organization must meet three tests.

- Purposes test: It must be organized and operated exclusively for specified purposes: "religious, charitable, scientific, testing for pub-

§ 170(f)(8)(A), (B) & (C). The Sklars did not present, prior to filing their tax return, a letter from the schools acknowledging their "contribution" and estimating the value of the benefit they received, as is required under the statute. As noted earlier, certain reporting requirements are not applicable where intangible religious benefits are received in exchange, but such exemptions apply only where the consideration consists solely of such benefits.

lic safety, literary, or educational purposes, or to foster national or international amateur sports competition (but only if no part of its activities involve the provision of athletic facilities or equipment), or for the prevention of cruelty to children or animals."

- Private inurement test: No part of its net earnings may inure to the benefit of any private shareholder or individual.

- Lobbying and political activities test: No substantial part of its activities may consist of attempting to influence legislation. In addition, it may not participate or intervene in any political campaign on behalf of or in opposition to any candidate for public office.

A 501(c)(4) must meet the same private inurement test. But the purposes for which it may be organized and operated are broader: it need only be operated "for the promotion of social welfare." Most importantly, it may lobby.

When we compare Code Section 170(c)(2) with Code Section 501(c)(3), we discover that all *domestic* 501(c)(3)'s except those dedicated to "testing for public safety" are eligible recipients for charitable contribution deduction purposes. *See* Rev. Rul. 65–61, 1965–1 C.B. 234. Corporate contributions are subject to one further limitation as to purpose: to be deductible, the contribution or gift must be intended for use for a permitted purpose within the United States or its possessions. By contrast, Code Section 170(c) contains no category of eligible 501(c)(4) recipients.

What this means is that most domestic tax-exempt organizations that do not lobby or engage in political activity can receive deductible contributions. A non-profit organization that wants to make lobbying a substantial part of its activities can still be tax-exempt, but cannot receive deductible contributions. The principal practical effect of the distinction drawn between 501(c)(3)'s and 501(c)(4)'s is to prevent donors from deducting their lobbying dollars by funneling them through tax-exempt recipients.

Sections 1 through 3 below explore the three requirements of Code Section 501(c)(3) in greater detail. In practice, however, the way donors resolve eligibility questions is simple: the IRS publishes an on-line list of organizations eligible to receive deductible contributions: Exempt Organizations Select Check, http://www.irs.gov/charities/article/0,,id= 96136,00.-html. More formally, the donor may request that the organization supply a copy of the IRS letter recognizing its exempt status and Code Section 170 eligibility.

SECTION 1: PURPOSES TEST

PLUMSTEAD THEATRE SOCIETY, INC. v. COMMISSIONER
74 T.C. 1324 (1980)

Respondent determined that petitioner does not qualify for exemption from Federal income tax as a charitable or educational organization under section 501(c)(3). The issue for our decision is whether petitioner is operated exclusively for charitable or educational purposes within the meaning of section 501(c)(3).

As stated in its articles of incorporation, petitioner was formed as a nonprofit corporation for the following specific and primary purposes:

"To cultivate, promote, foster, sponsor, develop, and encourage understanding of and public interest in the fields of theatre, dance, music, motion pictures, and the arts, all of the classic nature, whether ancient or contemporary;

To promote and encourage talent and ability in composition and creation of, as well as performance of, works in each of the said fields, through commissions for new and original works, awards and scholarships and grants to existing organizations and individuals active in these fields; to provide a training ground and workshop to develop dancers, choreographers, playwrights, writers, artists, composers, performers, designers, directors, musicians, technicians, and administrative personnel and the like in each of these fields;

To institute, organize and conduct workshops where the foregoing can meet, study, discuss, exchange and develop techniques in each of these fields;

To give recognition to experiments and achievements in each of these fields through citations, awards, scholarships and grants to individual writers, performers, organizations and the like; and to give public performances in each of the above fields.

To receive contributions and to make donations to, dispense contributions to, and otherwise aid and support those organizations qualified for exemption from federal income tax under the Internal Revenue Code of 1954, as now in effect or subsequently amended, that are organized and operated exclusively for the above mentioned purposes."

In addition, the articles of incorporation provide that petitioner is not organized and shall not be operated for pecuniary gain; that no part of its net earnings shall inure to the benefit of any private member or individual; that upon dissolution, any remaining assets shall be distributed to a nonprofit organization organized for the same purpose as petitioner and qualifying as tax exempt, under section 501(c)(3).

The members of the board of directors of petitioner are a diversified group of individuals interested in the performing arts. No officer or director is salaried in his or her capacity as an officer or director of petitioner. Several members of the board of directors advanced non-interest-bearing loans ranging from $100 to $250 to petitioner to cover initial costs of incorporation.

Initially, petitioner proposes to fulfill its purposes by presenting professional dramatic theatre productions of the classical nature, ancient and contemporary; by forming a workshop in the Los Angeles area for new

American playwrights; and by establishing a fund to assist new and established playwrights in writing new plays for petitioner to produce. During 1977, petitioner engaged in extensive negotiations with Ambassador International Cultural Foundation (the Ambassador Foundation), a nonprofit, cultural foundation, for joint sponsorship by petitioner and Ambassador College of a season of three family-oriented plays to be shown in the Ambassador Auditorium in Pasadena, Calif. Petitioner chose Ambassador Auditorium as the site for its resident theatre with the hope of rebuilding the theatre audiences from Glendale, San Gabriel, Orange County, and San Bernardino County after the demise of the Pasadena Playhouse. An agreement between petitioner and the Ambassador Foundation setting forth the respective rights and duties of each entity with regard to the production of the season of plays in Pasadena was executed on July 27, 1977.

Petitioner intends to use accomplished performers, directors, and technicians in its productions. Because petitioner is organized as a nonprofit corporation, it is able to operate under an Equity League of Resident Theatres Contract (LORT contract) which provides for lower compensation for the professionals used in its productions than that which is normally demanded of commercial theatre. As of December 1977, approximately 60 theatre companies in the United States, all tax-exempt, nonprofit corporations, used the LORT contract.

Petitioner plans to present its productions in Pasadena, Calif., and Washington, D.C., and in any other city where subscription prices and/or theatre guarantee will help defray the costs of production. Petitioner contemplates that contributions, donations, and low-cost loans will cover production costs and that ticket sales and/or theatre guarantees will cover the running costs. Any profits that may accrue to petitioner from specific performances will be used to fund future production projects, a playwriting commission for American playwrights, and an experimental workshop for actors and playwrights.

On August 15, 1977, petitioner entered into an agreement with the John F. Kennedy Center for the Performing Arts (Kennedy Center), a nonprofit tax-exempt organization, to coproduce the play, "First Monday in October" (First Monday). Under the agreement, petitioner and the Kennedy Center were each to provide one-half of the capitalization required for the production, and to share equally any profits or losses derived from the presentation of the play in Washington. Petitioner's president, Henry Fonda, starred in the play and agreed to accept a lesser salary than he would normally demand of commercial theatre, and to waive a royalty interest in the gross receipts. The play premiered at the Kennedy Center on December 26, 1977. The Washington, D.C., production of First Monday was petitioner's only theatrical production prior to the issuance of the final adverse letter ruling by respondent. Upon completion of the run of First Monday at the Kennedy Center, there remained over $90,000 in unrealized production costs with respect to the presentation of the play.

Prior to the premiere of First Monday at the Kennedy Center, petitioner encountered difficulties in raising its share of capitalization costs required for the production. In order to meet its obligations under the agreement with the Kennedy Center, petitioner sold a portion of its rights in First Monday to outside investors through a limited partnership entitled the First Monday in October Co. (the partnership). Petitioner is the general partner, and two individuals and Pantheon Pictures, Inc., a for-profit corporation, are the limited partners. The purpose of the partnership was to coproduce First Monday in Washington, D.C., and to individually produce or coproduce the play in New York or elsewhere. Under the partnership agreement, the limited partners were required to contribute capital to the partnership totaling $100,000. In return, they collectively received a 63.5 percent share in any profits or losses resulting from the production of First Monday. Petitioner was not required to make a capital contribution to the partnership. Petitioner closed First Monday on February 24, 1978, at a loss.

The issue for our decision is whether petitioner qualifies as a tax-exempt organization under section 501(c)(3). Respondent does not dispute that petitioner is organized for charitable and educational purposes, the first test an organization must pass in order to qualify for exemption. Rather, it argues that petitioner is not operated exclusively for charitable purposes within the meaning of section 501(c)(3), because petitioner has a substantial commercial purpose and is operated for the benefit of private, rather than public interests. Petitioner maintains that it is operated in a manner harmonious with the requirements of section 501(c)(3). We agree with petitioner that it is operated exclusively for charitable and educational purposes under section 501(c)(3).

Section 501(a) exempts from Federal income tax any organization which meets the criteria set forth in section 501(c). Section 501(c)(3) provides that a corporation which is organized and operated exclusively for charitable or educational purposes, among others, is an organization referred to in section 501(a), if no part of its net earnings inures to the benefit of any private individual or shareholder, and if it does not engage in other prohibited activity. It has long been recognized that the promotion and encouragement of the arts can be both charitable and educational. Cultural organizations such as museums, symphony orchestras, ballet, opera, repertory, modern dance, theatre, and other similar organizations may clearly qualify for tax-exempt status as educational and/or charitable organizations under section 501(c)(3), so long as the activities of the organization are in furtherance of its exempt purpose. These organizations are viewed as charitable and educational because they promote public appreciation of the arts, considered useful to the individual and beneficial to the community, as well as provide instruction and training to individuals for the purposes of improving or developing their capabilities.

Indeed, respondent has recognized in his revenue rulings that organizations devoted to the promotion of the arts may qualify for tax exemption. In Rev. Rul. 64–175, 1964–1 C.B. 185, respondent ruled that a nonprofit corporation organized and operated primarily for the purpose of developing the interest of the American public in the dramatic arts qualified for exemption under section 501(c)(3). The main activity of the organization described in the ruling was that of producing plays and making classical works of the theatre available in cities throughout the United States by means of a permanent touring repertory theatre company of the highest professional standards. In ruling that the theatre company qualified for tax exemption, respondent stated that the repertory company is educational, much in the same way a symphony orchestra is educational, for purposes of section 501(c)(3). Similarly, in Rev. Rul. 73–45, 1973–1 C.B. 220, respondent ruled that a nonprofit organization created to foster the development of an appreciation for drama in a particular community by sponsoring professional theatrical productions qualified for tax exemption under section 501(c)(3). The organization was not deemed to be operated for private rather than public benefit, even though it procured the theatre productions through a renewable contract with a commercial booking agency that had also played a major role in its creation.

In spite of public acknowledgment that nonprofit corporations which produce and present dramatic plays to the American public in furtherance of an exempt purpose of promoting cultural arts may qualify for tax exemption, respondent ruled adversely for petitioner in the instant case. First, respondent argues that petitioner has a substantial commercial purpose which defeats tax-exempt status under section 501(c)(3). Rephrased, respondent argues that despite the stated purposes in its articles of incorporation, petitioner is operating in a manner indistinguishable from a commercial enterprise involved in the business of producing plays, because its only activity thus far is coproducing (with the Kennedy Center) a play that has a commercial hue.

We do not believe the administrative record supports such a contention. It is clear from the record that petitioner's main focus is to organize a regional theatre in Pasadena, Calif., to produce and present plays for an area that lacks a community theatre. Toward this goal, members of the board of petitioner have spent countless uncompensated hours negotiating a contract with Ambassador College for the use of its auditorium to house a season of three dramatic productions. An arrangement was worked out with the Ambassador International Cultural Foundation to jointly sponsor the plays. A committee was formed to review and select appropriate dramatic plays in accordance with the highest literary and artistic standards.

We do not agree with respondent that because these productions, as well as the planned community workshops for actors and playwrights and the fund for American playwrights, have yet to materialize, they do not count as activities. Respondent took a still shot of what is an ongoing motion picture of many dimensions. It is quite clear that petitioner is anxious to effectuate its projects as soon as it can obtain funding. Especially in the formative years, a nonprofit community theatre needs a great deal of financial support in the form of contributions and donations before it can function. Until it is declared tax exempt, solicitation for foundation support and individual contributions is useless.

Nor do we agree with respondent that the activity of coproducing the play, "First Monday in October," with the Kennedy Center is indicative of a substantial commercial purpose. In fulfilling its goals of promoting and fostering the American dramatic arts, petitioner plans not only to resurrect past literary works, but to encourage and develop new and original theatre productions. Indeed, developing new works of artistic quality is considered one of the obligations of a nonprofit performing arts organization.

Respondent has not alleged that petitioner should not be allowed to produce and present original plays. Rather, it points to the manner in which First Monday was presented—that it was advertised in newspapers, that tickets were sold, that professionals were used in the productions—to argue that petitioner has a substantial commercial purpose.

We feel that respondent is completely misdirected in his objections. The Kennedy Center is a tax-exempt organization chartered by Congress and built partially with Federal funds. For major theatrical performances, it generally advertises in the newspaper, charges the public for tickets, and uses paid professionals. Symphony orchestras are considered per se educational under section 501(c)(3). *See* sec. 1.501(c) (3)–1(d)(3)(ii), example (4), Income Tax Regs. Yet, they too advertise performances, sell tickets, and pay their musicians, and such activity does not render them "substantially commercial." Indeed, all nonprofit performing arts organizations, from opera to ballet to theatre to symphony orchestras, depend upon ticket sales to cover a portion of their operating budgets. The purpose of presenting dramatic productions is for the public to see, to appreciate, to reflect, and to be educated. Nothing in section 501(c)(3) dictates that the public find out about petitioner's performances through word of mouth, that they be forced to watch amateurs act, or that they be seated totally free of charge. The kind of activity respondent deems objectionable in the instant case is no different from that which he has sanctioned on public record.

Admittedly, the line between commercial enterprises which produce and present theatrical performances and nonprofit, tax-exempt organizations that do the same is not always easy to draw. Indeed, the theatre is the most prominent area of the performing arts in which commercial enterprises coexist, often in the same city, with nonprofit, tax-exempt charitable organizations that also sponsor professional presentations.

However, there are differences. Commercial theatres are operated to make a profit. Thus, they choose plays having the greatest mass audience appeal. Generally, they run the plays so long as they can attract a crowd. They set ticket prices to pay the total costs of production and to return a profit. Since their focus is perennially on the box office, they do not generally organize other activities to educate the public and they do not encourage and instruct relatively unknown playwrights and actors.

Tax-exempt organizations are not operated to make a profit. They fulfill their artistic and community obligations by focusing on the highest possible standards of performance; by serving the community broadly; by developing new and original works; and by providing educational programs and opportunities for new talent. Thus, they keep the great classics of the theatre alive and are willing to experiment with new forms of dramatic writing, acting, and staging. Usually, nonprofit theatrical organizations present a number of plays during a season for a relatively short specified time period. Because of a desired quality in acoustics and intimacy with the audience, many present their performances in halls of limited capacity. The combination of the shortness of the season, the limited seating capacity, the enormous costs of producing quality performances of new or experimental works, coupled with the desire to keep ticket prices at a level which is affordable to most of the community, means that, except in rare cases, box office receipts will never cover the cost of producing plays for nonprofit performing arts organizations. We feel that petitioner has shown that it is organized and operated similar to other nonprofit theatre organizations, rather than as a commercial theatre.

Respondent's last argument is that because of the partnership petitioner entered into with two private individuals and a corporation, whereby the limited partners provided capital in exchange for an interest in the profits and losses of First Monday, petitioner is operated for private, rather than public interests. We do not agree. After entering into an agreement with the Kennedy Center, petitioner discovered it was in need of funds for its share of the capitalization costs of First Monday. The record shows that in an arm's-length transaction, it obtained those funds by selling a portion of its interest in the play itself, for a reasonable price. Petitioner is not obligated for the return of any capital contribution made by the limited partners from its own funds, and the partnership has no interest in petitioner or in any other plays it is planning to produce. The limited partners have no control over the way petitioner operates or manages its affairs, and none of the limited partners nor any officer or director of Pantheon Pictures, Inc., is an officer or director of petitioner. We find this arrangement, limited to one play produced by petitioner, is no more intrusive or indicative of private interests than the contractual, percentage arrangement approved of in *Broadway Theatre League of Lynchburg, Va. v. United States*, 293 F. Supp. 346 (W.D. Va. 1968).

Therefore, we find that petitioner is organized and operated exclusively for charitable and educational purposes under section 501(c)(3).

PROBLEMS FOR DISCUSSION

19–4. In *Plumstead*, the Tax Court views differences between the ways commercial theaters and tax-exempt theaters operate as relevant to whether petition is qualified for exempt status under Code Section 501(c)(3). How do tax-exempt universities operate differently from for-profit universities? What about tax-exempt as opposed to for-profit hospitals? What about tax-exempt as opposed to for-profit scientific research organizations?

SECTION 2: PRIVATE INUREMENT TEST

CHURCH BY MAIL, INC. v. COMMISSIONER

765 F.2d 1387 (9th Cir. 1985)

Church By Mail, Inc. appeals from the tax court's judgment on a stipulated administrative record denying the Church tax-exempt status pursuant to Internal Revenue Code §§ 501(a) and 501(c)(3). The Church contends that the tax court erred in finding that the Church is operated for the non-exempt purpose of providing a market for the services of Twentieth Century Advertising Agency (hereinafter Twentieth), a for-profit organization owned and controlled by Reverend James E. Ewing and Reverend M.R. McElrath, the same persons who serve and control the Church. The Church also argues that the tax court erred in finding that a substantial portion of the Church's net earnings inures to the private benefit of Reverend Ewing and Reverend McElrath and their respective families. Because the tax court's factual findings are supported by evidence in the record, we affirm.

Church By Mail, Inc. was incorporated under the laws of Oklahoma on November 28, 1978. The Church's primary activity has been the preparation, printing and mailing of various religious messages, most of which include a request for money. The Church is run by Reverend Ewing and Reverend McElrath. The Church also employs Reverend O.D. Snyder, Reverend D.R. Luce and Brenda Ewing.

The Church's mailing audience includes 3,393,055 homes, of which 167,698 are regular recipients. The Church mails at least one and sometimes as many as three sermons a month to its regular recipients. During the year ending December 31, 1980, the Church received $3,000,155 in donations from the recipients of its sermons.

Twentieth Century Advertising Agency provides the printing and mailing services for the Church's mass mailings. Twentieth is owned and controlled by Reverend Ewing and Reverend McElrath. Twentieth also employs Paul Ewing and Ray McElrath, the ministers' sons. Twentieth and the Church share office space in Beverly Hills, California.

Twentieth's services are provided to the Church under two contracts signed by Reverend Ewing on behalf of both Twentieth and the Church. Pursuant to the contracts, Twentieth subcontracts out the printing and bills the Church at cost plus a 15% commission. Any bills unpaid after ninety days accrue interest charges at a rate of 1 1/2% per month. In accordance with the contracts, Twentieth advanced $2,867,180 to the Church between April 1980 and February 1981. During this same period, the Church repaid principal of $1,757,178, and paid Twentieth $180,515 in commissions and $26,549 in interest. Approximately two-thirds of the time of Twentieth's employees is devoted to work for the Church.

In 1980, Twentieth received additional income from unrelated organizations for undisclosed services of approximately $1,144,000. Although Twentieth apparently has clients unrelated to the Church, Twentieth refuses to identify them. Twentieth does not advertise the availability of its services.

Since 1977, Reverend Ewing and Reverend McElrath have received the following amounts as compensation for services from the Church and Twentieth:

Reverend Ewing

Year	Church By Mail	Twentieth
1977	—	—
1978	none	none
1979	none	$10,600
1980	$48,600	$88.294.22
1981	$48,600	$111,600 (through August)

Reverend McElrath

Year	Church By Mail	Twentieth
1977	—	—
1978	None	None
1979	None	$10,600
1980	$46,500	$86,300
1981	$46,500	$111,600 (through August)

Both ministers also have the use of automobiles whose total value is $48,789. Since 1980, Brenda Ewing has received $8,550 per year from the Church, and Paul Ewing and Ray McElrath, Jr. have received $30,000 yearly from Twentieth.

On January 10, 1980, the Church filed an application with the Commissioner of the Internal Revenue Service seeking recognition of exemption from federal income tax pursuant to section 501(c)(3) of the Internal Revenue Code of 1954. The Commissioner denied the Church's application, finding that the Church was not operated for exempt purposes within the meaning of section 501(c)(3) because it served private rather than public interests and because part of its earnings inures to the benefit of private individuals.

The tax court upheld the Commissioner's determination, holding that (1) the Church was operated for the non-exempt purpose of providing a market for Twentieth's services, and (2) a substantial, if not principal, purpose of the Church's operations was to generate income for the private benefit of Reverend Ewing and Reverend McElrath and their respective families.

I.R.C. § 501(a) confers tax-exempt status on those organizations which are organized and operated exclusively for religious, charitable or other specified exempt purposes within the meaning of I.R.C. § 501(c)(3), provided that no part of the organization's net earnings inures to the benefit of any private shareholder or individual. The taxpayer has the burden to demonstrate that it is entitled to tax-exempt status pursuant to section 501(c)(3).

The dispositive issue in this case is whether the Church meets the "operational" test imposed by I.R.C. § 501(c)(3). The Treasury Regulations specify three criteria for this requirement. First, the organization must be primarily engaged in activities which accomplish one or more of the exempt purposes specified in section 501(c)(3), so that it is "operated exclusively" for exempt purposes. Second, the organization's net earnings must not be distributed in whole or in part to the benefit of private shareholders or individuals. (The first two criteria, though separate, frequently overlap. *Canada v. Commissioner*, 82 T.C. 973, 981 (1984)). Third, the organization must not be an "action" organization, *i.e.*, one which spends a substantial part of its time attempting to influence legislation. The Commissioner does not contend that the Church violated the "action" requirement, and our examination of the record shows that the Church had no involvement with legislation.

In order to establish that it meets the first criterion of the operational test, an organization must prove that it is operated for a public purpose rather than for the benefit of private interests, such as those of the creator or his family, shareholders, or designated individuals. The presence of a single non-exempt purpose, if substantial in nature, will destroy the exemption.

There is ample evidence in the record to support the tax court's finding that the Church was operated for the substantial non-exempt purpose of providing a market for Twentieth's services. The employees of Twentieth spend two-thirds of their time working on the services provided to the Church. The majority of the Church's income is paid to Twentieth to cover repayments on loan principal, interest, and commissions. Finally, the potential for abuse created by the ministers' control of the Church requires open and candid disclosure of facts bearing upon the exemption application. The failure to provide information concerning the identity of other clients for Twentieth's services, in combination with all of the other facts which are present in the record, supports an inference that the Church provides the primary market for Twentieth's services.

Moreover, the ministers' dual control of both the Church and Twentieth enables them to profit from the affiliation of the two entities through increased compensation. The income of each minister increased from approximately $10,000 per year in 1979 to approximately $135,000 per year in 1980 and $160,000 for eight months in 1981, apparently as a direct result of the 1980 contractual arrangements between the two organizations. In addition, Twentieth had retained earnings of $774,977 as of March 31, 1981, apparently due in large part to the contracts.

The Church contends that its business provides only a portion of Twentieth's income, and stresses the fact that the contractual arrangements between the two demonstrate that Twentieth is not attempting to profit at the Church's expense. The Church asserts that the tax court erred in refusing to assign primary importance to an examination of the reasonableness of the contracts between the Church and Twentieth.

The Church exaggerates the importance of the contracts. The critical inquiry is not whether particular contractual payments to a related for-profit organization are reasonable or excessive, but instead whether the entire enterprise is carried on in such a manner that the for-profit organization benefits substantially from the operation of the Church.

In short, the purpose and objective to which the income of the Church is devoted is the ultimate test in determining whether it is operated exclusively for an exempt purpose. The tax court's determination that the Church is operated for the substantial non-exempt purpose of providing a market for Twentieth's services is supported by evidence in the record and is not clearly erroneous.

In order to meet the second prong of the operational test, an organization must establish that no part of its net earnings inures to the benefit of a private person. Although reasonable salaries may be paid to clergy, the payment of excessive salaries constitutes inurement to the benefit of a private person.

There is evidence in the record supporting the tax court's finding that the combined salaries paid to Reverend Ewing and Reverend McElrath and their families by the Church and Twentieth were excessive. The ministers are responsible for drafting the sermons, conducting church services in various cities and handling the financial commitments of the Church, including the contractual arrangements with Twentieth. The ministers spend only 60% of their time working for the Church and Twentieth. As set forth above, for the first eight months of 1981 both ministers received income from the Church and Twentieth in excess of $160,000. During the same year, Brenda Ewing received $8,550 from the Church while Paul Ewing and Ray McElrath each received $30,000 from Twentieth. Other courts have considered salaries far less than these unreasonable, particularly where the clergy have control over the Church's financial affairs.

Moreover, we believe that services comparable to those performed by the ministers could be obtained from an outside source in an arm's length transaction at a more reasonable cost. It seems likely that a member of the clergy could be hired to perform the part-time duties for which the ministers are responsible at a salary of considerably less than $160,000 per year.

The Church argues that the tax court erred in examining the ministers' combined salaries from Twentieth and the Church, and contends that the proper inquiry is whether the salaries received by the ministers and their families from the Church alone are reasonable. (Reverend Ewing has received $48,600 per year since 1980 while Reverend McElrath has received $46,500 per year during the same period.)

We disagree. In *Hall v. Commissioner*, 729 F.2d 632 (9th Cir.1984), we held that when a second organization is created which serves to funnel income to the individual who controls the purportedly exempt organization and the income exceeds a reasonable salary, the income inures to the benefit of a private person within the meaning of I.R.C. § 501(c)(3). Because Twentieth funnels income received from the Church to the ministers and their families, it was proper for the tax court to consider evidence of the salaries received from Twentieth as well as those received directly from the Church.

Because there is evidence in the record to support the tax court's conclusion that the salaries and benefits paid to the Reverends by Twentieth and the Church were excessive, the court's finding that income from the Church inured to the benefit of private persons was not clearly erroneous.

Because the Church has failed to meet both the first and second prongs of the operational test under I.R.C. § 501(c)(3), the tax court's denial of exempt status was proper.

PROBLEMS FOR DISCUSSION

19–5. State University is a tax-exempt organization that provides undergraduate and graduate education, primarily for residents of the state in which is located, at several campuses across the state. The Board of Regents, State University's governing body, sets the salary of each campus's president. A controversy has arisen with regard to the presidents' salaries, which some view as excessive. In considering how to respond, should the Board of Regents be concerned that such salaries might place State U's tax-exempt status in jeopardy?

SECTION 3: LOBBYING AND POLITICAL ACTIVITIES TEST

(a) ATTEMPTING TO INFLUENCE LEGISLATION

Code: Sections 501(h) and 4911

Regulations: Section 1.501(c)(3)–1(c)(3) and (d)(3)

The statutory requirement that no substantial part of the activities of an organization exempt under Code Section 501(c)(3) consist of "carrying on propaganda, or otherwise attempting, to influence legislation ..." commonly arises in three different contexts.

First, an organization may constitute an "action organization" within the meaning of Treas. Reg. § 1.501(c)(3)–1(c)(3). The regulations provide:

> "An organization is an action organization if it has the following two characteristics: (a) Its main or primary objective or objectives (as distinguished from its incidental or secondary objectives) may be attained only by legislation or a defeat of proposed legislation; and (b) it advocates, or campaigns for, the attainment of such main or primary objective or objectives as distinguished from engaging in nonpartisan analysis, study, or research and making the results thereof available to the public."

For example, in 1995, the Republican Congressional leadership announced the formation of a "National Commission on Economic Growth and Tax Reform," to be financed by a 501(c)(3) fund. The IRS denied exempt status to the fund on the ground that it met both prongs of the regulation's "action organization" test: (a) it sought to encourage the implementation of a flat tax, a goal that could only be accomplished by legislation, and (b) it advocated for this goal. The courts upheld the IRS. *Fund for the Study of Economic Growth and Tax Reform v. IRS*, 161 F.3d 755 (D.C. Cir. 1998).

Second, an organization may exist for the purpose of advocating with respect to a politically controversial topic not necessarily tied to legislation. Instead of asking whether such organizations are "action organizations," the IRS and the courts generally ask whether their activities are "educational"—the exempt purpose such organizations typically invoke when seeking exempt status. Treas. Reg. § 1.501(c)(3)–1(d)(3) defines "educational" broadly to include:

> "The instruction of the public on subjects useful to the individual and beneficial to the community. An organization may be educational even though it advocates a particular position or viewpoint so long as it presents a sufficiently full and fair exposition of the pertinent facts as to permit an individual or the public to form an independent opinion or conclusion. On the other hand, an organization is not educational if its principal function is the mere presentation of unsupported opinion."

The question commonly asked, therefore, is whether the organization "presents a sufficiently full and fair exposition of the pertinent facts as to permit an individual or the public to form an independent opinion or conclusion." Resolving this question in a politically neutral manner is not easy. *Compare Big Mama Rag, Inc. v. United States*, 631 F.2d 1030 (D.C. Cir.1980) ("fair and full exposition" test unconstitutionally vague, reversing denial of exempt status to lesbian newspaper), *with National Alliance v. United States*, 710 F.2d 868 (D.C. Cir. 1983) (upholding denial of exempt status to organization dedicated to "arousing in white Americans of European ancestry 'an understanding of and a pride in their racial and cultural heritage and an awareness of the present dangers to that heritage'" for failure to meet "fair and full exposition" test). There are few cases in which the IRS has denied exempt status on this ground.

Third, at least in theory, an organization whose principal function is clearly exempt—for example, a church—may nevertheless lose its exempt status by engaging in "substantial" amounts of lobbying. Again, cases involving such facts are extremely rare. There are at least two possible reasons. First, Code Section 501(h) provides an elective safe harbor within which 501(c)(3)'s may lobby without risking their tax-exempt status. The safe harbor begins at 30 percent (150 percent of 20 percent) of "exempt purpose expenditures" for small organizations, declining in increments to 7.5 percent of such expenditures in excess of $1,500,000, capped in any event at $1,000,000. It is not clear whether any significant number of 501(c)(3)'s elect this safe harbor, but those that do presumably comply with its relatively straight-forward requirements. Second, although news outlets sometimes report that organizations whose principal function is clearly exempt have engaged in grassroots lobbying, the IRS rarely seems to pursue them. Its failure to do so is almost impossible to challenge for standing reasons, discussed in Section 3(c) below.

(b) POLITICAL ACTIVITIES

BRANCH MINISTRIES v. ROSSOTTI
211 F.3d 137 (D.C. Cir. 2000)

Four days before the 1992 presidential election, Branch Ministries, a tax-exempt church, placed full-page advertisements in two newspapers in which it urged Christians not to vote for then-presidential candidate Bill Clinton because of his positions on certain moral issues. The Internal Revenue Service concluded that the placement of the advertisements violated the statutory restrictions on organizations exempt from taxation and, for the first time in its history, it revoked a bona fide church's tax-exempt status because of its involvement in politics. Branch Ministries and its pastor, Dan Little, challenge the revocation on the grounds that (1) the Service acted beyond its statutory authority, (2) the revocation violated its right to the free exercise of religion guaranteed by the First Amendment, and (3) it was the victim of selective prosecution in violation of the Fifth Amendment. Because these objections are without merit, we affirm the district court's grant of summary judgment to the Service.

The Internal Revenue Code exempts certain organizations from taxation, including those organized and operated for religious purposes, provided that they do not engage in certain activities, including involvement in "any political campaign on behalf of (or in opposition to) any candidate for public office." Contributions to such organizations are also deductible from the donating taxpayer's taxable income. Although most organizations seeking tax-exempt status are required to apply to the Internal Revenue Service for an advance determination that they meet the requirements of section 501(c)(3), a church may simply hold itself out as tax exempt and receive the benefits of that status without applying for advance recognition from the IRS. 26 U.S.C. § 508(c)(1)(A).

The unique treatment churches receive in the Internal Revenue Code is further reflected in special restrictions on the IRS's ability to investigate the tax status of a church. The Church Audit Procedures Act ("CAPA") sets out the circumstances under which the IRS may initiate an investigation of a church and the procedures it is required to follow in such investigation. 26 U.S.C. § 7611. Upon a "reasonable belief" by a high-level Treasury official that a church may not be exempt from taxation under section 501, the IRS may begin a "church tax inquiry." *Id.* § 7611(a).

If the IRS is not able to resolve its concerns through a church tax inquiry, it may proceed to the second level of investigation: a "church tax examination." In such an examination, the IRS may obtain and review the church's records or examine its activities "to determine whether [the] organization claiming to be a church is a church for any period." *Id.* § 7611(b)(1)(A), (B).

Branch Ministries, Inc. operates the Church at Pierce Creek, a Christian church located in Binghamton, New York. In 1983, the Church requested and received a letter from the IRS recognizing its tax-exempt status. On October 30, 1992, four days before the presidential election, the Church placed full-page advertisements in *USA Today* and the *Washington Times*. Each bore the headline "Christians Beware" and asserted that then-Governor Clinton's positions concerning abortion, homosexuality, and the distribution of condoms to teenagers in schools violated Biblical precepts. The following appeared at the bottom of each advertisement:

> "This advertisement was co-sponsored by the Church at Pierce Creek, Daniel J. Little, Senior Pastor, and by churches and concerned Christians nationwide. Tax-deductible donations for this advertisement gladly accepted. Make donations to: The Church at Pierce Creek. [mailing address]."

The advertisements did not go unnoticed. They produced hundreds of contributions to the Church from across the country and were mentioned in a *New York Times* article and an Anthony Lewis column which stated that the sponsors of the advertisement had almost certainly violated the Internal Revenue Code.

The advertisements also came to the attention of the Regional Commissioner of the IRS, who notified the Church on November 20, 1992 that he had authorized a church tax inquiry based on "a reasonable belief ... that you may not be tax-exempt or that you may be liable for tax" due to political activities and expenditures. The Church denied that it had engaged in any prohibited political activity and declined to provide the IRS with certain information the Service had requested. On February 11, 1993, the IRS informed the Church that it was beginning a church tax examination. Following two unproductive meetings between the parties, the IRS revoked the Church's section 501(c)(3) tax-exempt status on

January 19, 1995, citing the newspaper advertisements as prohibited intervention in a political campaign.

The Church and Pastor Little commenced this lawsuit soon thereafter. The Church challenged the revocation of its tax-exempt status, alleging that the IRS had no authority to revoke its tax exemption, that the revocation violated its right to free speech and to freely exercise its religion under the First Amendment, and that the IRS engaged in selective prosecution in violation of the Equal Protection Clause of the Fifth Amendment. After allowing discovery on the Church's selective prosecution claim, the district court granted summary judgment in favor of the IRS.

The Church claims that the revocation of its exemption violated its right to freely exercise its religion. To sustain its claim, the Church must first establish that its free exercise right has been substantially burdened. We conclude that the Church has failed to meet this test.

The Church asserts, first, that a revocation would threaten its existence. The Church maintains that a loss of its tax-exempt status will not only make its members reluctant to contribute the funds essential to its survival, but may obligate the Church itself to pay taxes.

The Church appears to assume that the withdrawal of a conditional privilege for failure to meet the condition is in itself an unconstitutional burden on its free exercise right. This is true, however, only if the receipt of the privilege (in this case the tax exemption) is conditioned

> upon conduct proscribed by a religious faith, or ... denie[d] ... because of conduct mandated by religious belief, thereby putting substantial pressure on an adherent to modify his behavior and to violate his beliefs.

Although its advertisements reflected its religious convictions on certain questions of morality, the Church does not maintain that a withdrawal from electoral politics would violate its beliefs. The sole effect of the loss of the tax exemption will be to decrease the amount of money available to the Church for its religious practices. The Supreme Court has declared, however, that such a burden "is not constitutionally significant."

In actual fact, even this burden is overstated. Because of the unique treatment churches receive under the Internal Revenue Code, the impact of the revocation is likely to be more symbolic than substantial. As the IRS confirmed at oral argument, if the Church does not intervene in future political campaigns, it may hold itself out as a 501(c)(3) organization and receive all the benefits of that status. All that will have been lost, in that event, is the advance assurance of deductibility in the event a donor should be audited. Contributions will remain tax deductible as long as donors are able to establish that the Church meets the requirements of section 501(c)(3).

Nor does the revocation necessarily make the Church liable for the payment of taxes. As the IRS explicitly represented in its brief and reiterated at oral argument, the revocation of the exemption does not convert bona fide donations into income taxable to the Church. *See* 26 U.S.C. § 102 ("Gross income does not include the value of property acquired by gift...."). Furthermore, we know of no authority, and counsel provided none, to prevent the Church from reapplying for a prospective determination of its tax-exempt status and regaining the advance assurance of deductibility—provided, of course, that it renounces future involvement in political campaigns.

We also reject the Church's argument that it is substantially burdened because it has no alternate means by which to communicate its sentiments about candidates for public office. In *Regan v. Taxation With Representation,* 461 U.S. 540, 552–53 (1983) (Blackmun, J., concurring), three members of the Supreme Court stated that the availability of such an alternate means of communication is essential to the constitutionality of section 501(c)(3)'s restrictions on lobbying. The Court subsequently confirmed that this was an accurate description of its holding. *See FCC v. League of Women Voters,* 468 U.S. 364, 400 (1984). In *Regan,* the concurring justices noted that "TWR may use its present § 501(c)(3) organization for its nonlobbying activities and may create a § 501(c)(4) affiliate to pursue its charitable goals through lobbying."

The Church has such an avenue available to it. As was the case with TWR, the Church may form a related organization under section 501(c)(4) of the Code. *See* 26 U.S.C. § 501(c)(4) (tax exemption for "[c]ivic leagues or organizations not organized for profit but operated exclusively for the promotion of social welfare"). Such organizations are exempt from taxation; but unlike their section 501(c)(3) counterparts, contributions to them are not deductible. Although a section 501(c)(4) organization is also subject to the ban on intervening in political campaigns, *see* 26 C.F.R. § 1.501(c)(4)–1(a)(2)(ii) (1999), it may form a political action committee ("PAC") that would be free to participate in political campaigns. *Id.* § 1.527–6(f), (g) ("[A]n organization described in section 501(c) that is exempt from taxation under section 501(a) may, [if it is not a section 501(c)(3) organization], establish and maintain such a separate segregated fund to receive contributions and make expenditures in a political campaign.").

At oral argument, counsel for the Church doggedly maintained that there can be no "Church at Pierce Creek PAC." True, it may not itself create a PAC; but as we have pointed out, the Church can initiate a series of steps that will provide an alternate means of political communication that will satisfy the standards set by the concurring justices in *Regan.* Should the Church proceed to do so, however, it must understand that the related 501(c)(4) organization must be separately incorporated; and it must maintain records that will demonstrate that tax-deductible contributions to the Church have not been used to support the political activities conducted by the 501(c)(4) organization's political action arm.

That the Church cannot use its tax-free dollars to fund such a PAC unquestionably passes constitutional muster. The Supreme Court has consistently held that, absent invidious discrimination, "Congress has not violated [an organization's] First Amendment rights by declining to subsidize its First Amendment activities."

Because the Church has failed to demonstrate that its free exercise rights have been substantially burdened, we do not reach its arguments that section 501(c)(3) does not serve a compelling government interest or, if it is indeed compelling, that revocation of its tax exemption was not the least restrictive means of furthering that interest.

The Church alleges that the IRS violated the Equal Protection Clause of the Fifth Amendment by engaging in selective prosecution. In support of its claim, the Church has submitted several hundred pages of newspaper excerpts reporting political campaign activities in, or by the pastors of, other churches that have retained their tax-exempt status. These include reports of explicit endorsements of Democratic candidates by clergymen as well as many instances in which favored candidates have been invited to address congregations from the pulpit. The Church complains that despite this widespread and widely reported involvement by other churches in political campaigns, it is the only one to have ever had its tax-exempt status revoked for engaging in political activity. It attributes this alleged discrimination to the Service's political bias.

To establish selective prosecution, the Church must "prove that (1) [it] was singled out for prosecution from among others similarly situated and (2) that [the] prosecution was improperly motivated, i.e., based on race, religion or another arbitrary classification." *United States v. Washington*, 705 F.2d 489, 494 (D.C. Cir.1983).

At oral argument, counsel for the IRS conceded that if some of the church-sponsored political activities cited by the Church were accurately reported, they were in violation of section 501(c)(3) and could have resulted in the revocation of those churches' tax-exempt status. But even if the Service could have revoked their tax exemptions, the Church has failed to establish selective prosecution because it has failed to demonstrate that it was similarly situated to any of those other churches. None of the reported activities involved the placement of advertisements in newspapers with nationwide circulations opposing a candidate and soliciting tax deductible contributions to defray their cost. As we have stated,

> [i]f ... there was no one to whom defendant could be compared in order to resolve the question of [prosecutorial] selection, then it follows that defendant has failed to make out one of the elements of its case. Discrimination cannot exist in a vacuum; it can be found only in the unequal treatment of people in similar circumstances.

Attorney Gen. v. Irish People, Inc., 684 F.2d 928, 946 (D.C. Cir.1982); *see also United States v. Hastings*, 126 F.3d 310, 315 (4th Cir.1997) ("[D]efendants are similarly situated when their circumstances present no distinguishable legitimate prosecutorial factors that might justify making different prosecutorial decisions with respect to them.").

Because the Church has failed to establish that it was singled out for prosecution from among others who were similarly situated, we need not examine whether the IRS was improperly motivated in undertaking this prosecution.

For the foregoing reasons, we find that the revocation of the Church's tax-exempt status neither violated the Constitution nor exceeded the IRS's statutory authority.

REV. RUL. 2007–41
2007–1 C.B. 1421

Issue

In each of the 21 situations described below, has the organization participated or intervened in a political campaign on behalf of (or in opposition to) any candidate for public office within the meaning of section 501(c)(3)?

Law

Section 501(c)(3) provides for the exemption from federal income tax of organizations organized and operated exclusively for charitable or educational purposes, no substantial part of the activities of which is carrying on propaganda, or otherwise attempting to influence legislation (except as otherwise provided in section 501(h)), and which does not participate in, or intervene in (including the publishing or distributing of statements), any political campaign on behalf of (or in opposition to) any candidate for public office.

Whether an organization is participating or intervening, directly or indirectly, in any political campaign on behalf of or in opposition to any candidate for public office depends upon all of the facts and circumstances of each case. For example, certain "voter education" activities, including preparation and distribution of certain voter guides, conducted in a non-partisan manner may not constitute prohibited political activities under section 501(c)(3) of the Code. Other so-called "voter education" activities may be proscribed by the statute. Rev. Rul. 78–248, 1978–1 C.B. 154, contrasts several situations illustrating when an organization that publishes a compilation of candidate positions or voting records has or has not engaged in prohibited political activities based on whether the questionnaire used to solicit candidate positions or the voters guide itself shows a bias or preference in content or structure with respect to the views of a particular candidate. See also Rev. Rul. 80–282, 1980–2 C.B. 178, amplifying Rev. Rul. 78–248 regarding the timing and distribution of voter education materials.

The presentation of public forums or debates is a recognized method of educating the public. See Rev. Rul. 66–256, 1966–2 C.B. 210 (nonprofit organization formed to conduct public forums at which lectures and debates on social, political, and international matters are presented qualifies for exemption from federal income tax under section 501(c)(3)). Providing a forum for candidates is not, in and of itself, prohibited political activity. See Rev. Rul. 74–574, 1974–2 C.B. 160 (organization operating a broadcast station is not participating in political campaigns on behalf of public candidates by providing reasonable amounts of air time equally available to all legally qualified candidates for election to public office in compliance with the reasonable access provisions of the Communications Act of 1934). However, a forum for candidates could be operated in a manner that would show a bias or preference for or against a particular candidate. This could be done, for example, through biased questioning procedures. On the other hand, a forum held for the purpose of educating and informing the voters, which provides fair and impartial treatment of candidates, and which does not promote or advance one candidate over another, would not constitute participation or intervention in any political campaign on behalf of or in opposition to any candidate for public office. See Rev. Rul. 86–95, 1986–2 C.B. 73 (organization that proposes to educate voters by conducting a series of public forums in congressional districts during congressional election campaigns is not participating in a political campaign on behalf of any candidate due to the neutral form and content of its proposed forums).

Analysis of factual situations

The 21 factual situations appear below under specific subheadings relating to types of activities. In each of the factual situations, all the facts and circumstances are considered in determining whether an organization's activities result in political campaign intervention. Note that each of these situations involves only one type of activity. In the case of an organization that combines one or more types of activity, the interaction among the activities may affect the determination of whether or not the organization is engaged in political campaign intervention.

Voter Education, Voter Registration and Get Out the Vote Drives

Section 501(c)(3) organizations are permitted to conduct certain voter education activities (including the presentation of public forums and the publication of voter education guides) if they are carried out in a non-partisan manner. In addition, section 501(c)(3) organizations may encourage people to participate in the electoral process through voter registration and get-out-the-vote drives, conducted in a non-partisan manner. On the other hand, voter education or registration activities conducted in a biased manner that favors (or opposes) one or more candidates is prohibited.

Situation 1. B, a section 501(c)(3) organization that promotes community involvement, sets up a booth at the state fair where citizens can register to vote. The signs and banners in and around the booth give only the name of the organization, the date of the next upcoming statewide election, and notice of the opportunity to register. No reference to any candidate or political party is made by the volunteers staffing the booth or in the materials available at the booth, other than the official voter registration forms which allow registrants to select a party affiliation. B is not engaged in political campaign intervention when it operates this voter registration booth.

Situation 2. C is a section 501(c)(3) organization that educates the public on environmental issues. Candidate G is running for the state legislature and an important element of her platform is challenging the environmental policies of the incumbent. Shortly before the election, C sets up a telephone bank to call registered voters in the district in which Candidate G is seeking election. In the phone conversations, C's representative tells the voter about the importance of environmental issues and asks questions about the voter's views on these issues. If the voter appears to agree with the incumbent's position, C's representative thanks the voter and ends the call. If the voter appears to agree with Candidate G's position, C's representative reminds the voter about the upcoming election, stresses the importance of voting in the election and offers to provide transportation to the polls. C is engaged in political campaign intervention when it conducts this get-out-the-vote drive.

Individual Activity by Organization Leaders

The political campaign intervention prohibition is not intended to restrict free expression on political matters by leaders of organizations speaking for themselves, as individuals. Nor are leaders prohibited from speaking about important issues of public policy. However, for their organizations to remain tax exempt under section 501(c)(3), leaders cannot make partisan comments in official organization publications or at official functions of the organization.

Situation 3. President A is the Chief Executive Officer of Hospital J, a section 501(c)(3) organization, and is well known in the community. With the permission of five prominent healthcare industry leaders, including President A, who have personally endorsed Candidate T, Candidate T publishes a full page ad in the local newspaper listing the names of the five leaders. President A is identified in the ad as the CEO of Hospital J. The ad states, "Titles and affiliations of each individual are provided for identification purposes only." The ad is paid for by Candidate T's campaign committee. Because the ad was not paid for by Hospital J, the ad is not otherwise in an official publication of Hospital J, and the endorsement is made by President A in a personal capacity, the ad does not constitute campaign intervention by Hospital J.

Situation 4. President B is the president of University K, a section 501(c)(3) organization. University K publishes a monthly alumni newsletter that is distributed to all alumni of the university. In each issue, President B has a column titled "My Views." The month before the election, President B states in the "My Views" column, "It is my personal opinion that Candidate U should be reelected."For that one issue, President B pays from his personal funds the portion of the cost of the newsletter attributable to the "My Views" column. Even though he paid part of the cost of the newsletter, the newsletter is an official publication of the university. Because the endorsement appeared in an official publication of University K, it constitutes campaign intervention by University K.

Situation 5. Minister C is the minister of Church L, a section 501(c)(3) organization and Minister C is well known in the community. Three weeks before the election, he attends a press conference at Candidate V's campaign headquarters and states that Candidate V should be reelected. Minister C does not say he is speaking on behalf of Church L. His endorsement is reported on the front page of the local newspaper and he is identified in the article as the minister of Church L. Because Minister C did not make the endorsement at an official church function, in an official church publication or otherwise use the church's assets, and did not state that he was speaking as a representative of Church L, his actions do not constitute campaign intervention by Church L.

Situation 6. Chairman D is the chairman of the Board of Directors of M, a section 501(c)(3) organization that educates the public on conservation issues. During a regular meeting of M shortly before the election, Chairman D spoke on a number of issues, including the importance of voting in the upcoming election, and concluded by stating, "It is important that you all do your duty in the election and vote for Candidate W." Because Chairman D's remarks indicating support for Candidate W were made during an official organization meeting, they constitute political campaign intervention by M.

Candidate Appearances

Depending on the facts and circumstances, an organization may invite political candidates to speak at its events without jeopardizing its tax-exempt status. Political candidates may be invited in their capacity as candidates, or in their individual capacity (not as a candidate). Candidates may also appear without an invitation at organization events that are open to the public.

When a candidate is invited to speak at an organization event in his or her capacity as a political candidate, factors in determining whether the organization participated or intervened in a political campaign include the following:

- Whether the organization provides an equal opportunity to participate to political candidates seeking the same office;
- Whether the organization indicates any support for or opposition to the candidate (including candidate introductions and communications concerning the candidate's attendance); and
- Whether any political fundraising occurs.

In determining whether candidates are given an equal opportunity to participate, the nature of the event to which each candidate is invited will be considered, in addition to the manner of presentation. For example, an organization that invites one candidate to speak at its well attended annual banquet, but invites the opposing candidate to speak at a sparsely attended general meeting, will likely have violated the political campaign prohibition, even if the manner of presentation for both speakers is otherwise neutral.

When an organization invites several candidates for the same office to speak at a public forum, factors in determining whether the forum results in political campaign intervention include the following:

- Whether questions for the candidates are prepared and presented by an independent nonpartisan panel,
- Whether the topics discussed by the candidates cover a broad range of issues that the candidates would address if elected to the office sought and are of interest to the public,
- Whether each candidate is given an equal opportunity to present his or her view on each of the issues discussed,
- Whether the candidates are asked to agree or disagree with positions, agendas, platforms or statements of the organization, and
- Whether a moderator comments on the questions or otherwise implies approval or disapproval of the candidates.

Situation 7. President E is the president of Society N, a historical society that is a section 501(c)(3) organization. In the month prior to the election, President E invites the three Congressional candidates for the district in which Society N is located to address the members, one each at a regular meeting held on three successive weeks. Each candidate is given an equal opportunity to address and field questions on a wide variety of topics from the members. Society N's publicity announcing the dates for each of the candidate's speeches and President E's introduction of each candidate include no comments on their qualifications or any indication of a preference for any candidate. Society N's actions do not constitute political campaign intervention.

Situation 8. The facts are the same as in Situation 7 except that there are four candidates in the race rather than three, and one of the candidates declines the invitation to speak. In the publicity announcing the dates for each of the candidate's speeches, Society N includes a statement that the order of the speakers was determined at random and the fourth candidate declined the Society's invitation to speak. President E makes the same statement in his opening remarks at each of the meetings where one of the candidates is speaking. Society N's actions do not constitute political campaign intervention.

Situation 9. Minister F is the minister of Church O, a section 501(c)(3) organization. The Sunday before the November election, Minister F invites Senate Candidate X to preach to her congregation during worship services. During his remarks, Candidate X states, "I am asking not only for your votes, but for your enthusiasm and dedication, for your willingness to go the extra mile to get a very large turnout on Tuesday." Minister F invites no other candidate to address her congregation during the Senatorial campaign. Because these activities take place during official church services, they are attributed to Church O. By selectively providing church facilities to allow Candidate X to speak in support of his campaign, Church O's actions constitute political campaign intervention.

Candidate Appearances Where Speaking or Participating as a Non–Candidate

Candidates may also appear or speak at organization events in a non-candidate capacity. For instance, a political candidate may be a public figure who is invited to speak because he or she: (a) currently holds, or formerly held, public office; (b) is considered an expert in a non political field; or (c) is a celebrity or has led a distinguished military, legal, or public service career. A candidate may choose to attend an event that is open to the public, such as a lecture, concert or worship service. The candidate's presence at an organization-sponsored event does not, by itself, cause the organization to be engaged in political campaign intervention. However, if the candidate is publicly recognized by the organization, or if the candidate is invited to speak, factors in determining whether the candidate's appearance results in political campaign intervention include the following:

- Whether the individual is chosen to speak solely for reasons other than candidacy for public office;
- Whether the individual speaks only in a non-candidate capacity;
- Whether either the individual or any representative of the organization makes any mention of his or her candidacy or the election;
- Whether any campaign activity occurs in connection with the candidate's attendance;
- Whether the organization maintains a nonpartisan atmosphere on the premises or at the event where the candidate is present; and
- Whether the organization clearly indicates the capacity in which the candidate is appearing and does not mention the individual's political candidacy or the upcoming election in the communications announcing the candidate's attendance at the event.

Situation 10. Historical society P is a section 501(c)(3) organization. Society P is located in the state capital. President G is the president of Society P and customarily acknowledges the presence of any public officials present during meetings. During the state gubernatorial race, Lieutenant Governor Y, a candidate, attends a meeting of the historical society. President G acknowledges the Lieutenant Governor's presence in his customary manner, saying, "We are happy to have joining us this evening Lieutenant Governor Y." President G makes no reference in his welcome to the Lieutenant Governor's candidacy or the election. Society P has not engaged in political campaign intervention as a result of President G's actions.

Situation 11. Chairman H is the chairman of the Board of Hospital Q, a section 501(c)(3) organization. Hospital Q is building a new wing. Chairman H invites Congressman Z, the representative for the district containing Hospital Q, to attend the groundbreaking ceremony for the new wing. Congressman Z is running for reelection at the time. Chairman H makes no reference in her introduction to Congressman Z's candidacy or the election. Congressman Z also makes no reference to his candidacy or the election and does not do any political campaign fundraising while at Hospital Q. Hospital Q has not intervened in a political campaign.

Situation 12. University X is a section 501(c)(3) organization. X publishes an alumni newsletter on a regular basis. Individual alumni are invited to send in updates about themselves which are printed in each edition of the newsletter. After receiving an update letter from Alumnus Q, X prints the following: "Alumnus Q, class of XX is running for mayor of Metropolis." The newsletter does not contain any reference to this election or to Alumnus Q's candidacy other than this statement of fact. University X has not intervened in a political campaign.

Situation 13. Mayor G attends a concert performed by Symphony S, a section 501(c)(3) organization, in City Park. The concert is free and open to the public. Mayor G is a candidate for reelection, and the concert takes place after the primary and before the general election. During the concert, the chairman of S's board addresses the crowd and says, "I am pleased to see Mayor G here tonight. Without his support, these free concerts in City Park would not be possible. We will need his help if we want these concerts to continue next year so please support Mayor G in November as he has supported us." As a result of these remarks, Symphony S has engaged in political campaign intervention.

Issue Advocacy vs. Political Campaign Intervention

Section 501(c)(3) organizations may take positions on public policy issues, including issues that divide candidates in an election for public office. However, section 501(c)(3) organizations must avoid any issue advocacy that functions as political campaign intervention. Even if a statement does not expressly tell an audience to vote for or against a specific candidate, an organization delivering the statement is at risk of violating the political campaign intervention prohibition if there is any message favoring or opposing a candidate. A statement can identify a candidate not only by stating the candidate's name but also by other means such as showing a picture of the candidate, referring to political party affiliations, or other distinctive features of a candidate's platform or biography. All the facts and circumstances need to be considered to determine if the advocacy is political campaign intervention.

Key factors in determining whether a communication results in political campaign intervention include the following:

- Whether the statement identifies one or more candidates for a given public office;
- Whether the statement expresses approval or disapproval for one or more candidates' positions and/or actions;
- Whether the statement is delivered close in time to the election;
- Whether the statement makes reference to voting or an election;
- Whether the issue addressed in the communication has been raised as an issue distinguishing candidates for a given office;
- Whether the communication is part of an ongoing series of communications by the organization on the same issue that are made independent of the timing of any election; and
- Whether the timing of the communication and identification of the candidate are related to a non-electoral event such as a scheduled vote on specific legislation by an officeholder who also happens to be a candidate for public office.

A communication is particularly at risk of political campaign intervention when it makes reference to candidates or voting in a specific upcoming election. Nevertheless, the communication must still be considered in context before arriving at any conclusions.

Situation 14. University O, a section 501(c)(3) organization, prepares and finances a full page newspaper advertisement that is published in several large circulation newspapers in State V shortly before an election in which Senator C is a candidate for nomination in a party primary. Senator C represents State V in the United States Senate. The advertisement states that S. 24, a pending bill in the United States Senate, would provide additional opportunities for State V residents to attend college, but Senator C has opposed similar measures in the past. The advertisement ends with the statement "Call or write Senator C to tell him to vote for S. 24." Educational issues have not been raised as an issue distinguishing Senator C from any opponent. S. 24 is scheduled for a vote in the United States Senate before the election, soon after the date that the advertisement is published in the newspapers. Even though the advertisement appears shortly before the election and identifies Senator C's position on the issue as contrary to O's position, University O has not violated the political campaign intervention prohibition because the advertisement does not mention the election or the candidacy of Senator C, education issues have not been raised as distinguishing Senator C from any opponent, and the timing of the advertisement and the identification of Senator C are directly related to the specifically identified legislation University O is supporting and appears immediately before the United States Senate is scheduled to vote on that particular legislation. The candidate identified, Senator C, is an officeholder who is in a position to vote on the legislation.

Situation 15. Organization R, a section 501(c)(3) organization that educates the public about the need for improved public education, prepares and finances a radio advertisement urging an increase in state funding for public education in State X, which requires a legislative appropriation. Governor E is the governor of State X. The radio advertisement is first broadcast on several radio stations in State X beginning shortly before an election in which Governor E is a candidate for re-election. The advertisement is not part of an ongoing series of substantially similar advocacy communications by Organization R on the same issue. The advertisement cites numerous statistics indicating that public education in State X is under funded. While the advertisement does not say anything about Governor E's position on funding for public education, it ends with "Tell Governor E what you think about our under-funded schools." In public appearances and campaign literature, Governor E's opponent has made funding of public education an issue in the campaign by focusing on Governor E' s veto of an income tax increase the previous year to increase funding of public education. At the time the advertisement is broadcast, no legislative vote or other major legislative activity is scheduled in the State X legislature on state funding of public education. Organization R has violated the political campaign prohibition because the advertisement identifies Governor E, appears shortly before an election in which Governor E is a candidate, is not part of an ongoing series of substantially similar advocacy communications by Organization R on the same issue, is not timed to coincide with a non election event such as a legislative vote or other major legislative action on that issue, and takes a position on an issue that the opponent has used to distinguish himself from Governor E.

Situation 16. Candidate A and Candidate B are candidates for the state senate in District W of State X. The issue of State X funding for a new mass transit project in District W is a prominent issue in the campaign. Both candidates have spoken out on the issue. Candidate A supports funding the new mass transit project. Candidate B opposes the project and supports State X funding for highway improvements instead. P is the executive director of C, a section 501(c)(3) organization that promotes community development in District W. At C's annual fundraising dinner in District W, which takes place in the month before the election in State X, P gives a lengthy speech about community development issues including the transportation issues. P does not mention the name of any candidate or any political party. However, at the conclusion of the speech, P makes the following statement, "For those of you who care about quality of life in District W and the growing traffic congestion, there is a very important choice coming up next month. We need new mass transit. More highway funding will not make a difference. You have the power to relieve the congestion and improve your quality of life in District W. Use that power when you go to the polls and cast your vote in the election for your state senator." C has violated the political campaign intervention as a result of P's remarks at C's official function shortly before the election, in which P referred to the upcoming election after stating a position on an issue that is a prominent issue in a campaign that distinguishes the candidates.

Business Activity

The question of whether an activity constitutes participation or intervention in a political campaign may also arise in the context of a business activity of the organization, such as selling or renting of mailing lists, the leasing of office space, or the acceptance of paid political advertising. In this context, some of the factors to be considered in determining whether the organization has engaged in political campaign intervention include the following:

- Whether the good, service or facility is available to candidates in the same election on an equal basis,

- Whether the good, service, or facility is available only to candidates and not to the general public,

- Whether the fees charged to candidates are at the organization's customary and usual rates, and

- Whether the activity is an ongoing activity of the organization or whether it is conducted only for a particular candidate.

Situation 17. Museum K is a section 501(c)(3) organization. It owns an historic building that has a large hall suitable for hosting dinners and receptions. For several years, Museum K has made the hall available for rent to members of the public. Standard fees are set for renting the hall based on the number of people in attendance, and a number of different organizations have rented the hall. Museum K rents the hall on a first come, first served basis. Candidate P rents Museum K's social hall for a fundraising dinner. Candidate P's campaign pays the standard fee for the dinner. Museum K is not involved in political campaign intervention as a result of renting the hall to Candidate P for use as the site of a campaign fundraising dinner.

Situation 18. Theater L is a section 501(c)(3) organization. It maintains a mailing list of all of its subscribers and contributors. Theater L has never rented its mailing list to a third party. Theater L is approached by the campaign committee of Candidate Q, who supports increased funding for the arts. Candidate Q's campaign committee offers to rent Theater L's mailing list for a fee that is comparable to fees charged by other similar organizations. Theater L rents its mailing list to Candidate Q's campaign committee. Theater L declines similar requests from campaign committees of other candidates. Theater L has intervened in a political campaign.

Web Sites

The Internet has become a widely used communications tool. Section 501(c)(3) organizations use their own web sites to disseminate statements and information. They also routinely link their web sites to web sites maintained by other organizations as a way of providing additional information that the organizations believe is useful or relevant to the public.

A web site is a form of communication. If an organization posts something on its web site that favors or opposes a candidate for public office, the organization will be treated the same as if it distributed printed material, oral statements or broadcasts that favored or opposed a candidate.

An organization has control over whether it establishes a link to another site. When an organization establishes a link to another web site, the organization is responsible for the consequences of establishing and maintaining that link, even if the organization does not have control over the content of the linked site. Because the linked content may change over time, an organization may reduce the risk of political campaign intervention by monitoring the linked content and adjusting the links accordingly.

Links to candidate-related material, by themselves, do not necessarily constitute political campaign intervention. All the facts and circumstances must be taken into account when assessing whether a link produces that result. The facts and circumstances to be considered include, but are not limited to, the context for the link on the organization's web site, whether all candidates are represented, any exempt purpose served by offering the link, and the directness of the links between the organization's web site and the web page that contains material favoring or opposing a candidate for public office.

Situation 19. M, a section 501(c)(3) organization, maintains a web site and posts an unbiased, nonpartisan voter guide that is prepared consistent with the principles discussed in Rev. Rul. 78–248. For each candidate covered in the voter guide, M includes a link to that candidate's official campaign web site. The links to the candidate web sites are presented on a consistent neutral basis for each candidate, with text saying "For more information on Candidate X, you may consult [URL]." M has not intervened in a political campaign because the links are provided for the exempt purpose of educating voters and are presented in a neutral, unbiased manner that includes all candidates for a particular office.

Situation 20. Hospital N, a section 501(c)(3) organization, maintains a web site that includes such information as medical staff listings, directions to Hospital N, and descriptions of its specialty health programs, major research projects, and other community outreach programs. On one page of the web site, Hospital N describes its treatment pro-gram for a particular disease. At the end of the page, it includes a section of links to other web sites titled "More Information." These links include links to other hospitals that have treatment programs for this disease, research organizations seeking cures for that disease, and articles about treatment programs. This section includes a link to an article on the web site of O, a major national newspaper, praising Hospital N's treatment program for the disease. The page containing the article on O's web site contains no reference to any candidate or election and has no direct links to candidate or election information. Elsewhere on O's web site, there is a page displaying editorials that O has published. Several of the editorials endorse candidates in an election that has not yet occurred. Hospital N has not intervened in a political campaign by maintaining the link to the article on O's web site because the link is provided for the exempt purpose of educating the public about Hospital N's programs and neither the context for the link, nor the relationship between Hospital N and O nor the arrangement of the links going from Hospital N's web site to the endorsement on O's web site indicate that Hospital N was favoring or opposing any candidate.

Situation 21. Church P, a section 501(c)(3) organization, maintains a web site that includes such information as biographies of its ministers, times of services, details of community outreach programs, and activities of members of its congregation. B, a member of the congregation of Church P, is running for a seat on the town council. Shortly before the election, Church P posts the following message on its web site, "Lend your support to B, your fellow parishioner, in Tuesday's election for town council." Church P has intervened in a political campaign on behalf of B.

Holdings

In situations 2, 4, 6, 9, 13, 15, 16, 18 and 21, the organization intervened in a political campaign within the meaning of section 501(c)(3). In situations 1, 3, 5, 7, 8, 10, 11, 12, 14, 17, 19 and 20, the organization did not intervene in a political campaign within the meaning of section 501(c)(3).

(c) STANDING ISSUES

IN RE UNITED STATES CATHOLIC CONFERENCE
885 F.2d 1020 (2d Cir. 1989)

This appeal is before us for a second time. The Supreme Court has remanded the matter for a determination of whether the District Court had subject matter jurisdiction over the instant lawsuit that challenged the tax-exempt status of the Roman Catholic Church in the United States. The specific issue is whether the plaintiffs, who initiated this litigation to force the government to revoke the Catholic Church's tax-exempt status, satisfy the standing requirements of Article III. For the reasons discussed below, we hold that they do not.

Plaintiffs in this appeal are united in their commitment to a woman's right to obtain a legal abortion. The plaintiffs object to the Internal Revenue Service's (IRS) enforcement—or, as they describe it, nonenforcement—of § 501(c)(3)'s prohibition on lobbying and campaigning. Because this appeal arises from a motion to dismiss for want of standing, we must accept all of the plaintiffs' allegations as true and draw all inferences in their favor.

Plaintiffs first allege that the Catholic Church is repeatedly violating § 501(c)(3)'s prohibition on campaigning in order to promote the tenet that abortion is immoral and should therefore be made unlawful. For instance, plaintiffs point to the Church's "Pastoral Plan for Pro–Life Activities", which they claim is an organized effort to mobilize the entire Church in a "three-fold educational, pastoral and political effort to outlaw abortions in the United States." The complaint also alleges that through its priests and officials, the Catholic Church has endorsed or supported pro-life political candidates and opposed pro-choice candidates by publishing articles in its bulletins, attacking or endorsing candidates from the pulpit, distributing partisan letters to parishioners, and urging its members to donate to and sign petitions of "right to life" committees and candidates. Similarly, plaintiffs contend that the Church has contributed substantial sums of money to "right to life" and other political groups which have, directly or indirectly, supported the political candidacies for public office of persons favoring anti-abortion legislation.

Plaintiffs' other major contention is that the IRS knows about the Catholic Church's alleged political activities and has ignored these activities rather than either revoking the Church's tax-exempt status under § 501(c)(3), or not renewing the Church's annual exemption. They therefore assert that the government has "exempted the Roman Catholic Church from the strictures of the law and from the government's enforcement efforts," and that the IRS treats the Catholic Church more favorably than those organizations that are pro-choice. Yet plaintiffs do not allege that the IRS has penalized them for violating the Code; in fact, they assert that they have not violated § 501(c)(3) by electioneering, and do not intend to. Rather, they want the government to enforce the strictures of § 501(c)(3) against the Catholic Church. Thus, plaintiffs do not complain about their own tax status—their challenge is directed solely against the Catholic Church's exemption.

[The court recites the procedural history of the case.] Upon remand from the Supreme Court, we now must analyze whether plaintiffs have standing to sue the government for conferring tax-exempt status to the Catholic Church.

In *Allen v. Wright*, 468 U.S. 737 (1984), the Supreme Court made clear that standing is not merely a prudential inquiry into whether a court should exercise jurisdiction, but is rooted in Article III's "case" or "controversy" requirement and reflects separation of powers principles. Thus, when a plaintiff lacks standing to bring suit, a court has no subject matter jurisdiction over the case. Deceptively simple to state, standing entails a complex three-pronged inquiry. First, plaintiffs must show that they have suffered an injury in fact that is both concrete in nature and particularized to them. Second, the injury must be fairly traceable to defendants' conduct. Third, the injury must be redressable by removal of defendants' conduct. The second and third prongs—traceability and redressability—often dovetail; essentially, both seek a causal nexus between the plaintiff's injury and the defendant's assertedly unlawful act. To establish standing, a plaintiff must plead all three elements.

Standing in the case at hand is alleged under a number of theories that require a general overview in order to match the category of plaintiff to the asserted basis for standing. The prior proceedings have distilled standing theories that view plaintiffs as clergy, voters, and taxpayers. We first address those theories relied upon by the district court in finding that plaintiffs had standing, and then consider a fourth theory—competitive advocate standing—not explicitly addressed below.

1. Clergy Standing

Clergy plaintiffs claim standing under the Establishment Clause of the First Amendment. The amended complaint alleges that

> "The failure of the government defendants to apply the Code equally to the ... Church is in effect a subsidy of the Church's efforts to further its religious aims in the political sphere, a subsidy not granted to law-abiding ... plaintiffs, who hold contrary religious beliefs. This constitutes an unconstitutional establishment of religion."

It is true that an injury claimed to derive from a violation of the Establishment Clause can be spiritual in nature. Nonetheless, the injury must be particularized to the individuals who sue. The Establishment Clause does not exempt clergy or lay persons from Article III's standing requirements. Here, the clergy plaintiffs have not been injured in a sufficiently personal way to distinguish themselves from other citizens who are generally aggrieved by a claimed constitutional violation. For that reason, they lack standing.

Both *Valley Forge Christian College v. Americans United For Separation of Church and State, Inc.*, 454 U.S. 464 (1982), and *Allen v. Wright* support this conclusion. In *Valley Forge*, an organization dedicated to ensuring separation of church and state sued the Secretary of Health, Education and Welfare for conveying, without consideration, surplus government property to a religiously affiliated college. The *Valley Forge* plaintiffs made the same argument as the instant clergy plaintiffs—that by conferring a benefit to a third party that was a religious entity, the government had violated the Establishment Clause. The Supreme Court considered whether plaintiffs had been injured as taxpayers—a subject we address below—and as "separationists" bent on policing the Establishment Clause. Accepting the sincerity of plaintiffs' ire at the alleged violation of the Establishment Clause, it held that such distress was not cognizable unless plaintiffs could "identify any personal injury suffered by them as a consequence of the alleged constitutional error...." It was not enough to point to an assertedly illegal benefit flowing to a third party that happened to be a religious entity. Absent a particularized injury, plaintiffs could not maintain suit.

In *Allen v. Wright*, the plaintiffs were parents of black children who attended public schools. They sued the IRS, asserting that it was duty-bound to deny tax-exempt status to racially discriminatory private schools, and its failure to do so impaired desegregation of the public school system. In *Allen v. Wright*, as here, plaintiffs' complaint centered on the tax-exempt status of a third party. The parents asserted two injuries, only one of which is pertinent to this case—harm from the fact that the government was giving financial assistance to private discriminatory schools. The Supreme Court held that the parents did not have standing and made several points on the injury in fact requirement. Relying on *Schlesinger v. Reservists Committee to Stop the War*, 418 U.S. 208 (1974) (Reservists), the Court stated that "an asserted right to have the Government act in accordance with law is not sufficient, standing alone, to confer jurisdiction on a federal court." Parents did not derive standing by claiming "stigmatizing injury" caused by racial discrimination because "such injury accords a basis for standing only to 'those persons who are personally denied equal treatment' by the challenged discriminatory conduct." The Supreme Court then emphasized that when the injury asserted is an "abstract stigmatic injury," the requirement that a plaintiff be personally injured takes on heightened importance.

The clergy plaintiffs' complaint in the instant case suffers from the same defects as the parents' complaint in *Allen v. Wright* and the separationists' complaint in *Valley Forge*: The primary injury of which they complain is their discomfiture at watching the government allegedly fail to enforce the law with respect to a third party. As in *Valley Forge*, the instant plaintiffs state that defendants have violated their "sincere and deeply held belief in the separation of church and state." This injury can hardly be called personalized to the clergy plaintiffs. They can point to no illegal government conduct directly affecting their own ministries. Thus, the injury the clergy complain of could be asserted by any member of the public who disagrees with the views of the Catholic Church and the IRS in granting it a tax exemption.

Similarly, because the clergy have neither been personally denied equal treatment under the law nor in any way prosecuted by the IRS, their self-perceived "stigma" does not amount to a particularized injury in fact. To hold the clergy plaintiffs' injury cognizable would turn the federal court into " 'a forum in which to air ... generalized grievances about the conduct of government.' " Hence, the clergy's complaint collapses into that of an offended bystander, insufficient to meet Article III's standing requirements. A mere "claim that the Government has violated the Establishment Clause does not provide [plaintiffs] a special license to roam the country in search of governmental wrongdoing and to reveal their discoveries in federal court."

This analysis is unchanged by the fact that the plaintiffs in this case are clergy. To rebut the argument that they have not suffered a particularized injury, these plaintiffs contend that what distinguishes them from the ordinary member of the public who takes issue with the Church and

IRS is that they are members of the clergy. In our view, the holding in *Valley Forge* and its progeny would have been the same even had those plaintiffs been members of the clergy rather than Americans United For Separation of Church and State because "standing is not measured by the intensity of the litigant's interest or the fervor of his advocacy."

Moreover, granting standing to clergy qua clergy raises several troubling issues. Granting standing to the instant ministers and rabbis on the basis that they were directly and personally injured by the IRS' actions solely on account of their stature within their churches and synagogues would require us to give greater credence to the clergy's beliefs with the beliefs of their parishioners. Thus, to hold that a religious leader is more qualified to bring an Article III "case" or "controversy" than a member of his congregation seemingly entails an impermissible invasion into a church's or a synagogue's internal hierarchy and its autonomy. And, as the district court correctly noted, the Establishment Clause protects religions from secular interference.

Second, granting standing to enforce the Establishment Clause to clergy qua clergy might itself violate the same clause by constituting governmental favoritism of religion over non-religion. The Supreme Court has made clear that the Establishment Clause prohibits not only government endorsement of a given sect, but also forbids the government from generally favoring religion over secularism. Thus, the strength, intensity, or knowledge of one's religious beliefs obviously is not a criterion upon which to confer standing because such a rule would deny to non-believers the same benefits of maintaining suit. As Thomas Jefferson stated in his much quoted metaphor, the Establishment Clause was designed to build "a wall of separation between church and State." Plaintiffs point to no authority for a standing doctrine exception to this principle of separation between church and state. To read plaintiffs' complaint as stating a particularized injury simply because it is dressed in clerical garb would only weaken the foundation of Jefferson's metaphorical wall. As a consequence, stripped of the assertedly unique status of clergy, plaintiffs' injury is as generalized as that asserted in *Valley Forge* and *Allen v. Wright*, and their complaint must be similarly dismissed.

2. Taxpayer Standing

The taxpayer plaintiffs allege that they are "harmed because the government's subsidy of the . . . Church's illegal political activities is the equivalent of a government expenditure to establish a religion in violation of the First Amendment to the Constitution." In essence, they complain that not only is the government making illegal use of tax revenue, but also that they, as taxpayers, are forced to contribute to the government's asserted subsidy of the Catholic Church.

We set forth briefly the requirements for taxpayer standing, which are somewhat more specific than those for standing generally. The basic rule is that taxpayers do not have standing to challenge how the federal government spends tax revenue. *See Frothingham v. Mellon*, 262 U.S. 447,

488 (1923). In *Flast v. Cohen*, 392 U.S. 83 (1968), the Supreme Court created an exception to the *Frothingham* rule, holding that taxpayer standing is available to challenge Establishment Clause violations when the allegedly unconstitutional action was authorized by Congress under the taxing and spending clause of Art. I, § 8. Subsequent cases made clear the narrowness of *Flast*'s exception to *Frothingham*'s rule against taxpayer standing.

Then Valley Forge—handed down in the interim between the filing of the instant complaint and the motion to dismiss—caused some commentators to conclude that the taxpayer standing theory was virtually a dead letter. Hence, plaintiffs abandoned this theory in the district court. Following the Supreme Court's more recent decision in *Bowen v. Kendrick*, 487 U.S. 589 (1988) (holding that taxpayers had standing to challenge the application of the Adolescent Family Life Act (AFLA), plaintiffs renew before us their taxpayer standing arguments. In light of the protracted history of this litigation, it is appropriate to consider this issue now, if for no other reason than to prevent a third appeal.

The Supreme Court in *Kendrick* distinguished *Valley Forge* by emphasizing that in the latter case the decision by the executive agency to dispose of the surplus federal property—though made pursuant to a federal statute—was not a challenge to Congress' taxing and spending power because the statute's mandate derived from the property clause of Art. IV, § 3. In so doing, the Supreme Court clarified that taxpayer standing exists to challenge the executive branch's administration of a taxing and spending statute; the challenge need not be directed exclusively at Congress. But Kendrick's discussion of *Valley Forge* does not breathe new life into plaintiff's moribund taxpayer standing theory, as shall become evident.

In *Kendrick*, it was Congress that decided how the AFLA funds were to be spent, and the executive branch, in administering the statute, was merely carrying out Congress' scheme. Thus, the Supreme Court held that taxpayers had standing to challenge whether Congress' decision under the taxing and spending clause had violated the limits imposed by the Establishment Clause.

Plaintiffs in the instant case do not challenge Congress' exercise of its taxing and spending power as embodied in § 501(c)(3) of the Code; they do not contend that the Code favors the Church. The Supreme Court, as noted, has already upheld the constitutionality of that section. Instead, they argue that the IRS, in allegedly closing its eyes to violations by the Church, is disregarding the Code's mandate and the Constitution. The complaint centers on an alleged decision made solely by the executive branch that in plaintiffs' view directly contravenes Congress' aim. The instant case is therefore distinguishable from *Kendrick*. In that case, there was "a sufficient nexus between the taxpayer's standing as a taxpayer and the congressional exercise of taxing and spending power, notwithstanding the role the Secretary plays in administering the statute." Here, there is no nexus between plaintiffs' allegations and Congress' exercise of its taxing and spending power. Hence, *Kendrick* does not alter the requirements of taxpayer standing to allow the instant plaintiffs to challenge how the IRS administers the Code. Consequently, plaintiffs fall within *Frothingham*'s general rule denying taxpayer standing.

3. Voter Standing

The voter plaintiffs allege that they are injured because the IRS' refusal to revoke the Catholic Church's tax-exempt status "impairs and diminishes plaintiffs' right to vote." When it granted plaintiffs' "voter standing," the district court relied on *Baker v. Carr*, 369 U.S. 186 (1962). The district court's appellation of this theory as "voter standing" as applied to this case is a misnomer; plaintiffs' asserted basis for standing has nothing to do with voting. In *Baker v. Carr*, the Supreme Court held that disadvantaged voters had standing to challenge Tennessee's apportionment plan. The wrong that plaintiffs sought to vindicate in *Baker v. Carr* and in those cases that construed it was the dilution of their vote relative to the vote of other citizens of the same state—a direct, cognizable injury.

The Supreme Court has also held that disadvantaged voters may challenge an apportionment plan that is gerrymandered, that is, a plan whose voting district lines are drawn to reduce or eliminate the voting leverage of a given group of voters. It is undisputed that the instant plaintiffs do not allege that their vote has been diluted or that voting district lines have been gerrymandered to favor the Church or that anyone has "stuffed the ballot box" with votes for Church-backed candidates or that anyone has been prevented from voting. In short, plaintiffs here do not allege the particularized and objectively ascertainable injury in fact that sustained standing in the malapportionment cases. We therefore hold that *Baker v. Carr* and its progeny are inapposite and provide no basis for granting voter standing to these plaintiffs.

4. Competitive Advocate Standing

We consider finally whether the plaintiffs may have standing under a theory that the district court did not explicitly consider, yet which derives from its discussion of "voter standing." This theory may be labeled as "Competitive Advocate Standing." It is addressed separately from voter standing for analytical clarity and because it presents a closer question.

Plaintiffs allege that they are injured "by the unequal enforcement of the Code by [the government] . . . which constitutes an illegal, unfair and unconstitutional distortion of the political process by the government. . . ." They argue that their chance of electoral success is diminished because they do not receive the advantage that the Church receives from the government's asserted non-enforcement of the Code: The ability to campaign without losing tax-exemption under § 501(c)(3), and the ability nonetheless to offer their contributors a tax deduction for donating. "In the inherently competitive political arena an advantage granted to one competitor automatically constitutes a hardship to the others." The essence of this charge is that the IRS' non-enforcement of the Code creates an uneven playing field, tilted to favor the Catholic Church. The fatal flaw in the argument is that plaintiffs are not players in that arena or on that field.

The Supreme Court has found cognizable injuries to economic competitors. Implicit in the reasoning of those opinions is a requirement that in order to establish an injury as a competitor a plaintiff must show that he personally competes in the same arena with the party to whom the government has bestowed the assertedly illegal benefit. Only then does the plaintiff satisfy the rule that he was personally disadvantaged.

The economic competitor cases arose as banks diversified their functions, moved into new business areas, and became competitors of firms that had traditionally provided those services into which the banks sought to expand. The Supreme Court held that the organizations from which the banks sought to take away business—that is, with whom they sought to compete—had standing to challenge the banks' expansion into non-banking functions.

In each of these cases the banks obtained governmental rulings allowing them to compete on the same "playing field" as the plaintiffs. The results would have been different had the travel agents, for example, sought to complain about the bank's incursion into the data processing business. It is equally inappropriate to allow the present plaintiffs to challenge the IRS' treatment of the Church, since by their own admission they choose not to match the Church's alleged electioneering with their own. Therefore, they are not competitors.

Although the foregoing cases conferred standing to economic competitors, political competitors arguably should fare as well. Concededly, the *Association of Data Processing Serv. Orgs. Inc. v. Camp*, 397 U.S. 150 (1970), line of cases might extend to harms less concrete than diminution of profits. Plaintiffs' allegations of a political system biased against them by illegal government conduct are troubling. But, just as the Supreme Court has refused to recognize an Establishment Clause exception to standing doctrine, so must the requirements of Article III be applied with equal rigor to cases concerning participation in the political process. There is "no principled basis on which to create a hierarchy of constitutional values or a complementary 'sliding scale' of standing which might permit respondents to invoke the judicial power of the United States."

Like the claims of the clergy plaintiffs, the instant competitor claims lack particularized injury in fact. By asserting that an advantage to one competitor adversely handicaps the others, plaintiffs have not pleaded that they were personally denied equal treatment. They concede their tax status was correctly assessed by the IRS. Moreover, the complaint indicates that no plaintiff is currently a political candidate for public office. Plainly, the whole point of this lawsuit is plaintiffs' contention that it is illegal for the Catholic Church as a § 501(c)(3) recipient to participate actively in the political process. And, recognizing that potential illegality and the value of their own exemptions under §§ 501(c)(3) and (c)(4), plaintiffs state that they have refused to engage in electioneering to counter the Church's pro-life stance. Partly as a result of this self-imposed restraint, plaintiffs chose not to compete.

It may be argued that to qualify as competitor advocates plaintiffs need not go so far as to run for office or lobby; rather, they may simply advocate the pro-choice cause and stop short of supporting candidates. But that argument fails to answer the nagging question of why these individuals and organizations are then the appropriate parties to call a halt to the alleged wrongdoing. It is obvious that plaintiffs express their pro-choice views strongly and articulately. Yet such strongly held beliefs are not a substitute for injury in fact.

A further problem with recognizing a competitor advocate theory of standing in the present case is that it would be difficult to deny standing to any person who simply expressed an opinion contrary to that of the Catholic Church. Affording standing on that basis would lack a limiting principle, and would effectively give standing to any spectator who supported a given side in public political debate. This is precisely the problem the Supreme Court addressed in *Valley Forge* when it denied standing to plaintiffs who sued as taxpayers and citizens. We think that result would have been the same even had they called themselves "competitor advocates"—as proponents of a theory of the Establishment Clause different than that held by the government or the college that received the government benefit.

A similar theory was also initially raised in *Reservists*, where the plaintiffs sued as taxpayers, citizens, reservists and as opponents to the Vietnam War who sought to promote their viewpoint through lawful means. The district court found citizen standing. But "opponent standing" was too much, even for a court that thought the concept of standing had "been almost completely abandoned." Plaintiffs then withdrew the theory, and the Supreme Court therefore did not have an opportunity to address it when it ruled that the reservists did not have standing as citizens or taxpayers.

We do not foreclose the possibility that political competitors may state a cognizable injury; instead, we simply hold that the theory cannot be sustained here. Putting out into the stormy sea of this litigation, it is prudent to closely hug the shores of the pleaded facts and established law, and not venture out any further than we must. As a consequence, because we hold that plaintiffs have not pleaded a direct injury in fact, we need not decide whether the two other standing requirements of traceability and redressability have been met.

It could be argued that if no one among this diverse group of plaintiffs has standing to challenge the IRS' application of § 501(c)(3) to the Church, then perhaps no one could ever have standing to raise this issue. But such is irrelevant for determining whether the "case" or "controversy" requirement has been satisfied. Moreover, the lack of a plaintiff to litigate an issue may suggest that the matter is more appropriately dealt with by Congress and the political process.

Without reaching or deciding whether there are prudential reasons not to exercise jurisdiction, we conclude that plaintiffs have not met the Article III minimum requirements for standing. In sum, we hold that none of the plaintiffs has standing, that the district court therefore did not have subject matter jurisdiction, that the contempt adjudication must be vacated, and that the order denying the motion to dismiss the case must be reversed and the plaintiffs' complaint dismissed.

Problems for Discussion

19–6. What kinds of taxpayers may now challenge the tax-exempt status of the Catholic Church or demand that the IRS's tolerance of the Church's alleged violations of Code Section 501(c)(3) be extended to them as well?

Subchapter C: Limitations and Collateral Consequences

The mechanics of Code Section 170 are among the most complex of any in the Code. This subchapter offers only a cursory overview.

SECTION 1: PERCENTAGE LIMITATIONS

Code: Sections 170(b) and (d) and 509(a)

Code Section 170(b) imposes rules that limit the amount of charitable contribution deductions an individual taxpayer can take during any taxable year to specified percentages of his "contribution base"—adjusted gross income computed without regard to net operating loss carrybacks—for that year. For this purpose there are two categories of charitable donees: favored (listed in subsection (b)(1)(A)) and unfavored (listed in subsection (b)(1)(B)).

In general, donations to favored donees are deductible up to 50 percent of donor's contribution base, while donations to unfavored donees are deductible only up to 30 percent of donor's contribution base, and then only if that 30 percent has not already been used up by donations to favored donees. Code Section 170(b)(1). Deductions disallowed under this rule can be carried forward up to five years. Code Sections 170(d)(1) and 170(b)(1)(B), block language at end.

In practice, as a shorthand, the foregoing rule is more commonly stated in terms of gifts to "public charities" and "private foundations": Contributions to "public charities," it is said, are deductible up to 50 percent of donor's AGI, while donations to most so-called "private foundations" are deductible only up to 30 percent of donor's AGI, and then only if that 30 percent has not been used up by donations to "public charities."

To understand the distinction between public charities and private foundations, it is useful, yet again, to turn to the rules that govern the recipient organizations themselves. The term "public charity" never appears in the Code. The term is normally used, however, to refer to an organization described in clauses (1), (2), (3), or (4) of Code Section 509(a). There are two main types of organizations that fall into the "public charity" category.

Most general is the type described in clause (2): 501(c)(3) organizations that get the bulk of their funding from contributions from a broad public base—sometimes called "broadly supported charities." The second main type of "public charity" is described in clause (1), which refers back to Code Section 170(b)(1)(A), clauses (i) through (vi): churches, schools, hospitals, governmental units, and a few other categories. This type of 501(c)(3) is per se a public charity, regardless of where it gets its funding. All 501(c)(3)'s not described in Code Section 509(a), clauses (1) through (4) are "private foundations."

The reason for the distinction is to limit possible abuse by wealthy charitable donors. Assume that a rich would-be philanthropist creates his own charitable organization, appointing himself and his family and friends to the governing board, and makes a sizable charitable contribution to it— say a large chunk of stock in a corporation the philanthropist controls. Note that the charitable organization has not actually done anything with the contribution, which remains firmly under the would-be philanthropist's control. Yet the charitable organization is a separate legal entity and, by hypothesis, a qualified 501(c)(3). Should we treat this like any other charitable contribution?

Congress has approached this problem from two directions. First, it has imposed detailed regulations on the operation of private foundations. Second, it has imposed less favorable percentage limitation rules on contributions to most private foundations. (A few limited types of private foundations are treated as favored donees for percentage limitation purposes.)

In practice, the way donors determine whether a potential donee is favored or not is to check the IRS's website: Exempt Organizations Select Check, http://www.irs.gov/charities/article/0,,id= 96136,00.html.

SECTION 2: LIMITATIONS ON DEDUCTION OF FAIR MARKET VALUE

Normally, when our tax system allows a personal deduction for an item with basis, it limits that deduction to taxpayer's basis in the item. To give donors a further incentive to make charitable contributions, however, Treas. Reg. § 1.170A–1(c)(1) provides:

"If a charitable contribution is made in property other than money, the amount of the contribution is the fair market value of the property at the time of the contribution, reduced as provided in section 170(e)(1) . . ."

Assume, for example, that taxpayer contributes stock with a basis of $10,000 and a fair market value of $1 billion to an eligible recipient. Under Code Section 170, he is entitled to a deduction of $1 billion. His built-in gain of $999,990,000 is never recognized. This rule, not surprisingly, strongly favors charitable contributions of appreciated property.

Concern about this rule has not led to its repeal. Instead, Congress has enacted a number of exceptions and band-aids. Two are important.

First, in general, the rule that the amount of the contribution is measured by fair market value rather than by basis does not apply if (1) the gain would not be long-term capital gain if the property were sold, or (2) the property is tangible personal property not related to the donee's exempt purpose, or (3) the property is tangible personal property related to the donee's exempt purpose but is sold before the last day of the year in which the contribution is made, or (4) the donee is an unfavored donee for percentage limitation rule purposes, or (5) the contributed property is a patent, copyright, or like property. Code Section 170(e)(1).

Second, the percentage limitation for contributions of capital gain property given to favored donees is 30% rather than 50%.

Finally, in a number of contexts, it is possible to receive property without recognizing income. The IRS has held and the Seventh Circuit has confirmed that in at least one such context, claiming a charitable contribution deduction with respect to such property may trigger the previously excluded income.

HAVERLY v. UNITED STATES
513 F.2d 224 (7th Cir. 1975)

This case presents for resolution a single question of law which is of first impression: whether the value of unsolicited sample textbooks sent by publishers to a principal of a public elementary school, which he subsequently donated to the school's library and for which he claimed a charitable deduction, constitutes gross income to the principal.

During the years 1967 and 1968 Charles N. Haverly was the principal of the Alice L. Barnard Elementary School in Chicago, Illinois. In each of these years publishers sent to the taxpayer unsolicited sample copies of textbooks which had a total fair market value at the time of receipt of $400. The samples were given to taxpayer for his personal retention or for whatever disposition he wished to make. The samples were provided, in the hope of receiving favorable consideration, to give taxpayer an opportunity to examine the books and determine whether they were suitable for the instructional unit for which he was responsible. The publishers did not intend that the books serve as compensation.

In 1968 taxpayer donated the books to the Alice L. Barnard Elementary School Library. The parties agreed that the donation entitled the taxpayer to a charitable deduction in the amount of $400, the value of the books at the time of the contribution.

The parties further stipulated that the textbooks received from the publishers did not constitute gifts within the meaning of 26 U.S.C. § 102 since their transfer to the taxpayer did not proceed from a detached and disinterested generosity nor out of affection, respect, admiration, charity or like impulses.

There are no reported cases which have applied [the Code's and the courts'] definitions of income to the question of the receipt of unsolicited samples. In view of the comprehensive conception of income embodied in the statutory language and the Supreme Court's interpretation of that language, we conclude that when the intent to exercise complete dominion over unsolicited samples is demonstrated by donating those samples to a charitable institution and taking a tax deduction therefor, the value of the samples received constitutes gross income.

The receipt of textbooks is unquestionably an "accession to wealth." Taxpayer recognized the value of the books when he donated them and took a $400 deduction therefor. Possession of the books increased the taxpayer's wealth. Taxpayer's receipt and possession of the books indicate that the income was "clearly realized." Taxpayer admitted that the books were given to him for his personal retention or whatever disposition he saw fit to make of them. Although the receipt of unsolicited samples may sometimes raise the question of whether the taxpayer manifested an intent to accept the property or exercised "complete dominion" over it, there is no question that this element is satisfied by the unequivocal act of taking a charitable deduction for donation of the property.

The district court recognized that the act of claiming a charitable deduction does manifest an intent to accept the property as one's own. It nevertheless declined to label receipt of the property as income because it considered such an act indistinguishable from other acts unrelated to the tax laws which also evidence an intent to accept property as one's own, such as a school principal donating his sample texts to the library without claiming a deduction. We need not resolve the question of the tax consequences of this and other hypothetical cases discussed by the district court and suggested by the taxpayer. To decide the case before us we need only hold, as we do, that when a tax deduction is taken for the donation of unsolicited samples the value of the samples received must be included in the taxpayer's gross income.

This conclusion is consistent with Revenue Ruling 70–498, 1970–2 Cum. Bull. 6, in which the Internal Revenue Service held that a newspaper's book reviewer must include in his gross income the value of unsolicited books received from publishers which are donated to a charitable organization and for which a charitable deduction is taken. This ruling was issued to supercede an earlier ruling, Rev. Rul. 70–330, 1970–1 Cum. Bull. 14, that mere retention of unsolicited books was sufficient to cause them to be gross income.

The Internal Revenue Service has apparently made an administrative decision to be concerned with the taxation of unsolicited samples only when failure to tax those samples would provide taxpayers with double tax benefits. It is not for the courts to quarrel with an agency's rational allocation of its administrative resources.

SECTION 3: SUBSTANTIATION REQUIREMENTS

Code: Sections 170(a)(1), (f)(8), and (11)

Code Section 170(a)(1) now provides that "A charitable contribution shall be allowable as a deduction only if verified under regulations prescribed by the Secretary." In addition, Code Section 170(f) contains specific substantiation requirements for contributions in different types and amounts.

MOHAMED v. COMMISSIONER
T.C. Memo. 2012-152

Joseph and Shirley Mohamed donated extremely valuable real estate to charity in 2003 and 2004, but didn't follow the Commissioner' directions about how to document their donations. Even though the property was quite likely more valuable than the Mohameds reported on their tax returns, the Commissioner moved for partial summary judgment to deny them any deduction at all because of their failure to follow the regulation. The Mohameds reply that such a harsh result must mean that the regulation is invalid; or, if not invalid, should at least be read to imply an exception for substantial compliance—especially since, they argue, this problem was caused by the Commissioner himself, whose design of a tax form actively misled them.

Joseph Mohamed, Sr., is a real-estate broker, a certified real-estate appraiser, and a prominent Sacramento entrepreneur. During a long career he has amassed a fortune in real estate. He and his wife Shirley wanted to put their wealth to good use, and in 1998 they formed The Joseph Mohamed, Sr. and Shirley M. Mohamed Charitable Remainder Unitrust II. A charitable remainder unitrust, or CRUT, is a special kind of trust that allows taxpayers to claim an immediate deduction for a portion of the value of property settled in a trust, whose income goes to the donor for life or for a term not to exceed 20 years with the remainder to charity. The Mohameds intended that whatever was left in the Trust after their deaths would go to the Shriners Hospitals for Children, the Sacramento Food Bank & Family Services, and the Pacific Legal Foundation.

In 2003 the Mohameds donated five properties worth millions of dollars to the Trust. Four of the properties were on the same street corner in Rio Linda, California, a city just north of Sacramento (Rio Linda properties); the other one was 40 acres of subdivided land on Calvine Road south of Sacramento (Calvine Road property). Joseph filled out the 2003 tax return himself, including the Form 8283, Noncash Charitable Contributions. He admits that he did not read the instructions before completing the form, because he says it seemed so clear that he didn't think he needed to even though, in fairness to the Commissioner, the form does say right at the top and center: "See separate instructions." It's easy to see why Joseph thought so: The form says that section B, part I (the description of the donated properties) could be "completed by the taxpayer and/or appraiser." It also notes that "If your total art contribution deduction was $20,000 or more you must attach a complete copy of the signed appraisal. See instructions." The Mohameds were not donating art; they were donating real estate. Nowhere else on the form did it indicate that a taxpayer had to attach an appraisal. [The court summarizes how Joseph filled out Form 8283.]

The Commissioner started an audit of the 2003 return in April 2005, and was displeased at Joseph's self-appraisal of such high-dollar properties. So the Mohameds hired Woodrow Stephen Bowman to perform an independent appraisal of the Rio Linda properties and the Calvine Road property, and hired Robert R. Keeling to appraise the Elk Grove shopping center. The independent appraisals were similar, but not identical, to Mohamed's own:

Property	Mohamed appraisal	Independent appraisal
Rio Linda 1	$296,348.00	$296,000
Rio Linda 2	325,000.00	315,000
Rio Linda 3	125,000.00	140,000
Rio Linda 4	264,040.00	220,000
Calvine Road	14,873,921.00	16,380,000
Shopping center	2,642,190.62	2,926,246
Total:	18,526,499.62	20,277,246

After the Mohameds transferred the properties, the Trust sold some of them in arm's-length deals. Rio Linda parcel 3 sold for $125,000 in May 2003. Rio Linda parcel 4 sold for $265,000 in October 2003. The shopping center sold in April 2004 for $2,280,000. And by the end of 2004 the Calvine Road property was sold in two pieces for a total price of nearly $23 million.

Despite the relative consistency between the appraisals and the ultimate sale prices, the Commissioner thought the Mohameds had overstated the values of the properties, and these cases seemed set to become valuation battles. But then the Commissioner realized that the Mohameds had made several mistakes in filing their Forms 8283 for 2003 and 2004, and amended his answer to assert that these mistakes compel denying the Mohameds any charitable deductions for their CRUT at all. He also moved for partial summary judgment in both cases to settle this issue.

Section 170 governs the deductibility of charitable donations, and states that "A charitable contribution shall be allowable as a deduction only if verified under regulations prescribed by the Secretary." Sec. 170(a)(1). Paragraph (c)(2) of section 1.170A–13, Income Tax Regs., reads:

> "(2) Substantiation requirements—(i) In general.—Except as provided in paragraph (c)(2)(ii) of this section, a donor who claims or reports a deduction with respect to a charitable contribution to which this paragraph (c) applies must comply with the following three requirements:
>
> (A) Obtain a qualified appraisal (as defined in paragraph (c)(3) of this section) for such property contributed. If the contributed property is a partial interest, the appraisal shall be of the partial interest.
>
> (B) Attach a fully completed appraisal summary (as defined in paragraph (c)(4) of this section) to the tax return ... on which the deduction for the contribution is first claimed (or reported) by the donor.
>
> (C) Maintain records containing the information required by paragraph (b)(2)(ii) of this section."

The regulations further define what constitutes a "qualified appraisal." A qualified appraisal must be made no more than 60 days before the gift and no later than the due date of the return, must be signed by a qualified appraiser, must include specific information (such as a description of the property and certain disclosures by the appraiser), and must not involve a prohibited fee. The most important requirement is that the appraisal be done by a qualified appraiser, which the regulations say cannot be the donor or taxpayer claiming the deduction or the donee of the property. Joseph, who did the appraisals, was the donor and the taxpayer claiming the deductions. He was also, in his capacity as the trustee of the Trust, the donee. There is no way we can possibly find that he was a qualified appraiser for the gifts.

The Mohameds also have a second problem. Neither section B of the Form 8283 nor Joseph's attached statement qualifies as an appraisal summary. Section 1.170A–13(c)(4), Income Tax Regs., tells us what qualifies as an appraisal summary. One of the threshold requirements is that it be signed by the qualified appraiser who prepared the appraisal. Section 1.170A–13(c)(4)(ii), Income Tax Regs., says the summary also must include the following information:

- the name and Social Security number of the donor;
- a description of the property;
- a brief summary of the overall physical condition of tangible property;
- the manner and date of the donor's acquisition of the property;
- the cost or other basis;
- the name, address, and taxpayer identification number of the donee;
- the date the donee received the property;

- a statement about whether the contribution was made by bargain sale;
- the name, address, and identification number of the qualified appraiser;
- the appraised fair market value of the property;
- a declaration by the appraiser that he is an appraiser, with sufficient qualifications to make this appraisal, and not one of the people unable to be a qualified appraiser; and
- a statement by the appraiser that the fee charged was not of a prohibited type, and that the appraiser has not been barred from presenting appraisals to the IRS under 31 U.S.C. section 330(c).

Joseph failed to include information about several of these categories on his Forms 8283 and the attached statements. For instance, he didn't include his bases in the properties, there is no bargain-sale statement, and there are no statements from a qualified appraiser. In fact, the statements Joseph attached to the Forms 8283 don't indicate that they are appraisals at all. If Joseph had hired a qualified appraiser, the lack of appraisal summaries might not have been a problem—section 1.170A–13(c)(4)(iv)(H), Income Tax Regs., says that if a donor forgets to attach the appraisal summary, the IRS can request it and the taxpayer can still get the deduction if he submits the summary within 90 days of the request. But the underlying appraisal still has to be a qualified appraisal completed before the due date of the tax return, and the appraisal summary must still contain the information required by section 1.170A–13(c)(4)(ii), Income Tax Regs. Since Joseph didn't seek an independent appraisal until after the audits started (well after his returns were due), he can't even find refuge in this section.

We must conclude that there is no dispute that Joseph didn't follow the regulations. His appraisals weren't qualified because he did them himself, his attached statements weren't appraisal summaries, and his untimely independent appraisals came too late to be either qualified appraisals or remedial appraisal summaries. This means the Commissioner has to win unless we hold that the regulations are invalid, or unless we find that Joseph has raised a genuine dispute that he substantially complied with the regulations, or we find some legal merit in the peculiar problems that he points to in the appraisal form itself.

The Mohameds challenge the validity of the regulations, claiming they disallow deductions for verified and substantiated donations, whereas the statute permits the Secretary to disallow only unverified donations. They claim this is arbitrary and capricious because it lets a taxpayer keep some of the deduction if he follows the procedure but overvalues his donation, but takes away the entire deduction of the taxpayer who accurately values his donation but fails to follow the procedure.

Section 170(a)(1) reads, "A charitable contribution shall be allowable as a deduction only if verified under regulations prescribed by the Secretary." This language is an "express delegation of authority" to create rules about how a donation will be verified. *See Chevron, U.S.A., Inc. v. Natural Res. Def. Council*, 467 U.S. 837, 843–44 (1984); *see also Mayo Found. for Med. Educ. & Research v. United States*, 562 U.S. ___, 131 S. Ct. 704, 714 (2011). We can't invalidate regulations unless they are arbitrary, capricious, or manifestly contrary to the statute. We are also constrained in these cases by the Deficit Reduction Act of 1984 (DEFRA), Pub. L. No. 98-369, sec. 155, 98 Stat. at 691. DEFRA section 155 commanded the Secretary to issue regulations under section 170(a)(1) to require taxpayers to get a qualified appraisal and attach an appraisal summary to the first return on which the deduction is claimed for all donations of property for which the claimed value exceeds $5,000. DEFRA sec. 155(a)(1) and (2).

Under *Chevron*, we first ask whether Congress has directly spoken to the precise question at issue. If the answer is yes, we must give effect to congressional intent. If the answer is no, we don't replace the agency's interpretation with our own. Instead, we allow the agency interpretation to stand if it "is based on a permissible construction of the statute."

The Mohameds first disagree with the Commissioner's interpretation of the word "verified" in the regulation. They think the regulation is disallowing some deductions the Code allows—namely those that have been "verified" according to section 170, even though they don't meet the Commissioner's verification rules.

Although no courts have directly addressed whether section 1.170A–13, Income Tax Regs., fails the *Chevron* test, several courts have noted its "legislative history"—an odd concept, because regulations usually don't come from Congress. But courts have analyzed the interplay between DEFRA section 155 (in some sense a congressional interpretation of section 170(a)(1)), and the provisions in section 1.170A–13, Income Tax Regs. (which was the result of DEFRA). DEFRA is, after all, another law that we and the Secretary must follow, and it shows a clear congressional intent that contributions over $5,000 be verified via appraisal by a qualified appraiser to be deductible. DEFRA sec. 155(a). DEFRA section 155 also commands that the appraiser be someone other than the taxpayer or the donee. DEFRA sec. 155(a)(5)(A)(i), (iii). Therefore, we find that Congress has enacted one specific meaning of the term "verified" and the regulation accurately reflects that meaning.

Because the regulation matches the congressional definition, that should be "the end of the matter." But just in case the term "verified" was open to interpretation by the Commissioner, we proceed under *Chevron* step two to the question of whether his regulation was a permissible construction of the statute.

The Commissioner's regulation sets out a complicated way of verifying noncash donations worth more than $5,000. Taxpayers must hire an independent qualified appraiser, get a written appraisal document, and attach an appraisal summary with signed statements and detailed information to their tax return. We are also mindful of the apparent injustice the Mohameds point out on brief—some taxpayers who overvalue their property will still get a deduction, while others who accurately value their property may lose the entire deduction if they don't follow the regulation. But the Commissioner helpfully provided section 1.170A–13(c)(4)(iv)(H), Income Tax Regs., allowing a taxpayer who gets a qualified appraisal but doesn't follow the exact letter of the regulation to fix his mistake.

The essence of the regulation, and of DEFRA section 155, therefore, is that "verification" of a donation must be done by a qualified appraiser, and the rest of the rules are administrative means of conveying that appraiser's qualifications, honesty, and opinion on the matter to the IRS. The Commissioner's interpretation of "verified" is therefore something along the lines of "valued and documented by an independent appraiser." This serves the valuable government purpose of preventing tax evasion, both by overvaluation (Joseph's concern) and by undervaluation. This is not arbitrary or capricious—because the regulation matches the congressional interpretation in DEFRA section 155, the regulation is presumptively a permissible interpretation of the statute. The regulation is also "consistent with the statute's prescription," in this case to prescribe the form of the verification.

The Mohameds argue that even if the regulation is valid, and even if they didn't strictly comply with the regulation, they should still get deductions because they substantially complied. They draw their argument from a line of cases starting with *Bond v. Commissioner*, 100 T.C. 32 (1993), in which the taxpayers donated two blimps to charity. They hired an appraiser, who filled out the relevant parts of the appraisal summary in section B of the Form 8283, but left out his qualifications. He later provided a list of his qualifications—which were excellent—at the beginning of the audit. We found that the requirements of section 1.170A–13, Income Tax Regs., were directory rather than mandatory, and the Bonds had substantially complied because:

> "[The] petitioners ... met all of the elements required to establish the substance or essence of a charitable contribution, but merely failed to obtain and attach to their return a separate written appraisal ... even though substantially all of the specified information except the qualifications of the appraiser appeared in the Form 8283 attached to the return. ...."

Since *Bond*, few taxpayers have succeeded in showing substantial compliance. Their fatal mistakes have included:

- Failing to get an appraisal. See *Todd v. Commissioner*, 118 T.C. 334 (2002); *Hewitt v. Commissioner*, 109 T.C. 258 (1997), *aff'd without published opinion*, 166 F.3d 332 (4th Cir. 1998); *Jorgenson v. Commissioner*, T.C. Memo. 2000–38.

- Failing to fill out section B of Form 8283 (the appraisal summary). See *Hewitt*, 109 T.C. at 260, 264; *Smith v. Commissioner*, T.C. Memo. 2007–368, *aff'd*, 364 Fed. Appx. 317 (9th Cir. 2009).

- Having someone without expertise in appraisals complete the appraisal, *see Smith*, 2007 Tax Ct. Memo LEXIS, at *48 (CPA wasn't licensed appraiser); *D'Arcangelo v. Commissioner*, T.C. Memo. 1994-572 (high-school principal not qualified to appraise art supplies, and was employee of donee and therefore ineligible to be qualified appraiser).

- Having an appraisal prepared at the wrong time (*i.e.*, either more than 60 days before the gift or after the return was filed), *see Jorgenson* (appraisal prepared after tax return filed); *D'Arcangelo* (appraisal at least six years before gift).

- Including insufficient information or inappropriate information in an appraisal or appraisal summary, *see Smith* (appraisal of partnership shares "terse" and appraisal actually of assets held by partnership, not the shares themselves).

The cases make clear that substantial compliance requires a qualified appraisal. "Such a requirement is statutorily imposed by [DEFRA] section 155(a)(1)(A), and its impact is reflected in the legislative history of that provision." *Hewitt* quotes a House conference report stating:

> [N]o deduction is allowed for a contribution of property for which an appraisal is required under the conference agreement unless the appraisal requirements are satisfied.
>
> . . . .
>
> For donations of property as to which the donor appraisal requirements apply, the donor must obtain and retain a qualified written appraisal by a qualified appraiser for the property contributed and must attach a signed appraisal summary to the return on which the deduction is first claimed (with such other information as prescribed by regulations). [H.R. Conf. Rept. No. 98–861, at 995–96 (1984), 1984–3 C.B. (Vol. 2) 1, 249–50.]

This follows the related line of reasoning that a taxpayer can't substantially comply if he fails to comply with an "essential requirement" of the governing statute. Since it is an "essential requirement" of section 170(a)(1) and DEFRA section 155 that the taxpayer obtain a qualified appraisal, we can't excuse failure to do so as substantial compliance.

The Mohameds make one last-ditch effort to save their deductions. They point out that the Commissioner's Form 8283 for 2003 and 2004 didn't indicate anywhere on it that a taxpayer had to get an independent appraisal for contributions worth more than $5,000 and presented conflicting messages about what could be filled out by the taxpayer and what required an appraiser's signature. We won't try to explain away these difficulties, and note that the Commissioner has since changed his form to reduce confusion. Although sympathetic to the Mohameds' cause, we can't hold the form's failings against the Commissioner here, because "the authoritative sources of Federal tax law are in the statutes, regulations, and judicial decisions and not in such informal publications." Zimmerman

v. Commissioner, 71 T.C. 367, 371 (1978), *aff'd without published opinion*, 614 F.2d 1294 (2d Cir. 1979). A taxpayer relies on his private interpretation of a tax form at his own risk. Accordingly, we hold that the Mohameds are not entitled to any charitable deduction for 2003 or 2004.

We recognize that this result is harsh—a complete denial of charitable deductions to a couple that did not overvalue, and may well have undervalued, their contributions—all reported on forms that even to the Court's eyes seemed likely to mislead someone who didn't read the instructions. But the problems of misvalued property are so great that Congress was quite specific about what the charitably inclined have to do to defend their deductions, and we cannot in a single sympathetic case undermine those rules.

DURDEN v. COMMISSIONER

T.C. Memo. 2012–140

Petitioners resided in Texas at the time their petition was filed. During 2007, Mr. Durden was employed as an administrator by the Texas Department of Insurance and Ms. Durden was employed as an administrator by the Texas Department of Aging and Disability Services.

Petitioners timely filed their 2007 joint income tax return. On their attached Schedule A, Itemized Deductions, petitioners claimed a deduction of $25,171 for charitable contributions made by cash or check. Most of the contributions were made by check to petitioners' church, Nevertheless Community Church (NCC). Except for five checks totaling $317, the checks petitioners wrote to NCC were for amounts larger than $250. NCC is a section 501(c)(3) organization and is eligible to receive tax-deductible contributions under section 170(c)(2).

On April 13, 2009, respondent sent a notice of deficiency disallowing petitioners' claimed charitable contribution deductions for 2007. In response, petitioners produced records of their contributions, including copies of canceled checks and a letter from NCC dated January 10, 2008, which acknowledged contributions from them during 2007 totaling $22,517 (first acknowledgment). Respondent did not accept the first acknowledgment and informed petitioners that it lacked a statement regarding whether any goods or services were provided in consideration for the contributions.

Petitioners obtained a letter from NCC dated June 21, 2009 (second acknowledgment), that contained the same information found in the first acknowledgment as well as a statement that no goods or services were provided to them in exchange for their contributions.

Section 170(a)(1) allows a deduction for contributions to charitable organizations defined in section 170(c). Section 170(f)(8) provides substantiation requirements for certain charitable contributions. Specifically, section 170(f)(8)(A) provides: "No deduction shall be allowed under subsection (a) for any contribution of $250 or more unless the taxpayer substantiates the contribution by a contemporaneous written acknowledgment of the contribution by the donee organization that meets the requirements of subparagraph (B)."

For donations of money, the donee's written acknowledgment must state the amount contributed, indicate whether the donee organization provided any goods or services in consideration for the contribution, and provide a description and good faith estimate of the value of any goods or services provided by the donee organization. See sec. 170(f)(8)(B); sec. 1.170A–13(f)(2), Income Tax Regs. A written acknowledgment is contemporaneous if it is obtained by the taxpayer on or before the earlier of: (1) the date the taxpayer files the original return for the taxable year of the contribution or (2) the due date (including extensions) for filing the original return for the year.

Respondent argues that petitioners are not entitled to a deduction for the charitable contributions of $250 or more made to NCC during 2007 because neither the first nor the second acknowledgment from NCC satisfied the requirements of section 170(f)(8). Respondent contends that the first acknowledgment failed because it did not include a statement regarding whether any goods or services were provided to petitioners in consideration for their contribution and the second acknowledgment, which included the statement, was not contemporaneous.

Petitioners concede that they have not strictly complied with the statute. They argue, however, that they have substantially complied with the statute and are entitled to the claimed deductions.

In deciding this matter, we focus on whether petitioners' first acknowledgment, which the parties agree was contemporaneous, complied with the substantiation requirements of section 170(f)(8)(B). The second acknowledgment was not contemporaneous, and we do not consider it.

The doctrine of substantial compliance is designed to avoid hardship in cases where a taxpayer does all that is reasonably possible, but nonetheless fails to comply with the specific requirements of a provision. *Samueli v. Commissioner*, 132 T.C. 336, 345 (2009). This Court has held that "substantial rather than literal compliance may be sufficient to substantiate a charitable contribution deduction in certain instances." See *Consol. Investors Grp. v. Commissioner*, T.C. Memo. 2010–158.

Most often we have found substantial compliance in cases that involved procedural regulatory requirements where, despite a lack of strict compliance, the taxpayer substantially complied by fulfilling the essential statutory purpose. *See, e.g., Bond v. Commissioner*, 100 T.C. 32, 41–42 (1993) (although the taxpayers did not attach an appraisal summary to their tax return as required by regulations, they substantially complied with section 170 where virtually all required information was found on their attached Form 8283, Noncash Charitable Contributions); *Consol. Investors Grp. v. Commissioner*, T.C. Memo. 2010–158 (the taxpayer substantially complied with regulations under section 170 regarding a written appraisal for a contribution of property where the information provided to the Commissioner, although lacking in strict compliance with the regulatory requirements, was sufficient to permit evaluation of the contribution).

The essential statutory purpose of the contemporaneous written acknowledgment required by section 170(f)(8) is to assist taxpayers in determining the deductible amounts of their charitable contributions and to assist the Internal Revenue Service in processing tax returns on which charitable contribution deductions are claimed. *See Hewitt v. Commissioner*, 109 T.C. 258, 265–266 (1997), *aff'd without published opinion*, 166 F.3d 332 (4th Cir.1998); *DiDonato v. Commissioner*, T.C. Memo. 2011–153; H.R. Rept. No. 103–111, at 783, 785 (1993), 1993–3 C.B. 167, 359, 361.

Petitioners contend that they have fulfilled the essential statutory purpose even though their written acknowledgment does not include a statement regarding whether goods or services were provided in consideration for the contributions, as required by section 170(f)(8)(B)(ii). We have previously held that the specific statement is necessary for the allowance of a charitable contribution deduction. *See Friedman v. Commissioner*, T.C. Memo. 2010–45; *Kendrix v. Commissioner*, T.C. Memo. 2006–9.

Petitioners argue, in effect, that section 170(f)(8)(B) provides only "safe harbor" requirements in relation to the content of a written acknowledgment and does not establish the exclusive means by which a written acknowledgment may be deemed sufficient. This argument, however, fails to take into account the plain language of the preceding section 170(f)(8)(A), which states: "No deduction shall be allowed ... for any contribution of $250 or more unless the taxpayer substantiates the contribution by a contemporaneous written acknowledgment of the contribution by the donee organization that meets the requirements of subparagraph (B)." By referencing the requirements in section 170(f)(8)(B), one of which is that a statement is required regarding whether goods or services were provided in consideration for the contribution, section 170(f)(8)(A) makes the satisfaction of these requirements mandatory for a written acknowledgment properly to substantiate a charitable contribution.

Petitioners argue that the first acknowledgment was sufficient to enable a determination of their contribution amounts because their contributions were of cash and not of property that must be valued. Petitioners cite no caselaw in support of this position, and we have found none. Neither the statute nor its legislative history makes any distinction for purposes of substantiation between contributions of cash and those of property.

Even if contributions are of cash, such as petitioners', the statement regarding whether goods or services were provided is necessary to determine the deductible amount of the contributions. Petitioners' first acknowledgment stated the amount of their cash contributions to NCC for 2007 but included no statement indicating whether goods or services were provided to petitioners. It is impossible to determine from the amounts reported (or the checks produced) whether, for example, petitioners' payments were for meals or other goods or services provided by the church. Therefore, the first acknowledgment does not provide enough information to determine the deductible amount of petitioners' contributions.

Petitioners also argue that the omission of a statement regarding goods or services in the first acknowledgment was sufficient to indicate that no goods or services were provided in consideration for their contributions. The express terms of the statute require an affirmative statement. In addition, the legislative history of section 170(f)(8) confirms: "If the donee organization provided no goods or services to the taxpayer in consideration of the taxpayer's contribution, the written substantiation is required to include a statement to that effect." H.R. Conf. Rept. No. 103-213, at 565 n. 30 (1993), 1993-3 C.B. 393, 443.

Petitioners further contend that respondent should be required to consider information beyond that found in the first acknowledgment to determine whether petitioners received any goods or services as consideration. Petitioners cite *Addis v. Commissioner*, 118 T.C. 528 (2002), aff'd, 374 F.3d 881 (9th Cir. 2004), as an example of a case where the Commissioner looked to information beyond what was found in the written acknowledgment. In *Addis*, a charitable organization gave the taxpayers a written acknowledgment stating that no goods or services had been provided in consideration for a large cash contribution. The Commissioner investigated further and learned that the taxpayers actually had been provided with services by the charitable organization and that the value of the services had been intentionally misrepresented on the written acknowledgment. As a result, the taxpayers' charitable contribution deduction was disallowed.

This case is distinguishable. In *Addis*, the written acknowledgment contained all the statutorily required information although it was ultimately determined that the acknowledgment did not include a good faith estimate under section 170(f)(8). In contrast, petitioners' written acknowledgment lacks essential information required by the statute. Nothing in the statute or legislative history requires respondent to look beyond the written acknowledgment when on its face the acknowledgment fails to provide the information required to substantiate a charitable contribution deduction.

Petitioners have failed strictly or substantially to comply with the clear substantiation requirements of section 170(f)(8), and their deduction for the charitable contributions in issue for 2007 must be disallowed.

PROBLEMS FOR DISCUSSION

19–7. Sarah regularly attends her neighborhood church primarily for social reasons. As is customary, she makes a weekly contribution to the church; her contributions for the year total $1,000. She and her children attend the church's pot-luck supper every week. Her son is a member of a Boy Scout troop that meets weekly, free of charge, in one of the church's function rooms. In June of the year in question, her 17–year–old daughter was married in the church. Sarah made the required donation of $200; the church's minister officiated at the wedding ceremony conducted in the church sanctuary; the wedding reception was held in the church basement. Write the written acknowledgement on behalf of the donee church required by Code Section 170(f)(8).

INDEX

References are to Pages

ABILITY TO PAY
Generally, 419–530
Charitable contributions, 457–530
Family structure and income, 421
Nondiscretionary expenses and involuntary losses, 430–456
Taxation based on, 1

ABOVE-THE-LINE DEDUCTIONS
Generally, 96

ACCELERATED COST RECOVERY SYSTEM
See Capital Cost Recovery, generally, this index

ACCIDENT OR HEALTH INSURANCE
Exclusion of benefits. 167–170

ACCOUNTING METHODS
Generally, 117–152
Accrual method, 145–150
　See also Accrual Method of Accounting, generally, this index
Cash method, 118–145
　See also Cash Method of Accounting, generally, this index
Related party transactions, accrual deduction, cash inclusion 307

ACCRUAL METHOD OF ACCOUNTING
Generally, 145–150
All events test, 145–147
Economic performance, 147
Prepaid income, 148–150

ADJUSTED BASIS
Generally, 114–116

ADJUSTED GROSS INCOME
Generally, 96

ADMINISTRATIVE GUIDANCE
Chief Counsel Advice, 22
Field Service Advice, 22
Information letters, 22
Litigation bulletins, 22
Litigation guideline memoranda, 22
Non–Docketed service advice review, 22
Private Letter Rulings, 22
Regulations, 9–10
Revenue Procedures, 9–10
Revenue Rulings, 9–10
Service center advice, 22
Standards of review, 9–10

ADMINISTRATIVE GUIDANCE—Cont'd
Technical Advice Memoranda, 22
Written determinations, 22

ADVERTISING
Generally, 263

AGENTS
Assignment of income from services, 315–329

ALIMONY
"Married" couples, 304–305
"Unmarried" couples, 286–299

ALTERNATIVE MINIMUM TAX
Generally, 101–103

AMORTIZATION
Generally, 271–272
See also Cost Recovery, generally, this index

ANNUAL ACCOUNTING
Generally, 9

APPUCABLE FEDERAL RATE
Generally, 236
Below-market loans, 233–238
Original issue discount, 238–241

ARBITRAGE
Interest arbitrage, 104–107

ASSIGNMENT OF INCOME
Generally, 315–336
Agency triangle theory, 320–321
Income from property, 330–336
Income from services, 315–329
"Kiddie tax," 335–336
Section 482 reallocation distinguished, 323–328
Sham entity theory distinguished, 323–328

AUDITS AND DEFICIENCIES
Statutory notice of deficiency, 10

BAD DEBTS
Generally, 180–185

BALANCING ENTRIES
Generally, 224–229
Tax benefit rule, 225–227
Tax detriment rule, 227–229

BARGAIN PURCHASE RULE
Generally, 16

BARGAIN PURCHASES
Part gift/part sale transactions, 337

531

INDEX

References are to Pages

BARTER
Generally, 13–15
Nonmarket exchanges, 19–21

BASIS
Generally, 114–116

BEQUESTS
Basis, 337–339
Exclusion, 37–48

BELOW-MARKET LOANS
Generally, 233–238

BELOW-THE-LINE DEDUCTIONS
Generally, 96–97

BONUS DEPRECIATION
Generally, 265–266

BUSINESS EXPENSES
Bad debts, 180–185
See Capital Expenditures, generally, this index
See Cost Recovery, generally, this index
See Costs of Producing Income, generally, this index

CANCELLATION OF INDEBTEDNESS
See Debt, generally, this index

CAPITAL COST RECOVERY
See Cost Recovery, generally, this index

CAPITAL EXPENDITURES
Generally, 242–273
See Capitalization Requirement, generally, this index
Effective rates of tax, 242–252

CAPITAL GAINS AND LOSSES
Generally, 99–101

CAPITALIZATION REQUIREMENT
Generally, 252–267
Advertising, 263
Bonus depreciation, 265–266
Circulation expenses, 263–264
Exceptions, 263–267
INDOPCO regulations, 258
Research expenses, 264
Small business expensing election, 266–267
Software development expenses, 264–265

CASH METHOD OF ACCOUNTING
Generally, 118–145
Checks, 119
Cash equivalence, 126–129
Constructive receipt, 123–126
Credit cards, 120
Deferral of income, 125, 135–142
Economic benefit, 129–135
Letters of credit, 121
Methods of payment, 119–123
Prepaid expenses, 143–145

CASUALTY LOSSES
Generally, 451–456

CHARITABLE CONTRIBUTIONS
Generally, 457–530
"Contribution" defined, 458–476
Deduction of fair market value, 516–517
Equal protection issues, 471–476
Eligible recipient organizations, 476–515
"Excess payment" rule, 458
Gifts and scholarships compared, 47–48
Percentage limitations, 515–516
Substantiation requirements, 470, 519–530

CHECKS
Payment of deductions, 119

CHILDREN
Child credit, 426–427
"Dependent" defined, 421–424
Earned income credit, 427–429
Head of household status, 424–426
"Kiddie tax," 335–336
Personal exemptions, 421–424

CIRCULATION EXPENSES
Generally, 263–264

CLAIM OF RIGHT DOCTRINE
Generally, 9

CLAIMS COURT
Generally, 10

COHAN RULE
Generally, 285

COLLATERAL SOURCE RULE
Generally, 169

COMMUNITY PROPERTY
Generally, 287, 296–298

COMMUTING EXPENSES
Generally, 403–406

COMPLETE ACCOUNTING
Generally, 113–229
Basis, 114–116

COMPREHENSIVE TAX BASE
Generally, 57–65

CONSTITUTIONAL AUTHORITY AND LIMITATIONS
Generally, 166–167
Apportionment, 166–167
Direct vs. indirect taxes, 166–167
Uniformity, 166

CONSTRUCTIVE RECEIPT
Generally, 123–126

COST RECOVERY
Generally, 267–273
Amortization, 271–272
Advertising expenses, 263
Bonus depreciation, 265–266
Capitalization requirement, 252–267
Circulation expenses, 263–264
Depletion, 272
Depreciation, 267–271
See also Depreciation

COST RECOVERY—Cont'd
Expensing, 247–249
Nondistortive cost recovery, 249–252
Research expenses, 264–265
Small business expensing election, 266–267
Software development expenses, 264–265
Start-up expenses, 272–273

COSTS OF PRODUCING INCOME
Generally, 390
Activities not engaged in for profit, 345
Education expenses, 408–414
Entertainment and meal expenses, 391–402
Home office expenses, 417–418
Independent contractor vs. employee, 346–351
Legal expenses, 414–417
Non-business activities engaged in for profit, 344–345
"Ordinary and necessary" requirement, 369–380
Personal expenses distinguished, 380–382
Public policy, deductions contrary to, 382–390
Trade or business expenses, employee, 343–344
Trade or business expenses, non-employee 342–343
Trade or business vs. other for-profit activity, 351–355
Travel expenses, 402–408

COURTS
Court of Federal Claims, 10
District Court, 10
Tax Court, 10

CREDIT CARDS
Generally, 120

CRIMINAL TAX EVASION
Generally, 172–173

DAMAGES
Generally, 153–170

DEBT
Generally, 171–212
Bad debt deduction, 180–185
Below-market loans, 233–238
Contested liabilities, 177–179
Debt discharge income and exceptions, 173–180, 185–212
Deductibility of interest, 104–111
Gambling debt, 59–64, 197–212
Insolvency, 179–180
Original issue discount, 238–241
Purchase price adjustments, 175–177
Purchases of debt by related parties, 307–308
Nonrecourse debt, 185–197
Recourse debt, 197

DEDUCTIONS
Above-the-line deductions, 96
Accounting methods, 117–152
Accrual method, 145–150
See Accrual Method of Accounting, generally, this index
Advertising, 263
Alimony, 304–305

DEDUCTIONS—Cont'd
Amortization, 271–272
Bad debts, 180–185
Balancing entries, 224–229
Below-the-line deductions, 96–97
Bonus depreciation, 265–266
Cash method, 118–145
See Capital Expenditures, generally, this index
See Cash Method of Accounting, generally, this index
Casualty losses, 451–456
Charitable contributions, 457–530
Circulation expenses, 263–264
Cohan rule, 285
Commuting expenses, 403–406
See Cost Recovery, generally, this index
See Costs of Producing Income, generally, this index
Depletion, 272
Depreciation, 267–271
Economic performance, 147
Education expenses, 408–414
Entertainment expenses, 391–402
Expensing, 247–249
Gambling losses, 201
Hobby losses, 345, 355–368
Home mortgage interest, 109
Home office expenses, 417–418
Interest paid or accrued, 104–111
Itemized deductions, 96–97
Legal expenses, 414–417
Meal expenses, 391–402
Medical expenses, 430–450
Miscellaneous itemized deductions, 97–98
Net operating losses, 343
Non-itemized deductions, 96
Ordinary and necessary requirement, 369–380
Overall limitation on itemized deductions, 98
Passive activity loss limitation, 107–108
Personal exemptions, 421–424
Personal expenses, 57–65
Phase-outs, 97–99
Related party anti-abuse rules, 306–310
Research expenses, 264–265
Small business expensing election, 266–267
Software development expenses, 264–265
Standard deduction, 97
Start-up expenses, 272–273
State and local taxes, 450
Tax detriment rule, 227–229
Tax-related expenses, 354–355
Theft losses, 456
Travel expenses, 402–408
2–percent floor, 97–98
Wagering losses, 456

DEFENSE OF MARRIAGE ACT
Generally, 304–305

DEFERRED COMPENSATION
Generally, 135–142

"DEPENDENT" DEFINED
Generally, 421–424

DEPLETION
Generally, 272
See also Cost Recovery

DEPRECIATION
Generally, 267–271
Alternative depreciation, 270–271
Regular depreciation, 267–270

DIRECT TAXES
Generally, 166–167

DISABILITY INSURANCE
Generally, 167–170
Exclusion of benefits. 167–170

DISTRICT COURT
Generally, 10

DIVIDENDS
Generally, 99–100

DIVORCE and SEPARATION
Defense of Marriage Act, 304–305
"Married" couples, 303–305
Support obligations, 286–288
"Unmarried" couples, 299–303

EARNED INCOME CREDIT
Generally, 427–429
Tax expenditure, 93

EDUCATION EXPENSES
Generally, 408–414
Interest on educational loans, 110–111
Scholarships, 47

EDUCATION TAX CREDITS
Generally, 84

EFFECTIVE RATES OF TAX
Generally, 242–252
Computation of, 244–247
Internal rate of return, 242–244

EMINENT DOMAIN
Involuntary conversions, 218–222

EMPLOYEE
Independent contractor distinguished, 346–351

EMPLOYEE BENEFITS
Generally, 30–37

ENTERTAINMENT EXPENSES
Generally, 391–402
De minimis fringe benefits, 36–37
"Directly related" or "associated with" requirement, 395–397
50 percent disallowance rule, 397–402
Substantiation requirements, 397

ESTATE TAXES
Generally, 46–47

EXCHANGE OF PROPERTY
Realization, 7–8
Like-kind exchanges, 213–218
Nonrecognition, 213–223

EXPENSING
Generally, 247–249

FAIR MARKET VALUE
Definition, 16–17

FAMILIES, TAXATION OF
Generally, 275–339, 421–429
  See Assignment of income, generally, this index
Below-market loans, 233–238
Child tax credit, 426–427
Community property, 287
Defense of Marriage Act, 304–305
"Dependent" defined, 421–424
  See Divorce and separation, generally, this index
Earned income credit, 427–429
Entanglement, 277–305
Head of household status, 424–426
Joint filing, 310–315
Marriage bonuses and penalties, 310–315
"Married" couples, taxation of, 303–305
Personal exemptions, 421–424
Relative indifference, 306–339
"Unmarried" couples, taxation of, 277–303

FLOORS
Generally, 97–99

FOOD
See Meals and Lodging, generally, this index

FOREIGN CORPORATIONS, TAXATION OF
Generally, 12, 328

FORFEITABLE COMPENSATION
See Section 83, generally, this index

FRINGE BENEFITS
Generally, 30–37

GAMBLING
Debt, 197–212
Losses, 201

GENERAL WELFARE DOCTRINE
Generally, 48–56
Benefits held excludible, 54–55
Individual need requirement, 55
Social Security benefits, taxability, 55–56

GIFT TAXES
Generally, 46–47

GIFTS, BEQUESTS, AND INHERITANCES
Generally, 37–48
Basis, property acquired by gift, 336–337
Basis, property acquired by bequest or inheritance, 337–339
Gift and estate taxes, 46–47
Part gift/part sale transactions, 337
Employer gifts, 46
Transfer taxes, 46

GROSS INCOME
Generally, 96
Exclusions, 16–56

INDEX

HAIG-SIMONS DEFINITION OF INCOME
Generally, 57–65

HEAD OF HOUSEHOLD STATUS
Generally, 424–426

HEALTH INSURANCE
Exclusion of benefits. 167–170

HOBBY LOSSES
Generally, 345, 355–368

HOLDING PERIOD
Capital gains and losses, 99–100

HOME MORTGAGE INTEREST
Generally, 109

HOME OFFICE EXPENSES
Generally, 417–418

IMPUTED INCOME
Generally, 23–25
Haig–Simons definition of income, 64
Rental value of property, 25, 78–79

INCENTIVE COMPENSATION
See Section 83

INCOME
Generally, 4–56
Definition, 7
Employee benefits, 30–37
General welfare doctrine, 48–56
Gifts, bequests, and inheritances, 37–48
Haig–Simons definition, 57–65
Imputed income, 23–25
Non-market income, 19–22
Noncash receipts, 13–15
Psychic or incidental income, 25–29
Realization requirement, 7
Source, 1–12

INCOME SPLITTING
Generally, 310–315

INCOME TAXATION
Generally, 1–3
Constitutional authority and limitations, 166–167

INDEBTEDNESS
See Debt

INDEPENDENT CONTRACTOR
Employee distinguished, 346–351

INHERITANCES
Gifts and Inheritances, this index

INSOLVENCY
Debt discharges, 179–180

INSTALLMENT SALES
Generally, 156
Installment method purchases by related parties, 308–310

INSURANCE
Accident or health insurance benefits, 167–170
Collateral source rules, 169

INTANGIBLE PROPERTY
Amortization, 271–272

INTEREST FREE LOANS
Generally, 233–238

INTEREST PAID OR ACCRUED
Generally, 104–111
Educational loans, 110
Home mortgage interest, 109
Investment interest. 104–106
Passive activity interest, 107–108
Personal interest, 109
Incurred to purchase or carry tax exempt bonds, 106–107
Trade or business interest, 104

INTERNAL RATE OF RETURN
Generally, 242–244

INVOLUNTARY CONVERSIONS
Generally, 218–222

ITEMIZED DEDUCTIONS
Generally, 96–99

JOINT RETURN FILING
Generally, 310–315

LEGAL EXPENSES
Generally, 414–417
Attorneys fees, 332–335
Origin of claim doctrine, 415–416
Tax-related expenses, 354–355

LIKE-KIND EXCHANGES
Generally, 213–218

LOANS
See Debt, generally, this index

LOCAL TAXES
See State and Local Taxes, generally, this index

LOSSES
See Accrual Method of Accounting, generally, this index
Bad debts, 180–185
Balancing entries, 224–229
See Cash Method of Accounting, generally, this index
Casualty losses, 451–456
Gambling losses, 201
Hobby losses, 345, 355–368
Medical expenses, 430–450
Passive activity loss limitation, 107–108
Related party anti-abuse rules, 306–310
Theft losses, 456
Wagering losses, 456

MARKETS
Fair market value, 16–17
Income from non-market exchanges, 19–21
Role in measurement of income, 16–18

MARRIAGE
See Families, Taxation of

References are to Pages

MEAL EXPENSES
Generally, 391–402
See also Meals and Lodging Provided by Employer
De minimis fringe benefits, 36–37
"Directly related" or "associated with" requirement, 395–397
50 percent disallowance rule, 397–402
Substantiation requirements, 397

MEALS AND LODGING PROVIDED BY EMPLOYER
Generally, 30–36

MEDICAL EXPENSES
Deduction generally, 430–450
Cosmetic surgery, 436
Gender reassignment surgery, 436–447
"Medical care" defined, 430–436
Medical insurance premiums, 435
Qualified long-term care services, 435
Reproductive services, 447–450
Travel expenses, 435

MEDICAL INSURANCE
Exclusion of benefits. 167–170

MEDICARE TAXES
See Payroll Taxation

MISCELLANEOUS ITEMIZED DEDUCTIONS
Generally, 97–98

MORTGAGES
See Debt, generally, this index

MUNICIPAL BONDS
See Tax–Exempt Bonds, generally, this index

NET OPERATING LOSSES
Generally, 343

NONCASH RECEIPTS
Generally, 13–15

NON-ITEMIZED DEDUCTIONS
Generally, 96

NONMARKET EXCHANGES
Generally, 19–21

NONRECOGNITION
Generally, 213–222
Involuntary conversions, 218–222
Like-kind exchanges, 213–218

NONRECOURSE DEBT
Generally, 185–197

NONRESIDENT ALIENS, TAXATION OF
Generally, 12, 328

NOT-FOR–PROFIT ACTIVITIES
Generally, 345, 355–368

ORDINARY AND NECESSARY REQUIREMENT
Generally, 369–380
Capital expenses distinguished, 369

ORDINARY AND NECESSARY REQUIREMENT—Cont'd
Expenses contrary to public policy distinguished, 370
Personal expenses distinguished, 369, 380–382
Unreasonable expenses distinguished, 370
Unusual expenses distinguished, 370

ORIGINAL ISSUE DISCOUNT
Generally, 238–241

OVERALL LIMITATION ON ITEMIZED DEDUCTIONS
Generally, 98

PART GIFT/PART SALE TRANSACTIONS
Generally, 337

PASSIVE ACTIVITY LOSS LIMITATION
Generally, 107–108

PAYROLL TAXATION
Generally, 12
Independent contractor vs. employee, 346–351
Payroll tax safe harbor, 350–351

"PEASE"
Overall limitation on itemized deductions, 98

PENALTIES
Substantial authority, 22

PERSONAL CASUALTY LOSSES (AND GAINS)
Generally, 451–456
Personal casualty gains, 456
Theft losses, 456

PERSONAL EXEMPTIONS
Generally, 421–424
Phase-out, 99

PERSONAL EXPENSES
Generally, 57–65
Costs of producing income distinguished, 380–382
Alimony, 304–305
Casualty losses, 451–456
Charitable contributions, 457–530
Combined business and personal travel, 407–408
Commuting expenses, 403–406
Education expenses, 408–414
Hobby losses, 345, 355–368
Interest, 109
Legal expenses, 414–417
Medical expenses, 430–450
Meal expenses, 391–402

PHASE-OUTS
Generally, 97–99

POLITICAL ACTIVITIES
Effect on tax-exempt status, 506

PREPAID EXPENSES
Accrual Method of accounting, 147
Cash method of accounting, 143–145

PREPAID INCOME
Accrual method of accounting, 148–150

PRIMARY PURPOSE TEST
Generally, 25–29

PRINCIPAL RESIDENCE
Sale of, 222–223

PROPERTY
Acquisition, See Capital Expenditures
Disposition, See Capital Gains and Losses
Division on divorce, "married" couples, 303–305
Division on divorce, "unmarried" couples, 299–303
Forfeitable, received as compensation, See Section 83
Installment sales, 156
Involuntary conversions, 218–222
Like-kind exchanges, 213–218
Receipt as income, 13–15
Related party transactions, loss disallowance, 307
Sale of principal residence, 222–223

PSYCHIC OR INCIDENTAL INCOME
Generally, 25–29

PUBLIC POLICY, DEDUCTIONS CONTRARY TO
Generally, 382–390

QUALIFIED LONG–TERM CARE SERVICES
Generally, 169

RATES
Alternative minimum tax, 101–103
Capital gains, 99–101
Dividends, 99–101
Earned income credit, 427–429
Effective rates of tax, 242–252

REALIZATION REQUIREMENT
Generally, 7
Haig–Simons definition of income, 64

RECOVERIES
Generally, 153–170
Compensatory damages, 157–167
Installment sales, 156
Personal physical injury or sickness, 157–167
Recovery of basis, 153–156

REGULAR TAX
Generally, 96–97

REGULATIONS
Generally, 9
Judicial deference, 10

RELATED PARTY ANTI–ABUSE RULES
Generally, 306–310
Attribution, 309
Installment method purchases by related parties, 308–310
Purchases of debt by related parties, 307–308
Transactions between related parties, in general, 307

REPORTING REQUIREMENTS
Barter exchanges, 19

RESEARCH EXPENSES
Exception from capitalization requirement, 264–265
Tax expenditures, 70

REVENUE PROCEDURES
Generally, 9–10
Judicial deference, 9–10

REVENUE RULINGS
Generally, 9–10
Judicial deference, 9–10

RULINGS
Private letter rulings, 22
Revenue rulings, 9–10

SALES TO RELATED PARTIES
Disallowance of losses, 307
Part gift/part sale transactions, 337
"Spouses," sales between, 304

SCHEDULAR TAXATION
Generally, 12

SCHOLARSHIPS
Generally, 47

SECTION 83
Generally, 150–152

SECTION 482
Generally, 323–329
Correlative adjustments, 328–329

SECTION 501(C)(3) STATUS
Generally, 476–515
Lobbying and political activities test, 488–515
Private inurement test, 484–488
Purposes test, 477–484
Standing to challenge, 506–515

SECURITIES
Worthless securities, 456

SELF-EMPLOYMENT TAXES
See Payroll Taxation
Independent contract vs. employee, 346–351

SIXTEENTH AMENDMENT
Generally, 166–167

SMALL BUSINESS EXPENSING ELECTION
Generally, 266–267

SOCIAL SECURITY BENEFITS
Taxability, 55–56
Tax expenditure, exclusion of, 94

SOCIAL SECURITY TAXES
See Payroll Taxation

SOFTWARE DEVELOPMENT EXPENSES
Generally, 264–265

SOURCE OF INCOME
Generally, 4–12

INDEX

References are to Pages

STANDARD DEDUCTION
Generally, 97

START-UP EXPENSES
Generally, 272–273

STATE AND LOCAL TAXES
Generally, 450

STATE OR LOCAL BONDS
See Tax–Exempt Bonds, generally, this index

STATUTES OF LIMITATIONS
Generally, 9

TAX BENEFIT RULE
Generally, 225–227

TAX COURT
Generally, 10

TAX-EXEMPT BONDS
Generally, 106–107
Disallowance of related interest, 106–107
Tax expenditure, 94

TAX EXPENDITURES
Generally, 65–95
Baselines, 67–69
Armed Forces personnel, 69
Capital gains, 80
Charitable contributions, 86, 88
Child credit, 87
College tuition (American Opportunity), 84
Commerce and housing, 77–81
Community and regional development, 82–83
Depreciation, 80–81
Domestic production deduction, 81
Earned income credit, 93
Education, training, employment, and social services, 83–89
Employer-provided health insurance, 89
Employer-provided meals and lodging, 87
Energy, 71–74
Foreign earned income, 69
Health, 89–91
Home capital gains exclusion, 78
Home mortgage interest deduction, 78
Home property tax deduction, 78
Income of U.S.-controlled foreign corporations, 70
Imputed income on owner-occupied housing, 78
Income security, 91–94
Life insurance and annuity contracts, 77
Low income housing, 79
Medical care, 89
National defense, 69–70
Natural resources and environment, 75–76
Passive loss real estate exemption, 79
Present value, 67
Qualified dividends, 80
Pension and retirement plans, 91–92
Research and experimentation expenditures, 70

TAX EXPENDITURES—Cont'd
Science, space, and technology, 70–71
Self-employed health insurance, 89
Social Security benefit exclusion, 94
State and local bond interest, 94
State and local taxes, 95
Step-up in basis at death, 80
Transportation, 81–82
Veterans' benefits and services, 94–95
Workers' compensation benefits, 91

TAX HOME
Travel expenses, 403–406

TAX LITIGATION
Generally, 10

TAX-RELATED EXPENSES, DEDUCTION OF
Generally, 354–355

TAXABLE INCOME
Generally, 96–97

THEFT LOSSES
Generally, 456

TIME VALUE OF MONEY
Generally, 231–273
Below-market loans, 233–238
Cost recovery
Depreciation,
Effective rates of tax, 242–252
Expensing, effect of, 247–249
Internal rate of return, 242–244
Unstated interest, 233–241

TORT RECOVERIES
Generally, 157–166
Collateral source rule, 169

TRANSFER TAXES
Generally, 46–47

TRAVEL EXPENSES
Generally, 402–408
Change of tax home, 405–406
Combined business and personal travel, 407–408
Commuting expenses, 403–406
No additional cost service, 36–37
"Sleep or rest" rule, 402–403
Tax home, 403–406
Working condition fringes, 36–37

2–PERCENT FLOOR
Generally, 97–98

"UNMARRIED" COUPLES
See Families, Taxation of

WAGERING LOSSES
Generally, 456

WORTHLESS SECURITIES
Generally, 456

†